The
Research
Writer

Curiosity, Discovery, Dialogue

Van Rys ▪ Meyer ▪ Sebranek

WADSWORTH
CENGAGE Learning

The Research Writer
John Van Rys, Verne Meyer,
and Pat Sebranek

Publisher: Lyn Uhl

Acquisitions Editor: Kate Derrick

Editorial Assistant: Elizabeth Reny

Media Editor: Cara Douglass-Graff

Marketing Manager: Stacey Purviance
  Taylor

Marketing Coordinator: Ryan Ahern

Content Project Manager: Rosemary
  Winfield

Art Director: Jill Ort

Print Buyer: Betsy Donaghey

Rights Acquisition Specialist,
  Image: Jennifer Meyer Dare

Rights Acquisition Specialist,
  Text: Shalice Shah-Caldwell

Production Service: Sebranek, Inc.

Text Designer: Sebranek, Inc.

Cover Designer: Sebranek, Inc.

Compositor: Sebranek, Inc.

Sebranek, Inc.: Steve Augustyn,
  Colleen Belmont, Chris Erickson,
  Mariellen Hanrahan, Dave Kemper,
  Tim Kemper, Rob King, Chris Krenzke,
  Lois Krenzke, Mark Lalumondier,
  April Lindau, Jason Reynolds,
  Janae Sebranek, Lester Smith,
  Jean Varley

For product information and technology assistance, contact us at
Cengage Learning Customer & Sales Support, 1-800-354-9706.
For permission to use material from this text or product,
submit all requests online at **cengage.com/permissions.**
Further permissions questions can be e-mailed to
permissionrequest@cengage.com.

Library of Congress Control Number: 2010935802

ISBN-13: 978-0-618-75622-3

ISBN-10: 0-618-75622-1

Wadsworth
20 Channel Center Street
Boston, MA 02210
USA

Cengage Learning is a leading provider of customized learning solutions with office locations around the globe, including Singapore, the United Kingdom, Australia, Mexico, Brazil and Japan. Locate your local office at **international.cengage.com/region.**

Cengage Learning products are represented in Canada by Nelson Education, Ltd.

For your course and learning solutions, visit **www.cengage.com.**

Purchase any of our products at your local college store or at our preferred online store **www.cengagebrain.com.**

Credits begin on page 510, which constitutes an extension of this copyright page.

Printed in the U.S.A.
1 2 3 4 5 6 7 14 13 12 11 10

Contents

Tetra Images/Jupiter Images

I: Conducting and Writing Up Research

II: Research-Writing Forms and Projects

III: Systems of Documentation

Preface

The Research Writer helps students transition from writing "the research paper" to doing research writing, from reporting information to working with ideas. The subtitle—*Curiosity, Discovery, Dialogue*—signals this shift: this handbook promotes research as a curiosity-driven activity that leads to discoveries that are then shared through various types of dialogue.

With this practical and reader-friendly handbook, then, students will learn the research and writing skills needed for any research project and will be able to apply and transfer these skills to their own disciplines. Moreover, students can use *The Research Writer* to become more intelligent, ethically aware researchers, able not just to avoid plagiarism but to write with credibility while navigating the twenty-first century digital information landscape. For these reasons, *The Research Writer* is an excellent text for research-intensive Freshman Composition courses, as well as for advanced writing courses. In addition, students will find this handbook helpful throughout their college careers and beyond.

The Research Writer: How Is It Organized?

Divided into three parts, *The Research Writer* is structured around students' research and writing projects:

- **Part 1, Conducting and Writing Up Research,** gives students all the tools that they need to complete the research and writing process for any project. Starting with the thinking behind college-level research (the *curiosity, discovery, dialogue* pattern), this section helps students envision, plan, and complete their research, whether in the library, on the free Web, or in the field. But Part 1 also helps students make sense of their findings, develop their research writing through creative but careful engagement with sources, and polish their writing in order to present and publish it.

- **Part 2, Research-Writing Forms and Projects,** focuses on the most common forms of college-level research writing, from personal-research papers to literature reviews. Each chapter introduces the form, provides guidelines for writing the form, shows the form in a student model, and offers a set of focused projects, both traditional and multimedia.

- **Part 3, Systems of Documentation,** provides a complete introduction, full reference information, and a sample student paper for the dominant documentation systems across the disciplines: MLA, APA, Chicago, and CSE.

Each chapter in *The Research Writer* gives students easy access to solid instruction. Guided by the chapter introduction, with its initial "Query" and "What's Ahead" features, students will find instruction presented in manageable spreads filled with tables, illustrations, models, and lists—all focused on the students' own work.

Contents at a Glance

The Research Writer: What Are Its Distinctive Features?

If curiosity, discovery, dialogue offers the theme and guides the structure of *The Research Writer,* practical quality instruction is at the core of its distinctive features:

■ **Accessible, flexible handbook design.** *The Research Writer* has an attractive four-color design that helps students access exactly the instruction that they need as they work on research projects. Instruction is presented in a tight format with self-contained page spreads, annotated models, examples and illustrations, lists, graphic organizers, and cross-references. Moreover, a series of "Focus on" features draws students' attention to key material on recurring themes or topics: *Focus on Your Project, Focus on Your Major, Focus on Ethics, Focus on Research Essentials,* and *Focus on Multimedia.*

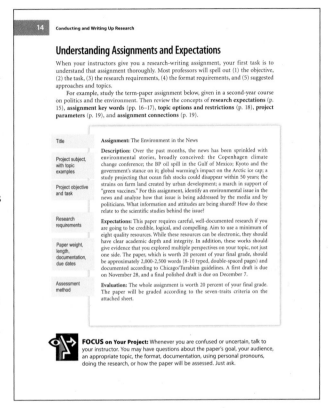

■ **Student writing and student project focus.** From beginning to end, *The Research Writer* helps students apply what they learn to their own research and writing projects. For example, the "Focus on Your Project" feature, the checklists, the end-of-chapter activities and projects, the guidelines for the forms of research writing, and the sample student papers all help students apply the text's instruction. Activities focus on exploration, application, and collaboration; projects offer opportunities to respond to the student models, to take a cross-disciplinary approach, to go multimedia, and to create real-world applications.

■ **Integration of the research and writing processes.** While showing that research projects unfold in broad phases, *The Research Writer* integrates research and writing activities, emphasizing fluidity, serendipity, and recursiveness within a larger structure.

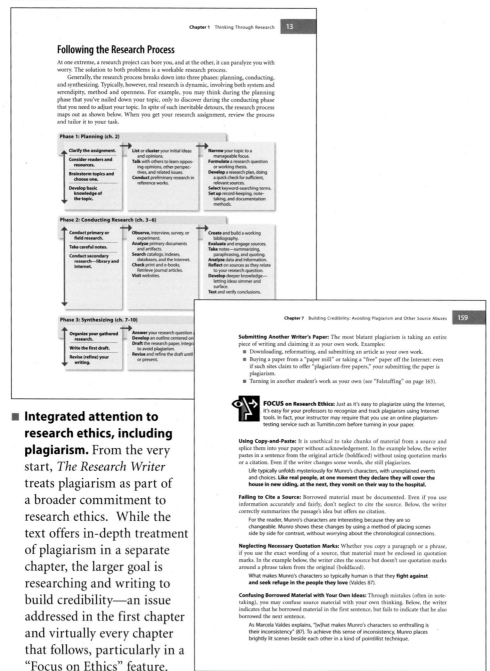

■ **Integrated attention to research ethics, including plagiarism.** From the very start, *The Research Writer* treats plagiarism as part of a broader commitment to research ethics. While the text offers in-depth treatment of plagiarism in a separate chapter, the larger goal is researching and writing to build credibility—an issue addressed in the first chapter and virtually every chapter that follows, particularly in a "Focus on Ethics" feature.

■ **Practical writing-in-the-disciplines (WID) emphasis.** Through a variety of strategies, *The Research Writer* stresses the value of research-writing skills in all college disciplines (and even beyond into other aspects of life). Using a recurring "Focus on Your Major" feature, the handbook also integrates illustrations and case studies across the disciplines: humanities (Jane Austen in fiction and film), social sciences (attachment disorder), and natural sciences (hybrid technology). In addition, end-of-chapter activities and projects, as well as the forms of research writing in Part 2 of the text, prompt students to apply effective research practices in their majors.

■ **Thorough treatment of research methods and writing with sources.** *The Research Writer* stresses both primary and secondary research methods, introducing students to the broad universe of resources to be found or developed for college-level projects. Moreover, this handbook shows students concretely how to work with sources in their own writing—from proper methods of summary, paraphrase, and quotation to correct citation to conversing with sources.

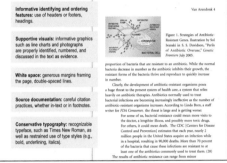

Chapter 10 Sharing Your Research Writing 249

Submitting an Academic Paper

For your research-writing project, submitting your paper (on time) may represent the most significant milestone. Turning in an academic research paper—whether a literary analysis, a psychology term paper, or an environmental-science experiment report—represents not only the completion of a course requirement but also your desire for educated feedback from your instructor. For these reasons, submit your academic paper according to accepted and respected conventions.

FOCUS on Your Major: Different disciplines follow standard formats for academic research writing, as well as standard submission guidelines related to the disciplines' for your major. Part 3 of this text introduces the main systems.

The Character of an Academic Paper

An academic paper aims to offer a substantive exploration of an issue, question, or problem. As such, your paper's format, design, and presentation should be fairly conservative, reflecting the seriousness of the topic and rhetorical situation. As shown in the sample page (formatted according to MLA guidelines), academic presentation is straightforward in order to accentuate content and thinking. While each system follows its own guidelines, all systems attend to features like these:

Informative identifying and ordering features: use of headers or footers, headings.

Supportive visuals: informative graphics such as line charts and photographs are properly identified, numbered, and discussed in the text as evidence.

White space: generous margins framing the page, double-spaced lines.

Source documentation: careful citation practices, whether in-text or in footnotes.

Conservative typography: recognizable typeface, such as Times New Roman, as well as restrained use of type styles (e.g., bold, underlining, italics).

Van Arendonk 4

Figure 1. Strategies of Antibiotic-Resistant Genes. Illustration by Sol Ivanski in S. S. Davidson, "Perils of Antibiotic Overuse," *Genetic Frontiers* July 2005.

proportion of bacteria that are resistant to an antibiotic. While the normal bacteria decrease in number as the antibiotic inhibits their growth, the resistant forms of the bacteria thrive and reproduce to quickly increase in number.

Clearly, the development of antibiotic-resistant organisms poses a huge threat to the present system of health care, a system that relies heavily on antibiotic therapies. Antibiotics normally used to treat bacterial infections are becoming increasingly ineffective as the number of antibiotic-resistant organisms increases. According to Linda Bren, a staff writer for *FDA Consumer*, the threat is large and is getting worse:

For some of us, bacterial resistance could mean more visits to the doctor, a lengthier illness, and possibly more toxic drugs. For others, it could mean death. The CDC [Centers for Disease Control and Prevention] estimates that each year, nearly 2 million people in the United States acquire an infection while in a hospital, resulting in 90,000 deaths. More than 70 percent of the bacteria that cause these infections are resistant to at least one of the antibiotics commonly used to treat them. (28)

The results of antibiotic resistance can range from minor

32 Conducting and Writing Up Research

Considering Information Sites

Where do you go to get the information you need? Your first instinct may be to hurry onto the Free Web, but don't limit yourself to that single research site. Consider the information "sites" listed below, and remember that resources may be available in different forms in different locations. For example, a journal article may be found in a library's holdings or in an electronic subscription database.

Information Source	Location	Example "Sites"
People	Experts (knowledge area, skill, occupation) Population segments or individuals (with representative or unusual experiences)	• Scholars and professionals • Reference librarians • An online discussion group
Libraries	**General:** public, college, online **Specialized:** legal, medical, government, business	• WorldCat/FirstSearch • Library of Congress • VERA (Virtual Electronic Resource Access): MIT libraries
Computer Resources	**Computers:** software, disks, CD-ROMs **Networks:** Internet and other online services (e-mail, limited-access databases, discussion groups, MUDs, chat rooms, Websites); intranets	• IPL.org • EBSCOhost (e.g., Academic Search Premier database) • LexisNexis (news databases)
Mass Media	Radio (AM and FM) Television (network, public, cable, satellite, Web) Print (newspapers, magazines, journals)	• National Public Radio (NPR) • *The Discovery Channel* • *Psychology Today* • *Bright Lights Film Journal* (e-zine)
Testing, Training, Meeting, and Observation Sites	Plants, facilities, field sites Laboratories, research centers, universities, think tanks Conventions, conferences, seminars Museums, galleries, historical sites	• The Smithsonian Institute • 20th Annual International Conference on Attachment and Bonding • Jane Austen Museum
Municipal, State, and Federal Government Offices	Elected officials, representatives Offices and agencies Government Printing Office (GPO <www.gpoaccess.gov>) websites	• Environmental Protection Agency • Census Data Online (www.census.gov) • FirstGov (www.firstgov.gov)
Workplace	Computer databases, company files Desktop reference materials Bulletin boards (physical/digital) Company, department Websites Departments and offices Associations, professional organizations Consulting, training, and information services	• Society for Automotive Engineers (www.sae.org) • American Academy of Childhood & Adolescent Psychiatry (www.aacap.org) • Jane Austen Society of North America (www.jasna.org)

■ **Full, thoughtful treatment of today's global, digital environment for research.**
Acknowledging the powerful presence of the free Web in students' lives, *The Research Writer* offers intelligent instruction for doing research both on and beyond the free Web. Stressing the centrality of the college library's digital resources, from catalogs to databases, this handbook nevertheless addresses the world of Google and Wikipedia so as to deepen students' understanding of the uses and limits of these tools. Moreover, *The Research Writer* offers full guidance for both evaluating digital resources and publishing digital, multimodal research writing.

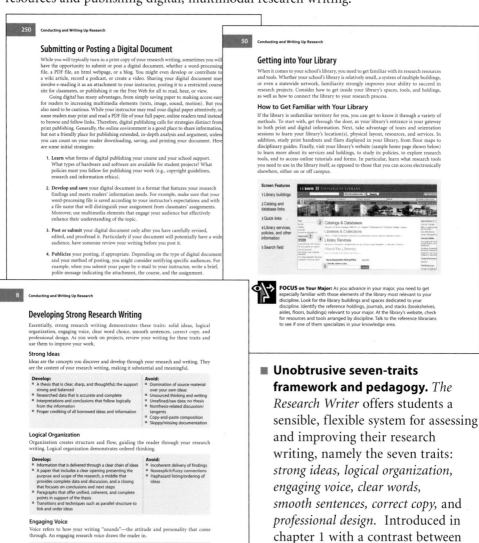

250   Conducting and Writing Up Research

Submitting or Posting a Digital Document

While you will typically turn in a print copy of your research writing, sometimes you will have the opportunity to submit or post a digital document, whether a word-processing file, a PDF file, an html webpage, or a blog. You might even develop or contribute to a wiki article, record a podcast, or create a video. Sharing your digital document may involve e-mailing it as an attachment to your instructor, posting it to a restricted course site for classmates, or publishing it on the Free Web for all to read, hear, or view.

Going digital has many advantages, from simply saving paper to making access easy for readers to increasing multimedia elements (texts, image, sound, motion). But you also need to be cautious. While your instructor may read your digital paper attentively, or some readers may print and read a PDF file of your full paper, online readers tend instead to browse and follow links. Therefore, digital publishing calls for strategies distinct from print publishing. Generally, the online environment is a good place to share information, but not a friendly place for publishing extended, in-depth analysis and argument, unless you can count on your reader downloading, saving, and printing your document. Here are some initial strategies:

1. **Learn** what forms of digital publishing your course and your school support. What types of hardware and software are available for student projects? What policies must you follow for publishing your work (e.g., copyright guidelines, research and information ethics).

2. **Develop and save** your digital document in a format that features your research findings and meets readers' information needs. For example, make sure that your word-processing file is saved according to your instructor's expectations and with a file name that will distinguish your assignment from classmates' assignments. Moreover, use multimedia elements that engage your audience but effectively enhance their understanding of the topic.

3. **Post or submit** your digital document only after you have carefully revised, edited, and proofread it. Particularly if your document will potentially have a wide audience, have someone review your writing before you post it.

4. **Publicize** your posting, if appropriate. Depending on the type of digital document and your method of posting, you might consider notifying specific audiences. For example, when you submit your paper by e-mail to your instructor, write a brief, polite message indicating the attachment, the course, and the assignment.

---

50   Conducting and Writing Up Research

Getting into Your Library

When it comes to your school's library, you need to get familiar with its research resources and tools. Whether your school's library is relatively small, a system of multiple buildings, or even a statewide network, familiarity strongly improves your ability to succeed in research projects. Consider how to get inside your library's spaces, tools, and holdings, as well as how to connect the library to your research process.

How to Get Familiar with Your Library

If the library is unfamiliar territory for you, you can get to know it through a variety of methods. To start with, get through the door, as your library's entrance is your gateway to both print and digital information. Next, take advantage of tours and orientation sessions to learn your library's location(s), physical layout, resources, and services. In addition, study print handouts and fliers displayed in your library, from floor maps to disciplinary guides. Finally, visit your library's website (sample home page shown below) to learn more about its services and holdings, to study its policies, to explore research tools, and to access online tutorials and forms. In particular, learn what research tools you need to use in the library itself, as opposed to those that you can access electronically elsewhere, either on or off campus.

Screen Features
1 Library buildings
2 Catalog and database links
3 Quick links
4 Library services, policies, and other information
5 Search field

FOCUS on Your Major: As you advance in your major, you need to get especially familiar with those elements of the library most relevant to your discipline. Look for the library buildings and spaces dedicated to your discipline. Identify the reference holdings, journals, and stacks (bookshelves, aisles, floors, buildings) relevant to your major. At the library's website, check for resources and tools arranged by discipline. Talk to the reference librarians to see if one of them specializes in your knowledge area.

---

8   Conducting and Writing Up Research

Developing Strong Research Writing

Essentially, strong research writing demonstrates these traits: solid ideas, logical organization, engaging voice, clear word choice, smooth sentences, correct copy, and professional design. As you work on projects, review your writing for these traits and use them to improve your work.

Strong Ideas

Ideas are the concepts you discover and develop through your research and writing. They are the content of your research writing, making it substantial and meaningful.

Develop:	Avoid:
■ A thesis that is clear, sharp, and thoughtful; the support strong and balanced	■ Domination of source material over your own ideas
■ Researched data that is accurate and complete	■ Unsourced thinking and writing
■ Interpretations and conclusions that follow logically from the information	■ Unrefined/raw data; no thesis
■ Proper crediting of all borrowed ideas and information	■ Nonthesis-related discussion/ tangents
	■ Copy-and-paste composition
	■ Sloppy/missing documentation

Logical Organization

Organization creates structure and flow, guiding the reader through your research writing. Logical organization demonstrates ordered thinking.

Develop:	Avoid:
■ Information that is delivered through a clear chain of ideas	■ Incoherent delivery of findings
■ A paper that includes a clear opening presenting the purpose and scope of the research, a middle that provides complete data and discussion, and a closing that focuses on conclusions and next steps	■ Nonexplicit/fuzzy connections
■ Paragraphs that offer unified, coherent, and complete points in support of the thesis	■ Haphazard listing/ordering of ideas
■ Transitions and techniques such as parallel structure to link and order ideas	

Engaging Voice

Voice refers to how your writing "sounds"—the attitude and personality that come through. An engaging research voice draws the reader in.

Develop:	Avoid:
■ A tone that is confident but also sincere, measured, and objective	■ Unreasonable/overconfident/ demanding voice
■ An attitude that objectively acknowledges uncertainty	■ Flat/boring/overly timid tone
■ A mature academic style	■ Use of personal pronouns I, we, and you (See your instructor about this.)

■ **Unobtrusive seven-traits framework and pedagogy.** *The Research Writer* offers students a sensible, flexible system for assessing and improving their research writing, namely the seven traits: *strong ideas, logical organization, engaging voice, clear words, smooth sentences, correct copy,* and *professional design.* Introduced in chapter 1 with a contrast between weak and strong research writing, these seven traits recur throughout the text without being obtrusive or prescriptive.

■ **Current and easy-to-navigate treatment of documentation systems.** *The Research Writer* covers MLA, APA, Chicago, and CSE documentation. Each system is presented for students' ease of understanding and use, starting with a directory, a Quick Guide providing an overview of the system, detailed citation and bibliographic guidelines (including samples), format guidelines, and a student model showing the system at work.

Directory to MLA Documentation

If you have a specific question about MLA style, use the directory below and on the next page to find the correct answer.

MLA Documentation: Quick Guide

In-Text Citations: The Basics 374	Works Cited: The Basics 375

Sample MLA Paper

Student Writer's Reflection 409	Sample Middle Pages 411
Sample First Page 410	Sample Works-Cited Page 418

MLA Format Guidelines

MLA Format at a Glance 401	Typographical Issues 403
Whole-Paper Format and Printing Issues 402	Page-Layout Issues 404

Endnotes and Footnotes in MLA Documentation

Content Notes 405	Format for Endnotes 405
Bibliographic Notes 405	

In-Text Abbreviations in MLA Format

General Guidelines for In-Text Abbreviations 406	Acceptable In-Text Abbreviations 406

Conventions for Names, Titles, and Internet Addresses

Names of People 407	Listing an Internet Address 408
Capitalization and Punctuation of Titles 407	

MLA In-Text Citations

General Guidelines for In-Text Citations 376
Guidelines for Sources without Authorship and/or Pagination 377
Sample In-Text Citations:

1. One Author: A Complete Work 378	10. A Series of Citations from a Single Work 380
2. One Author: Part of a Work 378	11. A Work Referred to in Another Work 380
3. Two or More Works by the Same Author(s) 378	12. A One-Page Work 380
4. Works by Authors with the Same Last Name 379	13. A Work without Page Numbers 380
5. A Work by Two or Three Authors 379	14. A Work in an Anthology or Collection of Texts, Essays, Letters, Etc. 380
6. A Work by Four or More Authors 379	15. An Item from a Reference Work 381
7. A Work Authored by an Agency, a Committee, or an Organization 379	16. A Part of a Multivolume Work 381
8. An Anonymous Work 379	17. A Sacred Text or Famous Literary Work 382
9. Two or More Works Included in One Citation 379	18. Quoting Verse 382
	19. Quoting Prose 383

Sample Student Paper: Analytical Research Writing

In the essay below, student writer Stevie Jeung analyzes an unusual topic: the cultural practice of giving condemned criminals a "last supper." As you study her analysis, explore how she thinks through the topic by drawing on various analytical modes.

Writer's Reflection

I wrote this essay for American Studies 101D: Crime and Punishment in American Culture. . . . We were required to choose two of three essay assignments, the first of which simply asked us to discuss "the iconography of the penitentiary." This intriguing first assignment sent so many half-baked ideas whizzing through my head that I almost gave up and resigned myself to the remaining two essay prompts. At just about the last minute, I stumbled upon a topic that compelled me. Suddenly, I just had to find out what was up with this whole last meal thing. Luckily for me, there was plenty to find. Really, who wouldn't love compiling research that included morbid cookbooks, mafia TV, and a poignant but absurd last request for Spaghetti-O's?

—Stevie Jeung

Preparing to read: What are your thoughts about attitudes toward capital punishment? How has this issue been treated in the media? What do you understand about the cultural meaning of crime and punishment?

Analytical Essay

> *A creative title offers a focus for the analysis.*

> *The writer opens with a chronological catalog of executed people and last suppers.*

> *The intro zeros in on the topic, focuses on what is odd or difficult to explain, and announces a search for explanations.*

**"I Did *Not* Get My Spaghetti-O's":
Death Row Consumption in the Popular Media**

Jesus Christ: Roast lamb, matzo, wine; around AD 30. Perry Smith and Richard Hickock: Identical meals of shrimp, french fries, garlic bread, ice cream and strawberries with whipped cream; 1965. Timothy McVeigh: Two pints of Ben & Jerry's mint chocolate chip ice cream; 2001. Tony Soprano: Holsten's onion rings; 2007. Karl Chamberlain: Final meal yet to be consumed; 15 days from now.

While executions historically demand a certain degree of morbid curiosity, the last meals of the condemned seem to stimulate heightened interest. Indeed, a prisoner's final feast has almost become an event in its own right, not only for the prisoner, but for the prison staff and the public. Web sites, novels, movies, television shows, newspapers, and even cookbooks report, dissect, criticize, and speculate regarding last meals real and imagined. When confronted with the ultimate consumption of dying people in so many areas of our popular media, the truth becomes alarmingly clear: This is odd behavior. There must be some reason that we institutionally allow our most hated and feared prisoners to choose and enjoy their final meal before we execute them, and there must be some reason that we like to watch and reproduce the event in popular culture.

■ **Intelligent coaching tone.** In *The Research Writer*, students are addressed directly in a thoughtful, supportive tone—by the authors and by fellow student writers.

The Research Writer: What Supplements Are Available?

Both students and instructors will find helpful supplemental support for the instruction offered in *The Research Writer.*

For the Student

The Research Writer E-Book: The e-book gives students online access to the entire text, along with video and audio explanations that enhance the text, research and writing tutorials, additional research-writing models, and links to carefully selected Web sites.

For the Instructor

Instructor Resource Manual (IRM): The IRM is available in a print version or is downloadable from the instructor's Web site; the document contains an overview of the course, sample syllabi, chapter summaries, and strategies for using the text.

Instructor's Web Site: This password-protected site is accessed at www.theresearchwriter.com. It provides the downloadable version of the Instructor's Resource Manual, assessment rubrics, learning objectives, and access to all materials in the student Web site.

Enhanced InSite for Composition™

Easily create, assign, and grade writing assignments with **Enhanced InSite for Composition.**

From a single, easy-to-navigate site, you can manage the flow of papers, use paperless grading tools, check for originality, and conduct peer reviews. Students gain access to an interactive e-book handbook, Personal Tutor, and resources for writers such as anti-plagiarism tutorials and downloadable grammar podcasts. Additional features include fully integrated discussion boards, streamlined assignment creation, and access to **InfoTrac® College Edition.** To learn more, visit www.cengage.com/insite. *Student access card required.*

Acknowledgements

The authors express their gratitude to the following people, who have contributed to the development of *The Research Writer.*

For their help and advice, thank you to our colleagues in the disciplines and in the library: Deborah Bowen, Hubert Krygsman, Marlene Power, Sheryl Taylor, Derek Schuurman, Jim Vanderwoerd, Marie Versteeg, and John Zwart.

John Van Rys, PhD
Verne Meyer, PhD
Pat Sebranek, MA

Part 1

Conducting and Writing Up Research

Chapters

Thinking Through Research

Q What is research, and what's involved in doing it well? Look around you. What do you see that is the product of research?

All of us do research to find answers to life's questions and to understand matters that matter to us. Whether we are checking out a movie review, following debates on climate change, or tracking down specifications about a car we want to buy, we are locating and using a range of different resources to access, think through, and work with ideas and information.

At first glance, your college research might look quite different. You may see it as a dry-as-dust business locking you into dim libraries and sterile laboratories—all so that you can churn out a dry-as-dust paper that regurgitates the facts you've found. But when it comes to research projects in your courses, nothing is further from the truth. Academic research isn't simply an academic exercise. It's a force for change in the world and in your life.

Ideally, academic research is about *curiosity, discovery,* and *dialogue.*

- **Curiosity:** Your research is driven by true inquiry—your desire to learn more, to know deeply, to solve puzzles that you've come to care about.
- **Discovery:** Conducting quality research, working with resources, and thinking through writing lead you into, what is for you at least, uncharted territory, where you can link what you have newly learned to what you already know.
- **Dialogue:** Through a variety of media, sharing your research findings engages various communities in testing, expanding, and applying knowledge.

While such academic research is perhaps more intense than practical research that we all do each day, they are closely related. In fact, your *personal* research is likely possible only because of someone else's *academic* research.

What's Ahead?

Research Rhetoric: Purpose, Audience, Context

In its simplest sense, research is about answering questions. It is your attempt to discover something through a trustworthy method—a careful, critical investigation that solves a puzzle or problem. In the classical sense, rhetoric refers to the art of persuasion— the impact of language and ideas on an audience. Rhetoric is about getting readers to understand and accept the answers you give them. Research rhetoric, which thus relates to how you *conduct* and *share* research, is at the core of any research project. The rhetorical situation includes three factors: (1) your *purpose* or reason for doing the research in the first place; (2) the *audience* who will read, listen to, or view the results of your research; and (3) the *context* for your research project (e.g., the course).

College research projects are highly diverse, differing not just from discipline to discipline but from course to course. Think about the research project described below, noting how the rhetorical situation directs the project.

> **Assignment:** In your textbook and in class, you were introduced to trauma theory as it relates to psychological disorders. In a 1,250–1,500 word paper, research one particular form of trauma in terms of its causes and effects on humans, and explore treatment methods that make sense for such trauma. Also prepare to present your research results in class.
>
> > *Purpose:* To deepen students' understanding of a complex psychological problem, going beyond introductory insights.
> >
> > *Audience:* Professor and classmates, an expert and fellow majors in Psychology
> >
> > *Context:* Meets course requirement of inquiry-focused learning; involves both written and oral presentation of learning

Research rhetoric emphasizes that research is not disinterested, objective, or disconnected from life. Rather, all research is *connected, directed,* and *applied:* connected to personal and cultural forces (including past research), directed by specific interests, and applied to concrete situations. Nevertheless, we can identify a range of research positions:

Biased research is distorted and foreclosed by a strongly slanted belief. **Backed research** is beholden to a particular group or organization. **Interested research** is guided by a particular set of values and may have a certain preferred set of results. **Independent research** is relatively unconstrained by special interests or allegiances.

Clearly, in your college research projects, you would hope to do either interested or independent research, governed by a distinct understanding of your *purpose, audience,* and *context*—topics addressed on the pages that follow.

Your Research Purpose

Your research purpose is what you hope to accomplish *in* and *through* your research. What exactly do you hope to discover, and why? What do you hope to do with your discoveries? Here are some tips for identifying your purpose:

- **Making Course Connections:** A research assignment usually relates to a course concept that your instructor wants you to learn more about. (See "Understanding Assignments and Expectations," p. 14.) For example, in an English course on literary fiction, your assignment may focus on postcolonialism, a phenomenon introduced in class.

- **Building Research Skills:** Strengthening your research skills is a key goal of your major assignments. Consider how a particular assignment will test your library skills, Internet capability, note-taking strategies, thinking patterns, and writing ability. For example, a history paper may require that you work with some primary documents and also learn to use the JSTOR database.

- **Aiming at Truth:** Your main goal is ultimately to discover the complex truth about a topic. Think about how you can discover and engage that truth, particularly by remembering, analyzing, contextualizing, intuiting, synthesizing, and/or arguing. For example, in an economics paper on the oil sector, you may need to analyze the complex cause-effect forces behind rising and falling oil prices.

- **Reaching Readers:** Know how you want to impact readers. Do you want to inform, persuade, or do both? Do you want to create understanding or change attitudes and behaviors? Do you want to entertain, share discoveries, answer a question, or offer a solution to a problem? For example, in a paper for a nursing course, you may intend to deepen your fellow students' understanding of dementia and persuade them to adopt certain best practices for treating patients with this illness.

 FOCUS on Research Essentials: Although it is something of a false distinction, scholars sometimes distinguish between *pure* and *applied* research. The purpose of the first is to seek answers to intellectual questions and puzzles; the purpose of the second is to put research answers to use. As you work on your college research projects, consider how they involve both pure and applied research.

Your Research Audience

You will be sharing your research results with other people, your audience. Smart researchers figure out where these people are coming from in terms of their values, needs, attitudes toward the topic, level of understanding, and expectations. Consider these potential members of your "research community":

- **Yourself:** In one sense, you are always your own research audience. You are researching and writing in order to discover and understand.
- **Your Professor:** Often, your audience may be limited to the instructor who will read, comment on, and grade your paper. The paper must speak to this reader's expectations.
- **The Academic Community:** Generally, your research writing addresses "the academic community"—curious, educated readers like your professor and classmates. In a sense, these readers function as your judge and jury. They are willing to acknowledge the truth when they hear it, but they are also restrained by some healthy skepticism that keeps demanding, "Prove it!"
- **An Interest-Based Community:** Your audience may be quite specific (e.g., fellow nursing majors or readers of J. R. R. Tolkien's work). As a group with common interests, you form a well-defined research community that shares knowledge, attitudes, and methods.
- **The Global Community:** On the Internet, anyone around the globe with access to a computer can potentially read your research.

FOCUS on Your Project: Who is the audience for your project—your professor, your classmates, or people searching the Web? With these readers in mind, consider the following questions:

1. What are your readers' values, needs, and priorities, and how do these relate to your research topic and findings? How would you answer the question "So what?" about your topic and your ideas?

2. What attitude do you think your audience has toward you and your topic? How would you characterize their level of curiosity about the matter?

3. What does your audience understand about the topic? What do they already know, and what do they need to know? How does this information impact your research and the way you share your research results?

4. What conventions of research writing (form, format, methods) does your audience expect you to follow?

5. What will your audience do with your research results? Will they use your writing to arrive at new understandings, to inform their choices, to adopt new attitudes, to take action?

The Context of Your Research

The research context refers to the conditions under which you are doing your research, writing it up, and sharing it with others. For your college research projects, the obvious context is the college course itself, with its requirements, expectations, and dynamics. Here are some key issues to think through:

- **Understand your own perspective.** You are a person with an identity, with interests, with values, and with experiences that you bring to any project. As you think about a research project for a specific course, ask yourself these questions:

  Where am I coming from as a researcher and a writer?

  What are my experiences with conducting research?

  What is my background and culture?

  What are my core values and my view of the world, and how do these relate to the research I must do?

- **Understand the practical limits or constraints of your project.** Considering your particular college or university context, ask yourself these questions:

  When must the project be finished, and how much time can I dedicate to it, given other course work and projects?

  What resources do I have available in terms of library access, online materials, software, and so on?

- **Understand the form of research writing required.**
  Research writing differs from discipline to discipline, assignment to assignment. It is crucial to know what research form you must follow— from the expected page margins to the paper's parts to the thinking patterns employed. Ask yourself these questions:

  What am I writing? A basic report supplying information, or a more complex essay or argument involving analysis, synthesis, and application?

  Which of the forms of research writing listed at the right am I producing, and what are its conventions?

Discipline Forms	
personal-research paper	(ch. 12)
analytical paper	(ch. 13)
argumentative paper	(ch. 14)
IMRAD report	(ch. 15)
literary analysis	(ch. 16)
review of literature	(ch. 17)

 FOCUS on Your Project: Try completing and expanding this statement: "In this research project on [topic], my main goal is to answer [essential question] so that my readers can [understanding or action statement]."

Developing Strong Research Writing

Essentially, strong research writing demonstrates these traits: solid ideas, logical organization, engaging voice, clear word choice, smooth sentences, correct copy, and professional design. As you work on projects, review your writing for these traits and use them to improve your work.

Strong Ideas

Ideas are the concepts you discover and develop through your research and writing. They are the content of your research writing, making it substantial and meaningful.

Develop:
- A thesis that is clear, sharp, and thoughtful; the support strong and balanced
- Researched data that is accurate and complete
- Interpretations and conclusions that follow logically from the information
- Proper crediting of all borrowed ideas and information

Avoid:
- Domination of source material over your own ideas
- Unsourced thinking and writing
- Unrefined/raw data; no thesis
- Nonthesis-related discussion/tangents
- Copy-and-paste composition
- Sloppy/missing documentation

Logical Organization

Organization creates structure and flow, guiding the reader through your research writing. Logical organization demonstrates ordered thinking.

Develop:
- Information that is delivered through a clear chain of ideas
- A paper that includes a clear opening presenting the purpose and scope of the research, a middle that provides complete data and discussion, and a closing that focuses on conclusions and next steps
- Paragraphs that offer unified, coherent, and complete points in support of the thesis
- Transitions and techniques such as parallel structure to link and order ideas

Avoid:
- Incoherent delivery of findings
- Nonexplicit/fuzzy connections
- Haphazard listing/ordering of ideas

Engaging Voice

Voice refers to how your writing "sounds"—the attitude and personality that come through. An engaging research voice draws the reader in.

Develop:
- A tone that is confident but also sincere, measured, and objective
- An attitude that objectively acknowledges uncertainty
- A mature academic style

Avoid:
- Unreasonable/overconfident/demanding voice
- Flat/boring/overly timid tone
- Use of personal pronouns I, we, and you (See your instructor about this.)

Clear Words

The words you use carry your meaning. Choose them with care.

Develop:
- Clear phrasing throughout the paper
- Language that readers will understand, using direct/plain English whenever possible
- Precise use of technical terms, defining them as needed

Avoid:
- Writing filled with obscure jargon
- Words chosen to impress
- Careless/confusing/incorrect use of terminology

Smooth Sentences

Sentences express complete thoughts and require careful construction.

Develop:
- Constructions that flow smoothly, with a good blend of sentence lengths (short and punchy, long and thoughtful) and patterns (loose, balanced, periodic)
- Sentences that carefully integrate source material

Avoid:
- Choppy or rambling constructions
- Nonsensical sentences
- Ineffective/clumsy integration of source material

Correct Copy

Correct writing follows the conventions of language, creating clarity and a positive impression.

Develop:
- Grammar, punctuation, mechanics, usage, and spelling that are correct—especially punctuation used with source material
- Documentation of research that is complete and correct, following an appropriate style (MLA, APA, CMS, CSE)

Avoid:
- Obvious/basic errors
- Faulty/confusing sentence structure
- Punctuation and spacing errors related to documentation

Professional Design

Document design refers to the appearance of your writing on the page, the poster, the screen, and so on. Professional design of your research writing builds credibility.

Develop:
- Correct document format (e.g., research paper, lab report, poster presentation, Web site)
- Attractive page layout making ideas and information accessible
- Reader-friendly typography (typefaces and sizes)
- Effectively presented data in discussions, lists, tables, charts, graphs, etc.

Avoid:
- Design that hinders access and understanding
- Design different from expected research form

Weak Research Writing: An Example

Read the poor research writing shown below, noting the trait-based sidenotes to the left. Simple editing will not make this piece acceptable; the paper must be thoroughly researched, rethought, and rewritten.

IDEAS
Generally in focus, but contains weak ideas, insight, and documentation: the writing asks readers to change their understanding and attitudes based on personal opinions alone, not researched evidence.

ORGANIZATION
Develops no clear research-based thesis, no orderly analysis or argument, and reaches no research-based conclusion.

VOICE
Uses informal street language; speaker seems uninformed; expresses personal opinions, not researched arguments.

WORDS
Uses slang words *(like)*, misused words *(do, whose)*, and cliches *(today's society)*; contains no research-based terminology.

SENTENCES
Some sentences are incomplete, choppy, or redundant.

CORRECTNESS
Contains usage errors *(whose)*, grammar errors *(they got)*, and incorrect punctuation *(!!)*.

DESIGN
Displays poor layout, margins, and spacing.

Give Animals a Break!

In today's society you hear lots of different ideas toward animals. Like, are they smart or not, or are they worth saving from extinction? Well, obviously, they're not as smart as us because even the stupidest people are smarter than the most intelligent animals.

But let's be fair and give animals their just do. You have to admit that animals do some things better than people and some things worse. That's the way to come to a fair assessment of the animal kingdom and not show prejudice.

Like bees, who knows what a bee thinks. In fact, I read somewhere that they got about 10,000 eyes and people just got two. So whose superior?

You know, people are always criticizing animals saying he's a pig or she's a dog or whatever. But if you're a cat, you can practically see in the dark, and if you're a dog you can hear high pitch whistles that people can't hear. In fact, even pigs are pretty smart, about equal to a horse. And dolphins—do I need to even talk about dolphins? Dolphins rock!!

FOCUS on Ethics: In the real world, sloppy research and untrustworthy ideas don't simply lead to a poor grade. Poor research fosters errors that can put people in harm's way. For example, for more than a decade a debate has been going on about the safety of childhood vaccinations—with some people claiming that immunizations are linked to autism. Poor understanding of the scientific issues and studies have led some parents to choose against immunizing their children, opening them and others to some serious illnesses. The lesson? In your own research and research writing, proceed with caution!

Strong Research Writing: An Example

The model below is an excerpt from an essay by student-writer Stevie Jeung. Her research focus is the cultural significance of condemned criminals' last meals. The full paper, a project that Stevie completed for an American Studies course focusing on crime and punishment, is on pages 301–307.

Jeung 1

Stevie Jeung

Professor Sasha Abramsky

American Studies 101D

17 February 2007

"I Did *Not* Get My Spaghetti-O's":

Death Row Consumption in the Popular Media

Jesus Christ: Roast lamb, matzo, wine; around AD 30. Perry Smith and Richard Hickock: Identical meals of shrimp, french fries, garlic bread, ice cream and strawberries with whipped cream; 1965. Timothy McVeigh: Two pints of Ben & Jerry's mint chocolate chip ice cream: 2001. Tony Soprano: Holsten's onion rings; 2007. Karl Chamberlein: final meal yet to be consumed: 15 days from now.

While executions historically demand a certain degree of morbid curiosity, the last meals of the condemned seem to stimulate heightened interest. Indeed, a prisoner's final feast has almost become an event in its own right, not only for the prisoner, but for the prison staff and the public. Web sites, novels, movies, television shows, newspapers, and even cookbooks report, dissect, criticize, and speculate regarding last meals real and imagined. When confronted with the ultimate consumption of dying people in so many areas of our popular media, the truth becomes alarmingly clear: This is odd behavior. There must be some reason that we institutionally allow our most hated and feared prisoners to choose and enjoy their final meal before we execute them, and there must be some reason that we like to watch and reproduce the event in popular culture.

IDEAS

Focuses on the author's fresh insight into a focused issue. Debts to others are suitably acknowledged.

ORGANIZATION

Each paragraph advances the analysis with information, ideas, and illustrations. Transitional phrases show the logic connecting sentences.

VOICE

Exhibits the confident voice of someone who has mastered the main subject and has thought both critically and creatively about it.

WORDS

Consistently uses mature vocabulary suitable to the topic and the reader; defines unfamiliar terms.

Jeung 2

SENTENCES
Author skillfully crafts sentences that express complex thoughts; sentence variety creates energy.

CORRECTNESS
Uses correct conventions in punctuation, spelling, capitalization, and grammar.

VISUAL DESIGN
Comfortable paragraph length creates order and rests the reader's eyes. The paper heading is correct and MLA formatting is followed throughout.

The last meal appears in almost every major arena of public entertainment. In *The Green Mile,* a motion picture based on Stephen King's novel of the same name, protagonist John Coffey is wrongfully executed in a heartbreaking, dramatic scene, but not before careful thought about his last meal: "Meatloaf be nice. Mashed taters with gravy. Okra, maybe. I's not picky." Prisoners are also served their last meals on the small screen. Take, for example, FOX's network TV show, *Prison Break,* in which Lincoln Burrows is served his last blueberry pancakes. In fact, on an episode of *The Simpsons,* a staple of American television, Homer eats Hans Moleman's last meal of lobster tail and raspberry tort just before Hans is executed, protesting, "But he ate my last meal!" Clearly, this animated man did not think it right to be executed without enjoying his final choice of cuisine. Of course, his expression of outrage is followed by, "Are you really allowed to execute people in a local jail?" reminding us that *The Simpsons,* however rich with American icons, is not real. Regardless of actual death row ceremony, the Americans who produce and consume these works of fiction expect that a special meal accompanies execution. . . .

FOCUS on Your Major: The seven traits of effective research writing transfer from one discipline to another, with modifications that fit the given discipline. For example, humanities research may be thesis driven, whereas science research is hypothesis driven, this difference naturally affecting how the ideas are expressed and organized within a paper. To learn how the seven traits are applied to writing in your field, do the following:

- Read the literature in your field, noting how it practices the traits.
- Visit the campus writing center and ask for an assessment of your writing.
- Ask a professor or upper-level student in your field to assess your writing and offer suggestions.
- Search online for OWLs (online writing labs) that post writing samples, rubrics, and instructional material for writing in your discipline. You could start with Purdue University's OWL: owl.english.purdue.edu.

Following the Research Process

At one extreme, a research project can bore you, and at the other, it can paralyze you with worry. The solution to both problems is a workable research process.

Generally, the research process breaks down into three phases: planning, conducting, and synthesizing. Typically, however, real research is dynamic, involving both system and serendipity, method and openness. For example, you may think during the planning phase that you've nailed down your topic, only to discover during the conducting phase that you need to adjust your topic. In spite of such inevitable detours, the research process maps out as shown below. When you get your research assignment, review the process and tailor it to your task.

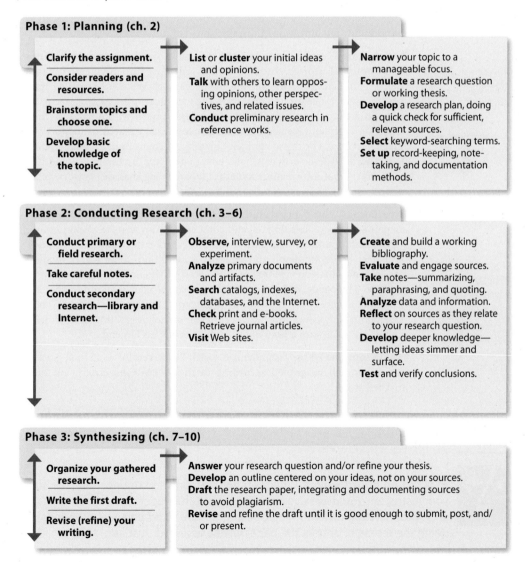

Phase 1: Planning (ch. 2)

Clarify the assignment.

Consider readers and resources.

Brainstorm topics and choose one.

Develop basic knowledge of the topic.

List or **cluster** your initial ideas and opinions.
Talk with others to learn opposing opinions, other perspectives, and related issues.
Conduct preliminary research in reference works.

Narrow your topic to a manageable focus.
Formulate a research question or working thesis.
Develop a research plan, doing a quick check for sufficient, relevant sources.
Select keyword-searching terms.
Set up record-keeping, note-taking, and documentation methods.

Phase 2: Conducting Research (ch. 3–6)

Conduct primary or field research.

Take careful notes.

Conduct secondary research—library and Internet.

Observe, interview, survey, or experiment.
Analyze primary documents and artifacts.
Search catalogs, indexes, databases, and the Internet.
Check print and e-books. Retrieve journal articles.
Visit Web sites.

Create and build a working bibliography.
Evaluate and engage sources.
Take notes—summarizing, paraphrasing, and quoting.
Analyze data and information.
Reflect on sources as they relate to your research question.
Develop deeper knowledge— letting ideas simmer and surface.
Test and verify conclusions.

Phase 3: Synthesizing (ch. 7–10)

Organize your gathered research.

Write the first draft.

Revise (refine) your writing.

Answer your research question and/or refine your thesis.
Develop an outline centered on your ideas, not on your sources.
Draft the research paper, integrating and documenting sources to avoid plagiarism.
Revise and refine the draft until it is good enough to submit, post, and/ or present.

Understanding Assignments and Expectations

When your instructors give you a research-writing assignment, your first task is to understand that assignment thoroughly. Most professors will spell out (1) the objective, (2) the task, (3) the research requirements, (4) the format requirements, and (5) suggested approaches and topics.

For example, study the term-paper assignment below, given in a second-year course on politics and the environment. Then review the concepts of **research expectations** (p. 15), **assignment key words** (pp. 16–17), **topic options and restrictions** (p. 18), **project parameters** (p. 19), and **assignment connections** (p. 19).

Title	**Assignment:** The Environment in the News
Project subject, with topic examples	**Description:** Over the past months, the news has been sprinkled with environmental stories, broadly conceived: the Copenhagen climate change conference; the BP oil spill in the Gulf of Mexico; Kyoto and the government's stance on it; global warming's impact on the Arctic ice cap; a study projecting that ocean fish stocks could disappear within 50 years; the strains on farm land created by urban development; a march in support of "green vaccines." For this assignment, identify an environmental issue in the news and analyze how that issue is being addressed by the media and by politicians. What information and attitudes are being shared? How do these relate to the scientific studies behind the issue?
Project objective and task	
Research requirements	**Expectations:** This paper requires careful, well-documented research if you are going to be credible, logical, and compelling. Aim to use a minimum of eight quality resources. While these resources can be electronic, they should have clear academic depth and integrity. In addition, these works should give evidence that you explored multiple perspectives on your topic, not just one side. The paper, which is worth 20 percent of your final grade, should be approximately 2,000-2,500 words (8-10 typed, double-spaced pages) and documented according to Chicago/Turabian guidelines. A first draft is due on November 28, and a final polished draft is due on December 7.
Paper weight, length, documentation, due dates	
Assessment method	**Evaluation:** The whole assignment is worth 20 percent of your final grade. The paper will be graded according to the seven-traits criteria on the attached sheet.

FOCUS on Your Project: Whenever you are confused or uncertain, talk to your instructor. You may have questions about the paper's goal, your audience, an appropriate topic, the format, documentation, using personal pronouns, doing the research, or how the paper will be assessed. Just ask.

Research Expectations

The elements below will likely be covered in your assignment description. After considering this information, ask your instructor for clarification as needed.

Primary and Secondary Sources: Should you avoid tertiary sources, such as general encyclopedias and Wikipedia? Can you start with such sources, without relying on them in your writing? Do you need to focus on secondary sources only, primary sources, or some blend of the two? (For more on these distinctions, see pages 34–37.)

Published and Personal Sources: Should you stick with published materials, or can you include personal observations and experiences?

Scholarly and Popular Sources: Should you limit yourself to academic and scholarly resources, or can you also use more popular sources?

Source Currency: For this particular project, how current should your sources be? Is there a restriction on how old a print or electronic source can be?

Print and Electronic Sources: Are you allowed to use narrowly defined Internet and free-Web resources? Or must you restrict yourself to print resources (or electronic resources available through subscription academic databases)?

Numbers of Sources: Must you use a certain number of books, journal articles, and so on? Are you restricted to one or two Web sites? What is the appropriate number of resources for this project?

Research Methods: Does the assignment specify or imply a particular research methodology? Does it require, for example, that you follow certain principles of text analysis, historical investigation, field research, human-subject study, or laboratory experimentation?

Research Style and Voice: Stylistically, are you allowed to use the first-person pronouns "I" and "we" or the second-person "you"? Or are you expected to remain strictly neutral and objective, using only "he," "she," "they," and "one"?

FOCUS on Your Major: As you begin to work on research assignments in your chosen major, pay attention to how research is done in your discipline. What types of resources are respected? What are the key scholarly journals and Web sites? What research methodologies are followed, and why? What materials are typically used?

Assignment Key Words

Key verbs in the assignment description will explain your main task. Generally, these tasks involve informing, analyzing, or persuading, with specific terms suggesting shades of emphasis. Study the list below and on the next page, noting the action each word calls for, which should become the focus of your research energy.

Terms That Call for Informing: With terms like these, your task is essentially to provide details or data in an orderly way. You are not required to interpret the meaning of that information or take a position on the issue.

■ **Describe:** To describe is to show in detail what something is like. Concerned with appearance and structure in the physical world, description appeals to the senses.

> Supplying specific details, **describe** the social conditions in France prior to the French Revolution.

■ **Find:** Finding refers to tracking down and sharing specific information.

■ **Review:** To review is to reexamine the key characteristics, major points, or varied positions on a topic. Generally, a review presents material in chronological order or in decreasing order of importance.

■ **Summarize:** Summarizing involves briefly presenting the main ideas or points of a topic. Details, illustrations, examples, and full explanations are usually left out. In your research writing, you may be asked to include a summary with your larger project.

Terms That Call for Analyzing: With terms like these, you are expected to make sense of a topic, information, or concepts through particular thinking principles or patterns. However, you are not necessarily required to take a position on the issue.

■ **Analyze:** To analyze is to break down a problem, a situation, an object, or a phenomenon into its constituent parts and then show how they relate to one another and/or the principles of how they work.

■ **Classify:** To classify is to sort out or arrange a broad group of related items (e.g., people, places, animals, plants, things, concepts), ordering them into comprehensive categories rooted in distinct characteristics.

■ **Compare and Contrast:** A comparison explains how things are similar in one or more important ways, while a contrast points out important differences. Sometimes instructors use "compare" to mean "compare and contrast." Ask for clarification, if needed, about the approach you need to take, including whether you ought to balance points of comparison with points of contrast or stress one over the other.

■ **Define:** Definition involves giving a clear, thoughtful explanation of what something means. In a research project focused on definition, you will likely be developing an extended definition that delves into a term's complexity, its history, its relationship to other terms, its importance, and so on.

- **Discuss:** To discuss is to explore an issue from all sides.
- **Examine:** To examine something is to look closely at it in order to understand more fully and deeply what it is, what makes it work, and so on.
- **Explain:** To explain is to bring out into the open, to make clear. This term is similar to *discuss* but places more emphasis on cause/effect relationships or step-by-step sequences.

> Based on your research into the forces that contribute to wellness, **explain** a major factor that impedes human well-being.

- **Interpret:** Interpretation involves explaining what something—a literary text, a historical event, a patient's psychiatric symptoms—means and how that meaning is produced. (Synonym: develop a reading of)
- **Investigate:** To investigate is to dig deeply to discover the facts and the truth, and to bring these to light for understanding. (Synonym: explore)
- **Reflect:** Reflecting involves sharing your well-researched and well-considered thoughts about a subject. Reflection makes room for musing in research writing.
- **Study:** Studying refers to looking closely at a topic in order to understand more fully its essential principles, its parts, its nature, and so on.
- **Synthesize:** Synthesis combines elements into a new whole, typically through predicting, inventing, redesigning, or imagining.
- **Trace:** To trace is to present—in a step-by-step sequence—a series of facts that are somehow related. Usually the facts are presented in chronological order; sometimes explaining the cause/effect relationships between steps is implied by the term *trace*.

Terms That Focus on Persuading: With terms like these, you are expected to take a position on an issue that is debatable or contested. Persuading in a research paper usually involves both informing and analyzing.

- **Argue:** To argue is to support a claim with logical reasoning backed up by valid evidence. You may be taking a position on an issue, persuading readers to act, or offering a solution to a problem.

> In recent years, cuts to education funding have led many high schools to trim or eliminate their music programs. Using reliable research, **argue** for or against these cuts.

- **Defend:** Defense involves adopting a particular stance on an issue and supporting that stance with the best evidence available, while acknowledging opposition.
- **Evaluate:** Evaluation involves making a value judgment by presenting pluses and minuses, positives and negatives, along with supporting evidence. (Synonym: judge)
- **Prove:** Proving involves marshalling strong evidence in favor of a specific claim.
- **Support:** Supporting a point involves marshalling the best reasoning and evidence to prove your claim.

Topic Options and Restrictions

The assignment often gives you topic or approach options, but it may also restrict those choices. Note the options and restrictions in the following assignment:

Assignment: Investigate how a natural disaster or major historical event has altered people's understanding of religion or government.

Options: You may choose any natural disaster or historical event. You may focus on religion or government. You may examine any kind of alteration related to any group of people.

Restrictions: You must examine closely a cause-effect relationship limited to people's religious or political understanding. The disaster must be natural and the historical event must be major.

Research assignments differ, then, in terms of how broadly or narrowly they specify your topic. On the one hand, an assignment may be wide open, giving you lots of freedom to formulate a topic, and on the other, it may spell out strict limitations that you must follow. Read the assignment carefully and look for the following types of restrictions:

Restriction Types	
Time Frame:	What period must you stay within, whether a century or a day?
Location:	Where must you stay, whether on a continent or in a town?
Political Body:	Must you limit your attention to a nation, state, province, county, municipality, or government agency?
Segment of Society:	Must you focus on a particular gender, ethnic group, race, class, or industry?
Depth of View:	Does the assignment restrict you to a limited, in-depth analysis or allow you to deal with the broader, bigger picture?
Portion of the Whole:	Are you restricted to a specific part of a larger topic?
Level of Seriousness or Significance:	Must you stick with a major, sober aspect of the topic, or can you handle the more lighthearted or ironic elements?

Project Parameters

Your research assignment may specify clear parameters concerning objectives, format, due dates, and so on: Pay attention to these requirements to keep your project in focus and on track.

The Rhetorical Situation: How does the assignment specify your goals for the project and describe the intended audience? See "Research Rhetoric," pages 4–7.

Form and Format: Ask, what are the assignment's requirements in terms of paper length (pages or words); due dates for choosing a topic, finishing research, completing a first draft, submitting a final draft, presenting your results; and format (parts, headings, spacing, margins, and so on)? Which presentation and documentation style must you use: MLA (ch. 18), APA (ch. 19), CMS (ch. 20), or CSE (ch. 21)?

Assessment: How will the assignment be evaluated and by whom? Can you obtain help (brainstorming, proofreading) and from whom (instructor, classmates, writing-center tutor)? At what stages during the process may you ask for help? Which of the seven traits, and which particular elements of each, will your instructor assess in your final work? (See pages 8–12.)

Assignment Connections

A useful strategy for thoroughly understanding your research assignment is to put it in perspective by linking it to other important issues.

Course Requirements:
- How much value (often expressed as a percentage of your final grade) has the instructor given this research assignment?
- What benefit does the assessment hold for you? (Understand course content more fully? Improve your research skills? Refine your ability to describe, explain, or persuade? Broaden understanding of workplace and societal issues? Increase your creativity?)
- How will this assignment help you achieve the course goals?

Other Research Assignments:
- How does this assignment build on previous research and writing assignments?
- How does it prepare you for the next assignment?

Your Major and Your Own Interests:
- How does the research assignment connect with topics that interest you?
- How does it connect with work in your other courses, particularly courses in your major? How does the research relate to the methods of your discipline?
- How does it connect with work that you may do in your career?
- How does it connect with local, national, or global issues?

Brainstorming and Refining Topics

Strong research starts with a strong topic. But what makes for a strong topic, and how do you arrive at one for your project? The process of arriving at a strong topic involves two seemingly opposite steps: (1) brainstorming many possibilities and (2) committing to the most promising option. You'll need some strategies for expanding your possibilities and then narrowing them to one workable topic.

Brainstorming Viable Topics

Finding a research topic that meets the assignment requirements grows out of a variety of explorations and preliminary searches. Employ the following strategies to begin your search:

1. **Check** your class notes and handouts for ideas related to the assignment.
2. **Search** the Internet. Type a keyword or phrase into a search engine or explore a subject tree. What topics turn up?
3. **Consult** indexes, guides, and other library references. An electronic database like EBSCOhost, for example, lists articles published on specific topics and explains where to find the articles (see pages 61–65). Typically, you'll find abstracts (summaries) and links to full-text versions, if available, so that you can scan material for topic ideas.
4. **Discuss** the assignment with your instructor, a librarian, or classmates.
5. **Attend** to your daily reading, listening, and viewing. Look for connections to your research subject.

In addition, generate research ideas with prewriting strategies like those described below and on the following pages. The value of these techniques is that they tap into your powers of association—your ability to mentally link topics and ideas.

Freewriting: Write nonstop for 10 minutes or longer to discover possible writing ideas. Use a key concept related to the assignment as a starting point. Soon you will discover potential writing ideas that you might otherwise not have considered. Write whatever comes to your mind—and don't stop to correct typos and other mistakes. In the example below, the student writer freewrites about reality TV shows for a project in a media studies course.

> *It seems like TV has gotten overrun with reality TV shows in the past few years—there's ones about love, like The Bachelor, and of course there's Survivor But why are there so many reality shows now, and what's that about? Is it just about ratings—these are shows that attract lots of viewers, and why is that? Maybe it's the voyeur in the viewer. Of course, reality tv in many ways isn't real at all but staged. The camera changes the way people act automatically, so the shows are "scripted" so to speak. Maybe that's what I could explore—the irony that reality tv isn't actually real.*

Listing: Freely list ideas as they come to mind, beginning with a key word or concept in the assignment. For example, if *water* appears in the assignment, write the word; then below it, list related terms like *rivers, drinking water, pollution, wells,* and so on. The key is to list whatever related terms come to mind: don't worry about judging or evaluating the choices right away. Here are three more examples:

Music	Housing	Genetics
Music therapy	Urban sprawl	Genetically engineered
Pop music	Affordability	food
Rap	Mortgage crisis	Cloning animals
R&B	Living in downtown	Reproductive
Music industry	Homelessness	technologies
Health	The suburbs	Gene therapies
Illegal downloads	Construction industry	The human genome
iPod development	Cottage	project
Concerts	Country	Genetics and crime
Crossover songs	Energy efficiency	Stem-cell controversies

Clustering: To begin the clustering process, write in the center of your paper a key word or idea from the assignment. Circle the word, and then cluster ideas around it. Circle each idea as you record it, and draw a line connecting it to the closest related idea. Keep going until you run out of ideas and connections. The value of the cluster is its ability to visually map out topics, subtopics, and relationships, as shown below in the cluster on "body art."

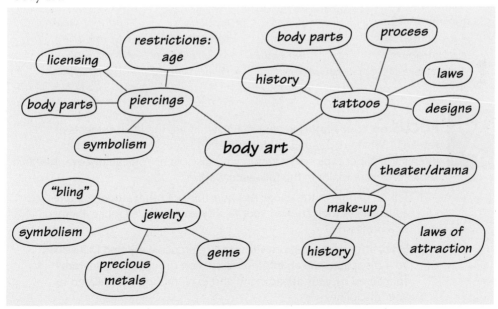

The Essentials of Life List: Below is a list of the major categories into which most essential things in our lives are divided. The list provides an endless variety of research topic possibilities.

Essentials of Life List

agriculture	clothing	friends	machines
animals	education	freedom/rights	measurements
art	emotions	fuel/heat	money/trade
books	energy	goals/purpose	music
careers	entertainment	health/medicine	natural resources
charity/	environment	housing	plants
citizenship	exercise	intelligence/mind	politics
communication	faith/religion	identity	recreation
community	family	land/property	science
computers	food	love	travel

Note how the highlighted categories can be grown into numerous research possibilities.

computers	education	identity	travel
• Google power	• Online	• Role of race	• Post 9/11
• PC vs. Apple	education	• Gender	security
• Online dating	• Funding	differences	• Occupational
• Internet crime	student loans	• Immigrant	mobility
• Online	• Learning	identity	• Energy
communities	disabilities	• Identity	conservation
• e-commerce	• Marvin Tromp,	formation in	• Commuting
• open-source	an influential	children	• National-
software	educator	• Brain trauma	park history

FOCUS on Your Major: In your major, what are the main subjects of research? What are the debatable, contested issues in the field? What interesting paper topics exist within your discipline? You can discover research subjects in your major in the following ways:

1. Talk to people in the know: Ask questions of other students more advanced in their studies, your faculty advisor, a reference librarian, or a professor.

2. Read, attend, and explore: Pick up a reference work that focuses on your discipline, join an Internet discussion group, attend lectures sponsored by your department, and explore Web sites related to your discipline.

Choosing a Narrow, Manageable Topic

Once you have brainstormed a set of possible topics, you need to assess those possibilities, choose the most promising topic, and focus on a specific feature or angle that allows for in-depth research. Use the strategies that follow to that end.

Choose Your Topic: From all the topics you have brainstormed, choose the best one for this particular research assignment.

A strong topic . . .

- ☑ meets the requirements of the assignment,
- ☑ is limited in scope rather than broad and encyclopedic,
- ☑ will appeal to and intrigue a knowledgeable audience,
- ☑ will require that you stretch yourself intellectually,
- ☑ seems practical (within your means to research), and
- ☑ sincerely interests you.

Refine the Topic You Have Chosen: As noted in the list above, a strong topic must be limited in scope so that you can aim for depth rather than breadth in your research and writing. Moreover, the topic must be manageable within the time and space constraints of your research assignment. To narrow your topic, zoom in for a closer look at it by taking steps like these:

1. **Check your topic.** Look in the *Library of Congress Subject Headings*, available in your library. Note "narrower topics" listed (see page 46).

2. **Read about your topic.** Consult specialized reference works to explore background that directs you to subtopics (see page 67–70). Also do a preliminary search of books and journal articles in your library. While books may offer broad information about a topic, individual chapters may address subtopics. Check the table of contents or index for interesting subtopics. Scan journal articles for insights into specific aspects of your topic.

3. **Check the Internet.** Do a keyword search or follow a subject directory to see where your topic leads (see pages 94–97). What intriguing dimensions of the topic show up?

4. **Return to brainstorming.** Continue freewriting (page 20) or clustering (page 21) to discover what aspect of the topic you are most interested in. Work to discover a fresh angle on the topic.

5. **Discuss your chosen topic.** Talk with classmates and your instructor, interview an expert, or raise the topic in an online discussion group.

6. **Focus your topic.** Consider specific methods of limiting your topic: addressing a local angle; exploring the topic's relevance for a particular group of people; linking the topic with a personal concern; or considering the topic in a particular time frame, space, or circumstance.

By following the brainstorming and selecting process described earlier, you will move from the assigned subject to a narrowed, manageable topic, as shown with the examples below.

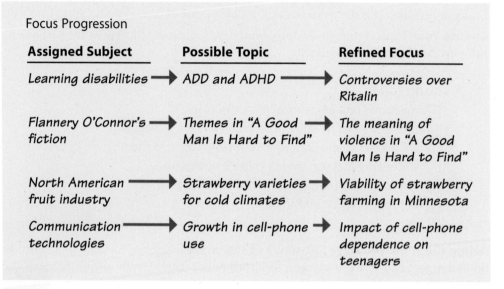

Focus Progression

Assigned Subject	**Possible Topic**	**Refined Focus**
Learning disabilities ➔	ADD and ADHD ➔	Controversies over Ritalin
Flannery O'Connor's fiction ➔	Themes in "A Good Man Is Hard to Find" ➔	The meaning of violence in "A Good Man Is Hard to Find"
North American fruit industry ➔	Strawberry varieties for cold climates ➔	Viability of strawberry farming in Minnesota
Communication technologies ➔	Growth in cell-phone use ➔	Impact of cell-phone dependence on teenagers

FOCUS on Your Project: The shift from a possible topic to a specific, refined focus is crucial to doing quality research. A refined focus points you toward the topic's complexities, its puzzles, the gaps and inconsistencies that evoke more intriguing research, writing, and reading. (Note, for example, how the refined topics above identity puzzles, challenges, and problems.) Such focus also helps you develop meaningful research questions as well as a working thesis and title.

Once you have identified your focus, you can test it, making sure that it will work for you and for your assignment. Take the following steps to assess whether you can commit to your topic and use it to complete your research assignment:

1. Do a quick search of the library catalog, electronic journal databases, and the Web to see if quality resources relevant to this narrowed topic are available. If you can, consult with a reference librarian. Then get started on developing a working knowledge of your topic by reading reference works, introductions to the subject, and basic articles in news sources.

2. Create a table entitled "Starting Points for Researching [Topic]." Label two columns "What I know" and "What I need to learn." Then fill in the columns as fully as you can until you have a sense of whether and how you might complete this research project successfully.

For ideas and help with selecting and refining research topics, visit our Web site at **www.theresearchwriter.com.**

Developing Research Questions

If you have to wear glasses or contacts, you understand blurriness. Blurry research is out-of-focus research. If you have refined your focus to a manageable topic (pages 23–24), things are getting less blurry for you. And now they can become even clearer by developing research questions. Such questions are important because they help direct you to meaningful information and ideas about your topic. Brainstorm a list of questions by following the strategies below.

Simple and Complex Questions Simple or basic questions aim for factual answers. More complex questions involve analysis, synthesis, and evaluation. Often, simple questions must be answered first, prior to delving into more complex questions of interpretation and debate. (Note that most of your college research projects will require you to focus on the complex questions.)

> **Simple Question:** How much fast food does the average person eat?
>
> **Complex Question:** How does eating fast food affect overall health?

Primary and Secondary Questions Ask a primary question about your topic—the main issue that you want to get at. Then brainstorm secondary questions that you need to research in order to answer your primary question.

> **Primary Question:** What are the primary causes of childhood obesity?
> **Secondary Questions** (who, what, when, where, why, how):
> **Who** experiences childhood obesity (specific socioeconomic groups)?
> **What** constitutes childhood obesity (medical definition)? What factors contribute to the condition? What are the consequences for children, families, and society?
> **When** did the childhood obesity trend begin? When did it gain attention?
> **Where** does this obesity happen (particular areas, regions, both urban and rural)?
> **Why** is childhood obesity increasing? Why is it a problem? (Is it problem?)
> **How** has the problem been addressed so far?

 FOCUS on Your Project: Once you have brainstormed a list of secondary questions, revisit and test your primary (main) research question:

_____ Is the question so narrow that I won't be able to find sources?

_____ Is the question so simple that it will be too easy to answer? Can the question be answered simply by going to a reference work?

_____ Does the question lead to significant sources, intellectual challenge, and more questions?

_____ Am I committed to answering this question? Does it interest me?

_____ Will the question and answer interest my readers?

Framing a Working Thesis

Before you dig into your research project more fully, you may decide to draft a working thesis. A working thesis (which can change as you conduct research) offers a preliminary answer to your main research question. It represents your initial perspective on the topic and keeps you focused, helping you decide whether to carefully read a particular book or just skim it, fully explore a Web site or quickly surf through it.

Drafting a Strong Working Thesis

Use the following formula to develop a thesis that is debatable, not a simple statement of fact.

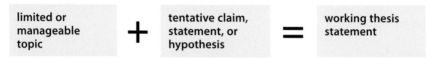

| limited or manageable topic | **+** | tentative claim, statement, or hypothesis | **=** | working thesis statement |

Poor Working Thesis: Such a thesis is a simple statement of fact that can be easily checked, or it is an opinion that cannot be argued or researched.

> Many auto manufacturers **are developing hybrid vehicles.** [fact]
>
> The fact that many celebrities are buying hybrid vehicles **is really great.** [opinion]

Strong Working Thesis: Such a thesis demonstrates higher-level thinking skills—analytical patterns such as compare/contrast or argumentative patterns such as problem/solution.

> The hybrid car **is part of a family of vehicles that combine two or more sources of power to create motion.** [analysis]
>
> Hybrid cars **are a positive step forward from the average internal-combustion car, but they won't make a large enough positive environmental impact.** [argument]

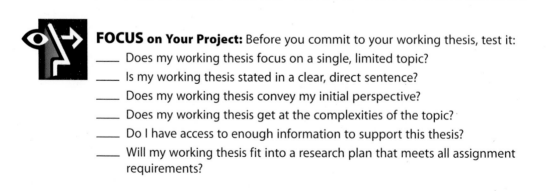

FOCUS on Your Project: Before you commit to your working thesis, test it:

____ Does my working thesis focus on a single, limited topic?

____ Is my working thesis stated in a clear, direct sentence?

____ Does my working thesis convey my initial perspective?

____ Does my working thesis get at the complexities of the topic?

____ Do I have access to enough information to support this thesis?

____ Will my working thesis fit into a research plan that meets all assignment requirements?

Focus on Ethics: Avoiding Plagiarism

Plagiarism—using source material without giving credit—is treated more fully elsewhere (pages 155–164). However, at the start of your research project, you need to focus particularly on avoiding *unintentional* plagiarism, which happens when you *accidentally* use a source's ideas, phrases, or information without documenting that material. You can prevent this problem by adhering to the principles of ethical research outlined below.

A Principled Beginning

Working ethically in the information age can be challenging, but a commitment to the following practices will result in honorable research.

- Author both the research and your paper honestly.
- Adhere to the research practices approved in your discipline (e.g., proper treatment of human subjects in psychology experiments).
- Conform to guidelines for working with people, resources, and technology—starting with your school's policy on academic integrity.
- Balance your research to honor the opposition and any contrary evidence.
- Present real, accurate data, not "fudged" or twisted facts.
- Treat source material fairly in your writing—no distortion, misquoting, or missing documentation.

Avoiding Unintentional Plagiarism

Conducting ethical research as it is described above will reduce the likelihood of unintentional plagiarism.

Begin by maintaining an accurate working bibliography (pages 136–138). When taking notes, distinguish source material from your own reflection by using quotation marks, codes, and/or separate columns or note cards. Then, as you draft your paper, transfer source material carefully. Coding material that you integrate into your discussion, use quotation marks, double-check your typing, or use copy-and-paste to ensure accuracy. Take the time to do your project right. Do not pull an all-nighter, which will not allow you to find, work with, and integrate sources properly.

Avoiding Internet Plagiarism

As with traditional print sources, Internet sources must be properly credited; Web material cannot simply be transferred into your paper without acknowledgement. So treat Web sources like print sources. Don't think, for example, that because something is on the Internet, it's free and can be used freely, or that because a Web source has no apparent author, it is yours to use as you please.

Practicing Your Research

1. **Explore:** Examine a research paper that you wrote recently for another course, assessing the following: (a) how well the paper is governed by the rhetorical situation—purpose, audience, context; and (b) how effectively the paper employs the seven traits of research writing. Then list issues that you want to work on in your future research writing.

2. **Apply:** From the list of broad research subjects below, select one and (a) brainstorm a list of related topics, (b) select and refine a topic, (c) list key research questions, and (d) formulate a working thesis.

   > Subjects: museums, organic foods, department stores, the entertainment industry, third-world struggles, comedy, wealth, mental illness, forests

3. **Collaborate on a Case Study:** As directed by your instructor, work with classmates on the following group project. (This project runs from chapter 1 to 11.) Clothing: we all wear it. But where does it come from, how is it made, why do we wear what we do, what do those choices mean? Using clothing as your group's broad subject, develop a focused topic for a paper and presentation on some aspect of clothing's significance in our lives.

4. **Focus on Your Major:** What subjects does your major explore? What are your discipline's contested issues? What kind of research is at its core? With these questions in mind and using the "Focus on Your Major" note on page 00, research your field of study.

5. **Focus on Your Current Project:** With your research assignment in front of you, use the instruction in this chapter and the checklist below to move your project from an analysis of the research rhetoric all the way to a working thesis.

Checklist:

- ☑ I have clarified the rhetorical situation behind my project and carefully studied the assignment—checking for key words, research requirements, topic options and restrictions, project parameters, and connections to my other work.
- ☑ I have a good sense of the ideas, organization, voice, word choice, sentence style, correctness, and design required in quality research writing.
- ☑ After brainstorming several topics, I have tentatively chosen one that fits the assignment, appeals to both my audience and myself, and is challenging yet doable.
- ☑ I have refined my chosen topic to a manageable focus and am committed to the research.
- ☑ I have chosen a main question, brainstormed secondary research questions, and developed a working thesis.
- ☑ I am committed to doing ethical research.

Planning Your Research

© Cengage Learning/Illustrated by Chris Krenzke

> In your experience, what planning is needed to make an event come together (e.g., a party, a date, a vacation, a job search)? How might similar planning strategies apply to research projects?

In a world of fast food and instant messaging, a college research project represents a significant commitment of time, attention, and mental energy. In fact, you may initially look at such an assignment as a torturous test of delayed gratification—or no gratification at all. However, while thoughtful research can't be rushed, the significant payoff is that it can seriously stimulate your gray matter—maybe even blow your mind.

On the surface, though, such a time-consuming project may look boring. You research a topic, analyze the information, and then present your findings to get the grade. A closer look tells you that such a research project may be your toughest, most mind-altering assignment. It may take months to complete, including weeks spent on the trail of facts, figures, and ideas. Research demands much of you, requiring challenging activities like these:

- Thoroughly organizing multiple tasks simultaneously
- Establishing a productive research path while remaining flexible enough to follow new leads as the project unfolds
- Digesting, debating, evaluating, and synthesizing source material while discovering and developing your own perspective

For these reasons, it pays to plan. In fact, a few hours of *planning* can save days of *doing* research and ensure that the research you do is fruitful.

What's Ahead?

Exploring Your Resource Options

To conduct thorough and creative research, you need a sense of what types of resources are available and which ones match up with your specific project. Study the table below, thinking about these three issues:

1. **Quality:** Which types of resources will give you the best information for your project?
2. **Balance:** How can you pursue a balanced range of resources for your project?
3. **Priorities:** Given time constraints, which resources should be at the top of your list?

Resources	Examples
Personal, Direct	Memories, diaries, journals, logs, experiments, tests, observations, interviews, surveys
Reference Works (print and electronic)	Dictionaries, thesauruses, encyclopedias, almanacs, yearbooks, atlases, directories, guides, handbooks, indexes, abstracts, catalogs, bibliographies
Books (print and electronic)	Nonfiction, how-to, biographies, fiction, trade books, scholarly and scientific studies
Periodicals and News Sources	Print newspapers, magazines, and journals; broadcast news and newsmagazines; online magazines, news sources, and discussion groups
Audiovisual, Digital, and Multimedia Resources	Graphics (tables, graphs, charts, maps, drawings, photos), audiotapes, CDs, videos, DVDs, Web pages, online databases, computer files and programs, CD-ROMs
Government Publications	Guides, programs, forms, legislation, regulations, reports, records, statistics
Business and Nonprofit Publications	Correspondence, reports, pamphlets, brochures, ads, instructions, handbooks, manuals, policies and procedures, seminar and training materials, Webinars, displays, presentations, demonstrations, catalogs, newsletters, news releases

FOCUS on Your Major: What types of resources must you or can you work with in your major? Study the discipline-specific examples below. Then begin compiling a list of the kinds of research resources valued in your field.

Discipline-Specific Examples

Humanities: Jane Austen's *Pride and Prejudice* in fiction and film	Social Sciences: the nature of and treatment for attachment disorder in children	Natural and Applied Sciences: hybrid cars as an environmental solution
Pride and Prejudice (novel and film) Interviews with film viewers or director	Interview with adoptive parents or psychologist Observation of child with attachment disorder	Test drive of Toyota Prius Survey of hybrid owners Interview with auto engineer
Critical Companion to Jane Austen: A Literary Reference to Her Life and Work	*Handbook of Preschool Mental Health: Development, Disorders, and Treatment*	Bureau of Transportation Statistics (www.bts.gov) *The Beaulieu Encyclopedia of the Automobile*
Kathryn Sutherland, *Jane Austen's Textual Lives: From Aeschylus to Bollywood*	Cathy Malchiodi, *Creative Interventions with Traumatized Children*	Myer Kutz (editor), *Environmentally Conscious Transportation*
Cathleen McGuigan, "Lights, Camera, Austen." *Newsweek* Jan. 21, 2008 Roberta Grandi, "The Passion Translated: Literary and Cinematic Rhetoric in *Pride and Prejudice* (2005)." *Literature Film Quarterly* (36.1)	Pat Wingert and Anna Nemtsova, "When Adoption Goes Wrong." *Newsweek* Dec. 17, 2007. Charles Zeanah and Anna Smyke, "Attachment Disorders in Family and Social Context." *Infant Mental Health Journal* (29.3)	Dennis Simanaitis, "Hybrids: High on the List." *Road & Track* June 2008. Craig Stephan and John Sullivan, "Environmental and Energy Implications of Plug-In Hybrid-Electric Vehicles." *Environmental Science & Technology* (42.4)
Miss Austen Regrets (biographical film) The Janeites online discussion group	*The Nature of Human Attachments in Infancy* (DVD) *John Bowlby: Attachment and Loss* (DVD)	Manufacturers' Web pages about hybrid vehicles and technology (www.honda.com) Chris Paine, *Who Killed the Electric Car?* (DVD)
Jane Austen Information Page from London Borough of Bexley (www.bexley.uk/service/lib-ebooks.html)	"Reactive Attachment Disorder of Infancy or Early Childhood." *Medline Plus* (service of U.S. National Library of Medicine and the National Institutes of Health)	"Fuel Cell Vehicles: Race to a New Automotive Future" (Report from the Office of Technology Policy) Zero Emissions Vehicle Mandate (California Air Resources Board)
Publishing company marketing material for Austen novels Movie studio promotional material for Austen films	"White Paper on Coercion in Treatment." *Association for Treatment and Training in the Attachment of Children* (ATTACh)	Manufacturer promotional materials (e.g., Ford's Web site information on its Escape hybrid and its statements about green vehicles)

Considering Information Sites

Where do you go to get the information you need? Your first instinct may be to hurry onto the free Web, but don't limit yourself to that single research site. Consider the information "sites" listed below, and remember that resources may be available in different forms in different locations. For example, a journal article may be found in a library's holdings or in an electronic subscription database.

Information Source →	Location →	Example "Sites" →
People	Experts (knowledge area, skill, occupation) Population segments or individuals (with representative or unusual experiences)	• Scholars and professionals • Reference librarians • An online discussion group
Libraries	**General:** public, college, online **Specialized:** legal, medical, government, business	• WorldCat/FirstSearch • Library of Congress • VERA (Virtual Electronic Resource Access): MIT libraries
Computer Resources	**Computers:** software, disks, CD-ROMs **Networks:** Internet and other online services (e-mail, limited-access databases, discussion groups, MUDs, chat rooms, Web sites); intranets	• IPL.org • EBSCOhost (e.g., Academic Search Premier database) • LexisNexis (news databases)
Mass Media	Radio (AM and FM) Television (network, public, cable, satellite, Web) Print (newspapers, magazines, journals)	• *National Public Radio (NPR)* • *The Discovery Channel* • *Psychology Today* • *Bright Lights Film Journal (e-zine)*
Testing, Training, Meeting, and Observation Sites	Plants, facilities, field sites Laboratories, research centers, universities, think tanks Conventions, conferences, seminars Museums, galleries, historical sites	• The Smithsonian Institute • 20th Annual International Conference on Attachment and Bonding • Jane Austen Museum
Municipal, State, and Federal Government Offices	Elected officials, representatives Offices and agencies Government Printing Office (GPO <www.gpoaccess.gov>) Web sites	• Environmental Protection Agency • Census Data Online (www.census.gov) • FirstGov (www.firstgov.gov)
Workplace	Computer databases, company files Desktop reference materials Bulletin boards (physical/digital) Company, department Web sites Departments and offices Associations, professional organizations Consulting, training, and information services	• Society for Automotive Engineers (www.sae.org) • American Academy of Childhood & Adolescent Psychiatry (www.aacap.org) • Jane Austen Society of North America (www.jasna.org)

Identifying Ethical Challenges

Research and research writing are principle-based activities. From the start, research involves choices that relate to results and consequences. Research ethics, more than simply avoiding unintentional plagiarism (see page 27), should be part of your planning. Here is an overview of the ethical challenges you face as you plan your project.

Ethical Practices: Your first challenge is to follow these sound practices to ensure that your research is done properly.

- **Maintain Self-Reliance:** Aim to do the research and write the paper yourself—not submit someone else's work. (See the fuller discussion of plagiarism in chapter 7, page 155.) Of course, such self-reliance doesn't rule out consulting with a librarian, your professor, a writing-center tutor, and so on. However, it does mean that you "own" the work you do and submit.

- **Attend to Standards:** Aim to follow school and discipline-related guidelines for working with people, resources, and technology. Specifically, follow the research practices approved in your discipline.

- **Treat Sources Fairly:** Aim to find the best sources—whether people, places, texts, or hypertexts—rather than relying on second-rate material. Also keep accurate records of the resources you consult. Finally, plan to show respect for intellectual property and copyright laws. (See page 163.)

Information Ethics: The second challenge relates to the proper handling of information.

- **Information Accuracy:** Aim to offer only reliable information and discussion in your research writing. Carefully evaluate and test the sources of information that you find. Present real, accurate data and results, not "fudged" or twisted facts and numbers nor "doctored" graphics. Also treat source material fairly in your writing—no distortion or misquoting.

- **Information Completeness:** Aim to offer the complete picture by doing well-rounded research. Avoid one-sided research by dealing openly with opposing viewpoints and contrary evidence. Also present your findings in a form that makes sense for your readers rather than mystifying them.

- **Information Confidentiality:** With certain types of research (e.g., working with human subjects), aim to respect people's privacy and to guard personal information as confidential. (For more on this issue, see page 109.)

Yuri Arcurs/www.shutterstock.com

Distinguishing Primary, Secondary, and Tertiary Sources

Information sources can be primary, secondary, or tertiary, depending on their proximity to the topic. With your college assignments, you will likely be expected to use primary and secondary sources but to avoid tertiary sources, except, perhaps, for gathering preliminary or general information. The following material explains the distinction between primary, secondary, and tertiary sources, as well as the symbiosis between them.

Primary Sources

A primary source is an original source, one that gives firsthand information on a topic: the source is close to the issue or question. This source (such as a log, a person, a document, or an event) informs you directly about the topic, not through another person's explanation or interpretation. Common primary sources are observations, interviews, surveys, experiments, documents, and artifacts. Frequently, you generate the primary source yourself, but sometimes primary information is available in published form. Consider how the sources below are primary for their close, direct relationship to the projects listed.

Project	Sources
Jane Austen's *Pride and Prejudice* in fiction and film	The text of the novel itself, the DVD of the 2005 film E-text of Jane Austen's letters Interview with a film scholar on novel-film adaptations
The nature of attachment disorder in children	Your case study of a child with attachment disorder Interview with adoptive parents of child with RAD Government-published statistics about RAD rates
Hybrid cars as an environmental solution	Test drive of hybrid-electric vehicle Interview with an automotive engineer about the technology Testing of hybrid fuel efficiency in real driving conditions

> **Tip:** If you are generating the primary information yourself, it is essential that you follow accepted methodologies for doing so. These methods are the subject of chapter 5, pages 105–134. If you are working with existing primary sources (e.g., an e-text), make sure these are authoritative and accurate.

Primary Sources ⊕ and ⊖

⊕ Primary sources produce information precisely tailored to your research needs—direct, hands-on access to your topic. For example, if your topic is the impact of tornados on communities, interviews with survivors would provide direct, firsthand information.

⊖ Primary research takes time, resources, and specialized skills (designing surveys, analyzing statistics, designing experiments).

Secondary Sources

In contrast to primary sources, secondary sources present secondhand information on your topic, information one step removed from its origin. Secondary information has been collected, compiled, summarized, analyzed, synthesized, interpreted, and evaluated by someone studying primary sources. Journal articles, encyclopedia entries, and documentaries are typical examples of secondary sources. Typically, you track down such resources in your library, through library databases, and on the Internet. Note how the sources listed below are secondary for their indirect relationship to the project.

Project	Sources
Jane Austen's *Pride and Prejudice* in fiction and film	Books and articles by scholars on Austen and on film, as well as by literary and film journalists; literary biographies about Austen's life; film reviews
The nature of attachment disorder in children	Books and articles by scholars sharing research done on the disorder; print and electronic manuals related to diagnosis and treatment
Hybrid cars as an environmental solution	Books and articles by engineers and environmental scientists sharing research about hybrid and other green technologies

Tip: Aside from determining how relevant the source is to your research question, it is crucial to determine the source's origin, perspective, and thinking. See pages 147–149 for more help with source evaluation.

Secondary Research ⊕ and ⊖

⊕ Secondary, or secondhand, does not mean "inferior." In fact, quality secondary sources—especially scholarly ones that have gone through a peer-review process—can offer expert perspectives on and analysis of your topic. Such sources can save you plenty of research labor while providing you with extensive data. In addition, secondary sources can help you see your topic from multiple angles as they tell you the story of research already done on your topic.

⊖ Because secondary research isn't written solely with you and your project in mind, you may need to do some digging to find relevant data. Moreover, the information that you do find may be filtered through the researcher's bias. In fact, the original research examined in the secondary source may be faulty, a point suggesting that the quality of secondary sources can vary greatly. (Peer review of secondary sources prior to their publication is, in this way, a form of quality control—a control missing from many free-Web resources.) Finally, because information about your topic can increase or radically change over time, secondary sources can become dated.

FOCUS on Research Essentials: Whether a source is primary or secondary depends on its refined topic. For example, if you were studying why brown-outs happen during heat waves, a newspaper editorial would be secondary. But if your focus were public attitudes toward brown-outs, the editorial could be primary. In other words, a given source is not always primary or always secondary.

Tertiary Sources

Some resources are tertiary—that is, thirdhand. They are essentially reports of reports of research. Writers of tertiary sources are pulling together their own thoughts based on a reading of secondary sources. If your project requires no primary research, and you use only secondary sources, then your paper becomes, in this sense, a tertiary source for your reader. Examples of tertiary sources would include some articles in popular magazines and entries in Wikipedia. (For a more in-depth discussion of Wikipedia, see page 86–89.) Note how the sources below function as tertiary sources because of their protracted relationship to the topic.

Project	Sources
Jane Austen's *Pride and Prejudice* in fiction and film	Online discussion group exchanging thoughts on a recent Austen biography; Wikipedia or other reference-work entry on Austen
The nature of attachment disorder in children	Blog by a parent of a child with attachment disorder explaining what she (the parent) has learned by reading a new book on the subject
Hybrid cars as an environmental solution	A literature review of all the research currently published on hybrid technologies; articles in trade or popular publications by science journalists

> **Tip:** Cautiously using tertiary sources as a starting point for your research—to find basic facts, ideas for narrowing your topic, or leads and links to further research—is acceptable. However, do not rely on these sources to complete your research paper.

Tertiary Sources ⊕ and ⊖

⊕ Tertiary sources are typically easy to find, easy to access, and easy to read. Note, for example, how a free-Web search of a specific topic frequently lists a Wikipedia entry in the first ten items.

⊖ The main weakness of tertiary sources is their distance from the original research and information. Because the information and ideas have been passed along in this way, errors, distortion, gaps, and oversimplification of complex issues may have been introduced. Generally, tertiary sources lack the reliability and depth necessary for college-level research projects.

The Primary-Secondary Symbiosis

In your research project, understanding the symbiotic relationship between primary and secondary sources is just as important as understanding the two source types themselves. In other words, you need to know the individual roles primary and secondary sources play in your writing as well as how they work together.

Consider how the main role of a primary source is to provide **raw material** and bring you into **close contact** with your topic. Then explore how a secondary source can **make sense** of primary-source information and help you to **work with** primary-source data. Finally, consider how a **blend** of primary and secondary sources can further your particular research project. (See "Research for Different Forms of Writing," page 42.)

Project	Symbiosis
Humanities: Jane Austen's *Pride and Prejudice* in fiction and film	In this project, secondary sources such as scholarly books and articles on Austen and on Austen in film or a literary biography on Austen play a supporting role: they supply ideas, analysis, and information that feed into your primary research of reading the text and viewing the film.

Tip: You may supplement your primary research by reading Austen's letters or studying interviews with the director and cast of the film.

Project	Symbiosis
Social Sciences: the nature of attachment disorder in children	In this situation, you will likely rely predominantly on finding and using quality secondary sources: books, articles, and other materials developed by qualified, trained scholars and professionals.

Tip: If your project does involve primary research, that primary study should be informed by a careful review of secondary sources (called a literature review).

Project	Symbiosis
Natural Science/ Technology: hybrid cars as an environmental solution	In this situation, you may do experimental primary research on hybrid technology. That primary research, driven by a hypothesis, should be informed by a systematic study of secondary sources, the previous experimental studies of your topic.

Tip: Your project goal will determine whether you need to do experimental primary research.

 FOCUS on Your Project: Identify the blend of primary and secondary sources that make sense for your project. How are primary and secondary research related, given your assignment and the research context?

Following Methods of Inquiry

As you begin to work on research projects in your major, part of your orientation to the discipline should involve learning the methods of inquiry used. The discussion below will help you locate your major and identify its research methods.

Locating Your Major Within the Division of Disciplines

The college curriculum is typically divided into three major divisions: humanities, social sciences, and natural and applied sciences. Each division is further divided into departments, which in turn house the major areas of study that you as a student declare. Some majors (e.g., Environmental Studies, Women's Studies) are interdisciplinary. The following chart lists the departments within each division.

Humanities: the study of human culture.	Art, English, History, Modern Languages, Music, Philosophy, Religion, Theater Arts
Social Sciences: the study of human behavior and societies	Business, Communication, Economics, Education, Political Science, Psychology, Sociology
Natural Sciences/Applied Sciences: the study of natural phenomena/applying the results to develop useful tools and artifacts	Astronomy, Biology, Chemistry, Computer Science, Engineering, Mathematics, Physics

Inquiry in the Humanities

In their study of culture, the humanities examine topics such as the history of civilization, cultural institutions and trends, religious beliefs and practices, languages and their use, and artwork and performance skills. The following information defines humanities research.

Purpose of Inquiry: Broadly, humanities research aims to understand more deeply some aspect of humanity's place and experience related to the artistic and imaginative, to the historical, to the spiritual, to the linguistic, or to the world of ideas and ethics.

Forms of Writing: Humanities scholars typically conduct research that is published in scholarly books and articles, such as interpretive analyses and arguments on a specific topic, theoretical studies of key concepts in the discipline, and book reviews or broader bibliographic surveys.

Methods of Research: The humanities involve carefully "reading" primary texts, artifacts, and events, as well as investigating past scholarship on a topic. With their focus on "reading," the humanities value the skills of interpretation—sensitivity to the primary text, consistent and thoughtful use of evidence, attention to the context, awareness of theoretical frameworks, ability to generate insightful theses, and thoughtful analysis and argument.

Inquiry in the Social Sciences

In their study of human behavior and societies, the social sciences examine topics such as economic systems, correctional programs, and personality disorders. The following information defines research in the social sciences:

Purpose of Inquiry: Broadly, social-science research aims to understand the laws and conventions that govern human behavior and societies.

Forms of Writing: With their focus on behavior and social laws, social scientists typically write experiment reports as well as reviews of the current literature on a topic, field reports, case studies, and clinical evaluations.

Methods of Research: Like scholars in the natural sciences, social scientists use the experimental method to test their observation-based hypotheses. Some social-science research, however, is more subjective, speculating about the mysteries of human consciousness, emotions, and the like. Because much social-science research is observation based, however, the thinking is often rooted in mathematics, particularly statistical analysis. Focused on testing hypotheses, such research pays careful attention to variables, controls, experiment replication, and case studies, and also values the objective analysis of all data.

Inquiry in the Natural and Applied Sciences

In their study of natural phenomena and the application of the resulting knowledge, the natural and applied sciences engage topics such as plant life, physical laws, the solar system, and molecular structures. The following information defines research in the natural and applied science.

Purpose of Inquiry: Broadly, natural science aims to explain observations in the light of current theories.

Forms of Writing: Normally, natural-science research involves sharing experiments and field reports in scholarly journals so that the broader scientific community can engage in a dialogue on the phenomena. However, such research may also involve reviewing and summarizing all the current research on a specific topic or writing studies that examine the theories themselves. Finally, applied research may involve writing technical reports that propose practical solutions to specific problems or challenges.

Methods of Research: Natural scientists practice two predominant research methods— laboratory experiments and field work. While both are rooted in objective attention to phenomena, laboratory research strictly follows the experimental method, and field work relies on careful, often quantifiable observation. Both forms of research value insightful hypothesizing, the careful collection and analysis of data, and the thoughtful connection of the results to past research and current theories.

Getting Organized

An organized approach to doing your research will save you time, help you work efficiently, and prevent frustration. To ensure success, remember to establish priorities, employ best study/work practices, and build a reasonable schedule.

Priorities

As you plan your work, you will soon realize the need to prioritize, to put first things first. Consider the project's requirements against the available resources and time by answering questions like these.

- How much research material do I need?
- What range of resources will give me quality, reliable information?
- What types of research does the assignment specify? How am I limited?
- What tasks does the project involve? Which tasks are primary? Secondary?
- What weight does the project carry in the course?
- How much time do I have to complete this project?

Answering these and similar questions will give you a clearer vision of your work and enable you to sort it out, to prioritize.

Tip: Writing down the answers to your questions will give you a list of tasks and ideas that you can then organize.

Best Practices

Using practical organizational skills like these explained below will lead efficiently to research writing and sharing.

Gathering Materials: You may choose to sign out library holdings or use interlibrary loan; photocopy book sections and journal articles; print, save, bookmark, or e-mail digital materials.

Taking Notes: Choose from the note-card, double-entry notebook, copy-and-annotate, and research-log methods (pages 140–143). Also set up a working bibliography (pages 136–138). Familiarize yourself with available note-taking software (page 143) and keep tools for writing within easy reach to capitalize on sudden insights.

Documenting Sources: It's likely that your instructor will designate a system such as MLA (page 371), APA (page 421), CMS (page 457), or CSE (page 483). If he or she does not do so, use a method that suits the subject matter and discipline. Whatever system you use, review its basic rules and strategies.

Schedule

Obviously, the time frame for completing a research project varies from one assignment to the next. The time between getting the assignment and turning it in may be two weeks or two months. You may also have intermediate deadlines for specific phases of the project (e.g., topic selection, project proposal, annotated bibliography, first draft). Generally, however, you should spend about half your time on research and half on writing. To stay on track, prepare a preliminary schedule with tentative deadlines for completing each phase of your work.

Sample Schedule

Notice the level of detail in this schedule. Ordered, detailed planning results in the effective use of available time.

This schedule template is available at our Web site .... www. theresearchwriter.com.

Course:
Weight:
Project:
Due Date:

Activity:	Completion Date:
Choose a topic	
Test topic with preliminary research and feedback (peer, instructor, others)	
Focus topic: research questions, working thesis	
Develop research plan	
Establish/submit working bibliography	
Complete primary/field research	
Complete library research	
Complete free-Web research	
Review, organize, synthesize findings/thinking: Refine thesis and develop paper outline	
Complete first draft, including initial documentation	
Seek feedback (peer, writing-center tutor, or instructor)	
Conduct further research, if needed	
Revise first draft for global changes (ideas, organization)	
Edit paper for word choice and sentence style	
Complete and check documentation: Parenthetical notes, works cited/references, footnotes	
Proofread paper for grammar, punctuation, spelling, mechanics	
Print, submit, publish, and/or present research paper/ findings	

FOCUS on Research Essentials:

1. Plan to gather more information than you could ever use in your paper. That richness gives you choices and allows you to sift for the crucial information.

2. Always start your project well before the due date so that your thinking can percolate. Pulling an all-nighter won't result in a good paper because doing so doesn't give you the time to research, read, think, write, revise, and edit your work.

Research for Different Forms of Writing

Different forms of college writing generally rely on specific research strategies. Here's an overview that refers to the forms of writing covered in part 2 of this manual, chapters 12–17. Use this table to plan the research for your next writing assignment.

Forms	Recommended Strategies
Personal Research Paper (chapter 12, page 283)	Focus on primary research: • Search your memories and reflect on your experiences. • Study artifacts such as photographs, diaries, old newspapers, and videos. • Observe locations and events. • Interview participants. Use secondary research as needed to clarify facts, background, definitions, and other details.
Analytical Research Paper (chapter 13, page 293)	Generally, start with primary research: • Study texts, documents, maps, objects, events, and videos. • Conduct observations, experiments, and tests. Use secondary research to support primary research: go to specialized reference works, journal articles, books, and online sources to create a context for and to clarify details of analysis.
Argumentative Research Paper (chapter 14, page 309)	Generally, rely on secondary research: • Review the literature on your topic. • Find authoritative, trustworthy information in reference works, journal articles, scholarly books, and credible Web sites. Use primary research in a supporting role: • Conduct interviews and surveys to get others' opinions on your topic. • Observe in order to "see for yourself." • Study primary texts and artifacts to get unbiased, objective information.
IMRAD Research Report (chapter 15, page 327)	For observation, survey, interview, experiment, and field reports, obviously rely on observing, surveying, interviewing, experimenting, and doing field work. However, collect background information from reference works and literature reviews of secondary sources to prepare for that primary research.
Analysis of a Literary Text (chapter 16, page 341)	As the title suggests, this form is a special application of the analytical research paper (an application that also shares characteristics with argumentative writing). Combine close analysis of the literary text itself (your primary text for the project) with fitting secondary research on the author, the form, criticism of the text, the historical or cultural background, theoretical perspectives, and so on.
Literature Reviews (chapter 17, page 359)	As the name of the form suggests, this writing relies exclusively on secondary research—surveying the work and the writing done on a specific topic. Such a review is often completed, however, in preparation for new primary research.

Writing a Research Proposal

For some research projects, you may need to submit a research proposal for approval before you actually undertake the full project. Typically the proposal relates to research you might do as part of an individual studies course, a group assignment, field research, a service-learning project, a co-op assignment, or a senior thesis project in a capstone course.

A project proposal seeks to explain what you plan to research, why, and how. In it, you show that the research is valid (makes good scholarly sense), argue that the research is valuable (will lead to significant knowledge), communicate your enthusiasm for the project, demonstrate that your plan is workable within the constraints of the assignment, and gain your instructor's approval.

The goals of a proposal, then, are to clarify your own thinking about a research topic, to convince your instructor that it is indeed a fruitful line of investigation, and to get helpful feedback about how to proceed.

Parts of a Research Proposal

For some projects, putting together a research proposal may involve completing a form or following a set formula. Whether you are following a form or drafting your proposal from scratch, here is an outline of the five elements of a proposal.

1. **Introduction:** Outline the subject and purpose of your research project. State why the topic is important and worthwhile, and provide any background or context that the professor needs to understand your line of thought.

2. **Project Description and Expected Results:** Provide a detailed discussion of what you propose to study. Declare the main topic or issue plus specific subtopics. List the key research question for your project plus a set of related questions that will guide your investigation of both primary and secondary material. These related questions should expand upon your key question, your initial hypothesis, or your theory. Project the outcomes that you expect from your research, including their value for yourself and for others.

3. **Project Plan (Research Methods and Procedures):** Explain how you plan to find answers to your questions, how you plan to research your topic. At this point, it would be useful to explain your primary research (the firsthand investigation) as well as the research tools you plan to use (e.g., catalogs, reference works, lab equipment, survey software). Include a working bibliography of your initial resources.

4. **Timetable or Schedule:** List deadlines that are part of the assignment and deadlines that you've set for yourself.

5. **Request for Approval:** Ask for feedback from your professor on your project plan and request approval to proceed.

Sample Research Proposal

Identify the course, yourself, and your research project's title.

Introduce your project in terms of its main focus.

Summarize what you propose to study and what you hope to learn: your focused topic, your questions, and your working thesis.

Explain how the research is both valid and valuable in terms of the outcomes.

Map out how you intend to carry out the research. Indicate both secondary and primary research.

Film Studies 302
Proposal: Jane Austen's *Pride and Prejudice* as Fiction and Film
Gwendolyn Mackenzie

For many years, I have been a Janeite, that is, a big fan of Jane Austen's novels and the film adaptations that have been made of them. For my term paper in Film Studies 302, I propose to study the 2005 film adaptation of Austen's *Pride and Prejudice*, the version directed by Joe Wright, in order to explore the Jane Austen phenomenon: her enduring fascination for readers, filmmakers, and filmgoers almost two centuries after her death.

Project Purpose, Description, and Outcome: What I would like to look at specifically is a comparison-contrast of how the novel and the film explore one of the key concepts captured in the title: prejudice. In particular, I plan to analyze the presentation of prejudice as it relates to gender. With this issue in mind, my main question is what sense do these texts (novel and film) make of prejudice as it relates to relationships between men and women? These would be secondary questions that I need to explore:

- What did prejudice mean for Austen, and what does it mean today?
- In the novel and the film, how is the problem of prejudice presented as an issue of gender, and is the problem ever solved?
- How do the novel and the film treat the issue similarly and differently? What do the similarities and differences mean about the past and the present, about fiction and film?
- How is prejudice central to the main relationship between Elizabeth Bennett and Mr. Darcy?
- What about secondary characters and secondary relationships: Is prejudice at work elsewhere in the story?

My working thesis is that the film highlights an issue of gender inequality already present in Austen's novel so that viewers can "read" that prejudice into their own experiences. In part, this potential in Austen's novel explains our continuing interest in her stories.

This study of gender prejudice will help me (1) develop new insights into the treatment of this theme in fiction and film, (2) understand better the nature of film adaptations, and (3) explain a small part of the Jane Austen phenomenon. In concrete terms, this project will lead to a 10-12 page paper and a 10-minute class presentation.

Project Plan: My primary research will involve rereading the novel and reviewing the film. Part of that research might involve searching an e-book version of the novel. In terms of secondary research, I have done an initial search of our library's online catalog, of WorldCat, and of EBSCOhost for books and articles relevant to my topic. While some of the works below predate the 2005 film, they should still provide me with useful ideas for my project.

Provide details demonstrating that you have a good grasp of fitting research methods.

Primary Sources

Austen, Jane. *Pride and Prejudice: An Authoritative Text, Background and Sources, Criticism.* Ed. Donald J. Gray. New York: Norton, 2001. Print.

---. *Pride and Prejudice. Project Gutenberg.* Project Gutenberg Literary Archive Foundation. 1 June 1998. Web. 1 Nov. 2011.

Pride and Prejudice. Dir. Joe Wright. Universal Pictures, 2005. Film.

Secondary Sources

Baker, William. *Critical Companion to Jane Austen: A Literary Reference to Her Life and Work.* New York: Facts on File, 2008. Print.

Cartmell, Deborah, and Imelda Whelehan. *The Cambridge Companion to Literature on Screen.* Cambridge: Cambridge UP, 2007. Print.

---. *Adaptations: From Text to Screen, Screen to Text.* London; New York: Routledge, 2004. Print.

Cohen, Paula Marantz. "Trends in Adaptation: Will and Jane Go Celluloid." *Michigan Quarterly Review* 44.3 (2005): 533-540. Print.

Crusie, Jennifer. *Flirting with Pride and Prejudice: Fresh Perspectives on the Original Chick-Lit Masterpiece.* Dallas: BenBella, 2005. Print.

Franklin, Nancy. "Everybody Loves Jane." *New Yorker* 21 Jan. 2008: 82-83. Print.

Grandi, Roberta. "The Passion Translated: Literary and Cinematic Rhetoric in *Pride and Prejudice* (2005)." *Literature Film Quarterly* 36.1 (2008): 45-51. Print.

McFarlane, Brian. "Something Old, Something New: 'Pride and Prejudice' on Screen." *Screen Education* 40: 6-14. Print.

Parrill, Sue. *Jane Austen on Film and Television: A Critical Study of the Adaptations.* Jefferson: McFarland, 2002. Print.

Stovel, Nora Foster. "From Page to Screen: Dancing to the Altar in Recent Film Adaptations of Jane Austen's Novels." *Persuasions: The Jane Austen Journal* 28: 185-198. Print.

Sutherland, Kathryn. *Jane Austen's Textual Lives: From Aeschylus to Bollywood.* Oxford: Oxford UP, 2007. Print.

Todd, Janet M. *The Cambridge Introduction to Jane Austen.* Cambridge. Cambridge UP, 2006. Print.

Troost, Linda V. "Filming Tourism, Portraying Pemberley." *Eighteenth Century Fiction* 18.4 (2006): 477-498. Print.

Supply a working bibliography indicating your preliminary survey of possible resources.

Format sources in the documentation system to be used in the paper.

To get a better sense of how Jane Austen fans react to this novel and film, I may research some Austen discussion groups.

Timetable for Project: Here is my schedule for completing this project:

1. Finish rereading the novel and reviewing the film: November 14.
2. Complete secondary research: November 21.
3. Develop outline for paper: November 24.
4. Finish first draft of paper: December 1.
5. Revise, edit, and proofread paper: December 6.
6. Develop presentation: December 7.
7. Submit paper and do presentation: December 9.

Map out a realistic research schedule indicating major milestones in the project.

Request both input and approval from the reader.

Project Approval: Dr. Rajan, I would appreciate your feedback on my proposed project, as well as your approval of my plan.

Preparing to Do Effective Keyword Searches

Keyword searching is a vital research skill. It helps you get at information in online library catalogs, online subscription databases for periodical articles, print indexes to periodical publications, books (both print and e-books), and Web resources. However, what you find and how fast you find it depends on the keywords you use. That's why it is important to develop strategies for doing effective keyword searching.

Keywords/Search Strategies

Because keywords give you "compass points" for navigating through a sea of information, you need to choose the best ones for your project.

The goal of a keyword search is generating quality results—a list of books, a set of journal articles, or a number of Web sites. To get those quality results, you need to build and refine your list of keywords and subject terms as you search various databases and resources. The four following strategies will help you do quality research.

■ **Brainstorm terms and synonyms.** Based on your current knowledge and/or background reading, brainstorm a list of possible keywords—topics, titles, and names. One technique is to generate a list by isolating the main terms in your research question or working thesis; then build a list of synonyms and related terms based on those key terms.

> **Question:** Should consumers embrace hybrid cars?
> **Key Terms:** hybrid cars
> **Related Terms:** hybrid vehicles, fuel cells, electric cars, automobiles, alternative energy, energy industry, automotive engineering

■ **Search Library of Congress subject terms.** LOC subject headings are the keywords that librarians use when classifying material, from books to articles to DVDs. For example, if you were to look up *hybrid vehicles* in the *Library of Congress Subject Headings* (big red volumes available in your library), you would find the entry below, advising you to use *hybrid electric vehicles*. Note the recommended keywords, broader terms, and narrower terms. Such an entry can also list related terms, subtopics, and tips for searching. This information is valuable because it shows the structure of your subject, tells you the best keywords to use in searches, and helps you narrow or broaden your project's search parameters.

Hybrid vehicles USE Hybrid electric vehicles

search tip ················	**Hybrid electric vehicles**
LOC call number ················	*[TL221.15]*
used for ················	UF Hybrid drive vehicles
	Hybrid vehicles
broader term ················	BT Electric vehicles
narrower term ················	NT Hybrid electric cars

■ **Use a shotgun approach.** Start your searches with the most likely keyword. If you get no "hits," choose a related term. Once you get some hits, check them carefully. The list of results might give you choices for directing and refining your search using related subject terms; and studying full citations might give you clues about other words to use as you continue searching.

■ **Use Boolean operators to refine your search.** Often, combining keywords by using Boolean logic leads to better research results. When you combine keywords with Boolean operators, the search string reads from left to right.

Boolean Operating Strategies

Narrowing a Search: To reduce the number of hits when a single word gives you too many, combine it with a related word **Use: and /+/not/-**	hybrid **and** car ➔ +hybrid +car	Both forms search for citations containing both keywords.
	hybrid **not** corn ➔ +hybrid -corn	Both forms search for citations containing "hybrid" but exclude those containing "corn" so that you eliminate material on hybrid corn.
Expanding a Search: To expand a search, combine a term providing few hits with a related word. **Use: or**	hybrid **or** electric➔	This form searches for citations containing either term.
Specifying a Search: Use quotation marks to indicate that you wish to search for the exact phrase enclosed. **Use: " "**	"fuel cells" ⟶	This form searches for the exact phrase "fuel cells."
Sequencing Operations: To indicate that the operations should be performed first before other operations in the search string, use parentheses. **Use: ( )**	(hybrid or ⟶ electric) and car or automobile	Searches first for citations containing either "hybrid" or "electric" and then checks results for either "car" or "automobile."
Finding Variations of a Word: Depending on the database, using truncation and wild card symbols will find variations of a word. **Use: $, ?, #**	electri# ⟶	This form searches for terms like *electric, electrical, electricity, electrify, electrifying.*

Practicing Your Research

1. **Explore:** In the past, which planning activities from this chapter have you typically used? Which "new" planning activities do you think would most improve your research experience?

2. **Apply:** Choose one of the subjects listed below. Using the tables on pages 00-00 as a guide, develop a list of possible resources for that topic. To create your list, you may first need to brainstorm about primary, secondary, and tertiary sources for such a topic as well as choose some keywords to do a quick search of your library catalog, library subscription databases, and the free Web.

   > Subjects: the history of comic films, the politics of free speech vs. political correctness, the health of our national forests.

3. **Collaborate on a Case Study:** As directed by your instructor, continue working with classmates on your clothing-focused project. With your research questions in mind, use the instruction in this chapter to (a) brainstorm a wide range of specific resource options and research "sites"; (b) debate the ethical challenges relevant to your project; (c) discuss the primary, secondary, and tertiary source blend you should aim for; (d) develop a list of keywords for your research; and (e) draft a research proposal.

4. **Research Your Major:** By talking with professors and advanced students in your major, gather answers to these questions: What resources are typically used and highly valued in this discipline? How does the primary-secondary distinction work for research projects? What planning activities work well for projects in this field?

5. **Work on Your Current Project:** With your main research question and working thesis in mind, use the instruction in this chapter to develop a solid research plan. Shape that plan into a research proposal to your instructor.

Checklist:

- ☑ I have explored potential resources and Web sites for my research.
- ☑ I have identified specific ethical challenges for my research project.
- ☑ I know what blend of primary and secondary research I need to do, particularly as these relate to my discipline and to the research methods and form required for my project.
- ☑ I have developed a research plan, including a schedule.
- ☑ If required, I have written a research proposal that explains my research problem, argues for my project's value and validity, and maps out a solid research method.
- ☑ I have developed a strong list of keywords for getting started on library and Internet research.

Doing Research in the Wired Library

3

© Cengage Learning/Illustrated by Chris Krenzke

 In which ways have you used or avoided libraries for research projects?

If you are like some students, you suffer from one or two research-related illnesses. First, you might have *libriphobia*, the fear of libraries. In serious cases, students experience the library as a maze without an exit. Second, you might have *print fever*, an allergic reaction to physical books and magazines. For a cure, many students turn to that miracle drug, the Web, with its active ingredient Google.

The problem with this miracle drug is the potential for overdependence. If it's done cautiously, free-Web research can be safe and productive, as the next chapter will discuss. But today's electronically oriented, Internet-connected library offers you fast and productive access to a greater proportion of quality resources than does the free Web. Here's why you should typically go first to library resources for your projects:

1. Library resources offer a higher degree of **reliability**. Before being published, most scholarly books and journal articles go through a rigorous review process, called *peer review*. Experts test the work and call for changes, if necessary, before the research is published.

2. Library resources tend to offer more **scholarly depth**. Most scholarly studies go well beyond the basics to explore the interesting complexities of a topic. In your research projects, that's where you want to be.

To help you find such reliable and scholarly resources, today's library is wired for research, as are the librarians who run it. It's the perfect place to plug into the research tools and resources that will power your research projects.

What's Ahead?

Getting into Your Library

When it comes to your school's library, you need to get familiar with its research resources and tools. Whether your school's library is relatively small, a system of multiple buildings, or even a statewide network, familiarity strongly improves your ability to succeed in research projects. Consider how to get inside your library's spaces, tools, and holdings, as well as how to connect the library to your research process.

How to Get Familiar with Your Library

If the library is unfamiliar territory for you, you can get to know it through a variety of methods. To start with, get through the door, as your library's entrance is your gateway to both print and digital information. Next, take advantage of tours and orientation sessions to learn your library's location(s), physical layout, resources, and services. In addition, study print handouts and fliers displayed in your library, from floor maps to disciplinary guides. Finally, visit your library's Web site (sample home page shown below) to learn more about its services and holdings, to study its policies, to explore research tools, and to access online tutorials and forms. In particular, learn what research tools you need to use in the library itself, as opposed to those that you can access electronically elsewhere, either on or off campus.

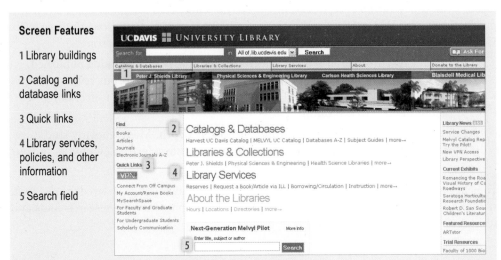

Screen Features

1 Library buildings

2 Catalog and database links

3 Quick links

4 Library services, policies, and other information

5 Search field

Source: University of California - Davis

FOCUS on Your Major: As you advance in your major, you need to get especially familiar with those elements of the library most relevant to your discipline. Look for the library buildings and spaces dedicated to your discipline. Identify the reference holdings, journals, and stacks (bookshelves, aisles, floors, buildings) relevant to your major. At the library's Web site, check for resources and tools arranged by discipline. Talk to the reference librarians to see if one of them specializes in your knowledge area.

An Overview of Library Resources and Services

Your library likely offers a full range of resources and services for completing your research projects. Here is an overview of what the library typically offers.

Librarians: These information experts manage the library's materials, guide you to resources, and help you perform online searches. To tap a librarian's help and expertise, make an appointment or stop by the reference desk. Consider, as well, electronic contact—using information at the library Web site, checking FAQs, or submitting an e-mail inquiry—as your library may offer a virtual reference service.

Collections: The library collects and houses a variety of materials.
- Books, videotapes, CD-ROMs, CDs, and DVDs
- Periodicals—journals, magazines, and newspapers in various formats
- Reference materials—directories, indexes, handbooks, encyclopedias, etc.
- Special collections—government publications, historical documents, etc.
- Clippings—"vertical files" of material on local or current interest

Research Tools: The library also contains research tools that direct you to materials.
- The online catalog allows you to search the library's holdings.
- Subscription databases identify periodical articles, providing many in full text.
- Internet access connects you with other library catalogs, online reference help, discussion groups, e-mail, and other Web resources.
- Tutorials, guides, and forms assist you in finding resources.

Special Services: These services may also help you complete research projects.
- Interlibrary loan gets books and articles not available in your library.
- "Hold" or "recall" allows you to request a book that is currently signed out.
- Photocopiers, CD burners, scanners, microform readers, bibliographic software, and presentation software help you do and share your research.

 FOCUS on Ethics: Your school's library is the common, shared space for conducting research on campus. As such, the library, its materials, and the people in it deserve your consideration. Follow these ethical guidelines:

- Treat shared items with respect, from chairs for reading to computer stations to books: avoid damaging items with ink, food, and drink stains.

- Avoid noise and socializing in quiet study and work areas.

- Follow your library's policies when it comes to keeping materials in certain areas or returning them for reshelving. Typically, you should simply place materials you have taken off a shelf on a reshelving cart or table; don't put the book back yourself.

- Respect print holdings by not annotating on them directly: if you wish to write notes on pages, use a photocopy instead.

Employing the Library

Every research project puts you on the trail of reliable and relevant resources. The simple practices that follow will help you stay on course to find useful resources in the library.

1. **Stay with the program.** As a general rule, allow your research questions, working thesis, and associated keywords (see pages 25–26) to guide you. Focusing on these central ideas helps you decide which resources to pursue and which to ignore.

2. **Take time to wander.** While staying focused is important, taking some time near the start of your project to both physically and electronically browse library resources can lead you to discoveries that will enrich your research.

3. **Start broad and end narrow.** Generally, begin with resources that give you a solid grounding in your topic (e.g., specialized encyclopedias), but gradually move toward the in-depth, scholarly books and journal articles on your topic.

4. **Follow that lead.** As you find resources—books, articles, and other media—study them carefully for clues that point to key studies, scholars, and research centers related to your topic. As you follow up on these leads, look for more.

   - In books, check footnotes or endnotes, as well as bibliographies and appendixes for clues on important sources and authorities.
   - In journal articles, check the early pages, which often include a review of previous research on the topic, as well as the notes and bibliography.
   - In database entries and at Web sites, check for promising links to related materials.

5. **Manage your findings.** As you work your way through your library research, you will be compelled to manage your findings. Good management includes developing a working bibliography, taking careful notes, and engaging and evaluating appropriate sources. See chapter 6 (pages 135–154).

FOCUS on Your Project: As you get into library research for your project, remember the **rhetorical situation:**

- What types of resources will help you achieve your **purpose,** whether to inform, entertain, analyze, or persuade?

- Which library sources will your **audience** understand and respect? Which would be irrelevant?

- How do library resources fit with the **assignment's requirements**? Does the assignment give clues about which resources to tap? Do you need primarily scholarly, peer-reviewed books and articles, or can you use popular magazines and Web sites?

Searching the Online Catalog

Library materials are cataloged so that they are easy to find within the library. In most college libraries, materials are cataloged in an electronic database, typically Web-based, and organized according to the Library of Congress classification system. Other libraries, especially public libraries, may use the Dewey decimal classification system. Your library's online catalog is a powerful tool for finding relevant, reliable books and other material on your topic, so learn to do productive searches that help you build a strong bibliography for your project. For help with keyword searching, see pages 46–47.

Starting Your Search

Below is a typical start screen for a Web-based catalog. Notice the different features that allow you to develop a successful search. Explore each feature, using the help function when necessary, and look for online tutorials about using the catalog.

Start Screen

1 Search options and levels

2 Search fields

3 Limiters

4 Helpful links for tailoring research

Source: Melvyl Catalog of the University of California Libraries

> *Note:* Not all research materials are indexed in the library catalog. You need to understand what materials you will and will not be able to find through searching it. (Some catalogs now integrate book and article search tools. See, for example, McMaster University's catalog at http://library.mcmaster.ca.)

Materials Typically Indexed

Books owned by the library, e-books available through databases ∣ Periodicals owned (journals, magazines, newspapers) ∣ Other media: CDs, audiotapes, videos, DVDs, microform

Materials Typically Not Indexed

Individual articles within periodicals owned by the library ∣ Web sites and other Internet materials

Searching the Catalog Using Distinct Methods

While online catalogs differ in appearance and features, typically your school's catalog will allow you to search the collection through a number of methods. Consider how the following options would be useful for your research project.

Author: If you have the name of a key writer on your topic, you can search the catalog for works published by that person.

Title: If you have discovered the title of a promising work, do a title search to see if your library has the book, to learn more about its content and relevance, and to locate it.

Subject: To locate all the works on your subject, use your topic as a keyword to identify those library holdings that have the topic in their subject list. Note that works in the catalog will be indexed according to the official Library of Congress subject terms: using these precise terms in your search will strengthen your results. For more on LOC subject terms, see pages 57–58.

Call Number: If you have identified a relevant Library of Congress call number for materials on your topic (see page 57), search your library's holdings for all works with that and closely related call numbers. In a sense, searching this way allows you to browse the library's shelves electronically.

Boolean Logic: Using quotation marks, multiple keywords, fields or boxes, parentheses, and Boolean operators such as "and" and "or," you can broaden or narrow your catalog search for more refined results. For example, by including the term "bibliography" along with your keyword or main topic, you may discover print bibliographies on your topic. Similarly, including the term "biography" along with the name of a person you are studying may locate biographies in the library's collection. See pages 46–47 for more on keyword searching.

Date and Medium Operators: Your catalog may have a variety of useful tools for limiting or expanding your search.

- Publication date: You may be able to restrict your findings to those works published after a given year or within a specific span of years.
- Medium: You may be able to restrict your findings to print books, DVDs, reference works, and so on.

Sample Search Using Subject Terms

Advanced Search: Entire Collection   Change Collection

			Words as Phrase	Results
Search :	Subject ▾	attachment disorder	○ No ☑ Yes	
and	Title ▾		◉ No ○ Yes	
and	Title ▾		◉ No ○ Yes	
	Search Clear		**View Search Results:**	

Optional Limits:
Library: ALL Libraries ▾

Tip: Want more or fewer results? Edit your search directly on this page .

Building on Your Initial Search Results

An initial keyword search will typically lead to a list of brief citations, such as the one shown below. Review the citations and do the following:

1. **Decide on the material's relevance for your project.** By briefly scanning each citation, you'll get a sense of whether the book or other resource relates to your focused topic and offers a quality discussion. For example, study the title for key terms related to your topic, the publication year for the currency of the resource, and the format for its usefulness (book, video, etc.).

2. **Expand or narrow your search.** If results are few, you may be restricting your search with terms that are too tightly focused, or you may not be using the best keywords. In this case, use expanders and add keywords (synonyms for your first term) by using the Boolean operator "or" or by adding keywords to search fields. Conversely, if your results are too numerous, use limiters to focus the results and make them manageable. For example, use the Boolean operator "and" with a narrower keyword, or limit the list by publication date.

3. **Try different keywords if the results are irrelevant.** If the citations are coming out of left field, you may need to switch search terms completely. Try other keywords from your brainstormed list or see the discussion of Library of Congress subject headings on page 58. LOC subject terms guarantee the best results, as these are the terms used to index material in the catalog.

4. **Mark citations that you wish to explore further.** By checking the appropriate box or icon, you generate a manageable list of citations to save and study more closely. You may also be able to export this list to a bibliography or e-mail it to yourself.

Sample Screen

1 Results summary

2 Select and save tools

3 Brief citation

4 View link for detailed citation

5 Google links for more info on books

Source: Melvyl Catalog of the University of California Libraries

Employing Full Citations

When you check the full citation for a book or other resource, the information will help you (a) determine whether the resource is worth exploring further, (b) locate the resource in the library, and (c) discover other research pathways.

Citation Components

1. **Author or Editor's Name:** With this detail, you can learn more about the author through some simple online research. In addition, by following the author link, you can find other resources authored by this person or organization.

2. **Title and Subtitle:** Clearly, the title's key words help you determine the resource's relevance to your project.

3. **Publisher and Copyright Date:** The publisher offers a crucial detail about the type of resource. Is this publisher a university press or a commercial press? The publication date helps you determine the resource's timeliness.

4. **Descriptive Information:** Aside from indicating a book's length, this information might indicate the presence of multimedia elements, such as photographs.

5. **Contents:** This citation component may give you chapter or section titles that can identify parts of the resource relevant to your project.

6. **Subject Headings:** This list indicates the LOC subject terms, sometimes called descriptors, for this particular resource—terms that may further your research if you (a) follow the links provided or (b) undertake a new search using these terms.

7. **Format and Location Information:** These crucial details identify the type of resource and allow you to locate it in the library. For print books, this key detail is the LOC call number; in fact, if the call number is a link, you may be able to "browse" other resources with similar call numbers and closely related subject matter. For e-books, as in the sample citation, the resource may be available through a link.

FOCUS on Research Essentials: The online catalog will likely allow you to save citation information through a print, save, export, or e-mail function. Use this feature to build your working bibliography (see page 136).

Locating Resources Using Call Numbers

Determined by the classification scheme, the call number is a resource's code. Library of Congress call numbers combine letters and numbers to specify a resource's broad subject area, topic, and authorship or title. Therefore, finding an item involves combining alphabetical and numerical order. Here is an example.

Sample Call Number: *The Neuroscience of Human Relationships: Attachment and the Developing Social Brain.*

QP360.C69 2006

| subject area | topic number | cutter number | publication date |

To find this resource, first determine its format (VIDEO, or REF, etc.) and go that specific location in your library. Once there, follow the call number elements one at a time:

1. Find the section on physiology, the "QP" designation.

2. Follow the numbers until you reach "360," a number within the span for neurophysiology and neuropsychology. If a subtopic number follows the topic number (e.g., 360.15), find that subtopic next—not shown in this example.

3. Use the cutter number "C69" to locate the resource alphabetically with "C" and numerically with "69."

Using the LOC System

In the LOC system, pay attention to subject-area letters, topic numbers, and subtopic numbers: Q4.6 comes before QP221; QM22 before QM178; QR74.M87 before QR74.5.M68. Note, as well, how tracking down a book or other resource in the stacks offers you the opportunity to do more browsing. Instead of browsing online (see page 54), you can physically browse the books on either side of the one you locate, and perhaps find more material relevant to your project.

Focus on Your Major: Finding Your LOC Classification Home

As you become more familiar with the subject matter of your major, you will learn how the LOC classification system treats that subject matter. In a sense, the LOC structures the knowledge embodied by your discipline and also relates it to other information.

LOC Subject Classes

The Library of Congress classification system combines letters and numbers, beginning with a letter indicating the subject class. The 21 subject classes are listed at the right. Identify the specific letters most closely aligned with your field of study, remembering that many fields include an interdisciplinary element that combines interests, approaches, and methods from more than one discipline. This is the case, for example, with environmental studies and cultural studies.

A General Works
B Philosophy, Psychology, Religion
C Auxiliary Sciences of History
D World History and history of Europe, Asia, Africa, Australia, New Zealand, etc.
E History of United States
F History of the Americas
G Geography, Anthropology, Recreation
H Social Sciences
J Political Science
K Law

L Education
M Music and Books on Music
N Fine Arts
P Language and Literature
Q Science
R Medicine
S Agriculture
T Technology
U Military Science
V Naval Science
Z Bibliography, Library Science, Information Resources (General)

Categories

Each subject class divides further into categories indicated by two- or three-letter combinations. These categories show the main areas of knowledge within the class. To become a more efficient researcher, explore thoroughly those categories related to your major, profession, or field. Learn the category breakdown, the range of call numbers for these categories, and the location of materials with these call numbers.

Class R – Medicine
R Medicine (General)
RA Public aspects of medicine
RB Pathology
RC Internal medicine
RD Surgery
RE Ophthalmology
RF Otorhinolaryngology
RG Gynecology and obstetrics
RJ Pediatrics

RK Dentistry
RL Dermatology
RM Therapeutics, Pharmacology
RS Pharmacy and materia medica
RT Nursing
RV Botanic, Thomsonian, and eclectic medicine
RX Homeopathy
RZ Other systems of medicine

Subcategories

Each main category breaks down into subcategories of knowledge—specific topics and subtopics studied in your major; in the LOC, these are arranged in a rough hierarchy, from general to specific, with each topic assigned a number or span of numbers. As shown in the example to the right (a partial list of subcategories), when you are working on a research project, this topical breakdown helps you identify relevant foci and the associated call-number ranges.

RJ – Pediatrics

RJ1-570	Pediatrics
RJ47.3-47.4	Genetic aspects
RJ50-51	Examination, Diagnosis
RJ52-53	Therapeutics
RJ59-60	Infant and neonatal morbidity and mortality
RJ91	Supposed prenatal influence, Prenatal culture, Stirpiculture
RJ101-103	Child health, Child health services
RJ125-145	Physiology of children and adolescents
RJ206-235	Nutrition and feeding of children and adolescents
RJ240	Immunization of children (General)
RJ242-243	Hospital care

FOCUS on Research Essentials: For a more detailed breakdown of the LOC system, check the print *Library of Congress Subject Headings* in your library or go to www.loc.gov/catdir/cpso/lcco/.

Connecting with Other Online Catalogs

From its Web site, your library may offer access to many other online catalogs. Such catalogs allow you to search for books and other resources not available in your own library, materials that may be available digitally or through interlibrary loan. Such access is especially important if your library has few resources on your topic. You can start by going to LIBCAT, www.librarysites.info, but you should also consider the following information:

NetLibrary

Your library may link you with this e-book collection. In fact, these e-books may be indexed through your college library's online catalog. With over 160,000 titles available (some free and some through your library's subscription), NetLibrary offers fully searchable books that can be "browsed" or "signed out." For more on e-books, see page 73.

State Libraries

Your library may provide links to a statewide system of libraries, giving you access to state, county, and city information, including government documents, reports, programs, and services. For example, North Carolina colleges, high schools, and public libraries are linked through NC LIVE: North Carolina Libraries for Virtual Education. For more examples of such state and regional systems, go to www.librarysites.info and search specific states under U.S. libraries.

Library of Congress

Your library may connect you with the Library of Congress catalog at www.loc.gov, which allows you to do basic and advanced searches of this national library, with links to a variety of other services for research writers.

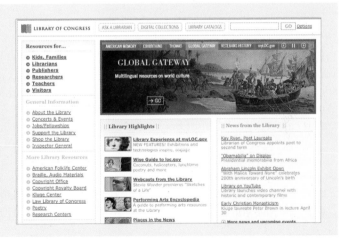

Library of Congress Prints and Photographs Division

FOCUS on Multimedia: You can also look for catalogs from other nations—a government's national library or the country's university libraries. For example, to gain access to Canadian libraries, you can enter the Canadian Library Gateway (http://www.collectionscanada.gc.ca/gateway/index-e.html).

Global Libraries: WorldCat

Especially helpful for your research is WorldCat, part of FirstSearch, a service provided by OCLC (the Online Computer Library Center). OCLC connects more than 60,000 libraries in 112 countries. Among other databases, FirstSearch includes OCLC libraries, ArticleFirst (an index of articles), ERIC (education field), GPO (U.S. government publications), MEDLINE (a medical, dentistry, nursing database), PapersFirst (conference papers index), and Proceedings (conference proceedings).

OCLC's FirstSearch WorldCat: Start Screen

1 Search options and database information

2 Search fields

3 Limiters

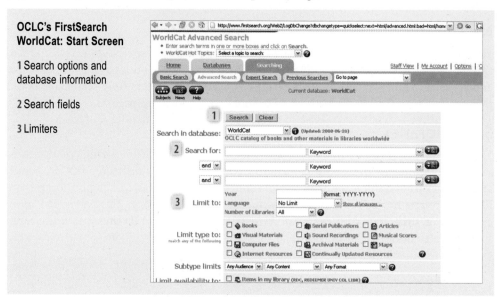

Source: http://www.worldcat.org/

Like your library's online catalog, WorldCat will generate a list of citations based on your keyword searching, searching that follows the same LOC rules. You can then mark specific citations, look at full citations, and save citations through a variety of methods. WorldCat also offers the following helpful services:

- It can generate a list of books and other materials that may be unavailable in your library—books you can order through interlibrary loan simply by making an e-mail request. In fact, WorldCat can give you a list of libraries worldwide that have a given book.
- It can indicate if a particular book or resource is available in your own library.
- It can give you a URL link for electronic books and other computer files.

FOCUS on Your Major: Your library may give you access to the catalogs of advanced research libraries specializing in specific fields. Here are two examples:

- Science and technology: the Massachusetts Institute of Technology (MIT) Libraries (http://libraries.mit.edu)
- Business: Harvard Business School's Baker Library (http://www.library.hbs.edu/)

Searching Subscription Databases for Periodical Articles

While your library's online catalog helps you find books and similar resources, subscription databases help you find periodical articles. As with the catalog and other library services, when it comes to database searching, take advantage of orientation sessions, tutorials, and librarian assistance so that your article searches will be productive. Note, too, that like the online catalog, subscription databases rely upon Library of Congress subject terms (see page 57).

Understand Periodicals

Periodicals are publications or broadcasts produced at regular intervals (daily, weekly, monthly, quarterly). Today, periodicals are distributed through virtually all communication media: print, television, radio, and the Internet. In fact, most print periodicals have an online version or complement. Although some periodicals are broad in their subject matter and audience appeal, most focus on a narrow range of topics for a particular audience.

- Daily newspapers and newscasts provide current information on events, opinions, and trends—from politics to natural disasters. **Examples:** *The Wall Street Journal, The Newshour, Thomson Reuters News* (www.reuters.com).

- Weekly and monthly magazines generally provide more in-depth information on a wide range of topics. **Examples:** *Time, Consumer Reports, Scientific American, 60 Minutes, Communication Arts* (plus online complement www.commarts.com).

- Scholarly and trade journals, generally published quarterly, provide specialized information for a narrowly focused audience. **Examples:** *Journal of Labor Economics, Literature Film Quarterly, Journal of Technology Education.*

Daily news publications and weekly or monthly magazines can prove useful for your research projects by capturing current events and interests, by offering an interesting introduction to your topic, or by expressing how an event or topic is relevant to people's lives. Articles in such periodicals, however, have limits: They tend to condense information rather than thoroughly address a topic; they are relatively brief; and they may lack documentation. For your research projects, then, you are better off attending to scholarly journals, which contain specialized, in-depth, carefully documented, peer-reviewed articles. *Note:* Online journals are discussed in chapter 4.

Identify Your Library's Subscription Databases

Typically, you'll find relevant articles for your project by searching article databases that your library subscribes to. These search services might include EBSCOhost, OCLC's ArticleFirst, JSTOR, and LexisNexis, as well as a host of specialized services and databases. These tools help you find citations of promising articles, often with links to full-text electronic versions. Start by going to your library's Web site to learn what databases and search tools your library subscribes to. Then study the sample search on the following pages.

Select and Search Databases

Based on your project's disciplinary focus, start your search for articles by selecting those databases that index articles in relevant journals. Typically, you might start with the general version of databases such as EBSCOhost and LexisNexis. For EBSCOhost, this database is Academic Search Premier, which provides access to over 4,100 scholarly publications covering all disciplines; for LexisNexis, this database is its News resource, which offers access to a range of articles and transcripts.

A more focused research strategy would involve turning to specialized databases, available for virtually every discipline and often an option within search services such as EBSCOhost (e.g., Business Source Elite, PsycINFO, ERIC, Humanities International Complete) and LexisNexis (e.g., Legal, Medical, and Business databases). If a basic search turns up little, turn to specialized databases, seeking help from a librarian if necessary. For a list of specialized databases, arranged by discipline, see page 66.

EBSCOhost Search Screen

The example below shows an EBSCOhost search screen for an article search focused on Jane Austen and film. Notice how limiters, expanders, and other advanced features help you find the highest quality materials.

Note: Such limiters can restrict the date and the type of journals.

Screen Features

1 Search fields

2 Database list

3 Limiters available

Generate a Citation List

Your database will generate lists of citations, brief descriptions of articles by way of keyword searches, subject terms, abstracts, and more. At this point, you must study the results and refine your list.

Refining Your List

Looking at all the features demonstrated in the following search screen, you can see how your list could easily grow out of control. Follow the three management strategies below to effectively evaluate citations and limit your list.

Search Features

1 Article links indicating article availability and format

2 Folder feature for "capturing" citations

3 "Sort" options

4 Numbered citations including titles, authors, journal information, length, and location notes

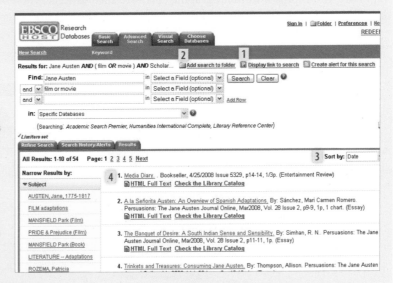

Management Strategies

1. If your results are too broad or numerous, limit them:
   - Use narrower search terms, especially LOC search terms that you might discover through studying full citations closely.
   - Follow links suggested by the search service: These may be provided in a list of subtopics, such as those shown at the left in the sample above.
   - Use additional limiters such as publication dates, full-text only, or scholarly articles only.

2. If your results are too narrow, too few, or irrelevant, expand your search by using different search terms until you discover the best ones, preferably the LOC subject terms. Consider using expanders available through the search service, trying different databases, or consulting with a librarian.

3. When you identify promising citations, mark them for "capture" or further study. After marking promising citations, you can then open citations to get complete information about the articles, as shown on the next page.

Study Citations and Capture Identifying Information

By studying a full citation, especially the abstract (article summary) included, you can determine three things: Is this article relevant to your research? Is an electronic, full-text version available? If not, does the library have this periodical? In the sample citation below, notice the helpful information about the author and her institutional affiliation, including the link to other articles written by the author. Also note the subject-term links that offer pathways to related resources.

To develop your working bibliography (see page 136), you should also "capture" the article's identifying details by using the save, print, or e-mail function; by importing the details into bibliographic software such as RefWorks; or by recording the periodical's title, the issue and date, and the article's title and page numbers.

Sample EBSCOhost Citation

1 Save options

2 Author links to other publications

3 Source link for more details or full text

4 Subject links for further research

5 Article summary

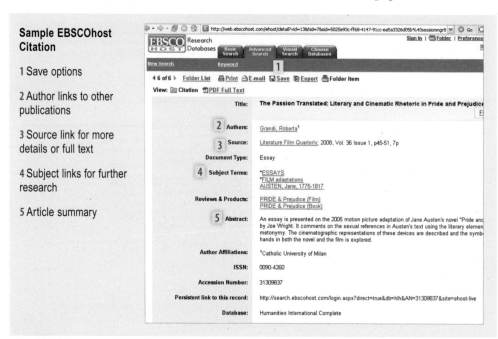

FOCUS on Research Essentials: As with other sources, you must evaluate articles and engage them critically (see pages 144–149). Consider especially the periodical's quality, goals, and intended audience, as well as the specific article's currency. In addition, because subscription databases have been indexing articles for a relatively short period, they do not point you to all periodical articles out there. If your project calls for articles published before 1985, for instance, you may need to use the *Reader's Guide to Periodical Literature* or another print index. While databases are rapidly digitizing pre-1985 articles (e.g., the JSTOR database), many excellent periodical articles are available only in print. To use the *Reader's Guide,* consult a librarian.

Retrieve the Article's Full Text

When a citation indicates that you have a promising article, you want to access the article as efficiently as possible. To do so, consider this procedure:

1. If available, retrieve the article through a direct link. Many citations contain a link to a full-text electronic copy. From there, you can print, save, or e-mail the article. Often, you will have the choice of accessing the article in *html* or *pdf* formats. The html version offers flexibility in working with the article text, but typically lacks page numbers and graphics. When documenting the article in your paper, you may have to identify borrowed material by indicating paragraph number rather than page number. The pdf version typically shows the article as it was published in the print periodical, showing all graphics and maintaining the pagination of the original.

2. If unavailable online, determine if your library has a copy of the periodical issue in which the article was published. If this availability is not already indicated in the citation, check your library's inventory of periodicals: Search the online catalog using the journal's title, or go to a list that is either printed out or posted on the library's Web site. As you check the lists, examine especially the periodical issues and dates available, the form (print or microform), and the library location (bound stacks, current-issues shelves, microform room).

3. To get the article, follow your library's procedure. You may have to submit a request slip so that a librarian can get the periodical, or you may be able to get it yourself in the current, bound, or microform collection. If the article is in microform, it means (as the word suggests) that the article has been captured photographically, shrunk down, and reproduced on film reels (microfilm) or rectangular sheets (microfiche). Once you retrieve the microform, you will need to find the article on the reel or sheet by using the microform machines in the library. These machines not only allow you to enlarge the image so that you can read the article but also may give you the option of printing out pages (probably for a charge comparable to a photocopier).

FOCUS on Research Essentials: Few libraries keep back issues of newspapers. If the full text of the article is not available through a database like LexisNexis, try going to an Internet resource such as <newspapers.com> or to the news source's own Web site (e.g., *Los Angeles Times* archives at http://pqasb.pqarchiver.com/latimes/search.html).

Focus on Your Major: Databases for Disciplines

Most libraries offer you access to periodical databases from a wide range of disciplines. Review the list below, identifying databases related to your major.

- **AGRICOLA** offers over 3 million bibliographic citations from the National Agricultural Library group—with materials about topics from animal science to nutrition.
- **ARTbibliographies Modern** abstracts articles, books, catalogs, and other resources on modern and contemporary art.
- **CAIRSS for Music** offers bibliographic citations for articles on music-related topics, from music education to music therapy.
- **Communication & Mass Media Complete** offers access to resources on topics like public speaking and TV broadcasting.
- **ERIC** offers citations, abstracts, and digests for over 980 journals in the education field.
- **First Search,** a fee-based information service, offers access to more than 30 scholarly databases in a range of disciplines.
- **GPO,** the Government Printing Office, offers access to more than 450,000 records for U.S. government documents (reports, hearings, judicial rules, addresses, etc.).
- **Health Source** (in Nursing and Consumer editions) offers access to almost 600 medical journals through abstracts, indexing, and full-text material on health topics.
- **Ingenta** offers citations for over 25,000 journals, particularly in the sciences.
- **JSTOR** offers full-text access to scholarly articles in a full range of disciplines, articles once available only in print.
- **Math Database** offers article citations for international mathematics research.
- **Medline** offers access to journals in medicine and medicine-related disciplines through references, citations, and abstracts.
- **MLA Bibliography** provides bibliographic citations for articles addressing a range of modern-language and literature-related topics.
- **National Environmental Publications Internet Site (NEPIS)** offers access to more than 6,000 EPA documents (full text, online).
- **PsycINFO,** from the American Psychological Association, offers access to materials in psychology and psychology-related fields (e.g., social work, criminology).
- **Scirus** indexes science resources by offering citations with article titles and authors, source publication information, and lines of text indicating the article's content.
- **Vocation and Career Collection** offers full-text access to over 400 trade- and industry-related periodicals.
- **Worldwide Political Science Abstracts** offers bibliographic citations in politics-related fields, from public policy to international law.

Using Print and Electronic Reference Works

Reference works are information-rich resources designed and organized to answer readers' specific questions. In general, such works supply information that you need for your project, or they function as tools for conducting research effectively. Reference works can be books, CD-ROMs, subscription databases, or Web sites—either general or specialized. While reference works may not end up on your final bibliography, they are crucial to your research for the following reasons:

1. **They provide an overview of your topic.** For example, an encyclopedia article on nuclear energy can give you the big picture of how this energy source works and what its history has been before you explore its pros and cons.

2. **They supply basic facts.** Reference works give you definitions, statistics, dates, names, and other details foundational to your topic. For example, a dictionary focused on the visual arts would give you a reliable definition of impressionism for a project on this movement's influence on American art.

3. **They share common knowledge about the topic.** Knowing what is common knowledge is important for two reasons: (a) you need to go beyond common knowledge in your project, and (b) you generally don't need to document common knowledge in your paper (see page 161).

4. **They offer ideas for focusing and furthering your research.** Frequently, reference works break down a topic into subtopics, introduce areas of complexity or controversy deserving more attention, or indicate key publications that you should use in your project.

How to Find and Use Reference Works

In your library, both print and digital reference works will likely be easy to find and access. Locate the reference works relevant to your project by following these steps:

- Find the reference and ready-reference areas in your library. Reference works are typically shelved separately from the main collection, with ready-reference texts (such as frequently consulted dictionaries) in a prominent location.

- Consult—you guessed it—a reference librarian for his or her expert advice.

- Through searching the online catalog, limit your results by using "reference" and identifying call numbers tagged with REF. If you are looking for a specific type of reference work (e.g., biographies), include that term in your search.

- Check the library's Web site for links to reliable, scholarly reference works available in digital, searchable form. In fact, your library may offer a virtual reference service: You submit your question, and the librarians send you the answer.

Use reference works productively by understanding their structure and coverage. Each reference work covers a certain amount and type of information. Learn these limits by checking forewords, prefaces, publication dates, FAQs, help screens, and instructions pages. Determine the work's usefulness by paying attention to these issues:

- The work's publication date, last update, and dates of coverage
- The actual material provided by the reference work (citations, abstracts, raw data in tables, full articles, bibliographic lists, and so on)
- The structure or organization of information (alphabetical, chronological, categorical, etc.)

Types of Reference Works

When you need basic information, foundational data, initial overviews, surveys of a topic, ideas for further reading, accurate definitions, guidance for research, direction to resources, and more—turn to reference works like those listed here and on the next two pages.

Abstracts direct you to articles on a topic. But abstracts also summarize those materials so you know whether a resource is relevant before you take time to locate and read it. Abstracts are usually organized into subject areas: *Computer Abstracts, Environmental Abstracts, Social Work Abstracts.* **Note:** Abstracts are often integrated into online database citations. (Depending on your project, you may have to write an abstract for your paper. For instructions on writing abstracts, see pages 238–239.)

Sample abstract for "Clarifying Core Characteristics of Attachment Disorders: A Review of Current Research and Theory," published in the *American Journal of Orthopsychiatry*, January 2006 (Volume 76, Issue 1), pages 55-64.

Reactive attachment disorder is a relatively new diagnosis that is not well studied. Conflicting ideas about its etiology and presentation pervade the theoretical, research, clinical, and popular literature. Clarifying core characteristics of this disorder and distinguishing them from comorbid conditions are critical for improved diagnosis and treatment of children with attachment problems.

Almanacs, Yearbooks, and Statistical Resources, normally published annually, contain diverse facts.

- *The World Almanac and Book of Facts* presents information on politics, history, religion, business, social programs, education, and sports.

Almanac Entry from 2008 *World Almanac:* "Influenza in the Off-Season"

Researchers at Penn State University and the National Institutes of Health reported that the influenza A virus migrates and mixes with other viruses during the summer, then returns to the Northern Hemisphere before winter as a genetically different virus. The scientists analyzed the genomes of influenza A samples from New Zealand, Australia, and New York State between 1998 and 2005, discovering that the New York viruses were related to viruses circulating during the winter in the Southern Hemisphere—implying a significant amount of traffic in both directions each season. The teams noted that the best protection against emerging, evolving viruses was the development of universal vaccines to protect against multiple strains of influenza.

■ The *Statistical Abstract of the United States* provides data on population, geography, social trends, politics, employment, business, science, and industry. For more information, go to http://www.census.gov/compendia/statab/index.html.

Statistical Abstract Entry

Table 711. **Retail Gasoline Prices—Selected Areas: 2005 to 2007**
[In cents per gallon. Prices are annual averages]

Area	Regular			Midgrade			Premium		
	2005	2006	2007	2005	2006	2007	2005	2006	2007
Boston, MA.........	225.7	256.3	271.0	236.3	268.2	283.6	246.4	278.7	294.2
Chicago, IL.........	231.8	266.3	294.1	241.9	276.6	305.1	251.9	286.8	315.4
Cleveland, OH.......	222.0	249.4	275.9	232.2	259.7	286.4	243.0	270.6	297.2
Denver, CO.........	223.9	253.1	276.8	235.4	264.7	289.0	245.4	274.5	299.7
Houston, TX	216.8	246.6	260.6	226.8	256.7	272.1	236.5	266.6	283.1
Los Angeles, CA	249.0	283.3	304.7	258.6	293.4	315.5	268.1	303.3	325.7
Miami, FL...........	238.9	267.1	286.0	249.3	277.9	299.1	258.5	286.9	309.8
New York, NY	230.0	263.1	278.9	241.5	275.8	293.3	251.3	286.4	304.4
San Francisco, CA.....	248.1	279.1	317.1	259.4	291.0	329.7	269.4	301.1	340.0
Seattle, WA.........	236.3	268.3	294.7	247.3	278.9	305.1	257.6	289.1	315.4

Source: U.S. Energy Information Administration, *Weekly U.S. Retail Gasoline Prices*, Gasoline Historical Data. See also <http://www.eia.doe.gov/oil_gas/petroleum/data_publications/wrgp/mogas_history.html>.

U.S. Energy Information Administration, Weekly U.s. Retail Gasoline Prices, Gaso line Historical Data.

Source: Central Intelligence Agency

Atlases contain maps, charts, and diagrams presenting data on geography, climate, and human activities. Generally, atlases present two types of map information. First, they can portray physical boundaries (land/water, rivers, mountains, etc.) and/or political boundaries (nations, states, counties). Second, atlases can offer thematic maps that represent topics like natural resources, climate, population density, etc. **Example:** *The New Rand McNally College World Atlas* provides global information useful in a variety of disciplines.

Bibliographies list resources on a specific topic or by a specific author. A good current bibliography saves you a lot of the work that goes into compiling your own bibliography on a topic. **Example:** *The Basic Business Library: Core Resources.* Remember to check for links to bibliographies at your library's Web site. You can also search for bibliographies within your library's collection by including "bibliographies" as a search term.

Biographical Resources supply information about people. General biographies cover a range of people. Other biographies focus on the deceased, the living, or people from a specific group (an industry, vocation, race, etc.). **Examples:** *Current Biography Yearbook, Contemporary Authors, Who's Who in America, Who's Who in Economics, World Artists 1980-1990.*

Directories supply contact information for people and organizations. **Examples:** *USPS ZIP Code Lookup and Address Information* (online), *Official Congressional Directory.*

Encyclopedias supply facts and overviews for topics arranged alphabetically.

- General encyclopedias cover many fields of knowledge: *Encyclopædia Britannica, Collier's Encyclopedia.*
- Specialized encyclopedias focus on a single area of knowledge: *Encyclopedia of Latin American History and Culture, Encyclopedia of American Film Comedy.*
- Wikis are, in a sense, electronic encyclopedias that evolve through collaborative authorship. For more on using and avoiding wikis, see pages 86–89.

Guides and Handbooks help you explore a knowledge area or work in a discipline.

- Guides to Fields or Disciplines: *Standard Handbook for Electrical Engineers, Treasurer's and Controller's Desk Book* (e-book), *Literary Research Guide.*
- Topical Guides: *Peterson's Graduate and Professional Programs, The Global Etiquette Guide to Mexico and Latin America, A Guide to Prairie Fauna.*

Indexes point you to useful resources. Some indexes are general, such as the *Reader's Guide to Periodical Literature,* while others specialize on a topic, such as the *Environment Index* and *Index to Legal Periodicals.* Note, however, that print indexes are often available electronically through your library's subscription databases. See pages 61–66.

Vocabulary Resources supply information on languages, information that can help you clarify and deepen your understanding of key concepts related to your topic.

- General dictionaries, such as the *Webster's Collegiate Dictionary* or the *Oxford English Dictionary Online* (to which your library might subscribe), supply definitions, pronunciations, and histories for a range of words.
- Specialized dictionaries and glossaries define words common to a field, topic, or group of people: *The New Harvard Dictionary of Music, Dictionary of Marketing Terms* (e-book), *Dictionary of Environment and Sustainable Development.*
- Bilingual dictionaries translate words from one language to another: *Diccionario Bilingüe de Negocios* (Bilingual Business Dictionary)
- A thesaurus presents synonyms—words with similar meanings.

Dictionary Entry for "hybrid" from *The American Heritage Dictionary of the English Language* (online)

NOUN: **1.** *Genetics* The offspring of genetically dissimilar parents or stock, especially the offspring produced by breeding plants or animals of different varieties, species, or races. **2a.** Something of mixed origin or composition. **b.** Something, such as a computer or power plant, having two kinds of components that produce the same or similar results. **3.** A word whose elements are derived from different languages. ETYMOLOGY: Latin *hibrida, hybrida,* mongrel

---

 FOCUS on Your Major: Each discipline has its own set of central reference works. As you advance in your major, identify the most relevant encyclopedias, dictionaries, biographical sources, and indexes for your research. Particularly important is finding a well-respected guide to the discipline.

Using Books: Trade, Scholarly, and E-Books

Your college library contains a range of books—technical publications, reference works, literature, and scholarly studies—available in print and/or digital form. Generally, these books will be excellent, authoritative texts, but you must still be discerning as you consider their content. As you track down books, you ought to identify their type and determine their value to your project.

Identifying Types of Books

Not all books are the same, so consider the distinctions below and how they are important to your project.

Trade books are typically written for a broad public and published by for-profit presses. Often written by experts and developed through a strong editorial process, such books can be filled with reliable, useful information for a lay audience, though quality, depth, and reliability can vary greatly.

> **Sample titles:** *Flirting with Pride & Prejudice: Fresh Perspectives on the Original Chick-Lit Masterpiece* (BenBella Books); *Parenting the Hurt Child: Helping Adoptive Families Heal and Grow* (Pinon Press); *Zoom: The Global Race to Fuel the Car of the Future* (Grand Central Publishing); *Write for Business* (UpWrite Press)

Scholarly books are typically written for a specialized audience and for college-level students. Having gone through a thorough peer-review and editorial process, such studies are typically published by university presses or other respected scholarly presses. Relevant to your topic, you might, for example, find books like these:

- a study written by an individual scholar or collaboratively by a team of scholars
- a collection of related essays written by a variety of scholars
- a book that is part of a larger scholarly series
- the published proceedings of a conference

> **Sample titles:** *Jane Austen on Screen* (Cambridge University Press); *Handbook of Preschool Mental Health: Development, Disorders, Treatment* (Guilford Press); *Environmentally Conscious Transportation* (Wiley Series in Environmentally Conscious Engineering); *The Century Handbook of Writing* (The Century Company)

Working with Print Books

Once you've found a good book, how do you use it? For many research projects, you simply don't have time to read the whole book. Instead, mine each book for its gold by using the strategies below.

Print Book Strategies

■ **Review front matter.** The title and copyright pages give the book's title and subtitle, the author's name, and publication information, including publication date and Library of Congress subject headings. Another page may contain a note about the author and/or sponsoring organization's credentials and other publications. Check this information for clues about the book's currency, focus, and credibility.

■ **Scan the table of contents.** To see what the book covers and how it is organized, review the table of contents. Note the sections and chapters that are relevant for your project.

■ **Search the index.** Using keywords, check the coverage for the topics most closely related to your project. Note the number of pages and their location.

■ **Skim the preface and/or introduction.** These pages often indicate the book's perspective, origin, and contents.

■ **Check appendixes, glossaries, endnotes, and bibliographies.** These are good sources for tables, graphics, definitions, and statistics. In addition, they often offer insights for further research.

BenBella Books

AVAVA/www.shutterstock.com

 FOCUS on Research Essentials: To confirm a book's quality, check reviews in the *Book Review Digest* or those available through online databases such as EBSCOhost or LexisNexis.

Working with E-Books

Library subscriptions to an e-book service such as NetLibrary offer you access to thousands of digital books. Similarly, you may find relevant e-books, which are flagged as electronic files with URLs, as you search your library's online catalog or WorldCat.

To determine the worth of an e-book to your project, review it in much the same way you would a print book. E-books can be electronically browsed, checked out, read online, or searched using keyword searches.

Caution: While it makes sense to search an e-book using keywords, be careful not to isolate a specific sentence or paragraph from the whole. Doing so decontextualizes the reading. Instead, read chapters or sections that relate to your topic.

Review the screen below. It shows the features, menus, and elements (e.g., an html version of the book's text) of a typical e-book.

Screen Features

1 Publisher identification

2 Book title and organizational author (link)

3 Search and navigation tools

4 Book page number and text

5 Text version choices (html or original print view)

6 Book table of contents links

Tip: As you work with an e-book, assess its reliability. What version of the text is this electronic edition? Who are the author and editor? Is the publisher respected?

FOCUS on Multimedia: Because it offers access to subscription databases, your library is likely your best source for finding quality e-books for your research. However, e-books are also available on the free Web (see page 84 for example Web sites that host e-books).

Practicing Your Research

1. **Explore:** Using the strategies in this chapter, get familiar with your school's library—its spaces, its services, and its Web site. Take notes on features most relevant to your work as a student, collect handouts that will help you with projects, and bookmark Web pages that you imagine yourself using frequently.

2. **Apply:** Identify two wars, two natural disasters, two works of literature, or two people—one from the past and the other current. Discover what your library has available on both topics by searching for books and other material in the online catalog, locating periodical articles through subscription databases, and identifying relevant reference resources. What are your conclusions about the library's value for researching quite different topics?

3. **Collaborate on a Case Study:** As directed by your instructor, continue to work with classmates on your clothing-focused project. Find four books through online catalogs and four periodical articles through subscription databases, making sure to determine the best LOC subject terms. Conduct preliminary and background research on your topic by accessing different reference works.

4. **Research Your Major:** Identify the library's materials and services related to your discipline: pertinent handouts or postings; call numbers of books and other media; reference works, including a disciplinary guide; important periodical databases and periodicals held; Web pages and links provided at the library's Web site. Report your findings as a kind of "how to" explanation of research in your discipline.

5. **Work on Your Current Project:** Conduct your library research:
   - Research your topic in reference works (print and electronic), looking for overviews, definitions, key facts, and insights for further research.
   - Using your library catalog and other online catalogs, find books and other materials—searching with the best LOC subject terms for your topic. Retrieve promising books from the stacks or through interlibrary loan.
   - Using your library's periodical databases, find quality articles on your topic. Retrieve promising articles through full-text links, by finding the periodicals in your library, or by ordering them through interlibrary loan.

Checklist:

☑ Using solid keyword searching strategies, I have effectively searched the library's holdings for items relevant to my topic.

☑ Using my library's access to other libraries, I have located and requested other items on my topic.

☑ I have tapped my library's print and electronic reference works for information.

☑ I have scoured my library's print and electronic periodical search tools and holdings for relevant articles on my topic.

Doing Research on the Free Web

4

© Cengage Learning/Illustrated by Chris Krenzke

 Q How much do you rely on free-Web tools such as Google, Yahoo, and Wikipedia to do research—for everyday concerns and/or for college work? How useful do you find such tools? What difficulties do you face in using them?

If you're young enough, it's probably hard for you to imagine a pre-Web world. Those of us old enough to remember life BI (Before the Internet) can testify that the digital revolution has radically transformed research—for good and ill. The Internet can be a great source of a wide range of information, or it can be a great waste of time as you face 2,251,817 hits for a keyword search or wander through a maze of fruitless links. For researchers both young and old, the trick is developing effective e-search skills and strategies, ones that quickly get you to relevant resources and help you sort the gold from the fool's gold.

If you typically do basic Google searches as your only Internet search method, developing these skills may be challenging. This chapter aims to help you meet that challenge. Let's begin with two reminders as you embark on free-Web research:

1. **Remember your research rhetoric:** Will free-Web research help you achieve your project's goal? Is this research fitting? Will your audience respond positively or negatively to various Web sources? Does the assignment disallow, discourage, encourage, or require Web sources? Does your topic lend itself to such research? How much time do you have to search on the free Web?

2. **Remember your library's portal to the Internet:** As we discussed in chapter 3, the library often offers the kind of guidance to Internet sources that will get you to scholarly, reliable, in-depth information on your topic. Start there.

What's Ahead?

Understanding the Web: A Primer for Research

It's likely that you already understand the basics of the Web—either through the experience of using it regularly or through some instruction in grade school and high school. But what do you need to recall or learn about the Internet in order to use it for college-level research? The following discussion offers a primer for such use.

What Is the Internet?

The **Internet** is a worldwide network of connected computers and computer networks, a network that allows computers to share information with each other. Often abbreviated to **Net,** the Internet essentially allows networks to share Web pages, send e-mail, provide text chat, transfer files, conduct video and audio conferencing, and more.

What Is the World Wide Web?

The **World Wide Web** is a set of interconnected documents, files, and databases, all accessible by a Web browser. Here's how it works:

- Millions of **Web pages** are available because of **hypertext links.** These links appear as clickable words or icons or as Web addresses. (See the sample Web page below.)
- **Web sites** are groups of related Web pages posted by the same sponsor or organization. A **home page,** a Web site's "entry" page, typically provides main links and access to information about the sponsor. **Directories, search engines,** and **metasearch tools** are special Web sites that provide searchable listings of many resources on the Web.
- A **Web browser** such as Internet Explorer, Firefox, Safari, or Opera is a graphical program that accesses files on the Web.

Sample Web Page with Research Features:

1 Site name

2 Search field

3 Title bar

4 Navigation buttons

5 Drop down menus

6 Page title

7 Text links and menus

American Psychological Association

What Does an Internet Address Mean?

An Internet address, called a URL (Uniform Resource Locator), includes the protocol indicating how the computer file should be accessed—often http: or ftp: (followed by a double slash); a domain name—often beginning with www; and additional path information (following a single slash) to access other pages within a site.

http://www.nrcs.usda.gov/news/index.html#csp_watershed2

In the example above, the URL (www.nrcs.usda.gov) is made up of the Web designation, the subdomain "nrcs" the domain "usda," and the domain-name extension "gov." Everything after the extension designates a folder or file hosted by the domain. Domain name extensions (technically called TLDs, or top-level domains) are a key part of an address because, as shown below, they indicate what type of organization created a site and give you clues about the site's purpose (e.g., to educate, sell, and/or entertain).

Domain Type & Description		Example
.com	a commercial organization or business	Honda Hybrid Page http://automobiles.honda.com/alternative-fuel-vehicles
.gov	a US government organization—federal, state, or local	Transportation Technology R&D Center for the Argonne National Laboratory, US Dept. of Energy: http://www.transportation.anl.gov
.edu	an educational institution	ARC: Automotive Research Center, U of Michigan: http://arc.engin.umich.edu
.org	a non-profit organization	Society of Automotive Engineers: http://www.sae.org/servlets/index
.net	an organization within the Internet's infrastructure	eiNET Directory: http://www.einet.net
.mil	a military site	United States Transportation Command: (TRANSCOM) http://www.transcom.mil
.biz	a business site	Advantica (global engineering consultancy in energy industry): http://www.advantica.biz
.info	any site primarily providing information	Alternative Energy News: http://www.alternative-energy-news.info

What Is the Free Web vs. the Deep Web?

The free Web refers to anything posted on the Web that is openly accessible to anyone. The deep Web refers to material on the Internet not readily found by search engines or in some way restricted in terms of access. Content on the deep Web is estimated to be several times larger than what is on the free Web. As the previous chapter discussed, your library tends to take you into the deep Web: restricted-access reference tools, subscription databases, the WorldCat catalog, the NetLibrary of e-books, and so on. This chapter focuses on free-Web research.

Using the Free Web for College Research

Depending on your interests, you likely use the free Web for a wide range of your communication and entertainment needs: e-mail, Facebook, MSN, music downloads, online shopping, YouTube, eBay, gaming, and so on. The list seems endless and the possibilities keep expanding. Moreover, you likely use Google for searches, and you readily navigate to Wikipedia when you need some basic information. In fact, these may have been your primary tools for doing research in high school.

But how well does the free Web support your college-level research and writing projects? For this work, the free Web is changing. More and more scholarly, reliable material is moving onto the free Web; however, finding those reliable resources among the mediocre or misleading material can be difficult and time-consuming. For that reason, your instructors may restrict you in certain projects from using any resources from the free Web. When you are allowed to use free-Web resources, make decisions based on their benefits and drawbacks.

Benefits of Free-Web Research

Imagine that in a cultural-studies course, you are researching the cult of celebrity in our society—the public fascination (obsession) with actors and other prominent people, with entertainment television, and so on. You might be interested in the psychology of such fascination, with the effects on celebrities, with the phenomenon of the paparazzi, with a specific celebrity's story, or with reality TV shows that relate to this cult. Doing a basic "cult of celebrity" search with a search engine such a Google would lead to the results shown partially below.

As a researcher into the cult of celebrity, you might capitalize on these strengths of the free Web for such a project:

- **Information Volume.** Obviously, the free Web contains a great wealth of information on virtually every topic imaginable (almost 400,000 hits in our example). Even though the free Web covers a relatively small portion of the whole Web, you are nevertheless likely to find information for your research project, regardless of the topic.

- **Information Currency.** Because the free Web is electronic, it can help you find information posted only seconds earlier—the most current news on your topic, such as a journal article being prepared for print publication, a speech presented this morning and posted this afternoon, statistical analysis of last month's gas-price changes, or the most recently edited version of a wiki document.

- **Information Flexibility.** The free Web contains information in text, sound, and visual formats, offering you many choices for your research needs. In addition, free-Web tools such as wikis allow you to collaborate on research projects and post research results in creative ways.

- **Information Democracy.** Virtually anyone can contribute to the material on the free Web: from the average citizen to any government agency, from an entrepreneur to a global corporation, from a person riding a hobby-horse interest to a scholar with a Ph.D. That information—virtually accessible to anyone around the globe—can be shared in highly structured and carefully linked Web sites or in informal blogs and amateur videos. Varied people anywhere can add their two-cents-worth on your topic.

- **Information Accessibility.** Because the information is digital, it can be searched quickly and conveniently, with a whole range of continually-evolving search tools that make that information accessible. Moreover, that material can be conveniently copied, saved, and sent as you do your research. And of course, the Web is always open—even at 2:00 a.m. when you are sitting in your home or dorm room.

- **Information Popularity.** Depending on the search tool that you are using, searching on the free Web takes you to popular information, that is, information that people contributing to and searching the free Web determine to be most popular through linking, visiting, and other means (including commercial). In the "cult of celebrity" search, for example, top hits include a Wikipedia entry, news articles, a network site focused on the topic, and blogs.

- **Information Variety.** Free-Web searching takes you to Internet sites coming from a wide range of perspectives and posted for a wide range of reasons—educational, informative, commercial, personal, and much more.

Drawbacks of Free-Web Research

In many ways, the strengths of the free Web are also its weaknesses. Consider again a search on the cult of celebrity, with the partial list of results shown on the previous pages. What does that basic search show about the drawbacks of free-Web research? Consider these issues:

- **Search Difficulties.** Because of the large amount and relative disorganization of material, finding useful information on the free Web can be time-consuming. Whereas library catalogs and subscription databases involve searching well-cataloged and well-indexed materials organized by Library-of-Congress subject terms, searching the free Web requires a lot more experimental use of keywords and can lead to a large number of hits unrelated to your specific topic or relatively useless for your project.

  In our sample search, notice what resources Google's ranking algorithms put at the top of the results list: a Wikipedia article, some magazine articles, a network site dated 2003-2006, a blog entry, and so on. While the Wikipedia entry and the magazine articles might offer a helpful starting point for a project, they will likely have limited use for an academic paper on some aspect of the cult of celebrity. Moreover, without using advanced search techniques, a researcher would find it impossible to deal with all 396,000 results, most of which would also likely be of little use for a scholarly research project.

  If we look more closely at the Wikipedia article ranked first by Google in this search, this challenge of free-Web research becomes clear. While Wikipedia does contain many solid articles (Wikipedia is discussed more fully on pages 86–89), this particular article contains very little information, though the basic definitions and explanations may offer you a starting point and the links might provide helpful avenues of further research.

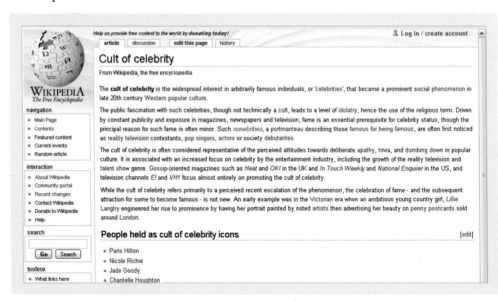

■ **Information Reliability.** Simply put, to a large degree the free Web lacks quality control (the kinds of editorial and peer-review controls used in scholarly publishing). While the Open Access movement is leading to more scholarly research being posted on the free Web, virtually anybody can post virtually anything on the free Web. For this reason, some experts have called the free Web the Wild West of the Internet. In this situation, it's researcher beware! Because you are ultimately responsible for the sources that you use in your research writing, you must use caution with free-Web sources, carefully evaluating what you are finding. (See pages 90–92 for more on evaluating Web resources.)

In the Wikipedia article on the cult of celebrity, for example, how do we determine the reliability of the information presented? While many Wikipedia articles offer strong in-text citations, a list of references, and suggestions for further reading, this particular article is thin in citations and sources, as Wikipedia's editors indicate at the end of the article.

■ **Unclear Authorship.** A key factor in determining source reliability is authorship: who wrote and posted the material? What are this person's credentials? Much of the material on the free Web is published anonymously or by individuals whose credentials are unclear. This is the case with the Wikipedia article, for example. Such articles are written and edited through collaboration, which can be explored through the "history" and "discussion" tabs; however, while editorial principles are at work, we as readers do not really know who wrote the article, and we cannot check the original author's credentials, or those of anyone who has edited the article.

■ **Information Depth.** While the surface Web contains many in-depth resources (reports, e-books, open-access journal articles), the Web medium often works against depth of discussion. The average Web page tends to present information in small blocks that can be skimmed, not in a sustained discussion or analysis of the topic. For this reason, many Web resources may provide some useful information but be too basic for your college-level research writing, which emphasizes in-depth analysis and argument. The Wikipedia article on the cult of celebrity, for example, offers basic information in short paragraphs and lists that are heavily filled with links inviting readers to leave the article to find related information.

■ **Information Stability.** The free Web changes rapidly—what's here today may be gone, modified, or outdated tomorrow. For your research projects, you must use caution in relying on such changing resources, and you must keep careful records. This is the case, for example, with the Wikipedia article, which may look very different in another hour or another day.

■ **Counterproductive Research Practices.** Free-Web searching and surfing can produce shallow research. Skimming and scanning is easier than carefully reading and thinking through the material. Copying and pasting big chunks of material into a paper is easier than digesting the material first, and then using its ideas to develop and refine your own. In other words, the free Web makes plagiarism—unintentional and deliberate—easy.

Guidelines for Researching the Free Web

Given the strengths and weaknesses of free-Web research described on the previous pages, you should approach such research with the commonsense guidelines described below.

1. **Limit your reliance on free-Web resources.** Even if your instructor doesn't forbid or restrict your use of free-Web material, make sure that you do not use it exclusively or even over-rely on it. As a researcher, your credibility suffers if your bibliography lacks balance or is dominated by sources with questionable credentials. Exception: Certain topics (for example, some aspect of the Internet itself) warrant relying on Web sources.

2. **Use advanced research tools and strategies.** First, learn to do more than basic Google, MSN, or Yahoo! searches. Research into research suggests that most free-Web researchers do little more than simple keyword searches and rarely check beyond the first few hits. (We discuss this issue further on page 98 in the section or search engines.) Even learning to do advanced Google searches, or to use Google Scholar or the Google Directory, is a step in the right direction. Similarly, learn to get beyond Wikipedia articles as your main resources. (More on this topic is on pages 86–89.)

3. **Evaluate material you find.** Assessing the credibility and reliability of Web material is crucial to deciding its usefulness for your project. On pages 90–92, you'll find a full discussion of these evaluation criteria.

4. **Look for sources with depth.** While for some projects business and commercial sites make sense, generally search for educational sites (.edu), government sites (.gov), and nonprofit organizations (.org). (Note: while some .info sites are reliable, some are actually spammers or other less-than-trustworthy sites). Look for identifiable, trusted organizations, not personal sites and blogs. Look, too, for information beyond the tertiary, that is, sources that are primary or secondary with respect to your topic (see pages 34–37 for a discussion of the differences). Exceptions: If your topic is commercially focused in some way or relates to the Web itself, traditional Web sites may offer valuable information.

Matthias Pahl/www.shutterstock.com

5. **Consider stable and recommended sites.** As mentioned in the previous chapter, your library's Web site may offer you links to recommended free-Web sites, sites that information experts have themselves reviewed. Consider, for example, LII, the Librarians' Internet Index (a subject directory discussed on pages 94–97), or WorldCat's "Internet" limiter, giving you the power to search Web materials indexed by librarians. Your library's Web site might also point you to reliable reference resources on the free Web, from dictionaries to news sites, as well as to some discipline-specific Web resources. Finally, for college research projects, consider the free-Web resources recommended on the next two pages.

 FOCUS on Multimedia: For more on debates over free-Web research, visit www.theresearchwriter.com. There, you'll find links to stories on Google, Wikipedia, Open Access journals, multitasking, and more.

Focus on Your Project: Saving Web Information

Accurately saving Web addresses and material is an essential part of good research. Moreover, you may want to revisit sites and embed URLs in your research writing. As you work on your project, save addresses and material through methods like these:

- **Bookmark:** If you are working on your own computer, use your browser to save a site's address through a "bookmark" or "favorites" function on your menu bar, remembering that sites change. Do this by setting up a separate "favorites" folder for each project. Some online services, such as Delicious.com, allow URLs to be saved in an account to be re-accessed from any computer.

- **Print:** If a document looks promising, print a hard copy. Look especially for a print button on the page that will allow you to print a well-formatted version of the document. Remember to capture details needed for citing the source—author, title, site sponsor, database name, publication or posting date, access date, and other publication information—if these do not automatically appear on the printout.

- **Save:** To keep an electronic copy, save the document to your computer. Beware, however, of large, space-eating files with many graphics. Look for a text-only save feature, or copy and paste the text into a word-processing document.

- **E-mail:** If you're not at your own computer, e-mail the document to yourself or use copy-and-paste to send yourself an e-mail containing the document's URL.

Recommended Web Resources for College Research

Given the size and complexity of the Web, offering a comprehensive list of Web sites and Web tools for your research is impossible. However, this page and the next offer helpful resources that will take you to the best free-Web information.

Search Tools

Note: Searching a search engine using your topic or subject area plus the term "database" may help you locate searchable databases for your topic or major.

ipl2: http://www.ipl2.org This site, a merger between the Internet Public Library and the Librarians' Internet Index, offers access to electronic reference resources, to e-books and electronic articles, and to special collections. This site's chief value is its subject collections of Web resources, which have been reviewed by experts for content quality and relevance.

SearchEdu.com: http://www.searchedu.com Besides offering links to reference resources, this search tool allows you to search educational sites (.edu) on the Web. (Warning: Use this site with caution, as it is a commercial site with some questionable links and connections.)

Infomine: http://infomine.ucr.edu Subtitled Scholarly Internet Resource Collections, this librarian-built site is designed for college and university faculty and students; the site offers researchers access to databases, electronic journals and books, and more, including government information.

WWW Virtual Library: http://vlib.org Started in 1991 by Tim Berners-Lee, the man credited with creating the Web (Vint Cerf is credited with fathering the Internet), the Virtual Library is the oldest catalog on the Web and one that aims to direct users to quality sources.

E-Books and Other Electronic Documents

Note: Because of copyright restrictions, possibly only older books with expired copyrights are available for free. Check if your library subscribes to NetLibrary.

Project Gutenberg: http://www.gutenberg.org One of the oldest and largest e-book sites, Project Gutenberg indexes more than 25,000 electronic texts freely available on the Web, with more than 100,000 texts available through PG's partners, affiliates, and resources.

Bartleby.com: http://bartleby.com This site publishes literature, poetry, and reference texts for students and researchers.

Electronic Text Center: http://www.lib.virginia.edu/scholarslab This site houses an online archive of humanities-focused texts and images.

Google Books Search: http://books.google.com This site offers bibliographic or full-text access to texts made available through a large-scale digitization project.

Articles

Reminder: You are more likely to discover and access quality articles through your library's subscription databases than on the free Web. (See pages 61–66.)

Directory of Open Access Journals: http://www.doaj.org Part of a growing movement in academics, this site lists over 3500 scholarly journals, with search capability at article level for almost 1200 journals.

LookSmart Find Articles.com: http://findarticles.com This commercial site can give you citations for articles on your topic, although getting full-text access may involve fees.

HighBeam Research: http://www.highbeam.com Like LookSmart, this is a commercial search site, particularly strong in newspapers and magazines, as well as reference information.

Newspapers.com: http://newspapers.com Another commercial site, this one can help you find and search specific newspapers.

Google Scholar: http://scholar.google.com While it indexes just a small portion of all published articles, Google Scholar can help you build citations from a variety of sources, citations you can then find in your library's subscription databases. Moreover, it ranks articles by weighing the full text, the author, the publication, and frequency of citation in other sources.

Government Resources

Tip: When searching for government info, consider the branch (e.g., legislative, judicial, executive) and the level (federal, state, municipal).

USA.gov: http://www.usa.gov This is the US government's official Web site, allowing you to search government information through keywords, by topic, by agency, by level of government, and so on.

Google US Government Search: http://www.google.com/ig/usgov

50States.com: http://www.50states.com This site allows you to search for state-specific information, as well as information on US commonwealths and territories.

United Nations: http://www.un.org The UN's Web site offers you access to UN documents and activities, to resolutions, to its different bodies, to its programs (e.g., UNICEF, its Environment Programme), and to world statistics.

Research Centers, Laboratories, Societies, and Associations

Note: Offering a full list of institutions is not possible, but you may locate one relevant to your project by searching your topic keywords with "research center" or a synonym.

Argonne National Laboratory: http://www.anl.gov A US Department of Energy laboratory started in 1946, the ANL carries on many research projects in a range of sciences, in energy, in environmental management, and in national security.

The PEW Charitable Trusts: http://pewtrusts.org Pew is a nonprofit organization focused on civic life—on improving society through public policy support, through information and education, and through arts and culture support. Pew also has a research center: http://pewresearch.org.

National Institutes of Health: http://www.nih.gov As part of the US Department of Health and Human Services, NIH is responsible for conducting and supporting medical research.

The Hastings Center: http://www.thehastingscenter.org This site is an example of a think tank dedicated to a specific issue: bioethics.

Statistical Resources

Note: While these sites give you access to a wide range of local, national, and international statistics, much of the data will be politically, economically, and socially focused. (Statistics are a large part of research in the social sciences.)

Fedstats: http://www.fedstats.gov This official government site allows you to search for statistics on specific topics; and for statistical profiles of states, counties, cities, and so on. It also links you to statistical agencies and allows you to search across agencies.

US Census Bureau 2008 Statistical Abstract: http://www.census.gov This site offers the official summary of social, political, and economic statistics about the US.

Statistical Resources on the Web: http://www.lib.umich.edu/govdocs/statsnew.html This University of Michigan site functions as a gateway to a wide range of statistics available on the Web.

STAT-USA/Internet: http://www.stat-usa.gov A service of the US Department of Commerce, this site gives you access to the Federal Government's business, trade, and economic information.

UNData: http://unstats.un.org/unsd This site supported by the United Nations Statistics Division of the Department of Economic and Social Affairs (DESA) brings together UN statistical databases for searching at one entry point.

Using Wikis in Your Research

Like blogs and podcasts, wikis have become enormously popular on the Web in recent years. For example, you may use wikis as a place to publish your research writing: We address this topic on page 254. However, here, we discuss wikis as research resources.

Understanding Wikis

The term *wiki* is a Hawaiian word meaning fast. When used to refer to the Internet, *wiki* refers to a *fast*-Web format—a Web page that can be quickly and easily created, posted, and *changed*. A wiki page, then, is one that can be read and changed by a variety of people on the Web, not just one person. A wiki site is typically a collection of wiki pages all focused on a particular project or subject. Many wiki sites are open, meaning that anyone on the Web can create and edit pages; other wikis are restricted in terms of who can post and change content, while some are completely private.

As wikis relate to research, they are collaborative sites for building content on a range of topics. Wikis tend to build knowledge and share information openly so that the result is a searchable database that has been developed by a group of people and that can continue to grow and change. Typically, as well, wiki content is built using links between pages so that related material is easy to navigate. In other words, when you search a wiki site, you are accessing knowledge developed through collaboration, open to change, and organized for easy access and searching.

Wikipedia as a Resource: Strengths

It's likely that you recognize the screen on the next page—an article from Wikipedia, a collaboratively written Web encyclopedia. From Wikipedia's beginning in 2001 to today, a large population of volunteer writers and editors from around the globe has made it a top-ten Internet-traffic site. As of 2008, more than 684 million visitors had accessed a Wikipedia article, articles that number more than 10 million in over 250 languages. As a student, you are likely one of those 684 million visitors: you may have found Wikipedia articles useful for projects in high school, and you undoubtedly have noticed Wikipedia articles appearing in the top-ten hits for Web searches of many topics. But what about Wikipedia for college-level research? Put simply, Wikipedia is a controversial resource for academic research. First let's consider Wikipedia's strengths for research.

- **Consensus Model of Knowledge:** Because articles develop through diverse input, they can represent a collaborative agreement about a topic—a topical knowledge base that is fair and fairly comprehensive. Generally, articles improve over time, offering researchers a source of what might be called "open-source" knowledge.
- **Currency of Information:** Because they are Web-based, articles are regularly monitored and updated—a distinct advantage over print encyclopedias.
- **Breadth of Information:** Given its size, and global community of contributors, Wikipedia offers articles on a wide range of topics. And because of its contributor demographic, it is quite strong in pop culture, current events, computer, and science topics.

■ **Links:** Articles tend to be heavily linked throughout so that readers can pursue associated topics, sources, recommended reading, and related categories.

Example: The article on Angelina Jolie is partially protected from vandalism (lock icon), and it is one of Wikipedia's featured articles—deemed high quality by editors (star icon). The article offers a full, up-to-date introduction to this pop-culture icon's acting, humanitarian work, and personal life.

Screen Features

1 Featured article icon

2 Semi-protected article icon

3 History tab

4 Discussion page

5 Title

6 Introduction

7 Links

8 Wikipedia's search field

9 Wikipedia's menus

10 Contents Menu

11 Essential facts

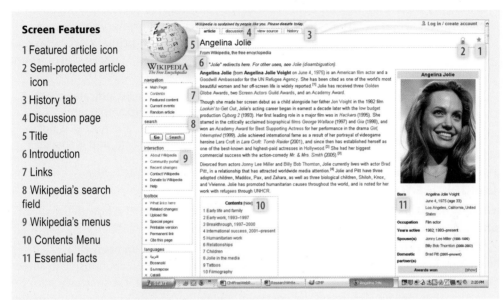

Source: Wikipedia

Wikipedia as a Resource: Weaknesses

In some ways, Wikipedia's strengthens are closely related to its weaknesses for college-level research. Consider these issues:

■ **Popularity Model of Knowledge:** The dark side of the consensus model of knowledge is knowledge dictated by popularity, and the dynamics of popularity can lead to bias, imbalance, and errors. In some ways, this approach minimizes the value of training, education, and expertise while promoting a kind of democracy of knowledge as opposed to a true encyclopedia of knowledge.

■ **Anonymity of Authorship:** Wikipedia allows contributors to remain anonymous. Researchers thus have little way of checking the credentials and credibility of authors.

■ **Variable Quality of Content:** While many well-established articles are quite stable, balanced, and comprehensive, other articles (particularly new ones) can be partial, driven by a biased perspective, erroneous, and poorly sourced.

■ **Variable Coverage:** Because of its open nature and volunteer contributors, Wikipedia's strength in some content areas is matched by gaps and incompleteness in other content areas. Unlike more traditional reference works, Wikipedia's topical coverage is not determined by a particular plan.

- **Vulnerability to Vandalism:** Wikipedia has a number of processes in place to limit people from harming articles with misinformation. Regular monitoring, posting of recent changes, partially protecting specific pages—such steps typically mean that most vandalism is corrected within hours, if not within minutes. However, some errors have persisted for months, and at any given moment, the article you are looking at may have been vandalized.

- **Tertiary Nature of Information:** For most of your research projects, Wikipedia articles function as tertiary sources—twice removed from primary sources, or reports of reports of research. (See pages 34–37 for more on primary, secondary, and tertiary distinctions.) As with most print encyclopedias, Wikipedia articles are not substantial enough for academic projects.

  Example: The "Cult of Celebrity" article shown in part on page 80 indicates some of the possible weaknesses of a Wikipedia article. As another example, note that in contrast to the article on Angelina Jolie, the article on Jane Austen is not protected from vandalism, is not a featured (highest rated) article, and is shorter than the Jolie article.

Guidelines for Using Wikipedia

Given Wikipedia's strengths and weaknesses, you can judge when and how to use specific articles. However, here are some guidelines:

1. **Respect your assignment.** Because of Wikipedia's nature as an open wiki encyclopedia, your instructors may give you varied instruction about using it: some restricting you from using it at all, others cautioning you that it is a tertiary source that shouldn't appear in your bibliography, and still others making it an assignment to write or thoroughly edit a Wikipedia article. Respect these guidelines.

2. **Use other sources to verify Wikipedia information.** If you are going to use information from Wikipedia in your research writing, also use other more traditional sources to verify that information.

3. **Use Wikipedia as a semi-authoritative reference source, but not as a significant resource.** Generally, the more academic and scholarly your research assignment, the less you should rely on Wikipedia. Just as most general encyclopedias would not be central to your college research projects, look at Wikipedia articles for what they are: encyclopedia reference articles, sources of basic and background information for your research (in this case, a little more open and unstable than traditional encyclopedias).

4. **Use Wikipedia as one starting point.** Because of their accessibility, currency, coverage, and links, Wikipedia articles can offer a good place to get started on a research project: You can learn what is considered "open-source" knowledge on your topic, gather ideas for developing and narrowing a topic, find links to related topics and other resources (both within and outside Wikipedia), and begin to build a bibliography of resources for your project.

5. Study individual articles to get a sense of their reliability. When you find a Wikipedia article relevant to your research project, check the article for quality and stability. While the instructions on the next pages for evaluating Web resources will help, consider these issues as well:

- Scan the article to assess its overall coverage. Do the contents look thorough and balanced?
- Check the article's history by clicking the history tab at the top. How old is the article, and what were the most recent changes? How many people have contributed to the article? Have they identified themselves or are they anonymous? Is there any evidence of a kind of "war of words" between contributors and editors—changes back and forth? Is there evidence of vandalism?
- Check the discussion page for the article, if it has one. Do the discussions raise concerns about the trustworthiness of the article?
- Check for tags, icons, and messages indicating the state of the article. For example, you might find an icon indicating that the article is semi-protected from vandalism or that the article is considered strong or good. Similarly, you might find notes that an article needs to be cleaned up, that it lacks sources, that some information has not been verified, or that the article is new.
- Check the "what links here" link in the toolbox at the left of the screen. This feature will show you other Wikipedia articles that link to the article you are reading—a general indication of the article's significance within Wikipedia.

Finding Other Wikis

While Wikipedia may be the biggest and most popular wiki, it is not the only one available to researchers. Consider these possibilities:

Other Wiki Encyclopedias: A number of wiki encyclopedias are being developed in response to the perceived weaknesses of Wikipedia:

- Veripedia http://en.veropedia.com: Developed by a group of Wikipedia editors, this wiki takes Wikipedia articles, strengthens the quality, and saves them in a stable form.
- Citizendium http://en.citizendium.org: This Citizen's Compendium wiki offers modest control of articles by experts in order to minimize vandalism and errors. Citizendium also has a project called Eduzendium that encourages professors and their students to contribute to Citizendium.
- Scholarpedia http://www.scholarpedia.org: A peer-reviewed encyclopedia written by scholars who are experts on the topics, Scholarpedia uses a system by which the experts who initially write articles function as their curators.

Specialized Wikis: As wikis become popular tools for collaboration, a number of specialized wikis are emerging, often developed by scholars in a specific field. To find a wiki relevant to your topic, type the relevant subject or discipline plus "wiki" into a search engine. For more details and recommended wikis, check our Web site: www.theresearchwriter.com.

Evaluating Free-Web Resources

Source evaluation is critical regardless of what resources you are using. While general guidelines for such evaluation are outlined on pages 147–149, evaluation of free-Web resources is particularly challenging, given the Wild-West nature of the Web. While a healthy sense of caution and your common sense should guide you, consider as well the suggestions below and on the next page.

Signs of a Quality Web Site

When it comes to the free Web, appearances can be deceptive. A graphically sophisticated site can hide a lack of content, significant bias, or outright deception. Nevertheless, you can learn to read some signs of a quality versus a suspect Web site, in terms of whether or not the sites are valuable for college research projects. Study the two Web pages below, noting the signs.

Quality Page

Trustworthy URL

Depth and breadth of information

Clear navigation

Quality links to research, news, and information

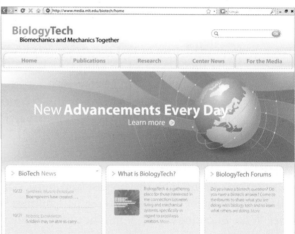

Suspect Page

Suspicious URL

Sparse information

Biased language

Errors in editing

Testing a Web Site's Quality and Reliability

Assessing whether a particular Web resource is suitable for your research begins with recalling your research purpose. Given your goals, your topic, your use of the information, and so on, what types of Web resources would fit your assignment? Once you have your purpose in focus, you can then evaluate each Web resource in two ways: (1) Is the source worth looking at more closely? (2) If yes, what is the resource's level of quality and reliability? To answer these questions, take these steps:

1. **Interpret the URL.** Studying the resource or page's URL can give you clues about the type of information it offers. What is the domain-name extension: edu, com, org, gov, mil, net, info, biz or something else? As discussed on page 77, the domain-name extension will give you clues about the purpose of the site. Similarly, a tilde (~) plus a person's name in the URL usually indicates that the resource is personal rather than institutional. Be cautious about personal sites.

2. **Learn more about the site.** Aside from looking for obvious clues about the site's nature, such as pop-ups and advertising, spend some time identifying the server that is hosting this Web resource. Often, you can learn more by searching the site's "home" or "about us" pages: Is the organization reputable? What is its mission? What sort of agenda does the site serve or promote? Is it a commercial site, a special-interest advocate, a site with a particular political or philosophical agenda, a professional organization, a museum? Why is it making this resource available? In addition, review the site's content through menus provided: How information-rich is the site? How current is the content? For an external view of the site sponsor, you can conduct research into the organization itself using About.com at http://www.about.com/ or WhoIs at http://www.whois.net. To learn more about what other Web resources and sites link to this site and resource, search Alexa at http://www.alexa.com/ using the URL of the site or specific resource.

3. **Identify and learn more about the author.** Authorship is a crucial element to deciding a resource's authority. With some Web resources, authorship is anonymous, with the site's sponsoring organization serving as the authority for the content. When an author is indicated, learn what you can about his or her credentials: What is this person's training and level of education with respect to the topic? What is the author's institutional affiliation? Where is the author coming from in terms of perspective? Often, author information will be provided in the resource itself, but you can also research the person by doing a Web search, checking his or her home page, or e-mailing the author, if the resource offers an address.

4. **Put the resource in context.** How did you find or learn about this resource? Was it recommended by another resource? Do other resources link to it for positive reasons? Do the source's own links take you to quality resources? What form does the resource take? For example, is it an open-source scholarly journal article, a list-server discussion posting, or an individual's blog? Consider, in other words, how the resource fits into the web of resources available: are there signs that the piece is respected, not just that it is or is not popular?

5. **Study the content.** As you examine the resource's content, explore these issues:

- Is the discussion itself neutral and objective, or biased? Is the tone reasonable, the language moderate?
- Is the information substantive or thin? Is the reasoning sound? Does the writer support his or her claims with reputable evidence? Do arguments appeal primarily to logic or to emotion?
- Does the resource contain accurate, quality information gained through sound research methods, or does it contain errors and misinformation?
- Does the resource clearly document its own sources of information with references and a bibliography? Can the information be verified elsewhere?
- Is the resource an electronic version of a print source, a supplement to a print source, or a resource from a reputable online publisher (e.g., educational publisher)—suggesting a degree of authority and stability?
- Is the source current and timely with respect to your topic? Or does the source need updating?
- For your project, is this source primary, secondary, or tertiary? In terms of the evidence provided, how distant is it from your topic? (See pages 34–37.)

Locating Information: URLs, Menus, Links, & Site Searches

For your research projects, the basic rule about doing research on the free Web is this: Use a variety of methods and search tools in order to locate valuable resources. In other words, don't settle for doing a basic search of one search engine or a five-minute surf from link to link. Instead, be systematic, creative, and intuitive by tapping into a variety of directories and search engines, as discussed on the following pages. But first, here's a reminder about the simple but powerful navigation tools available to you.

Work with URLs

Finding useful Web resources can be as easy as typing in and working with URLs. If you know the address of the Web site that you want to visit, simply type or copy-and-paste it into the address bar of your Web browser. If you don't have the exact URL of an organization you would like to visit, sometimes you can guess it. Try the organization's name or a logical abbreviation plus the likely domain-name extension to get the home page. For example, most government-agency Web sites use the agencies' acronym or initialism in the Web address (e.g., http://www.usda.gov for United States Department of Agriculture). If that doesn't work, search a search engine using the company's name.

> **Formula:** <http://www.organization-name-or-abbreviation.domain-name-extension/>
>
> **Examples:** www.nasa.gov, www.honda.com, www.habitat.org, www.ucla.edu

Remember, too, that if you find yourself deep in a Web site and want to surface at the site's home page, backspace part by part on the URL in the address bar.

Follow Helpful Links

Undoubtedly, one of the most convenient ways of navigating and locating information on the Web is through surfing—following links between parts of pages, separate pages within a site, or from one site to another. As you research by following links, keep these issues in mind:

- Pay attention to whether a link is internal to the site or external. If you need to explore this site more fully, you may want to save the external link for later.
- Your browser keeps a record of the pages that you visit during a search session. While the back and forward arrows will help you navigate this search "history," you'll have to explore how your browser displays this history, as each browser does so differently. This feature is useful as you make decisions about using sites, revisiting them, and bookmarking them for your project.

Reminder: Sponsored links listed at a Web site are essentially a form of advertising. Their purpose is primarily commercial, though they may contain useful information.

Explore Menus

Most sites offer rich menu options for navigating the site. These menus are typically to the right or left of the screen, or near the top (often as drop-down menus). When you find a site that looks promising for your project, take a few minutes to study these menus to see what the site offers. This practice is the Web equivalent of browsing a bookshelf or browsing your library's online catalog: Such browsing may lead you to discoveries you hadn't anticipated. Just be careful that you don't get distracted by all the choices, go off on complete tangents, and lose track of time!

Try the Site's Search Feature

Many sites allow you to search their pages by conducting keyword searches. Look for this feature at the top or side of the page, and use it if the site looks promising in terms of content but no link or menu item jumps out as an obvious choice.

Remember that keyword searching on the Web, whether internally to a specific site or with a search engine, involves some special strategies, particularly because Web resources are not indexed and ordered systematically according to standard search terms such as Library of Congress subject headings. Here are specific tips:

- Enter a single word to seek pages that contain that word or a derivative of it. *Example:* The term "apple" yields pages containing the word "apple," "apples," "applet," and so on.
- Enter more than one word to seek pages containing any of those words. *Example:* The words "apple" and "pie" yield sites containing "apple" only and "pie" only, as well as those containing both words (together or not).
- Use quotation marks to find an exact phrase. *Example:* The term *"apple pie"* (together in quotation marks) yields only pages with that phrase.
- Look for advanced search instructions at the site in order to make the most of what the site offers.

Locating Information: Subject Trees or Directories

A *subject tree,* sometimes called a *subject guide* or *directory,* lists Web sites organized into categories by experts who have reviewed those sites. It's important to note that this human input distinguishes subject directories from search engines. Use subject trees or directories for the following reasons: (1) You need to narrow a broad topic, (2) you want evaluated sites, or (3) you desire quality over quantity. For example, if you are researching film adaptations of Jane Austen's *Pride and Prejudice,* you might want to use a subject directory to zero in on reviewed sites about film so as to weed out commercial sites and personal blogs that would appear with a search engine.

As for good subject directories available, your library may subscribe to a service such as NetFirst, a database in which subject experts have catalogued Internet resources by topic. Similarly, WorldCat has directory features that you can follow. However, here are some common subject directories that you can access on the free Web. As you check them out, explore which directories lead to sites most suitable for college research.

About.com (channels list)	http://www.about.com
BUBL Link	http://bubl.ac.uk/link/subjectbrowse.html
DMOZ Open Directory Project	http://www.dmoz.org
Google Directory	http://www.google.com/dirhp
ipl2	http://ipl2.org
Magellan	http://www.magellan.cc
WWW Virtual Library	http://vlib.org/Overview.html
Yahoo! Directory	http://dir.yahoo.com

The Structure of a Subject Tree

How does a subject tree work? Essentially, it allows you to select from a broad range of subjects or "branches." With each topic choice, you narrow your selection through subtopics until you arrive at a list of Web sites. In addition, a subject directory may allow you to keyword-search selected Web sites—in the whole directory, in one branch (category), in one topic, and so on. The diagram below shows just one small part of a large subject tree broken down from main category to subcategories to topics to specific sites, based on one category in the Yahoo! Directory, Science.

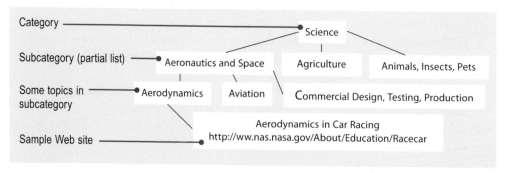

Subject Trees: A Sample Search

While each subject directory uses slightly different categories and breaks these down into subcategories and topics according to different rules, conducting a directory search essentially involves tracing and exploring the branches that seem most relevant to your research project until you arrive at a list of Web resources that you can explore individually.

For example, imagine that your research project is focused on understanding, analyzing, and constructing an argument concerning some form of hybrid-technology transportation. The following directory search shows how you might proceed.

Step 1: Study the subject tree below provided by the Librarians' Internet Index (LII). To find reviewed Web sites containing information on hybrid transportation, you could select from this start page a range of categories, depending on the angle that you want to explore: *Business,* if you wish to focus on the commercial aspect of hybrids; *Government,* if you are looking for government's involvement in hybrid technology; or *Science,* if your focus is understanding hybrid technology itself. Each of these starting points will lead to a different but possibly overlapping listing of relevant sites. Another option would be to use the keyword search feature shown.

Screen Features

1 Sponsor or site information

2 Keyword search field

3 Main subject categories, with subcategories indicated in short form

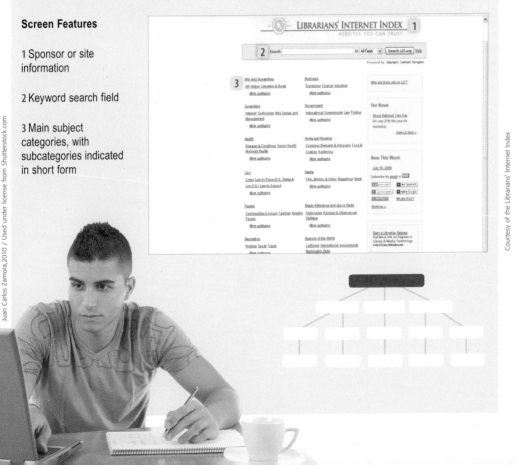

Step 2: If you chose *Science,* the subcategories shown below would appear. Note the alphabetical arrangement first across columns and then downward. At this point, you would again have several choices. You could select from the subcategories of *Environment, Energy,* or *Technology;* or you could do a keyword search, perhaps of the whole *Science* category. Again, each choice might lead to a distinct set of Web sites. In fact, you may benefit by trying all these options.

Screen Features

1 Keyword search field

2 Category

3 Specific subcategories arranged alphabetically, with number of Web sites in subcategory indicated in parentheses

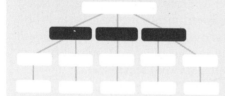

Step 3: If you were to choose *Technology* in this example, the next screen would be the one shown partially below. Notice the new features at this point. While you still have the option of searching LII (the entire collection or part of it) using keywords, a list of topics within the *Technology* subcategory is now provided at the left. In the middle right, a list of Web sites now begins to appear. For each Web site, the directory offers a site title, a site description, a URL, and the date the site was added to the directory.

Screen Features

1 Category and subcategory

2 Topics and Web site count

3 Web sites

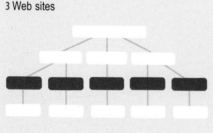

Step 4: Because the results from *Technology* were still large (more than 2,300 sites), you might next scan the topics under technology and find *Transportation* as a good choice. Clicking on this subtopic would then lead to the results below, more than 600 Web sites with a further breakdown of transportation-related topics. Another option would be to search these transportation Web sites with the phrase "hybrid technology," as shown in the search field.

Screen Features

1 Category, subcategory, main topic

2 Subtopics with number of sites in parentheses

3 Web site descriptions and links

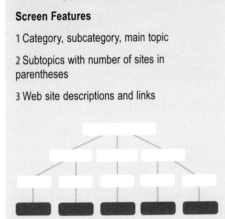
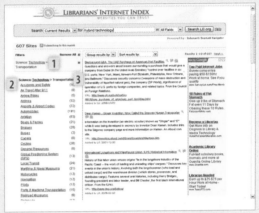

Courtesy of the Librarians' Internet Index

Step 5: If you were to search the more than 600 transportation Web sites using "hybrid technology," you would get the results shown below: three Web sites that offer content on hybrid technology. These sites, remember, have all been recommended by librarians for the sites' quality, though you still need to evaluate what you find. Notice that the directory offers not just links to each site, but a button for additional information, one for adding your own comment about each site, and one for e-mailing the information about each site to yourself. In this example, notice that the first site is a government site (State of California), while the second is a well-known and respected online buying guide, and the third site takes you to a report on hybrids published in a science journal.

Screen Features

1 Search field

2 Directory branches

3 Web site descriptions and links

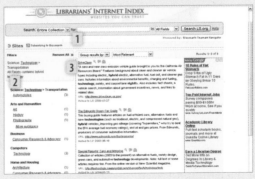

Courtesy of the Librarians' Internet Index

Locating Information: Search Engines and Metasearch Tools

Search engines such as Google and Yahoo! are clearly among the most popular and most powerful search tools available on the Web. Like millions of people around the globe, you probably "Google it" when you have a question that you need answered. But how should you use search engines in the larger context of the research you need to do for academic projects in college or university? Answering that question is the focus of the following pages.

© Karl-Josef Hildenbrand/dpa/Corbis

Understanding Search Engines as Research Tools

Unlike a subject directory, which is built through human evaluation of Web resources, a search engine is a program that automatically scours a large amount of Web material using keywords and commands that you submit. In that respect, the search is only as productive as the terms you use, the quality of the search program used by the engine, and the amount and areas of the Web that the engine searches—and all of these issues differ from one search engine to the next. When you use search engines, be aware of these factors in how they work:

Web Coverage: Even though the largest search engines search billions of Web resources, those pages represent just a portion of the Web—as little as 20 percent, though that 20 or less percent often leads to more than enough hits for your research. The point to keep in mind is that any given search engine is not searching the entire Web for you and may be focusing on particular kinds of pages and documents, likely in the free Web rather than the deep Web. Moreover, a given engine may not be searching each resource in its entirety but only certain portions (citations, Web address, page description, etc.) or up to a certain size of the document.

Resource Ranking: When you search, a search engine returns results in a ranking of resources based on complex mathematical algorithms—a weighing of a variety of criteria that differ from one engine to the next. One criterion used is the number of times your keywords appear in a given resource. A second criterion might be the number and type of links to a given page—a measure, in other words, of the site's importance or popularity on the Web. While these algorithms are highly sophisticated, the point is that the results returned to you are a particular measure of the relevance of particular pages: the hits are not necessarily for resources that are truly relevant and reliable for academic research. That's why the results of a basic search tend to be a mishmash of Web pages that you need to sort through. Moreover, knowing how these rankings work, organizations on the Web work very hard to make sure that their pages get ranked near the top of searches; some companies hire consultants to help achieve this result or even try to fool the programs. In other words, what you are getting in your search is not necessarily an objective listing of the best, most useful resources for your project.

Search Habits: Using search engines is complicated not just by algorithms but by the habits of users themselves. Studies suggest, for example, that very few users look past the first three hits returned by a search, in fact, that only one percent of searchers go past the first ten hits. (You can understand, then, why some organizations work so hard to get into that top-ten list for specific keyword searches.) Moreover, very few users go on to refine their search after the initial results, supposedly satisfied with what they have found, although studies also suggest that few users can effectively evaluate the returned resources in terms of their quality, authority, objectivity, and timeliness (currency of information). The implications for your college research projects are clear: such search habits rarely lead to quality resources that you can use in an academic project.

Guidelines for Using Search Engines

What conclusions can we reach about how college students should use search engines to conduct research? Here are four guidelines:

1. **Restrict search-engine use to specific purposes.** Generally, a search engine is useful for college research projects in these circumstances:

   - You have a very narrow topic in mind or an exact question you need answered.
   - You have a highly specific word or phrase to use in your search.
   - You want a large number of results.
   - You are looking for a specific type of Internet file.
   - You have the time to sort the material for reliability.

2. **Learn to do advanced searches.** Basic searches tend to lead to basic results. Most search engines actually allow you to do quite complex searches through advanced-search screens. With these, you can employ Boolean logic to a degree, use limiters and expanders, and refine your results in other ways. Study the search engine's help pages for instructions on how to benefit from these advanced-searching techniques. Such an advanced search is also shown on pages 101–103.

3. **Approach results with a high degree of suspicion.** Perhaps *suspicion* is too strong a word, but given the wide-ranging quality and reliability of material on the free Web, given the varied reasons that people and organizations post resources on the free Web, it is imperative that you scrutinize and evaluate resources that you find through search engines. See "Evaluating Free-Web Resources" on pages 90–92.

4. **Use search engines that seem to give you more quality results.** Try out a variety of search engines using the same search, and compare the results. While you generally want to choose search engines that cover a large portion of the Web, offer quality indexing, and give you high-powered search capabilities, you also want to consider a search-engine's information focus: try out search engines whose goals seem more obviously focused on academics. Essentially, you gain the most by becoming familiar with a few search engines—what areas of the Web they search, what elements of Web pages they search, what rules you should follow to ensure successful searches, and how they rank results.

Choosing Search Engines for College Research

When it comes to search engines, the Web landscape is constantly changing. However, here is an overview of your choices: first, the most popular search engines; second, some advanced metasearch and deep Web tools; and third, some recommended tools and strategies that are more academic in focus.

Basic Search Engines: Search millions or billions of pages automatically; return results ranked according to specific search algorithms.

All the Web	http://www.alltheweb.com
Alta Vista	http://www.altavista.com
Ask.com (formerly Ask Jeeves)	http://www.ask.com
Gigablast	http://www.gigablast.com
Google	http://www.google.com
HotBot	http://www.hotbot.com
Vivísimo	http://www.vivisimo.com
Yahoo!	http://www.search.yahoo.com

Metasearch and Deep-Web Tools: Search several search-engines at once, generally returning results that overlap between search engines; or search Internet databases and other Web resources not accessible to basic search engines.

Dogpile (metasearch)	http://www.dogpile.com
Library Spot (deep Web)	http://libraryspot.com
Metacrawler (metasearch)	http://metacrawler.com
OAIster (deep Web)	http://oaister.org
Scirus (deep-Web science)	http://scirus.com

Some Scholarly Tools and Strategies: On pages 84–85 is an overview of free-Web resources recommended for your research projects (including, for example, using Google Scholar, Infomine, and the Internet Public Library). However, here are some specific tips on getting the most from search engines:

- To find a search engine or database relevant to your topic, subject area, or discipline, query one of the search engines above using your subject plus the terms "database" or "search engine." For example, if you were interested in Canadian Studies, such a search would take you to, among other sites, the University of California at Berkeley's "Research Tools for Canadian Studies" page.
- Generally, you won't use blog and list-server postings as academic sources, but if they are useful for your project, check a search engine for the option to search for these types of Web documents (e.g., Google blog search).
- To find a bibliography on your topic on the Web, query a search engine with your topic and the term "bibliographies."

Conducting Advanced Searches with Search Engines

Because search engines differ, there is no simple recipe for conducting advanced searches that will yield higher quality results than a basic search. Reading the engine's description of itself, getting familiar with its advanced search functions, and referring to help pages will strengthen your searching. In addition, you can study the sample advanced search on the following pages to see how Advanced Search works with the most popular search engine, Google.

Step 1: If your project were focused on attachment disorder, you might go to Google as a supplement to your library research into books and journal articles after you had sufficiently narrowed the topic. For example, you may have decided to look at particular methods of treating attachment disorder in children. Using the advanced screen in Google, you might begin by shaping your search according to the following factors (shown in the screen below):

- Looking for resources containing the exact wording "attachment disorder"
- In that set of results, finding pages that include at least one of the synonyms "treatment" and "therapy"
- Restricting sites to ones in English
- Restricting results to resources that are educational (.edu) (Note that you could consider restricting results to .gov and .org sites, as well, depending on your information needs.)
- To keep information current, restricting results to resources from the past year

Note some of the other options in the advanced-search screen, options that allow you to refine your search in other ways. In particular, note the box at the bottom of the screen allowing you to find resources similar or linked to a page that you find helpful.

Screen Features

1 Search string created by choices

2 Keyword fields

3 Search limiters

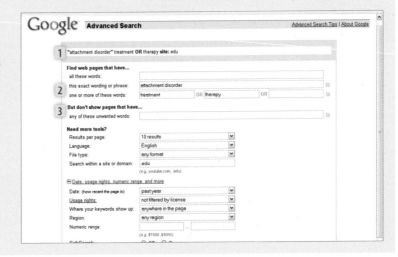

Courtesy of Google.com

Step 2: The results of the initial search are shown below. Note that this search already yields far fewer and more relevant results than a basic search: 134 resources. At this point, you have several choices:

- Work through the 134 hits, using the resource titles, brief descriptions, and URLs to decide whether to study closely or bookmark sites.
- Search the "Sponsored Links" listed to the right—remembering that these three results are essentially advertising results tailored to the search you conducted.
- Using these initial results as a starting point, study them and then refine the results using additional advanced-search tools.

Screen Features

1 Search string

2 Results summary

3 Highest ranked results: page date, page title (link), text excerpts where keywords appear, URL link, link to "cached" (saved) version of page, link to similar pages

4 Sponsored links (primarily advertising)

Courtesy of Google.com

In this example, you might notice in studying the results that the phrase "family therapy" keeps recurring. Deciding to pursue that research line as a narrower aspect of your topic, you might then use the "search within results" tool shown below to pull out those resources that explore some aspect of family therapy for attachment disorder, as opposed to other forms of therapy.

Courtesy of Google.com

Step 3: By your searching for "family therapy" within the initial set of results, the resources would be narrowed to 52 resources. Again, you would have a variety of choices:

- Study the 52 resources to find ones that seem relevant. For example, you might notice that a number of the initial hits include documents from courses and the curriculum vitas (academic resumés) of individuals: you might like to further weed out these sites unless course materials and specialist credentials are part of your focus.

- When you find a helpful site, find similar sites through the "similar pages" feature or by using the feature that lets you find pages that link to this particular page. By taking this approach, you begin to explore a web of related resources likely of equal importance and quality, sources that are in a kind of dialogue.

- Further refine your search with additional keywords, again through the "search within results" tool.

In our example, you might notice that some resources focus especially on therapy for adoptive families. Using that focus as a cue, you might search within the results to find resources focusing on adoption as a factor within family therapy. That step would result in the hits below—a workable 23 resources. Note that while some of them are still course-related documents, many of them are citations for or links to reports, educational documents, and scholarly books and articles. At this point, of course, you would study relevant resources to assess where the information comes from, whether the information is reliable, and how it relates to your research questions.

Practicing Your Research

1. **Explore:** Describe your current use of the free Web—for communication, for entertainment, for research, and more. Based on that description and your review of this chapter, what skills will help you use the free Web productively for college-level research projects? What skills and habits do you need to strengthen? What research tools do you need to learn how to use or use better? As directed by your instructor, record and share your reflections.

2. **Apply:** Using the variety of methods outlined in this chapter, conduct a free-Web search for information on a controversial topic, event, person, or place (e.g., a civil-rights leader such as Martin Luther King, Jr.; rising gas prices; debates surrounding smoking; the War on Terror; Hurricane Katrina and New Orleans; the seal hunt in Atlantic Canada; disputes over Arctic sovereignty; same-sex marriage). Analyze and evaluate the range of Web resources you find—the quality, objectivity, depth, perspective, reliability, and currency. As directed by your instructor, develop a report and/or presentation of your findings.

3. **Collaborate on a Case Study:** As directed by your instructor, continue work with classmates on your clothing-focused project. Determine what types of Free-Web resources might make sense for your focused topic. Then use the advanced search strategies described in this chapter to find and evaluate Web resources from educational, governmental, organizational, commercial, and informational domains, as fits your project.

4. **Research Your Major:** Starting with your library Web site's introduction to Web research in different disciplines, explore what quality research tools and resources the Web offers for your major. Using a variety of search strategies, identify relevant search engines and databases, wikis, professional organizations, government resources, educational sites, research institutes, electronic reference tools, and more. Than draft an informal report to share with your instructor and classmates about Web resources available in your discipline.

5. **Work on Your Current Project:** With your narrow topic in focus and library research in hand, do free-Web research using a range of tools described in this chapter: recommended Web tools, subject directories, and search engines. Evaluate and save the best resources that you find, while comparing and contrasting how different tools lead to different resources.

Checklist:

☑ I have used Internet search tools intelligently—from URL addresses to subject trees to search engines—to find quality, reliable information on my topic.

☑ I have carefully saved free-Web information through bookmarking, printing, file saving, copying-and-pasting, or e-mailing.

☑ I have carefully evaluated each Web resource for authorship, site sponsorship, objectivity, currency, logic, and depth.

© Cengage Learning/Illustrated by Chris Krenzke

5

Doing Primary Research

Q What types of primary research have you done for past writing projects? For other areas of your life? What makes primary research primary?

Primary research brings you into close contact with material directly related to your topic. When you work with primary sources, you engage firsthand information, rather than information that has already been interpreted or analyzed by someone else and then presented to you from that person's perspective. As the saying goes, you get it straight from the horse's mouth—from a source involved with the issue that you are researching.

What form might primary research take for your project? It might involve finding primary sources already published, or it might include generating your own primary information through interviews, observations, experiments, and more. It might take you back into the library, into an archive, onto the Internet, into a lab, or out to the "field" (a community, a business, a park, a lake, etc.). It might involve studying an historical document, analyzing a short story, responding to a piece of jazz music, interviewing a disaster survivor, observing animal behavior, or surveying senior citizens. Whatever the form, such primary research gives you an inside view of your topic.

Doing valid and reliable primary research is an important part of many courses in the humanities (such as journalism), as well as most courses in the social sciences and natural sciences. This chapter, then, focuses on how primary research complements library and free-Web research. To start with, you might review the differences between primary, secondary, and tertiary sources discussed on pages 34-37. Then dig into this chapter, with its overview of primary research and its instruction on conducting specific types of such research.

What's Ahead?

Planning for Primary Research

Because primary research is hands-on research, it requires carefully planning. If you hope to gather truly useful information for your project, you need to be aware of the proper methods of doing specific forms of primary research, as well as the strengths and weaknesses of these forms—what each method can and cannot give you, how that primary information should and should not be used in your research writing. You need to choose the methods that will gather information directly related to your main research question and that will complement your secondary research. To select the best methods for your project, review the issues below and on the next page.

Considering Primary Research

Several factors should weigh into your choice to do primary research, as well as the methods to use:

- **The assignment:** Does the assignment dictate a particular form of primary research? For example, a literary-analysis paper requires close textual analysis, a history paper may require a review of primary documents, and an education project may include a classroom observation. Similarly, the form of research writing (e.g., lab report) may dictate the main method of research.

- **The course, major, or discipline:** Does the course's subject matter point you towards particularly valued methods of primary research? For example, social-science disciplines tend to value surveys, natural sciences tend to focus on experiments, and humanities typically involve analysis of various texts.

- **The topic and your research questions:** How might your understanding of the topic deepen with information gathered through a particular method? Are there gaps in the secondary information that you need to fill? For example, would interviewing film viewers add a human-response component to your analysis of good-and-evil dynamics in *The Dark Knight?*

- **The timing:** How much time do you have for doing primary research? How much secondary research have you done to prepare the way for primary research? How familiar are you with the methods—what would your learning curve be? Many forms of primary research can be quite time consuming, so make choices based on the time available to you.

- **The audience for your research writing:** What forms of primary research will the audience for your research writing or presentation expect, respect, or value? For example, in a paper about the presidential electoral process, will your political-science professor respect evidence gathered from interviews with one or two campaign workers? If yes, what would your professor see as the limits of such evidence?

Choosing a Method of Primary Research

Using the factors discussed on the previous page, you can select methods of primary research. Each method is briefly described below, with instruction on the pages that follow.

Interviews (pages 110–115) involve consulting people through a question-and-answer dialogue. Interviewees can be either experts on your topic or people who have had a particular experience with the topic, either witnessing it or involved in some way.

> *Value:* First, interviewing experts can add authoritative input, though experts sometimes disagree. Second, interviewing someone with experience of your topic can give an inside perspective into its causes and effects, as well as personal dimensions.

Requests in Writing (pages 116–118) through e-mail or discussion groups can gather information to review and analyze. Depending on the writing medium used, such requests can function as a type of written interview.

> *Value:* As with interviews, you can gather both expert insight and personal experiences through written requests. Moreover, respondents can take time to formulate and shape a coherent answer.

Surveys (pages 119–123) gather information from representative groups of people as responses you can review, tabulate, and analyze, most often statistically.

> *Value:* Such research can give you strong insights into how the group thinks about your issue; however, it may not be able to gather complex responses.

Analyses of Texts, Documents, Records, and Artifacts (pages 124–127) involve studying original correspondence, reports, legislation, images, literary works, tools, and so on.

> *Value:* Such research provides a direct experience of your topic and insights into its immediate nature, products, or remnants, but the quality of research depends on how fully and effectively you analyze the "text" in question.

Observations (pages 128–131) involve systematically examining and analyzing places, spaces, scenes, equipment, work, events, and other sites or phenomena.

> *Value:* Such research provides a range of information—from personal impressions to precise data (measurements, etc).

Experiments (pages 132–133) test hypotheses—predictions about why things are as they are or happen as they do—so as to arrive at conclusions that can be tentatively accepted, related to other knowledge, and acted upon.

> *Value:* Such testing often explains cause-effect relationships for varied natural, social, or psychological phenomena, offering a degree of scientific certainty about the forces at work in your topic.

Doing Effective Primary Research

Whatever method of primary research you choose, you should conduct that research in a systematic, careful manner in order to generate valid, reliable primary information and ideas. While specifics for each method are presented later in this chapter, here are some principles that are common to all methods of primary research:

1. **Locate a reliable source.** Make sure, in other words, that the person, place, group, document, or image is the real thing—an authoritative, representative, respected source of information. Whether you find your source in a print publication (e.g., a version of a Shakespeare play published by a scholarly press), on the Internet (e.g. a piece of legislation), in an archive or museum (e.g., a sculpture), through personal contact (e.g., a home visit), or through exploration (e.g., a ravine in your city)—make sure that the source matches your research need and has the right "weight" for your project.

2. **Aim for objectivity.** For any researcher, complete objectivity is not only impossible but also undesirable, as intuition, imagination, and beliefs play a role in any project. You should, nevertheless, approach most primary research with an objective frame of mind: remain open to the evidence that arises by keeping your subjective wishes and impressions in check; otherwise, your research will be slanted and your readers will recognize the biases and gaps in your thinking.

3. **Root your primary research in a foundation of knowledge.** That is, don't go cold into your primary research. Do your homework first—learning the key concepts and perspectives on your topic, the theories debated, and the knowledge that has already been built by others. That way, your primary research will grow out of some foundational thinking and be driven by a specific purpose and specific questions.

4. **Use the right tools.** Each method of primary research requires tools—physical tools (e.g., lab notebook, field notebook, instruments), software (e.g., survey software, spreadsheet software), and analytical tools (e.g., the ability to compare and contrast, sort out causes and effects). Moreover, these tools tend to be used in particular ways in different disciplines. Make sure that you are using reliable tools and are using them effectively.

5. **Gather and work with data carefully.** Primary information is only as good as the care with which it was gathered and the care with which it is interpreted and presented. Keep accurate, complete records of your research; in some projects, you may even have to include such records and "raw data" in an appendix to your writing. Above all, as discussed on the next page, work ethically with your data by avoiding errors, gaps, and omissions, and by not fudging your data or doctoring graphics to make them fit the results you want.

Focus on Ethics: Respecting and Protecting Your Sources

Because primary research brings you into close contact with your topic, such research involves a range of complex ethical challenges. In fact, most colleges have a research-ethics committee that reviews, approves, and oversees research by scholars. Ethical review ensures that primary research is sound, safe, and beneficial. As a student undertaking primary research, strive to meet these ethical standards in your work.

Doing Primary Research with Integrity

Whatever primary research you are doing, be honest and truthful in these ways:

1. **Research Trail:** Through careful note-taking, create a record of your primary research methods, the data and information you collect, and your calculations and analyses. This record serves as verification of your research activities.

2. **Research Accuracy:** Gather information through respected methods, and keep your results real. No data should be fudged or omitted because they don't agree with the results you want; people's statements should not be misquoted or taken out of context; graphics should not be doctored or manipulated.

Handling People with Care

Primary research often involves working directly with people—"human subjects," in the language of research ethics. Such research should be guided by these rules:

1. **Do no harm.** Strive to prevent not only the physical harm of participants but also other forms of damage—psychological, social, financial, and so on. While some primary research does involve risk, dangers should be minimized and weighed against potential benefits for the participant, others, and society.

2. **Respect individual autonomy.** Essentially, respect participants' rights and dignity as individuals by keeping private information confidential, as appropriate; keeping identities anonymous, in some cases; and protecting vulnerable populations, such as children. In the end, it also means never coercing people to participate. Participation should be voluntary, granted in writing after a full disclosure of what participation entails: the nature of your project, its purposes and methods, the risks, and the possible benefits for participants and others.

 FOCUS on Your Major: For additional information on research ethics related to your discipline, check sites like these:

- Arts and Humanities: MLA Statement of Professional Ethics
  http://www.mla.org/repview_profethics

- Social Sciences: APA Research Ethics & Regulation
  http://www.apa.org/science/research/regbiblio.html

- Natural Sciences: Department of Health & Human Services Office for Human Research Protections
  http://www.hhs.gov/ohrp/irb/irb_guidebook.htm

Conducting Interviews

A good interview is essentially a focused, productive conversation with someone about your research topic. That "someone" could be (1) an expert on your topic, (2) someone who experienced your topic (e.g., a participant, an eyewitness, a person affected by your issue), or (3) a combination of types 1 and 2.

But why might you interview people? What can interviews add to your research? Interviews are about people—their wisdom, experiences, insights, opinions, concerns, struggles, stories, and voices. Through interviews, then, you can gain this personal angle on your topic. You can explore things that puzzle you about your topic and get feedback on issues that your traditional research hasn't addressed.

Choosing and Finding People to Interview

Because interviews can take a lot of time to plan and conduct, you want to select interviewees carefully so as to get useful material. For some projects, you may have access to already-published interviews (e.g., of authors, politicians, entertainers, scientists, and so on—available in periodicals, in books, and at Web sites). The downsides, of course, of such published interviews are that you are not in control of the questions, and the interviewee's statements may have been edited or summarized by the interviewer. To choose and locate people to interview, take these steps:

1. **Decide what types of people to interview.** Should you interview experts, people with experiences of your topic, or both? For example, if your project focused on attachment disorder's causes, should you interview a psychologist, a parent who has adopted a child diagnosed with the disorder, and/or the child? If your focus were on effects or treatments, which interviewees would you prefer?

2. **Decide how many interviews to do.** For some projects, a single interview might be sufficient to get the personal input you need. For other projects, several interviews covering a variety of perspectives on the issue would be more appropriate. For example, if you wanted representative feedback from viewers who have just seen the film *Pride and Prejudice,* two or three interviews might be sufficient.

3. **Tap a variety of resources to find people's names and contact information.** Think creatively about locating people to interview:
   - Consider your campus: Are there professors with a relevant expertise? Would specific students fit your project? Check different departments and associations.
   - Consider groups connected to your topic: Is there an online discussion group focusing on your subject? Is there a company or nonprofit organization in your community or online with a spokesperson you could interview?
   - Consider your sources: Do the resources you are reading point you to possible people? Do you have connections through family and friends? Have you tried the Yellow Pages or online directories? Have you explored the author links for articles and Web pages?

4. **Consider your choices of interview medium.** Whenever possible, interview people in person: face-to-face exchanges are not only much more personable but also give you the opportunity to read facial expressions, hand gestures, and other body language. If distance is an issue, consider a phone interview. If neither of these options is possible, you might choose to request information in writing: this topic is addressed on pages 116–118.

Preparing for an Interview

Once you have identified a person you wish to interview, you need to carefully prepare for the interview in order to ensure that it goes smoothly and proves productive. Take these steps:

1. **Make sure that you have done sufficient preliminary research.** Not having done your homework about the topic shows in an interview, so get ready by reading into your topic. That way, you will ask informed questions and get from the interviewee material that can't be found in other sources. Prepare, as well, by learning as much as you can about the interviewee—the sources of his or her expertise, the nature of his or her experiences.

2. **Identify your purpose.** Based on your preliminary research, identify why you think you should interview this person. What can an interview with this person about this topic add to your research? Complete a statement like this: *By interviewing [name], I hope to learn. . . .*

3. **Contact the potential interviewee and explain your request.** Whether you make your request in person, on the phone, or through e-mail, your request should always be polite rather than demanding, clear rather than vague. Include the following elements in your request:

   - Identify yourself and describe the research project you are working on.
   - Ask the person if he or she would be willing to grant an interview on the particular issue. Explain how you learned about the person and (as it relates to your goal for the interview) why the interview would be important for your project. State why you would value the person's insights.
   - Address practical details about the interview, showing attention to the interviewee's convenience: the time commitment involved, possible dates and times, and preferred medium (in person or on the phone). If appropriate, briefly outline the questions you might ask and request permission to record the interview.
   - Provide contact information so that the potential interviewee can reach you. He or she needs that information in order to answer your request. In addition, the interviewee may have follow-up questions or may need to contact you to cancel or reschedule the interview if a conflict or problem arises.

4. **Brainstorm questions.** With your purpose, preliminary research, and specific interviewee in mind, develop possible questions:
   - Consider the five or six key issues that you want to get at in the interview—gaps in your knowledge, issues of conflict or misunderstanding, the interviewee's central link to your topic. Then use the five W's and H *(who, what, when, where, why, and how)* to draft questions about these issues.
   - Understand open and closed questions. Closed questions ask for straightforward answers, such as "yes" or "no"; open questions ask for an explanation.
     Closed: *Did you watch* Pride and Prejudice *in a theater or on television? Approximately how many patients with attachment disorder have you treated? How many hybrid vehicles has your dealership sold in the past year?*
     Open: *Which moment between Elizabeth and Darcy sticks out in your mind, and why? How can adoptive families faced with attachment disorder best cope with the day-to-day challenges? How do your customers explain their interest in a hybrid vehicle?*
   - Avoid slanted or loaded questions that suggest you want a specific answer

     > *Slanted:* What's your judgment of the blatant sexism shown in *Pride and Prejudice*?
     >
     > *Better:* What portrait of gender relations did the film create for you?

5. **Select and order your questions.** After brainstorming questions, you'll likely need to pare back and organize your list. While you should be cautious about over-scripting the interview so that it becomes a rigid, flat question-and-answer period rather than a conversation, map out the key questions you want to cover and arrange them for a logical flow. Consider these tips:
   - First record identifying information about the interview and interviewee: name, position or title, contact information; the interview date, time, and location.
   - Start with a straightforward question that your interviewee will be able to answer comfortably and that will establish rapport between you.
   - Select five-to-ten main questions (depending on the length of your interview), but also imagine the follow-up issues that the earlier questions might prompt.
   - Consider concluding with an open question that allows the interviewee to offer whatever information, comments, or insights that he or she finds relevant.
   - Write or type the questions on the left side of the page. Leave room for quotations, information, and impressions on the right side.

6. **Get practical.** To ensure a smooth interview, do the following:
   - Rehearse the questions, visualizing how the interview might go.
   - Gather pens, paper, and other recording equipment, making sure that you have back-ups, batteries, and so on in case something breaks down or runs out.
   - If you are unfamiliar with the location, examine it prior to the interview.

Doing the Interview

If you are well prepared (as described earlier), the interview should go smoothly; however, you should also observe the guidelines that follow.

1. **Be natural, sincere, and professional:**
   - Respect the interviewee's time by being on time, efficient, and courteous.
   - Relax so that both you and the person can be open.
   - Introduce yourself, remind the interviewee why you've come, thank the person for the interview, and provide whatever background information will help him or her feel comfortable and focused.
   - Listen much more than you talk, and avoid impolite interruptions.

2. **Create a record of the interview:**
   - If the person has given permission, tape the interview and take pictures. Use a recorder with a counter so that you can jot down the number when the interviewee makes an important point.
   - To make recording equipment less intrusive, place it slightly off to the side.
   - Write down key facts, quotations, and impressions, even if you are using a recorder. Doing so keeps you engaged and creates a second record if something goes wrong with the recording.
   - Note, in particular, sources that the interviewee may suggest. If necessary, ask for identifying details that will allow you to find such sources yourself.

3. **Listen actively.** Use body language (nods, smiles, and eye contact). Pay attention to not only what the person says but how he or she says it—tone, context, and his or her body language.

4. **Be tactful and flexible.** If the person avoids a difficult question, politely rephrase it or ask for clarification. If the person looks puzzled by a question, rephrase it or ask another. If the discussion gets off track, gently redirect it. But don't limit yourself to your planned questions. Instead, ask pertinent follow-up questions like these:
   - *Clarifying:* Do you mean . . . ?
   - *Explanatory:* What do you mean by . . . ?
   - *Detailing:* What happened exactly? Can you describe that?
   - *Analytical:* Did that happen in stages? What were the causes? The outcomes?
   - *Probing:* What do you think that meant?
   - *Comparative:* How was that similar to or different from . . . ?
   - *Contextual:* What else was going on? Who else was involved?
   - *Summarizing:* Overall, what was the net effect?

5. **End positively.** Conclude by asking if the person wants to add, clarify, or emphasize anything. (Note: important points may come up late in the interview.) Thank the person, gather your notes and equipment, and part with a handshake.

Sample Interview Note-Taking Sheet

Below, note how the researcher sets up questions for an interview with an automotive engineer regarding hybrid technology. The interviewer begins with identifying information for future reference, and then moves from a basic "connecting" question into the technology's principles, strengths, challenges, and future. On the right, he would leave room (approximately half the sheet) for taking notes.

Interview with Jessica Madison, automotive engineer for Future Fuel Corporation (e-mail jmadison@futurefuel.com; phone 555-555-5555)
January 22, 2009: 2:30 p.m.

Notes, quotations, observations:

Preliminaries: thanks/appreciation; introduction of myself; background, purpose, hoped-for outcome of research (report on hybrids' environmental potential)

Initial Question
1. Please tell me about your research into hybrid technology. When and how did you become interested? What discoveries have you made?

Hybrid Technology: Principles
2. How does hybrid technology actually work? What's the principle behind the hybrid vehicle?

3. How is the hybrid engine different from the traditional internal-combustion engine?

Strengths and Challenges
4. What are the strengths of hybrid vehicles?

5. What are some of the challenges of hybrids? Some of the weaknesses?

The Future/Viability
6. Where is hybrid technology going? What's the next generation of clean-car technology?

7. What are the benefits or drawbacks of society investing in hybrids? Why should the average person care about hybrid technologies?

8. Would you like to add or clarify anything about hybrid technologies?

Closing: thank for taking time, offering insights

Following Up the Interview

Effectively following up the interview is almost as important as effectively planning the interview. Follow up is what you make of the interview itself. Consider these tips:

1. **Study your notes and records.** As soon as possible, review all your notes and fill in responses you remember but couldn't record at the time. If you recorded the interview, replay or review it, looking carefully for key ideas, information, quotations, anecdotes, and so on.

2. **Analyze the results.** Study the information, insights, and quotations you gathered. What do they reveal about the topic? How does the interview confirm, complement, or contradict other sources on the topic? What has the interview added to your larger project?

3. **Reconnect with the interviewee, if appropriate.** Contact the interviewee by note, e-mail, or phone to address these issues:

   - Thank the person for his or her time and help.
   - If necessary, ask the interviewee to confirm statements, details, and quotations.
   - Offer to let the person see the interview's outcome—the research paper, for example.

FOCUS on Ethics: Because an interview is a direct research encounter between yourself and another person, it involves critical ethical considerations. While these ethical issues are discussed more fully on page 109, follow these practices as you conduct interviews and use the information you gather:

- Observe interview etiquette. Respect the person even while pressing for answers. Avoid being invasive, instigating an argument, questioning the interviewee's honesty, or making unreasonable time demands.

- Use the interviewee's statements fairly. Avoid taking statements out of their context, misquoting them, or using sarcasm when you present them.

- If fitting, respect the interviewee's right or need for privacy and anonymity, both within the body of your writing and your bibliography of resources.

- As you analyze what your interview gathered, consider the interview dynamics: did your interaction with the interviewee slant his or her responses in particular ways?

FOCUS on Your Major: Consider these discipline-focused issues:

- Interviewing is foundational research in many disciplines, particularly in the social sciences where people are the focus. However, interviews can be useful in any discipline. Consider how interviews make sense for the subject matter of your major.

- For information on how interviews are documented, check these pages: MLA (pages 393 and 399), APA (pages 428 and 438), and Chicago (page 468).

Requesting Information in Writing

Sometimes, it makes sense to request information in writing from people—as with interviews, people with expertise or experiences related to your topic. Such a request falls between a personal interview and a formal survey. When you contact people by e-mail or letter with your request or questions, you give them time to think about and formulate a response: the result may be highly thoughtful insights for your project from people closely related to the topic. Moreover, you can fairly efficiently send your request to many people, if need be, and gather many responses.

Finding Contacts

Depending on your project and your information need, you might write to a scholar, someone in a profession, a representative of an organization, or a member of a group (online or otherwise). You can find people to contact by following many of the tips discussed on page 110 for finding interview subjects: depending on your information need and goals, consider people on your campus, in your community, or online. It is especially important that you find an e-mail or physical address for making contact. For this purpose, use various links and directories:

- Directories of people, departments, and groups on your campus
- The Yellow Pages and other business directories, directories for government offices, directories of nonprofit organizations, etc. in your community
- Author links for Web resources
- Directories of people online: Yahoo! People Search (www.people.yahoo.com)
- Directories for faculty at colleges and universities (Yahoo! Educational Directory)
- Directories for online chat groups, list servers, and other groups: Yahoo! Chat; Yahoo! Groups; MSN Chat; Google Directory; Google Groups; Cata-List; Tile.net; Directory of Scholarly and Professional E-Conferences.

Making Your Request

Once you have identified a person to contact, develop your request message by following the steps below and studying the sample request message on page 118.

1. **Think through the context.** Consider your own and your reader's situation:
   - What is your goal in writing this person? Record what you hope to gain.
   - Who exactly is the person? Jot down details like these: the nature of your relationship, the person's training and experiences, the contact's professional affiliations, the means by which you learned about the person.
   - Consider practical details: the deadline by which you need a response, the best medium for contact (e-mail, letter, etc.).

2. **Draft your message.** Making your message courteous, draft your request:
   - In the *opening,* identify yourself as a student from a specific school, describe your project, and state why you need the reader's help.

- In the *middle*, outline the specifics of your request: the information or items that you need, or the questions you would like answered. Restrict your request to three or four items or questions: to increase the likelihood that your reader will respond positively, you need to make your request reasonable (not demanding, burdensome, or time-consuming).

- In the *closing*, explain details related to the reader's response. If possible, encourage the reader to respond by stressing benefits of the research and of his or her responding. Then indicate a date by which you need a response, as well as the preferred method and address. Finally, thank the reader for *considering* your request (do not assume a positive answer).

3. **Revise and edit your message.** Before sending your request, carefully review it to make sure that it is polished and professional. Have you used a polite, person-to-person tone, including a simple "please" and "thank you"? Is the tone confident but not pushy? Concerning what you have requested, have you used precise and understandable terms? Are grammar, punctuation, and spelling correct? Is the message properly and attractively formatted?

FOCUS on Research Essentials: If your request takes you into an online writing environment (discussion group, etc.), you need to observe Netiquette. When online, people don't have visual cues, and they can't hear tone of voice. Therefore, the intent of a message can be easily misunderstood. In addition, you may be jumping into the middle of an ongoing "conversation." As outlined below, Netiquette practices help you be considerate of others when you are online

- **Lurking:** When you join a mailing list or newsgroup, it's best to lurk before you leap. That is, listen to the conversations for a while before contributing or making a request. Also, check out the group's FAQ (frequently asked questions) page, or search available archives to see if the information that you need is already there.

- **Message Politeness:** Online groups can be diverse in terms of nationality, race, gender, and so on. Be sensitive to such differences in your messages. Moreover, avoid *flaming*—the practice of sending or posting an angry, abusive message. On the Net, words in capital letters mean SHOUTING, so don't use all caps.

- **Message Professionalism:** Because you are communicating with someone about an academic research project, your message should meet professional standards. As you likely know from your own experience, people writing online often write informally: they add "smileys" such as ☺ (also called "emoticons") to be friendly, and they use abbreviations (e.g., LOL for "laughing out loud") to speed the flow of communication (especially in IM or chat environments). However, when you are making requests for an academic project, you should avoid emoticons and abbreviations: instead, develop your message as an electronic letter, with a courteous, fairly formal tone.

Sample Request Message

The sample message below shows what a written request might look like for an academic project. In the example, the student writer contacts a scholar whose name she got from an online academic discussion group and seeks this academic's expert opinion on Jane Austen's popularity in fiction and film.

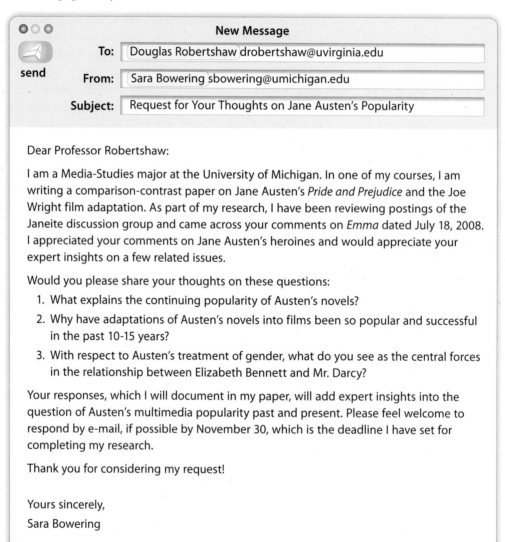

○ ○ ○   **New Message**

To: Douglas Robertshaw drobertshaw@uvirginia.edu

send

From: Sara Bowering sbowering@umichigan.edu

Subject: Request for Your Thoughts on Jane Austen's Popularity

Dear Professor Robertshaw:

I am a Media-Studies major at the University of Michigan. In one of my courses, I am writing a comparison-contrast paper on Jane Austen's *Pride and Prejudice* and the Joe Wright film adaptation. As part of my research, I have been reviewing postings of the Janeite discussion group and came across your comments on *Emma* dated July 18, 2008. I appreciated your comments on Jane Austen's heroines and would appreciate your expert insights on a few related issues.

Would you please share your thoughts on these questions:

1. What explains the continuing popularity of Austen's novels?
2. Why have adaptations of Austen's novels into films been so popular and successful in the past 10-15 years?
3. With respect to Austen's treatment of gender, what do you see as the central forces in the relationship between Elizabeth Bennett and Mr. Darcy?

Your responses, which I will document in my paper, will add expert insights into the question of Austen's multimedia popularity past and present. Please feel welcome to respond by e-mail, if possible by November 30, which is the deadline I have set for completing my research.

Thank you for considering my request!

Yours sincerely,
Sara Bowering

FOCUS on Your Major: For information on how written responses to requests (e.g., e-mail messages, IM, chat) are documented according to different systems, check these pages: MLA (page 399), APA (page 428), and Chicago (page 467).

Conducting Informal Surveys

Surveys are useful tools for collecting primary information, especially statistical data, because they allow researchers to gather and analyze responses from large numbers of people. While collecting complex responses from people (as you might with an interview or a written request for information) is difficult, surveys work well to measure the attitudes, opinions, and experiences of representative members of identifiable groups of people. So if your project might benefit from understanding a particular group's thinking, consider conducting a survey. Think about these examples:

- For a project on film adaptations of Jane Austen's novels, a survey of film viewers could gather their reactions to the presentation of gender issues.

- For a project on attachment disorder, a survey of professionals could gather information on their preferred methods of treatment.

- For a project on hybrid vehicles, a survey of fellow students could measure their knowledge of hybrid technology and likelihood of purchasing a hybrid.

 FOCUS on Research Essentials: Surveys are common research tools in the social sciences, where responses to well-crafted questions offer researchers the opportunity to develop statistical analyses related to human behavior, social institutions, public attitudes, political participation, consumer practices, and the like. With this reality in mind, consider these two issues:

- **Training:** The science of crafting formal research surveys and analyzing the statistical significance of the results is beyond the scope of this book: whole courses are dedicated to this topic. The directions that follow will simply allow you to do informal surveys, the types of surveys that might complement your main research but not function as central evidence in your analysis or argument. If you wish to make survey research a major component of your project, consult with your instructor and seek help from an expert in the social sciences.

- **Online resources:** If you wish to do serious survey research, a number of survey programs are available on the Web. These help you develop and administer your survey, as well as tabulate and analyze the results. Popular commercial sites include SurveyMethods.com, Zoomerang.com, SurveyMonkey.com, WebSurveyor.com, and QuestionPro.com. A good open-source choice is LimeSurvey.org.

Finding and Selecting People to Survey

Your first step in conducting a survey involves considering possible respondents. As with interviews (page 110) and written information requests (page 116), you should consider contacting people on campus, in your community, or online, again depending on your research goals. Following the tips on those pages about locating research subjects, tailor your search to an identifiable group with the questions on the next page.

- What population of people can provide the information that you need?
- What can they offer that you can't find in other sources?
- How can you contact people from that group—by e-mailing individuals, soliciting participants through a notice on campus, meeting with the representative of an organization for permission and contact information of members, or by posting a notice in a discussion group?

Once you have identified your target group and contact methods, decide how to distribute your survey. (Generally, a 60 to 70 percent response rate is considered good, although lower rates are common.) Use methods like these to distribute your survey:

- **Systematic random sampling:** Choose a cross section of people from the target audience (for example, by picking every tenth student from the college directory).
- **Stratified random sampling:** If your target audience has a number of subgroups, pick a proportionate cross section of people from each group—for example, a proportionate number of male and female students.
- **Quota sampling:** In this method, you choose a number of representative individuals from the group, without a clear system—for example, the first 25 students leaving an auditorium.

Developing a Sound Survey

A well-crafted survey convinces respondents of its importance, asks clear questions, and is easy to complete and submit. To craft such a survey—one that effectively and efficiently gathers the information you need—take these steps:

1. **Do some planning.** Sort out your initial thinking on these issues:
   - *Purpose:* What is the limited, measurable goal of your survey? What research issue will it address? What information will it provide?
   - *Respondents:* Who are the respondents you have chosen? What are their experiences, education, values, and attitudes to your topic? What is the nature of the group to which they belong? Are there distinct subgroups within the larger population? What can they offer that you can't get elsewhere? What would be a reliable sampling of this group?
   - *Context:* How should you distribute and collect the survey—in person, through the mail, via e-mail, through a Web site? By when do you need responses? What conditions would encourage objective responses and a high return rate? For example, should your survey be anonymous?

2. **Draft relevant, reliable, and valid questions.** Relevant questions clearly address the survey's topic. Reliable questions are understandable. Valid questions give you data that are relevant and accurate. To write such questions, do the following:
   - Phrase questions precisely, in language that readers understand, with answer options that are both complete and without overlap.
   - Make questions objective and manageable for your readers—neither too broad nor slanted toward a specific answer; neither insulting nor time-consuming and complicated.

- Make your questions efficient: each question should cover one item only, and no questions should be duplicated.
- Draft some questions that distinguish your respondents in ways that help you analyze subgroups within your target audience (e.g., by gender, major, occupation, age). Draft other questions focused on your topic, questions that get at the key issues of attitude, understanding, and belief that you want answered by your target audience.

3. **Choose fitting questions.** Consider both open-ended and closed questions:
   - Open-ended questions ask respondents to provide written responses. While such questions can collect in-depth and varied information (perhaps useful quotations and surprising insights), responses take time to complete and can be difficult to summarize and code during tabulation.
   - Closed questions give respondents a limited number of clearly distinguished answer options. Questions are easy to answer and tabulate:
     Yes/No: Answers divide respondents into two groups.
     True/False: Answers indicate respondent attitudes, beliefs, understandings.
     Multiple Choice: Answers show respondents' preferences, knowledge, actions, or behaviors.
     Ranking: Answers indicate respondents' order of priority, sense of importance.
     Likert Scale: Answers show respondents' level of feeling, type of judgment, frequency of activity, etc.

4. **Select a limited number of questions.** Restrict your survey to approximately six to ten questions, or a maximum of one page. While some questions may be needed to distinguish the segments of your survey population (e.g., gender, age, major in college), include only relevant, non-intrusive questions, and limit the number of open-ended questions. Unless conditions are favorable and respondents highly motivated, a long survey will yield a low return.

5. **Organize your survey with the respondent in mind.** These features make a survey easy to complete:
   - The title suggests the survey's purpose.
   - The introduction (a) states who you are and who is authorizing the survey; (b) indicates why you need the information; (c) suggests benefits for completing the survey; and (d) explains how to complete it, by when, and how to return it.
   - Numbers, instructions, white space, headings, boldface, and underlining guide the reader through the survey.
   - Questions are grouped logically—moving smoothly from one topic to the next. Typically, first questions are ones that identify the respondent within your target audience (e.g., gender, major, age).

6. **Test your survey.** Ask someone for feedback on a draft. To debug the survey, do a trial run with a small group similar to the target group.

Doing Your Survey

Administering your survey involves distributing it, collecting completed ones, tabulating responses, and analyzing results. Take these steps:

1. **Contact respondents and distribute or post your survey.** Depending on the potential respondents you have identified, the number of surveys you wish to distribute, the location of respondents, and so on, make sensible choices about contacting potential respondents and sending out the survey:

   - Choose your contact medium based on the distribution method you have chosen (see page 120).

   - Whenever possible, make your contact with potential respondents personal. Doing so may involve dropping off the survey or even completing it with the respondent. Or it might involve sending the survey with a cover message that uses the respondent's name, identifies yourself and your project, explains the survey's purpose and importance, politely requests the respondent's participation, explains when to complete it and how to return it, and thanks the potential respondent for considering your request. In other words, make each potential respondent feel knowledgeable and valued.

   - Send or post the survey in a convenient format. If, for example, you distribute a paper survey, include a return envelope (postage included, if appropriate). If you distribute the survey by e-mail, make it an attachment that is easy to open, complete, and return. Or you might post the survey at a Web site in a format that is easy for respondents to complete (and using software that automatically imports responses into a spreadsheet).

2. **Collect and tabulate responses.** If you are conducting your survey using survey software, tallying results should be a function of the software itself. Another option might involve creating a spreadsheet for survey responses. However, if you are doing a simple survey, you can tally responses manually by following this process:

   - Make a separate tally sheet for each question. Write the question at the top, and establish columns for (a) the respondent (either the person's name or a code number), (b) each answer option, and (c) "no response."

   - List respondents by code or name in the left column, and begin checking off responses to that question by reviewing each returned survey.

   - When you have checked that question on each survey, total the responses at the bottom of the columns and then calculate percentages.

3. **Analyze results and draw conclusions.** Survey software helps in this regard, but such analysis also relies on training in reading and understanding statistics. For your informal survey, simply do the following:

   - Study the numbers for trends. What do respondents' answers to specific questions mean? What does the percentage breakdown mean about the population's beliefs, attitudes, values, and behaviors? Looking at subgroups of respondents, can you discern differences in response (e.g., between male and female)? How might these differences be explained?

- Measure the results against your expectations. For specific questions and the overall survey, what responses had you anticipated? Did the survey offer support to your theories? If results were contrary to your expectations, what might explain this difference?
- With open-ended questions, study responses for patterns, themes, and quotations. What insights do these written responses offer? How do these responses relate to the numbers for the closed questions?

Sample Informal Survey

In the following informal survey, a student gathers information about fellow students' reactions to Patricia Rozema's film adaptation of Jane Austen's *Mansfield Park*. After putting on a screening for respondents who volunteered for her study, she had students answer the questions below. Notice that responses are anonymous.

Survey on Patricia Rozema's *Mansfield Park*

Thank you for your willingness to contribute to my project on film adaptations of Jane Austen's novels. Your feedback on Rozema's *Mansfield Park* will help me understand the film's attention to a variety of social and moral issues. Note that all of your responses will be treated anonymously.

1. What is your gender? ___ male ___ female

2. What is your age? ___ 20 or under ___ 21-30 ___ 31-40 ___ 41 or over

3. What is your ethnic identity? ___ Black ___ Asian ___ Hispanic ___ White ___ Other ___

4. What is your area of study? ___ Humanities ___ Social Sciences ___ Natural Sciences

5. How much did you enjoy Rozema's *Mansfield Park*?

Strong dislike   Strong appreciation

       1   2   3   4   5

6. How would you respond to this statement: "I identified with Fanny Price's character—her struggles, her situation, her dreams." ___ True ___ False

7. How would you rank the film's presentation of social and moral issues, with 1 most important and 5 least important? ___ wealth and poverty ___ race ___ gender ___ class ___ fidelity/honesty

8. What was the film's main message about life, past and present?

Analyzing Texts, Documents, Records, and Artifacts

People make "texts." In their various cultural activities, past and present, humans have produced and continue to produce written texts, official records, unofficial documents, art works, transcripts, a variety of tools and objects, and much more. Researchers can study such texts so as to understand human culture more fully (artistically, literarily, philosophically, sociologically, historically, scientifically, etc.).

When such a text is directly related to the event, issue, object, or phenomenon that you are researching, that text is called a primary text. This text might be any one of the following: a poem, a novel, a letter, a diary, a speech, a painting, a piece of legislation, a transcript of a trial, a film, or an e-mail message—a whole range of works created and left behind by people. When you analyze such texts, you interpret them: you put them in context and closely examine their parts in order to arrive at conclusions about what these texts say and mean in relation to your research questions. Consider these examples:

- In a project on Jane Austen's treatment of gender, you interpret the dynamics of character and plot in *Sense and Sensibility*.
- In a project on attachment disorder, you study drawings and paintings done by children as part of their therapy.
- In a project on hybrid vehicles, you study marketing texts (magazine ads, television commercials, Web sites) to understand how the science of hybrids is being applied, popularized, and "sold."

Choosing Primary Texts

Often, your project itself will specify a primary text. For example, a literary-analysis paper (see pages 341–358) requires a close reading of one or more poems, short stories, novels, or plays: these literary texts are your research project's primary texts. Similarly, a history paper might require that you examine original texts—government records, business reports, eyewitness accounts, and so on. In fact, many humanities projects center on primary texts, whether art works, philosophical writings, sacred texts, or historical documents. Texts—often verbal but sometimes visual—are the focus of study.

However, when you are free to choose primary texts for your project, brainstorm options by answering this question: What texts, documents, records, and artifacts originated from or grew out of your topic? Then select materials that directly relate to your research questions about this topic.

> **Example:** If you were studying English labor riots of the 1830s, you could investigate these primary sources:
> - to understand what rioters were demanding, copies of speeches given at demonstrations.
> - to know who the rioters were, names from police reports or union-membership lists.
> - to learn the political response to the riots, political speeches or legislation.
> - to get at the attitudes of people from that time, newspaper reports, art works, or novels from that period.

Locating Primary Texts

Once you have identified primary texts to study, you must locate them. For some projects, this task may be simple, as the primary texts may be included in your course texts or placed on reserve by your instructor. However, for other projects, locating and accessing primary texts might be difficult. Obviously, you may find what you need by researching within your library and through your library's online resources and search tools (see pages 49-66). In addition, you might be able to access a text in e-book format (see page 73), or you might find primary government documents via the Web (see page 85). However, you could also explore archival resources such as these, as archives typically collect letters, journals, personal papers, and other texts:

1. **Local archives:** If appropriate for your project, check the archives of your college's library, or of your city, county, or state libraries, which typically collect documents of local interest. In addition, local and regional museums, clerk or records offices, county courthouses, and historical societies can help you get at a local angle on many research topics. For example, if you are researching the Civil Rights movement, such libraries, museums, and offices might have archival material and records that could help you analyze how the movement was experienced in your city, county, or state.

2. **National and international archival sources:** A helpful resource for researching archival holdings around the globe is the University of Idaho's "Repositories of Primary Resources," a guide to more than 5,000 Web sites that describe, index, or provide full-text versions of a whole range of primary texts: www.uidaho.edu/special-collections/Other.Repositories.html. In addition, here are some useful national sites:

   - U.S. National Archives (with information about regional archives): www.archives.gov
   - Archives Canada: www.archivescanada.ca
   - The National Archives of the United Kingdom: www.nationalarchives.gov.uk

As libraries, museums, and government agencies put more and more material online, you can expect to do some archival research from the comfort of your computer. One example is the British Library's "Turning the Pages" project, an online resource that allows you to study or "leaf through" digitized versions of the library's rare books. Check it out at www.bl.uk/onlinegallery/ttp/ttpbooks.html.

 FOCUS on Research Ethics: However you access primary texts, the rule of thumb is "handle with care." Obviously, if you are physically working with letters, diaries, manuscripts, and similar archival documents, you need to respect those resources, taking great care not to mark them or damage them in any way. In addition, your actual analysis of a primary text, even if it is not rare or you are working with a digital version, should respect the text's origin and context, and interpret the piece thoroughly and fairly. For a fuller discussion of primary-research ethics, see page 109.

Analyzing Primary Texts

Typically, analyzing or interpreting primary texts is a thoughtful process that involves establishing the text's context, closely reading and rereading the text, and developing and testing a thesis about the text's meaning in relation to your topic. When interpreting primary texts, follow these practices:

1. **Frame your examination with questions.** To make sense of the text, document, record, or artifact, understand what you are looking for and why. Identify the central question you wish to answer (the question at the heart of your research project). Then list the secondary questions that you want to answer in relation to the main question. All of these questions function as the analytical "tool" or method guiding your reading of the text.

   Example: Historical research involves discovering significant change, the reasons for the change, and the consequences or implications of that change. If you were examining Mary Wollstonecraft's *A Vindication of the Rights of Woman* as a primary text for a history paper, these might be some framing research questions:

   What is this book's relationship to the age of revolution out of which it came? How are Wollstonecraft's ideas related to Enlightenment rationalism, as well as the growing emphasis on liberty, individual rights, and individualism during the eighteenth and nineteenth centuries? How does this document relate to the changing situation of women in Europe during this time? What effects did her book have?

2. **Put the document or artifact in context.** So that the material takes on meaning, clarify its external and internal nature. First, consider its external context—the five W's and H: What exactly is it? Who made it, when, where, why, and how? Second, consider its internal nature—what the document means, based on what it can and cannot show you: What does the language mean or refer to? What is the document's structure? What are the artifact's composition and style?

   Example: If you were examining Mary Wollstonecraft's *A Vindication of the Rights of Woman* in a history or women's studies course, you would examine the following:

   - External context: *Who was Mary Wollstonecraft, and what are the major facts of her life? When did she write* A Vindication of the Rights of Woman, *and under what conditions? Why did she write it, and for whom? How did her contemporaries, both male and female, respond to her? What type of document is her* Vindication?

   - Internal context: *What is Wollstonecraft's argument? What are her key ideas and themes? What is her evidence? Does her* Vindication *represent the views of all late eighteenth-century women? Does her text address the situation of all women? Can we expect Wollstonecraft to speak the language of twentieth- or twenty-first-century feminism?*

3. **Draw coherent conclusions about meaning.** Make sense of the source in relation to your research questions. What connections does the source reveal? What important changes or developments? What cause-and-effect relationships? What themes? With what voice does it speak?

   Example: With respect to Wollstonecraft's *Vindication,* you might draw conclusions about the connections between her discussion of women's rights and rationalism, revolution, and individualism; about her sense of what constitutes womanhood; about the effects that her text had on her society; about the character of late-eighteenth-century feminism; or about the debt of contemporary feminism to her thinking.

 FOCUS on Your Major: Discipline-Specific Questions. Studying primary documents and artifacts is central to many disciplines: e.g., history, literature, theology, philosophy, political studies, and archaeology. Such study requires effective interpretation of primary sources—a process that the researcher directs by asking questions appropriate to his or her discipline. With the English labor riots of the 1830s again as an example, here are possible framing questions from four disciplines:

- *History* would ask what process or change these riots were part of. How did they reflect and respond to the ideas and social structure of their time? What were the reasons for the riots? How did they turn these ideas and structures in new directions? What consequences did their actions have?

- *Political science* might ask what political theories the rioters held, what political structure gave rise to their grievances or contributed to the conflict or injustice the rioters protested, how politicians responded to rioters' claims, how the political structure affected the resolution of the riots, and what assumptions about public justice were implemented or evident in the resolution.

- *Sociology* might ask what the living conditions and class of the rioters were, how relations within and between different social institutions (e.g., the family, business, the church, government) affected the rioters and contributed to the conflict, what changes in social structures or attitudes were or are needed in order to solve the problems that contributed to the riots.

- *Art or literature* might ask how the concerns of the rioters were embodied in the new "realist" style of the mid-1800s, how artists and writers sympathized with and addressed an alienated working-class audience, and how they commented on the social structure of their time.

Making Observations

Observation is a form of research that places you at a site directly related to your topic. Whether you are examining people's behavior, natural phenomena, or a location's features, observation can help you gather a range of information—subjective impressions, sensory data, various recordings (photos, sound, film), or concrete measurements. And such observations can help you formulate and/or test concepts, ideas, or theories.

Finding a Site for Your Project

If a particular observation site is not already specified for your project (as it often is for field research in the sciences), brainstorm possible sites by considering these questions: What places, objects, and events are directly related to my topic? What natural sites or people places? What sites are within range for me, given the time and resource restrictions of my project? Here are three examples:

- For a theater project on Shakespeare's *Othello,* a student might attend a production of the play and observe scenic, directorial, and acting choices, as well as audience reactions to various moments in the story.
- For a project addressing ADD (attention deficit disorder) in the classroom, an Education student might visit an elementary school classroom to observe ADD's effects on students and teachers.
- For a project on white-tail deer behavior, an Animal-Science student might visit a state park to document feeding habits and social interaction.

Getting Ready to Observe

As with most forms of primary research, preparation will make your observations productive. Prepare for your observation by addressing these issues:

1. **Know what you want to accomplish.** That is, what is the point or goal of your observation? Do you need to understand a place or a process? Solve a problem? Answer a question? What kind of information do you want to gather?

2. **Consider possible perspectives and vantage points.** To think through possible angles of vision, explore these questions:
   - To get a full perspective on your topic, should you visit one site or several? For a given site, should you plan multiple visits in order to gather comprehensive information? Or will one visit to one site give you a sufficient view?
   - Should you observe the site passively or interact with it? For example, if you are observing horses, do you want to stay back and observe how they interact with each other or do you want insights into how they interact with you?
   - Should you remain objective as you record data, or include impressions? For example, does your assignment require that you scientifically assess the results of a forest fire, or is your task to register your impressions of such destruction?
   - Should you observe from one position or several? Close up to the object of observation, or at a distance?

3. **Make your observations informed.** Undertake your observation after having done sufficient background and contextual research on your topic. For example, your observations of people's buying habits in a mall would benefit from reading about the sociology of consumerism and consumption. This reading will give you questions that direct your observations and focus your analysis.

4. **Plan your observation.** Preparation involves both academic and practical issues:
   - Based on your purpose for observing and your background research, create a list of questions to answer and things to look for.
   - If the observation site isn't public, seek permission. Even if it is public, you may need to inform someone in authority concerning your plans.
   - Ensure your safety if the site involves dangerous conditions. Consider observing with a partner, taking safety equipment, wearing appropriate clothing, and having a means of contacting people if you run into trouble.
   - Consider the timing of your observations. When would be a good time to visit? How much time should you set aside?
   - Assess how the type of site, the weather conditions, and your data-collection activities might require special transportation, clothing, and equipment.

5. **Gather observation tools.** Thinking about the site and your purpose, pull together the tools you need to conduct your observations. Collect tools like these:
   - note-taking tools (pens, pencils, paper; field notebook; palm device or laptop).
   - recording equipment (camera, video recorder, tape recorder, sketch book).
   - measuring equipment (maps, counter, tape measure, watch, etc.).
   - other tools (containers for samples, a flashlight, geologist's hammer, etc.).

 FOCUS on Research Ethics: Conducting observations ethically means more than getting permission to observe. Two other issues are significant:

1. **Recognize the limits of your own powers of observation.** No one person can catch everything in an observation. Moreover, while perfect objectivity may be your aim, the reality is that perfect distancing is not possible (nor always desirable). You observe from and out of a particular perspective, to a greater or lesser degree conscious and controlled. As you use your observations in your research writing, recognize the limits of your information and perspective.

2. **Measure the effects of your presence.** It's a general principle of research that the presence of the researcher changes the object of study. Be aware that during observation, your presence as the observer can alter what you observe in both subtle and drastic ways. First, you want to make sure that your presence does no harm to the people, creatures, or natural environment. But you also want to consider how your presence might alter the behavior, words, and appearance of what you are observing. Factor these possible effects into your conclusions.

Conducting Your Observation

Once you have arrived at your observation site, get ready to observe. If appropriate, start by informing your contact person of your arrival and reviewing your research plan. Then set up your equipment and follow guidelines like these:

1. **Be flexible.** Follow your plan, but be open to surprises. For example, while your task might be to observe student behaviors at a football game, perhaps you might become aware of some interesting student-senior citizen interactions.

2. **Identify your position.** Where are you in the site? What is your angle? More broadly, what is your personal and/or cultural stance here—your gender, socioeconomic background, religious beliefs, nationality, age, and so on? For example, if you are attending a cultural festival, your stance might be defined as both literal spectator (at the sidelines) and a cultural "visitor" (someone from the outside looking in).

3. **Stay focused.** Pay attention to the big picture (the context, time frame, and surroundings), but focus on your observational goal by filtering out unnecessary details. In other words, pay attention to the people, objects, and events related to your research questions, but remember the background and edges of your view. Zoom in on your object of study, but occasionally pull back and pan out to the larger scene.

4. **Take notes on specific details and impressions.** While being careful not to miss too much, jot down data for later review—conditions, appearances, actions, events, and so on. At a play, for example, record details about lighting, sound, costuming, acting, etc. If appropriate for your goal, focus on your five senses:
   - *Sights*—record colors, shapes, and appearance; see the large view and the little details.
   - *Sounds*—listen for loud and subtle, harsh and pleasant, natural and mechanical sounds; if people are present, record relevant conversations.
   - *Smells*—check out both pleasant and unpleasant odors: what's spicy, sweaty, pungent, and rancid.
   - *Textures*—safely test things for temperature, smoothness, and roughness.
   - *Tastes*—if your site permits, test tastes for sweet, sour, bitter, etc.

5. **Gather other forms of evidence.** If appropriate, explore your sixth sense—thoughts, feelings, associations, and intuitions. Or take measurements, record images and sound, gather samples, interview people, study event programs, get brochures—do whatever you can to collect material for further study and analysis.

Making Sense of Your Observations

Once you have completed your observations and left the site, spend some time in reflection that makes sense of what you have gathered. While you will clearly also be processing what you are observing during the observation, do the following after the fact:

1. **Complete and review your notes and evidence.** As soon as possible, flesh out your notes a bit more fully—while your memory is still good. Then examine closely everything that you have written, recorded, and collected, looking for patterns and themes in the information you've gathered. Relate the evidence to your research questions and working ideas about your topic.

2. **List your conclusions.** Describe what has been clarified about your topic through the observation. Record the conclusions that you have reached, along with supporting details from your observations.

3. **Relate your observations to other research.** Specifically, do the following:
   - Explore how your observations confirm, contradict, complement, or build on other sources of information.
   - Assess the overall value of the observation for your research.
   - Consider ways that you can use the evidence in your research writing.

 FOCUS on Your Major: If you are in the Natural Sciences, your main observation tool will be the field notebook. While your science instructors will likely give you specific instructions about keeping a field notebook in their classes or in your discipline, here is some general advice to get you started:

- **Content:** Your field notes should be rich in content—data and analysis. Your content should be driven by the specific question or questions for your field trip. Those questions should lead you to record data such as these: field trip identification (trip title, date, time, specific site, weather conditions, partner or team members); to-scale and labeled map of location; description of site, including key features; measurements and methods used; any other observable data; and notes on on-site presentations.

- **Visuals:** Your field notes should be rich in graphical information. In addition to developing maps, gather information visually by arranging data in tables, sketching key objects and samples, and taking photographs. Fully label each graphic.

- **Practical Practices:** Because you will use your notebook outdoors at various sites in all sorts of weather, take care of it. In case you mislay it, make sure that it is a bright color and has your contact information inside the front cover. To keep your notes from getting ruined by water, routinely cover the pages in clear contact paper; as insurance, regularly photocopy your field notes and put them in a safe place.

Conducting Experiments

Experimenting is the way researchers gather primary information in the scientific disciplines. Many science courses devote prime time to lab work. Why? Because scientific research involves more than getting up to speed about a topic by reading about it—whether in a textbook or in journal articles. For scientists, experimentation is the prime way of getting at primary information.

 FOCUS on Research Essentials: While a full treatment of the topic is beyond the scope of this book, the instruction that follows serves as a brief introduction to the complex process of scientific investigation through experiments. Review this information to help you with lab work in your courses; however, to design your own experiments as part of research projects, consult with the experts—professors in the social and natural sciences.

Understanding Experimentation

An experiment is the process of testing a hypothesis—a prediction about why something does what it does, happens in a particular way, or is structured according to particular laws. Well-tested hypotheses are eventually refined into theories—overarching explanations that make sense of observations. Technically, experiments do not prove hypotheses to be correct; rather, experiment results can either "agree with" or disprove the theory. Thus, scientists conduct experiments for one or more reasons: (1) to make sense of new data and observations, to relate these to existing hypotheses, concepts, and theories; (2) to verify the results of previous experiments; or (3) to challenge current theories or concepts in order to correct and improve our knowledge.

Following the Experimental Method

Many introductory college lab courses focus on individual aspects of the experimental method rather than presenting the whole process. This lab work gives you practice in research methods. These labs may also simplify the scientific method into three steps: (1) state a hypothesis, (2) test the hypothesis with an experiment, (3) accept or reject the hypothesis based on the results. However, actual empirical science—the process of experimenting or doing primary research—is more complex. The overall procedure involves moving from observation to explanation, as shown below:

1. **Observation:** In the course of your investigations into some element of the social or natural worlds, you observe something interesting (often while looking for something else), something (a behavior, process, phenomenon) for which you currently have no explanation or understanding.

2. **Literature Review:** You check to see if any other scientist has made the same observation, has tested it, and has an explanation for it. Typically, this step in the experiment process is called a literature search or literature review, as you research and review the published literature on this topic.

3. **Hypothesis:** Depending on what you learned through your literature review, you pull together your observations into a summary statement and then generalize them into a hypothesis—a working theory explaining the phenomenon observed. Your hypothesis must be something testable, in other words a prediction about what will happen under specific conditions.

4. **Test:** To test your hypothesis, you design the actual experiment. This test must map out highly precise details of materials to be used, equipment needed, data to be collected, variables to be isolated, and controls to be used.

5. **Results Analysis:** Based on the data collected and your analysis of that data, you accept, reject, or modify your hypothesis.

6. **Publication:** When you feel that you understand what is going on with the observed phenomenon you have tested, you write a paper so that other scientists can respond to and build on your work. Most experiment reports include these parts (shown in the IMRAD model on pages 330-338):

   - an abstract (summary)
   - an introduction and theory section (including literature review)
   - an explanation of the experimental method
   - the results and an analysis of these data
   - a discussion of conclusions
   - references

Here are a few additional points about this process. First, the aim is to get a deeper understanding of the phenomenon you originally observed. Second, to get there, you will probably have to go through steps 3-5 several times. Third, if the scientific community agrees with your explanation and believes that it was well tested, your explanation helps build a scientific theory—adding to your specific discipline's *paradigm* (its pattern of thinking and knowing its particular area of investigation).

 FOCUS on Your Major: The Lab Notebook A general rule of science note-taking is replication: your notes should so clearly record what you have done as a researcher that another researcher could repeat your experiment precisely. The lab notebook is the instrument that scientists use to keep this record, collate their data, and reflect about their research. While your science instructors will likely give you specific instructions about keeping a lab notebook in their classes or in your discipline, here is some general advice to get you started:

- **Standard Practice:** Use a bound book, not a three-ring binder or a notebook with removable pages—the notebook must be a true record of all research, even failed experiments. Thus, pages should never be removed.
- **Note-Taking Content:** Identify experiment goals, discussing them as fully as needed; in detail, describe procedures, materials used, equipment, and conditions, providing rationale and sketches as needed; record or insert all data collections.

Practicing Your Research

1. **Explore:** Study a print, television, or online news source that interests you. Examine three or four articles or stories covered by this source for evidence of different forms of primary research. What is your sense of how much this writing relies upon primary research and how well that primary research has been done? Then list examples of primary research that you have done for past projects, from interviews to experiments: What primary-research skills have you learned? What skills do you need to strengthen?

2. **Apply:** Imagine that you are enrolled in an environmental writing course and need to complete a project on some aspect of urban life and the environment. Drawing upon this chapter's instruction in different methods of primary research, sketch out a plan for at least one form of primary research.

3. **Collaborate on a Case Study:** As directed by your instructor, continue work with classmates on your clothing-focused project. Given your group's focus, what forms of primary research would complement your library and free-Web research? Develop and implement a primary-research plan.

4. **Research Your Major:** Develop answers to these questions: (a) What methods of primary research are practiced and valued in my discipline? (b) What skills are needed to do that primary research effectively? You can find answers to these questions by studying scholarly books and articles published in your discipline, and by talking to others in the discipline: students more advanced in your major, graduate students, or professors.

5. **Work on Your Current Project:** Review your assignment (its purpose, audience, and context). Then considering the different forms of primary research outlined in this chapter, develop a plan for including primary research in your project, if appropriate. What primary information would complement your secondary research?

Checklist:

- ☑ I have chosen methods of primary research that fit the project and discipline.
- ☑ I have effectively prepared to do the research, whether conducting interviews, making written requests, conducting surveys, analyzing documents, doing observations, or conducting experiments.
- ☑ I have systematically and carefully gathered primary information.
- ☑ I have followed up in fitting ways to understand the research results.
- ☑ I have conducted the primary research according to ethical standards.

Working with Sources and Taking Notes

© Cengage Learning/Illustrated by Chris Krenzke

Q What note-taking tools and techniques do you use for research? How do you approach sources, and what do you look for?

Gathering good resources for your project is one thing. Working with these sources effectively is another. In fact, how thoughtfully you read your sources and how well you take notes on them can make or break your research project. That's because research writing requires careful management of material—especially with so much information and powerful technology at our fingertips. It's easy to become overwhelmed, to lose track of things, to gather materials without really making sense of them.

Effectively engaging sources takes time, but that time investment pays off by strengthening your thinking and getting you prepared to write. Essentially, strong critical-reading and note-taking practices will help you do the following:

1. **Keep good records.** Developing accurate records, identifying and distinguishing between sources, and separating source material from your own ideas will keep your research in order and help prevent plagiarism. You will work efficiently and flexibly with a wide range of resources—primary and secondary, print and electronic, verbal and visual. And your notes will be rich and complete so that you need not reread sources and can efficiently develop your paper's outline and first draft.

2. **Engage sources critically and creatively.** Good practices help you make sense of sources—their information, ideas, reasoning, and evidence. Specifically, they help you relate sources to your research question or working thesis, and relate different sources to each other. In the process, your thinking grows and deepens as it is affirmed, challenged, and altered.

3. **Evaluate your sources.** By carefully examining sources, you will be able to assess the quality and reliability of what you are reading and thinking.

What's Ahead?

Maintaining a Working Bibliography

A working bibliography keeps track of resources as your research unfolds—sources that you have located, plan to read, and have already read.

Setting Up Your Bibliography

You can establish and maintain a working bibliography by following these guidelines:

1. **Choose an orderly method.** Select an efficient approach for your project:
   - **Paper note cards:** use 3" by 5" cards, and record one source per card.
   - **Paper notebook:** use a small, spiral-bound book to list sources.
   - **Computer software:** record source information electronically, either by capturing citation details from online searches or by recording bibliographic information. Consider using research software such as Refworks (see page 138).

2. **Include complete identifying information for each source.** Consider giving each source a code number or letter: doing so will help you when drafting and documenting your paper. Then include specific details for each kind of source, listed below and shown on the facing page.
   a) **Print books:** author, title and subtitle, publication details (place, publisher, date).
   b) **Print periodical articles:** author, article title, journal name, publication information (volume, number, date), page numbers.
   c) **Online sources:** author (if available), document title, site sponsor, database name, publication or posting date, access date, other publication information.
   d) **Primary or field research:** date conducted; name and/or descriptive title of person interviewed, place observed, survey conducted, document analyzed.

3. **Add locating information.** Because you may need to retrace your research footsteps, include details about your research path:
   a) **Print books:** include the call number, plus any additional direction regarding a specific library, building, location, or collection.
   b) **Print periodical articles:** note where and how you accessed them (stacks, current periodicals, microfilm, database).
   c) **Online sources:** carefully record the complete URL, not just the broader site address; if available, record the document's DOI (digital object identifier). For both the URL and DOI, use copy and paste to ensure accuracy.
   d) **Field research:** include research dates, sites, and contacts, including their telephone numbers, e-mail addresses, and other appropriate information.

4. **Add a note about the source.** Depending on whether you have or have not already read the source, note its potential or actual usefulness, its content and focus, its perspective and reliability. Consider listing its main topics or indicating how the source fits into your larger research plan or what it offers (e.g., perspective on issues, types of evidence, primary or secondary relationship to topic, background).

Sample Working Bibliography Entries

A. Print Book	Cozolino, L. J. 2006. *The neuroscience of human relationships: Attachment and the developing social brain*. New York: Norton. LOC: QP360.C69 2006 This in-depth study looks at the brain science of attachment—how attachment happens, what interferes with it.
B. Print Periodical Article	Zeanah, C. H. & Smyke, A. T. (2008). Attachment disorders in family and social context. *Infant Mental Health Journal, 29*(3), 219-233. Current periodicals Article reviews current research on attachment disorder and explores what the research means for children and families.
C. Online Source	Reactive attachment disorder. (2008). In *Facts for Families*. Retrieved November 10, 2010, from the American Academy of Child & Adolescent Psychiatry. http://www.aacap.org Offers definition of a.d., advice to parents, and useful links.
D. Primary or Field Source	Zeanah, C. H. E-mail interview. 20 November 2010. czeanah@tulane.edu As follow-up to reading Zeanah & Smyke article, contacted Dr. Zeanah and received additional information on common family dynamics for adoption situation.

FOCUS on Research Essentials: An orderly working bibliography helps you get your project off to a good start and keep it on track. To keep on top of your bibliography, follow these tips:

1. Record bibliographic details for each source in the format of the documentation system that you will be using in your paper. Note that some research software allows you to import or record bibliographic information, save it, and then format your bibliography according to the desired system. (See page 138.)

2. If using paper note cards or computer software, keep your working bibliography in alphabetical order: use the authors' last names or, if authorship isn't indicated, the titles of sources. Doing so now will save time later.

3. As you conduct your research and work with sources, keep your working bibliography up to date. Your working bibliography should evolve to reflect your most current assessment of those sources. As you track down new resources, add them to your bibliography. When you discover that a source will not be useful for your project, move that citation to a list of "discarded sources" or a "not used" file.

Developing an Annotated Bibliography

For some projects, your instructor may require an annotated bibliography on your topic. Each entry in your annotated bibliography includes two parts: identifying details for the source plus a statement about the source. The statement, or annotation, which can range from one sentence to a paragraph, can include a variety of information: a summary of the source's content, an assessment of its value for your project, a review of its perspective, and an evaluation of its quality. Check the sample annotated bibliography entry below, excerpted from a student's project on short-story writer Alice Munro. A full annotated bibliography is available at www.theresearchwriter.com.

> Howells, Coral Ann. *Alice Munro.* Contemporary World Writers. Manchester and New York: Manchester UP, 1998. Print. This scholarly study offers a good introduction to Munro's work, analyzing her fiction book by book up to *Open Secrets.* Because of its publication date, Howells' study does not directly discuss *Runaway,* the volume of short stories that I am examining.

Focus on Multimedia: Using Bibliographic Software

In recent years, bibliographic software—both commercial and open source—has emerged to help researchers build bibliographies. Such programs typically allow you to do the following tasks:

- Import automatically or copy-and-paste source information from online databases and catalogs, from text files, and from similar electronic sources.
- Manually enter bibliographic details for sources.
- Save bibliographic entries in files and folders, as well as sorting, viewing, editing, and searching sources.
- Format sources according to the desired documentation system (MLA, APA, Chicago, CSE, etc.).

One popular software is RefWorks, a program that your school may make available for your research project. The screen below shows you a bibliographic entry whose details have been exported from a research database.

Developing a Note-Taking System

Good note taking is systematic but flexible. Being systematic ensures good record-keeping, which is crucial for documenting sources and creating a research trail. Being flexible within your system keeps you open to discoveries and makes your research intuitive rather than robotic. As explained more fully below and on the following pages, such flexible, systematic note taking creates a rich resource of ideas and information to draw upon when drafting your paper.

Note-Taking Strategies

What are you trying to do when you take notes on sources? What you are NOT doing is (a) collecting quotations to plunk in your paper, (b) piling isolated grains of data into a growing stack of disconnected facts, or (c) intensively reading and taking notes on every source you find. Instead, use these strategies:

1. **Be selective.** Guided by your research questions and working thesis, focus on sources that are central to your project. From these sources, record information clearly related to your limited topic, but also note what surprises or puzzles you. Be moderate and selective, avoiding notes that are either too thin or too extensive.

2. **Read different sources for different reasons.** As you read a source, quickly identify what it offers for your topic—background information, context, analysis of key issues, a particular position—and then take notes accordingly.

3. **Read for leads.** As you work with sources, note other sources mentioned, referenced, or linked. Do particular sources get mentioned frequently—either positively or negatively? Does a particular writer seem to be an authority? Keep track of promising resources that can extend and deepen your research.

4. **Develop a shorthand of keywords.** As you read into your topic, certain concepts will emerge as important. List those concepts, and then use them to label and organize your research notes. This organizational thinking will help you later on when outlining and drafting your paper.

5. **Be smart with your writing technologies.** Obviously, working electronically to take notes offers great flexibility in terms of creating and working with a record of ideas and information; however, in some circumstances, you may need to or even prefer to take handwritten notes (e.g., a lab or field notebook, annotating print versions of resources). Whatever technologies you choose, use them to create an efficient, orderly, and accurate record of ideas and information that you can easily access and understand the next day or the next month.

6. **Aim for a standard of verifiability.** Your note taking should create a research record that functions as backup for your research writing, as verification of that work. Technically, for all your projects, that research record should be accessible to your readers and later researchers, but for some projects and in some disciplines, you may have to submit your notes and raw data or append them to your research writing.

7. **Make space for your own thoughts.** While much of your note taking will involve summarizing, paraphrasing, and quoting from sources, build a lot of reflective source "dialogue" into your notes. Explore what you are discovering, make connections between different sources and between sources and your own experience, identify different perspectives on an issue, and reflect on your evolving conclusions. Whether you integrate your thoughts into source notes or keep them separate, always mark your own thoughts with a code or symbol, whether your initials, "my response," "my idea," or something else you'll remember.

Note-Taking Systems

Using an article on Jane Austen in film as an example, four note-taking systems are described and modeled on the following pages.

The Computer Notebook or Research Log. This method involves note taking on computer or on sheets of paper. Here's how it works:

1. Establish a central location for your notes—a notebook, file folder, binder, or electronic folder.

2. Take notes one source at a time, making sure to identify the source fully. Number your note pages.

3. Using your initials or some other symbol, distinguish your own thoughts from source material.

4. Use codes in your notes to identify what information in the notes relates to which topic in your outline. Then under each topic in the outline, write the page number in your notes where that information is recorded. With an electronic notebook or log, you may be able to rearrange your notes into an outline by using copy-and-paste—but don't lose source information in the process!

Upside: Taking notes feels natural without being overly systematic.
Downside: Outlining and drafting may require time-consuming paper shuffling.

Grandi, Roberta. "The Passion Translated: Literary and Cinematic Rhetoric in *Pride and Prejudice* (2005)." *Literature Film Quarterly* 36(1): 45-51.

- Overall, the article looks at the sexual references in Austen's novel and how the 2005 film adaptation of P&P translates those verbal references to visual references.

- 45: first two paragraphs offer overview of other resources that look at rhetorical devices related to the presentation of sexuality – check Chandler reference especially.

- 46: Grandi's thesis: "The use of tropes, such as synecdoche and metonymy, and of the stylistic technique of focalization, finds its effective counterpart in the filmic grammar that includes close-ups, insert shots, subjective shots, eyeline matches, and reaction shots." – very helpful list of comparative fiction and film techniques: think about specific passages and scenes to analyze in P&P.

The Double-Entry Notebook. The double-entry notebook involves parallel note taking—notes from sources beside your own brainstorming, reaction, and reflection. Using a double-entry notebook or the columns feature of your word-processing program, do the following:

1. Divide notebook pages in half vertically.

2. In the left column, record bibliographic information and take notes on sources.

3. In the right column, write your responses. You can generate these responses as you take notes on the source. Or you can complete your note-taking on the source, and then go back to work on your reflection. Think about what the source is saying, why the point is important, whether you agree with it, and how the point relates to other ideas and other sources. Consider questions like these:

   ■ How does this source relate to your research question and/or working thesis?
   ■ How do specific ideas, explanations, and pieces of evidence strike you?
   ■ Does the source affirm, challenge, or build your thinking? How?
   ■ How does the source connect with your own experiences, values, and beliefs?
   ■ How might this source material might be useful in your paper?

Upside: This method creates accurate source records while encouraging thoughtful responses; also, it can be done on computer.

Downside: Organizing material for drafting may be a challenge.

Grandi, Roberta. "The Passion Translated: Literary and Cinematic Rhetoric in *Pride and Prejudice* (2005)." *Literature Film Quarterly* 36(1): 45-51.

• 46: technique of synecdoche in Austen: one part of the body stands for the whole – eyes, locks of hair, hands, feet: in P&P, it begins with Elizabeth's eyes for Darcy.	*Do the parts of the body represent particular attractions? On the surface this sounds a bit clinical, a bit biology 101 – or is it more about associations for readers and viewers, about imagining and seeing the whole person through just one small image?*
• 46: after tracing the "eyes" references in the novel, Grandi concludes "When love and passion need no longer be hidden, the 'indirection' can finally be redressed and the truth can be confessed without fear or repression: the eyes can finally be again a part of a whole body." – argument that the synecdoche is a strategy for indicating growing attachment and feeling fulfilled in the end.	*The eyes are the window to the soul—does this popular saying help explain the focus on the eyes? Is the focus on the eyes as much spiritual as it is romantic or sexual?*
• 46-47: film's equivalent of synecdoche for eyes = the close-up of the heroine – in PP film, frequent shots of Keira Knightley's eyes as "the centre of the public's attention" (47).	*Hmmm …yes, this is true about Elizabeth in the film, but is it also true of Darcy – aren't his eyes also a repeated focus in close-ups?? If not, why not?*

Copy (or Save) and Annotate. The copy-and-annotate method involves working with photocopies, print versions, or digital texts of sources. Here's how to do it:

1. Selectively photocopy, print, and/or save important sources. Copy carefully, making sure that you have full pages, including page numbers.

2. As needed, add identifying information on the copy—author, publication details, and date. Each page should be easy to identify and trace. When working with books, keep copies of the title and copyright pages with your notes.

3. As you read, mark up the copy and highlight key statements. In the margins or digital file, record your ideas:
   - Ask questions. Insert a "?" in the margin, or write out the question.
   - Make connections. Draw arrows or make notes like "see page 36."
   - Add asides. Record what you think and feel while reading.
   - Define terms. Note important words that you need to understand.
   - Create a marginal index. Write key words to identify themes and parts.

Upside: Copying, printing, and/or saving helps you record sources accurately; annotating encourages careful reading and thinking.

Downside: Organizing material for drafting is inconvenient; when done poorly, annotating and highlighting involve skimming, not critical thinking.

---

helpful examples

At Rosings Park:

His eyes had been soon and repeatedly turned toward them with a look of curiosity. (XXXI, 143)

And at Pemberly:

It was not often that she could turn her eyes on Mr. Darcy himself; but whenever she did catch a glimpse, she saw an expression of general complaisance. (XLIV, 214)

Control: camera eye and director's choices

The focalization is visually translated by the cinema through subjective (point-of-view) shots: the camera eye, in fact, allows the film director to have total control over point of view and over what the spectator can see (contrary to what happens in the theatre, where the audience is able to choose where to focus attention). The subjective shots make spectators see through the characters' eyes or, in the case of mental point-of-view shots, through their minds. The film does not employ this technique very often but two episodes are worth noticing. A classic subjective shot is performed with

Focalization examples from P & P

1 a pan during an interlocutory scene: in order to communicate the cycle of the seasons and the passing of time between the announcement of Charlotte's marriage with Mr. Collins and Elizabeth's visit at their parsonage, the scene depicts Elizabeth sitting on a swing in her garden and, as she turns, the camera

2 pan shows us through her eyes the changing landscape and

FOCUS on Research Essentials: If you're not careful, too much highlighting or underlining becomes a means of evading rather than engaging the text. Excessive highlighting might be your brain saying "I'll learn this later." Moreover, excessive highlighting can make the text difficult to work with when you are drafting your paper.

Paper or Electronic Note Cards. Using paper note cards is the traditional method of note taking; however, note-taking software is now available with most word-processing programs and special programs like TakeNote, EndNote Plus, and Bookends Pro. Here's how a note-card system works:

1. Establish one set of cards (3 x 5 inches, if paper) for your working bibliography (page 136).

2. On a second set of cards (4 x 6 inches, if paper), take notes on sources:
   - Record one point from one source per card.
   - Clarify the source: list the author's last name, a shortened title, or a code from the matching bibliography card. Include a page number.
   - Provide a topic or heading: called a slug, the topic helps you categorize and order information.
   - Label the note as a summary, paraphrase, or quotation of the original.
   - Distinguish between the source's information and your own thoughts, perhaps by using your initials or recording your ideas on separate cards.

Upside: Note cards are highly systematic, helping you categorize material and organize it for an outline and first draft.

Downside: The method can be initially tedious and time-consuming.

Focus on Multimedia: Using Note-Taking Software

As shown in the example above, the traditional note-card method once practiced extensively by scholars and students with paper note cards can now be practiced electronically with software such as TakeNote and OneNote. Such programs allow you to record notes, save them, organize them, and search them. If you wish to take notes in a highly systematic way—which is advisable for many big projects—consider whether such software would help you get and stay organized.

Engaging Your Sources through Critical Reading

Rich research notes grow out of engaged reading. As you read, your curiosity directs you into a dialogue with your sources, a mental conversation with what they are saying. Such engaged reading is the opposite of passive reading, which makes these mistakes:

- treating all sources the same—worthy of the same attention.
- skimming each resource—no deep, attentive reading.
- swallowing whole what's in the material—no processing, questioning, critiquing.
- ignoring the information context—extracting isolated bits of information.
- selecting only that evidence supporting one's position—ignoring opposition.

By contrast, full engagement involves practices like those that follow.

Testing Each Source for Value

As you began working with resources, gauge how each might fit within your project. Revisit your project's goals, your intended audience, and the assignment's context. Then ask questions like these, which will help you determine how to approach each source:

- *How closely related to my topic is this source?* Is the connection direct? Is the source primary or secondary? If the source is indirectly related to my topic, might it still prove useful in giving me ideas or a bigger picture?
- *Is this source too basic, overly complex, or just right?* Given the level of my project, is this resource respectable? Is the level of language and argument a manageable stretch of my understanding, or well beyond my current comprehension?
- *What could this source add to my overall balance of sources?* Does it supply useful background—historical or cultural context, useful definitions, an overview of key issues? Does it point me toward interesting, pertinent research questions? Does it provide crucial evidence? Does it offer a helpful window into opposing interpretations or arguments? (Note: don't reject a source simply because it disagrees with your perspective. Good research engages rather than ignores opposition.)

Example: If you were writing on film adaptations of Jane Austen's fiction and if your goal were to understand the filmic techniques used to convey male-female relationships, a fifteen-page article in *Persuasions*, a scholarly Jane Austen journal, would likely be more valuable than a newspaper film review or an Austen fan's blog.

FOCUS on Research Ethics: To a degree, active research reading means engaging the text on its own terms. Why approach such a dialogue ethically, that is, with commitment and concern? To start with, what you are seeking to discover is truth, truth that may shape your values, beliefs, choices, actions, and relationships. In addition, when your reading impacts your writing, two powers stand out: first, your potential power to affect others with what you've read by shaping their perceptions, values, and actions; and second, the power to build your credibility by treating the text fairly and thoughtfully or to destroy your credibility by distorting or abusing the text.

Reading Key Sources Systematically and Critically

Once you have determined that a source is valuable for your project, you need to engage that source both systematically and critically in order to fully understand it, learn from it, and question it. With key sources, follow these steps:

1. **Survey the Source.** Start by looking for main ideas. Read introductory and concluding paragraphs, and the topic sentences of intermediary paragraphs. Pay special attention to headings, chapter titles, illustrations, and boldfaced type. Also check out any graphics—charts, maps, diagrams, illustrations—that visually reinforce key points. In addition, ask questions of the text, questions that you hope to answer as you read. Here are some ways to generate questions:

   - Turn any headings and subheadings into questions. For example, if the subhead says, "Methods," ask, "What methods did the researcher use?"
   - Ask why the author makes key points and how these points will be elaborated, developed, and supported. Ask what evidence would be convincing.

   Benefits: Surveying gives you the big picture, while also stabilizing and directing your thoughts. In addition, asking questions will keep you actively thinking about what is coming up and will help you to maintain an appropriate critical distance.

2. **Read to Understand the Source.** As you work through the source, focus on understanding what the source is saying, using questions like these:

   - What does this mean? What is clear, and what is confusing?
   - What is the larger context or framework for the information provided?
   - How do the ideas relate to each other and to what I know?
   - What ground have I covered, and what's coming next?

   Keep track of your answers and other key ideas by annotating the text, summarizing passages, paraphrasing key points, and recording quotations. Read difficult parts slowly; re-read them if necessary and look up unfamiliar words.

   Benefits: Understanding what a source is saying builds your knowledge of the topic and lays the groundwork for engaging the source critically.

Mapping: You may understand a text best by graphically mapping out its important parts. One way to do so is by "clustering." Start by naming the main topic in a circle at the center of the page. Then branch out using lines and "balloons," each balloon containing a word or phrase for one major subtopic in the source. Branch out in further layers of balloons to show subordinated points. For example, the cluster below maps out an article entitled "Is Google Making Us Stupid?"

Impact of Internet Use on Thinking

Online reading habits, info decoding, not deep reading

Technology, reading, and writing: metaphors of self; brain changes

Taylor's algorithm of efficiency, Google, artificial intelligence, and the human mind

Outlining: Another method of understanding a source is an outline, which shows all the major parts, points, and sub-points in a text. An outline uses parallel structure to show coordinated points and indented structure to show subordinate points. Some outlines use only phrases; in full outlines, each item is a complete sentence. Here is a sample outline for the article "Is Google Making Us Stupid."

Introduction: our minds are changing because of our online habits
1. The Net is affecting our abilities to concentrate and contemplate.
    - Evidence from bloggers and from research into online reading habits
    - Perspective of developmental psychology: deep reading replaced by info decoding
2. The importance of technologies to our experiences of reading and writing
    - Example of Nietzsche using typewriter when eyesight deteriorated
    - The plasticity of adult brain: taking on the qualities of technologies (e.g., clock)
    - Adaptability to technologies reflected in metaphors people use to describe the self
    - The Internet's power to absorb and re-create other media in a "crazy quilt": scattering viewer's attention and diffusing concentration
3. Frederick Winslow Taylor's algorithm of efficiency
    - His system applied to human production in manufacturing
    - His system now being applied to the human mind in relation to the computer
    - Google's ambition to systematize everything
    - Google's unsettling ambition to supplement human brain with artificial intelligence
Conclusion: while it is common to resist and question technological change, the resistance in this case is warranted because deep reading and contemplative thought are at stake.

3. **Read the Source Critically.** As you gain understanding of the source, enter into an imaginary dialogue with it. Express agreement, lodge complaints, ask for proof—and imagine the writer's response or look for it in the text. Making sure to take notes on your thinking, engage the source critically through questions like these:

   - What is the purpose and audience? Was the piece written to inform or persuade? Is it aimed at the general public, specialists, supporters, or opponents?

   - How do you react to the material? What does it make you think, feel, or believe? How does the source affirm or challenge your ideas?

   - What is the nature of the source's argument? What is the essential thesis, the main points in support of that thesis, the type of reasoning used, and the foundational evidence provided? Do you find the thinking compelling? Why or why not? Are there gaps or errors in the evidence and reasoning?

   - How does this source relate to or compare with other sources you have read?

   Benefits: Engaging critically with the text in this way will deepen your thinking about your topic and generate key ideas for your writing.

4. **Review the Source and Your Notes.** As soon as you finish reading and taking notes, double-check the questions that you posed in the "survey" stage. Can you answer them? Study your notes from the source, and assess what this source contributed to your project.
   Benefits: Reviewing helps you process information, move it to your long-term memory, and assess how the information relates to other sources' assertions and your own evolving conclusions.

Evaluating Your Sources

An essential part of working with your sources, reading critically, and taking notes is evaluating each source's quality and reliability, its strengths and weaknesses. By doing so, you learn the limits of the information and ideas you are working with; these judgments will prove crucial when you develop your paper. Assess each source using the criteria that follow.

A Rating Scale for Source Reliability and Depth

You should judge each source on its own merit. Generally, however, types of sources can be rated for reliability and depth, as shown in the table below, based on their authorship, length, topic treatment, documentation, publication method, review process, distance from primary sources, allegiances, stability, and so on. Use the table to

1. target sources that fit your project's goals,

2. assess the approximate quality of the sources you're gathering, and

3. build a strong bibliography that readers will respect.

Deep, Reliable, Credible Sources	**Scholarly Books and Articles:** largely based on careful research; written by experts for experts; address topics in depth; involve peer review and careful editing; offer stable discussion of topic. Examples: *The Neuroscience of Human Relationships,* published by Norton; "The Passion Translated: Literary and Cinematic Rhetoric in *Pride and Prejudice* (2005)" in *Literature Film Quarterly.*
	Trade Books and Journal Articles: largely based on careful research; written by experts for an educated general audience. Sample periodicals: *Atlantic Monthly, Scientific American, Nature.*
	Government Resources: Books, reports, Web pages, guides, statistics developed by experts at government agencies; provided as service to citizens; relatively objective. Example: *Statistical Abstract of the United States*
	Reviewed, Official Online Documents: Internet resources posted by legitimate institutions— colleges and universities, research institutes, service organizations; although offering a particular perspective, sources tend to be balanced.
	Reference Works and Textbooks: provide general and specialized information; carefully researched, reviewed, and edited; lack depth for focused research (e.g., general encyclopedia entry).
	News and Topical Stories from Quality Sources: provide current affairs coverage (print and online), introduction-level articles of interest to general public; may lack depth and length. Sample sources: *The Washington Post, The New York Times; Time, Psychology Today;* NPR's *All Things Considered.*
	Popular Magazine Stories: short, introductory articles often distant from primary sources and without documentation; heavy advertising. Sample Sources: *Glamour, Seventeen, Reader's Digest.*
	Business and Nonprofit Publications: pamphlets, reports, news releases, brochures, manuals; range from informative to sales focused.
	List Server Discussions, Usenet Postings, Blog Articles, Talk Radio Discussions: highly open, fluid, undocumented, untested exchanges and publications; unstable resource.
Shallow, Unreliable, Not Credible Sources	**Unregulated Web Material:** personal sites, joke sites, chat rooms, special interest sites, advertising and junk e-mail (spam); no review process, little accountability, bias present.
	Tabloid Articles (print and Web): contain exaggerated and untrue stories written to titillate and exploit. Sample Source: *The National Enquirer.*

Criteria for Assessing Sources

Evaluating a particular source involves examining it for clues about its quality and its perspective, and reading the source with an eye to the strength of its content, analysis, and argument. The criteria that follow apply to both print and online sources; note, however, the additional tests offered for Web sources because of the particular difficulty of assessing their quality. For more on evaluating free-Web sources, see pages 90–92.

_____ **Credible Author:** An expert is an authority—someone who has mastered a subject area. Is the author an expert *on this topic* (as opposed to an unrelated topic)? What are his or her credentials, and can you confirm these? What are the author's professional affiliations or connections? Do these connections strengthen or weaken his or her authority? For example, an automotive engineer would be an expert on hybrid-vehicle technology, whereas a celebrity in a commercial would not.

Web test: Is an author indicated? If so, are the author's credentials noted and contact information offered (e.g., an e-mail address)?

_____ **Reliable Publication:** Has the source been published by a scholarly press, a peer-reviewed professional journal, a quality trade-book publisher, or a trusted news source? Did you find this resource through a reliable search tool (e.g., library catalog or database)?

Web test: What individual or group posted this page? Is the site rated by a subject directory or library organization? How stable is the site—has it been around for awhile and does material remain available, or it the site "fly-by-night"? Check the site's home page, and read "About Us" pages and mission statements, looking for evidence of the organization's perspective, history, and trustworthiness.

_____ **Unbiased Discussion:** While all sources come from a specific perspective and represent specific *commitments,* a *biased* source may be pushing an agenda in an unfair, unbalanced, incomplete manner. Watch for bias toward a certain region, country, political party, industry, gender, race, ethnic group, or religion. Be alert to connections between authors, financial backers, and the points of view shared. For example, if an author has functioned as a consultant to or lobbyist for a particular industry or group (oil, animal rights), his or her allegiances may lead to a biased presentation of an issue.

Web test: Is the online document one-sided? Is the site nonprofit (.org), government (.gov), commercial (.com), educational (.edu), business (.biz), informational (.info), network-related (.net), or military (.mil)? Is the site U.S. or international? In other words, is this organization pushing a cause, product, service, or belief? How do advertising or special interests affect the site? You might suspect, for example, the scientific claims of a site sponsored by a pro-smoking organization.

_____ **Current Information:** How timely is the source's information in relation to your topic? A recent date is not always the measure of currency. While a five-year-old book on computers may be outdated, a 40-year-old book on Abraham Lincoln could still be relevant. Given your needs, is the source up to date?

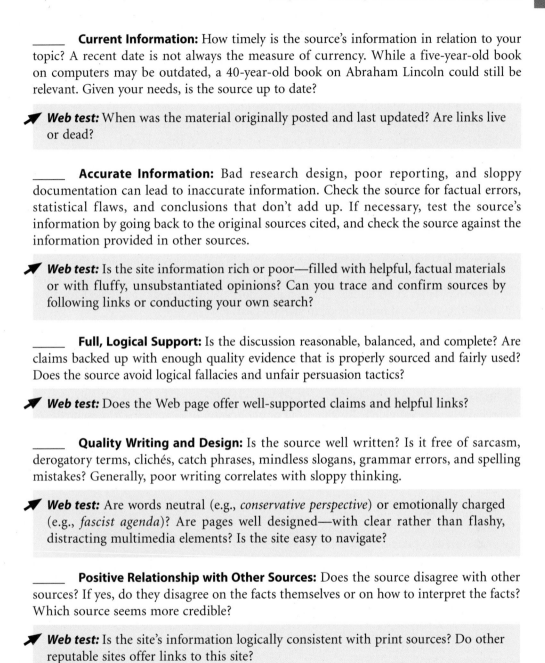 **Web test:** When was the material originally posted and last updated? Are links live or dead?

_____ **Accurate Information:** Bad research design, poor reporting, and sloppy documentation can lead to inaccurate information. Check the source for factual errors, statistical flaws, and conclusions that don't add up. If necessary, test the source's information by going back to the original sources cited, and check the source against the information provided in other sources.

Web test: Is the site information rich or poor—filled with helpful, factual materials or with fluffy, unsubstantiated opinions? Can you trace and confirm sources by following links or conducting your own search?

_____ **Full, Logical Support:** Is the discussion reasonable, balanced, and complete? Are claims backed up with enough quality evidence that is properly sourced and fairly used? Does the source avoid logical fallacies and unfair persuasion tactics?

Web test: Does the Web page offer well-supported claims and helpful links?

_____ **Quality Writing and Design:** Is the source well written? Is it free of sarcasm, derogatory terms, clichés, catch phrases, mindless slogans, grammar errors, and spelling mistakes? Generally, poor writing correlates with sloppy thinking.

Web test: Are words neutral (e.g., _conservative perspective_) or emotionally charged (e.g., _fascist agenda_)? Are pages well designed—with clear rather than flashy, distracting multimedia elements? Is the site easy to navigate?

_____ **Positive Relationship with Other Sources:** Does the source disagree with other sources? If yes, do they disagree on the facts themselves or on how to interpret the facts? Which source seems more credible?

Web test: Is the site's information logically consistent with print sources? Do other reputable sites offer links to this site?

 FOCUS on Research Essentials: The quality of a source doesn't necessarily indicate its usefulness for your project. For example, a source containing errors, faulty logic, or unsubstantiated opinion might serve as a form of opposition in your paper—something you write against.

Focus on Multimedia: Interpreting and Evaluating Visuals

Whether you find them in scholarly articles or at Web sites, graphics—tables, line graphs, flow charts, photographs, maps, and so on—appear in a whole range of resources. Such graphics are typically packed with information, and they powerfully convey ideas. For this reason, you should engage and evaluate visual resources as thoroughly as verbal materials. Study graphics for what they "say" by focusing on these issues:

- **Purpose:** What are the visual's goals? Does it aim to be informative, illustrative, revelatory, instructive, persuasive, entertaining—or some combination of these?
- **Medium:** What type of visual is this—table, graph (line, bar, pie), flow chart, map, line drawing, photograph? What kinds of information does this type of visual effectively share? What are the limits of this medium? Does the writer's use of the visual exceed these limits?
- **Message:** What main point or theme does the visual convey? What does the graphic include and exclude in terms of information? Does the visual create a valid or manipulative central idea? For example, does the image seek to bypass logic by appealing to sexual impulses or to stereotypes?
- **Context:** How does the visual relate to the written text? Does it support the text or contradict it? How effectively is the visual discussed by the writer?
- **Quality:** Is the visual well designed and easy to understand—or cluttered and distorted?
- **Reliability:** Who developed this visual? Where did it come from? Is it current? Is a reliable source provided? In what kind of publication or resource is it presented?

Sample Visual and Analysis

Mary Evans/Working Title Films/Ronald Grant/Everett Collection

This image is of one of several within the article "The Passion Translated: Literary and Cinematic Rhetoric in *Pride and Prejudice* (2005)." Taken from the sculpture-gallery scene in the film, the image captures Elizabeth Bennett face to face with Raffaele Monti's *Veiled Vestal Virgin*. In the article, Roberta Grandi analyzes the scene in terms of the visual identification created between the character and the figure in the statue. The image serves an illustrative and instructive purpose, as it "freezes" the moving images of the actual film. Isolated from the larger scene, the image also serves a persuasive purpose in support of the author's argument about the sexual visual language of the film. As you study the image in relation to the article, you might explore alternative interpretations of the image: is the author right that this scene is filled with "unmistakable erotic suggestions"?

Summarizing, Paraphrasing, and Quoting Source Material

As you work with sources, you must decide what to put in your notes and how to record it—as a summary, paraphrase, or quotation. Use these guidelines:

- How relevant is the passage to your research question or working thesis?
- How strong and important is the information offered?
- How unique or memorable is the thinking or phrasing?

The more relevant, the stronger, the more memorable the material—the more likely you should note it.

The passage below comes from an article on GM's development of fuel-cell technology. Review the passage; study how the researcher summarizes, paraphrases, and quotes from the source; and then practice these same strategies as you take notes on sources. Such effective note taking will help you when you integrate source material into your draft (see pages 190–194).

From Burns, L.D., McCormick, J.B., and Borroni-Bird, C.E. "Vehicle of Change." *Scientific American* **287:4 (October 2002): 10 pp.**

When Karl Benz rolled his Patent Motorcar out of the barn in 1886, he literally set the wheels of change in motion. The advent of the automobile led to dramatic alterations in people's way of life as well as the global economy—transformations that no one expected at the time. The ever increasing availability of economical personal transportation remade the world into a more accessible place while spawning a complex industrial infrastructure that shaped modern society.

Now another revolution could be sparked by automotive technology: one fueled by hydrogen rather than petroleum. Fuel cells—which cleave hydrogen atoms into protons and electrons that drive electric motors while emitting nothing worse than water vapor—could make the automobile much more environmentally friendly. Not only could cars become cleaner, they could also become safer, more comfortable, more personalized—and even perhaps less expensive. Further, these fuel-cell vehicles could be instrumental in motivating a shift toward a "greener" energy economy based on hydrogen. As that occurs, energy use and production could change significantly. Thus, hydrogen fuel-cell cars and trucks could help ensure a future in which personal mobility—the freedom to travel independently—could be sustained indefinitely, without compromising the environment or depleting the earth's natural resources.

A confluence of factors makes the big change seem increasingly likely. For one, the petroleum-fueled internal-combustion engine (ICE), as highly refined, reliable and economical as it is, is finally reaching its limits. Despite steady improvements, today's ICE vehicles are only 20 to 25 percent efficient in converting the energy content of fuels into drive-wheel power. And although the U.S. auto industry has cut exhaust emissions substantially since the unregulated 1960s—hydrocarbons dropped by 99 percent, carbon monoxide by 96 percent and nitrogen oxides by 95 percent—the continued production of carbon dioxide causes concern because of its potential to change the planet's climate.

Summarizing Useful Passages

Summarizing condenses a passage's main points into a unit of thought expressed in your own words. Summarize when the source provides relevant ideas and information on your topic. Follow these steps:

1. Re-read the passage, jotting down a few key words.

2. State the main point in your own words. Add key supporting points, leaving out examples, details, and long explanations. Be objective.

3. Check your summary against the original, making sure that you use quotation marks around any exact phrases you borrow.

Sample Summary: While the introduction of the car in the late-nineteenth century has led to dramatic changes in society and world economics, another dramatic change is now taking place in the shift from gas engines to hydrogen technologies. Fuel cells may make the car "greener," and perhaps even more safe, comfortable, unique, and cheap. These automotive changes will affect the energy industry by making it more environmentally friendly; as a result, people will continue to enjoy mobility while transportation moves to renewable energy. One factor leading to this technological shift is that the internal-combustion engine has reached the limits of its efficiency, potential, and development—while remaining problematic with respect to emissions, climate change, and health.

 FOCUS on Your Major: In some disciplines, *writing* summaries (also called *abstracts*) is routine. In addition, source summarizing is required within literature reviews. For more, see pages 238 and 360.

Paraphrasing Key Passages

Paraphrasing puts a whole passage *in your own words*. Paraphrase passages that present important points, explanations, or arguments but that don't contain memorable or straightforward wording. Follow these steps:

1. Quickly review the passage to get a sense of the whole.

2. Go through the passage carefully, sentence by sentence. State the ideas in your own words, defining words as needed, and edit for clarity, but don't change the meaning. If you borrow phrases directly, put them in quotation marks.

3. Check your paraphrase against the original for accurate tone and meaning.

Sample Paraphrase of the Second Paragraph in the Passage: Automobile technology may lead to another radical economic and social change through the shift from gasoline to hydrogen fuel. By breaking hydrogen into protons and electrons so that the electrons run an electric motor with only the by-product of water vapor, fuel cells could make the car a "green" machine. But this technology could also increase the automobile's safety, comfort, personal tailoring, and affordability. Moreover, this shift to fuel-cell engines in automobiles could lead to drastic, environmentally friendly changes in the broader energy industry, one that will be now tied to hydrogen rather than fossil fuels. The result from this shift will be radical changes in the way we use and produce energy. In other words, the shift to hydrogen-powered vehicles could promise to maintain our society's valued mobility, while the clean technology would preserve the environment and its natural resources.

Quoting Crucial Phrases, Sentences, and Passages

Quoting records statements or phrases in the original source word-for-word. As you work with a source, be careful not to over-quote or to quote large chunks without reason. Instead, quote key statements that (a) are especially well phrased, (b) express a convincing authority, (c) speak directly to your research question, or (d) help show different views on your topic. *Note:* As an exception to this caution, remember that some projects involve close analysis of primary texts, meaning that your notes may involve a great deal of quotation. To quote effectively, follow these guidelines:

1. Note the quotation's context—how it fits in the author's discussion.

2. Copy the passage word for word, checking its accuracy. To indicate that it is a quotation, enclose the passage within distinguishing marks, whether quotation marks, a letter, or a symbol. Or you might highlight the quotation or put it in a different color. Use this practice consistently throughout your notes.

3. As long as you do not contort the meaning of the original, you can make changes to the quotation. Signal changes in these ways:

   ■ If you omit words, use a bracketed ellipsis [. . .]. (See page 192.)

   ■ If you change any word for grammatical reasons or to clarify a term, put changes within brackets. (See page 192.)

   ■ If the quotation contains an error (e.g., a typo), keep the mistake but place "[sic]" after it in the original.

Sample Quotations:

"[H]ydrogen fuel-cell cars and trucks could help ensure a future in which personal mobility [. . .] could be sustained indefinitely, without compromising the environment or depleting the earth's natural resources."

> *Note:* This sentence captures a key claim about the benefits of fuel-cell technology.

"[T]he petroleum-fueled internal-combustion engine (ICE), as highly refined, reliable and economical as it is, is finally reaching its limits."

> *Note:* This quotation offers a well-phrased statement about the essential problem.

FOCUS on Research Essentials: Whether you are summarizing, paraphrasing, or quoting, keep your notes in order by doing the following:

1. Whenever possible, include a page number, paragraph number, or other locating detail. Such identification at this stage is crucial to avoiding plagiarism down the road (see pages 155–164).

2. Be true to the source by respecting the context and spirit of the original. If you were to claim that the sample passage is arguing that the internal-combustion engine was an enormous engineering and environmental mistake, you would be twisting the passage to serve your own writing agenda.

Practicing Your Research

1. **Explore:** Reflect on the typical note-taking practices and methods that you have used for research projects in the past. How have you worked with, kept track of, taken notes on, and evaluated sources? Compare and contrast your practices with the guidelines outlined in this chapter: what do you plan to change? In addition, study the bibliography for one of your recent research projects. Evaluate the range and quality of the sources that you used: what would you do differently?

2. **Apply:** (a) Using the rating scale on page 000, find three resources on the same topic: one from a resource near the top of the scale, one from the middle, and one near the bottom. Compare and contrast the types of information found in each resource, as well as the depth and reliability. (b) Using your research skills, track down the following article: "When Adoption Goes Wrong," by Pat Wingert and Anna Nemtsova. Assuming that you are researching attachment disorder's impact on adoptive families, take notes on the article using this chapter's instruction on note-taking systems, critical reading, and source evaluation.

3. **Collaborate on a Case Study:** As directed by your instructor, continue work with classmates on your clothing-focused project. Together, develop a shared working bibliography and adopt a note-taking system that allows for individual contributions to group exchanges. Select key sources and evaluate their quality.

4. **Research Your Major:** By talking with professors and upper-level students in your major, explore your discipline's methods of working with sources.

5. **Work on Your Current Project:** Advance your work by doing the following:

   - Establish and keep current a working bibliography.
   - Establish a note-taking system, one of the four introduced in this chapter or a hybrid system that helps you work well with your resources.
   - Read your sources selectively but carefully, taking notes that will lead to a first draft of your paper. Keep your main research question or working thesis in focus, periodically taking stock of how your thinking is developing.

Checklist:

- ☑ I have established and am maintaining an accurate working bibliography.
- ☑ I have taken notes carefully in order to prevent unintentional plagiarism.
- ☑ I have established a note-taking system that keeps track of resources, helps me gather key ideas and information from these sources, and encourages me to build my own thinking.
- ☑ I have carefully engaged and evaluated all my sources, both print and electronic.
- ☑ I have responsibly summarized, paraphrased, and quoted sources in my notes.

Building Credibility:

Avoiding Plagiarism and Other Source Abuses

 What is credibility, and why does it matter in research? What makes a piece of research writing credible? How does plagiarism relate to credibility?

"That's incredible!" is normally a positive exclamation of amazement. But maybe it's an exclamation that you do not want to hear about your research writing, if incredible means *unbelievable*. If your paper is unbelievable, your credibility as a researcher and a writer is seriously damaged.

Obviously, you want to create a credible discussion of your carefully researched topic. While the next chapter focuses on drafting such a paper, this chapter prepares you for drafting by offering instruction in building and maintaining credibility, beginning with these principles:

1. **Write the paper yourself.** It's acceptable to consult with others, but in the end the paper must be yours. Take ownership of your thinking and writing.
2. **Be honest, accurate, and measured.** Make sure that what you write is correct, not false, spun, or distorted. Moreover, make realistic claims.
3. **Show respect.** Treat your reader, the topic, and opposing viewpoints with care. Indicate awareness of the impacts and consequences of your claims.
4. **Establish and strengthen your credentials.** Your credibility is rooted in your credentials—your authority, training, and experience. By demonstrating that you have done thorough, careful research, you will earn your reader's trust.

What's Ahead?

Developing Credibility through Source Use

Your credibility—how fully your readers trust and believe you—is partly rooted in how well you treat your sources in your writing. While plagiarism does the most serious damage to your credibility (as discussed on the following pages), a range of source abuses can undermine your credibility. Conversely, several good practices enhance it. Check the differences between the passages below and on the next page.

Writing with Poor Use of Sources

What does poor source use look like? A poor paper might read like a recitation of unconnected facts, unsupported opinions, or undigested quotations. It may contain contradictory information or illogical conclusions. A source's ideas may be distorted; source statements may be taken out of context. In fact, sources may be absent, or they may so dominate the writing that the writer disappears. At its worst, poor source use involves plagiarism, sources used without credit.

The writing offers weak generalizations in several spots.

Material from sources is clearly borrowed but not referenced through in-text citation.

A passage from an online source is copy-and-pasted into the paper without credit.

The writer uses a visual from the Internet without indicating the source or effectively discussing the graphic's meaning.

It goes without saying that cell phone usage has really increased a lot, from the beginning of the cell phone's history until now. How many people still don't have a cell—basically, no one! The advantages of cell phones are obvious, but has anyone really thought about the downside of this technological innovation? For example, there's "rinxiety," where people believe that their cell phones are ringing but they're not. Two-thirds of cell users have reported this feeling, which some experts believe to be a rewiring of the nervous system similar to phantom limb pain, while other experts thinks it's about the pitch of cell rings. It's not good.

But the most serious problem with cell phones is without a doubt driving while talking or texting. Due to the increasing complexity of mobile phones –often more like mobile computers in their available uses– it has introduced additional difficulties for law enforcement officials in being able to tell one usage from another as drivers use their devices. This is more apparent in those countries who ban both hand-held and hands-free usage, rather those who have banned hand-held use only, as officials cannot easily tell which function of the mobile phone is being used simply by visually looking at the driver. This can mean that drivers may be stopped for using their device illegally on a phone call, when in fact they were not; instead using the device for a legal purpose such as the phones' incorporated controls for car stereo or satnav usage – either as part of the cars' own device or directly on the mobile phone itself.

The question arises, is the cell phone even being used as a phone? And are these other uses legitimate or just gimmicks. This chart makes the point.

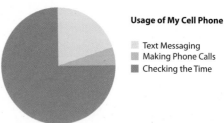

Usage of My Cell Phone

- Text Messaging
- Making Phone Calls
- Checking the Time

Writing with Strong Use of Sources

A strong paper centers on the writer's ideas, ideas advanced through thoughtful engagement with and crediting of sources. It offers logical analysis or a persuasive argument built on reliable information from quality sources that have been treated with intellectual respect. Note these features at work in the excerpt below from student writer Brandon Jarritma's essay on cell-phone dependency.

Facts and ideas are credited through in-text citations.

The writer builds on and reasons with source material.

Direct quotations from sources are indicated with quotation marks.

A case study from a source makes a concept concrete through cause-effect reasoning.

This dependency on cells is reflected in the phenomenon that has come to be termed "rinxiety." Frequent cell phone users are reporting numerous instances of either hearing their phones ring or feeling them vibrate, even if their phones are not around. Two thirds of cell phone users in a recent survey report having experienced this ("Phantom Ringing"), which is thought by some to be a rewiring of the nervous system similar to phantom limb pain (Lynch). Others theorize that it is a result of the pitch of typical cell rings being similar to elements of commonplace sounds, such as running water, music, traffic, and television (Lynch, Goodman). Regardless of the particular explanation, the experience of rinxiety is more common among young, frequent users of cell phones, which seems to indicate a constant expectation of calls ("Phantom Ringing"). This expectation is damaging to relationships because someone expecting a phone call or e-mail to arrive at any moment is not mentally present in other interactions he or she may be involved in. We've all experienced being around someone who was waiting on a phone call. How much more distracted would that person be if he or she were subconsciously expecting a phone call every hour of the day?

The corollary of constantly expecting incoming cell communication is the constant impulse to send out messages. Fifty-two percent of respondents to an informal survey at CSU, Fresno, admitted to being "preoccupied with the next time they could text message," and forty-six percent of students "reported irritability when unable to use their cell phones" (Lui). In a study of an international sample of cell phone users, some respondents recounted how they felt anxiety if they forgot to take their phone out of the house with them (Jarvenpaa 12). Even when the phone was not anywhere near them, they couldn't escape its demands on their attention. The phone has moved from being an object of utility to being one of psychological necessity, which constantly demands attention from its user regardless of its proximity or restrictions on its use. Lauren Hawn, a student at Pennsylvania State University, reports that when she is near her cell, she does the following: "I seem to look at it a lot and check the time [on the phone's digital display] even when I don't need to" (qtd. in Lynch). Hawn does not consciously think that there is a phone call or text message that might require her attention, but she is nevertheless prompted to stop whatever activity she is currently engaged in and have a private moment with her phone.

Imagine you were having a conversation with her. . . .

Recognizing Plagiarism

The road to plagiarism may be paved with the best intentions—or the worst. Either way, the result is a serious academic offense. To stay off that road, start by reviewing your school's student handbook and your instructor's course materials for policies on plagiarism and other academic offences. Then study the following pages.

What is Plagiarism?

Plagiarism refers to borrowing someone's words, ideas, or images (what's called intellectual property) without crediting the source: you use the material so that it appears to be your own. By presenting source material, whether published in print or online, without acknowledging the debt, you're stealing. Plagiarism thus refers to a range of thefts:

- Submitting a paper that you didn't write yourself.
- Pasting chunks of a source into your paper and passing them off as your own work.
- Using summaries, paraphrases, or quotations without documenting the origins.
- Using the exact phrasing of a source without quotation marks.
- Mixing up source material and your own ideas—failing to distinguish the two.

FOCUS on Research Essentials: Plagiarism refers to more than "word theft." Because plagiarism is really about failing to credit someone else's work, the rules also apply to ideas, visual images, tables, graphs, charts, maps, music, and so on. Moreover, simply listing in a bibliography the resources that you used in your paper is not good enough: within the paper, you must cite your borrowing in order to acknowledge how your work relies on your sources.

What Does Plagiarism Look Like?

Plagiarism is sometimes obvious, sometimes not. Read the passage below, and then review the five types of plagiarism that follow, noting how each misuses the source.

Original Article

The passage below is from page 87 of "Some Stories Have to Be Told by Me: A Literary History of Alice Munro," by Marcela Valdes, published in the *Virginia Quarterly Review* 82.3 (Summer 2006).

> What makes Munro's characters so enthralling is their inconsistency; like real people, at one moment they declare they will cover the house in new siding, at the next, they vomit on their way to the hospital. They fight against and seek refuge in the people they love. The technique that Munro has forged to get at such contradictions is a sort of pointillism, the setting of one bright scene against another, with little regard for chronology.

FOCUS on Multimedia: For activities on understanding and recognizing plagiarism, visit our Web site at www.theresearchwriter.com.

Submitting Another Writer's Paper: The most blatant plagiarism is taking an entire piece of writing and claiming it as your own work. Examples:

- Downloading, reformatting, and submitting an article as your own work.
- Buying a paper from a "paper mill" or taking a "free" paper off the Internet: even if such sites claim to offer "plagiarism-free papers," your submitting the paper is plagiarism.
- Turning in another student's work as your own (see "Falstaffing" on page 163).

 FOCUS on Research Ethics: Just as it's easy to plagiarize using the Internet, it's easy for your professors to recognize and track plagiarism using Internet tools. In fact, your instructor may require that you use an online plagiarism-testing service such as Turnitin.com before turning in your paper.

Using Copy-and-Paste: It is unethical to take chunks of material from a source and splice them into your paper without acknowledgement. In the example below, the writer pastes in a sentence from the original article (boldfaced) without using quotation marks or a citation. Even if the writer changes some words, she still plagiarizes.

> Life typically unfolds mysteriously for Munro's characters, with unexplained events and choices. **Like real people, at one moment they declare they will cover the house in new siding, at the next, they vomit on their way to the hospital.**

Failing to Cite a Source: Borrowed material must be documented. Even if you use information accurately and fairly, don't neglect to cite the source. Below, the writer correctly summarizes the passage's idea but offers no citation.

> For the reader, Munro's characters are interesting because they are so changeable. Munro shows these changes by using a method of placing scenes side by side for contrast, without worrying about the chronological connections.

Neglecting Necessary Quotation Marks: Whether you copy a paragraph or a phrase, if you use the exact wording of a source, that material must be enclosed in quotation marks. In the example below, the writer cites the source but doesn't use quotation marks around a phrase taken from the original (boldfaced).

> What makes Munro's characters so typically human is that they **fight against and seek refuge in the people they love** (Valdes 87).

Confusing Borrowed Material with Your Own Ideas: Through mistakes (often in note-taking), you may confuse source material with your own thinking. Below, the writer indicates that he borrowed material in the first sentence, but fails to indicate that he also borrowed the next sentence.

> As Marcela Valdes explains, "[w]hat makes Munro's characters so enthralling is their inconsistency" (87). To achieve this sense of inconsistency, Munro places brightly lit scenes beside each other in a kind of pointillist technique.

Avoiding Source Misuse

Research writing requires that you treat your resources with respect. But what does *disrespecting* your sources mean? What types of misuse do you want to avoid, and how do you avoid them? The following pages address these questions.

Why Is Plagiarism So Serious?

Perhaps the answer is obvious. But some people believe that because they have "free" access to Internet material (whether text, visual, or sound), they can use it as their own in research writing. After all, they reason, a lot of stuff on the Web doesn't even list an author, so what's the harm? Here's some food for thought:

Plagiarism is Academic Dishonesty. At its heart, plagiarism is cheating—stealing intellectual property and passing it off as one's own work. Colleges take such dishonesty seriously. Plagiarism, whether intentional or unintentional, will likely be punished in one or more ways:

- Failing grade for the assignment or even for the course.
- A note on your academic transcript that failure resulted from academic dishonesty (a note that could be seen by potential employers, as well as graduate-school and professional-program entrance committees).
- Expulsion from college.

Plagiarism Robs the Academic Community. The research paper represents your dialogue with other members of the academic community—classmates, the instructor, others in your major, past researchers of your topic, and people who might read and rely upon your writing. When you plagiarize, you short-circuit the dialogue:

- You gain an unfair advantage over your classmates, those who follow the rules and earn their grades.
- You disrespect other writers, researchers, and scholars by lip-syncing them.
- You disrespect your readers by passing off others' ideas as your own.
- You insult your instructor, a person whose respect you need.
- You harm your college by risking its reputation and its academic integrity.

Plagiarism Robs *You* Now. Not only does plagiarism disrupt real academic dialogue, but it also negates the real curiosity and true discovery that should motivate your research. Because research projects help you learn course-related concepts and writing skills, plagiarism steals your opportunity to learn both. Moreover, you rob yourself of your integrity and reputation. After all, as a student you are seeking to build your credibility within the broader academic community, your major, and your future profession.

Plagiarism Robs You in the Future. Research projects often train you for your future work in terms of research, thinking, and writing skills, skills that you will need to succeed in the workplace. If you do not learn the skills now, you will enter the workplace without them—a situation that your employer will, at some point, find out.

How Do You Avoid Plagiarizing in Your Writing?

As discussed in earlier chapters (see pages 27, 33, and 136), preventing plagiarism begins the moment that you get an assignment. Essentially, prevention requires your commitment and diligence throughout the project. Follow this advice:

Resist temptation. With the Internet, plagiarism is mouse clicks away. Avoid last-minute all-nighters that make you desperate; start research projects early. Note: it's better to ask for an extension or accept a penalty for lateness than to plagiarize.

Play by the rules. Become familiar with your college's definition, guidelines, and policies regarding plagiarism so that you don't unknowingly violate them.

Take orderly, accurate notes. From the start, carefully keep track of source material and distinguish it from your own thinking. Do so by maintaining an accurate working bibliography (page 136); adopting a decent note-taking system (page 139); and accurately summarizing, paraphrasing, and quoting (pages 151).

Document borrowed material. Credit information that you have summarized, paraphrased, or quoted from any source, whether that information is statistics, facts, graphics, phrases, or ideas. Readers can then see what's borrowed and what's yours, understand your support, and do their own follow-up research.

> *Common Knowledge Exception:* Common knowledge is information—a basic fact, for instance—that is generally known to your particular readers or easily found in several sources, particularly reference works, that themselves feel no need to source. Because it's common, such knowledge need NOT be cited. However, when you go beyond common knowledge into research findings, interpretations of the facts, theories, explanations, claims, arguments, and graphics—you MUST document the source. Study the examples below, but whenever you are in doubt, document.

> *Examples:*
> - The fact that Jane Austen wrote *Pride and Prejudice* is common knowledge, whereas the details of the novel's composition are not.
> - The idea that attachment is key for emotional well-being is common knowledge, whereas the clinical effects of attachment disorder are not.
> - The fact that automakers are developing hybrid electric cars is common knowledge, whereas the precise details of GM's AUTOnomy project are not.

Work carefully with source material in your paper. See pages 190-194 for more on integrating and documenting sources, but here, briefly, are your responsibilities:
- Distinguish borrowed material from your own thinking by signaling where source material begins and ends.
- Indicate the source's origin with an attributive phrase and a citation (parenthetical reference or footnote, consistent with an appropriate documentation system).
- Provide full source information in a works-cited or references page.

What Other Source Abuses Should You Avoid?

Plagiarism, while the most serious offense, is not the only source abuse to avoid when writing a paper with documented research. Consider these pitfalls, which refer again to the sample passage on page 158.

Using Sources Inaccurately: When you get a quotation wrong, botch a summary, paraphrase poorly, or misstate a statistic, you misrepresent the original. *Example:* In this quotation, the writer carelessly uses several wrong words that change the meaning, and adds two words that are not in the original.

> As Marcela Valdes explains, "[w]hat makes Munro's characters so appalling is their consistency. . . . They fight against and seek refuse in the people they say they love" (87).

Using Source Material Out of Context: By ripping a statement out of its context and forcing it into yours, you can make a source seem to say something that it didn't really say. Instead of respecting the source and engaging it fairly in terms of its overall argument, you distort the source for your own benefit. *Example:* Below, the writer uses part of a statement to say the opposite of the original.

> According to Marcela Valdes, while Munro's characters are interesting, Munro's weakness as a fiction writer is that she shows "little regard for chronology" (87).

Overusing Source Material: When your paper reads like a string of references, especially quotations, your own thinking disappears. *Example:* The writer takes the source passage, chops it up, and splices it together.

> Anyone who has read her stories knows that "[w]hat makes Munro's characters so enthralling is their inconsistency." That is to say, "like real people, at one moment they declare they will cover the house in new siding, at the next, they vomit on their way to the hospital." Moreover, "[t]hey fight against and seek refuge in the people they love." This method "that Munro has forged to get at such contradictions is a sort of pointillism," meaning "the setting of one bright scene against another, with little regard for chronology" (Valdes 87)

"Plunking" Quotations: When you "plunk" or "drop" quotations into your paper by not preparing for and following them up, the discussion becomes disconnected. *Example:* The writer interrupts the flow of ideas with a quote "out of the blue." In addition, the quotation hangs at the end of a paragraph with no follow-up or transition.

> Typically, characters such as Del Jordan, Louisa Doud, and Almeda Roth experience a crisis through contact with particular men. "They fight against and seek refuge in the people they love" (Valdes 87).
>
> Violent disruptions sometimes play a large role in the lives of Munro's women. . .

Relying Heavily on One Source: If your writing is dominated by one source, readers may doubt the depth and integrity of your research.

Using "Blanket" Citations: Your reader shouldn't have to guess where borrowed material begins and ends. For example, if you place a parenthetical citation at the end of a paragraph, does that citation cover the whole paragraph or just the final sentence?

Failing to Match In-Text Citations and Bibliographic Entries: All in-text citations must clearly refer to accurate entries in the Works-Cited, References, or Endnotes page. Mismatching occurs when an in-text citation refers to a source that is not listed in the bibliography, or a bibliographic resource listed is not referenced anywhere in the paper.

Fabricating or Falsifying Research: Simply put, making up sources or data, fudging the facts, reading an abstract but implying that you read the whole source, and altering graphics to improve results—all these practices violate principles of research honesty.

What Other Academic Violations Should You Avoid?

Double-Dipping. When you submit one paper in two different classes without permission from both instructors, you take double credit for one project.

Falstaffing. This practice refers to a particular type of plagiarism where one student submits another student's work. Know that you are guilty of Falstaffing if you let another student submit your paper.

Copyright Violations. When you copy, distribute, and/or post in whole or in part any intellectual property without permission from or payment to the copyright holder, you commit a copyright infringement, especially when you profit from this use. To avoid copyright violations in your research projects, do the following:

- **Observe *fair use* guidelines:** Quote small portions of a document for limited purposes, such as research. Avoid copying large portions for your own gain.
- **Understand what's in public domain:** You need not obtain permission to copy and use public-domain materials—primarily documents created by the government.
- **Observe *intellectual property* and *copyright laws:*** First, know your college's policies on copying documents. Second, realize that copyright protects the expression of ideas in a range of materials—writings, videos, songs, photographs, drawings, computer software, and so on. Always obtain permission to copy and distribute copyrighted materials.
- **Avoid changing a source** (e.g., a photo or graph) without the permission of the creator or copyright holder.

 FOCUS on Research Ethics: Source-use standards apply to all researchers, not just undergraduate students. Graduate students, professors, and people in the workplace are also bound by these ethical guidelines. Why? Honest, fair treatment of other people's work is a foundational principle of doing research in any social context. For more on this issue, as well as information on the Creative Commons movement and debates about copyright, visit our Web site at www.theresearchwriter.com.

Practicing Your Research

1. **Explore:** Reflect on the consequences of unethical research. In the wider world, what happens when research is shoddy or deceptive? Research a story of unethical research that happened in the past decade.

2. **Apply:** Find three articles on the same topic, articles from different media (e.g., newspaper, magazine, Web site). Explore how each writer attempts to establish and build credibility. How well does each succeed?

3. **Collaborate on a Case Study:** As directed by your instructor, continue work with classmates on your clothing-focused project. Together, review the sources that you have been working with as well as the notes that you have generated. Discuss what strategies and practices you will use to build credibility and avoid plagiarism when you write up your research.

4. **Research Your Major:** What does *credibility* mean in your discipline? What ethical practices for treating sources are emphasized in your major? Research these questions by (a) interviewing instructors in your major; (b) examining scholarly books, trade books, and journal articles in the field; and/or (c) studying statements of research ethics published by professional organizations related to your discipline (e.g., check the MLA, APA, or CSE manuals or Web sites).

5. **Work on Your Current Project:** Advance your current research project by carefully reviewing your research notes for clarity and accuracy. By referring back to the sources themselves, determine whether your notes (a) reflect a fair "dialogue" with those sources and (b) properly distinguish source material—summaries, paraphrases, and quotations—from your own thoughts. Then identify strategies that you will use to build credibility and avoid plagiarism when you write your research paper.

Checklist:

- ☑ I plan to establish and build my credibility as a research writer by being honest, making measured claims, backing up my claims, and showing respect.
- ☑ I am avoiding accidental plagiarism by (a) starting early and completing work on time, (b) continuing to work carefully with sources, and (c) taking accurate notes.
- ☑ When writing my paper, I know how to avoid plagiarism through careful citation of all borrowed material—from phrases quoted to passages summarized to ideas relied upon.
- ☑ I will make sound judgments about what information is and is not common knowledge with respect to my topic and my specific readers.
- ☑ I know how to avoid other source abuses when I draft my paper: from inaccurate transfer of information into my paper to violating copyright rules.

Drafting Papers with Documented Research

© Cengage Learning/Illustrated by Chris Krenzke

Q When you sit down to draft a paper, what practices work for you? What challenges do you face? How does writing with sources complicate your task?

"Writing," suggests author Peter Stillman, "is the most powerful means of discovery available to all of us throughout life." This claim to writing's power for discovery is equally true of research writing. During your research, you have been making meaningful discoveries by pursuing your curiosity about a topic and engaging your sources in a kind of conversation. Now in your research writing, your aim will be twofold: first, to clarify and deepen the discoveries and dialogue for yourself as the writer; and second, to appeal to your readers' curiosity, leading them to their own discoveries and inviting them into the conversation.

But as you contemplate planning and writing your research paper, this ideal may seem farfetched. Instead, you may feel intimidated—faced with a kind of paralysis in the face of the task ahead. You may be surrounded by your stack of sources, buried under a mass of notes, or lost in a labyrinth of conflicting ideas. The step from research to writing may feel more like an impossible leap across a canyon.

Don't panic. This chapter will give you practical strategies for taking this step and making it a step in the right direction, a step toward discovery for both you and your readers.

What's Ahead?

Shifting from Research to Writing

With every research project, the time comes when you must transition from exploration to sharing discoveries, from research to writing. As emphasized earlier (see page 000), research writers need to build into their projects a healthy amount of time for planning, drafting, and revising their papers. This is the right time to reconsider your project's rhetorical situation and get a grip on the writing process.

Revisiting Your Research Rhetoric

When you revisit your project's rhetorical situation, you set a direction for your research writing, whatever the form. You can begin to think of your writing as a kind of double conversation, first with your sources and secondly with your reader. While key rhetorical issues are outlined fully on pages 4–7, here are brief reminders:

1. **Your Purpose:** What are your general goals—to inform the reader about your topic, to analyze it in depth, to construct an argument about it? What are your specific aims in terms of your own learning and your reader's? As you think about the research that you have completed, which sources are most closely tied to your goals and aims? Which sources should be featured in your writing?

2. **Your Audience:** Who are your readers? Your instructor and classmates? The college community? The general public? An online group? What are their values and attitudes concerning your topic? What is their level of knowledge about it? What have you discovered that would connect with their needs? Which resources will help you create credibility and clarify the topic for your audience?

3. **Your Writing Role:** What approach and tone should you adopt as a research writer? Should you be completely serious and objective, lighthearted and personal, or somewhere in between? Consider, too, these roles:

   - *Reporter or Informer:* Your task is to supply information within a framework or structure that makes sense of it.
   - *Analyst or Interpreter:* Your task is to explain your topic so that your reader understands it in greater depth—through analytical modes such as definition, classification, and cause and effect.
   - *Advocate or Persuader:* Your task is to convince the reader of your point of view or position and to bring the reader to act on your claims.

4. **The Context:** Revisit the parameters of your project by considering these issues:

   - *The subject:* In what ways has your research taken you more deeply into the assigned subject? What dimensions have you explored most fully?
   - *The assignment:* What are the requirements you must follow for your written paper in terms of length, voice, content, number of sources, and so on?
   - *The form of writing:* What type of document are you creating with this project, and what are the specifications or conventions of this form? Are you writing an essay, a lab or field report, a Web page, a seminar presentation?
   - *The documentation system:* What method of documentation are you expected to follow in this paper—MLA, APA, Chicago, CSE?

Understanding the Writing Process

At the beginning of this book, we outlined the stages of the research process (see the diagram on page 13). Writing, too, is a process with distinct phases. You have already used writing to engage sources, record information, and explore your own thinking; now you will use writing to discover new meaning for yourself and to dialogue with your reader. Below is an overview of the writing process, which is addressed in detail on the pages that follow.

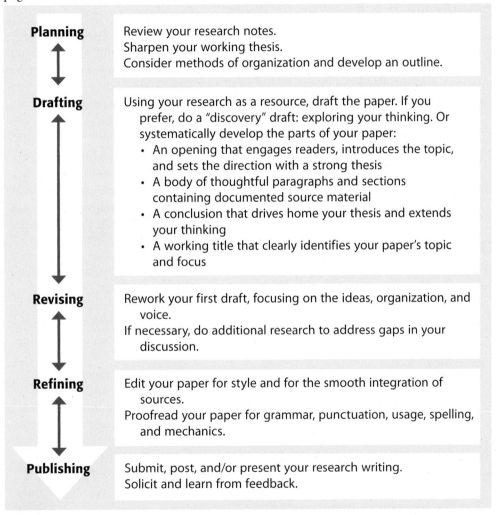

Planning
- Review your research notes.
- Sharpen your working thesis.
- Consider methods of organization and develop an outline.

Drafting
- Using your research as a resource, draft the paper. If you prefer, do a "discovery" draft: exploring your thinking. Or systematically develop the parts of your paper:
  - An opening that engages readers, introduces the topic, and sets the direction with a strong thesis
  - A body of thoughtful paragraphs and sections containing documented source material
  - A conclusion that drives home your thesis and extends your thinking
  - A working title that clearly identifies your paper's topic and focus

Revising
- Rework your first draft, focusing on the ideas, organization, and voice.
- If necessary, do additional research to address gaps in your discussion.

Refining
- Edit your paper for style and for the smooth integration of sources.
- Proofread your paper for grammar, punctuation, usage, spelling, and mechanics.

Publishing
- Submit, post, and/or present your research writing.
- Solicit and learn from feedback.

FOCUS on Research Essentials: While the writing process can unfold systematically in the phases outlined above, writing can also be fluid, intuitive, and recursive—as indicated by the arrows. Experiment with the process to develop an approach productive for you. But whatever steps you follow, carefully track and document source material during all stages.

Reviewing Your Findings

The planning stage of the research-writing process involves a great deal of sorting and weeding source material as it relates to your thinking. While you may feel the urge to draft right away, take time to review and order your notes, using them to stimulate your thinking and planning. Go over your notes many times—until the ideas percolate and the information makes sense. In addition, try the strategies below that follow.

Conducting Q & A

Early in your project, you may have generated a set of questions, with a primary question directing your research (see page 25). Now that you have completed the bulk of your research, you might do the following Q & A activity to clarify how your research has impacted your thinking:

- **Review your primary research question:** What essential answers has your research produced? How thorough are your answers? Are the answers engaging—or unsettling?
- **Review your secondary research questions:** What information have you found to answer these questions? How do the answers enhance your thinking about the primary question?
- **List questions generated by your research:** As you engaged resources, new questions may have occurred to you. Add these to your list and then answer them.

Deepening Your Thinking on the Topic

During note taking, you focused on making sense of what individual sources said about your topic. Now, take these steps to deepen and expand your thinking:

- **Identify key discoveries.** What central ideas and new facts have you learned through research? What conclusions have you reached, and why? How has your research changed your thinking? By answering these questions, you are clarifying what you think about the topic, as well as what your reader might think.
- **Identify connections between sources.** How are your sources related to each other? Do they share similar points of view and similar conclusions? Do some sources build on other sources? Which one was published first, second, third, etc.? By answering questions like these, you can synthesize your findings, discovering what your sources share or agree upon.
- **Identify differences between sources.** In what ways and on what issues do sources disagree? Why? What sense do you make of the differences? By focusing on differences, you can balance your thinking and locate problematic issues and conflicts to explore in your own writing.
- **Identify limits and gaps.** What issues do your sources neglect to cover? What evidence would you find useful if it were available? What questions remain unanswered? How much of your information comes from primary sources, and how much from secondary sources? How important is this distinction to your conclusions? By exploring questions like these, you identify limits that you may need to acknowledge in your writing.

Imagining Your Paper

As you review your findings, you can also prepare to write your paper by imagining what it might include. Consider these strategies:

1. **Look for organizational clues.** How do your sources organize their discussions of your topic? Are there particular patterns that make sense of the issues? Would similar patterns work for your own writing?

2. **Anticipate how you might use source material.** As you study your notes, imagine how the particular points you have recorded (summaries, paraphrases, quotations) could be used in your writing. Here are some ways you might use source material:

   - *Background, historical context, definitions:* foundational information creating a framework for understanding your topic and its issues
   - *Principles and theories:* idea "tools" that you can use as part of your exploration of the topic, especially your analysis of the issues
   - *Expert insights, points of view, and reasoning:* the thinking of those people most knowledgeable about your topic; the arguments your sources make
   - *Examples and case studies:* illustrations that vivify an abstract idea
   - *Concrete evidence:* the facts, numbers, statistics, measurements, statements, and so on that support your claims

 FOCUS on Your Project: What might imagining your paper mean? Consider writing a "discovery draft" simply by taking what your research has taught you and engaging it in an exploratory dialogue. That conversation can deepen your thinking to the point of discovering what you truly want to say. Out of such a quick, rough draft you can then pull the ideas around which your more polished writing will develop.

Sorting Out Your Notes

Reviewing your notes should also involve sorting and weeding them. If you have done a good job of note taking, you likely have far more material than you need for your writing. That's good, because it means that you have a wealth of information from which to draw. Try crossing out the obviously not useful material in printed notes or highlighting it in electronic files. But be careful: Keep everything that you may need for your paper, and don't cut material simply because it disagrees with your thesis.

At this point, you can also begin ordering source material by labeling and clumping. As you review your notes, generate a list of key terms, concepts, and phrases that emerge. Then use these concepts to label individual notes or to group them—physically or electronically. This activity is particularly helpful for developing an outline (see page 178).

Sharpening Your Working Thesis

As you move toward drafting your research paper, decide how to set your paper's direction—ask a question, identify issues to be discussed, establish critical background and definitions, or revisit and revise your thesis. On page 26, you learned about the working thesis. Now, informed by your research, you can strengthen that thesis and use it to develop an outline.

Deepening Your Thesis

Review your working thesis. Given the research that you have completed, does this thesis stand up? Has your thinking changed? It is possible, of course, that your research has led you to a conclusion that is opposite of your original working thesis. If this is the case, rewrite your thesis accordingly. However, you may also stick with your original thesis, but strengthen it by using these strategies:

1. **Use richer, clearer terms.** Test your working thesis for vague, broad, or inappropriate terms or concepts. While plain English is always a good choice, use terms in your thesis that have rich meanings, that are respected in discussions of your topic, and that refine your original thinking.

2. **Introduce qualifying terms where needed.** With qualifying terms such as "normally," "often," and "usually," as well as with phrases that limit the reach of your thesis, you are paradoxically making your thesis more reasonable and thoughtful.

3. **Stress your idea through opposition.** You can deepen your working thesis by adding an opposing thought (usually placed in a dependent clause). The contrast often emphasizes your own idea through contrast.

> **Original Working Thesis:** In Alice Munro's "An Ounce of Cure," infatuation messes with the narrator's head, so her life gets turned upside down.
>
> **Revised Working Thesis:** While Alice Munro's "An Ounce of Cure" tells a simple story of infatuation leading to confusion and trouble, the story is more importantly about the "plots of life"—the ways in which the narrator experiences life as a competing set of stories (romance, fairy tale, farce), none of which does justice to the complexity of real life.

 FOCUS on Research Essentials: The working thesis is your key discovery about the topic, a statement that answers a meaningful question. Make sure that your writing is guided by such a thesis and NOT by one of the following types of statements (though such content may be part of your paper's opening):

- **Statement of topic, purpose, or plan for the paper:** In this paper, I plan to explore infatuation in Alice Munro's "An Ounce of Cure" by examining plot and character.
- **A question:** What is important about the narrator's infatuation?

Questioning Your Thesis

Another method of sharpening your working thesis involves questioning it; that is, viewing it from your reader's point of view. What would the reader think of it? Would the thesis encourage further reading? Specifically, what questions might the reader formulate, given the key words, phrases, and concepts within your thesis? Look at this example:

> **Working Thesis:** While Alice Munro's "An Ounce of Cure" tells a simple story of infatuation leading to confusion and trouble, the story is more importantly about the "plots of life"—the ways in which the narrator experiences life as a competing set of stories (romance, fairy tale, farce), none of which does justice to the complexity of real life.

Reader's Questions:

- In what ways is the story primarily about infatuation? What kinds of trouble flow from the infatuation? What confusions?
- What do you mean by the phrase "plots of life," and where does it come from?
- What is the nature of each type of story listed? In what ways do these story types "compete"?
- How is real life more complex than these fictional stories? Does the narrator experience real life? If so, where and how?

This thesis questioning can guide your planning in at least three ways:

1. Are these questions really the ones you want to answer in your paper? If yes, your working thesis is on target. If not, revise your working thesis until it clarifies the idea that you truly wish to elaborate and support.

2. Does the thesis answer the reader's "So what? Why is this idea important?" If not, revise your thesis to better appeal to your reader's curiosity.

3. Do the questions suggest a structure for your paper? In other words, would it help the reader to have the questions answered in a particular order? Can the questions be sequenced logically from basic to complex? If yes, you can use your thesis questioning to develop an initial outline for your drafting.

FOCUS on Your Project: The strategies above show you how to sharpen your working thesis in preparation for outlining and drafting your paper. Before you proceed with your current project, test your thesis with this checklist:

_____ My working thesis offers a clear answer to my specific research question, an answer that is consistent with what I discovered through research.

_____ My thesis is phrased in a way that fits the assignment.

_____ My thesis uses precise terms and appropriate qualifiers.

_____ My thesis substantively answers my reader's question: "Why is this idea important?"

Considering Methods of Organization

Before drafting, explore which methods of organization would work well for your paper. While some assignments specify the organizational pattern (e.g., compare-contrast or problem-solution), often you need to determine the patterns that will work best for your project. In fact, even when an assignment requires an overall pattern, you will still need to make choices about ordering particular sections and paragraphs. The discussion that follows will help you make good choices.

Organizational Practices to Avoid

College-level research writing generally aims to offer an advanced, thoughtfully rich discussion of a complex issue. As such, your paper should avoid the following simplistic patterns or templates:

1. **The five-paragraph essay:** Popularly known as the high school hamburger, this structure is too basic and limiting for most college research projects. The pattern of introduction (bun), three supporting points in three paragraphs (the beef), and conclusion (bun) is too restrictive and prescriptive for discussing complex issues.

2. **Information regurgitation:** Generally, college-level research writing requires analytical thinking about information. When you organize your paper by simply sharing information from your sources, it will resemble something of a subject report without the complexities of thoughtful research.

3. **A series of source summaries:** While there is definitely room in your writing for summarizing sources (sometimes called a literature review, see page 359), your whole paper should not be structured as a discussion of one source after another. Such an overall structure shows no real synthesis or analysis of material.

4. **Writer-friendly patterns:** It's important to start by organizing your thinking about the issue so that the pattern reflects and deepens your own understanding of the topic. However, you need to go beyond that step and structure the discussion with your reader in mind. For example, what background and context does the reader need in order to understand your thinking? How should you order your points so that your reader can grasp them and be effectively persuaded to adopt your position?

 FOCUS on Your Major: Each discipline has its own conventions for structuring research writing (e.g., an experiment report vs. a literary analysis paper). Learn the structures that are respected in your discipline, and be careful not to carelessly transfer those structures to research projects you may complete in other disciplines.

Organizational Practices That Consider Sources

Because the writing you are doing is research based, it makes sense to factor your sources into the organization. Here are some ideas that may work with your project.

Consider where to position primary and secondary sources. Different writing projects require different approaches to using, balancing, and integrating primary and secondary sources. (See pages 34-37 for more on this distinction.) As you plan your writing, ask these questions:

- Where and how should I work in primary sources—interview material, survey data, textual and artifact analysis, observation results, experiment results?
- Where and how should I bring in secondary sources—scholarly books, journal articles, and the like?

Example: In a literary analysis, you might rely on primary textual analysis of a novel throughout your paper, but support that analysis with secondary-source biographical information placed early in your paper.

Order your writing around key sources. As discussed on the previous page, you shouldn't organize your whole paper as a series of source summaries. However, sometimes your writing can take direction specifically from the sources that you have researched. Consider these options:

- *Make one of your key points a response to a specific source.* Did a particular source stand out as especially strong or especially contrary to your own thinking? Shape part of your paper as an affirmation of the strong source's authority, or as a rebuttal to the contrary source's claims.
- *Structure your paper around a dialogue with sources.* Do your sources offer multiple, divergent, even contradictory perspectives on your topic? If they do, consider organizing your paper around a dialogue with these sources—a he-says, she-says, and here's-my-say approach. This strategy may work especially well with writing that addresses a complex or controversial topic requiring multiple perspectives.

Map out relationships between sources and ideas. Having reviewed your findings and sharpened your working thesis, you might consider how your sources support that thesis. To visualize your options, create a diagram, map, or flowchart that shows where particular sources speak to particular points.

Put your discussion in context. Often, the early part of your paper will involve establishing a context for exploring your topic. Consider, then, tapping your sources to present necessary background, explain key terms, describe the big picture, set out key principles, or establish a theoretical framework for your discussion. For example, if your paper will explore the problem of teen homelessness in Atlanta, you might present your analysis in light of the national trends, general causes of homelessness, sociological definitions of homelessness, and so on.

FOCUS on Your Major: In most disciplines, it is common practice early in the paper to "survey the literature" on the topic. In a literary analysis, you might survey common interpretations before you relay your own. In a botany field report, you might review other studies done on the topic before you present your own.

Basic Essay or Paper Structure

While the shape of your research writing should be dictated by the form (e.g., analytical essay, field report) and the medium through which you publish your work (e.g., presentation, Web page, printed paper), a good starting point is the structure of the traditional academic paper. The chart below lists some of the main writing moves that you can use to develop your paper. You don't need to use them all nor employ them in a particular order. Rather, consult the chart as a general guide, adapting it to your project.

Opening

■ *Engage your reader.* Stimulate and hold the reader's attention.
■ *Establish your direction.* Identify the topic and put it in perspective.
■ *Get to the point.* Narrow your focus by clarifying the specific issue; then state your thesis or offer a meaningful question.
■ *Point forward.* Forecast how your discussion of the thesis or question will unfold.

Middle

■ *Create a foundation.* Put your discussion of the topic in context by providing necessary background (e.g., historical, social), establishing principles and definitions, clarifying the issue's importance, and/or surveying the literature.
■ *Develop a line of reasoning.* Explain and elaborate your thesis with a series of points that create depth, substance, and interest. Raise and answer the questions that lie behind your main research question or working thesis.
■ *Be supportive.* As you make points (claims) that support your main point (thesis), use sound logic based on convincing evidence and plenty of detail.

Ending

■ *Reassert your main point.* Rephrase your thesis to reflect how your discussion has deepened your thinking and the reader's.
■ *Explain implications of the thesis.* Elaborate on why this main idea matters in a broader context. Help the reader look outward from the idea and apply it in different contexts.
■ *Point the reader forward.* Explore where the research might lead, what further research may be inspired, or what steps should be taken.

Patterns of Reasoning

Because college-level research writing typically aims to offer a reasonable discussion of an issue, understanding patterns of reasoning can contribute to your thinking about organization. Details of how to map out your reasoning at the paragraph level are offered on page 186, but here are some strategies for your whole paper.

Allow your thesis to dictate the structure. Your thesis sets the direction for your paper, so your paper's structure should be in line with that direction. With your thesis and a list of possible supporting points in front of you, ask yourself how best to sequence that support. Should you move from simpler to more complex points, from accepted points to arguable ones, from causes to effects? Notice how the thesis statement below provides direction and shape for the writing that follows.

> **Thesis:** The best solution to controlling deer populations is to stay as close as possible to nature's ways, and managing the population by hunting meets this criterion.
>
> **Discussion:** This thesis points to a problem-solution structure, meaning that the first part of the paper will likely identify the problem, establish its causes and effects, and argue for its significance. The paper will then offer a specific solution in the context of alternatives and defend that solution.

Choose between inductive and deductive patterns. Inductive logic reasons from specific information (your research evidence and findings) toward general conclusions (supporting points and thesis). Deductive logic reasons from general principles toward specific applications. Notice in the diagram below that inductive reasoning starts with specific information, details, or observations (concrete evidence) and then moves "up" to broader ideas and eventually to a concluding generalization (your thesis about the issue or topic). In contrast, deduction starts with a general principle (your thesis, claim, conclusion, or point) at the top and then works down, applying the principle to explain particular instances.

Paragraphs and whole papers can be organized inductively, deductively, or with some combination of both. The traditional structure is deductive: place your thesis up front and then elaborate it, apply it, and defend it with reasoning and evidence. However, inductive structure can work well if you begin your essay by asking a question or raising an issue, and then work toward an answer or solution by the end of the paper (thesis placed in the conclusion).

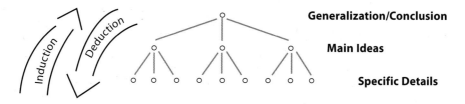

Induction   Deduction   Generalization/Conclusion

Main Ideas

Specific Details

Traditional Organizational Patterns

As shown in the "writing moves" chart on page 174, organizing your paper into an opening, a middle, and an ending can involve a variety of strategies. Particularly for the middle part, the traditional patterns work well for developing your thinking. Each choice offers a basic structure for your paper, but several patterns may be used within the body of your paper.

Analysis clarifies how something works by breaking the object or phenomenon into parts or phases and then showing how they work together.

> *Example:* In a study of Mark Twain's *The Adventures of Huckleberry Finn,* you analyze the changing relationship of Huck and Jim in the beginning, middle, and end of the narrative.

Argumentation asserts and supports a main claim with supporting claims, logical reasoning about each claim, and concrete evidence to back up the reasoning. This pattern also includes acknowledging and countering any opposition, as well as reasserting the main claim (perhaps in a modified form).

> *Example:* In an environmental policy paper, you take a position for or against wind farms.

Cause-effect organization can (1) explore the factors that led to an event or phenomenon, (2) explore the consequences of an event or phenomenon, or (3) do both.

> *Example:* In a psychological study of attachment disorder, you trace the lifelong effects of attachment problems established in infancy.

Chronological order arranges items in a temporal sequence (order of events, steps in a process).

> *Example:* In a political science paper, you map out the phases of Barack Obama's education and career leading up to his presidency.

Classification places items within categories. Each category is characterized by what the items share with each other and by what makes them different from items in the other categories.

> *Example:* In an economics paper, you categorize the types of solutions that economists and others have proposed to deal with the 2008-2009 recession.

Compare-contrast organization examines two or more items for similarities, differences, or both. Such a study typically holds the items side by side, comparing or contrasting traits point by point.

> *Example:* In a computer-science paper, you compare and contrast the user interfaces of Macs and PC's.

Definition clarifies a term's meaning through appropriate strategies: explaining the term's origin and history, offering examples and illustrations, elaborating key concepts at the heart of the term, and so on.

Example: In a sociology paper, you explore traditional definitions of marriage in light of current challenges to that tradition.

Description orders details in terms of spatial relationships, color, form, texture, and so on.

Example: In an urban-planning paper, you explore the relative positioning, size, style, and symbolism of several key national monuments at the heart of the capital, Washington, DC.

Evaluation measures the strength or quality of something against particular standards, standards that are already accepted or that are established prior to the evaluation.

Example: In a media-studies class, you evaluate a reality-TV show that focuses on radical makeovers of women in light of the American Psychological Association's research on healthy self-image.

Order of importance arranges items from most to least important, or from least to most.

Example: In a history paper on post-WWII prosperity in the U.S., you arrange prosperity indicators from least significant to most significant.

Partitioning breaks down an object, a space, or a location into ordered parts, or a process into steps or phases.

Example: In a paper explaining how hybrid-vehicle technology works, you partition the vehicle's power sources.

Problem-solution organization describes a problem, explores its causes and effects, surveys possible solutions, proposes the best one, and defends it as desirable and doable. This pattern may also involve explaining how to implement the solution.

Example: In a global-issues paper, you examine the problem of worldwide human trafficking and propose a range of political and legal solutions.

Question-answer organization moves back and forth from questions to answers in a sequence that logically clarifies a topic.

Example: In an ethics paper, you ask and answer questions about the rise of tolerance in post-WWII Netherlands and what led to the current crisis in that society.

 FOCUS on Your Project: As you work toward developing an outline for your paper, consider which of the organizational patterns above would (a) offer a structure for the whole paper and (b) be useful for a particular part of the paper. Note, too, that the list above functions as a brief overview of possibilities. In chapters 12–17, the organizational patterns fitting for different forms of research writing (from the personal research paper to the literature review) are discussed more fully and shown graphically. Review those chapters for a pattern that fits your project.

Developing an Outline

According to writer Ken Macrorie, "[G]ood writing is formed partly through plan and partly through accident." Macrorie's point is that planning is important, but it must leave room for discovery through writing. That's where the outline for your research writing comes in. A good outline sets a course for your drafting but allows you to redirect that course as you write.

If you have revisited the rhetorical situation for your project (especially the form of writing and any expectations about organization), reviewed your findings, sharpened your working thesis, and explored organizational options, you should be ready to develop an outline for your paper. Simply put, an outline lists the points that you want to cover in the order that you plan to cover them. However, developing a strong outline requires that you consider the following complexities:

- **Sequence:** The order of your points should represent a line of reasoning that elaborates and supports your working thesis. The points should logically and effectively build on each other; they should not be a random list of ideas.
- **Weight:** Your outline can indicate through the presentation of points and subpoints the relative weight or importance of particular ideas.
- **Connection to Research Notes:** Your outline is not simply a reorganized version of your research notes, nor can it replace your notes. Rather, your notes supply the raw material (evidence, illustrations, quotations, statistics, etc.) you will draw on as you draft your paper.
- **Format and Depth:** Depending on your own drafting style, your preferences, and the type of writing you are doing, you can choose from several outline styles: a basic list, a graphic organizer, a topic outline, or a sentence outline. Each of these options is discussed below.

Choosing a Type of Outline

An outline can be simple or complex, brief or highly detailed. Here are your main choices, along with the benefits of each and the format to follow.

Basic List

This outline reduces your drafting plan to the key terms that encapsulate your thinking. As such, the basic list requires you to do a great deal of development during drafting. On the plus side, the basic list offers you the creative flexibility to expand your thinking while drafting.

> **Example:**   *Approaches to Talking About Literature*
> *text centered*
> *audience centered*
> *author centered*
> *ideologies*

Graphic Organizer

If you are a visual person, you may prefer to order your ideas with a graphic organizer. Such organizers can map your thinking in a nonlinear, more spatial display. Below is a classification chart that would work well for a paper that categorizes information. **Note:** Software such as Inspiration (www.inspiration.com) might prove helpful in creating visual outlines.

Sample:

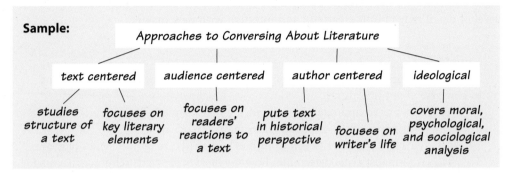

Approaches to Conversing About Literature

| text centered | audience centered | author centered | ideological |

studies structure of a text — focuses on key literary elements — focuses on readers' reactions to a text — puts text in historical perspective — focuses on writer's life — covers moral, psychological, and sociological analysis

Topic Outline

The topic outline states the thesis and then maps out main points, supporting points, and details written succinctly as phrases in parallel format. When items are parallel, they are expressed in similar grammatical form (for example, a series of noun phrases or verbal phrases). Drafting from an outline that uses brief phrases rather than full statements requires hard work to develop your thinking; nevertheless, the topic outline does set a fairly strong direction for writing.

Sample:
Thesis: Approaches for conversing about literature
   I. Text-centered approaches
      A. Also called formalist criticism
      B. Emphasis on structure of text and rules of genre
      C. Importance placed on key literary elements
   II. Audience-centered approaches
      A. Also called rhetorical or reader-response criticism
      B. Emphasis on interaction between reader and text
  III. Author-centered approaches
      A. Emphasis on writer's life
      B. Importance placed on historical perspective
      C. Connections made between texts
   IV. Ideological approaches
      A. Psychological analysis of text
      B. Myth or archetype criticism
      C. Moral criticism
      D. Sociological analysis

Formal Sentence Outline

This outline uses complete sentences not only for the thesis statement but also for all the main points and supporting points that will comprise the paper's body. In fact, the outline may include the key supporting evidence. In this way, the sentence outline lists full ideas, setting a strong direction for your drafting: specific points can function as topic sentences for sections or paragraphs of the paper. The one drawback is that this level of detail may cramp creativity and interfere with new insights.

Sample:

Thesis: Depending on their interests, readers can use four different perspectives to converse about literature.

    I. A text-centered approach focuses on the literary piece itself.
       A. This approach is often called formalist criticism.
       B. This method of criticism examines text structure and the rules of genre.
       C. A formalist critic determines how key literary elements reinforce meaning.
    II. An audience-centered approach focuses on the "transaction" between text and reader.
       A. This approach is often called rhetorical or reader-response criticism.
       B. A rhetorical critic sees the text as an activity that is different for each reader.
   III. An author-centered approach focuses on the origin of a text.
       A. An author-centered critic examines the writer's life.
       B. This method of criticism many include a historical look at a text.
       C. Connections may be made between the text and related works.
    IV. The ideological approach applies ideas from outside of literature.
       A. Some critics apply psychological theories to a literary work.
       B. Myth or archetype criticism applies anthropology and classical studies to a text.
       C. Moral criticism explores the moral dilemmas portrayed in literature.
       D. Sociological approaches include Marxist, feminist, minority, and postcolonial criticism.

Connecting Your Outline and Your Notes

Once you have developed your outline, whatever the format, you can go back to your notes and begin to "clump" material or link it to points in the outline. Depending on the note-taking method you have used, try the following techniques. (Also be careful to avoid plagiarism by identifying source material as you draft.)

- **Reorder** your notes: For electronic notes, try copy-and-paste. For notes on paper, try the old-fashioned cut-and-paste, using scissors and tape.
- **Code material** in your notes by using numbers or letters corresponding with points in your outline.
- With books, articles, and other resources, **apply post-it notes** to key pages.

Considering Drafting Strategies

With research writing, developing the first draft involves exploring your own thinking in relation to the ideas and information that you have discovered through research. Your goal is to develop and support your ideas—referring to and properly crediting sources, but not being dominated by them. Such drafting requires both creativity and care: the creativity to see connections and to trace lines of thinking, and the care to respect ideas and information that you are borrowing from sources.

Choosing a Drafting Method

Before starting your draft, choose a drafting method that makes sense for your project (its complexity, formality, etc.) and your writing style. Consider these two options (the first orderly and the second creative) or something in between:

Writing Systematically

1. Develop a detailed outline, including supporting evidence, such as the formal outline on page 000.
2. Arrange all your research notes in a precise order in relation to your outline.
3. Write methodically, following your thesis, outline, and notes. However, be open to taking your writing in an interesting new direction and modifying your outline as you write.
4. Cite sources as you draft.

Writing Freely

1. Review your working thesis and notes. Then set them aside.
2. If you need to, make a brief outline, such as the basic list on page 000.
3. Write away—get all your research-based thinking down (on the screen or on paper) without stressing about details and flow.
4. Going back to your notes as needed, explore your draft for what is valuable, develop it further, and carefully integrate and document source material.

Respecting Your Sources While Drafting

Research writing involves handling your sources with care, including during the first draft. While drafting, try to have source material at your fingertips so that you can integrate summaries, paraphrases, and quotations without disrupting the flow and energy of your drafting. Moreover, take care not to overwhelm your draft with source material. As you draft, keep the focus on your own ideas:

- Avoid strings of references and chunks of source material without your discussion, explanation, or interpretation in between.
- Don't offer entire paragraphs of material from a source with a single in-text citation at the end: when you do so, your thinking disappears.
- Be careful not to overload your draft with unexplained, complex information.
- Resist the urge to copy-and-paste big chunks from sources. Even if you document the sources, your paper will quickly become a patchwork of source material with a few stitches (your slim contribution) holding the paper together.

Drafting the Introduction

Your paper's opening is a crucial part of the whole. For this reason, some writers actually draft the introduction after they have drafted the body and developed a stronger sense of their overall message about the topic. Other writers start by drafting the introduction in order to get the paper effectively focused. Whatever method you choose, you want your opening to accomplish at least four things: (1) engage the reader, (2) establish the focus and scope of your writing, (3) set the tone and diction level, and (4) introduce your line of thinking about the topic.

Engaging Your Reader

Traditional research writing has a reputation for being boring—focused on just the facts. However, college-level writing should focus on entering and advancing a conversation on complex and intriguing issues. Your opening should reflect that engagement in a way that fits the topic, the audience, and the form of writing. To hook your reader, particularly in the first sentences, follow this advice:

Avoid bland openings. Your first words should not be flat, general, broad, awkward, drawn out, clichéd, or pompous.

Examples:

- *Society today involves people making very interesting choices about their lifestyles.*
- *Throughout history love has been in the air.*
- *There are serious problems in today's economy.*
- *In this paper, I plan to discuss an important problem for today's society, the very serious problem of how fat our children are getting because of problems with fast food, families eating on the run, unhealthy diets, and spending too much time in front of the TV or computer.*

Make your opening interesting, concrete, and specific. While the first sentences should always be pertinent to your topic (not just gimmicks to get the reader's attention), make the opening engaging through strategies like these:

- Offer a pithy, thought-provoking, or startling quotation.
- Give a problematic or controversial statement or fact from a source.
- Pose a puzzling or challenging question.
- Share an anecdote (an illustration or story) that makes the issue concrete.
- Describe an important scene, perhaps focusing on a contrast.

Examples:

- *The American art museum suffers from a multiple-personality disorder. It is a strange hybrid, both public and private in nature. . . .*
- *Antibiotics are one of modern medicine's proudest achievements. The accidental discovery that led to this achievement occurred in 1928. A scientist named Alexander Fleming noticed an unusual occurrence. . . .*

Establishing Focus and Scope

Once you have engaged your reader, you need to set a direction for your paper and, if appropriate, describe the limits of your study. To do so, consider this pattern, modifying it for your own writing purposes:

1. **Identify the topic of your research writing.** Describe the topic in a way that helps the reader recognize it and identify with it. To do so, think about the common ground you and your reader share concerning the topic: What do you both know and feel about the topic? Focus on this shared perspective.

2. **Narrow the discussion to your specific research focus.** Explain what dimension or aspect of the topic constitutes the focus of your writing. If necessary, explain what you are not examining in your paper and offer any important background information the reader needs to grasp your focus.

> *Example:*
> . . . Antibiotics have greatly enhanced the treatment of many human sicknesses caused by bacterial infections. Strep throat, sinus infection, urinary tract infection, and ear infection are all less serious now than in the past because antibiotic therapies are available. For example, while tuberculosis, pneumonia, and gastrointestinal infections, all caused by bacteria, were the three major causes of death near the beginning of the twentieth century, respiratory-tract infections were the only bacterial infection remaining in the top ten causes of death by the end of the twentieth century (Wenzel and Edmond 1961). The availability and use of antibiotics was in most part responsible for this impressive change. . . .

Establishing Your Voice

From the first words, your writing establishes a particular voice that expresses an attitude toward the topic, your reader, and yourself. That voice is created by a variety of factors: the tone (humorous, casual, serious, etc.); the level of language, from slang to formal diction; the use or avoidance of the personal pronouns *I, we,* and *you;* the simplicity or complexity of sentence syntax; the use or avoidance of contractions; and even punctuation style, from a primary use of commas and periods to a more emotional use of question marks and exclamation points to the academic use of semicolons and colons. While many of these style issues are addressed in the next chapter (pages 203-240), as you draft your introduction, focus especially on the level of your language, setting a tone appropriate for your rhetorical situation.

- **Formal English,** modeled on this sentence, is worded correctly and carefully so that the language can withstand repeated readings without seeming tiresome, sloppy, or cute.
- **Informal English** (the type of language you are reading now) sounds like one person talking to another person in a somewhat relaxed setting. It sounds comfortable and real, not affected or breezy.

Introducing Your Line of Thinking

After engaging the reader and establishing your voice and focus, you must introduce the essential thinking that will drive your paper forward. This last part of your introduction, after you have created common ground, creates a kind of cognitive dissonance. How? You introduce the question, puzzle, debatable issue, or problem at the heart of your research. Consider these strategies:

1. Choose between an inductive or deductive approach. Your instructor may require the deductive approach, in which case you need to state your thesis after identifying the issue or problem behind your research. However, if the inductive approach is acceptable, you may end your opening with the question, puzzle, or problem, using your writing itself to build toward the thesis later in the paper. The following example introduces the problem at the heart of the paper.

   Example: However, after all of this success with antibiotic use, a phenomenon called antibiotic resistance is now seriously threatening the effectiveness of antibiotic use in medicine.

2. Consider a forecasting statement. Once you have posed your question or stated your thesis, you may end your introduction with a sentence that briefly outlines the structure of your paper—the main points or issues that you will address to answer the question or support the thesis.

   Example: This study will explain the science behind antibiotic resistance, clarify why it is happening, and offer some solutions.

A Strong Opening

The opening below effectively gets the reader's attention, establishes a proper voice, creates a focus, and sets out a line of reasoning.

As recently as 150 years ago, the middle of the North American continent was a treeless prairie covered by tall grasses and populated by roaming buffalo and aboriginal peoples. When European settlers came, they called this area "the Great American Desert." Today, this desert is covered with bright green circles: fields of wheat, corn, and alfalfa made by center-pivot irrigation. As this description and the name indicates, center-pivots spray water on crops by slowing rotating around a center point. Traveling through Nebraska, for example, one might see water arcing high through the air onto the thirsty crops, making crop agriculture possible. However, where does this water come from? It has been pumped up from a body of water formed over millions of years: the Ogallala Aquifer. Studies of the Aquifer's use to irrigate farmland indicate a serious problem: the Ogallala is being overused. While the center-pivot system is partly to blame, a variety of farming practices, urban water uses, public attitudes, and government policies must change so that the Aquifer can remain a sustainable water resource keeping the Great American Desert green.

Drafting the Body: Reasoning with Evidence

The body of your paper presents the weight of your research findings in light of your best thinking. Here you support your thesis with a line of reasoning that is carefully thought out and backed up by evidence. For help, see the strategies outlined below and on the following pages.

Featuring Research in Your Discussion

The body of a paper needs to feature research findings in particular ways. Here are a few tips:

Follow your lead. If you have already drafted an opening, you have set a direction for the body, either by raising an issue, problem, or question, or by presenting a thesis. The first point in your paper's body should be a natural outgrowth of that introduction. Here are some helpful ways to follow the opening's lead:

- *Fundamental Support:* Offer a basic supporting point backed up by foundational evidence. Doing so eases the reader into your line of reasoning with something understandable and straightforward.
- *Context:* Start by explaining the background information, history, key terms, and important theories that are needed to follow and understand your discussion. Doing so creates "common ground" on which you can build your message.
- *Overview of Findings:* Start by digesting or summarizing what you discovered through research—the most important evidence; key studies published; or the main positions, points of view, interpretations, or explanations of the issue. An overview starts a dialogue that prepares the reader for your contribution to the conversation on the topic.
- *Staying the Course:* Writing that wanders loses its hold on the essay's purpose—and on the reader. Keep your thesis in mind as you draft and integrate source material: All parts of the body should clearly address that main idea.

Draw on source material. As you draft, pull in source material in a variety of ways:

- *Various Uses:* Draw on your sources when you need ideas—ideas that you either agree with or argue against, explanations that lie at the heart of your own reasoning. In addition, use authoritative source material when you need to back up your own idea with the voice of a credible expert. Most importantly, use concrete evidence from your sources to bolster your point with details.
- *Scratch Outlines:* Depending on the level of detail in your outline, you will likely make choices that you didn't foresee when you began. Use scratch outlines (informal jottings) along the way to map out particular points from your outline or to show where your new ideas may take you.
- *Points and Paragraphs:* Your past experience with writing may have led you to believe that you should have one paragraph per point in your outline. That approach is too restrictive. Instead, envision your body as a series of paragraph clusters—one cluster of paragraphs for each main point. Depending on the relative importance of points, clusters will vary in length.

The Full-Bodied Paragraph

Drafting the body means drafting body paragraphs. A typical body paragraph starts with a topic sentence that makes a point in support of your thesis, then elaborates that point with careful reasoning and detailed evidence, and finishes with a concluding sentence that reiterates and advances the idea in the topic sentence.

Sample Body Paragraph Showing Reasoning with Evidence:

Topic sentence: idea elaborating and supporting thesis.	Antibiotics are effective only against infections caused by bacteria and should never be used against infections caused by viruses. Using an antibiotic against a viral infection is like throwing water on a grease fire—water may normally put out fires but will only worsen the situation for a grease fire. In the same way, antibiotics fight infections, but they only cause the body harm when used to fight infections that are caused by viruses. Viruses cause the common cold, the flu, and most sore throats, sinus infections, coughs, and bronchitis. Yet antibiotics are commonly prescribed for these viral infections. *The New England Journal of Medicine* reports that 22.7 million kilograms (25,000 tons) of antibiotics are prescribed each year in the U.S. alone (Wenzel and Edmond 1962). Meanwhile, the CDC reports that approximately 50 percent of those prescriptions are completely unnecessary ("Antibiotic Overuse" 25). "Every year, tens of millions of prescriptions for antibiotics are written to treat viral illnesses for which these antibiotics offer no benefits," says the CDC's antimicrobial resistance director David Bell, M.D. (qtd. in Bren 30). Such misprescribing is simply bad medical practice that contributes to the problem of growing bacterial infection.

Where in the left column: "Development of idea through reasoning." and "Support of idea through reference to evidence from source material." and "Concluding statement of idea." appear as labels.

FOCUS on Research Essentials: As your writing unfolds, make sure that your thinking is sound. To that end, consider these points:

- **Supporting Ideas:** The supporting idea in your topic sentence is essentially a claim—an idea that explains or argues a point. Make sure that your claim is clearly and logically tied to your thesis.

- **Reasons:** These sentences elaborate, develop, and deepen the claim in the topic sentence. However, reasoning also functions to explain the evidence when you present it. Just remember that the evidence does not generally speak for itself: your reader is likely seeing it for the first time.

- **Evidence:** This material is foundational to your thinking—the facts, statistics, quotations, artifacts, illustrations, case studies, and more that you have gathered through research. Choose evidence that clarifies and convinces, and aim for providing a level of detail that makes your discussion concrete, clear, and convincing.

Choosing and Using Evidence

As you draft your paper, you are constantly choosing and using evidence to ground your thinking. What choices should you consider, and how should you use the evidence that you do choose? Consider these issues:

Choose evidence that fits your reasoning. Several types of evidence gathered through research can support your reasoning.

Observations and anecdotes share what people (including you) have seen, heard, smelled, touched, tasted, and experienced. Such evidence offers an "eyewitness" perspective shaped by the observer's viewpoint, which can be powerful but may also prove narrow and subjective.

> *Example:* Most of us have closets full of clothes: jeans, sweaters, khakis, T-shirts, and shoes for every occasion.

Primary-text quotations present original words from literary texts and other documents in support of your analysis. Such direct, word-for-word evidence can powerfully illustrate and focus your analysis, while also creating a shared text for your reader's own interpretation. Simply take care not to overquote.

> *Example:* Hulga blames this affliction for keeping her on the Hopewell farm, making it plain that "if it had not been for this condition, she would be far from these red hills and good country people" (O'Connor 1944).

Statistics offer concrete numbers related to your point—amounts and proportions gathered through surveys and studies, numbers often related to analysis, comparison, and prediction. If properly generated, statistics can offer scientific, measurable evidence in support of your reasoning. However, numbers don't "speak for themselves." They need to be interpreted and compared properly—not slanted or taken out of context. The numbers also need to be up-to-date, relevant, and accurate.

> *Example:* Pennsylvania spends $30 million annually in deer-related costs. Wisconsin has an estimated annual loss of $37 million for crop damage alone (Blumig).

Test or experiment results provide hard data developed through the scientific method, data that must nevertheless be carefully studied and properly interpreted. Well-designed experiments can provide strong cause-effect evidence that supports or disproves a hypothesis; they can also point effectively to practical applications and project likely outcomes. However, some tests are not well designed, are not relevant to your point, or may conflict with other tests and evidence.

> *Example:* According to the two scientists, the rats with unlimited access to the functional running wheel ran each day and gradually increased the amount of running; in addition, they started to eat less (McGovern 1-2).

Visuals provide information in graphic form—from tables presenting data in rows and columns to charts, maps, drawings, photographs, and video clips. Clearly, visual evidence allows you to powerfully convey complex information related to your point. However, when poorly or improperly done, visuals can distort the truth. For more on using and integrating visuals, see page 198.

> **Example:** This process is shown in more detail in Figure 1 below, where antibiotic resistant genes are shown (a) creating efflux "pumps" that get rid of antibiotics, (b) creating enzymes that break down antibiotics, or (c) changing the antibiotic chemically in order to make it ineffective.

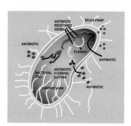

Analogies compare two things, creating clarity by drawing parallels. However, every analogy breaks down if pushed too far.

> **Example:** Look what happened in Southeast Asia with the Tsunami: 150,000 lives lost to the misnomer of all misnomers, "mother nature." Well, in Africa, 150,000 lives are lost every month, a tsunami every month. And it's a completely avoidable catastrophe. – Bono

Expert testimony offers insights from an authority on your topic and the point you are making. Experts have certification and insight based on training and experience. However, such testimony always has limits as evidence: Experts don't know it all, and they work from distinct perspectives, which means that they can disagree.

> **Example:** One specialist opposed to drilling is David Klein, a professor at the Institute of Arctic Biology at the University of Alaska-Fairbanks. Klein argues that if the oil industry opens up the ANWR for drilling, the number of caribou will likely decrease because the calving locations will change (McCarthy).

Illustrations, examples, and demonstrations support general points with specific instances, making such statements seem concrete, vivid, and observable. However, an example can be puzzling, unfamiliar, or misleading: A single case, by itself insufficient to prove a general idea or establish a trend, may deflect attention from several examples against the claim.

> **Example:** Think about how differently one can frame Rosa Parks' historic action. In prevailing myths, Parks—a holy innocent—acts almost on whim. . . . The real story is more empowering: It suggests that change is the product of deliberate, incremental action.

Predictions offer insights into possible outcomes or consequences by forecasting what might happen under certain conditions. To be plausible, prediction must be rooted in a logical analysis of the present facts.

> **Example:** While agroterrorist diseases would have little direct effect on people's health, they would be devastating to the agricultural economy, in part because of the many different diseases that could be used in an attack.

 FOCUS on Research Essentials: As you do research projects in your major, learn which forms of evidence are valued and which are generally considered suspect. Moreover, learn to think and work with the accepted types of evidence. For example, in history, primary documents, statistics, expert testimony, and illustrations may be valued forms of evidence, whereas personal anecdotes and experimental data may be less relevant or treated differently than they would be in a discipline like psychology.

Test your evidence using standards of support. Your evidence is foundational to your reasoning; if your reader questions or rejects your evidence, then your reasoning itself will collapse. For the reader to accept your evidence, it should have these qualities, like evidence presented to a jury in a court case:

- **Accurate:** Each detail is correct and precise, preferably verifiable in more than one source. The evidence is solid.
- **Authoritative:** The evidence clearly comes from a credible, reliable source, based on the identity of the author, the institutional affiliation, the publisher, and so on. The witness is reliable, so to speak.
- **Close to the original source:** At best, the evidence is your direct "report of the evidence," and hence is already filtered for your reader. However, if your evidence is two or three times removed from the original source (a report of a report of evidence), the risk of distortion increases, and the evidence becomes hearsay.
- **Current:** The evidence is reliably up-to-date, a measurement that is determined by the nature of the topic.
- **Relevant:** The evidence is clearly related to the point that you are making; the information isn't "beside the point."
- **Representative:** The evidence is actually typical of the whole body of evidence available, not an unusual anomaly that you are putting forward as the rule rather than the exception.
- **Sufficient:** The evidence you are providing is complete enough to make the point clearly and convincingly for the reader. In other words, the amount of evidence is neither too skimpy nor too extensive (overkill). The weight of evidence is compelling.

Drafting the Body: Smoothly Integrating Source Material

As you draft body paragraphs, you need to not only reason with evidence (as discussed on the previous pages) but also integrate source material properly. As you develop your first draft, track borrowed material by marking it carefully with codes, highlighting, brackets, or other symbols that will allow you to identify that material and distinguish it from your own thinking. Then, as you work with that draft, make sure that any source material is smoothly integrated and properly documented. The instruction that follows explains how to do so.

A Pattern for Integrating Sources

Source material—whether a summary, a paraphrase, or a quotation—can be pulled into your discussion in a variety of ways, depending on your need. You might start a paragraph with a strong source reference to focus on an issue, concept, or problem. Similarly, you might build a paragraph toward a source reference that clinches or summarizes your point. Generally, however, you will work source material into the middle of a paragraph, folding it into your discussion as you relate it to your own thinking. Let your ideas guide the way by using this pattern:

1. State, explain, and develop your idea, creating a context for the source.
2. Identify and introduce the source: link it to your discussion and use an attributive phrase, if appropriate.
3. Summarize, paraphrase, or quote the source, providing a citation in an appropriate spot.
4. Discuss the source by explaining, expanding, or refuting it in relation to your idea.
5. As needed in the paragraph, repeat this pattern with additional source material.
6. Finish with commentary and conclusions built on your reasoning about the source material.

Sample Passage: Note the integration pattern at work in the paragraph below.

Writer's ideas	The motivation and urgency to create and improve hybrid-electric technology comes from a range of complex forces. Some of these forces are
Attributive phrase	economic, others environmental, and still others social. In "Societal Lifestyle Costs of Cars with Alternative Fuels/Engines," Joan Ogden, Robert Williams,
Quotation	and Eric Larson argue that "[c]ontinued reliance on current transportation fuels and technologies poses serious oil supply insecurity, climate change,
Citation commentary	and urban air pollution risks" (7). Because of the nonrenewable nature of fossil fuels as well as their negative side effects, the transportation industry is confronted with making the most radical changes since the introduction of the internal-combustion automobile more than 100 years ago. Hybrid-
Conclusion	electric vehicles are one response to this pressure.

Practices for Smoothly Integrating Quotations

Working with direct quotations of source material in your writing requires special care and attention. Follow these guidelines.

Limit the number of quotations. In most research writing, restrict the amount of direct quoting you do and the size of individual quotations. Quotations should be nuggets:

- Key statements by authorities (e.g., the main point that a respected Jane Austen scholar makes about the plot dynamics of *Pride and Prejudice*).
- Well-phrased claims and conclusions (e.g., a powerful conclusion by a psychologist about the moral reasoning of adults who suffered from attachment disorder as children).
- Passages in which careful word-by-word analysis and interpretation are important to your argument (e.g., an excerpt from a speech made by a politician about support for green transportation initiatives—a passage that requires careful analysis for the between-the-lines message).

    Exception: When a primary text (a novel, a poem, a piece of legislation, a historical document) is a key piece of evidence or the actual focus of your project, careful analysis of many quoted excerpts may be necessary and expected.

Limit the length of quotations. Quotations, especially long ones, must pull their weight, so generally paraphrase or summarize source material instead, unless the material is a nugget, as described above. A paper dominated by a series of long quotations lacks the quality of conversation with sources that should characterize a thoughtful paper.

Work quotations into sentence syntax. Work quotations smoothly into your writing by paying attention to sentence syntax, style, and punctuation.

- Avoid quotations that are simply "plunked" into your writing.

    Example: For hydrogen cars to become a reality, changes to the fuel delivery system must be factored into planning. "Because fuel infrastructure changes are costly, the number of major changes made over time should be minimized" (Odgen, Williams, and Larson 25). Hydrogen fuel stations currently do not exist, so developing fuel delivery capacity will be a major undertaking.

- Work the quotation into the syntax of your sentence by using a pattern that creates emphasis and stylistic variety. Always use enough of the quotation to make your point without changing the meaning of the original, and always place quotation marks around words taken directly from the source.

    Quotation after introductory clause: According to Ogden, Williams, and Larson, "[b]ecause fuel infrastructure changes are costly, the number of major changes made over time should be minimized" (25).

Quotation after lead-in clause and colon: Odgen, Williams, and Larson explain that any development of hydrogen-fueled vehicles must include planning about fueling stations: "Because fuel infrastructure changes are costly, the number of major changes made over time should be minimized" (25). Note: The clause that leads up to the colon should be independent.

Quotation split by attributive phrase: "Because fuel infrastructure changes are costly," argue Odgen, Williams, and Larson, "the number of major changes made over time should be minimized" (25).

Quoted phrases woven into sentence: Ogden, Williams, and Larson conclude that the hydrogen fuel-cell vehicle is "a strong candidate for becoming the Car of the Future," given the trend toward "tighter environmental constraints" and the "intense efforts underway" by automakers to develop commercially viable versions of such vehicles (25).

Properly mark any necessary changes to quotations. You may shorten or change a quotation so that it fits more smoothly into your sentence—but don't alter the original meaning. Use an ellipsis within square brackets to indicate that you have omitted words from the original. An ellipsis is three periods with a space before and after each period.

Example: In their projections of where fuel-cell vehicles are heading, Ogden, Williams, and Larson discuss GM's AUTOnomy vehicle, with its "radical redesign of the entire car. [. .] In these cars steering, braking, and other vehicle systems are controlled electronically rather than mechanically" (24).

Use square brackets to indicate a clarification or to change a pronoun or verb tense or to switch around uppercase and lowercase.

Example: As Ogden, Williams, and Larson explain, "Even if such barriers [the high cost of fuel cells and the lack of an H2 fuel infrastructure] can be overcome, decades would be required before this embryonic technology could make major contributions in reducing the major externalities that characterize today's cars" (25).

FOCUS on Your Major: The discussion and examples above demonstrate how to integrate and document sources using MLA practices, the system followed predominantly in the Humanities. Note that referring to sources is handled differently from one discipline to the next. For example, in Humanities disciplines, a source reference might foreground the author's name, his or her credentials, and the source's title; conversely, a source reference in the Social or Natural Sciences might foreground the year that the study was done or published. Nevertheless, the essential principles remain the same for all systems: Clearly indicate all borrowed material, your debt to other studies. For instruction on the documentation system associated with your discipline, go to the appropriate chapter in part 3 of this text.

Guidelines for Correctly Documenting Sources

Just as you need to integrate source material carefully into your writing, you must also carefully document where that source material comes from. From your first word to your last, the reader should be able to recognize what material is yours and what facts and ideas come from other sources. The principles that follow will ensure effective documentation.

Identify clearly where source material begins. Your discussion must offer a smooth transition to source material. To achieve such a transition, follow these guidelines:

- For first references to a specific source, use an attributive statement that indicates some of the following information: the author's name and credentials, the title of the source, the nature of the study or research, and helpful background.

    Example: *Joan Ogden, Robert Williams, and Eric Larson, members of the Princeton Environmental Institute,* explain that modest improvements in energy efficiency and emissions reductions will not be enough over the next century because of anticipated transportation increases, especially in current Third World countries (7).

- For subsequent references to a source, use a simplified attributive phrase, such as the author's last name or a shortened version of the title.

    Example: *Ogden, Williams, and Larson* go on to argue that "[e]ffectively addressing environmental and oil supply concerns will probably require radical changes in automotive engine/fuel technologies" (7).

- In some situations, such as quoting straightforward facts or providing an overview of research, simply skip the attributive phrase. The parenthetical citation supplies sufficient attribution.

    Example: Various types of transportation are by far the main consumers of oil (¾ of world oil imports); moreover, these same technologies are responsible for ¼ of all greenhouse gas sources (Ogden, Williams, and Larson 7).

- The verb you use to introduce source material is a key part of the attribution. Use fitting verbs, such as those in the table on the facing page, noting how different verbs indicate a specific direction or emphasis (e.g., informing, arguing). Normally, use attributive verbs in the present tense (called the historical present in this context). Use the past tense only when you want to stress the actual time frame of a source.

    Example: In their 2004 study, "Societal Lifecycle Costs of Cars with Alternative Fuels/Engines," Ogden, Williams, and Larson *present* a method for comparing and contrasting alternatives to the traditional internal-combustion engine. In an earlier study, these authors *had made* preliminary steps toward this analysis. . . .

Sample Attributive Verbs—Beyond "Says": Verbs indicating how the source. . .

Informs		Analyzes		Persuades	
adds	lists	believes	hypothesizes	accepts	disagrees
confirms	outlines	cautions	interprets	acknowledges	insists
declares	points out	compares	shows	affirms	maintains
discusses	responds	concludes	speculates	argues	praises
enumerates	shares	considers	stresses	asserts	proposes
emphasizes	states	contrasts	studies	claims	proves
highlights	suggests	describes	supports	contradicts	refutes
identifies	summarizes	explains	verifies	criticizes	rejects
				defends	urges
				denies	warns

Indicate where source material ends. Closing quotation marks and a citation, as shown below, indicate the end of a source quotation. Generally, place the citation immediately after a quotation, paraphrase, or summary. However, you may also place the citation early in the sentence or at the end if the parenthetical note is obviously obtrusive. When you discuss several facts or quotations from a page in a source, use an attributive phrase at the beginning of your discussion and a single citation at the end.

> *Example:* As the "Lifestyle Costs" study concludes, when greenhouse gases, air pollution, and oil insecurity are factored into the analysis, alternative-fuel vehicles "offer lower LCCs than typical new cars" (Ogden, Williams, and Larson 25).

Set off longer quotations. If a quotation is longer than four typed lines, set it off from the main text following these guidelines: Generally, introduce the quotation with a complete sentence and a colon. Indent the whole quotation one inch (10 spaces) and double-space it, but don't put quotation marks around it. Put the parenthetical citation outside the final punctuation mark.

> *Example:* Toward the end of the study, Ogden, Williams, and Larson argue that changes to the fuel delivery and filling system must be factored into planning:
>
> > Because fuel infrastructure changes are costly, the number of major changes made over time should be minimized. The bifurcated strategy advanced here—of focusing on the H2 FCV for the long term and advanced liquid hydrocarbon-fueled ICEVs and ICE/HEVs for the near term—would reduce the number of such infrastructure changes to one (an eventual shift to H2). (25)

 FOCUS on Your Project: As you draft, test each body paragraph.

____ The paragraph effectively follows or varies from this pattern: topic sentence, reasoning, presentation of evidence, concluding sentence.

____ The points, reasoning, and evidence are logically linked to the thesis.

____ The variety of evidence used is accurate, close to the original source, authoritative, sufficient, representative, relevant, and current.

____ Material from sources is smoothly integrated and properly documented.

Drafting the Conclusion

If your opening invites the reader into the world of your paper, the closing does the opposite: it helps the reader exit that world with the substance of your discussion in hand. As such, closing paragraphs can be important for tying up loose ends, clarifying key points, or signing off with the reader. In a sense, the entire paper is preparation for an effective ending that helps the reader reconsider the discussion with new understanding and deeper appreciation. The conclusion might even offer the reader fresh food for thought. To draft such a strong conclusion, consider the strategies that follow.

FOCUS on Research Essentials: As with your opening, you want to put special effort into your conclusion. Don't just dash it off in a state of writing fatigue and use it—your first and only effort. Follow this advice to get your closing right:

- Draft a variety of possible endings. Choose the one that flows best from the whole.

- If you are having trouble expressing your conclusion, go back to your thesis. Strengthening a weak or unclear thesis can help you develop a satisfactory ending.

- Make your conclusion (1) flow naturally from the last body paragraph; (2) match the paper's tone, style, voice, and language level; and (3) fit proportionately with the paper, neither too abrupt nor drawn out.

- Avoid endings that begin weakly, with phrases such as "In conclusion," "To conclude," "In short," "In summary," or "This discussion has shown."

Deepen Your Thesis

Whether you have worked inductively or deductively, the closing is the place where you deepen the essential idea of your paper—the thesis. If the paper is fairly long and the thinking complex, the reader may need clarification and reminders of how you have fulfilled the promises and the plan that you laid out in your opening. Consider these strategies:

1. **Remind the reader.** Recall what you set out to do; check off the key points you've covered; or answer any questions left unanswered. In other words, summarize your main research findings.

2. **Rephrase and solidify your thesis.** If you offered your thesis in the introduction, restate it now in fresh language that reflects the most important support you have given. If possible, sharpen the thinking offered in the opening thesis statement.

    Example: It is time to think about future generations. To do the right thing with the Ogallala Aquifer, the nation must uphold the standard of conservation—the sustainable use of Ogallala water. The survival of this amazing underground sponge, as well as the farms and towns of the Great American Desert, depends on it.

Complete and Unify Your Discussion

Your ending is your last opportunity to refocus, unify, and otherwise reinforce your message. Moreover, the conclusion is your final chance to convince a reluctant reader to accept your analysis or embrace your argument. Consider these strategies:

1. **Show the implications of your thesis.** Simply put, why should your reader care about your central idea? Why does it matter in terms of understanding the issue, changing oneself and the world, making choices, and so on? What are the benefits of accepting or applying the idea? What does it add to the dialogue on the topic? Try to express some of these implications after restating your thesis.

2. **Return to your opening.** If you began with a quotation, an anecdote, or a description, remind the reader of that opening and elaborate it in terms of your paper's message.

3. **Point forward or outward.** With your specific issue now fully discussed, locate the issue within its larger context or explore connections between it and other issues. Similarly, predict where the issue is going next, or outline possibilities for additional or related research.

4. **Save the best for last.** In order to finish strong, consider setting aside an especially thought-provoking statement, a quotation, or an anecdote for your conclusion. Doing so might clinch your analysis or argument, or it might leave your reader with provocative food for thought.

A Strong Conclusion

The conclusion below shows commitment to the paper's main idea by restating that idea and elaborating its significance.

> Art museums that have long suffered from their public-private hybrid nature may now take advantage of it. As the Brooklyn Museum controversy has shown, museums are best able to serve a broad audience if they are allowed to take risks and invite private sponsorship. While the risk for controversy increases as audiences expand, the very growth in attendance confers legitimacy upon the museum enterprise. Private dollars and public interests need not be at odds, as both parties reap the benefits of more programs and more diverse exhibitions. If museums are careful to choose their offerings based on aesthetic considerations rather than on mere profit-making concerns, private commercial involvement may prove to be a public blessing.

FOCUS on Your Project: As you prepare to draft your conclusion, review your introduction, read through the body, and scan your research notes. Ask yourself what you have left to say or what you still need to say about the issue. Once you have drafted the ending, check it.

____The ending effectively restates but deepens my original thinking.

____The conclusion effectively summarizes my paper's discussion.

____The closing points toward the discussion's larger implications.

Drafting the Title

At any point during the research and writing process, you may want to jot down possible titles for your paper, titles that capture your focused topic, the central issue or problem, your discoveries, and your main idea. As you complete a first draft of your paper, the time is right to review possible title choices.

The Purpose of the Title

What exactly do you want the title to accomplish? That depends on the type of writing you are doing—whether, for example, the paper is an informal personal essay, a magazine article, a blog, a Web site, or a traditional academic paper. For more informal writing, your title can be fairly brief and imaginative—"The Stream in the Ravine," "Scab!," or "Three Family Cancers." However, titles for academic papers should more often follow these principles:

Establish an engaging focus. Your title is the first place to engage your reader's attention and indicate your paper's essential issue. Avoid broad, vague, boring, or farfetched titles—titles that simply indicate the assignment, a broad subject, or the literary work you are researching. Note: No title or an unfocused title often indicates no thinking or unfocused thinking in the paper—at least, that's the message sent to the reader!

Above all, be precise. While a title should be concise, it need not be brief. It is more important that the title be clear and accurate. Your title is your first opportunity to locate or situate your research study within the larger conversation on this topic. Therefore, your title should contain the key words that your reader may be looking for, the terms plugged into the reader's mental or digital search engine.

Weak titles:	**A strong title:**
History Research Paper	Our Roots Go Back to Roanoke:
The Novel *Pride and Prejudice*	Investigating the Link between
Attachment Disorder	the Lost Colony and the Lumbee
Hybrid-Electric Vehicles	People of North Carolina

Patterns for Academic Titles

With the principles above in mind, you can develop a title according to these patterns:

The main topic + your specific type of study and/or focus

> *Examples:* The Threat of Antibiotic Resistance
> An Apology for the Life of Ms. Barbie D. Doll
> Economic Disparities Fuel Human Trafficking

The main topic or theme + a colon + a subtopic, focus, or question

> *Examples:* An American Hybrid: The Art Museum as Public-Private Institution
> The Ogallala: Preserving the Oasis of the Great American Desert
> Guy Vanderhaeghe's *The Englishman's Boy:* Cross-Border Encounters

Focus on Multimedia: Using and Integrating Visuals

In a digital culture, complementing and connecting research writing with visual information is possible for most research projects. While traditional research papers may still communicate very well through text alone, many research papers and certainly other forms of research writing (e.g., wikis, poster sessions, presentations, and Web sites) can effectively mesh words and images to powerfully communicate research findings. That's because visuals "picture" information so that the reader can see relationships (like percentages of data), qualities (like shapes), and appearances (like facial expressions). Should you use visuals in your research writing? Decide by reviewing the discussion and instruction that follows.

Uses of Visuals in Your Research Writing

When should you use visuals? Obviously, if the assignment and the writing form restrict their use, you need to respect those limits. However, research writing benefits from visuals when they are used to do the following:

- Make information readable—mapping out relationships between details
- Clarify complex ideas—"showing" in support of your "telling"
- Focus your analysis—"picturing" what you are carefully studying in your written message (e.g., a painting, a film shot, data from an experiment)
- Dramatize important points—developing sight impact for your ideas
- Condense information—letting an image save a thousand words
- Add persuasive energy—supplementing an argument with multimedia evidence

Planning Visuals for Your Paper

To effectively integrate visuals into your research writing, first plan the "visual story" of your paper and then address presentation issues.

Map out your paper's visual story. Given your topic and line of reasoning, where and how might visuals contribute to your discussion? What mix of writing and visuals should you use—primarily writing, primarily visuals, or a balance of the two? In what order should visuals appear? Will later visuals build on earlier ones?

Effectively relate written text to visuals. Connect words and images by following these two principles:

- *Placement:* Consider the size and importance of visuals when deciding where to place them. Place a small visual on the same page as the written reference, a large visual on a facing page or the following page.
- *Discussion:* Unless the visual is essentially separate from the verbal text (e.g., a thematic photo for a Web page), discuss the visual directly. To lead in to your discussion, explain key ideas that the visual shows. Then refer to the visual by noting its number, title, and location in your paper. Finally, comment on the visual to help the reader understand the information.

Parts of a Visual

While each type of visual has its own guidelines and features, all visuals share some common elements, especially when they appear in academic research writing. Study the visual below and review the discussion of its parts: title, body, and caption.

The Title: Each visual needs a descriptive title that clearly indicates its topic and purpose. If a document contains more than one visual, each visual should be numbered as well. Organize tables in a set called "tables" (Table 5), and place graphs, charts, and images in a second set called "figures" (Figure 3).

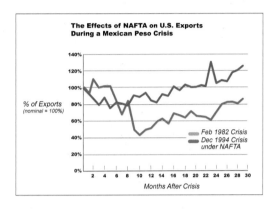

The Effects of NAFTA on U.S. Exports During a Mexican Peso Crisis

 FOCUS on Your Major: The different academic paper styles offer different guidelines about where to place and how to punctuate and present visual numbers and titles. See part 3 of this text for details.

The Body: Provide what is needed for the type of visual: columns, rows, bars, lines, arrows, boxes, and so on. For clarity, include labels (written horizontally whenever possible), numbers and units of measurement, and a legend for symbols and colors.

Note or Caption: To explain information in the visual and to connect it to the text around it, provide a footnote or caption. The caption should be brief and clear, helping the reader understand the significance of the visual.

 FOCUS on Research Ethics: While visuals and other media offer distinct benefits, use them carefully in your research writing.

- Generally avoid filling academic writing with flashy, merely decorative visuals. Use quality visuals.
- Avoid filling visuals themselves with "chartjunk"—flashy but useless features.
- Don't create or use visuals that distort and hence falsify ideas.
- Get permission to use a visual created by someone else, particularly if your document has a nonacademic purpose.
- Acknowledge a borrowed visual with *Source:*, *Adapted from:*, or *Used with permission of.* As with borrowed text, credit visuals to avoid plagiarism.

Types of Visuals

What types of visuals will best support your research writing? Answer this question by considering these issues:

- Who are your readers, and what visual support do they need?
- What kinds of visuals will illuminate the topic?
- What types of visuals are used in your sources? How?
- What types of visuals are used in the discipline? How?

To select visuals, first note that traditionally visuals are divided into two categories: tables (numerical and text) and figures (graphs, charts, and images). Then review the specific types of visuals described below.

Tables arrange data in a grid of rows and columns to show the intersection of two factors. Each slot in the grid contains data where two factors intersect (for example, type of trip and the number of days taken). Use tables when you want to categorize data for easy comparison of several factors; provide many exact figures in a compact, readable format; or present raw data that are the foundation of later line, bar, or pie graphs.

Numerical Tables: provide amounts, dollars, percentages, and so on.

Text Tables: use words, not numbers.

Types of Weekend Trips in the United States in 2004			
	Length of Trip		
Type of Trip	**1–2 Nights**	**3–5 Nights**	**Total**
Number			
Total trips	252,581	188,804	441,385
Business	32,358	33,172	65,530
Pleasure	186,219	134,659	320,878,
Visit friends and relatives	104,438	74,151	178,589,
Leisure	81,781	60,508	142,289
Personal Business	34,004	20,970	54,974
Percent			
Number	100.0	100.0	100.0
Total trips	12.8	17.6	14.8
Business	73.7	71.3	72.7
Pleasure	41.3	39.3	40.5
Visit friends and relatives	32.4	32.0	32.2
Leisure	13.5	11.1	12.5
Personal Business			

Conjunctions			
Coordinating		**Correlative**	**Subordinating**
and	for	both/and	after	than
but	so	either/or	although, though,	that, so that
or	yet	neither/nor	as, as if	unless
nor		not only/but also	because, since	until
		whether/or	before	when, whenever
			if	where, whereas

Graphs show relationships between numbers—differences, proportions, or trends. When properly designed (without distortion), graphs can clearly portray complex ideas, from patterns in U.S. immigration for the past 50 years to the proportion of the student body in each major at your school this year.

- Line graphs reveal trends by showing changes in quantity over time.
- Bar graphs compare amounts by using a series of vertical or horizontal bars.
- Pie graphs divide a whole quantity (a circle or "pie") into parts ("pie wedges") to show proportions.

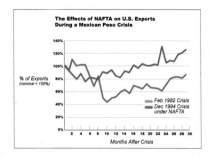

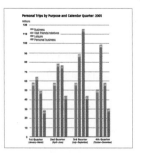

Charts show relationships between parts, steps, or stages. In other words, charts are useful for showing at a glance how something is structured or how a process works.

■ Organizational charts picture structures and relationships within a group.

■ Flowcharts map out steps in a process.

■ Gantt charts provide an overview of project tasks and phases.

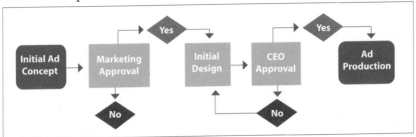

Images visualize places, objects, or people. By stressing certain details, these images help the reader understand ideas, see concepts concretely, and organize information.

■ Maps present information oriented on geography: communication and transportation links, distances, directions, regions, zones, natural and urban features, and so on.

■ Photographs and other visual images can provide a wealth of vivid, informative details. Traditional photographs, black-and-white or color, show the surface appearance of what's pictured—from people to objects to landscapes. Other photographic technologies can show external and internal images: infrared pictures, X-rays, ultrasounds, CAT scans, 2-D and 3-D computer-generated images, and so on.

■ Line drawings present simplified images of objects, images that screen out unnecessary details.

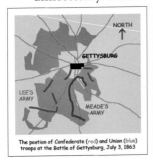

The position of Confederate (red) and Union (blue) troops at the Battle of Gettysburg, July 3, 1863

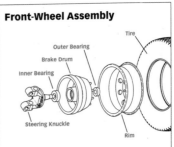

Front-Wheel Assembly

Sebranek inc.

Note: This discussion of visuals can be applied to other media useful for research projects—video clips, audio clips, and so on. For more instruction on using multimedia in your research writing, visit our Web site at www.theresearchwriter.com. Other useful sites are listed here:

■ www.writersatwork.us/

■ labwrite.ncsu.edu/www/res/gh/gh-bargraph.html

■ writing.colostate.edu/guides

Practicing Your Research

1. **Explore:** Think about your past writing practices. How productively have you used the whole writing process outlined on page 167? What organizational patterns have you used in past projects? Have you relied exclusively on the "high school hamburger," the five-paragraph essay? What types of outlines do you typically create before drafting? With these questions and the chapter content in mind, identify three strategies that will improve your organizing and drafting habits.

2. **Apply:** Develop a formal sentence outline for an article or book chapter that you used as a source. What organizational patterns has the writer used? What other patterns might he or she have chosen?

3. **Collaborate on a Case Study:** As directed by your instructor, continue work with classmates on your clothing-focused project. After reviewing your project's rhetorical situation and the notes you have generated as a group, discuss and debate the key discoveries you have made, agree upon a main idea, and plan your paper's sections. Then assign group members to draft sections, leaving the introduction and conclusion until the body is drafted.

4. **Focus on Your Major:** Through reading, studying assignments, talking with other students, and asking instructors, discover what forms of research writing are done in your discipline. Study those forms carefully to determine (a) the typical organizational patterns used in those papers and (b) the patterns of reasoning and evidence valued.

5. **Focus on Your Current Project:** Advance your current research project by making the transition from research to writing. Liberally use the strategies in this chapter, from reviewing your research rhetoric to integrating visuals. As you do so, refer to the checklist below.

Checklist:

Prior to drafting, I have

- ☑ reviewed the rhetorical situation to keep on track.
- ☑ reviewed my research findings and sharpened my working thesis.
- ☑ explored methods of organization that might work for my paper.
- ☑ developed an outline that fits with my writing habits, relates my thinking and my notes, and effectively prepares me to write my first draft.

Following these preparatory tasks, I

- ☑ drafted an introduction that engages the reader, establishes my voice, establishes the focus and scope of my paper, and introduces my line of thinking.
- ☑ drafted the body so as to reason with the evidence and smoothly integrate and document source material.
- ☑ drafted a conclusion that deepens my thesis and completes my discussion.
- ☑ drafted a working title that creates an engaging focus but is precise.
- ☑ effectively chose and integrated needed visuals into my paper.

© Cengage Learning/Illustrated by Chris Krenzke

Revising and Refining Your Research Paper

9

Q What do you normally do with your research writing once you have completed a first draft? What makes for effective revising, editing, and proofreading? Why does this work matter?

Once you've completed a first draft of your paper, you might be tempted just to turn it in. After all, you may need a break, or you may have other pressing projects to get at. But giving in to this submit-the-first-draft temptation would be a mistake because that draft likely contains mistakes—a variety of problems that can be fixed with time and effort.

Aside from getting a better grade, why expend that time and effort? First, revising, editing, and proofreading allow you to cook the raw thinking of your first draft. Second, reworking your writing allows you to strengthen what you are saying by improving how you are saying it: style becomes central to expressing your thinking, not just an adornment to it. Finally, this refining work quite simply shows respect for your readers. You want to have a positive conversation with your readers when you submit, post, or publish your writing: strengthening your first draft so that the thinking is sound, the organization strong, the style engaging, and the prose correct helps you start a quality conversation with your readers.

Doris Lessing has said of the writing process that "the more a thing cooks, the better." This chapter offers you some key cooking lessons for your research writing. (lessons rooted, once again, in the seven traits of effective research writing outlined on pages 8-12).

What's Ahead?

Practical Strategies for Improving Your First Draft

How do you move your writing from a rough first draft to a polished final draft? For starters, you can use the practical strategies described below.

Break Down Revising and Refining into Manageable Steps

Improving your first draft involves reworking it several times, with each review focusing on different issues so as to progressively strengthen the paper. Here is a recommended process, which you can adjust to your own practices and projects:

1 **Revising:** Begin by strengthening global issues in your first draft—the quality and clarity of your ideas and your support for those ideas; the organization or line of reasoning in your draft; and the overall tone or voice. At this stage, you cut, condense, expand, and add material. By addressing these whole-paper issues first, you can edit and proofread more efficiently later. After all, what's the point of carefully editing a passage for style and grammar when in the end, you cut the passage?

> *Timing Tip:* Leave forty-eight hours or more between completing your first draft and working on revision. That time allows you a fresh view of your draft.

2 **Editing:** Once you are fairly confident about the global traits of ideas, organization, and voice, begin strengthening sentence style and word choice. At this stage, your aim is to make your writing clear, concise, energetic, and varied. Because your attention is focused more locally or microscopically on your writing, you can also fix obvious errors, though that task is really the focus of the next phase, proofreading.

> *Timing Tip:* Between revising your paper and editing it, leave at least 24 hours. Again, this time lapse allows your brain to get ready for a different kind of writing task and to come to the revised draft fresh.

3 **Proofreading:** This phase focuses on correctness—accuracy of information and research references; and correct grammar, punctuation, mechanics, usage, and spelling. At this stage, your goal is to make your already edited writing clean.

> *Timing Tip:* Again, leave about 24 hours between editing and proofreading, if possible. Moreover, because proofreading takes focused attention at the local level of your writing, do it for relatively short periods, rewarding yourself with breaks.

 FOCUS on Research Essentials: The process outlined above breaks down strengthening your first draft into distinct phases and different rewriting activities. In actual practice, you might find the process more fluid, with revising, editing, and proofreading activities happening simultaneously or woven together more organically. However you work through this process, remember to save multiple drafts of your paper: doing so creates a record of important changes that you may need to retrieve and revise.

Review Your Draft from Multiple Points of View

Part of effectively reworking your first draft is learning to look at it from multiple perspectives. Each fresh view creates an opportunity to freshen your thinking, your organization, your style, and more. Here are some choices:

Work with your draft on screen. Reading print on screen is generally more difficult than reading print on paper; however, on-screen review of your draft offers you tremendous power and flexibility. You can revise and edit by cutting and pasting large chunks of prose, quickly reworking passages, and freely testing different phrasings and word choices to see which ones work best. Try strategies like these:

- Enlarge the view of your writing using the zoom function.
- Reformat the paper temporarily by increasing line spacing or placing paragraphs on separate pages.
- Use highlighting or a different font color to distinguish source material.

Work with your draft printed on paper. At some point in your reworking of the draft, you need to see your words in physical print on the page, to feel the "weight" of your writing. Practically speaking, the printed page is easier to read than words on a screen. In addition, working on paper allows the power for change to flow from your mind through your pencil onto the page—a dynamic quite different from working with a keyboard. When working with a print copy, try strategies like these:

- Reformat the paper to increase type size, margins, and line spacing—creating "white space" to see your writing and to write in changes.
- As you read the paper, carry on a kind of conversation with it. In the margins and between the lines, note what seems confusing, incomplete, or misplaced.

Work with the oral version of your paper. Simply put, read your paper aloud or have someone else read it aloud, and consider recording either event. Hearing your words will help you identify where your thinking stumbles, your writing voice falters, your sentence style falls flat, or your grammar breaks down.

 FOCUS on Research Essentials: A crucial strategy for improving your paper is peer review—either with a classmate or in your school's writing center. This process mirrors the process of peer review that happens in the world of academic research writing. See page 276 for a full discussion of peer review.

Use Your Software's Editing Tools as an Aid

Your writing software likely has several helpful tools: spell check, grammar check, a thesaurus for finding synonyms, find-and-replace functions, a "track changes" tool, split screens for placing two pieces of writing side by side on the screen, document mapping, and so on. The key is to use these tools wisely while not relying on them exclusively. For example, spell check will not catch usage errors such as *it's* versus *its*. In the end, you need to manage the rewriting process, including your writing tools.

Revising in Action: Fixing Global Issues

The example below shows revising in action. After setting aside her draft for a few days, the student writer carefully looked at global issues—her ideas, the paper's organization, and her voice. She wrote notes to herself to record her ideas for revision.

Stevie's revision notes:

I need to give my opening more energy and concrete detail—a bit abstract now.

What's weird? Clarify/ offer thesis as precise questions.

This historical overview delays look at pop culture— the real focus of my paper. Move this paragraph down.

Make this topic sentence more precise—flat, basic idea here.

Consider these last, pre-execution meals. . . .

Death Row and the Popular Media

∧Executions historically are associated with a certain degree of morbid curiosity. The last meals of the condemned seem especially to stimulate heightened interest. A prisoner's final feast has almost become an event in its own right. This is true for the prisoner. But also true for the prison staff and the public. The media talk about last meals real and imagined. When confronted with the ultimate consumption of dying people in so many areas of our popular media, the truth becomes alarmingly clear:⟨This is really weird!⟩ *? There's got to be some reason* ∧*that we. . .*

For a long time Americans have been fascinated with not just execution, but the ritual of a condemned criminal's last day. They would turn up for all the proceedings and rituals, not just the actual execution, and the public loved, just loved to read all the morbid details. In fact, publishers would make up last words even if the convict didn't say anything (source: Atwell 8). Whhile the death penaly gradually got less popular people would still get into the spectacle of it all wherever and whenever it happened. It seems that the death penalty remained most popular in the South for a long time: theres lots of reporting the last days of convicts in gross detail. *almost every major arena of Public entertainment*

The last meal appears in ~~pop culture~~ ∧ In The Green Mile, a motion picture based on Stephen King's novel of the same name protagonist John Coffey is wrongfully executed in a heartbreaking, dramatic seen, but not before careful thought about his last meal: "Meatloaf be nice. Mashed taters with gravy. Okra, maybe. I's not picky. Prisoners are also served their last meals on the small screen, take for example FOX's network tv show, Prison Break, in which Lincoln Burrows is served his

Editing in Action: Fixing Local Issues

Once the student writer had revised her draft for global issues, she began editing the paper for local issues of style and correctness. Some of her editing is shown below.

The writer revises her title.

"I Did Not Get My Spaghetti-O's":
Death Row ~~and~~ the Popular Media
Jesus Christ: roast lamb. . . . ^Consumption in
~~Consider these last, pre-execution meals:~~ Perry Smith and Richard

She tightens her opening paragraph into a surprising list.

Hickock ~~had~~ identical meals of shrimp, french fries, garlic bread, ice
cream and strawberries with whipped cream. ; 1965 (In The Sopranos, Tony
Soprano ~~had~~ Holsten's onion rings. ; 2007 ~~In 2001,~~ Timothy McVeigh had two

pints of Ben & Jerry's mint chocolate chip ice cream. Karl Chamberlein:

final meal yet to be consumed; 15 days from now.

She rewrites and combines some choppy sentences, adding transitions where needed.

While
^Executions historically are associated with a certain degree of

morbid curiosity. The last meals of the condemned seem especially to
Indeed,
stimulate heightened interest. ^A prisoner's final feast has almost become
, not only
an event in its own right. ~~This is true~~ for the prisoner. But also ~~true~~ for
Web sites, novels, movies, television shows, newspapers, and even
the prison staff and the public. ~~The media talk about~~ last meals real
cookbooks report , dissent, criticize, speculate regarding
and imagined. When confronted with the ultimate consumption of

She adds words to make her points clear, precise, and energetic.

dying people in so many areas of our popular media, the truth becomes
odd behavior   must
alarmingly clear: This is ~~really weird!~~ There's ~~got to~~ be some reason that
to choose and enjoy their final meal before execution   there must
we institutionally allow these prisoners ~~one last meal~~, and ~~their has got~~
like to watch and reproduce the event in popular culture.
be some reason that we ~~are obsessive about it in our society~~

She corrects all spelling, grammar, punctuation, and mechanics errors.

The last meal appears in almost every major arena of public

entertainment. In The Green Mile, a motion picture based on Stephen

King's novel of the same name, protagonist John Coffey is wrongfully
scene
executed in a heartbreaking, dramatic ~~seen~~, but not before careful thought

about his last meal: "Meatloaf be nice. Mashed taters with gravy. Okra,
"
maybe. I's not picky. Prisoners are also served their last meals on the small

screen, take for example FOX's network tv show, Prison Break, in which

Lincoln Burrows is served his last blueberry pancakes. In fact, on

Testing Your Ideas and Organization

To test your paper's thinking and structure, you need to approach your draft with the critical eyes of a reader. How will your readers react to your ideas—with understanding or confusion, with agreement or rejection? Does your line of reasoning establish a clear path for readers to follow, or might they get lost in the thickets of your thinking? The strategies that follow will help you identify writing weaknesses.

Improving Your Reasoning

Is your thinking sound? Does it work? Does your writing encourage readers to think thoroughly and deeply about your topic? Test your thinking in these ways:

Test the strength of your essential thinking. To get a sense of how well your overall thinking works, highlight your initial thesis statement and your restatement of the thesis in your conclusion. Then also highlight the main points along the way from thesis statement A to thesis statement B: these points are likely featured in your paragraphs' topic sentences. Do the thesis statements relate well to each other? Is the line of reasoning from A to B solid, or are there weak links that need repair? Is your thinking logical and convincing from start to finish? Moreover, does your thinking have an energy or urgency to it: Are reasons that your ideas are important clearly stated or implied? Have you answered your readers' questions: Why do these ideas matter? Why should we care about them?

Test the balance of reasoning and support. Examine the big picture of how you have used source material in relation to your own discussion of the issue. Highlight all source material in your draft and weigh that material against your own thinking. If your draft includes claims that lack needed support you need to either scale back the claims or add information and evidence.

Conversely, your draft may be dominated by source material, not your own thinking. If your paper reads like a series of source summaries or loosely stitched together quotations, if it contains big patches of copy-and-paste material, if your paragraphs all seem to start and end with source material, or if your writing is dense with detailed but almost incomprehensible data, deepen your own contribution to the paper by trying the following:

1. **Expand your discussion.** Before diving into source material within a paragraph or section of your paper, flesh out your thinking more fully. Offer reasoning that elaborates the claim and effectively leads into the evidence.

2. **Elaborate the evidence.** As you present evidence from source material, build on it by explaining what it means. Evidence doesn't typically speak for itself: through analysis, synthesis, illustration, contrast, etc., you need to show how or why your sources advance your thesis.

3. **Clarify the significance.** After you have presented evidence that elaborates and supports your idea, extend your thoughts by answering the reader's "So what?" or "Why does this matter?"

Test your evidence. Review your draft by examining how well your researched information elaborates and backs up your points or claims. Will readers accept your sources and how you use them, or will they question your evidence? That evidence should be solid enough to encourage readers to accept your ideas; conversely, weak evidence will lead readers to reject your analysis or argument. As discussed in chapter 8 on page 189, your evidence should meet these seven criteria: (1) accurate, (2) authoritative, (3) close to the original source, (4) current, (5) relevant, (6) representative, and (7) sufficient.

Test the warrants connecting your reasoning and evidence. To make sense, the elements of an analysis or argument must connect logically. In other words, each point you make should be logically linked to its supporting evidence, just as each point that you make should be logically linked to other points in the development of your thinking. In formal logic, these links or connections are called *warrants*—the often unspoken principles or assumptions that lie behind reasoning. If the warrants are valid, the elements hold together to create one unified line of reasoning. However, if the warrants are faulty, the analysis or argument falls apart.

For example, read the two-sentence argument below, which is built out of a claim, supporting evidence, and understood (but unstated) warrants connecting the two. The question is, which of the warrants are valid and which weak?

Argument: Emeryville should immediately shut down its public swimming pools (claim). The reservoir is thirty-four feet below normal, and DNR officer Ted Licken said that if current trends continue, the reservoir will be empty in two years (evidence).

Unstated Warrants or Assumptions:
- It is not good for the reservoir to be empty.
- The swimming pools draw significant amounts of water from the reservoir.
- Emptying the pools would help raise the level of the reservoir.
- No other action would better prevent the reservoir from emptying.
- It is worse to have an empty reservoir than an empty swimming pool.

Test for plagiarism. Going back to your notes and sources as needed, check that you have clearly indicated what material in your draft is summarized, paraphrased, or quoted from a source. In particular, check that your attributive phrases and citations set off all source material except that which is common knowledge. (For more help, see pages 190-194.)

FOCUS on Research Essentials: If you find major weaknesses in your thinking—in the content of your draft—you may need to step back rather than move forward toward editing. At the very least, you might have to go back to your research notes to locate more food for thought. More seriously, you may have to do more research.

Eliminating Logical Fallacies

Logical fallacies are false arguments: bits of fuzzy, misleading, or incomplete thinking. You might recognize fallacies in advertising, political debates, editorials, talk-show discussions, and blogs—in fact, in any writing in which people are analyzing an issue or constructing an argument. These fallacies, then, may also be present in your own writing. Examine your draft to weed out fallacies like those below.

Distorting the Issue. This type of fallacy falsifies an analysis or argument by twisting the logical framework. For example, your writing might make a *bare assertion,* a claim that "That's just how it is," regardless of any evidence. You might be guilty of *oversimplification,* claiming that "It's a simple question of. . . ." when the issue is more complex. Or you might *beg the question,* i.e., offer circular reasoning by assuming in your discussion the point that you need to prove. Similarly, you might exaggerate or misrepresent an opposing position, setting it up as a *straw man* to knock down; or you might ignore a fundamental or basic question by posing a *complex question.* Here is another distorting-the-issue fallacy to remove from your writing:

- **Either/Or Thinking:** Also known as black-and-white thinking, this fallacy reduces all options to two extremes. Frequently, the fallacy evolves from a clear bias.

  > Either this community develops light-rail transportation or the community will not grow in the future. (**Objection:** The claim ignores the possibility that growth may occur through other means.)

Sabotaging the Argument. These fallacies falsify the argument by twisting it. They replace reason with something hollow or misleading. For example, you might derail your discussion with *misused humor,* humor that distracts or mocks rather than contributes to the point. Or you might *appeal to pity* (a misleading tug at the heartstrings), *popular sentiment* (associating your claim with something popularly loved, like Mom and apple pie), or *bandwagon mentality* (asserting that majority support makes something true). Even more seriously, your writing might rely upon *threats,* often implied, that if the reader doesn't agree with your claim, grim consequences will follow; in some writing, this fallacy might be called fear-mongering. Here is another such fallacy:

- **Red Herring:** This strange term comes from the practice of dragging a stinky fish across a trail to throw tracking dogs off the scent. If you present a volatile idea that pulls readers away from the real issue, readers become distracted. Suppose you are addressing drilling for oil in the Arctic National Wildlife Refuge (ANWR) of Alaska, and you made this statement:

  > In 1989, the infamous oil spill of the Exxon Valdez led to massive animal deaths and enormous environmental degradation of the coastline. Drilling in the ANWR could be disastrous. (**Objection:** Introducing this notorious oil spill distracts from the real issue—how oil drilling will impact the ANWR.)

Drawing Faulty Conclusions from the Evidence. This group of fallacies falsifies an analysis or argument by short-circuiting proper logic in favor of assumptions or faulty thinking. You might, for example, construct a slippery slope argument, stating that a single step will start an unstoppable chain of events. Or you appeal to ignorance, suggesting that because no one has proven a particular claim, it must be false; or, because no one has disproved a claim, it must be true. By doing so, you unfairly shift the burden of proof onto someone else, not yourself as the writer. Here are two more such fallacies:

- **Hasty or Broad Generalization:** Such a claim is based on too little evidence or allows no exceptions. In jumping to a conclusion, you may use intensifiers such as *all, every,* or *never,* or phrases such as *everywhere in today's society.*

   > Today's voters spend too little time reading and too much time being taken in by 30-second sound bites and YouTube videos. (**Objection:** Some voters may spend too little time reading about the issues, but it is unfair to claim this of everyone.)

- **False Cause:** This fallacy confuses sequence with causation: If *A* comes before *B*, *A* must have caused *B*. But *A* may be one of several causes, or *A* and *B* may be only loosely related, or the connection between *A* and *B* may be coincidental.

   > Since that new school opened, drug use among young people has skyrocketed. Better that the school had never been built.

Misusing Evidence. These fallacies falsify an analysis or argument by abusing or distorting the evidence. For example, you might be guilty of *impressing with numbers,* drowning your readers in statistics that overwhelm them into agreement without proper interpretation. You might be offering *half-truths,* leaving out "the rest of the story" in favor of that part that supports your point. You might have created a *false analogy,* a comparison between two things where the grounds for comparison are weak or vague, resulting in an unclear or exaggerated idea. Or your point may be based on an *attack against the person,* also known as an *ad hominem* argument based on a person's character, lifestyle, or beliefs rather than the issue. Here are two more such fallacies:

- **Unreliable Testimonial:** An appeal to authority has force only if the authority is qualified in the proper field. If he or she is not, the testimony is irrelevant. Note that fame is not the same thing as authority.

   > On her talk show, Alberta Magnus recently claimed that most pork sold in the United States is tainted with H1N1. (**Objection:** Although Magnus may be an articulate talk show host, she is not an expert on food safety.)

- **Hypothesis Contrary to Fact:** This fallacy relies on "if only" thinking. It bases the claim on an assumption of what would have happened if something else had, or had not, happened. Being pure speculation, such a claim cannot be tested.

   > If only multiculturalists hadn't pushed through affirmative action, the U.S. would be a united nation.

Improving Organizational Flow

Good research writing has structure, whether that organization is foregrounded through devices such as headings, implied more fluidly in the progression of paragraphs, or presented creatively through cross-references and hyperlinks. In each approach, the structure leads readers logically and clearly from one point to the next, sometimes in a straight line and other times through a mapping out of connections and associations. And at an essential level, that structure is always linking specific points, paragraphs, and parts back to the central question or thesis. To strengthen the structure of your first draft, then, test it in the following ways:

Test the overall design of your draft. Look closely at the sequence of ideas that you have developed in your draft. Does that sequence advance your thesis? Do the points build effectively? Does your thesis lack consistent support? Do tangential points stray from your main point? Is your organization unclear and difficult to follow? If you find such problems, consider the following actions:

1. **Refine** the focus, emphasis, or sequence by rearranging material within the draft, whether specific points, individual paragraphs, or larger sections.

2. **Fill** in the gaps by drafting new material, drawing on your research notes and findings, as needed.

3. **Cut** material that wanders tangentially from your purpose. (However, consider saving this tangential material in a file of ideas for future projects. Tangents often represent your mind pursuing an interesting idea connected to your current discussion.)

4. If your paper or a portion of your paper lacks focus or unity, **find** an organizational pattern that refocuses the message. Go back to "Considering Methods of Organization" on pages 172-177.

5. **Feature** the structure of longer papers with these techniques:

   - Indicate distinct sections with descriptive, parallel headings. For example, a paper on a film version of Jane Austen's *Pride and Prejudice* might use these headings: *The Discourse of Love in the Novel, Visual Gazes in the Film, The Film Language of the Body, The Ritual of Dance in Word and Image.*

   - To link sections of your paper, add brief transitional paragraphs (two to three sentences) that summarize the prior discussion and point forward to the next section of your paper.

   - To help readers navigate a substantial research document, add an outline or a table of contents, menus, helpful cross-references and links, or an index.

Test the flow of ideas and information. Generally, your writing with source material should follow the known/new principle. Because readers "build" meaning as they proceed through your writing, your paper's overall structure, its sections, and its paragraphs should all be built so that new information comes gradually and is linked to information that the reader already knows. Check that your draft unfolds this way.

Improving Paragraphs

In drafting, you may have constructed paragraphs that are loosely held together, poorly developed, unclear to readers, or weak in the blending of your thinking and source material. To revise your drafted paragraphs, review the principles for opening paragraphs, body paragraphs, and closing paragraphs shared in the previous chapter (pages 182-196). Then test your paragraphing in the following ways.

Test your introduction and conclusion. Review your paper's opening and closing to judge how well your paper begins and ends.

- Place the opening and closing side by side. How effectively do these "bookends" frame your paper? Do the opening and closing match in terms of emphasis, ideas, and tone? If they seem mismatched, look for ways to link the wording, ideas, and images of the conclusion back to the introduction.
- Does your opening effectively "tug" your readers out of their world into the world of your paper? Does the introduction (1) engage the reader; (2) establish the focus and scope of your writing; (3) set the tone and diction level; and (4) introduce your line of thinking about the topic? If not, rework the opening.
- Does your closing effectively "transition" your readers from the world of your paper back into their own worlds? Does the conclusion (1) deepen your thesis, and (2) complete and unify your thinking? If not, rework the closing.

Test body paragraphs for the basics. As discussed earlier, your body paragraphs should generally follow a pattern (page 186) that smoothly integrates sources (page 190). While you needn't be too rigid, test each body paragraph against this pattern:

- ☑ A topic sentence that offers a controlling idea for the paragraph and that links the paragraph with the paper's thesis
- ☑ Sentences that develop the topic-sentence idea through reasoning
- ☑ Support of the reasoning through reference to source material, effectively integrated and cited, along with further reasoning with that evidence
- ☑ Commentary that brings the topic-sentence idea to a close

Test body paragraphs for unity. A unified paragraph is one in which every statement and all evidence help to develop a single idea. In other words, all supporting sentences relate to the topic sentence. (The topic sentence is usually the first sentence, but sometimes you can place it elsewhere for effect: in the middle to build up to the idea and then lead away from it, as in a paragraph contrasting two items; or at the end to build to a climax, as in a persuasive or narrative paragraph.) Revise a paragraph lacking unity in one of these ways:

- Delete the extraneous material from the paragraph.
- Rewrite the material so that it clearly supports the topic sentence.
- Create a separate paragraph based on the tangential material.
- Revise the topic sentence so that it better unifies all the material.

Test body paragraphs for completeness. An incomplete paragraph is a fragmentary or underdeveloped paragraph. The supporting sentences don't fully elaborate the main idea in the topic sentence: the discussion and evidence provided are not sufficient to fully clarify the thought. Examine your draft for particularly brief or thin body paragraphs— ones that run only a few sentences. When you find such paragraphs, complete them in one of these ways:

1. **Combine them.** Fuse two or more short paragraphs to create one more full-bodied paragraph. However, make sure that the new paragraph has a strong topic sentence that unifies the discussion.

2. **Complete the paragraph fragment.** Develop any partial paragraph by (a) deepening your own thinking about the main point and/or (b) adding more evidence in support of that main point. For ideas, see the full discussion of types of evidence on pages 187-189, but here is quick list of your choices:

Observations and anecdotes	Analogies
Primary-text quotations	Expert testimony
Statistics	Illustrations, examples, demonstrations
Test or experiment results	Predictions
Visuals	

Test body paragraphs for coherence. When a paragraph is coherent, the parts hold together. The paragraph flows smoothly because each sentence is connected to others by patterns in the language such as repetition, synonyms, pronouns, and transitions. Check your paragraphs for choppiness or disconnection, and check the links from one paragraph's ending to the next paragraph's beginning. Then repair problems with strategies like these:

1. **Creating patterns of related words:** Create patterns of related words: Improve coherence by repeating key terms as you move from sentence to sentence. To make sure that the repetition doesn't get repetitive, use synonyms for these terms. When well done, this linking of sentences through key words helps readers understand your thinking. How? By connecting the new statement back to what you have already said, you create a "known-new" pattern in which new discussion or information becomes clear in the context of what readers have earlier come to know. Note these patterns of related words below:

> The first public gallery was, in fact, founded in 1773 in Charles Town, South Carolina, by the city's Library Society, whose membership was largely drawn from the professional and landowning ranks. Soon, historical societies and colleges had gotten in on the act, amassing their own collections of art and curiosities for public display. As Meyer describes it, "each of these institutions was the fruit of spontaneous citizen initiative" (24). Nearly all of these early museums were organized as not-for-profit organizations controlled by private boards of trustees, setting "a pattern of local initiative and private control" that still prevails (25). It is not, Meyer contends, the organization of museums that has changed over the years but the ways in which they are funded.

2. **Create clear transitions within and between paragraphs:** Linking words and phrases like "next," "on the other hand," and "in addition" connect ideas by showing the logical connection between them. Test your writing for strong transitions in two ways:

   - In the first sentence of each paragraph, make sure that you offer a clear transition from the previous paragraph. That transition can be a linking word like "however" or "moreover"; or the link can be made by pulling a key word or phrase from the end of the previous paragraph into the first sentence of the next.

   - Within each paragraph, look for places where transitional words would better signal the logic of your thinking. As shown in the table below, consider links that show location or time, that compare or contrast things, that emphasize a point, that conclude or summarize, that add information, or that clarify.

Note the transitional words at work in the passage below:

> As in *Cool Hand Luke*, this public spectacle of punishment and revenge is a self-serving institution of the prison system itself.
>
> The public, however, has its own incentives for gobbling it all up, so to speak. Revenge is probably one of them, as is pure, unabashed voyeurism. American people tend to take the idea of the last meal to heart, though, and somehow make it their own. Many visitors to the "Dead Man Eating" Web site and message boards all over the internet do this by submitting their own "last meal requests," as if they were going to die tomorrow. Apparently, then, this fixation on the last meal is not limited to intrusive consumption of execution records; it extends to the public and their own final food choices. In fact, the subject of hypothetical last meals has given this icon. . . .

Transitions and Linking Words: The words and phrases below can help you connect sentences and paragraphs within your writing. Choose the link that fits your logic.

Linking logic	Examples
Location	above, across, against, along, among, around, away from, behind, below, beneath, beside, between, beyond, by, down, in back of, in front of, inside, into, near, off, on top of, onto, outside, over, throughout, to the left, to the right, under
Time	about, after, afterward, as soon as, at, before, during, finally, first, immediately, later, meanwhile, next, next week, second, soon, then, third, today, tomorrow, until, when, yesterday
Similarities	also, as, in the same way, like, likewise, similarly
Differences	although, by contrast, but, even though, however, on the other hand, otherwise, still, unlike, yet
Emphasis	again, even, for this reason, in fact, particularly, to emphasize, to repeat, truly
Conclusion or Summary	all in all, as a result, finally, in conclusion, in summary, last, therefore, to sum up
Addition	additionally, again, along with, also, and, another, as well, besides, equally important, finally, for example, for instance, in addition, likewise, next, second
Clarity	for instance, in other words, put another way, that is

Checking the Voice of Your Writing

Generally, readers more fully trust research writing that speaks in an informed voice, a voice that is committed and energized but also measured. If your writing voice has this tone, it helps build your credibility as a researcher; if instead your voice is flat, pompous, insecure, aggressive, or chummy, your credibility will be damaged, and your readers disengaged.

Testing Your Level of Confidence

In research writing, establishing the right level of confidence can be difficult. As you revise your draft, test the confidence level of your voice by examining your writing's degree of commitment and use of qualifiers.

1. **Revise for commitment and intensity.** To what degree does your writing show that you care about the topic, your research, and your readers? Does your writing show an appropriate level of intensity, even passion? All writing, including academic research writing, connects better with readers when it communicates care, curiosity, and concern. In the original passage below, the voice demonstrates little interest in the topic. In contrast, the revised version expresses a committed energy.

   Original Passage: Motz says that Barbie dolls contribute to the issues that women face in today's society. It is more likely that other things are causing these issues in today's society.

   Revised Version: In other words, Motz uses Barbie as a scapegoat for problems that have complex causes. However, a girl's interest in romance is no more Barbie's fault than the fault of books like *On the Shores of Silver Lake*. Fashion magazines targeted at adolescents are the cause of far more anorexia than is Barbie. And mothers who encourage daughters to find security in men teach female dependency, not Barbie.

2. **Keep your thinking appropriately qualified and balanced.** Qualifiers are words and phrases that make points more reasonable by limiting them in logical ways. The goal in your writing is to appropriately qualify your thinking: on the one hand, you don't want your claims to be so sweeping that your reader judges them faulty; on the other hand, you don't want your points to be over-qualified so that your thinking comes across as insecure. Aim to place accurate limits on your thinking, based on your research. Here is an example:

   Unqualified: All these star athletes are taking way too many academic shortcuts.

   Qualified: Some star athletes are allowed to take improper academic shortcuts in specific circumstances.

   Qualifiers: almost, frequently, likely, many, maybe, might, often, probably, some, tends to, typically, usually

Testing for an Academic Style

Most college-level research writing calls for an academic style. Such a style isn't stuffy; you're not trying to impress readers with ten-dollar words. Rather, you are using language that facilitates a thoughtful, evidence-focused, and engaged discussion of the topic. To test your draft for a fitting academic voice, consider the issues below.

1. **Examine your use of personal pronouns.** In some academic writing, the personal pronouns *I*, *we*, and *you* are acceptable, especially in a limited way. (See, for example, the personal-research paper, pages 283-292.) Generally, however, you are expected to avoid these personal pronouns in traditional academic research writing. By restricting pronouns to *he*, *she*, *they*, and *one*, you are foregrounding the topic, not yourself; you are letting your attitude be revealed indirectly.

   Too Personal: I really think that the problem of home foreclosures is at a crisis level, given how many people in my family this is happening to.

   More Academic: The rise of housing-foreclosure rates has reached critical levels. This increase has not only contributed significantly to the nation's economic recession but also created enormous stress at personal and familial levels.

   Note: Use the pronoun *one* carefully. When it means "a person," *one* overused can lead to an awkward style. Moreover, the pronoun *their* (a plural pronoun) should not be used with *one* (a singular pronoun). Example: When *one* views a film adaptation of a Jane Austen novel, *one* (not *they*) needs to know the language of dance.

2. **Examine the formality level of your prose.** Most college-level research writing should adhere to the standards of formal English. As you revise your draft, bring the writing to an appropriate level of formality by examining the following issues:

   - Is the language standard English rather than slang (e.g., *strength* vs. *guts*)?
   - Have you avoided contractions (e.g., *it is* vs. *it's*, *does not* vs. *doesn't*)?
   - Do some sentences have complex syntax reflecting complex thinking, as opposed to a predominance of simple sentences? (See sentence variety on page 000.)
   - Does your writing adhere to the traditional conventions of spelling, grammar, mechanics, and punctuation? Does your writing avoid exclamation marks; does it use semicolons and colons effectively?

   Informal: Your avg. American art museum has serious issues with a kind of craziness, something like multiple personality disorder. It's really a bizarre mix, both kind of public and kind of private. And not just that but it's hooked into such different groups of people who've got totally at-odds goals. That's why it's tough to see what the whole point of museums now is.

   Formal: The American art museum suffers from a multiple-personality disorder. It is a strange hybrid, both public and private in nature, and beholden to a constituency varied in its interests.

Editing for Sentence Smoothness

When you feel fairly confident about the global issues in your research writing (the ideas, organization, and voice), it's a good time to focus on more local issues, starting with sentence style. As you work with specific sentences, your goal is to improve their clarity and energy. In particular, you want to examine whether source material, especially direct quotations, is smoothly integrated into sentence syntax. While the appropriate practices are addressed fully on pages 191-192, check the example below:

> **Poor Integration:** The use of antibacterial soaps, detergents, lotions, and other household items is becoming increasingly common so that "there has never been evidence that they have a public health benefit" (Bren 31).
>
> **Effective Integration:** The use of antibacterial soaps, detergents, lotions, and other household items is becoming increasingly common. Stuart Levy, M.D., president of the Alliance for the Prudent Use of Antibiotics, says that "there has never been evidence that they [antibacterial products] have a public health benefit" (qtd. in Bren 31).

Smooth integration of source material into sentence syntax is one key editing issue, but your sentences can be strengthened a number of ways, as discussed on the following pages. By using these techniques, start to recognize problem sentences:

- Read aloud your sentences, or have someone read them aloud to you. Listen for sentences that sound convoluted, rough, or flat.
- Highlight sentence openings to look for repetitive patterns.
- Estimate sentence lengths, looking for patterns of overly short and overly long sentences, as well as lack of variety in length.

Fixing Primer Style

Primer style refers to a series of short, choppy sentences, such as the passage below. You can fix primer style in these ways.

1. Combine shorter sentences using techniques like these:
   - Create a series of words, phrases, or clauses listing parallel items or concepts.
   - Subordinate secondary ideas and integrate them into a main idea.
   - Put some ideas in introductory phrases or clauses before the main idea.
2. Expand and enrich individual sentences within the primer passage by adding modifying words, phrases, or clauses.

> **Primer Passage:** The water flows through a narrow pipe. The water activates a mechanism. The mechanism makes the out-end tower roll in a large circle. The rest of the towers follow. All the towers spray water.
>
> **Edited Passage:** As it flows through the narrow pipe, the water activates a mechanism that causes the outer-end tower to roll in a large circle. The rest of the towers follow, spraying water as they go. This system thus causes the crops to grow in the shape of an enormous circle, as the corners of the 160-acre square plots of land are not irrigated.

Fixing Rambling Sentences

Rambling sentences pile up more information than readers can easily comprehend. The rambling sentence is particularly problematic in research writing, in which presenting complex information requires that you carefully control the info flow.

Recognizing Ramblers: To recognize ramblers in your writing, scan your writing for sentences two or more lines long—longer than 20 words. Read these sentences aloud, listening for confusion and for an overpopulation of coordinating conjunctions (*and, but, or,* etc.), subordinating conjunctions (*although, because, since, when,* etc.), and/or relative pronouns (*who, whom, which, that*).

Repairing Ramblers: Once you've identified a rambler, consider these fixes.

1. Ask: What's my basic point here? Then state that point directly, clearly.
2. Ask: What can my reader comfortably comprehend in one sentence? Then
   - divide your material into comprehensible pieces—one sentence per piece.
   - order information by shaping it into parallel lists or numbered steps.
   - locate and cut say-nothing material from the sentence.
3. After circling coordinating conjunctions, subordinating conjunctions, and relative pronouns, use them to decide how to pull apart the sentence.

A Rambling Sentence: There's no question that tumor cells can hurt the body in a number of ways, one of which is that a tumor can grow so big that it takes up space needed by other organs, or some cells may detach from the original tumor and spread throughout the body, creating new tumors elsewhere, as does lymphatic cancer, which is so hard to control because it spreads so quickly.

Rambling Sentence Fixed: Tumor cells can hurt the body in a number of ways. First, a tumor can grow so big that it takes up space needed by other organs. Second, some cells may detach from the original tumor and spread throughout the body, creating new tumors elsewhere. This happens with lymphatic cancer—a cancer that's hard to control because it spreads so quickly.

Fixing Unparallel Structures

Coordinated sentence elements should be parallel. That is, they should be written in the same grammatical forms. Parallel structures save words, clarify relationships, and present information in a sensible sequence—all important goals in your research writing.

Weak Parallelism: As an organization, MADD promotes severely punishing drunk driving, not to mention the outright elimination of it, because this offense leads to a large number of deaths, in addition to the sorrow people experience.

Strong Parallelism: As an organization, MADD promotes eliminating and severely punishing drunk driving because this offense leads to many deaths and untold sorrow.

Fixing Sluggish Sentence Structures

Some sentences fall flat. Because of the way they are constructed, these sentences lack energy and drive. Look for and fix the sluggards below.

Reworking Nominal Constructions: In a nominalized construction, a strong verb (e.g., *describe* or *explain*) is used in a noun form (e.g., *description* or *explanation*) so that the sentence typically contains a weaker verb (the linking verb *be* or verbs such as *give* or *provide*). The nominal construction is both sluggish and wordy.

Nominal Constructions (noun form underlined):	**Strong Verbs:**
Engineer Tim McAllister *gives a description* . . .	McAllister describes . . .
Scholar Lydia Balm provides an *explanation* . . .	Balm explains . . .

Rewrite sentences heavy with nominal constructions by turning the nominalizations into verbs.

Sluggish: In her study of Austen film adaptations, Lydia Balm provides an explanation for the narrative power of dance scenes. Dances offer a symbolization and visualization of characters in situations of mutual attraction but nonverbalization.

Energetic: In her study of Austen film adaptations, Lydia Balm explains the narrative power of dance scenes. Dances symbolize visually the attraction characters feel for each other but cannot verbalize.

Eliminating Expletives: Typically, sentences beginning with the expletives "It is" and "There is" are wordy and unnatural. Expletives are essentially fillers that serve no purpose in most sentences: an occasional expletive for emphasis can work, but frequent use of expletives deadens your writing. So find them and remove them, as shown below.

Sluggish: It is believed by some people that childhood vaccinations can cause autism. There are several Web sites that promote this point of view quite forcefully. In fact, it is also the case that some celebrities advocate this cause.

Energetic: Some people believe that childhood vaccinations can cause autism. Several Web sites promote this point of view forcefully, along with some celebrities.

Turning Negatives into Positives: Sentences constructed upon the negatives *no, not, neither/nor* can be wordy and difficult to understand. Stating what is the case instead of what is not creates stronger, clearer sentences.

Negative: Hybrid vehicles are not completely different from traditional cars, as hybrids cannot run without gas and cannot rely only on battery power that has not been created by the gasoline engine.

Positive: Hybrid vehicles are similar to traditional cars, as hybrids do require gas in order to power an internal-combustion engine that in turn powers batteries.

Using Active and Passive Voice of Verbs

Verbs in your research writing should be energetic—indicating what happened, how something works, what should be done, and so on. However, the story of verbs is somewhat complicated. Some verbs are not action verbs but linking verbs (the most common is *to be*): these linking verbs create vital connections in your writing. But even action verbs are complicated in that they can be in the active or passive voice. When the verb is active, the sentence's subject performs the action: the sentence pattern moves from subject to verb to object, from actor to action to receiver-of-action. When the verb is passive, the subject is acted upon or receives the action: what was originally the verb's object, the receiver of the action, is in the subject position.

Active: Given the global connections between national economies, when U.S. consumers **stopped buying** automobiles, Japanese carmakers **shared** in the rapid economic downturn.

Passive: Given the global connections between national economies, when automobiles **were** no longer **being bought** by U.S. consumers, the rapid economic downturn **was shared** by Japanese carmakers.

Generally rely on the active voice. The passive voice tends to be wordier (requiring helping verbs and "by" phrasing) and more sluggish than the active voice because the verb's action is directed backward, not forward. In addition, passive constructions can be impersonal in that the true actors of the verb can disappear: the actor need not be in the sentence. Normally, then, avoid extended passages using the passive voice.

Poor Passive: As a sign of a deepening recession, job losses were experienced by 600,000 workers in January 2009.

Better Active: As a sign of a deepening recession, 600,000 workers lost their jobs in January 2009.

Use the passive voice in particular circumstances. The passive voice has some important uses: (1) if you wish to stress the object or person acted upon, and (2) if the actual actor is understood, unknown, or unimportant. These uses are particularly recommended in the social and natural sciences. Yet even here, restrict passive voice to actions describing research methods; avoid it when discussing hypotheses and results.

Poor Active: The federal governments of both the U.S. and Canada **bailed out** both GM and Chrysler, two struggling automakers.

Better Passive: Both GM and Chrysler, two struggling automakers, **were bailed out** by the U.S. and Canadian governments. (stress on receiver of action)

Active: As part of the study, participants **drove** hybrids for six months.

Passive: As part of the study, hybrids **were driven** for six months. (emphasis on receiver; actor understood)

Editing for Sentence Variety

When you edit your sentences, consider the overall variety of your style. If all your sentences seem to begin the same way, be the same length, or follow the same pattern, rework them to create more engaging, nuanced prose.

Vary sentence openings: If a series of sentences begin the same way, create variety by moving modifying words, phrases, or clauses to the front of some sentences.

> **Unvaried:** The problem is not just about wasteful irrigation, though. The problem is also about resistance to change. The problem is that many people have fought against restrictions when governments have tried to pass regulations.
>
> **Varied:** However, the problem is not just about wasteful irrigation. It is about resistance to change. When governments have tried to pass regulations controlling water use, many people have fought against restrictions.

Vary sentence lengths: Short sentences (5-15 words) make points crisply. Medium sentences (15-30 words) should carry the bulk of your information. When well-crafted, occasional long sentences (more than 30 words) can deepen ideas.

- **Short:** Museum exhibitions have become increasingly commercial in nature.
- **Medium:** To the extent that "access" is an adequate measure of museum performance, art as entertainment "has proven a resounding triumph" (Meyer 268).
- **Long:** Shows featuring motorcycles, automobiles, the treasures of King Tutankhamen, the works of Van Gogh, and other blockbuster favorites not only have proven immensely popular but have also offered the promise of corporate underwriting and ample commercial tie-ins (Meyer 116).

Vary sentence kinds: In research writing, the bulk of your sentences should be declarative—focused on making, elaborating, and supporting points. However, edit your writing so that it effectively uses other types of sentences.

- **Declarative:** Historical records indicate that the lost colonists of Roanoke may have been harboring a dangerous virus: influenza.
- **Conditional:** If the influenza virus was not present in the New World before the arrival of Europeans, then it is highly probable that the lost colonists of Roanoke made contact with the indigenous groups of North Carolina and served as vectors for the influenza disease (Mires, 1994).
- **Interrogative:** That being said, we must now turn to a different question: What happened to those lost colonists? (Note: do not overuse rhetorical questions.)
- **Imperative:** Let us take steps to ensure that the Lumbee People do not share the fate of the colonists who disappeared from the island of Roanoke.
- **Exclamatory:** Just as John White found upon his belated return to the deserted colony over 400 years ago, something is terribly wrong! (Note: generally avoid exclamatory sentences in traditional academic writing.)

Vary sentence arrangements: Where do you want to place the main point of your sentence? You make that choice by arranging sentence parts into loose, periodic, balanced, or cumulative patterns. Each pattern creates a specific effect.

Loose: Men are frequently mystified by women, with their unfamiliar rituals, their emotional vitality, and their biological clocks—issues often addressed in Romantic Comedies.
Analysis: This pattern is direct. It states the main point immediately, and then tacks on extra information in a series of phrases.

Periodic: While Western culture celebrates and idolizes romantic and sexual forms of love, seen powerfully in the films that it creates and the romance novels it produces, such attraction between a man and a woman, no matter how strong initially, in the end fails to sustain a relationship for a lifetime.
Analysis: This pattern postpones the main point until the end. The sentence builds to the point after a series of dependent clauses and additional phrases, creating an indirect, dramatic effect.

Balanced: The modern Romantic Comedy often portrays male characters as resistant to or hopelessly clueless about love; however, in Jane Austen's narratives, while male characters do exhibit these features to a degree, men's behavior is complicated by traditional codes of honor that have now largely vanished.
Analysis: This pattern gives equal weight to complementary or contrasting points; the balance is often signaled by a comma and a conjunction *(and, but)*, or a semicolon. Often a conjunctive adverb *(however, nevertheless)* or a transitional phrase *(in addition, even so)* will follow the semicolon to further clarify the relationship.

Cumulative: In spite of his initially limiting pride and his confused, resistant adoration of Elizabeth Bennet, *Mr. Darcy,* now properly proud and still handsome, *emerges* finally *as the consummate romantic hero,* the anonymous savior of Elizabeth's family, a man capable of correcting his faults when they are revealed to him, a true gentleman.
Analysis: This pattern places the main idea in the middle, surrounding it with modifying words, phrases, and clauses. The result is a sentence that cushions, qualifies, or elaborates a point. Here are seven ways to expand a main idea:

- With adjectives and adverbs: *now properly proud, still handsome, finally*
- With phrases: *in spite of his initially limiting pride; his confused, resistant adoration of Elizabeth Bennet; the anonymous savior of Elizabeth's family; a true gentleman*
- With clauses: *when they are revealed to him*

Editing for Energetic Word Choice

As you rework your draft, ask this fundamental question: *Have I chosen the best words to clearly communicate my research findings to these readers?* To improve your writing at the level of word choice, edit it for the problems that follow.

Eliminate Wordiness

Wordy writing taxes the reader's attention. While your paper itself may be long, the writing itself should be *concise*—tightly phrased so that each word counts. To tighten your research writing, cut the following types of wordiness:

- **Deadwood:** filler material or verbal "lumber" that serves no vital purpose
- **Redundancy:** words that say the same thing, like these common repetitive phrases: *combine together, new discovery, green in color, round in shape, visible to the eye, small in size, end result, brief in duration, repeat again*
- **Unnecessary modifiers:** Adjectives and adverbs typically clarify nouns and verbs; however, excessive modifiers make prose dense. Generally, replace multiple modifiers with one; avoid the need for modifiers by using precise nouns and verbs; avoid intensifying adverbs (*very, extremely, intensely, awfully, especially*); and cut meaningless modifiers (*kind of, sort of*).
- **Long phrases and clauses:** Often, a long phrase or clause can be replaced by a single word or at least a shorter phrase. For example, replace *in many cases* with *often, aware of the fact that* with *aware that,* and *at the present time* with *presently.*

Wordy Passage: Among a variety of different possible devices, an extremely interesting one is LEPA, also known by many as low-energy precision application, hence the acronym. With this LEPA device, the nozzles of the center-pivot are especially close to the ground of the field. Because of the fact that low-energy precision application uses water pressure that is lower and gives off water drops that are larger in size than the traditional center-pivot system, this LEPA device reduces and lessens the evaporation of water by a lot in that it goes up to about 98 percent.

Concise Passage: A second device that prevents water waste is LEPA, or low-energy precision application. With LEPA, the center-pivot nozzles are close to the ground. With less water pressure and bigger drops than the traditional center-pivot system, LEPA reduces evaporation by as much as 98 percent.

Replace Vague Wording with Precise, Concrete Terms

In research writing, the best words are those that clearly, precisely, and directly communicate your meaning. These are quality words. By contrast, weak words are vague and imprecise. As novelist Mark Twain puts it, "The difference between the right word and the almost right word is the difference between lightning and the lightning bug." While you may sometimes need to use general, abstract terms to convey complex ideas, you should use concrete, specific terms to flesh out more precisely what you mean. For example, check the differences between the statements that follow.

Vague: In Austen's works, things usually work out satisfactorily.

Precise: In novels such as Austen's *Pride and Prejudice,* the plot's denouement normally involves satisfying forms of closure. The right men and women marry (Darcy and Elizabeth, Bingley and Jane), while characters of questionable conduct pay for their errors and folly (e.g., Lydia and Wickham are each other's punishment). Moreover, deserving female characters such as Elizabeth and Jane are rescued from a possible poverty unfairly dictated by the rules of a patriarchal society.

1. **Make nouns specific.** Some nouns are general *(footwear, movement, fruit)* and give the reader a vague picture. Other nouns are specific *(flip flops, Civil Rights, mango)* and give the reader a clear, detailed picture. In your research writing, replace or supplement general terms with specific, precise terms.

2. **Make verbs vivid.** Like nouns, verbs can sometimes be too general to create a vivid word picture (e.g., *work out*). By contrast, vivid verbs make your writing clear (e.g., *marry, pay, are rescued*). That's because verbs are the engines that drive your sentences forward: the stronger and more efficient your verb "engines," the more powerful and economical your sentences. Edit your verbs using these guidelines:

   ■ Use precise rather than general verbs. For example, *brush, scrub, sanitize, dissolve,* and *sweep* are all more precise and vivid than *clean.*

   ■ Use action verbs instead of linking verbs. When your writing is dominated by linking verbs, the result is flat, listless writing.

3. **Make modifiers strong.** Modifiers can be adjectives, adverbs, or prepositional phrases. To use strong modifiers, follow these guidelines.

   ■ Use specific adjectives to modify nouns: one strong adjective is better than several weak ones.

   ■ Use adverbs only when needed to clarify the verb's action. Don't use a verb-adverb combination when one vivid verb would be better.

   ■ Avoid tired adjective and adverbs like those listed.

Tired Adjectives: bad, big, certain, cute, fun, funny, good, great, improved, long, neat, new, nice, old, several, short, small, various

Tired Adverbs absolutely, basically, certainly, essentially, exceptionally, extremely, greatly, highly, hopefully, incredibly, kind of, perfectly, sort of, very

Hit the Right Diction Level

Diction level refers to the formality level of your word choice. While most research writing is formal in tone and language level (page 183), your diction level might be different, depending on the rhetorical situation. Edit your writing for a consistent diction level:

Formal: Environmentally-concerned citizens should consider purchasing a hybrid-electric vehicle.

Informal: People worried about the environment should think about buying a hybrid.

Slang: Gen-X or Yuppies—doesn't matter—need to get a green set a wheels.

Replace Slanted Terms with Neutral Ones

Words typically have two levels of meaning. First, words have denotations—essentially, their neutral dictionary definitions. Second, words have connotations—personal, cultural, and historical associations coloring readers' reactions. Such associations can be positive, negative, or anywhere in between, often depending on the context in which the word is used. For example, the word *cute*, which has an objective dictionary definition, would have different connotations when used to describe a child as opposed to a grown man or woman. To edit for connotations, follow these guidelines:

1. **Make sure connotations fit the context.** For example, the words *liberal* and *conservative* might be used with fairly neutral connotations in an academic research paper on a political topic, whereas these same words might take on highly charged associations in a newspaper editorial.

2. **Normally replace words having negative connotations:** For example, words such as *neglect, gullible,* and *foolish* have negative connotations: they are strong but loaded words. When possible, find more neutral substitutions.

> **Loaded Terminology:** Senator Radinsky, acting pretty shifty behind the podium, dodged the reporters' questions about the environmental devastation that would undoubtedly result from the ill-conceived dam.
>
> **Neutral Terminology:** Senator Radinsky, clearly uncomfortable behind the podium, offered vague answers to reporters' questions about the environmental impact of the dam.

Cut Clichés

A cliché or trite expression is a phrase that has become tired from overuse. As a reader, you probably recognize clichés: *easy as pie, burn bridges, can of worms, go for broke, pay through the nose.* Whereas many clichés were once fresh comparisons, through overuse they have ceased to communicate anything surprising or insightful. Thus, research writing dominated by clichés conveys a lack of thoughtfulness—an impression the exact opposite of what you wish to make. As a result, readers tune out of the research conversation. To fix clichéd writing, consider editing choices like these:

1. **Replace clichés with straightforward terms.** Once you have identified a cliché, think of simple, direct terms that will make the same point. For example, instead of describing the *tough economic road ahead,* simply state that *the near future will be economically stressful.*

2. **Replace clichés with fresh comparisons.** In research writing, a fresh comparison can (a) deepen an idea by connecting it with something unexpected or (b) clarify a complex idea by relating it to something familiar. Try replacing a clichéd comparison with a creative comparison. For example, instead of saying "There's a beehive of activity under the grass," writer Annie Dillard explains that "The world is a wild wrestle under the grass."

Rework Pretentious and Flowery Language

You might think that style is something that you add to your research writing to sound impressive—a slick phrase here, a highbrow term there. But style as it relates to word choice has nothing to do with adornment that just clutters things up. Instead, strengthen your style by choosing simple and direct language.

Pretentious language aims to sound intelligent but comes off sounding phony—like the writer is trying to sound smarter than he or she actually is. Such language calls attention to itself rather than its meaning; in fact, pretentious words can be so high-blown that meaning is obscured altogether.

> **Pretentious:** Liquid precipitation in the Iberian Peninsula's nation-state of most prominent size experiences altitudinal descent as a matter of course primarily in the region characterized by minimal topographical variation.
>
> **Plain:** The rain in Spain falls mainly on the plain.

Flowery phrases contain language that is overblown, exaggerated. As such, the wording is unnecessarily fancy and often sentimental. It is wording that draws attention to itself and hence gets in the way of direct communication.

> **Flowery:** The gorgeous beauty of the Great Barrier Reef is fantastically displayed in coral formations of all the colors of the rainbow and in its wondrous variety of delightful tropical fish.
>
> **Fresh:** The beauty of the Great Barrier Reef is displayed in rainbow-colored coral formations and in a wide variety of tropical fish.

Eliminate Jargon

Although it depends upon the context, your research writing naturally relies upon the specialized vocabulary of the subject area. However, be careful that your writing isn't dense with unnecessarily technical terminology. Similarly, jargon—popular buzzwords and catchphrases such as *rightsize* and *deconstruct* (especially when used incorrectly)—deaden your ability to communicate effectively.

1. **Replace jargon with plain terms.** Identify terms that have crept into your writing as popular catchphrases. Then identify plain English replacements, if possible. For example, replace *When the political message is deconstructed* with *When the political message is analyzed . . . .*

2. **Use technical terms when readers are "insiders."** If your readers are topic experts, technical terms function as an acceptable shared shorthand. Example: The *rising action* of the *gothic novel* normally introduces potent *gender-specific conflicts . . . .*

3. **Define technical terms unfamiliar to your reader.** If a precise technical term is needed in your discussion but you know readers are unfamiliar with the term, offer a definition when you first use the term. Example: A hybrid vehicle, *any mode of transportation that combines two or more sources of power. . . .*

Focus on Research Ethics: Plain and Fair English

Ethical research writing involves more than avoiding plagiarism. It also requires that you choose language that shows respect for people's intelligence and for their diverse identities. Such language strengthens the dialogue by keeping it at a level fitting the topic, standards of clarity and honesty, and cultural norms of discourse. So carefully edit your research writing to show the kinds of respect described below.

Striving for Plain English

In many ways, plain English is the product of the principles discussed on the previous pages: avoiding jargon, technical language, flowery phrasing, and pretentious wording. However, plain English also counters these ethically questionable uses of language:

Obfuscation involves using fuzzy terms like *throughput* and *downlink* to muddy the issue. These words may make simple ideas sound more profound than they really are, or they may make false ideas sound true.

> **Example:** Through the fully functional developmental process of a streamlined target-refractory system, the U.S. military will successfully reprioritize its data throughputs. (**Objection:** What does this mean?)

Ambiguity (especially deliberate) makes a statement open to two or more interpretations. While desirable in some forms of writing (like poetry and fiction), ambiguity is usually disruptive in traditional research writing because it obscures and muddies issues.

> **Example:** Many women need to work to support their children through school, but they would be better off at home. (**Objection:** Does *they* refer to *children* or *women*? What does *better off* mean? These words and phrases are unclear.)

Euphemisms are overly polite expressions that avoid stating an uncomfortable truth. In your research writing, you generally want to choose neutral, tactful phrasing, but avoid euphemisms.

> **Example:** This economically challenged neighborhood faces some issues concerning mind-enhancing substances and scuffles between youths. (**Translation:** This impoverished neighborhood is being destroyed by drugs and gangs.)

Doublespeak is phrasing that deliberately seeks either to hide the truth from readers or at least to understate the situation. Such slippery language is especially a temptation when the writer wields authority, power, or privilege in a negative situation (e.g., a hospital administrator writing a report, as shown in the sentence below). Avoid such verbal misdirection; be clearly honest by choosing precise, transparent phrasing.

> **Example:** The doctor executed a nonfacile manipulation of newborn. (**Translation:** The doctor dropped the baby during delivery.)

Note: Plain English is particularly important when your readers are English-Language-Learners, people for whom English is not their first language. Unfamiliar cultural references and sayings, word connotations, clichés, slang: these all give your ELL readers trouble as they seek to enter the dialogue of your research paper.

Striving for Respectful Language

In the many cultural situations where language is used, including research writing, words carry power. Given that research writing tends to focus on debatable issues, the concern here isn't political correctness: it's respect. Research writing should adhere to standards of respect within the research community and the broader culture.

The principles below address how language identifies and distinguishes people. However, the first principle of showing respect is this: unless necessary to your discussion, avoid identifying a person's sex, age, race, religion, sexual orientation, ethnicity, or disability. Treat people as individuals, not group representatives.

Respect the names. Start, quite simply, with correct spelling—spelling of your instructor's name, as well as of the names of researchers you are referencing and people you are discussing. While it depends on the type of research writing and the documentation system (particularly the MLA and Chicago systems), follow these practices as well:

1. With your first reference to a person, give the person's full name: *During his inauguration address, President Barack Obama. . . .*

2. With second and subsequent references, use the person's last name only: *In his most recent address on the economic crisis, Obama. . . .*

3. Avoid referring to people by their first names only: *Barack faced three main challenges during his first year in office. . . .*

4. In traditional research writing, generally avoid using titles such as *President, Reverend, Sir, Dr., Professor, Mr., Ms., Senator,* and so on, unless, in the first reference, the title is needed to identify the person's office. In second and subsequent references to the person, the title can generally be dropped, unless the writing situation calls for a high formality.

5. With the names of organizations, give the full name in the first reference (possibly followed by an acronym or initialism in parentheses). For subsequent references, use an accepted shortened form or the acronym or initialism: *The North Atlantic Treaty Organization (NATO) has been tested by Afghanistan. . . . In 2009, Obama encouraged NATO allies. . . .*

Respect sexual orientation. While cultural attitudes concerning sexual orientation continue to evolve, generally follow these guidelines:

1. Start by avoiding derogatory terms designating sexual orientation and differing attitudes toward sexual orientation. Note, as well, that *sexual orientation* is now preferred over *sexual preference* as being a more accurate phrase.

2. In much research writing, especially in the social sciences and the natural sciences, these would be accurate terms describing orientation with respect to sexual identity and behavior: *heterosexual, bisexual,* and *homosexual.*

3. In other forms of research writing (particularly in the humanities), it is acceptable to use these terms: *straight* for heterosexual individuals, *gay* for homosexual men, and *lesbian* for homosexual women.

Respect gender. Avoid sexist language, which stereotypes both males and females or slants your discussion toward one gender. These practices will help:

1. Take care with occupations. Some words imply that given occupations are restricted to one sex. Use *salesperson* instead of *salesman*, *firefighter* instead of *fireman*, and so on. In addition, avoid using *man*, *woman*, *lady*, *male*, or *female* as adjectives modifying occupations (e.g., male nurse, female minister).

2. Generally use *men* and *women* when discussing gender-specific issues; use *male* and *female* when examining statistical differences or animal species.

3. Use parallel language for both sexes. Look for subtle differences in the way you treat men and women—attention to appearance, attitudes toward work, etc. For example, don't say *Percy Bysshe Shelley and his authoress wife Mary. . . .* but *Poet Percy Shelley and novelist Mary Shelley. . . .*

4. Use neutral terms and expressions rather than gendered ones. When a term implies that only one gender is included, use a more inclusive term. Use *people* or *humanity* rather than *mankind*, for example.

5. Avoid masculine-only pronouns (*he*, *his*, *him*) when referring to people in general. While this practice was once considered acceptable, such pronoun use now seems restrictive.

Sentence with gender problems: A good **congressman** seeks input from all **mankind** affected before **he** brings forward legislation.

Solutions: Start by making specific nouns gender neutral. Then fix the pronouns by using one of the options below.

■ Make the pronouns and their antecedents (the nouns to which they refer) plural. Change verbs as needed, and check that pronoun references remain clear. Before good **congressional representatives** bring forward legislation, **they** seek input from all **people** affected.

■ Use "he or she" with care. Overuse sounds awkward and actually draws attention to gender. Example: "When *he or she* does the laundry, *he or she* must separate *his or her* clothes in darks, brights, and whites."
A good **congressional representative** seeks input from all **citizens** affected before **he** or **she** brings forward legislation.

■ Rewrite the sentence to eliminate pronouns altogether.
A good **congressional representative** seeks input from all **constituencies** affected before bringing forward legislation.

Respect age. Avoid age-related terms that are too familiar or that carry negative connotations: *kids*, *juveniles*, *yuppies*, *old man*, or *old woman*. In addition, use these terms for general age groups:

up to age 13 or 14	boys, girls, child, children
between 13 and 19	youth, young people
late teens and early 20s	young adults, young women, young men
20s to age 60s	adults, men, women
65 and older	seniors, senior citizens

Respect ethnicity and race. Don't use words that reflect negatively on an ethnic or racial group. In addition, avoid clichés, stereotypes, and extraneous references to cultural characteristics, as well as dated terms. For example, use *person of color* rather than *nonwhite, person of mixed race* rather than *mulatto, white* rather than *Caucasian.* Choose words that show your respect for all people and cultures:

1. Use acceptable general and specific terms. Follow the practices below in order to respect racial and ethnic diversity within the United States.

   ■ For citizens of African descent, use *African American* or *black.* The first term is now widely accepted, though some people prefer the second.

   ■ To avoid the notion that *American* by itself means *white,* use *Anglo-American* (for English ancestry) or *European Americans.* More specific terms would be *Irish Americans* or *Ukrainian Americans.*

   ■ Avoid using the term *Orientals.* Instead, use *Asian,* and when appropriate, *Asian Americans,* and the specific terms *Japanese Americans* and *Chinese Americans.*

   ■ As a general term, use *Hispanic Americans* or *Hispanics.* For specific terms, use *Mexican Americans, Cuban Americans,* etc.

   ■ As a general term, use *Native Indians* or *Native Americans.* Note, however, that some native peoples prefer to be called by their tribe: *Cherokee people, Inuit.*

2. Use the term *American* carefully. When writing to other U.S. citizens, the terms *America* and *American* are acceptable. However, anyone living in North or South America is also an American. Therefore, when communicating with people outside the U.S., use *United States* and *U.S. citizen* in place of *America* and *American*

> **Poor:** In her novels, Amy Tan, a petite Oriental woman, explores the experiences of Orientals in America.
>
> **Better:** In her novels, Amy Tan explores the experiences of Asian-Americans in the United States.

Respect disabilities and impairments. The first rule when writing to or about people with disabilities or impairments is to refer to a condition only if it's relevant to the message. In addition, follow the two guidelines below.

1. Put people first. Avoid referring to people as if they are their condition rather than people who simply *have* that condition. Put the person first, the disability second. For example, use *students with dyslexia* rather than *dyslexics; participants* or *patients* rather than *subjects* or *cases; people with disabilities* rather than *the disabled.*

2. Avoid negative labels. Do not use obviously degrading labels such as *crippled, deformed, maimed, idiot,* and *invalid,* but also avoid phrases with negative connotations, for example, labeling people as *victims of, suffering from,* or *confined to.* Use *disabled* not *handicapped, congenital disability* not *birth defect, speech impairment* not *lisp, cleft lip* not *harelip, person with AIDS* not *AIDS victim.*

Proofreading for Correctness

When proofreading your research writing, you sweat the small stuff (accuracy, grammar, punctuation, mechanics, spelling, usage). Of course, the small stuff can become big stuff if you are not careful. While a full treatment of grammatical correctness is beyond the scope of this chapter, the following pages address the key issues.

Test Your Draft for Accuracy

It's essential that your paper contain accurate research findings and information. Careful note-taking, transcription, and copy-and-paste should ensure a high degree of this correctness with respect to source information: your paper should have accurate facts, figures, names, dates, and so on. However, double-check these issues as well:

Respect for Sources. Your draft needs to speak respectfully both to the sources you've used and to your readers. Test your writing for lapses, especially when you disagree with a source or press your reader to accept a position. And when the evidence itself is contradictory, incomplete, or uncertain, signal those limits through qualifiers such as *possibly, usually,* and *might.* (See page 216 for more.)

> **Weak:** The arguments that such slaves of the oil companies use to attack climate change are simply way out there, completely ignorant of massive evidence.
>
> **Strong:** While researchers are right to be cautious about interpreting the climate-change evidence, the arguments of those who question climate change are flawed.

Correct Summaries, Paraphrases, and Quotations. Check your use of sources for accuracy. Are summaries and paraphrases true to the original? Are your quotations word-for-word the same as the original? Have you attributed source material to the right source, with the author's name spelled correctly? Is the page number correct?

Proper Acknowledgement of Changes to and Errors in Quotations. Sometimes, you need to signal changes that you have made to quotations, changes that do not seriously change the meaning of the original but may be needed for clarity and conciseness. Brackets [] signal changes to words and letters; ellipses [...] signal that you have omitted words from the original; and the Latin [sic.] signals that the preceding word contains an error (e.g., spelling) that was in the original source, not in your own writing. See page 192 for more details.

> *Example:* As she explores her spiritual attraction to monasteries, Kathleen Norris clarifies that "[she is] not a monk, although [she has] a formal relationship with the Benedictines as an oblate . . . of a community of about sixty-five monks" (17).

Proper Match of Citations and Bibliography. Check to ensure that every source that you reference within your paper is indeed listed in your bibliography. Conversely, double check that every source listed in your bibliography actually is referred to in your paper. If you find a mismatch in either direction, correct it so that your documentation reflects your actual use of specific resources.

Check Quotation Integration and Punctuation

Because research writing, especially in the Humanities, relies on direct quotation of sources, you should carefully check that as quotations are integrated into your sentences, the syntax and punctuation are correct. Check especially for these issues:

- Proper use of commas and colons before source material, as well as end punctuation after source material.
- Proper pronoun reference: using a direct quotation within your sentence sometimes creates a pronoun shift in that the pronouns in the quotation don't match in person the nouns and pronouns in the first part of the sentence.
- Proper content, format, and punctuation for citations.

> **Incorrect:** Kathleen Norris clarifies that: "I am not a monk, although I have a formal relationship with the Benedictines as an oblate." (page 17)
>
> **Correct:** Kathleen Norris states, "I am not a monk, although I have a formal relationship with the Benedictines as an oblate" (17).

Quotations within Quotations. When the source passage that you are quoting contains within it words within quotation marks, place the entire passage within regular quotation marks ("") and place the quoted material within the quotation in single marks (' ').

> *Example:* According to psychologist Leonard Kravitz, "clinical depression manifests itself in Hamlet-like expressions of life as 'flat' and 'stale'" (32).

Quotations, Commas, and Periods. Generally, place commas and periods inside quotation marks; however, when a quotation is followed by an in-text citation in parentheses, place the punctuation outside the closed parenthesis.

> *Example:* "If pumped out over the United States," Jack Lewis of the EPA writes, "the High Plains aquifer would cover all 50 states with one and one-half feet of water" (423).

Quotation Marks, Semicolons, and Colons. Always place semicolons and colons outside quotation marks. If a quotation is followed by an in-text citation, the semicolon or colon goes after the closed parenthesis.

> *Example:* Teri Edelstein contends that "as educational institutions, museums succeed when they bring thought-provoking art before the public"; this includes making available works owned by private collectors who may stand to benefit from the exposure (113). The issue turns, says Edelson, on "reasonable perception" (174): would the average citizen see the private-public collaboration as artistically or financially motivated?

Quotation Marks, Question Marks, and Exclamation Points. If a question mark or exclamation point punctuates the quotation, place the mark inside the quotations; if the mark punctuates your sentence, place it outside the quotations.

> *Example:* In her report, McAllister asks, "Is the hybrid vehicle a truly significant green transportation solution?" (35). Perhaps more importantly, is she accurate when she describes the hybrid as "only an interim solution" (42)?

Check Titles of Works

Research writing frequently refers to the titles of a wide range of resources. Check your writing to make sure that you have formatted titles correctly.

Works That Are Placed within Quotation Marks. Generally, titles of shorter works, portions of larger works, or individual postings on a site are put within quotation marks.

Short story: "Araby"
Short poem: "Birches"
Newspaper article: "The New Admissions Game"
Magazine or journal article: "Is Google Making Us Stupid?"
Online article: "Wikipedia and the Meaning of Truth"

Chapter or article in a book: "Reflections on Advertising"
Lecture title: "Multiculturalism and the Language Battle"
Song: "Disturbia"
Television episode from a series: "Force of Nature" (from *Star Trek: The Next Generation*)

Works That Are Italicized. Generally, titles of longer works, collections of works, and sites are italicized.

Novel: *Gilead*
Play: *Much Ado About Nothing*
Film: *Slumdog Millionaire*
Sculpture: *The Thinker*
CD: *The Joshua Tree*
Television program: *Nightline*

Web site: *GeoCities*
Periodical: *The Atlantic*
Scholarly book: *Jane Austen on Screen*
Report: *Writing, Technology and Teens*
Legal case: *ACLU v. State of Ohio*
Pamphlet: *College Loans*

Titles within Titles. Sometimes, one title appears within another title—a book title within an article title, and so on. Follow these guidelines:

- Title of longer work within title of shorter work: "The Passion Translated: Literary and Cinematic Rhetoric in *Pride and Prejudice* (2005)"
- Title of longer work within title of longer work: *Flirting with* Pride and Prejudice: *Fresh Perspectives on the Original Chick-Lit Masterpiece*
- Title of shorter work within title of longer work: *James Joyce's "Araby": Case Studies in Criticism*
- Title of shorter work within title of short work: "Narrative Implosions in Alice Munro's 'Carried Away'"

Check Your Use of Historical Present Tense

Even though the sources you are using were written in the past, in a sense they still "speak" in the present. That's the logic behind what's called the historical present tense. Unless you are emphasizing the pastness of a source or its publication date in relation to other sources, use the present tense when conveying what a source says.

Example: In his review of Alice Munro's 1996 *Selected Stories*, John Updike *offers* [not *offered*] the following assessment of Munro's composite heroine. . . .

Check for Common Grammar Errors

Spelling mistakes and typos top the list of common errors to fix in your writing. However, focus on proofreading your paper for these additional errors:

Pronoun-Antecedent Agreement: A pronoun doesn't match its antecedent (the noun to which it refers) in number, person, or gender (sex).

> *Example:* When a consumer purchases clothing at the department store, ~~they have~~ *he or she has* little knowledge of where the fabric was woven or where the garment was made.

Ambiguous, Indefinite, or Broad Pronoun Reference: It is unclear which word or phrase a pronoun in the sentence refers to.

> *Example:* When President Obama and Prime Minister Harper met, ~~he~~ *Harper* extended his hand in friendship. This *gesture* was good diplomacy, given talk of protectionism.

Subject-Verb Agreement: The verb doesn't match the subject in terms of person (first, second, or third) or number (singular or plural).

> *Example:* The hybrid vehicle, along with other green technologies such as wind and solar power, ~~are~~ *is* part of a larger movement to reduce people's carbon footprint.

Misplaced and Dangling Modifiers: Either an adjective or adverb (word, phrase, or clause) is distant from the word being modified (misplaced modifier), or the modifying phrase has no term to be modified in the sentence (dangling modifier).

> *Example:* *When it remains* ~~Remaining~~ untreated with therapy, Dr. Berger explains that attachment disorder only leads to stress within families increasing as the child grows.

Unparallel Construction: Words, phrases, or clauses arranged in a series are not phrased according to the same syntactic pattern.

> *Example:* Most consumers remain unaware of where their food originated, how it was grown or raised, ~~as well as that it was processed and needed transportation.~~ *how it was processed, and how far it was transported.*

Sentence Fragment: A phrase or clause lacking a subject, verb, or some other vital part is presented as a complete sentence.

> *Example:* Although, as the New York Times article explained, *Slumdog Millionaire* received positive reviews, *it was not initially seen as an Oscar contender.*

Comma Splice: Two independent clauses are connected with only a comma.

> *Example:* *Pride and Prejudice* is likely Austen's most popular novel; arguably, however, *Persuasion* is her most mature accomplishment.

Comma Omission: A comma is missing when needed to (a) set off introductory material from the main clause, (b) separate two independent clauses joined by a coordinating conjunction, or (c) set off phrases or dependent clauses unnecessary to the sentences' basic meaning.

> *Example:* According to the study, the meaningful presence of a father in a child's life seems connected with higher educational achievement and career stability, but a father's absence, whether short- or long-term, correlates with high-risk social activities and lower grades.

Check for Common Usage Errors

In English, there are a number of commonly confused and misused words. Use the brief glossary below and on the next page to check your writing for the most common problems.

among, amongst, between *Among* and *amongst* are typically used when emphasizing distribution throughout a body or a group of three or more, although *among* is preferred in U.S. English; *between* is used when emphasizing distribution to individuals.

> There was discontent **among** the relatives after learning that their aunt had divided her entire fortune **between** a canary and a favorite waitress at the local cafe.

amount, number Amount is used for bulk measurement. *Number* is used to count separate units. (See also "fewer.")

> The **number** of new instructors hired next year will depend on the **amount** of revenue raised by the new sales tax.

can, may In formal contexts, *can* is used to mean "being able to do"; may is used to mean "having permission to do."

> **May** I borrow your bicycle to get to the library? Then I **can** start working on our group project.

compare with, compare to Things in the same category are *compared with* each other; things in different categories are *compared to* each other.

> **Compare** Christopher Marlowe's plays with William Shakespeare's plays.

> My brother **compared** reading *The Tempest* to visiting another country.

continual, continuous *Continual* often implies that something is happening often, recurring; *continuous* usually implies that something keeps happening, uninterrupted.

> The **continuous** loud music during the night gave the building manager not only a headache, but also **continual** phone calls.

fewer, less *Fewer* refers to the number of separate units; *less* refers to bulk quantity.

> Because of spell checkers, students can produce papers containing **fewer** errors in **less** time.

good, well *Good* is an adjective; *well* is nearly always an adverb. (When used to indicate state of health, *well* is an adjective.)

> A *good* job offers opportunities for advancement, especially for those who do their jobs *well*.

imply, infer *Imply* means "to suggest without saying outright"; *infer* means "to draw a conclusion from facts." (A writer or a speaker *implies*; a reader or a listener *infers*.)

> Dr. Rufus **implied** I should study more; I **inferred** he meant my grades had to improve or I'd be repeating the class.

it's, its *It's* is the contraction of "it is." *Its* is the possessive form of "it."

> **It's** not hard to see why my husband feeds that alley cat; **its** pitiful limp and mournful mewing would melt any heart.

like, as *Like* should not be used in place of as. *Like* is a preposition, which is followed by a noun, a pronoun, or a noun phrase. *As* is a subordinating conjunction, which introduces a clause. Avoid using *like* as a subordinating conjunction. Use *as* instead.

> You don't know her **like** I do. (Incorrect)
>
> You don't know her **as** I do. (Correct)
>
> **Like** the others in my study group, I do my work **as** any serious student would—carefully and thoroughly. (Correct)

medium, media, median When *medium* refers to a means by which something is communicated, *media*, not *mediums*, is the correct plural. (*Mediums* can refer to people claiming to communicate with the spirits of the dead.) *Median* means "in the middle."

> As Frances ambled across the **median**, he considered what **media** by which to share the love letter that he had composed to Becky Sharp. Ruling out **mediums** given Becky's fictional nature, he chose a blog as the best **medium**.

oral, verbal *Oral* means "uttered with the mouth"; *verbal* means "relating to or consisting of words and the comprehension of words."

> The actress's **oral** abilities were outstanding, and her pronunciation and intonation impeccable; but after trying to decipher the play's meaning, I doubted the playwright's **verbal** skills.

principal, principle As an adjective, *principal* means "primary." As a noun, it can mean "a school administrator" or "a sum of money." A *principle* is an idea or a doctrine.

> His **principal** gripe is lack of freedom. (adjective)
>
> My son's **principal** expressed his concerns to the teachers. (noun)
>
> After 20 years, the amount of interest was higher than the **principal**. (noun)
>
> The **principle** of caveat emptor guides most consumer groups.

than, then *Than* is used in a comparison; *then* tells when.

> Study more **than** you think you need to. **Then** you will probably be satisfied with your grades.

their, there, they're *Their* is a possessive personal pronoun. *There* is a pronoun used as a function word to introduce a clause or an adverb used to point out location. *They're* is the contraction for "they are."

> Look over **there**.
>
> **There** is a comfortable place for students to study for **their** exams, so **they're** more likely to do a good job.

who's, whose *Who's* is the contraction for "who is." *Whose* is a possessive pronoun.

> **Whose** car are we using, and **who's** going to pay for the gas?

your, you're *Your* is a possessive pronoun. *You're* is the contraction for "you are."

> If **you're** like most Americans, you will have held eight jobs by **your** 40th birthday.

Focus on Your Major: Developing a Summary or Abstract

Summarizing is clearly an important skill for effective note-taking during research (see page 152). However, this skill is also crucial for doing effective research writing. In fact, the summary portion of a research paper may be the most read, most prominent part of the document. Therefore, writing a strong summary is crucial to your research writing's success. Frequently, as well, the summary is the last portion of the paper written, so now that you have revised and refined your draft, it's a good time to focus on the summary. Let's start with basic definitions and distinctions:

- A *summary* extracts from a larger document, a discussion, a presentation, or a meeting the key points and significant information needed by particular readers.
- Essentially, the word *abstract* is a synonym for *summary* in that an abstract also describes the content of a larger paper and pulls out and gathers together the original's key points. However, *abstract* is a more technical term that tends to refer to summaries published as part of official research in academic disciplines, especially in the natural and social sciences. Such abstracts are published along with or even separate from the longer research study. For example, abstracts appear in database descriptions of articles, at the beginnings of research articles, and in separate published indexes such as *Personnel Management Abstracts*.

The Content and Style of a Summary

As you develop a summary for your research project, consider the following issues:

What to include in your summary. Depending on the summary's purpose and readers, the content can vary greatly—from a basic review of the topics covered in your paper to more in-depth coverage of your main points, claims, analysis, and arguments. Generally, however, include key points, conclusions, recommendations, and the most significant information—the heart of your paper's discussion and argument. Conversely, exclude specific examples, supporting details, and extensive numerical data—all the material and evidence used to back up the main claims you made.

The length of your summary. The length should be tied specifically to how you see your readers using your summary. Generally, however, a summary should be about ten percent as long as the paper itself.

The stylistic features of a good summary. Above all, your summary must be clear to readers. For that reason, your summary should

- have a stand-alone, self-explanatory quality.
- use objective wording, plain English, and keywords readers are looking for.
- be written in brief sentences that have strong transitional words.
- maintain the focus and tone of the original document.
- avoid references to the writer and the document such as "The writer says" or "In the next section. . . ."

Writing a Summary

Your goal when writing a summary is to boil down the information in your paper to its basic ingredients—the main points, reasoning, conclusions, and so on. To write an effective summary, follow these steps:

1. **Remember your main points.** Skim your paper to remind yourself of your overall analysis or argument: review your opening and closing paragraphs, headings, topic sentences of paragraphs, graphics, and so on.

2. **Review the paper carefully to take note of important points.** Skip background, examples, descriptions, and most supporting details. Instead, zero in on essentials—conclusions, recommendations, main points, key facts and numbers—signaled by key words like the following:

   - *Enumerating words:* first, second, third, in addition, furthermore, finally
   - *Contrasting points words:* although, however, by contrast, not only . . . but also, on the other hand
   - *Significance words:* basically, central, crucial, essential, fundamental, indispensable, important, key, leading, major, principal, serious, significant, main point, conclusion, result, problem, solution, cause, effect

3. **Draft** the summary by identifying the topic and focus of the paper, stating its central point, and clarifying the line of reasoning or supporting points in the same order presented in the paper.

4. **Revise and refine** your summary by checking it against these questions:

   - Are all the ideas accurately conveyed, using the key words that your reader would be looking for?
   - Does the organization of the summary reflect the organization of the original?
   - Do the sentences read smoothly, not like a choppy series of extracted sentences strung together? If necessary, add transitions and reword long or awkward sentences.
   - Is your summary free of obvious grammar, punctuation, and spelling errors?

Sample Abstract

While remaining something of a mystery, the disappearance in the late sixteenth century of a group of colonists from Roanoke Island off North Carolina is likely related to the mystery of the ancestry of the North Carolina's Native American Lumbee tribe. Using evidence from the parallel example of the Catawba Indians, as well as evidence related to bald cypress tree rings, historical analysis, immunology, genetic studies, and linguistic patterns, one can tentatively conclude that the lost colonists were perhaps captured by, intermarried with, and were absorbed by the sixteenth-century ancestors of the Lumbee. This conclusion points to the need for further study, as the Lumbee People's status as Native American is currently contested and needs to be resolved in order for them to be recognized by the federal government.

Practicing Your Research

1. **Explore:** Patricia O'Connor has said that "[a]ll writing begins life as a first draft, and first drafts are never any good. They're not supposed to be." Do you agree or disagree with O'Connor? Given the discussion in this chapter of reworking a first draft, what does it take to develop a polished piece of research writing?

2. **Apply:** Find an informal piece of writing that you have previously developed—a reading response in a course, a writing-journal entry, an e-mail to a friend. Then using the revising, editing, and proofreading strategies in this chapter, turn your "first draft" into a more formal piece of academic prose.

3. **Collaborate on a Case Study:** As directed by your instructor, continue work with classmates on your clothing-focused project. Using the different talents and points of view in your group, take your group's first draft through the process of revising, editing, and proofreading. (See chapter 11 for more on peer review.)

4. **Research Your Major:** What does a polished piece of writing look like in your discipline? Talk to instructors and students further along in the program about expectations; check the library, the writing center, and online resources for style guides; and review important journals in the field by skimming articles and gathering information about publishing expectations at journal Web sites. Synthesize your research by developing a list of the 10 key features of writing in your discipline (anything from type and placement of thesis to punctuation practices).

5. **Work on Your Current Project:** Take stock of your first draft—its strengths and weaknesses in light of the assignment, your purpose, and your readers. Using the strategies in this chapter, revise and refine your paper to the point that it offers a quality discussion of the topic, a discussion into which readers can enter. As you do this work, refer to the checklist below.

Checklist:

☑ I have revised my first draft for global issues:

- *Ideas:* the thinking, content, and use of source material are sound.
- *Organization:* the overall structure and the paragraphing create a sound progression of support for the thesis.
- *Voice:* the tone is consistently credible and measured.

☑ I have edited my paper for local (or style) issues:

- *Sentences:* constructions are energetic and varied, with sources integrated smoothly.
- *Word Choice:* wording is clear, precise, and concise—free of jargon, clichés, euphemisms, flowery language, doublespeak, and biased language.

☑ I have proofread my paper for *correctness:*

- Accurate research findings and documentation.
- Correct grammar, punctuation, mechanics, spelling, and usage.

© Cengage Learning/Illustrated by Chris Krenzke

10

Sharing Your Research Writing

Q How is research writing traditionally shared in an academic environment? How is research shared (published, posted, presented, and so on) in other environments (e.g., workplace, media)? What strategies make the sharing of research effective?

Sharing your research-based analysis and results is one key goal of any research project. This sharing with real readers advances the dialogue on your topic, a dialogue that started with curiosity and led to discoveries.

Typically and traditionally, this sharing has meant submitting an academic research paper to your instructor for his or her review, evaluation, and feedback. Today, however, sharing your research writing can mean developing other conversations: presenting your findings textually, orally, and visually to classmates or community groups; posting your writing on a Web site or in a blog; developing a video record or a podcast of your findings; or contributing to a wiki through collaboration with other researchers and writers. In the digital age, you have fresh opportunities for publishing your research-based thinking—as well as new challenges for doing this well.

Communication scholar Marshall McLuhan famously claimed that the medium is the message. Whether you share your research in print or digitally, in a 400-page dissertation or a 140-character "Tweet," the medium-message relationship is central to presenting your research findings. Negotiating that relationship effectively is the focus of this chapter.

What's Ahead?

Designing Your Research Document

Reader-friendly document design is about effective presentation. Whether you are writing a traditional academic research paper or creating a Web page, strong design aims to (1) create a sense of professionalism, (2) invite readers into your document, (3) help them navigate the content, (4) map out the structure of your thinking, and (5) promote understanding of that thinking. What follows introduces the basics of such reader-friendly design.

Making Rhetorically-Driven Design Choices

To ensure that the document's design helps achieve your research-writing goals, root the design in your project's rhetorical situation:

- **Purpose:** What do you want your document to accomplish? Is it informing, analyzing, persuading—or all of these? Is your document clarifying complex information? Are you aiming to set a particular tone with your document (e.g., scholarly, entertaining)?

- **Audience:** What are your readers' needs, values, and experiences? What will they be looking for, and how will they use it? How will readers access, transport, and store the document? Will they be reading vertically (digging deeply) or horizontally (searching for sections, skimming, following links)? Will readers be focused or distracted, motivated or reluctant? What reading skills will they bring to the task?

- **Context:** What kind of document are you writing, following what conventions? Will the document be print, digital, or both? How will it be produced and shared? Where will it be shared, posted, or published?

Consider, for example, this fact sheet about Swine Flu published at the Centers for Disease Control Web site. The goal of this digital document (with only its beginning shown here) is to efficiently share accurate information on a disease that a highly diverse readership (various ages, cultures, regions, and so on) might find frightening, given possibilities of deadly pandemics. The fact-sheet format calls for minimal color and graphics; instead, information is laid out through clear headings, a Q&A structure, and short paragraphs. Such a design supports the online document's intended purpose and audience, just as the effective design of an academic paper on the same topic would support that paper's intended purpose and audience.

Planning Your Research Document's Format

Document format refers to the shape of the whole piece. With some research projects, the format will be specified by your assignment and the document's conventions (e.g., academic essay, lab report, poster presentation). Other times, you will have some freedom about format. To develop a format that fits your research project and findings, think through the issues below.

Consider delivery methods. Developing a document format begins with choosing a delivery method: paper, digital, or both. Which medium will best deliver your message, and what document type will best embody that message?

- *Paper* documents are stable, portable, traditional, and familiar; moreover, such documents can be easily created, copied, distributed, and posted. Readers tend to give paper more in-depth attention. With paper, you can be creative in your format choices: paper of different sizes, colors, and weights; standard sheets or pamphlet-like folded pages; and various bindings (from paper clips to binders to spiral binding).
- *Digital* documents are flexible; are easy to create and modify; may include dynamic multimedia elements; can be quickly posted, distributed, accessed, downloaded, and printed; and allow for rapid response. With digital formats, you can be highly creative and engaging. However, readers tend to skim digital documents rather than read them in depth.

Make format choices that create document access for readers. Access elements help readers enter your research document easily, find what they need, and exit smoothly. Consider these options:

- *Heading system:* A system of parallel, informative headings and subheadings consistently used throughout a document shows readers the structure of your thinking and offers them quick access to specific elements.
- *Headers and/or footers:* A definitive header or footer quickly identifies the document, chapter, or section. A header supplies a name, title, phrase, or other identifying word above the text on each page; a footer runs that information at the bottom of each page.
- *Page numbering system:* A print document longer than one page should use numbering. In digital documents that are not pdfs of print documents, consider numbering paragraphs or sections.
- *Tables of contents, menus, and indexes:* For longer and more complex documents, these are indispensable tools for locating topics and information quickly. For example, a strong Web page typically offers readers a menu of links.
- *Dividers and tabs:* In longer documents, dividers and tabs help readers quickly find what they need. Dividers are typically pages of different paper weight and color from regular pages, and they may have tabs for identification.
- *Icons:* Clear, well-placed icons guide readers by alerting them to key information; however, be careful not to overuse icons to the point of creating confusion.

Thinking through Page Layout

Page layout—how you arrange material on a page—determines whether your document is attractive, readable, and accessible. Generally, aim to avoid dense blocks of prose and cluttered pages. For most research writing, you aim is to develop a page layout that reflects the conventions of the discipline and that features your content, a layout that avoids distracting glitz. Such a layout exhibits balance on the page, creates a flow from left to right and top to bottom, emphasizes important content, and creates a consistent layout pattern for the whole document. The guidelines below will help you achieve such layout.

Choose your page orientation. Standard orientation for most pages is vertical, called portrait; such orientation is used for traditional academic research writing. However, some documents, such as pamphlets and Web pages, follow a horizontal orientation, called landscape. Select the orientation that best presents your research findings, meets readers' needs, and supports their use of the document.

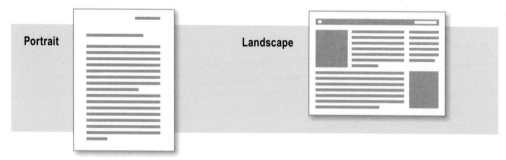

Choose numbers and types of columns. Number of columns can range greatly—from the one-column format of traditional academic papers to three or more columns for pamphlets, newsletters, and Web pages. Moreover, multiple columns can be newspaper or parallel. With newspaper columns, text runs continuously from the bottom of one column over to the top of the next. With parallel columns, the text in each column remains separate. As you plan the layout for your research document, consider these options:

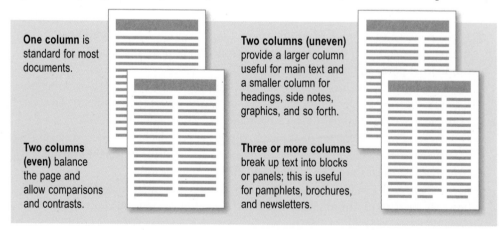

One column is standard for most documents.

Two columns (even) balance the page and allow comparisons and contrasts.

Two columns (uneven) provide a larger column useful for main text and a smaller column for headings, side notes, graphics, and so forth.

Three or more columns break up text into blocks or panels; this is useful for pamphlets, brochures, and newsletters.

Use white space. To balance dark print, build white space into your page layout. Used well, white space rests readers' eyes, "chunks" related information, and highlights key ideas and details. Frame your page with generous margins, generally 1 inch or 1½ inches on all sides of a standard 8½- by 11-inch sheet. In addition, keep your prose from getting heavy and dense on the page by increasing line spacing, adding space between paragraphs, using headings, presenting information in bulleted or numbered lists, placing key text in boxes, and separating text with rules (horizontal or vertical lines).

Format lines effectively. In a standard, one-column document such as a traditional research paper, your lines should average 50-80 characters (about 10–15 words). Overly long lines make reading difficult, whereas overly short lines suggest lack of substance. With respect to alignment, most text should be left justified (aligned) but right ragged.

Avoid layout problems. Use your word-processing program's tools to avoid *widows* (single lines of text that sit alone at the top of a page), *orphans* (first lines of paragraphs left alone at the bottom of a page), and *tombstones* (headings sitting alone at the bottom of a column or page, detached from the text to which they refer).

Develop consistent visual cues. Page layout should distinguish between main and secondary points, as well as show how the points are connected. Create clear design patterns, and stick with them, by following these principles:

1. *Stress content connections through design similarities.* Closely related content in your research writing should be graphically connected through proximity on the page and similar treatment in terms of headings, typography, and color. Repetition of parallel features will create a clear pattern.

2. *Stress content contrasts through design differences.* Contrasting ideas can be made graphically distinct through opposing typography, paragraphing, lists, and color.

3. *Emphasize primary content through bold design features.* The most important content will jump off the page through prominent headings, boxes, background and text colors, listing, icons, tables, rules, and the like.

4. *De-emphasize secondary content through subdued design features.* Less important information might be relegated to smaller print, subsections, and footnotes.

5. *Supply readers with visual signals.* Generally, create a focal point for each page and design the rest of the page around that focus. Your heading system, indenting practices, paragraphing, listing, icons, visuals, and more—all of these announce the page's information structure and guide readers through the page.

Using Color

Color choices are central to strong document design. Depending on the situation, black and white is generally flexible and conservative—fitting for the academic research paper. However, color—whether in paper, type, background, or graphics—might improve your research document by both grabbing your reader's attention and communicating content more clearly.

Make color choices rooted in the color wheel. Design theory as it relates to color is based in the color wheel, which pictures the relationships between colors. Primary colors (red, blue, and yellow) are foundational—not made from blending other colors. Secondary colors result from the blending of the two primary colors between which they lie. Endless color variations can be created from these building blocks. Select colors for your document based on the principles below:

1. *Use complementary colors to create energy.* Colors opposite each other on the wheel are complementary. Placed together, these colors "complete" each other, making each appear deeper and richer. Offering a good foundation for your document's color scheme, complementary colors energize your design.

2. *Use related colors to create harmony.* Colors close together point to similarities and subtle variations in content. When brought together, related colors keep things calm and balanced.

3. *Work with color associations.* Different colors have different associations for different people. Generally, however, some colors are warm (yellow, orange, red, brown), whereas others are cool (purple, blue, green). This difference refers, in part, to the emotional tone the colors create. Moreover, colors have both personal and cultural associations—red with passion, blood, and warnings; blue with sky, water, and stability; green with nature, growth, and cheerfulness. However, color associations in one culture don't necessarily translate well in other cultures. For example, in European-rooted cultures, black is associated with mourning, whereas in China the color of mourning is white.

Use color for different design elements. As you develop your overall design, consider where you can use color and for what effects. Here are some choices:

- *Paper:* Generally, use white or off-white paper, especially in a standard academic research paper. For special sections, dividers, and covers, use colored paper. However, choose wisely: subtle, traditional colors (like tan, blue, or green) imply strength and stability; pastels lightness; neon colors "advertising."

- *The Computer Screen:* For digital applications such as word processing and e-mail, an off-white background works best. However, Web pages and presentation software tend to use brighter and deeper colors to attract attention.

- *Visuals:* Graphs, charts, photographs, and drawings—if your document includes visuals like these, they can be powerfully enhanced by effective color combinations.

- *Text and Background:* Traditionally, print on paper or on screen is black against a neutral background. Consider, however, varying from this practice at specific points in your document in order to create emphasis—in headings, boxes, menus, lists, and so on. You can vary the text color, the background color, or both. The first rule, however, is to use text and background combinations that make text legible.

Make color purposeful. Tie your color scheme to an analysis of the purpose, audience, and context for your research writing.

1. *Use color carefully in academic research writing.* Conservative colors are suitable for research papers, poster presentations, and slide shows. Brighter colors may be appropriate for less formal research writing.

2. *Use color to feature material.* Draw readers' attention to key elements and establish patterns that create a visual logic. Focus on headings, bullets, text boxes, and so on.

3. *Use a limited color palette consistently.* Once you've established a color pattern, use it throughout the document. Avoid a confusing look and clashing colors (such as pink and orange).

Example: The sample shown is the first page of a four-page brochure promoting solar technology. Notice the conservative, calm color choices, specifically the blue and greens, typically associated with nature. Note, as well, how the leaves on the left anchor the two photographs. The harmony is completed by a strong blue and green logo, blue type in the headings, and black serif type for the text. A quote is added for visual and intellectual interest.

Making Typographical Choices

Typography refers to the actual print on the page or screen. With print, your aim is to create a positive impression, make reading easy, and clarify content.

Select fitting typefaces. Typeface refers to the look shared by the letters and other symbols of a specific type. These typefaces cluster in families—Arial, Courier, and Times Roman, for example. In addition, typefaces are designated as serif or sans serif. Serif typeface, like this, has finishes on the letters. Sans serif typeface, like this, has no finishes. Follow these guidelines for choosing typeface:

1. Use a serif typeface for main text, a sans serif for headings. Note that you would reverse this practice for digital documents—sans serif for main text, serif for headings—because computer-screen resolution makes sans serif cleaner, crisper.

2. Select an attractive typeface that is readable, given the document type. For example, a French script might make reading difficult in an academic research paper.

Vary type size. For normal reading conditions, make main text 10 or 12 points. For titles, headings, and subheadings, increase size 2–4 points; 12, 14, 16, or 18 are good choices. Make the jump noticeable but not drastic. For documents read under difficult conditions and for document parts that are critical (e.g., warnings in instructions), consider larger type. And for material projected onto a screen, think big—18–36 points or even larger.

# The Future of Hybrid Transportation	title (18 points)
## History of Hybrid Technologies	heading (16)
### Recent Legislation on Clean Air and Climate Change	subheading (14)
Beginning in the 1980s, legislators in North America . . .	main text (12)

Use different type styles. Type style refers to special effects like those shown below. Use each stylistic effect for a reason, not for dazzle. Moreover, be moderate: avoid combining several techniques. Generally, use effects to set off special text.

UPPER CASE IS MORE PROMINENT THAN LOWER CASE BUT HARDER TO READ IN EXTENDED PASSAGES.

Underlining is useful for indicating subheadings, key words, and key sentences, but avoid using it for extended passages.

Highlighting and similar techniques such as shading and **outlining** draw attention to key words and statements.

Boldface causes print to jump out. It's especially useful for headings, subheadings, and other key information.

Italics indicates book titles, terms and words designated as words, and key statements. Avoid it, however, for extended passages because it is difficult to read.

Color helps highlight headings, warnings, tips, and other key material. However, make sure that color combinations work well.

Submitting an Academic Paper

For your research-writing project, submitting your paper (on time) may represent the most significant milestone. Turning in an academic research paper—whether a literary analysis, a psychology term paper, or an environmental-science experiment report—represents not only the completion of a course requirement but also your desire for educated feedback from your instructor. For these reasons, submit your academic paper according to accepted and respected conventions.

FOCUS on Your Major: Different disciplines follow standard formats for academic research writing, as well as particular submission guidelines related to the disciplines' for your major. Part 3 of this text introduces the main systems.

The Character of an Academic Paper

An academic paper aims to offer a substantive exploration of an issue, question, or problem. As such, your paper's format, design, and presentation should be fairly conservative, reflecting the seriousness of the topic and rhetorical situation. As shown in the sample page (formatted according to MLA guidelines), academic presentation is straightforward in order to accentuate content and thinking. While each system follows its own guidelines, all systems attend to features like these:

Informative identifying and ordering features: use of headers or footers, headings.

Supportive visuals: informative graphics such as line charts and photographs are properly identified, numbered, and discussed in the text as evidence.

White space: generous margins framing the page, double-spaced lines.

Source documentation: careful citation practices, whether in-text or in footnotes.

Conservative typography: recognizable typeface, such as Times New Roman, as well as restrained use of type styles (e.g., bold, underlining, italics).

Van Arendonk 4

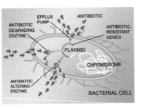

Figure 1. Strategies of Antibiotic-Resistant Genes. Ilustration by Sol Ivanski in S. S. Davidson, "Perils of Antibiotic Overuse," *Genetic Frontiers* July 2005.

proportion of bacteria that are resistant to an antibiotic. While the normal bacteria decrease in number as the antibiotic inhibits their growth, the resistant forms of the bacteria thrive and reproduce to quickly increase in number.

Clearly, the development of antibiotic-resistant organisms poses a huge threat to the present system of health care, a system that relies heavily on antibiotic therapies. Antibiotics normally used to treat bacterial infections are becoming increasingly ineffective as the number of antibiotic-resistant organisms increases. According to Linda Bren, a staff writer for *FDA Consumer,* the threat is large and is getting worse:

> For some of us, bacterial resistance could mean more visits to the doctor, a lengthier illness, and possibly more toxic drugs. For others, it could mean death. The CDC [Centers for Disease Control and Prevention] estimates that each year, nearly 2 million people in the United States acquire an infection while in a hospital, resulting in 90,000 deaths. More than 70 percent of the bacteria that cause these infections are resistant to at least one of the antibiotics commonly used to treat them. (28)

The results of antibiotic resistance can range from minor inconveniences, to higher health-care costs, and even to death. This

Submitting or Posting a Digital Document

While you will typically turn in a print copy of your research writing, sometimes you will have the opportunity to submit or post a digital document, whether a word-processing file, a PDF file, an html Web page, or a blog. You might even develop or contribute to a wiki article, record a podcast, or create a video. Sharing your digital document may involve e-mailing it as an attachment to your instructor, posting it to a restricted course site for classmates, or publishing it on the free Web for all to read, hear, or view.

Going digital has many advantages, from simply saving paper to making access easy for readers to increasing multimedia elements (texts, image, sound, motion). But you also need to be cautious. While your instructor may read your digital paper attentively, or some readers may print and read a PDF file of your full paper, online readers tend instead to browse and follow links. Therefore, digital publishing calls for strategies distinct from print publishing. Generally, the online environment is a good place to share information, but not a friendly place for publishing extended, in-depth analysis and argument, unless you can count on your reader downloading, saving, and printing your document. Here are some initial strategies:

1. **Learn** what forms of digital publishing your course and your school support. What types of hardware and software are available for student projects? What policies must you follow for publishing your work (e.g., copyright guidelines, research and information ethics).

2. **Develop and save** your digital document in a format that features your research findings and meets readers' information needs. For example, make sure that your word-processing file is saved according to your instructor's expectations and with a file name that will distinguish your assignment from classmates' assignments. Moreover, use multimedia elements that engage your audience but effectively enhance their understanding of the topic.

3. **Post or submit** your digital document only after you have carefully revised, edited, and proofread it. Particularly if your document will potentially have a wide audience, have someone review your writing before you post it.

4. **Publicize** your posting, if appropriate. Depending on the type of digital document and your method of posting, you might consider notifying specific audiences. For example, when you submit your paper by e-mail to your instructor, write a brief, polite message indicating the attachment, the course, and the assignment.

 FOCUS on Ethics: Digital publishing can take you out of the comfort zone of submitting a paper to an instructor for a grade. Online, readers may rely on your research not only to understand something but to make decisions. For this reason, take your online responsibilities seriously: post only credible, reliable information and thoughtful discussion.

Developing a Web Site

Developing a Web site requires that you be concise, focused, and visually appealing. After all, people don't read Web sites so much as scan them, so information should be presented in short chunks of text that quickly and clearly get to the point, and pages should be designed to minimize scrolling and maximize use of available screen space. Start with the fundamentals that follow.

Understand Web Page Elements. Page elements are defined primarily by purpose—headings, body text, and so forth. Before developing your site, consider these elements:

- *Headings* (also called headers) come in six levels and are used to separate different sections and subsections of Web documents. Heading 1 is the largest; heading 6 is the smallest. All are bold black serif font by default.
- *Body text* is organized into chunks, called paragraphs, which are separated by white space. Unlike printed text, paragraphs on the Web do not generally have a first-line indentation. By default, body text is a black serif font roughly the same size as a heading level 4 (though not bold).
- *Preformatted text* is "monospaced"; it displays all characters at the same width. It is used primarily to show mathematical formulas, computer code, and the like.
- *Lists* can be formatted in three types: Ordered lists are numbered, unordered lists are bulleted, and definition lists present pairs of information—usually terms alongside their definitions, which are indented.
- *Images* can include photographs, clip art, graphs, line drawings, cartoon figures, icons, and animations.
- *Background color* for a Web page is white by default (medium gray in older browsers), which makes the standard headings and text easily legible.
- *Tables* are grids of rows and columns that allow designers to control where various elements appear on a page.

Understand Web Page Functions. On the Web, readers can browse pages in almost any order, send messages and files, and much more. Before developing your site, consider these functions common to Web pages:

- *Hyperlinks*—links for short—are strings of specially formatted text that enable readers to jump to another spot on the Web. Internal links take you to another section of the same Web page or to another Web page on the same site. External links lead to pages on other Web sites. "Mail to" links allow readers to address e-mail to recipients.
- *Menus* offer structured lists of links that operate like a Web site's table of contents. Menus are typically presented in a column or row at the edge of a Web page. Good Web sites include a standard site menu on every page so readers don't get lost.
- *Forms* enable the host of a Web site to interact with the site's readers. Web forms can be used for surveys, complaints, requests, or suggestions.

Plan Your Web Site. Once you understand Web site elements and functions, you can begin planning your Web site. Take the following steps:

1. *Focus your site.* Analyze the rhetorical situation by asking yourself these questions:
   - What is the primary purpose of the Web site? Am I creating a library of informative reference documents, or am I arguing a position on an issue?
   - Who is the site's audience? What people will seek out this site? Why? What do they need with respect to my topic? What level of language formality is appropriate? What graphics, colors, and design will appeal?
   - What is the site's central topic? What is the most important information that I have? How will I demonstrate that the information is credible and reliable? How can I divide the information into brief segments? What visual elements would help present my message? What other Web sites address this topic, and should my Web site link to them?

2. *Establish your site's central message.* State the main idea that you want your site to communicate—its theme or "mission statement." As shown below, use a key verb like inform, explain, provide, or persuade, plus a precise topic statement.

> The purpose of this Web site is to inform fellow students and the general public about current research into hybrid-vehicle transportation.

3. *Create a site map.* Web sites can be as simple as a personal site or as complex as a government site. As you develop a site map, consider these principles:
   - No one will read your entire site. People curl up with books, not Web sites.
   - Your site will likely have many small audiences. A site's audience may include anyone with a computer, an Internet connection, and an interest in some aspect of your site's topic. Keep all potential readers in mind.
   - Web sites are nonlinear. A single "home page" or "splash page" introduces the site, which branches out like tree limbs into pages with varied content.

Sample site map: A map for a simple site might include only four items—a home page, page A, page B, and page C (as shown in white on the diagram). Users can jump between any of the secondary-level pages or back to the home page. A more complex Web site typically needs more levels (as shown in green on the diagram). Likewise, its menu will offer more navigation choices. Related pages might be connected with links (as represented by the dotted lines).

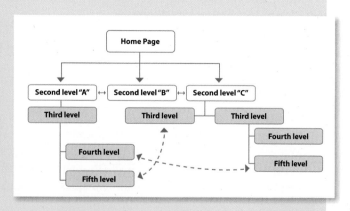

Develop Individual Web Pages. When you create individual pages, consider both the design and content—specifically how to make the two work well together.

1. *Consider design principles.* In particular, apply these principles to your pages:
   - Like many other publications (e.g., magazines), most Web pages are designed on grids of columns and rows. Some rows may span multiple columns, while some columns may overrun several rows.
   - Good Web pages demonstrate simplicity and balance. You might balance light elements with dark ones, open space with full space, text with images, etc. Similarly, keep pages uncluttered by using short paragraphs, headings, and visuals.
   - Web sites may contain a variety of pages to present a combination of informative and persuasive content. Use each page's purpose to guide your choices.

2. *Draft the content.* Relying on your research findings, write and revise the prose for specific pages, carefully testing and refining them before posting them. In particular, do the following:
   - Identify the site. Write an introductory sentence or brief paragraph for your site's home page that lets visitors know immediately the site's purpose.
   - Provide clear links. Create links for your pages, using clear descriptors such as "History of Hybrid Transportation." If necessary, add a descriptive sentence to further identify the link. Let visitors know precisely where each link will take them.
   - Introduce each page. Search sites may deliver some visitors to a page other than your home page. Give each page a brief introduction that clearly identifies it. Also, remember to provide a link back to your home page.
   - Title each page. Atop the browser window is a title bar, where the current page should be identified. This title is used in browser bookmarks, search engine listings, and the like. So be sure to give every page on your Web site a descriptive title.

3. *Keep the content fresh.* Your Web site should be a living thing. Monitor your site and seek feedback, making adjustments and updates, especially to keep your research and information current.

Sample Web page: The Web page below is from an online journal that publishes undergraduate research.

Source: The Journal of Young Investigators

Contributing to a Wiki

Wikis are becoming a popular method of building and sharing information. There's Wikipedia, of course, but educational groups, government agencies, and businesses are all beginning to use wikis as online sites for collaboration. (See pages 86-89 for a discussion of wikis as research resources.) But what about your own research project? How might contributing to a wiki fit with your research writing? Here are some possible scenarios:

- *Within Your Course:* The courseware used at your school and in your course could have a wiki feature. Your instructor might ask you to collaborate with classmates to develop a wiki presentation of your research findings.

- *A Free-Web Wiki Project:* As a component of or choice within your research project, your instructor might ask you to contribute to a free-Web wiki encyclopedia such as Wikipedia or Citizendium (e.g., its Eduzendium project). You might develop an article on a topic that is currently absent or is simply a "stub" (incomplete); conversely, you might do a careful edit of an existing article.

- *Research-Project Follow-Up:* After you have completed your course research project, you might contribute your newfound knowledge to a wiki such as Wikipedia. At a more advanced state of your education, you might contribute to more specialized, discipline-specific wikis.

Such a wiki project might involve developing distinct documents from the same research. You might, for example, write a traditional research paper, but also write an encyclopedia entry on the same topic for a wiki. Whatever your reason for contributing to a wiki, follow these guidelines:

Before contributing, become familiar with the site. While wiki software is quite simple, you do need to learn how to use it. Similarly, each wiki site typically has its own rules for contributing—guidelines for drafting articles and for making editorial changes to existing articles. Study these expectations carefully so that you can contribute without disrupting or offending the wiki community. To this end, it is also helpful to study the structure, tone, style, and documentation methods of well-developed articles in the wiki. Doing so will give you a good sense of the writing conventions for this particular wiki.

Draft your content according to reference-work conventions. Wiki entries are typically NOT analytical or argumentative research papers, so you cannot simply post your paper to the wiki. In fact, if you do so you are likely to have your paper removed. Instead, develop wiki contributions that have these features of electronic reference works:

- Supply reliable, well-researched information, explanations, and narratives. Your wiki writing should center on what is the accepted, agreed-upon knowledge on your topic.

- Break down information into small, discrete subtopics. Because readers are typically looking for a particular piece of information, you need to make that information accessible through the clear organization of your article, informative headings, short paragraphs, and lists.

- Maintain a neutral tone throughout your article. Your approach to the topic needs to be objective; therefore, discussions should not be biased, and language should be free of negative connotations.
- Create helpful links and indicate your sources. By using strategic keywords, link your discussion at each point with other parts of your article, with other articles in the wiki, and with external sources. Wiki articles rarely contain original, primary research; instead, focus on carefully indicating your secondary sources, providing links and URLs whenever possible to verify your information. (Note that your wiki article thus becomes a tertiary source of information on the topic. See pages 34-37 for clarification of the primary, secondary, tertiary distinction.)

Collaborate constructively. One strength of a wiki is that it encourages collaborative development of knowledge. No single writer claims authorship rights but posts what he or she has drafted, understanding that others within the writing community may revise and edit that material with the aim of correcting, deepening, and extending the content. The wiki's writing community might be as small as your project's group of fellow students or as large as anyone on the free Web (e.g., Wikipedia). Whatever the nature of the wiki's writing community, collaborate constructively by doing the following:

- Be open to the editing of others. Respect and study the changes made by others, letting those changes be reviewed by additional editors while resisting the urge to change the content back to your original draft.
- Be a respectful editor. When you wish to revise or edit an existing article, first make sure that you are familiar with the editing protocols you must follow. Then carefully study the editorial history of the article to see how the article has changed through time. In particular, have the changes you are planning been introduced and then rejected in the past? If yes, why?

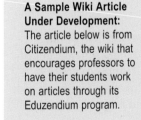

A Sample Wiki Article Under Development: The article below is from Citizendium, the wiki that encourages professors to have their students work on articles through its Eduzendium program.

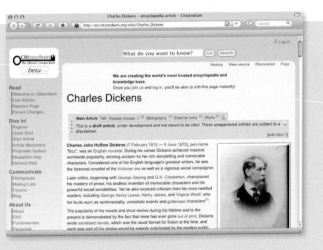

Source: WikiMedia

Sharing Findings in a Blog

A blog (short for "Web log") is essentially an online journal posted to a Web page. The writer's thoughts, shaped into what are called blog posts or entries, are usually displayed in reverse chronological order—from most recent entry back to the earliest post. Posts can contain written text, images, and links. While a writer's blog can be quite personal, often a blog is focused on an area of interest to the writer, from fashion to green technology to horror films to a medical disorder. This area of interest is typically something that the blogger regularly experiences, reads about, and researches. As a researcher, should you develop your research findings into a series of blog postings? The advice below will help you decide.

Decide whether blogging matches your topic and interests. You may already be a blogger in the sense that you post a personal journal on the Web for your friends and family. It might be, however, that you are ready to develop a topical blog based on your research, if your research has (a) revealed what you consider fascinating and helpful findings that you want to share, and (b) piqued your interest in and passion for the topic to the point that you can see yourself continuing to read and research in this area. Blogging involves a certain level of commitment: commitment to writing regularly, to receiving and responding to feedback from readers, and to taking criticism. Before committing to developing a blog on your topic or topic area, consider these questions:

- Do you have the interest and resources to develop postings over the long term? Can you deepen your knowledge through additional experiences and more research?
- What kind of audience might there be for your blog? What would the needs and interests of your readers be? Would they be looking for information, instruction, entertainment, debate? What blogs on your topic already exist, and what might you add to the field? Research current blogs online, using resources such as Bloglines and Blog Pulse.

Develop blog postings that engage and attract readers. These guidelines will help:

1. *Offer quality information and ideas.* In each post, aim to provide interesting, reliable discussion. While blogs typically don't require formal documentation of sources, refer to your sources so that readers will judge your findings credible. When possible, offer links to these sources and to supporting sites. Consider, too, how your discussion might be helpful for your readers—and stress that value or those benefits (the "so what?" of your posting).

2. *Focus on your personal insights.* In the traditional academic paper, you are largely expected to be neutral and objective. In your post, you certainly want to be measured when it comes to the evidence, but you also want to express your own passion and interest, even your own position. Blog readers are looking for your point of view.

3. *Make your title engaging but brief.* Your title (as well as the posting itself) should contain the keywords that search engines and specific readers are looking for, like a newspaper headline or a magazine article title. But your title should also get readers' attention to the extent that they will move into the posting itself. Caution: the title should not, however, be a trick. The blog must deliver on the title.

4. *Keep individual postings relatively brief.* Depending on the topic and audience, individual postings should be in the range of 250 words—what takes about one and a half minutes to read. Online readers are unlikely to remain attentive beyond that point. A key strategy, then, is to map out a series of related topical postings by breaking down your research topic into subtopics, writing a blog entry that introduces a given subtopic and its issues, and then proceeding with two, three, or more postings for the given subtopic. By doing so, you build your blog gradually, avoiding long, rambling postings that discourage a readership.

5. *To make postings inviting, use effective organization, writing style, and design.* Place your main point up front in most posts, and follow with an orderly exploration of that point. Moreover, keep your writing voice engaging, using relatively short sentences and energetic, precise language. Build your credibility as a writer by editing and proofreading carefully before posting the message. Finally, make information in your blog accessible by keeping paragraphs short, creating "white space" on the screen, using headings, shaping points into lists, and integrating related visuals.

Sample blog posting:
To the right is a sample blog post by an officer of a Wisconsin poetry society. The post engages other poetry fans by comparing the work of a pair of modern Midwestern poets with that of a famous twentieth-century English poet.

Photo from Susan Law Cain 2010/www.shutterstock.com

 FOCUS on Multimedia: If you decide that you don't have the time or commitment to develop a topical blog, consider instead starting or joining an online forum or discussion group related to your topic. The forum might be with classmates or with a global online community.

Preparing Research Presentations

Your research project might involve an oral and/or visual presentation, in addition to or even instead of a written paper. While presenting your research findings can be a powerful opportunity for sharing, educating, and conversing, presenting can also be a painful experience—for both presenter and audience—when nerves kick in, the voice stutters, the material becomes disordered or too dense, or technology fails to work.

Essentially, an effective research presentation is both engaging and substantial: the delivery holds the audience's attention, and the content offers something of value, whether new understanding, practical instruction, or a position to debate. To deliver valuable content, start with the instruction below and on the following pages.

Planning Your Presentation

A strong presentation requires effective planning and preparation:

Analyze the presentation situation. Consider the rhetorical context:
- *Purpose:* Are you trying to inform, teach, analyze, inspire, persuade? What exactly do you want your audience to take away (mentally and physically) from your presentation on this topic?
- *Audience:* What are your listeners' knowledge of and attitudes toward your topic? What are their ages, interests, and reasons for attending the presentation?
- *Context:* What are the possibilities and constraints for your presentation—the physical or digital setting, the time limits, the hardware and software available? How complex is your topic, the information, and the reasoning you need to share? What media make sense for this presentation: text, image, sound, video? Should you offer a print handout, project content on a screen, use your voice alone, or perform a demonstration? What level of formality is expected? What degree of audience involvement do you desire?

Choose a fitting format for your presentation. Occasionally, you might be asked to report informally and spontaneously on your research findings, perhaps during a class discussion or a Q&A session at a meeting. In this situation, you need to quickly organize and deliver your thoughts. Generally, however, you have time to prepare your presentation according to a particular format:
- *List:* Use a list for a short, informal presentation. Write out the first sentence or two; create a summary phrase for each of your main points; and write out your closing sentence.
- *Outline:* Use an outline for a more complex topic or formal presentation. With an outline, you can organize material in greater detail without tying yourself to a word-for-word presentation. You might write the opening statement as complete sentences, phrase all main points as complete sentences, include supporting points as phrases or clauses, write out any quotations word-for-word, and state your conclusion as complete sentences. If you have visual aids, other multimedia elements, or handouts, make sure that you refer to these in your outline.

■ *Manuscript:* For highly formal presentations in which your words must be carefully chosen, develop a manuscript. Make sure to double space your speech, number all pages, mark difficult words for pronunciation, mark the script for interpretation and emphasis using boldface or italics, and clearly indicate references to visual aids and other resources.

Organizing and Developing Your Presentation

Think about your presentation having three distinct parts: an introduction, a body, and a conclusion. The common advice here is tell your audience what you are going to say, say it, and tell them what you've said. However, here is a bit more advice on shaping the three parts of your presentation:

Introduction: Explore possibilities for greeting your audience, identifying yourself if needed, getting listeners' attention, identifying your topic and its importance, framing your key question or idea, and forecasting the parts of your presentation. Consider a variety of creative strategies for opening: stating a little-known fact, asking a probing question, telling a relevant anecdote, offering a thought-provoking quotation, describing a problem, projecting an engaging image, playing a short video or audio clip, or making a short demonstration.

Body: Shape your essential message—main points, reasoning, and evidence—so clearly that your audience will understand it after hearing it only once. To do so, consider these tips:

■ Use a straightforward organizational pattern such as problem/solution, cause/ effect, chronology, order of importance.

■ Provide clear, emphatic transitions such as *first, second, third; therefore, however, by contrast; in summary.*

■ Structure your presentation around a limited number of memorable points (3–4), rather than around many smaller points.

■ Avoid overwhelming listeners with complex details and dense explanations. Instead, make information clear through visuals and handouts.

■ Make abstract ideas concrete by offering examples and illustrations.

■ Whenever possible, use plain English and a direct, vigorous sentence style rather than jargon and convoluted sentence syntax.

Conclusion: Create a bookend for your introduction by reinforcing your main idea and supporting points, re-emphasizing the importance of the ideas, and focusing your audience on what it might take away from your presentation in terms of new understanding, changed attitudes, or possible actions. In addition, you might outline what further research could happen and where listeners might get additional information. Finally, make sure that your conclusion also thanks the audience.

Delivering Your Presentation

A presentation involves much more than creating a script: you have to effectively deliver that script by bringing it to life through communicating with the audience. To do so, consider the tips below.

Rehearse your presentation. Whatever format you choose for the script (list, outline, manuscript), carefully rehearse your presentation for clarity, emphasis, and pacing. If you are using a microphone, handouts, projections, or other visuals, practice with these elements as well. When you practice, time yourself and adjust your presentation to fit within your allotted time. In addition, record your presentation or have a classmate or friend offer feedback on your rehearsal: doing so will give you a more objective view of your presentation's content and delivery.

Get set up prior to your presentation. If possible, test the room and equipment prior to your presentation. Check the following:

- Are tables and chairs set up in an arrangement that will work?
- Is your equipment set up so that you can deliver your presentation comfortably (from lectern or otherwise), without blocking the audience's view of the screen?
- Is the AV hardware and software working, and are any visual elements ready to go?
- Is your script in the right order and in place?
- Do you have drinking water?

Be professional and engaging. As you deliver your presentation, aim to communicate in a clear and engaging manner:

- Be confident, positive, and energetic in your speaking; don't rush, mumble, or trail off. Remember the listeners at the back of the room.
- Maintain eye contact with various listeners around the room; don't look down at your script constantly.
- Use gestures and movement during your presentation in a natural way; maintain good posture.
- Provide for audience participation, even if in a small way (e.g., a show of hands in response to a question).
- If your audience looks confused, then pause, reword, and clarify your discussion. Improvise an illustration, example, or comparison.

Follow up with Q&A. After your presentation, you may want to invite your audience to ask questions. A Q&A session is a good opportunity for the group to clarify, elaborate, and apply points from your discussion. Respond to questions by following these tips:

- Listen carefully, think about each part of the question, and repeat or rephrase the question for the whole group, if needed.
- Answer the question concisely, clearly, and honestly. Avoid rambling, but make your answer a kind of dialogue or exploration with the questioner and the audience.

FOCUS on Your Major: Developing a Poster Session

Poster sessions are a common type of research presentation in the social and natural sciences. Through well-organized text and graphics, a poster (either a single poster or a series of panels) effectively summarizes your research so that you can engage an audience moving among a whole series of displays. Readers can study your display to understand what you have researched and why, the methods that you used, the results you found, and the conclusions you reached. Moreover, they can engage you in a conversation, based on what you have written and visualized in your display. Here are some initial guidelines:

Focus on visual communication supported by text. Graphics, whether line charts, maps, photographs, or diagrams, should carry the weight of your message. Written text, presented in small blocks, should support and elaborate the visual content. Typically, written text might be a much-condensed version of your fuller research report.

Make your poster visually appealing. Using columns, headings, and white space, keep your poster clean, uncluttered, and balanced. Use colors that attractively combine, restricting yourself to two or three complementary colors. For titles and headings, use type sizes that can be easily read from a distance of three to six feet.

Structure the poster to feature conclusions and results. While you do want to include attention to methods, stress your research results and the conclusions you draw from them. In addition, the research question or problem behind your research should be quickly apparent in the title and introductory material. Finally, remember to indicate sources for your research. For people interested in additional details about your research, it is wise to provide a supplementary handout that includes contact information.

GQ 2010/www.shutterstock.com

FOCUS on Multimedia: Using Presentation Software Effectively

Presentation software can aid an effective presentation, but not substitute for it. With the popularity of presentation software such as PowerPoint, certain bad habits have crept into presentation practices. As you consider using presentation software to develop and deliver you presentation, avoid these pitfalls:

1. Avoid reducing your thinking to a list of bulleted points.
2. Avoid filling your slides with small, dense text without visual relief.
3. Avoid simply reading slide after slide to your audience.

Should you use presentation software for your research presentation? If yes, how should you use it? The advice below is a place to start.

Enhance Your Oral Presentation with Slides. An effectively developed slide show can deepen and strengthen your speaking in a number of ways. Use slides to do the following:

- *Feature your organization:* Slides can forecast what your presentation will cover and can highlight the main points as you proceed. Consider, for example, how your opening slide can identify your presentation, set the tone, and identify your focus and approach. Similarly, your last slide can review the territory you have covered and help your audience apply the ideas to their own situations.

- *Share complex information:* While you don't want slides to be dense with small text or numbers, you can use them to share information that might be too hard to process simply through hearing it. Such information might be shown, for example, in table form so that you can point out comparisons, or two images might be placed side by side for discussion of links.

- *Control the flow of ideas:* With its slide structure and animation tools (dissolves, fades, wipes, etc.), you can focus listeners' attention on one point, gradually unfolding your points so that relationships become clear. However, make sure that the tools you use are not distracting.

- *Add multimedia impact to your ideas:* Photos, illustrations, charts, diagrams, etc. visually enhance slides to provide information not communicated through your words alone. In addition, you can link to or embed audio and video files to provide illustrations, examples, and demonstrations.

- *Create a tone:* The colors, background features, and animation all create a mood for your presentation—from lighthearted and humorous to scholarly and serious.

Additional Information on Presentations: For additional tips and instruction on developing presentations, visit our Web site at www.theresearchwriter.com. There, you'll find additional help for turning your research into poster presentations, slide shows, podcasts, videos, and other types of presentations.

Sample Presentation Slides: The slides below show an effective use of presentation software's possibilities. Text is kept to a minimum as reference points for talking; visuals offer a focused form of information that complements spoken words and creates an opportunity for explanation; and the slide's design conveys a tone fitting the subject matter.

■ *Opening Slide:* The first slide identifies the presentation occasion, the topic, and the speaker. Visuals set a tone.

A Picture before a Thousand Words:

Art Therapy and the Treatment of Anorexia Nervosa

Rubi Garyfalakis

English 201

sniegirova mariia /www.shutterstock.com

■ *Middle Slide:* A middle slide offers textual and visual information that enhances the spoken presentation.

Interpreting Artworks Made by People with Eating Disorders

The axorexic-bulimic patient's artwork can be understood symbolically:

- Issues of artistic restraint vs. feelings of lack of control
- Isolated figures in a dark or stormy environment
- Representations of emotions difficult to verbalize

qvist/www.shutterstock.com

■ *Closing Slide:* The final slide focuses on the "So what?" of the presentation—why the speaker's analysis matters in terms of thinking and application.

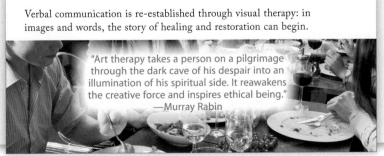

Verbal communication is re-established through visual therapy: in images and words, the story of healing and restoration can begin.

"Art therapy takes a person on a pilgrimage through the dark cave of his despair into an illumination of his spiritual side. It reawakens the creative force and inspires ethical being."
—Murray Rabin

corepics/www.shutterstock.com

Building Your Research-Writing Portfolio

For your research project, submitting your paper, posting your findings, or presenting your ideas may bring a sense of relief and of closure. However, in a larger sense, these steps are simply mile markers on your research and writing journey. Sharing your writing signals your deepening participation in the world of research and research writing, participation that can be extended by adding your project to your portfolio—or starting a portfolio, if you haven't done so already.

What is a portfolio? While the term's literal meaning is a bundle of papers, in our digital age, *portfolio* also refers to the various documents (paper and electronic) that you create and then collect for reflection, future review, evaluation, and/or display. To make portfolio building productive, follow the guidelines below.

Explore Your Project's Fit in Your Portfolio

Building your portfolio is a progressive activity closely related to the rhetorical situation of your research project: your goals, readers, and subjects. For example, getting feedback from real readers helps you know whether you have achieved your goals, whether those goals are to entertain, inform, analyze, or persuade. Similarly, adding the paper to your portfolio helps you see the range of subjects that you have addressed. Think especially about the following rhetorical issues:

- **Your Goals:** How has writing this paper and adding it to your portfolio helped you achieve specific aims as a researcher and a writer? Have you strengthened certain research skills, become familiar with important research tools, or learned of key resources? Have you improved your ability to think and write with researched information? Have you become more familiar with a specific form of research writing (e.g., literary interpretation, historical analysis, field report)?
- **Your Readers:** How has sharing your research writing deepened your participation in your major? How have you entered into or continued a dialogue with a specific research community (e.g., others in the discipline, experts on your topic, students on your campus, people looking for information on the Web)?
- **Your Subjects:** How has writing on your topic added to the range of subjects on which you have written? How has researching this topic modified your understanding of other topics you have researched? Has this research project piqued your interest in further research into this topic? Did you come across other interesting topics during research, topics you might research and write about in the future?

Add Your Paper to Your Portfolio

When you add research writing to your portfolio, pay attention to helpful strategies such as these.

Create easy-to-find-and-identify print and digital copies. Because your research writing might originate in quite different courses at different stages of your academic career, give each document a distinct file name and a clear submission or posting date.

Moreover, collect copies of all these writings in a portfolio folder distinct from individual course materials—both a digital folder and a print folder or binder. Digital copies create flexibility and portability; print copies promote careful study and review.

Analyze feedback on your paper. Your writing doesn't stop with placing your paper in a portfolio. Study all the feedback you can get: your instructor's marginal notes and concluding comments, peer discussion of your research and thinking, or responses to your online posting or Web site. What do these responses tell you about what you did well, what you need to work on, and what it means to participate in this research community? If appropriate, further revise or update your document.

Reflect on your research in a cover sheet. Instead of just placing a final copy of your paper in your portfolio, take time to reflect on what went well in your research and writing and what needs to be improved. Reflect on the project as a process of discovery and dialogue. Save these reflections and revisit them at the start of your next research project.

Save and track resources you used. Keep more of your research project than just the final copy of the paper. For comparison purposes, hold onto the first draft: that way, you can revisit what major changes you have to make. Moreover, keep a full bibliography of resources on the topic, including key reference works, books, journal articles, and Web pages. In fact, if you have hard copies, printouts, and electronic copies of sources, collect these in folders (paper and/or electronic). You can use such bibliographies and folders not only to create a record of your research but also to establish a resource that might prove useful for future research and writing.

FOCUS on Your Major: Writing into Your Discipline
When you turn in research writing in your major and when you add that writing to a portfolio, you achieve important goals in your discipline:

1. By writing a paper that carefully follows the format and documentation guidelines used in your major (e.g., MLA or APA style; business case study or chemistry lab report), you
   - work within your role as a scholar in the discipline.
   - show respect for your discipline's research methods.
   - participate in your discipline's research community.

2. When you collect your papers in a portfolio of writing in your major, you
   - show the range of discipline-specific subjects with which you are getting familiar through in-depth research and analysis.
   - generate a foundation of research writing on which to build in future projects, such as a senior thesis.
   - add to the writing samples that you can use for profession preparation, for an application for advanced training, or for a job search.

Practicing Your Research

1. **Explore:** As this chapter indicates, research findings can be shared, presented, and published in different formats for a range of audiences. Studying concrete examples of different publications and postings (e.g., academic article, Web site, wiki article, news article, video documentary) on the same topic, reflect on how different formats and media treat information and ideas similarly and differently.

2. **Apply:** Study an academic research paper that you wrote in the past, and do the following: (a) strengthen the paper's format and design as an academic paper; (b) rework elements of the paper as a digital document such as a Web page or blog; and (c) shape some part of the paper into a five-minute presentation.

3. **Collaborate on a Case Study:** As directed by your instructor, continue work with classmates on your clothing-focused project. For example, you might refine the format and design of your research writing as an academic paper. But you might also shape your research findings into a Web site or wiki reference article. Based on your group's written text(s), develop a presentation on your research findings.

4. **Research Your Major:** How is research shared within your discipline? Talk with advanced students and instructors about practices and expectations for submitting research writing and making presentations. Similarly, explore scholarly journals in the major, discipline-specific Web sites or blogs, specialized wikis, and discussion groups: what do these reveal about presenting research in your field?

5. **Work on Your Current Project:** Complete your research project by doing the following: (a) refining the format and design of your paper; (b) planning a digital version of your project; and (c) developing a presentation of your research.

Checklist:

☑ My research document is effectively designed in terms of format, page layout, and typography—in ways consistent with my purpose, audience, and research context.

☑ My academic research paper correctly follows all the format and documentation conventions for the appropriate system: MLA, APA, Chicago, or CSE.

☑ My digital document (Web site, wiki contribution, blog) is effectively written and designed to meet the needs of online readers.

☑ My presentation has been effectively shaped into an introduction, body, and conclusion, using a format (list, outline, manuscript) that fits the occasion; in addition, my presentation aids (handout, poster, slides) have been designed to enhance my oral delivery.

☑ I have placed my research writing in my portfolio, reflecting on how the project has added to my knowledge and skills, as well as where the project might lead with respect to further research and writing.

Completing Team
Research Projects

© Cengage Learning/Illustrated by Chris Krenzke

What is team research, and what does it involve? What team projects have you done and with what success? How might team research be part of your college work and your future profession?

"Two heads are better than one," some sage said long ago. But that adage still applies to most college research projects today: multiple heads working as a team do produce better results than one head working alone. This is true not only for individual projects when two or three people team up to respond to each other's writing but also for other groups (small or large) who share the research/writing process more fully—from selecting the topic to submitting the polished text. In either case, success depends on the group's ability to work as a team—to achieve a shared goal through a shared effort.

Such effort takes time, patience, and knowledge—and sometimes a thick skin. However, if done well, the benefits are great. Working together combines peoples' different skills and perspectives, and it gives writers feedback before they get it from actual readers. In fact, because the consequences of poor research writing can be serious, no important study should be published without input from others.

This collaborative approach to research and writing is one that you might find valuable in many contexts. For example, research projects in upper-level courses in your major may be team projects, reflecting the way that research often happens for scholars within the discipline. Moreover, in business, industry, and government, research is often such a team effort. With this big picture in mind, this chapter will help you develop your team-writing skills. The instruction supports the adage: two heads are always better than one when their collaboration is focused, cooperative, and generous.

What's Ahead?

Understanding Collaboration

Research writing done as a group depends on healthy teamwork. To strengthen your teamwork skills, adopt the principles below and use the types of collaboration explained on the following page.

Principles of Collaboration

To successfully contribute to a group-research project, participants should practice foundational principles such as those that follow:

1. **Authority.** In any team-writing situation, be clear about where the authority and responsibility lie for the document. For example, if a peer gives you feedback, assess its value and decide whether to use it. However, if your group leader or instructor supplies feedback, consider it informed counsel (or a directive) and follow the advice.

2. **Perspective.** Any collaboration on a research project should happen in the larger context of the group's welfare. Specifically, all team members should share the team's (or course's) values and goals, and seek to achieve those goals. In addition, all members should follow the instructor's research policies and guidelines, as well as those of the department or school.

3. **Direction.** The team's work must move the project toward the group's goal. Collaboration fails when members lose sight of that goal by getting bogged down in details or getting mired in conflicts or personality issues. Good leadership helps keep the group focused and productive.

4. **Differences.** To be successful, colleagues must practice cooperation and professionalism during collaboration. Such productive behavior includes both respecting and embracing differences. Consider these differences:

   Conflict: Within bounds, a group's conflicts can support its collaborative work. For example, by listening to and considering contrasting opinions, the group can learn from multiple viewpoints, test their reasoning, and tap their creative potential. The key is to manage the conflict through respectful listening, probing, and negotiating. (For tips on dealing with conflict, see page 275.)

   Criticism: To improve their writing, writers need in-depth, constructive criticism—not wishy-washy generalities. However, to be productive and avoid needless conflict, the criticism must be directed to the document, not to the writer—to fixing problems, not griping about the problems. (For tips on giving and taking criticism, see page 274; for tips on requesting or offering advice, see 276-277.)

5. **Audience.** Whether you are the writer or reviewer, put yourself in your reader's shoes during collaboration. Your own personal reactions, no matter how valid, are secondary to the potential responses of real readers.

Types of Collaboration

The forms of teamwork described below can help you research and write well.

Informal Teamwork: Informal collaboration follows no prescribed pattern. For example, you might brainstorm with your instructor regarding research topics, confer with a classmate about how to document a quotation, ask a friend to evaluate the tone of a two-page report, or ask a tutor in the writing center to check your first draft for clarity.

> **Media:** Informal teamwork can happen face to face, over the phone, by e-mail, or in a course chatroom or discussion board.
>
> **Suitable Projects:** traditional essays, lab or field reports, course presentations
>
> **Examples:** A lab partner reviews the technical content of your lab report. A friend reviews the tone of your e-mail response to your group leader or instructor.

Formal Review: Formal collaboration occurs when writers take an important document through a systematic review and/or revision process. For example, collaborative projects intended for publication in a journal or presentation at a conference might be reviewed by advisers or review committees.

> **Media:** Formal reviews are usually structured processes that include communication by e-mail, telephone, and sometimes face-to-face meetings.
>
> **Suitable Projects:** major research or capstone projects; documents that are topically or thematically aligned with a publication or conference
>
> **Example:** Students in an upper-level accounting course survey members of the state's professional organization of CPAs regarding how the quality of business-related e-mail impacts their efforts to complete projects. The students then analyze survey responses, write a report, and submit it to the program committee that selects presentations for the CPAs annual conference.

Group Projects: Group collaboration relies on the contributions of many writers to complete research, prewriting, drafting, revising, and refining tasks. The group may include a mix of participants with different majors, skills, and experiences.

> **Media:** Group projects usually require multiple face-to-face meetings, constant correspondence, and use of file sharing and editing software.
>
> **Suitable Projects:** large research projects; projects requiring a range of skills such as scholarly and technical expertise
>
> **Example:** Five students majoring in environmental studies or digital design study a fungus that deforms and ultimately kills brook trout. The students gather data regarding the fungus, photograph fish at various stages of their illness, design digital models of the fish and their environment, and then write a report and create a documentary film that chronicle the causes and effects of the fungus. The report is published, and the film is broadcast.

Leading a Team Research Project

Leading a team research project requires many skills, including the ability to help individuals understand and complete their tasks, and to inspire and guide members to work cooperatively on their shared project.

Leading Individuals

One leadership strategy is to periodically discuss with the group each individual's responsibility to do the following:

1. Stay focused on the goals of the group and the purpose of the project.
2. Contribute fully by identifying what research-writing skills he or she brings to the group, sharing those skills liberally, and honoring the skills and contributions of other group members.
3. Respect the group's deadlines and your assignments. To ensure smooth development of the document, get work done correctly and on time.
4. Work efficiently. Help keep meetings productively on track. Use e-mail and other technologies to share ideas, research leads, and develop and revise drafts.

Leading the Group

Leading a group includes helping it function as a team while doing all of the following: articulating its goal, budgeting its resources, developing a schedule, gathering materials, conducting research, measuring the outcomes, drafting the project document, revising and editing the document, and submitting it for evaluation. To complete these tasks efficiently, work through the planning and control steps that follow.

Note: Because the subject matter, research strategies, and goals of research projects vary, be ready to adapt the steps to your own group's needs.

Planning steps:	Questions to ask:
1. Assess needs	Why (purpose)—and for whom (audience)—are we doing this project?
2. Define the project goals	What specific goals does this project need to achieve? What related goals are beyond the scope of this project? (Those can be addressed another time.)
3. Create a cohesive team	What expertise and contributions are required? What are the main assignments? How can the work be fairly and effectively shared?
4. Select appropriate delivery media	What media—print, audio, video, or Web—are best suited for our purpose, audience, and topic? How much will each medium cost? How much time is needed to develop content for each selected medium? What style guidelines shall we follow?

5. Schedule and allocate resources	How much can we spend? Who's available to help? Who will do what? Who's in charge? What are the technical requirements—software, hardware, and personnel? How much time do we have before each deadline? When—and how often—should we schedule meetings? How will members of the project communicate?

Control steps

1. Conduct research	What is our research plan? How should we divide research tasks? What primary research should we do (e.g., interviews, surveys, textual analysis)? What secondary research should we do (e.g., books, articles)? How will we share or post research findings and build a working bibliography?
2. Create and develop the content	Have we addressed specific elements of document design—layout, headings, text formats, images, etc.? What are the specific writing guidelines? Does our topic require a style guide for grammar, punctuation, acronyms, abbreviations, or special terminology? How will we organize the document and divide drafting duties? What about possible workflow bottlenecks? Is there content that can't be created until other tasks are done?
3. Review and revise	Are we missing anything? What could be condensed or cut? Does the content support the project's goals? Are we communicating the right ideas? Is the voice appropriate? How do visuals support our goals?
4. Publish	How is the content being delivered? Are we developing materials in the formats required by potential publishers? How long does the printer—or Web developer—need to publish the content? Are we controlling quality and costs?
5. Evaluate	Were we successful? Were we on time (and on budget)? Can we be proud of the quality of this work? What have we learned from this project that we can apply to other projects? Have we celebrated completion and success?

Communicating in a Group

To advance a research project, groups can use many communication activities, especially *brainstorming* and *problem solving*. For example, if a group gets stuck problem solving, it may take 10 minutes to brainstorm new ideas before going back to problem solving. The following pages describe these two activities, plus *making decisions, giving criticism, taking criticism,* and *resolving conflicts*. Effective use of all these communication practices will help your team advance its research and writing.

Brainstorming

Brainstorming is an activity that generates ideas quickly. For this reason, your group can brainstorm to plan research and writing activities; produce new ideas based on your research, experience, and thinking; list problems that you must address; or explore possible solutions to problems. Such brainstorming usually includes three steps: *generating, discarding,* and *evaluating*.

Generating: Group members have one objective—to generate as many good ideas as possible.

- The leader states the discussion topic or problem.
- Someone records the ideas on a board, computer screen, or flip chart.
- Participants pitch ideas as quickly as they come to mind.
- All ideas are welcome: the goal is quantity as well as quality.
- Members listen carefully so that one idea can trigger another.
- Nothing is allowed to slow or block new ideas. No one judges—all ideas are equally valuable. Similarly, no one makes negative or evaluative comments such as "That's not possible" or "Wouldn't this cost too much?"

Discarding: Group members review the gross list of ideas generated, looking for patterns, associated points, and overlap. The group then discards duplicate ideas.

Evaluating: Group members discuss the value of each idea, weeding out the weaker ones, keeping stronger ones, and perhaps combining several ideas.

Solving Problems

Group discussion is an effective method of problem solving for a research team because discussion enables individuals to listen to ideas, evaluate them, and reach a mutually acceptable solution. Problem-solving discussions should work through these steps:

1. **Define the problem.** What exactly is the problem? Do group members agree on what lies at the heart of the disagreement?
2. **Analyze the problem.** How did the problem arise? What are its essential causes? Why is it important in terms of advancing and completing the project? What are the problem's effects on the team and its work?

3. **Discuss criteria for choosing the best solution.** What should a solution accomplish? Will the solution create other problems? What will the solution cost the group in terms of time, effort, compromise, quality of the research and writing, and so on?

4. **Identify possible solutions.** What solutions have already been tried—with what degree of success? What new solutions might resolve the issue?

5. **Select the best solution.** Using the criteria your group identified, evaluate which of the possible solutions best solves the problem while also being workable within the constraints of your project (e.g., deadlines).

6. **Implement and test the solution.** Set guidelines for how and when work must be done. Then assign specific group members to carry out the solution. Plan, as well, for follow up that tests how effective the solution has been: set guidelines and dates for the evaluation, and assign people to do the task.

Making Decisions

To make decisions, groups might choose one of these methods: *consensus, authority, minority,* or *majority.*

Consensus: Group members discuss an issue until there is general agreement. All members agree to support the decision even though some individuals have reservations about it. While a consensus decision takes time, members might support it more willingly than other types of decision.

Authority: The group discusses issues and might make a recommendation; however, one authority figure (the team leader, an invited expert, the instructor, the lead researcher or writer for the project) makes the decision. Although this method is efficient, members might feel that it usurps their authority.

Minority: A vocal or powerful minority might make a decision that the majority disagrees with yet feels forced to accept. This "minority-rule" often leaves the majority feeling resentful or uncooperative.

Majority: The group votes, and the side with the *majority* (most votes) wins. However, a majority is not necessarily more than half the votes. For example, if 10 members choose between two options, a majority is 6 votes (more than half of 10). If the same group chooses between 3 options, option one may get 3 votes, option two 3 votes, and option three 4 votes. In this case, the majority is 4 (fewer than half of 10).

While majority rule is common and efficient, it has problems. Whether the vote is between two or more choices, a close vote may mean that the majority may not be able to gain the cooperation of the minority. To avoid this problem, a group might decide *before it votes* that it will not accept a choice that does not receive a large majority (e.g., 60 percent). Or it might agree to vote twice: first to determine the two most popular choices, and second to choose one of these two.

Giving Criticism

Effectively offering criticism is a difficult skill, but one that is crucial for the success of a research project that involves any form of collaboration. If you are required to offer criticism, make it constructive by following the guidelines below.

Think about your goal: What do you want to happen *after* you speak?

Think about the issue: Limit criticism to an issue that the listener can (1) understand and (2) address and change through action. Think about *what* the problem is, what *caused* it, and *how* the listener can solve it.

Think about the listener: How will the person benefit from the criticism? Does he or she have special needs that you must consider?

Think about the message: How can you state the message so the listener knows that you're trying to correct the *problem* and not the *person*?

Think about the setting: Is this the best time and place to give the criticism? Should this criticism be offered one-on-one in private, rather than in a group setting? Should the criticism take place in person or through electronic communication?

Think about your group: Are you criticizing in order to help the team in its work on the research project, or to promote yourself?

Rehearse and deliver the message: If the situation allows it, say the criticism out loud first to yourself prior to discussing the issue with the individual. When you deliver the criticism, speak in a positive tone while you watch if the listener understands the problem and takes ownership of it, is committed to working toward a solution, and feels your support in achieving the solution.

Taking Criticism

While offering constructive criticism is difficult, taking criticism graciously, positively, and productively can be equally difficult. Make the most of criticism that you receive during a research project by following these guidelines:

Listen for the message: Prepare to listen by asking, "What is the problem?" Listen to the solution by asking, "How could this fix the problem?"

Respect the speaker: Regardless of how the speaker states the criticism, think about the person's ideas rather than how to defend yourself from those ideas.

Value criticism: Remember, criticism helps you understand that a problem exists, why it exists, and how it can be resolved.

Respect yourself: Practice being a person who takes criticism calmly, evaluates it carefully, uses what is good, and courteously disposes of the rest.

Resolving Conflicts

The six guidelines below will help you resolve most conflicts constructively within your research team so that the project will benefit.

1. **Listen carefully and think clearly.** Listen to competing arguments to get the information you need; then think through the information to gain a win/win solution. (For a definition of win/win solutions, see below.)

2. **Be honest, clear, and direct.** If others think you're dishonest, they won't invest the effort needed for a constructive solution.

3. **Avoid harsh or slanted language.** Whereas harsh words might help you blow off steam, they will cost you the team's respect and your own self-respect.

4. **Avoid spiraling combat.** Conflicts out of control get extremely destructive as both parties abandon hope for a constructive solution and seek victory at all costs.

5. **Show goodwill even if your position or solution isn't accepted.** Goodwill earns the other person's respect—something you want and need in the future.

6. **Know when to defer, compromise, compete, or cooperate.** Choose the approach that fits the situation:

   - Consider **deferring** to the other person when you learn that you are wrong, the issue is more important to the other person than it is to you, or the cost of winning isn't worth the potential conflict (particularly in relation to the project's success).

   - Consider **compromising** when there is not enough time to seek a win/win outcome, the issue doesn't warrant lengthy negotiations, the person isn't willing to seek a win-win outcome, or the research project's context requires compromise.

   - Consider **competing** when the outcome is important to the research project, the other person will exploit your noncompetitive approach, or other choices violate your principles or the policies of the course or your school (e.g., academic integrity, plagiarism, research ethics).

   - Consider **cooperating** when the issue is too important for a compromise, your long-term relationship with the other person or the team is important, or the other person is willing to cooperate.

FOCUS on Research Ethics: When giving criticism, taking criticism, or resolving conflicts, generally seek a win/win solution. In such a solution, both parties gain something, whether that be their own goal, mutual good will, or others' respect. However, if criticism or conflicts become contentious and personal, know what processes you should follow to appeal or protest the situation. For example, you may need to confer with your instructor, ask a third party to attend a meeting, or follow your school's grievance procedure.

Using Peer-Review and Peer-Editing Strategies

To give and receive helpful feedback, both writers and peer reviewers need to know their roles (shown below) as well as peer-review strategies (shown on the following page). In addition, both should be familiar with the research and writing process, and they should make requests or offer suggestions at fitting points in that process. For example, during early drafts, peer reviewers should focus on the paper's ideas, organization, and voice. When refining the paper, they should focus on sentence structures, word choice, correctness issues, and design. (For more on these Seven Traits, see pages 8-12; for more on drafting, revising, and refining techniques, see pages 165-240.)

Writer's Role

1. Share a paper copy—or an electronic format that's easy to read, print out, and respond to orally and/or in writing. On the first page, indicate the document's status by printing **"DRAFT"** in caps and boldfacing.
2. Introduce the context of your piece, but let the writing speak for itself.
3. Use the Seven-Trait terms to specify the kind of feedback that you want and give a reasonable deadline. Example: *"I think the report's ideas and organization are fine, but I'd like you to look at the voice. Could you return the paper (with your suggestions) by Wednesday?"*
4. Remain open to reviewers' comments. Take brief notes, asking for clarification when necessary. Then reflect on those responses and develop a revision plan.
5. Raise any specific concerns.

Reviewer's Role

1. Consider the document's purpose and reader. Then listen to and/or read the draft attentively.
2. Take brief notes. Annotate the draft with comments and questions.
3. Use the Seven-Trait terms to make specific, focused statements about what you hear in the writing. Balance constructive criticism with praise of good material. *Example:* "The overall organization works well, but you could add transitions that more clearly link the four middle paragraphs."
4. Ask questions to help the writer think and talk about the draft.
5. In a group session, listen carefully and, if helpful, add to others' comments; however, avoid needlessly repeating others' comments.
6. Focus on the success of the writer, the document, the project, and the group.
7. For a first-draft review, focus on improving ideas, organization, voice, and the overall format. Avoid commenting extensively on word choice, sentence style, and grammatical correctness. In addition, focus on the writing, not the writer, offering praise or criticism that suggests revisions rather than forcing your opinion. (A fellow student should make suggestions, whereas a group leader, instructor, or review committee can give directives.)

Peer-Review Systems

Effective peer review of an early draft goes beyond "It looks okay." Instead, effective feedback offers specific, systematic suggestions aimed at strengthening the writing. Here are two systems that help peer reviewers give practical feedback:

Reacting to Writing: In *Writing Without Teachers,* Peter Elbow offers four strategies for reacting to a draft.

1. **Pointing** refers to highlighting words, phrases, and ideas that make a positive or negative impression. This technique alerts writers to both strong and potentially weak passages in the draft.

2. **Summarizing** refers to a general reaction to or understanding of the draft. List the main ideas, or focus on a key word or sentence. This strategy helps the writer sense if the paper is communicating the necessary content.

3. **Telling** refers to what happens as you read: *First, this happens; then this;* and so on. "Telling" helps the writer hear the draft from the reader's perspective.

4. **Showing** refers to expressing feelings about a piece by using a comparison. For example, you might say the following: *The organization seems like a meandering path. I think that I could follow the argument more easily if it followed a straighter, more clearly unified line of reasoning.* A good comparison offers a tool for understanding a quality of the draft.

Practicing OAQS: A four-part reviewing scheme—Observe, Appreciate, Question, Suggest—helps you make productive comments about an early draft. Such comments can help the writer map out a revision plan.

1. **Observe:** Note the document's purpose, and then note something about the content and design as it relates to that purpose: *Your goal is to prove that the computer program improves the reading scores of children with dyslexia. Inserting a table showing that improvement could strengthen your argument.* This strategy helps a writer revise content to meet his or her writing goal.

2. **Appreciate:** Praise something in the piece: *Your opening paragraph really grabs my attention!* This strategy helps writers see what's already good in the draft.

3. **Question:** Ask questions that help writers think about the draft's content.
   - Reflect on purpose and audience: *What was the goal of your research? What is the aim of your writing, and what does your reader need?*
   - Focus the ideas: *What essential point are you making? How does your paper explain and support that point?*
   - Consider organization: *What do you need to share in the opening? What's the best way of ordering the middle? What should happen at the end?*
   - Hear their voice: *What tone do you want to adopt, and why?*

4. **Suggest:** Give thoughtful, courteous, specific advice about possible changes: *Your discussion of the potential benefits of counseling services is strong. But you might consider summarizing those benefits up front.*

Integrating Teamwork into the Research and Writing Process

Like an individual writer, your team needs to work through a research and writing process that helps it produce an effective document. To get started, review the diagram of the research process on page 13 and the overview of the writing process on page 167. Then adapt these processes to your group project by following the advice below.

Dividing Tasks

You might divide tasks evenly, based on the amount of time that each task could require. Or you might assign tasks based on group members' specific interests in the topic, their types and levels of skills, or their available time. Assigning tasks based on members' skills can build on individuals' strengths but put the bulk of work on one or two people. This page and the next include tips for assigning tasks.

Prewriting

Work with others to get the project in focus, develop a research plan, conduct research, review results, and generate ideas.

- Discuss the project's purpose, the document's readers, and the context (format, deadlines, resources) so that everyone is "on the same page."
- Explore the project's research requirements, brainstorming where and how your group might find quality resources. Develop a research plan that divides tasks.
- Building a working bibliography as you research, share notes and findings. Review the findings together, focusing on what the group is discovering.
- Brainstorm initial content thoughts for the document. Encourage full participation, recording all points uncritically. However, do consider focusing discussion on potential ideas, possible organization, and the best tone for the document. After reflection, select your best options and "clump" points together.
- Review model documents, working towards an outline. With the outline settled, make drafting assignments.
- If the drafting process is shared, each writer benefits by doing his or her own research and outlining the assigned section. However, to keep everyone on the same target, share tips, finds, outlines, and progress reports before drafting.

Drafting

Generally, having individuals draft separate sections works best. This approach enables each writer to focus on a specific topic, to do a thorough job within this boundary, and to create content quickly. One weakness of this approach is that extensive revision could be needed to blend writers' different voices or to fuse their different writing styles. To minimize such problems, each writer should remember the big picture while working on his or her section, follow the outline selected by the group (but still exercise some creativity), concentrate on getting down the ideas and information needed in the section, and adhere to whatever style guidelines the team has adopted.

FOCUS on Research Essentials: Other approaches to dividing drafting duties can be used. All team members could research and write their own drafts of the document; or all members could share the research, with one writer using their findings to do the first draft. However, these methods are generally less efficient than the one described above.

Revising

First-draft feedback is vital. Honest, constructive criticism helps the team move the draft forward. However, the group must agree on routing procedures before the review process begins. These questions will help you establish a procedure:

- Will we route a single print copy of the document, photocopies, or a digital copy?
- If we use electronic files, how will we safeguard the original draft?
- Will all comments be written on one copy of the document, attached as comments to an electronic file, or submitted on separate copies?
- How will we make sure that everyone is reading the most recent version?
- How will we compile comments in order to review them? Will we use a "track changes" feature in our software?

There are two common strategies for circulating documents during the review process, and each may be suitable for print or digital distribution:

- **Round robin** routing involves passing a single copy of the draft from one team member to the next. This method is the slower of the two, as each person must wait his or her turn to comment, although it has the advantage of keeping everyone's comments in one place. Problems with this method can include delays and disagreements as the draft moves from one team member to the next.
- **Centralized routing** means that one team member distributes copies of the document to the rest of the group. Everyone reviews the document at the same time and has the same deadline for submitting comments. The quicker of the two methods, this strategy also ensures that reviewers don't get distracted by others' comments. Compiling reviewers' comments can be labor-intensive, though less so when the routing is done digitally.

Refining

After revision, one or more editors should check the master document for

- accuracy, consistency, and clarity of information.
- appropriate tone and smooth flow throughout.
- consistent formatting (page layout, heading system, numbering, etc.).
- correct and consistent spelling, punctuation, grammar, and mechanics.

FOCUS on Multimedia: Digital tools and software can make the research and writing process both creative and efficient. Explore how word-processing software, e-mail, desktop publishing, course software's collaboration features, and wikis might support your project.

Practicing Your Research

1. **Explore:** Interview a person in an organization's Human Resources Department regarding how and why employees collaborate on projects.

2. **Apply:** Reflect on a group project that you participated in during the course of your college work. Assess (a) whether the project succeeded or failed, (b) why it succeeded or failed, and (c) how your work affected the outcome.

3. **Collaborate:** Work with three classmates to (a) choose an issue in the news that affects you and about which you could write an 8-10 page report, (b) use this chapter to collaborate on the paper, and (c) present your report to the class.

4. **Research Your Major:** To what extent is research in your discipline collaborative? Talk with senior students and instructors in the field. In addition, look at scholarly books and articles for examples of coauthorship.

5. **Work on a Current Project:** Work with a classmate to (a) exchange pieces of writing, (b) respond to each other's writing using one of the systems on page 277, (c) edit your partner's writing for style and grammar issues, and (d) write your partner a response explaining the value of his or her advice.

Checklist: Peer-Review and Peer-Editing

Writer

☑ I used the reader's time well by developing the writing as far as I could, arriving on time, and providing a clear copy in an appropriate format (paper or electronic).

☑ I treated the reader professionally by introducing my writing (purpose, topic, and audience) and citing precisely the help I wanted (e.g., editing for sentence style).

☑ I listened carefully to the reader's response, taking notes and asking appropriate questions for clarification.

☑ I thanked the reviewer; but I showed no defensive body language, and I did not argue about her suggestions.

Reader/Listener

☑ I made the writer feel welcome and offered my help freely.

☑ I listened to the writer's concerns and focused on those issues.

☑ I evaluated whether the document's content, style, and voice matched the writer's purpose, topic, occasion, and audience.

☑ For early drafts, I focused on issues related to content (ideas, organization, and voice); for later drafts, I also focused on sentence fluency, word choice, correctness, and design.

☑ I balanced deserved praise with specific, constructive criticism.

☑ Wherever possible, I phrased my criticism as a question: *You say here that the TV ad is weak, but could you support that point with specific details?*

Part 2

Research-Writing Forms and Projects

Chapters

© Cengage Learning/Illustrated by Chris Krenzke

12

The Personal Research Paper

Q What distinguishes a personal research paper from other research-writing forms? What topics are addressed in such papers? What research methods are used, and how do they impact the writing process?

A personal research paper is one that grows out of your interests and experiences. Because of its history, nature, or impact on you or people you know, the topic and its related issues are things that you want to learn more about: to experience more fully, to think through more carefully, or to understand more clearly. For this reason, such a paper is sometimes called an I-search paper.

Like your other research projects, your immediate audience for this paper is likely your instructor and classmates. However, because the topic and tone of the paper are somewhat more personal and informal than most academic research writing, you might aim to write for a much broader secondary audience. For example, you could consider posting the paper at your own Web site, shaping it as a series of blogs, or submitting it to a magazine or ezine as a journalistic article or personal essay.

Topics to Consider To generate topics, consider how you or someone close to you has wrestled with or experienced the following:

- **Identity:** How has this person's identity been affected by issues related to religion, ethnicity, gender, education, aging, community, or a disability?
- **Justice or Injustice:** How has she or he been shaped by policies related to adoption, imprisonment, voting rights, tax assessments, lawsuits, or politics?
- **Employment:** How has this person's success been affected by hirings, firings, promotions, lay-offs, sexual abuse, or company practices or policies?
- **Institutions:** How has she or he been influenced by institutions such as prisons, K-12 schools, colleges, city government, libraries, hospitals, or places of worship?

What's Ahead?

Guidelines for Writing a Personal-Research Paper

When you have chosen a topic, work through the research and writing process briefly outlined below. (As needed, go to the in-depth instruction in chapters 1-11.)

1. **Use free writing or listing to probe your topic:**
   - Briefly describe what you want to write about and why.
   - Explain how you learned about this topic, and why it is important to you.
   - List questions (like those below) that you hope your research writing will answer:
     - What is at the heart of this topic, issue, or phenomenon?
     - What have I experienced related to this topic?
     - How has this issue impacted me or others close to me?
     - What economic, political, or ethical issues are related to this issue?
     - What are the origins of this issue, and where is it going in the future?
     - How will learning more about this topic help me (or others)?

2. **Focus your thinking.** Do a few hours of research to answer the questions that you drafted in step 1. Then based on this preliminary research and writing, draft a working thesis (you may revise it later) that introduces the topic, along with related issues that you plan to discuss.

3. **Gather and analyze information.** Research your topic thoroughly, looking for details that help you describe the topic and explain its relevance. If possible, deepen your personal experience of the topic or connect with people having personal experience. Search for reliable evidence that clearly relates to specific conclusions about the topic, issue, or phenomenon—taking care to avoid broad generalizations from limited experience and evidence.

4. **Get organized.** Consider structuring your paper around your personal experience and evolving insights (e.g., your initial beliefs followed by your research-revised thinking). Conversely, you might use a traditional structure like those outlined on pages 176–177. Here are additional organizational strategies for personal research writing:

   Opening: Start by gaining your readers' attention and orienting them to your topic. You might try engaging readers through a memory, an image, a conflict, a puzzling idea, an anecdote, or an illustration related to the topic and/or your experience of it.

   Middle: Consider organizing the body of your writing fairly fluidly, looking for ways to mix narration, description, discussion of sources, and personal reflection so as to build interest and deepen understanding. Consider these strategies:
   - Introducing and intensifying various forms of conflict or confusion and then resolving them
   - Creating a vivid, engaging puzzle that is then explored and solved
   - Moving from a broad view of the topic or situation to a more narrow, focused close-up
   - Alternating passages of reflection and source discussion with anecdotes and illustrations

   Closing: Bring the end of your essay to a resolution that gives readers room to think about their own knowledge of and experiences with your topic. While avoiding trite moralism and simplistic conclusions, consider these strategies:
   - Offering natural and authentic reflection on how your understanding has been deepened
   - Returning to an image, anecdote, memory, puzzle, or illustration in the opening
   - Taking a surprising twist or turn in thought

5. **Draft the essay.** Rough out the essay before attempting to revise it. As you write, show how specific details relate to specific conclusions. Where appropriate in your essay, indicate your personal interest in, connection to, and/or experience with the topic. Make sure that you use strong transitional words to link paragraphs and sentences (see the table of transitions on page 215).

6. **Revise the essay.** Whatever organization pattern your draft follows, use the checklist below to strengthen and refine your discussion.

> ☑ The opening clearly introduces the topic and clarifies its relevance (including personal importance, if appropriate).
> ☑ The thesis succinctly states the main point and indicates the essay's pattern.
> ☑ Elements of the discussion (e.g., personal experiences, comparisons, descriptions) are clearly presented, fully discussed, and smoothly woven together.
> ☑ Supporting details are well researched, relevant, and strong.
> ☑ Smooth transitions lead into and out of quotations and personal insights, showing their relevance.
> ☑ The conclusion restates the main insight and unifies the essay.
> ☑ All source material is clearly and correctly documented.

7. **Get feedback.** Ask a peer reviewer or someone from the college's writing center to read your essay for the following:
   - An engaging opening and a clear and logical thesis
   - Clear and convincing reasoning—no logical fallacies
   - A closing that wraps up the discussion, leaving no loose ends

8. **Edit the essay** for clarity and correctness. Check for the following:
   - Precise, appropriate word choice
   - Complete, smooth sentences
   - Clear transitions between paragraphs
   - Correct names, dates, and supporting details
   - Correct mechanics, usage, grammar, and documentation practices

9. **Publish your essay.** Share your writing with others:
   - Submit it to your instructor.
   - Post it on a Web site: the class's, the department's, or your own.
   - Submit the paper for presentation at an appropriate event or group meeting.
   - Send it as a service to relevant nonprofit agencies.

Sample Student Paper: Personal-Research Essay

Lured by her personal interest in cultural issues, Michelle Winkler researched Native American religious practices and visited the Pi-Nee-Waus Powwow. In her essay below (documented using the MLA system), she uses both her personal experience and secondary sources to develop her thesis that the Native American powwow is a powerful community-building ritual. Note that the argument proceeds inductively with the thesis stated most clearly in the last paragraph.

Writer's Reflection

At a young age, I remember asking my father, "Hey, what religion are we anyways?" His response: "I guess we're Christians, like everyone else." Since then, I've often wondered what beckons individuals to religious institutions. A comparative religion class in my senior year of college granted me the opportunity to explore the nature of spirituality in its many and varied contexts. For our final assignment, we were asked to attend a religious ceremony that was outside our frame of reference. Being a devout agnostic, myself, made it so that any religious ceremony was "outside my frame of reference." I chose to attend the Pi-Nee-Waus Powwow because I've always felt an innate reverence for indigenous religions. Nervous and excited, I adopted a passive role as I eagerly documented the sights, sounds, and smells of a robust and passionate community. (But, alas, no fry bread.) In the resulting paper, I attempted to bridge the gap between academic and creative-nonfiction writing and, ultimately, gained a greater appreciation for the faith of the Native American culture and a more nuanced understanding of my own humanity.

—Michelle Winkler

Preparing to Read: What do you know about Native American culture? What have you experienced of it? Have you participated in or attended a powwow?

Personal-Research Essay

The title introduces her thesis.

Present-tense verbs create a personal tone and draw readers into the experience.

A transitional phrase links the paragraphs and the experiences they describe.

The Pi-Nee-Waus Powwow: A Place to Gather

Driving over the I-5 Bridge, I see the grey clouds hang low in the sky, as our view is obscured by an opaque layer of rain. The car antenna buzzes and vibrates with the thrust of the wind, and the tires whoosh through the thin layer of water that has collected on the roadway. The semi truck in front of us kicks up this moisture and spatters it onto our windshield as our wiper blades keep time with the rhythmic raindrops. This is the kind of day my husband and I live for. Most people in the Pacific Northwest worship the sun, but not us. We long for the moist grey days that beckon, "Relax, come on, take it easy for awhile." As we cross the 405 Bridge, I notice the old Union Pacific switchyard. It looks dirty, wet, and dark; yet, somehow, it inspires a wave of nostalgia in me, as we descend into the city. I feel like I'm coming home.

Across the street from the Native American Center stands the first little basement apartment that my husband and I shared together nine years ago.

As I approach, a flood of memories trickle back to me, as palpable as the raindrops on my face: the time we played catch with my nephew in the mud and then hosed off my husband in the front yard, the snow head we built that first winter, crazy bubble games, our first pet, first garden, encounters with city wildlife, our days together before we had a car or a house. I enter the campus of Portland State University heavy with an intangible longing for something just past my reach.

As we proceed through the doors of the gym, there is a great bustle of bodies and voices, and I am plagued by an unexpected sense of guilt and shame, as I notice that I am different from so many of the people around me. "Oh no, I'm white," I think to myself. Although I called ahead to make sure that the powwow was open to the public, it did not occur to me that I would be physically different from most of the people at the event and that I would feel like an outsider. I wonder if I will be accepted by this community or rejected for my "otherness." This worries me for about fifteen seconds, until I realize that no one else seems to notice my difference, and I am relieved. Feeling more comfortable now, my next thought is, "I want fry bread." The gym is lined with booths displaying feathered headdresses, beaded jewelry, purses, blankets, lithographs, dream catchers, and drums of various sizes. There is a food booth selling hotdogs, chili, nachos, and pop; but, to my dismay, no fry bread. I notice the multitude of people, ranging from the very young to the very old. I am impressed by the diversity and number of people attending the powwow, and I begin to become aware of a familiar sense. Fisher asserts that for many indigenous people "community is paramount," and therefore, "everything is experienced as family" (55). I ponder this sense of family as my husband and I find a place to sit in the bleachers.

We remain silent for a few moments, taking it all in. I notice a low, droning hum in the air, reverberating like the pulse of a drum or a heartbeat. Seated in front of us is a Native American girl who looks to be about 16 years old. Her long, black hair is parted into two braids that are intertwined with iridescent sequined strands that end at her waist in beaded tassels. She is wearing an ornately beaded headdress, which bears the title, "Jr. Miss Ma'Klas Queen." Her dress is white with light and dark blue details and features several eagles and roses. She is carrying a staff that is adorned with five large feathers that fan out at its apex. Every inch of her attire is embellished with beads, sequins, and jewels. She's beautiful. I am impressed with the intricacy and artistry of her garments, and I can't help but compliment her. She tells me that her mother handmade her entire ensemble. "It must have taken her hundreds of hours to make," I suggest. She affirms my assumption. A drum begins to beat as a muted chorus of singers responds from across the room. The Native American woman behind me jests about her Krispy Kreme addiction. People all around us hug and greet each other. The "royalty" is called to the front stage to sign in so that they may receive recognition during the ceremony.

The stage is at the head of the gym and is approximately eight by sixteen

---

Sidebar notes (left margin):

The writer both describes what she sees and reflects on what she feels.

She links insights gained from primary sources with those gained from secondary sources.

She observes multi-cultural elements: a girl wearing native dress with a western-style title, and a woman celebrating the native powwow while acknowledging her Krispy Kreme addiction.

She integrates what she senses from the drums with what her other sources assert about drum use.

The writer describes "the roundness of things"—a core postulate in the traditional Native American worldview.

The writer feels the drum's lure and cites a secondary source that confirms this sensation.

Details about how the circular symbols of dance, smoke, beads, and anklets sensually draw the group together develop the thesis: the powwow is a community-building ritual.

feet, with two six-foot folding tables lined up end to end. Five stackable chairs rest behind the tables. There are two flags on each side of the modest stage. A large statured man, the announcer, dressed entirely in black, is seated at the table and holds a microphone in one hand; in the other hand, he balances a young toddler on his lap. Six large drums, each approximately two and a half feet in diameter, are lined up at the base of the bleachers. Around each drum is a circle of chairs. Georges Niangoran-Bouah explains that the drums' "primal discourse carries the sacred consciousness of ancient ways, [. . .] much as holy books do for other faiths" (qtd. in *Anthology* 44) and can be "a precious element of communication" for indigenous cultures (45). Within the African sacred liturgy of the talking drum, worshipers summon the drum, chanting, "Speak, speak to us" (45). I think about the drum's circular shape mirrored in the ring of chairs, and it reminds me of how Roy Wilson taught us that the medicine wheel is also composed of a circle, with each element contrasted and balanced by its opposite (Wilson). Fisher contends that, like other indigenous religions, Native Americans see "everything in the cosmos [as] intimately interrelated" (50). For this reason, the circle has become a profound symbol of harmony and unity (50). "Everything is a medicine wheel," Wilson contends, "the universe, our star system, the earth, the nation, state, county, family, individual, everything." The interconnectedness of these circular systems, for the Native American, is evidenced in Wilson's proclamation, "I am the wheel, and the wheel is me" (Wilson). This thought comforts me.

A small girl, about four or five years old, in a bright-yellow silk dress accented with blue, red, and white, the bodice bedazzled with sequins, begins to jump rhythmically up and down, as if she is dancing. The motion reminds me of playing *Double Dutch* and *Chinese jump* rope as a child. A group of three men is seated around one of the large drums at the far end of the gym. They begin to play and sing. A woman stands beside them and joins in the warm-up. They are drumming softly, and their voices are muted. They sound far away, from a distant past, as the voices of drum and singers reflect off the far wall. Again, I feel the weight of an inexpressible nostalgia growing inside me, and I wonder if there is truth in Fisher's assertion that the "drumming creates a rhythmic environment in which [. . .] people can draw close to the unseen powers" (62).

Vince Wannassay, an elder in the Native American community, takes the microphone and explains that the theme of tonight's powwow is "gathering of community strengths." The ceremony begins with the Eagle Staff Song to honor the tradition of the Pi-Nee-Waus Powwow. A group seated around one of the large drums begins to play and sing. The "whip man" directs the ceremony. He has long, straight, black hair to his waist and is wearing a cranberry silk shirt adorned with a breastplate made of tubular, white bone beads, cream colored leather breeches with fringe along the seams, tan moccasins, and anklets made of percussive hooves. The whip man slowly dances the perimeter of the gym, rhythmically stomping as he carries the Eagle Staff. The Staff is shaped like a large shepherd's crook wrapped in fur and leather that ends in a dream catcher at the crest, with feathers and blue, yellow, and red swaths tied at the top. Vince explains that a new feather is added each year at the opening of the powwow. The whip man then circles the gym with a smudge and a feather for wafting the smoke, allowing individuals to direct the smoke around their bodies. Fisher explains that indigenous groups often "gather for ritual purification and spiritual renewal" (69). Smudges of sage or sweetgrass are burned to produce a smoke that is believed to cleanse the air and body (69).

At 7:00 p.m., the Grand Entry is announced. The previously boisterous crowd instantly falls silent. Everything is still, including the air. Then, it begins, and I am literally overwhelmed by the influx of color, tassels, feathers, ribbons, sequins, beads, drumming and singing. It is simply spectacular, beyond description. The announcer explains that the participants are dancing to show respect for the elders, to acknowledge their wisdom and their teachings. Barre Toelken maintains that "with certain Native American tribes, dance may be the most religious act a person can perform" (qtd. in *Anthology* 56). The Grand Entry is succeeded by a Lutheran prayer invocation to request the blessing of the Great Spirit and honor the four sacred directions. Next, a Victory Dance is performed, followed by a rendition of "Taps" played on a Native American flute. Finally, the veterans and royalty are recognized, and then the real fun begins. In the novel *Fools Crow,* while the characters are participating in the Sun Dance festival, the narrator interjects, "And always there were the drums, the singing and dancing" (Welch 114). What comes next is a procession of dances, each accompanied by drumming and singing. Fisher contends that "body movements are a language in themselves expressing the nature of the cosmos, a language that is understood through the stories and experiences of the community" (*Anthology* 63). At the powwow, there are so many dances, so many stories being told: the Round Dance, Friendship Dance, Intertribal Time, Tiny Tot Dance, Fancy Dance, Fast and Fancy Dance, Traditional Dance, Grass Dance, Hoop Dance, Jingle Dance, and the Owl Dance.

About half way through the powwow, I spy Ed Edmo making his rounds among the crowd. He is smiling and obviously enjoying himself as he visits with various participants. Watching from a distance, I notice him talking with two young children. I wonder if he is telling them some of the Native American stories that he shared with our class, maybe one about Coyote or Beaver. Fisher reminds us that, as the Native American religion is an oral tradition, "teachings are experienced rather than read from books" (46). Storytelling can play an integral part in helping to form a young child's sense of self; I hope Ed is, indeed, passing on these stories to the younger generation.

What I find most striking about the powwow is a drum group by the name of Northwest Connections. They are unique in that all members are teenagers or youth in their early twenties. They stand out from the crowd, and I notice them right away. There are five other drum groups, but these powwow drummers are something special. Unlike the other groups,

---

The writer explains how the ceremony melds the Grand Entry (another circular symbol) with a Lutheran prayer, colorful costumes, and story-telling Native American dance.

To develop her thesis that the powwow is a community-building event, she describes someone who visited her class and quotes a source.

She describes how the drum group's actions and name (Northwest Connections) reflect their identification with the crowd.

each time Northwest Connections plays they are surrounded by a second circle of supporters. Together, they make a colorful bunch. Many visible piercings: nose, eyebrows, tongue. They wear baggy pants and jersey jackets and share jive handshakes between them. They are so cool! I find myself totally engrossed with this group of young kids. At first, I can't figure out why I am so taken by them. Then I realize that they represent a part of the population that is so often absent from church in mainstream religions, such as Christianity. In my experience, church goers are often comprised of elderly members, middle aged couples, and families with young children. When these children reach their teens and that infamous stage of rebelliousness, it seems more often than not that they leave the church in an attempt to discover the real *Truth* about the world. I am stuck by Northwest Connections because they are a "connection"; they bridge the gap between the generations. I can't help but see them as the saviors of their faith. This realization fills me with a sense of pride for what they and their community have accomplished. Again, I feel a longing, a creeping desire to belong to something greater than myself.

The writer tests her thesis by describing her own skepticism.

Save for a few announcements, the powwow consists of nearly three solid hours of drumming, singing, and dancing. The events are concluded with a Flag Song and a Victory Dance. My husband and I have been sitting in the bleachers for four-and-a-half consecutive hours. I am overwhelmed by the power of it all, and as we rise to leave, I feel weak and exhausted but deeply moved; yet, I still can't quite resist my inherent nature. A consummate skeptic myself, I am reminded of a song written by a local singer-songwriter named Bill Bloomer. Upon returning home, I put on his CD, sit back, and listen. He croons,

She quotes a song that mirrors her skepticism.

> If wishes were horses, we'd all take a ride.
> Tall in the saddle, our heads held up high.
> Then off in the sunset, hats pulled down tight.
> If wishes were horses, we'd all take a ride [. . .]
> But wishes aren't horses; we all walk alone.
> I'm empty, I'm lonely, I'm scared to the bone.
> Just wondering if I can ever get home.
> Wishes aren't horses; we all walk alone.

She re-states her thesis by quoting Fisher, her most influential secondary source.

I think about how Bill has traveled the globe, searching for something that he still hasn't found. I guess I am still searching, as well. However, I am glad that I took the opportunity to attend a Native American powwow. I think that the most valuable thing I learned is how vibrant and connected the Native American community is, in this area. Fisher reminds us that "through group rituals, traditional people not only honor the sacred but also affirm their bonds with each other and all of creation" (68). For me, my experience at the powwow kindled a longing to regain something from my past, a desire to return home. I'm not sure where this feeling will take me; however, I know that what Rigoberta Menchu contends is true: "The indigenous community is not a vestige of the past, nor is it a myth. It is full of vitality and has a course and a future" (qtd. in *Living Religions* 77).

Works Cited

Bloomer, Bill. "If Wishes Were Horses." *Temple Dogs.* TDP Records, 1998. CD.

Fisher, Mary Pat. *Living Religions.* 5th ed. Upper Saddle River, NJ: Prentice Hall, 2002. Print.

Fisher, Mary Pat, and Lee W. Bailey, Ed. *An Anthology of Living Religions.* Upper Saddle River: Prentice Hall, 2000. Print.

Niangoran-Bouah, Georges. "The Talking Drum: African Sacred Liturgy." Fisher and Bailey 44-7.

Toelken, Barre. "Seeing with a Native Eye." Fisher and Bailey 55-6.

Welch, James. *Fools Crow.* New York: Viking, 1986. Print.

Wilson, Roy. Humanities 350 Class Lecture. Washington State University, Vancouver, WA. 22 Jan. 2004.

Reading Research Writing: Questions

To deepen your understanding of personal-research writing, consider these questions about Michelle's paper:

1. How does Michelle's title introduce and face the essay?

2. Review her opening two paragraphs, noting examples of narrative voice, first-person pronouns, and present-tense verbs. What tone and style do these choices create?

3. Examine three paragraphs in which the writer blends personal observations with references to secondary sources. How are the two types of evidence related to each other?

4. Citing examples to support your argument, identify the writer's main idea or thesis and explain how she uses inductive reasoning to develop this idea. (For an explanation of inductive reasoning, see page 175.)

5. Review Winkler's explanation of how Native Americans' observance of the circular design (or roundness) of things reflects their worldview. How does Michelle deepen and illustrate this idea?

6. Note how Winkler closes the essay by acknowledging her skepticism regarding the powwow's real significance or value. What does this acknowledgement add to the essay?

Practicing Your Research

1. **Respond to the model.** Review Michelle Winkler's paper, "The Pi-Nee-Waus Powwow: a Place to Gather." Identify elements that you find convincing/ unconvincing, or clear/unclear and explain why. Then list related topics that you could research and write about, thereby continuing the dialogue. For example, you might do the following:
   • If you disagree with Winkler's ideas, develop your own.
   • You might research other Native American activities.
   • You might visit and research cultural or religious events for another group.

2. **Take a cross-disciplined approach.** Choose a topic that you are personally connected to that you can also analyze from two or more disciplinary perspectives. For example, if you have relatives living in Mexico City, you could examine the outbreak of the H1N1 virus (also called "Swine Flu") from perspectives like these: biological—what the virus is and how it spreads; sociological—societal impact within Mexico of this virus-related pandemic; or economic—costs to Mexican tourism of H1N1.

3. **Make it multimedia.** Write a personal-research paper that includes multimedia to convey its message. For example, to help her readers vicariously experience a powwow, Michele Winkler might have included in her essay one or more of the following: photographs, a video, or an audio recording. **TIP:** Make sure that multimedia content advances your thinking and fits the tone.

4. **Take it to the streets.** When in our lives we are faced with a big decision or we are touched by some crisis or tragedy, we often do personal research in order to make sense of what's happening or to make a decision. With this idea in mind, write a personal-research report for one of the following situations:
   • A major decision: a consumer purchase, a move to another city.
   • A major crisis: an illness faced by a relative, a death in the family, a family conflict, a financial problem, an experience of a natural disaster.

Checklist: Use these seven traits to check the quality of your writing:

☑ **Ideas:** The paper explores the topic in a clear, well-reasoned discussion driven by personal interest and/or experience.

☑ **Organization:** The structure helps readers understand the topic and effectively weaves together experiences and sources.

☑ **Voice:** The tone is informed; personal and researched elements blend seamlessly.

☑ **Words:** Terms are precise, clear, and defined when necessary.

☑ **Sentences:** Structures are clear, varied, and smooth.

☑ **Correctness:** The writing is free from glaring and confusing errors in grammar, punctuation, spelling, and mechanics.

☑ **Design:** Format and documentation follow the assigned guidelines.

The Analytical
Research Paper

© Cengage Learning/Illustrated by Chris Krenzke

13

Q When people analyze something, what are they doing? What makes for sound analysis? What do you, yourself, analyze in your daily life? In your major?

The word *analyze* literally means "to loosen or undo." When you analyze something, you take it apart, examine it, and seek to understand the logical relationships between the facets. For example, you might analyze the influences on a particular impressionist painter, the forces that turn a healthy cell into a cancerous cell, the potential impact of a rapid-transit system expansion in your city, or the differences between two religious sects. An analysis can involve a range of modes: definition, classification, chronological process, compare-contrast, cause-effect, and so on. In fact, virtually all analytical writing blends these modes, even if one mode dominates.

An analytical research paper thus aims to understand a topic at a structural level, going beyond surface knowledge to an underlying logic. The research, both primary and secondary, aims to create that deeper knowledge of the topic, and the paper aims to share it with the reader. In this sense, the analytical research paper goes beyond the informational report but stops short of the fully argumentative paper that persuades the reader to take a position on some issue.

Topics to Consider: Analyze a cultural event, practice, or phenomenon. What is the meaning of this phenomenon? How is it related to other phenomena? What forces created it? What are its effects? Topics can range from reality TV to organic farming—anything requiring in-depth thinking. Consider choices in these categories:

- **Society:** e.g., financial stresses and family life, the cult of celebrity
- **Politics:** e.g., post 9/11 security, the 2008 presidential election
- **Business and economics:** e.g., financial-system crises, unemployment impacts
- **Environment:** e.g., wind farms, impact of climate change on polar regions
- **Health:** e.g., the H1N1 flu (Swine Flu), stem-cell research
- **Sports and leisure:** e.g., Jamaica's sprint team's success, extreme vacationing
- **Technology:** e.g., social network sites, changes in automotive technology

What's Ahead?

Guidelines for Writing an Analytical Paper

When you have chosen a topic, work through the research and writing process briefly outlined below. (As needed, go to the in-depth instruction in chapters 1-11.)

1. **Probe your topic.** By reading and using techniques like freewriting, listing, and clustering, explore and deepen your current understanding of the topic. How would you define it or illustrate it with examples? What are its key parts, and how do they connect, relate, or work? How is the topic related to a larger group of topics, and how does it compare with these other topics? What cause-effect forces are at work in the topic?

2. **Choose your analytical approach.** If an approach isn't specified in the assignment, select an analytical mode based on the questions you wish to answer. Your writing may draw on a range of modes, but one will likely dominate. Here is an overview of analytical modes:

   - *Definition* analysis explains the essential meaning of a term—at its heart, what it is (and isn't). Such analysis distinguishes or clarifies the term.
   - *Process* analysis examines the chronology of a phenomenon, whether naturally occurring or man-made. By breaking down the "event" into stages, phases, or steps, such analysis shows how the process works or is completed.
   - *Classification* analyzes large or complex sets of things by placing them in distinct categories based on their key features. Such analysis orders information and allows the reader to better understand individual items within the larger scheme.
   - *Compare-contrast* analysis examines the similarities and/or differences between two or more subjects (objects, processes, people, ideas, and so on). Such analysis clarifies each subject through connections and distinctions.
   - *Cause-effect* analysis asks why a phenomenon happens and/or what its results are. Such analysis gets at the root forces governing the phenomenon.

3. **Conduct your main research.** Undertake both primary and secondary research, taking careful notes:

   - *Primary:* Depending on your topic, closely examine the specific object of your study—a text, an artifact, a film, experimental data, and so on.
   - *Secondary:* Support your primary research with secondary research that supplies context, background, expert analysis, theoretical clarity, and more.

4. **Refine your thinking.** Reviewing all your notes, synthesize your findings by exploring connections, relationships, and distinctions—both within the object of analysis and between resources. In addition, determine the conclusions you have reached and draft a working thesis for your paper. Here are contrasting analytical theses:

   - *Weak thesis* (statement of fact, taste, or opinion): The practice of shunning is not very nice.
   - *Good thesis* (thinking with analytical sophistication): Shunning, a practice

that crosses ethnic and cultural boundaries, happens on three levels: the physical, the psychological, and the social.

■ *Strong thesis* (thinking with risk, tension, surprise, depth): Americans most often associate shunning with foreign cultures and unfamiliar religions; however, shunning—more broadly understood—is both a painful and productive practice that happens daily in most American communities.

5. **Organize your analysis.** What sequence of points will deepen the reader's understanding of and support for your working thesis? What pattern is suggested by the analytical mode(s) you are using? While no one order fits all analytical research writing, consider this template as a starting point:

■ *Introduction:* Present the topic and focus; indicate an analytical approach or mode; offer your thesis; forecast the discussion of the thesis.

■ *Needed background:* Offer a framework for analysis, key definitions, critical survey or literature review, an overview of the analytical approach or issue.

■ *Ordered analysis:* Break down the actual analysis into a sequence of points that elaborate and support the thesis.

■ *Conclusion:* Summarize the results of analysis (insights gained); suggest the importance or relevance of this deeper understanding of the topic.

6. **Draft your paper.** Using your outline, write a first draft. Refer carefully to your research notes, as well as to primary materials, in order to keep the focus on the object of analysis and to accurately integrate secondary sources. As you draft, write to refine your thinking and use examples to illustrate your points.

7. **Revise the paper.** Review your draft for global issues like these:

■ *Ideas:* Is the analytical logic sound throughout the paper?

■ *Organization:* Does the sequence of points effectively develop the analysis?

■ *Voice:* Is the tone neutral, consistent, and fitting for the topic and audience?

8. **Edit and proofread the paper.** Carefully review your writing for these issues:

■ *Word choice:* Are terms used accurately and clearly within the analysis?

■ *Sentence smoothness:* Do sentences read well and clearly communicate the thinking involved? Do transitions effectively signal analytical logic?

■ *Correctness:* Is the writing free of errors in grammar, spelling, punctuation, and mechanics?

■ *Design:* Are the paper's format, presentation, and documentation effective, accurate, and reader-friendly?

9. **Share your findings.** Whether through submitting your paper, posting it, or presenting your findings—find ways to engage an audience with your analysis.

FOCUS on Research Essentials: In one sense, an analytical paper constructs an argument that deepens understanding of a topic. However, an argumentative paper (see chapter 14) typically takes a position on a controversial issue or problem. If necessary, clarify with your instructor the approach you are expected to take.

Analytical Modes: An Overview

Taken together, the analytical modes seek to clearly explain the logical workings of a given topic. But each mode involves a distinct mental operation. For that reason, understanding the individual modes will help you choose and combine those that will best clarify your thinking about a topic. The instruction below and on the pages that follow provides an overview of each mode.

Definition

Definition clarifies meaning through an equation: *term x = explanation y.* As an analyst, your task is to show that the explanation on the right amounts to the same thing as the term (or referent) on the left. While definitions come in various forms, they range from formal to extended. Sometimes a definition within a piece of writing is necessary to the greater analysis. Always use transitions to lead smoothly into and out of the definition.

A formal single-sentence definition offers a term's precise, denotative meaning: term = larger class + distinguishing features or characteristics.

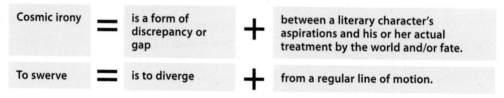

| Cosmic irony | = | is a form of discrepancy or gap | + | between a literary character's aspirations and his or her actual treatment by the world and/or fate. |
| To swerve | = | is to diverge | + | from a regular line of motion. |

To write an effective formal definition, make the larger class fairly narrow: if it's too broad, it will require too many distinguishing features. Moreover, these features should focus on the term's key or unique properties, its action or function, its appearance or substance. Finally, avoid these errors:

- Repeating the term in the definition: e.g., **Breakeven** *is the point at which sales income and production costs* **break even.**
- Using the phrase *is when,* which creates an ungrammatical structure: e.g., *Importing* **is when** *you purchase goods and services from other countries.*

An extended definition offers an expanded discussion of a term. While a formal definition can relate a term to the greater essay in a few explanatory sentences, the extended definition offers an even closer examination, requiring one or several paragraphs, or comprising an entire piece of writing. Explore the possibilities suggested by the diagram. Besides discussing the class and the distinguishing features of a term, the extended definition can provide examples, comparisons, applications, and visuals that make the term concrete and familiar.

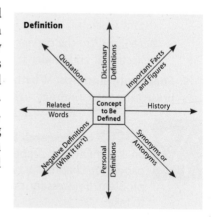

Definition

Quotations — Dictionary Definitions — Important Facts and Figures — Related Words — Concept to Be Defined — History — Negative Definitions (What It Isn't) — Personal Definitions — Synonyms or Antonyms

Process

Analytical writing is often time related. You need to map out sequences, steps, or events in order to explain how something happens, works, is made, or is done—so that your reader thoroughly understands the process. The process may be natural (a phenomenon that occurs in nature, including human nature), performative (mechanical, something people do), or historical/cultural (events in time and/or within communities or groups). Whatever the process, your analysis should follow these guidelines:

Be clear and complete. Shape the analysis based on how readers will use it and how much they already know about the process. Aim to deepen their current knowledge about how the process unfolds and what principles are at work.

Give an overview first. In order to understand individual parts of or moments in the process, readers generally need to have the big picture. Start, then, by explaining the process's essential principle, its goal, or its main product and/or result. That overview statement about the process's principle, result, or importance can often serve as the thesis statement. Example: *When a cell begins to function abnormally, it can initiate a process that results in cancer.*

Make the process manageable. A process analysis unfolds effectively and clearly when it is presented in manageable sections. First identify the process's major phases or stages (perhaps limiting these to three or four). Then break each stage into discrete steps or events, grouping actions in clear, logical ways.

Make the process familiar. In your analysis, use precise terms, well-chosen adjectives, and clear action verbs. Consider, as well, using comparisons for unfamiliar parts of the process, likening, for example, the growth of hair to the growth of grass. Finally, design graphics such as flowcharts, time lines, or sequential drawings to visualize the process. (See the sample flowchart below.)

Signal clear temporal relationships. Because process analysis is time related, you need to use time cues effectively. Consider terms such as *step, phase, stage;* transition words such as *first, second, next, finally;* or actual numbering systems *(1, 2, 3).*

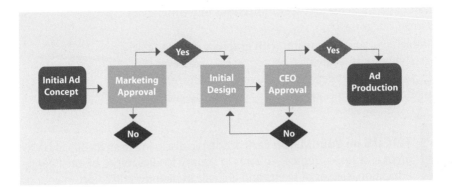

Classification

In writing rooted in classification, you create logical categories into which people, places, things, or concepts can be grouped. Categorization makes sense of a body of information by showing how members of the group are both related and differentiated. Classification, then, can reveal something about the overarching structure of the whole, the nature of a particular category, or the distinctive features of one member of the group. Follow these principles:

Establish a principle for grouping. Given your purpose for classification, find a basis or principle for categorizing items. This principle becomes the "common denominator" for your ordering scheme. For example, you could group or divide trees based on principles like these:

- Size: types of trees grouped by height categories
- Geography: trees common to different areas, zones, or elevations
- Structure or composition: division by leaf type (deciduous vs. coniferous)
- Purpose: windbreak trees, shade trees, flowering trees, fruit trees, etc.

Develop the classification scheme systematically. The following guidelines will keep your categorization orderly:

- Start with a limited number of main categories. (Two to five main categories are manageable, whereas six or more are unwieldy.)
- Make sure that the main categories you designate do cover the topic or body of information completely.
- Devise subcategories to distinguish the units or elements that comprise a category. To further distinguish elements within the whole, break these subcategories into smaller groups.
- Keep your groups exclusive. Make sure that your groups are distinct, not overlapping in any way.
- In presenting your scheme, order the categories and subcategories according to a sensible principle, not just haphazardly. What sequence will help the reader digest the classification scheme and see connections and differences between categories?
- Complement your discussion with graphics such as tables, charts, diagrams, drawings, photographs—whatever can help your reader understand the overall structure of the classification scheme, as well as individual categories.

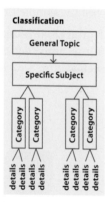

FOCUS on Your Major: Each academic discipline uses classification to a greater or lesser degree—genres in literary studies, types of intelligence in education, classes of plants and animals in biology, and so on. In your own major, discover the classification schemes that make sense of the larger body of knowledge.

Compare-Contrast

Compare-contrast analytical writing holds two or more things, phenomena, or concepts side by side—with comparison focusing on similarities, contrast on differences. By looking at subjects beside each other, we more clearly see their unique and shared traits. Follow these guidelines:

Know your purpose. Are you comparing in order simply to understand one or both subjects better? In your comparison, what weight will you give to similarities versus differences, what will you emphasize, and what direction will your analysis take?

Make sure that the items have a solid basis for comparison. Comparable items are types of the same thing (e.g. two rivers, two bodies of water, the atmosphere and oceans). Moreover, the subjects are of the same order—one cannot simply be an example of the other (e.g., rivers and the St. Lawrence in particular: such a discussion would work as an example or illustration, but not as a true comparison).

Develop criteria (standards, features, etc.) on which to base the comparison. For example, a comparison of two characters in a play might focus on their backgrounds, their actions in the play, their psychology, their fate, and so on. Once you have chosen the criteria, apply them consistently, perhaps using a Venn diagram.

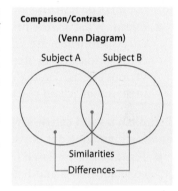

Comparison/Contrast

(Venn Diagram)

Subject A   Subject B

Similarities
Differences

Consider how to use comparison and contrast within your research project.

- The framework for an entire essay, offering a compare-contrast thesis and structuring the discussion around appropriate points of comparison
- A strategy used in a paragraph or a section of an essay, comparing and contrasting details to illuminate an idea

Phrase a compare-contrast thesis to clarify relationships. Consider these templates:

- *Emphasizing similarities:* Although [subjects A and B] appear quite different in terms of their _____, they show important similarities in that _____.
- *Emphasizing differences:* Although [subjects A and B] appear quite similar in terms of their _____, they are essentially different in _____.

   Sample thesis: Although independent films with their smaller budgets rely less on expensive special effects than do blockbusters, indies tell more compelling and complex stories.

Organize your comparison to clarify similarities and differences for readers. Decide how to sequence points in your comparison so as to illuminate the topics.

- Whole vs. whole discusses items separately, giving a strong overview of each. Use this pattern with short, simple comparisons.
- Point by point discusses items together, criterion by criterion. This pattern stresses fine distinctions, making sense for long, complex comparisons.

Cause-Effect

Cause-effect thinking can move in two directions. First, it can explore the effects of a particular event, action, or phenomenon—the logical results, actual or anticipated. Second, it can trace backward from a particular result to those forces that created the results—the causes. As you think through causes and effects, your job is to establish and explain solid cause-effect links.

Explore the cause-effect evidence. Test all possible explanations for a given phenomenon's causes and effects. Consider these options:

- *Causes:* What forces can be designated primary or root causes? What forces are secondary or contributing causes? What factors are only enabling conditions for the phenomenon? Which causes are immediate (near), and which are remote (distant)? What cause-effect "evidence" is simply coincidental? What evidence—measurements, testimony, and so on—supports or disproves the causal links? Can the links be tested?

- *Effects:* What are the primary, secondary, and ripple effects? Which are main effects and which are side effects, which immediate and which long-term? What is the seriousness or strength of each effect? What aspects of the cause led to the various effects? Do the effects themselves become causes of a different set of effects in a kind of "chain reaction"?

Establish a solid cause-effect claim as your thesis. A cause-effect thesis is phrased as an insight growing out of your careful study of the topic. Here are templates:

- *Focus on causes:* Based on a close examination of the forces at work, we can conclude that A and B are the fundamental causes of C.

- *Focus on effects:* Based on a close examination of the forces at work, we can conclude that the most important results of A have been B, C, and D.

   Example: When people around the globe watch Hollywood blockbuster films, they absorb a distorted vision of U.S. culture that fuels misunderstanding and, in fact, undermines the government's "war on terror."

Supply reliable evidence that supports the logical connection. Cause-effect analysis stands on your logical interpretation of the evidence. When you present your cause-effect analysis, avoid these problems: (1) relying extensively on circumstantial evidence, (2) drawing firm conclusions without adequate support, and (3) mistaking sequence for a cause-effect link. (Even though A came before B, A didn't necessarily cause B.)

Organize your cause-effect analysis to feature your chain of reasoning. The phrasing of your thesis implies a certain method of developing and supporting the thesis—a way of proceeding with and handling the cause-effect evidence. It is often necessary, for example, to begin by exploring the background, the larger context for the topic, in order to situate your cause-effect analysis. Generally, structure your essay according to the direction of your analysis (from effect to causes or from cause to effects).

Sample Student Paper: Analytical Research Writing

In the essay below, student writer Stevie Jeung analyzes an unusual topic: the cultural practice of giving condemned criminals a "last supper." As you study her analysis, explore how she thinks through the topic by drawing on various analytical modes.

Writer's Reflection

I wrote this essay for American Studies 101D: Crime and Punishment in American Culture. . . . We were required to choose two of three essay assignments, the first of which simply asked us to discuss "the iconography of the penitentiary." This intriguing first assignment sent so many half-baked ideas whizzing through my head that I almost gave up and resigned myself to the remaining two essay prompts. At just about the last minute, I stumbled upon a topic that compelled me. Suddenly, I just had to find out what was up with this whole last meal thing. Luckily for me, there was plenty to find. Really, who wouldn't love compiling research that included morbid cookbooks, mafia TV, and a poignant but absurd last request for Spaghetti-O's?

—Stevie Jeung

Preparing to read: What are your thoughts about attitudes toward capital punishment? How has this issue been treated in the media? What do you understand about the cultural meaning of crime and punishment?

Analytical Essay

A creative title offers a focus for the analysis.

The writer opens with a chronological catalog of executed people and last suppers.

The intro zeros in on the topic, focuses on what is odd or difficult to explain, and announces a search for explanations.

"I Did *Not* Get My Spaghetti-O's": Death Row Consumption in the Popular Media

Jesus Christ: Roast lamb, matzo, wine; around AD 30. Perry Smith and Richard Hickock: Identical meals of shrimp, french fries, garlic bread, ice cream and strawberries with whipped cream; 1965. Timothy McVeigh: Two pints of Ben & Jerry's mint chocolate chip ice cream: 2001. Tony Soprano: Holsten's onion rings; 2007. Karl Chamberlain: Final meal yet to be consumed; 15 days from now.

While executions historically demand a certain degree of morbid curiosity, the last meals of the condemned seem to stimulate heightened interest. Indeed, a prisoner's final feast has almost become an event in its own right, not only for the prisoner, but for the prison staff and the public. Web sites, novels, movies, television shows, newspapers, and even cookbooks report, dissect, criticize, and speculate regarding last meals real and imagined. When confronted with the ultimate consumption of dying people in so many areas of our popular media, the truth becomes alarmingly clear: This is odd behavior. There must be some reason that we institutionally allow our most hated and feared prisoners to choose and enjoy their final meal before we execute them, and there must be some reason that we like to watch and reproduce the event in popular culture.

The last meal appears in almost every major arena of public entertainment. In *The Green Mile,* a motion picture based on Stephen King's novel of the same name, protagonist John Coffey is wrongfully executed in a heartbreaking, dramatic scene, but not before careful thought about his last meal: "Meatloaf be nice. Mashed taters with gravy. Okra, maybe. I's not picky." Prisoners are also served their last meals on the small screen. Take, for example, FOX's network TV show, *Prison Break,* in which Lincoln Burrows is served his last blueberry pancakes. In fact, on an episode of *The Simpsons,* a staple of American television, Homer eats Hans Moleman's last meal of lobster tail and raspberry tort just before Hans is executed, protesting, "But he ate my last meal!" Clearly, this animated man did not think it right to be executed without enjoying his final choice of cuisine. Of course, his expression of outrage is followed by "Are you really allowed to execute people in a local jail?" reminding us that *The Simpsons,* however rich with American icons, is not real. Regardless of actual death row ceremony, the Americans who produce and consume these works of fiction expect that a special meal accompanies execution.

Compulsory inclusion of a last meal in fictional executions is one thing, but our fascination does not stop there. Where convicts are executed, the state documents and even publishes details of the last meal and last words before they administer capital punishment. Until recently, Texas, the number one execution state, posted prisoners' last meals on their Justice Department's Web site ("Death Row Information"). They discontinued this practice for unclear reasons, but the archived lists from 2003 and earlier are still readily available, and the department continues to publish names, execution dates, case records, and even pictures of the dead and soon-to-be-dead (like Karl Chamberlain, mentioned above). Oklahoma, ranked third among execution states, takes a more voyeuristic approach: "The local newspaper [prints] a blow-by-blow account. Time of injection. Facial expressions. Final meal requests" ("Artist"). While this might seem like a gruesome practice on the state's part, the public does not shy away. In fact, commercial reproduction of this information proves that it's not just reporting; it's entertainment.

It is evident not only that people read this stuff, but that they actually use available execution and last meal information to create and market their own masterpieces of morbid exposition. It becomes at once blatantly, amusingly, and disgustingly clear when you stumble across Web sites like "Last Suppers: Famous Final Meals from Death Row," "Meals to Die For," and "Dead Man Eating," which faithfully posts the last meal (along with "the skinny" on the day's events and case details) of every person executed in the United States since 2002. The most shocking part is that the Web site also sells T-shirts, coffee mugs, and even thong underwear, all of which read "Dead Man Eating: looking for a killer meal?" and feature a crude drawing of a dead man hanging with an ice-cream cone in his

The analysis focuses on specific examples in film and television.

The analysis turns to real executions and state practices.

The writer explores the presence of "last supper" interest on the Web, using concrete details and examples.

hand. A more tasteful, if just as morbid strategy is to publish a "last meal" cookbook or coffee-table book. A quick search for "last meal" on Amazon. com yields at least four such books (along with Snoop Dogg's album, which is entitled *The Last Meal* for reasons I unfortunately could not find). According to its description, one of the books, *Last Suppers: Famous Final Meals from Death Row* (Ty Treadwell and Michelle Vernon), both lists the gritty details of last meals and uses the public's "appetite" for this last-minute courtesy to comment on the death penalty. *Meals to Die For* comes from Brian D. Price, a former inmate who personally cooked eleven years' worth of final meals for Texas death-row inmates. His book reveals recipes, pictures, and even handwritten last-meal requests he received during his incarceration (Amazon.com). The last things that our allegedly deadliest murderers eat, then, are not only published for the public, but published *again* with extra details for *sale* to the public. This doubly consuming public just eats this stuff up.

The more closely we look at it, the more bizarre this cycle of consumption and death appears: a man kills, he eats, we kill him, and then we eat it up. Where does it really begin, though? The "last meal" has a symbolic and ritualistic significance since, well, Jesus and the Last Supper (Peck). At some point, between Jesus and today's American megaprisons, we began to recognize the last meal as a ritual of institutionalized execution.

Since the early nineteenth century, Americans have been fascinated with not just execution, but with the ritual of a condemned criminal's last day. A large crowd would turn up to hear the death warrant, sermon, and last words before a hood was slipped over the offender's head and he was hanged by the neck. Still more people read the details of the execution as it was published, and "if the offender could not or would not utter any memorable last words, the publisher had no compunction against compositing them" (Atwell 8). The 1840s brought the American death penalty's first decline in a trend of fluctuating popularity that would continue to the present day, but wherever there was a spectacle, there was an audience. As the death penalty remained popular in the South, so did reporting the last days of convicts in gross detail.

Each of the states that employ capital punishment uses its own set of rules and procedures. Some states enforce a price limit, while Texas limits a last meal to the things accessible by the regular prison kitchen staff. In 1995, the federal government administered its first execution since 1969. Timothy McVeigh's execution prompted development of a 56-page "Execution Protocol," "meant to ensure that all executions are carried out 'in an efficient and humane manner.'" This document clearly outlines a last meal choice as a scheduled step in the execution process: "At least seven days prior to the execution, the warden or designee will contact the condemned individual to arrange for his/her last meal," and "The condemned individual will be served a final meal at a time

The analysis draws conclusions from the examples discussed.

With a question, the writer explores possible origins of the phenomenon and offers a chronological survey.

The analysis compares and contrasts the capital-punishment practices of different government bodies (federal, states).

determined by the warden" between twelve and three hours prior to the execution (Fritsch). In Texas, according to death row chef Brian Price, the meal would be ready at 3:45 p.m. and delivered at 4 p.m., two hours before lethal injection. This last tray of food, which would become very public following the execution, was covered in paper "for privacy." Price reveals that although an inmate could request anything, he often received something different: "The local newspaper would always say they got 24 tacos and 12 enchiladas, but they would actually get four tacos and two enchiladas" ("Confessions"). After all of this procedure, the report sensationalizes the last meal, much as early publications sensationalized the last words.

So why does the state even allow a last meal? Bob Greene argues that "inviting" prisoners to choose a last meal is "hypocritical and insulting to the memory of the victims" because, he poignantly argues, murderers take that foresight and choice from their victims. Perhaps, Tony Karon of *Time* suggests, the prisoners accept a last bit of freedom and humanity to make up for the "grim act of violence of the state" that is about to occur. Especially considering that prisoners don't always get what they ask for, this seems unlikely. Daniel LaChance notices that although execution practices have historically moved toward anonymity and bureaucracy, the last meal and final speech have incongruently been sustained. His recent paper, "Last Words, Last Meals, and Last Stands: Agency and Individuality in the Modern Execution Process," argues that in giving the prisoners choice in their final meals and words, the state portrays them as autonomous agents who have chosen their deeds and accepted their fates. In other words, the prison system denies a prisoner individuality until his or her last day of life in order to feel righteousness in executing him or her. In the midst of a vengeful prison system (Abramsky), this makes perfect sense. It is much more satisfying to exact revenge on a person than on a number. In fact, despite the moves toward more humane and less painful execution, the state can treat mentally ill patients with antipsychotics so that they're "sane enough to be executed" ("Confessions"). Clearly, the "ideal candidate" is an irredeemable individual, sane enough both to feel and participate in the death. In other words, if they can choose the last thing they eat, they must have chosen to murder, in which case they deserve to die. Furthermore, resemblance to the biblical Last Supper might justify vengeful treatment in the name of religion, especially for prison staff like Oscar Dees, who believed that God intended him to punish criminals. This powerful, righteous moral logic is published and extended to the public, creating a sense of justice that maintains support for the death penalty. As in *Cool Hand Luke,* this public spectacle of punishment and revenge is a self-serving institution of the prison system itself.

The public, however, has its own incentives for gobbling it all up, so to

---

A "why" question pushes forward the analysis.

Disagreeing with one source's explanation, the writer turns to another source.

The writer analyzes the moral psychology of the execution rituals, including the last meal.

speak. Revenge is probably one of them, as is pure, unabashed voyeurism. American people tend to take the idea of the last meal to heart, though, and somehow make it their own. Many visitors to the "Dead Man Eating" Web site and message boards all over the Internet do this by submitting their own "last meal requests," as if they were going to die tomorrow. Apparently, then, this fixation on the last meal is not limited to intrusive consumption of execution records; it extends to the public and their own final food choices. In fact, the subject of hypothetical last meals has given this icon of criminality and death a fresh, not-so-morbid vantage point. James L. Dickerson's book, *Last Suppers: If the World Ended Tomorrow, What Would Be Your Last Meal?* asks popular celebrities and political figures to divulge their last meal of choice. Bill Clinton, for instance, would like to enjoy chicken enchiladas before his hypothetical death, and professional football coach Mike Ditka fancies pigs in a blanket. *My Last Supper,* by Melanie Dunea, asks the same of chefs.

(margin note: She turns her attention to the motivations of the public in its obsession with last meals and other execution details.)

Still others forego the macabre enjoyment and the distant speculation and use the vivid image of eating for the last time to protest the death penalty through art. Photographer Jacquelyn C. Black organizes pictures of inmates and their meals in a book entitled *Last Meal,* in which she also includes statistics: 10 of the 12 states without the death penalty have homicide rates below the national average, for example. University of Oklahoma professor Julie Green paints a series of dinner plates, each depicting what was on the last plate of a particular inmate. Reading about the executions in the newspaper "humanized death row" for her and struck her as an invasion of privacy ("Artist"). Whether they seek revenge or redemption, Americans see the last meal as a symbol in the life-or-death of justice, on death row and in their living rooms.

(margin note: The writer turns to artistic renderings of last meals, works that make political statements.)

The final episode of *The Sopranos* illustrates the place of "The Last Supper," generally speaking, in the American psyche. Mob leader Tony Soprano sits down at Holsten's diner in New Jersey and tension builds around him as the other characters bustle about in their respective scenes. The viewer gets the distinct feeling that they are preparing to kill Tony, who looks nervous, as though he knows that his criminal career is about to end in execution. Tony's family arrives at the diner and he offers a basket of onion rings around the table, but before we find out whether or not he dies, the scene cuts to black. The end. No more Tony, no more *Sopranos.* This could just be another cliffhanger, but many fans see it as Tony's "Last Supper," and "If Holsten's onion rings—round, crunchy, and, according to one influential diner, the best in the state—didn't symbolize communion wafers, as some viewers of the final scene of 'The Sopranos' have theorized, they do now" (Erminio). The point is that the subsequent pilgrimage to Holsten's taken by many fans of the show proves one of two things. Either (a) the megahit show *did* intend to showcase a symbolic "last meal" for its main character or (b) all of these people are making it

(margin note: Exploring an example from television, the writer pulls together the strands of her analysis.)

up. Either case gives powerful support to the idea that this last ritual of consumption is popularly recognized as the appropriate ending to a life, whether fictional, criminal, or biblical.

The interplay between the public, the media, and the criminal justice system gives the last meal a unique importance to each. The criminal system perpetuates the tradition in its own interest and uses the media to lend righteousness to its questionable and somewhat manipulative actions, but the media and the public interact to derive much greater religious, social, emotional, and political meaning, thus creating a pervasive and lasting icon which permeates popular culture and popular perception. Thomas J. Grasso, executed by lethal injection in Oklahoma (1995), seemed to appreciate the significance of a last meal in the public eye when he gave his last speech (reported in "Last Words"): "I did not get my Spaghetti-O's, I got spaghetti. I want the press to know this."

> In her conclusion, the writer answers her original questions and offers a final quotation that drives home her point and revisits her title.

> The paper's bibliography lists a range of scholarly books, trade books, scholarly articles, popular articles, and Web sites on the topic.

> Each entry provides complete identifying information, properly formatted according to MLA practices.

Works Cited

Abramsky, Sasha. *American Furies: Crime, Punishment, and Vengeance in the Age of Mass Imprisonment.* Boston: Beacon, 2007. Print.

"Artist Serves 'Last Supper' on Plates." *LJWorld.com. Lawrence Journal* 29 Oct. 2006. Web. 5 Feb. 2008.

Atwell, Mary Welek. *Evolving Standards of Decency: Popular Culture and Capital Punishment.* New York: Peter Lang, 2004. Print.

Black, Jacquelyn C. . . . *Last Meal.* Monroe: Common Courage, 2003. Print.

"Confessions of a Death Row Chef." *guardian.co.uk: TheObserver. Guardian News* 14 Mar. 2004. Web. 5 Feb. 2008.

"Death Row Information." *Texas Department of Criminal Justice.* TDCJ 7 Nov. 2007. Web. 5 Feb. 2008.

Dickerson, James L. *Last Suppers: If the World Ended Tomorrow, What Would Be Your Last Meal?* USA: Citadel, 2004. Print.

Dunea, Melanie. *My Last Supper.* USA: Bloomsbury, 2007. Print.

Erminio, Vinessa, "Chewing Over Tony's Last Meal." *nj.com: Sopranos Archive.* New Jersey On-Line, 23 June 2007. Web. 5 Feb. 2008.

Fritsch, Jane. "Word for Word/Execution Protocol; Please Order Your Last Meal Seven Days in Advance." *New York Times.* New York Times, 22 Apr. 2001. Web. 5 Feb. 2008.

Greene, Bob. "They didn't get to choose their last meals." *Jewish World Review. Jewish World Review,* 12 June 2001. Web. 5 Feb. 2008.

Karon, Tony. "Why We're Fascinated by Death Row Cuisine." *TIME. Time,* 10 August 2000. Web. 5 Feb 2008.

LaChance, Daniel. "Last Words, Last Meals, and Last Stands: Agency and Individuality in the Modern Execution Process." *Law & Social Inquiry* 32 (2007): 701-24. *JSTOR*. Web. 5 Feb 2008.

"Last Meals on Death Row." *Dead Man Eating.* Bohemian Catfish, 2005. Web. 7 Feb. 2008.

"Last Words on Death Row." *CNN.com: The Best of Court TV.* Cable Network News, 31 Dec. 2007. Web. 5 Feb. 2008.

March, Ray A. *Alabama Bound: Forty-Five Years Inside a Prison System.* Alabama: U Alabama P, 1978. Print.

Peck, John. "Last Meals." *Tucson Weekly. Tucson Weekly,* 5 Jan. 2006. Web. 5 Feb. 2008.

Price, Brian D. *Meals to Die For.* USA: Dyna-Paige, 2001. Print.

Treadwell, Ty, and Michelle Vernon. *Last Suppers: Famous Final Meals from Death Row.* Port Townsend: Loompanics, 2001. Print.

Reading Research Writing: Questions

To deepen your understanding of analytical research writing, consider these questions about Stevie Jeung's paper:

1. How do the opening two paragraphs create a focus and direction for analysis? Do you find Stevie's writing strategies successful?
2. How would you characterize the tone of Stevie's analysis? Is this tone fitting?
3. In what ways does the paper deepen your understanding of execution rituals? What questions does the paper leave unanswered?
4. Analytical papers tend to mix analytical modes (definition, process, cause-effect, etc.). Identify two different analytical modes employed by the writer. How effectively are these modes used?
5. How would you characterize the strength of the writer's research and her use of sources? To answer, study both the in-text citations and the works-cited list.

FOCUS on Research Essentials: For more examples of analytical research writing, consider the following:

- Literary Analysis: "Stephen Dedalus: Finding Identity in Myth" (pages 351-357)
- MLA Paper: "A Picture before a Thousand Words: Art Therapy and the Treatment of Anorexia Nervosa" (pages 410-418)

Practicing Your Research

1. **Respond to the model.** In her paper, Stevie Jeung draws links between crime and punishment, popular culture, and religion. In response, research and write your own analysis of a related topic, such as one of these:
   - Another dimension of crime and punishment in popular culture (e.g., organized crime in film and television, corporate crime, serial killers)
   - Crime, punishment, religion, and art (e.g., the gospel stories of Jesus' execution; works of art on crime and punishment, such as Da Vinci's *The Last Supper* or Margaret Atwood's *Alias Grace*; the moral dimensions of a specific condemned person's case)

2. **Take a cross-disciplined approach.** Many topics (e.g., the food we grow and eat) can best be analyzed using an interdisciplinary approach. Analyze a focused food topic from two disciplinary perspectives (e.g., agriculture, psychology, history).

3. **Make it multimedia.** While many analytical essays rely solely on written words, analysis can be accomplished through other media. For example, you could analyze the topic of culture-shaping technologies by developing a digital document that includes text, photographs, audio, and video.

4. **Take it to the streets.** Analysis is a natural part of public life, the workplace, and home. Practical projects of this sort typically involve applied research—analyzing in order to do something with the results. Focusing on a personal choice, purchase, or decision (e.g., career path, city to live in, vehicle to purchase), write a research report that gathers and analyzes the topic to provide objective thinking that might inform such a choice.

Checklist: Use this checklist to review your analytical research paper.

- ☑ **Ideas:** The analytical thinking is sound, with appropriate analytical modes used to elaborate and support a thesis that clearly reveals or unfolds the topic.
- ☑ **Organization:** The writing moves effectively from an opening that identifies the topic and analytical approach, to a middle that develops the topic by breaking it down into points that support the thesis, to a closing that shares the significance of the conclusions.
- ☑ **Voice:** The voice is fittingly neutral but interested, given the topic, reader, and context for the writing.
- ☑ **Words:** Language is careful and precise, with important terms defined as needed.
- ☑ **Sentences:** The prose reads smoothly, with well-crafted sentences advancing the analytical thinking within the paper.
- ☑ **Correctness:** The writing is free from glaring and confusing errors in grammar, punctuation, spelling, and mechanics.
- ☑ **Design:** The document—essay, report, Web page, etc.—is effectively, clearly designed for readers and/or viewers and is formatted and documented correctly.

© Cengage Learning/Illustrated by Chris Krenzke

The Argumentative Research Paper

14

When you think of an argument, what comes to mind? What does an argument look like in daily life? What does one look like in college writing?

"I wasn't convinced." Maybe you've said something similar while watching a political debate, viewing an ad, listening to a presentation at work, or discussing an issue in class. You simply didn't find the argument logical, believable, or persuasive.

In a sense, all research writing is argumentative in that it seeks to convince readers that the information is accurate and has been carefully researched, that conclusions drawn from the evidence are sound, and that the analysis is insightful and complete. But some research writing is argumentative in a more particular sense: the writing takes a position on a debatable, perhaps even controversial issue; it may even seek to sway readers to adopt the position themselves or to change their attitudes, beliefs, and actions. This chapter focuses on such research writing.

Topics to Consider: Debatable issues, controversies, and problems center on ideas about which thoughtful people can reasonably disagree. For your research paper, consider an issue related to one of the categories below.

- **Current Affairs:** Explore recent trends, new laws, and major changes discussed in the news media, journals, blogs, and discussion groups.
- **Burning Issues:** Which issues related to family, work, education, recreation, technology, the environment, or popular culture do you care about?
- **Dividing Lines:** What dividing lines characterize the communities to which you belong (e.g., city, state, ethnic group, age group, gender)? Which issues set people against each other or cause problems? Religion, gender, money, class?
- **Major Issues:** What controversies are typically tackled in your discipline? Which disagreements do experts debate? What problems are solved in your major?
- **Fresh Fare:** Sometimes an unexpected topic offers the most potential. Avoid tired and polarized issues unless you can revive them with a fresh perspective.

What's Ahead?

Guidelines for Writing an Argumentative Paper

When you have chosen a topic, work through the research and writing process briefly outlined below. (As needed, go to the in-depth instruction in chapters 1-11.)

1. **Take stock.** What do you currently know about the issue? What is your current stance on it? What do you hope to accomplish through researching and writing about it? Who will read your argument, and what might be their positions? To explore various points of view on your issue, read some magazine articles and blogs.

2. **Consider an argumentative approach.** If an approach isn't specified in the assignment, think through which argumentative mode makes sense:

   - *Taking a position* involves exploring all possible stands on an issue, committing to the strongest, and convincing readers of your position's strength.
   - *Persuading readers to act* involves urging readers to change their behavior or to take action on an issue.
   - *Arguing against a claim* involves countering a commonly held idea by showing weaknesses in that claim and perhaps by arguing for an alternative.
   - *Proposing a solution* involves describing a problem, explaining its importance, exploring possible solutions, and arguing for the best solution.

3. **Conduct research to get inside the issue.** Undertake significant research that gets at underlying sources of difference and disagreement. Investigate all possible positions, explanations, and alternatives. Look for secondary sources that are authoritative and credible, but also consider doing primary research that will help you speak with inside knowledge. As you research, try setting up "opposing viewpoints" columns and then tracking various arguments in each column.

4. **Refine your thinking.** With the bulk of your research complete, review your reasoning about the issue: how has it been affirmed, deepened, and changed? In addition, test your thinking for logic and evidence: Is your thinking free of fallacies such as broad generalizations, either/or thinking, or oversimplification? Do your ideas have a range of reliable support, from statistics to expert testimony? Finally, push your thinking toward a working thesis (a claim about the issue). Here are some examples:

   - *Position statement:* Barbed fishing hooks should be banned in favor of smooth hooks so that fish stocks can be protected.
   - *Persuading readers to act:* It's time for all consumers to learn more where their food comes from and how it gets to their table.
   - *Arguing against a claim:* Contrary to Motz's contention, Barbie play does not make girls victims of gender stereotypes.
   - *Proposing a solution:* Because the potential for agro-terrorism is real, the government should take steps to protect food at all stages of production.

5. **Organize your argument.** Sometimes, you might want to be direct in your argument: make your claim and then support it. Other times, you might want to be indirect: first lay out the issue and then build toward your essential claim. Whether you choose to be direct or indirect, consider this template as a starting point:

- *Introduction:* Seize the reader's attention and imagination through a pertinent and vivid anecdote, image, example, question, personal confession, quotation, or similar strategy. Raise concern for the issue, narrow the focus, and make your claim (if you are being direct).

- *Needed background:* Help readers understand the issue by putting it in context. Supply facts about the issue's starting point, its significance, its causes and effects, its relationship to other issues. Clarify concepts crucial to your argument.

- *Ordered argument:* In a logical and compelling sequence of points, build the case for your claim. Support each point with careful reasoning and convincing evidence. Within this structure, address opposing points of view and alternatives with concessions and counterarguments.

- *Conclusion:* End on a lively, thoughtful note that stresses your commitment, presses home your claim, and urges readers to accept that claim—whether a position, a call to action, or a solution.

6. **Draft your paper.** Using your outline, write a first draft of your argument. Refer carefully to your research notes in order to keep the argument on track and to accurately present compelling evidence.

7. **Revise the paper.** Review your draft for global issues like these:

- *Ideas:* Does the argument hold water? Is the reasoning sound, the evidence solid?

- *Organization:* Does the overall flow and direction of the argument work?

- *Voice:* Is the tone compelling and urgent but reasonable? Does the writing show respect for opposing points of view?

8. **Edit and proofread the paper.** Carefully review your writing for these issues:

- *Word choice:* accurate, understandable terminology free of jargon, double-talk, and negative connotations

- *Sentence smoothness:* both energetic and thoughtful sentence structures that convey committed and subtle thinking

- *Correctness:* writing free of errors in grammar, spelling, punctuation, and mechanics

- *Design:* reader-friendly format and accurate documentation

9. **Share your argument.** Whether through submitting your paper, posting it, or presenting your findings—find ways to engage an audience with your argument.

Argumentation: A Primer

Formally, an argument is a series of statements arranged in a logical sequence, supported with sound evidence, and expressed powerfully so as to sway an audience. Virtually all research writing is argumentative to a degree. After all, its use of logic and evidence aims to convince readers that the information is reliable and the thinking sound. However, some research writing is more intensively and intentionally argumentative. It makes bold claims about controversial, multi-sided issues and seeks to persuade readers to a particular conclusion or action. Such persuasive arguments stand or fall on three types of appeal made to readers:

1. **An appeal to character** (Greek term *ethos*) calls on readers' perceptions of the one making the case or argument. Does he or she seem trustworthy, credible, fair, authoritative, intelligent, respected, wise? What credentials does the writer bring to researching and discussing the issue?

2. **An appeal to emotion** (Greek term *pathos*) works on the readers' feelings, using word connotations, examples, stories, symbols, allusions, and descriptions to sway the reader's heart in relation to the issue. Does the writer successfully but ethically sway the reader to care about the issue, to accept the claim, and possibly to act?

3. **An appeal to reason** (Greek term *logos*) calls on logic, thoughtful treatment of evidence, and common sense. Do the principles of thought applied to the issue make sense? Do the conclusions follow naturally from the evidence?

While research-based, scholarly arguments seek to rely primarily on appeals to reason, virtually all arguments also invoke some appeals to character and emotion.

Appealing to Character

A persuasive argument is credible partly because of the perceived character of the advocate for the specific claim. As an advocate, you want to come across as admirable (i.e., decent, courageous, moral, generous), authoritative (i.e., up-to-date, well informed, knowledgeable), careful (i.e., thorough, accurate), fair (i.e., objective, nonpartisan), and safe (open, nonthreatening). To create this character, do the following:

Be thoroughly honest. Demonstrate integrity toward the topic—don't falsify data, spin evidence, or ignore facts. Document your sources meticulously.

Be realistic. Make measured claims, projections, and promises. Avoid emotionally charged statements and pie-in-the-sky forecasts.

Develop and maintain trust. From your first word to your last, develop trust—in your attitude toward the topic, your treatment of readers, your presentation of sources, and your respect for opposing viewpoints.

Lean on the experts. You deepen your own credibility by relying on credible, authoritative sources.

Appealing to Emotion

While appeals to character prompt readers to connect with and trust the writer, appeals to emotion connect with readers' feelings surrounding the issue. To prompt readers to change their minds or act, writers must often appeal to emotion. Emotion, motivate, movement: all these terms come from the same root, which means "to push." Persuasion pushes readers from a standstill or point of resistance. The best persuasion makes that movement emotionally satisfying. Consider these guidelines:

Picture readers as resistant. Who are your readers—peers, professors, fellow citizens? What are their allegiances, worries, and dreams? On what points might you agree or disagree? Accept that your readers, including those inclined to agree with you, need convincing. Think of them as alert, cautious, and demanding—but also interested.

Aim to motivate, not manipulate. Whereas you do want readers to accept your viewpoint, you don't want to win at all costs. Avoid bullying, guilt-tripping, and tugging heartstrings.

Use appeals that match readers' needs and values. Your argument may support or challenge readers' needs and values. To understand those needs, study the table below, which is based loosely on the thinking of psychologist Abraham Maslow. Maslow's hierarchical theory ranks people's needs on a scale from the most basic to the most complex. The table begins at the bottom with having necessities (a basic need) and ends at the top with helping others (a more complex need). For example, if you're writing to argue for stricter regulations regarding home mortgages, you would argue differently to legislators (whose focus is on helping others) than to home owners (whose focus is on having necessities). Create effective emotional appeals to readers' needs and values by following these strategies:

- Use appeals that match the foremost needs and values of your readers.
- If appropriate, constructively challenge readers' needs and values.
- Whenever possible, phrase your appeals in positive terms. Avoid appeals geared to play on readers' ignorance, prejudices, selfishness, or fears.
- Based on your analysis of readers' needs, choose a persuasive theme for your argument: a positive benefit, advantage, or outcome that readers can expect if they accept your claim. Use this theme to help readers care about your claims.

Reader Needs	Persuasive Appeals
To make the world better by helping others	values, ethics, and social obligations
To achieve by being good at something or getting recognition	self-fulfillment, reputation, appreciation, status
To belong by being part of a group, by loving and being loved	self-fulfillment, reputation, appreciation, status
To survive by avoiding threats and having necessities	safety, security, physical needs (food, water, shelter, sleep, clothing)

Appealing to Reason

The heart of your research-writing argument will likely be an appeal to reason. A reasonable argument follows rules of logic, evidence, and common sense. It makes clear claims, supports those claims with sound reasoning, provides solid evidence for the reasoning, and effectively addresses opposing points of view. To appeal logically in your argument, follow the guidelines below.

Make and qualify reasonable claims. An argument centers on a claim—a debatable statement drawn from logical thought and reliable evidence. A claim is not simply a personal opinion, a taste, a preference, or an attitude. The claim functions as the thesis being defended by your argument. Here are guidelines for developing a sound claim:

1. **Distinguish three types of claims.** Fact, value, and policy—these are the types of claims made in an argument. Their differences are important because each type has a distinct goal and calls for distinct reasoning and supporting strategies.

   ■ *Claims of fact* state that something is or is not the case. As a writer, you want readers to accept your claim as trustworthy and responsible. After all, accepting or not accepting it can have serious consequences.

   Example: The current rate of climate change will result in more storms each year, storms that are also more severe.

   ■ *Claims of value* state that something does or does not have worth. As a writer, you want readers to accept your judgment. To that end, value claims must be supported by referring to a known standard or establishing an agreed-upon standard.

   Example: Many music videos fail to present positive images of women.

   ■ *Claims of policy* state that something ought or ought not to be done. As a writer, you want your readers to approve a course of action. To get there, you might first have to establish certain facts and values.

   Example: President Obama should take three steps to help resolve the conflict between Israelis and Palestinians.

2. **Press yourself to make a strong claim.** A strong argument begins with a strong claim—one that expresses rich thinking about the issue. Here are examples of weak, good, and strong argumentative theses to guide your own efforts:

   ■ *Weak thesis* (statement of taste or opinion): Internet pornography is serious.

   ■ *Good thesis* (thinking with sophistication): Given the prevalence of Internet pornography and evidence of its impact on young people, governments should fund research into technologies that truly restrict access.

   ■ *Strong thesis* (thinking with risk, tension, surprise, depth): While parents, educators, employers, and others should certainly continue to create technologies that restrict access to Internet pornography, given the global nature of the Internet and the multiple means of access for young people, we would be much further ahead to include elements of gender respect in sex education. After all, the root of the pornography problem is the objectification of human beings, particularly of women and children.

3. **Develop a defensible claim.** An effective claim balances confidence with common sense. Refine your claim using these strategies:

- Avoid all-or-nothing, extreme claims. Propositions using words that are overly positive or negative (e.g., all, best, never, worst) may be difficult to support.

  Example: Anyone caught DUI should never be allowed to drive again.

- Make a truly meaningful claim. Avoid claims that are obvious, trivial, or vague. No such claim is worth the energy needed to argue the point.

  Example: The college's gym is a good place to exercise.

- Use qualifiers to temper your claims. Qualifiers are words or phrases that make claims more reasonable. Examples: almost, frequently, likely, many, maybe, might, often, probably, some, tends to, typically, usually

  Poorly qualified: Star athletes take far too many academic shortcuts.

  Effectively qualified: Some star athletes take improper academic shortcuts.

Support claims logically. A claim stands or falls on its support. It's not the popular strength of your claim that matters, but the strength of your reasoning and evidence. Much of that instruction in logical support is found earlier in this text, primarily in chapters 8 and 9: "Patterns of Reasoning" (pages 175-177), "Drafting the Body: Reasoning with Evidence" (pages 185-189), "Improving Your Reasoning" (pages 208-209), and "Eliminating Logical Fallacies" (pages 210-211). However, the following outlines offer some starting templates for your own line of reasoning:

Outline 1: **Present your supporting arguments, then address counterarguments, and conclude with the strongest argument.**
   Introduction: question, concern, or claim
      1. Strong argument-supporting claim
        • Discussion and support
      2. Other argument-supporting claims
        • Discussion of and support for each argument
      3. Objections, concerns, and counterarguments
        • Discussion, concessions, answers, and rebuttals
      4. Strongest argument-supporting claim
        • Discussion and support
   Conclusion: argument consolidated—claim reinforced

Outline 2: **Address the arguments and counterarguments point by point.**
   Introduction: question, concern, or claim
      1. Strong argument-supporting claim
        • Discussion and support
        • Counterarguments, concessions, and rebuttals
      2. Other argument-supporting claims
        • Discussion and support for each argument
        • Counterarguments, concessions, and rebuttals for each argument
      3. Strongest argument-supporting claim
        • Discussion and support
        • Counterarguments, concessions, and rebuttals
   Conclusion: argument consolidated—claim reinforced

Engage opposing points of view. Think of an argument as an intelligent, lively dialogue with resistant readers. Anticipate their questions, concerns, objections, and counterarguments. Then use these strategies:

1. **Establish points of agreement.** Before you focus on disagreements, lay out the common ground. Doing so establishes rapport, mutual respect, and a shared logical foundation.

   Example: Many women—regardless of their current career standing and their adult attitude toward dolls—have fond childhood memories of playing with Barbie.

2. **Make concessions.** When you offer a concession, you acknowledge a legitimate point or concern of those on another side of the issue. Doing so (a) shows that you understand others' points of view, (b) locates truth in other positions, and (c) acknowledges the limits of your own argument. Paradoxically, such concessions strengthen your overall argument by making it seem more balanced and credible. Concede points graciously, using words like these:

Admittedly	Granted	I agree that	I cannot argue with
It is true that	They're right	I accept	No doubt
Of course	I concede that	Perhaps	Certainly it's the case

   Example: Granted, Barbie's physical appearance isn't realistic. As Motz explains…

3. **When appropriate, develop rebuttals.** When you concede a point, you can often answer the objection by rebutting it. A good rebuttal is a tactful argument aimed at a weak spot in the opposing argument. Rebuttal strategies include the following:

   - Point out the opposition's limits by putting the point in a larger context. Show that the other argument leaves something important out of the picture.
   - Tell the other side of the story. Offer an opposing interpretation of the evidence, or counter with stronger, more reliable, more convincing evidence.
   - Address logical fallacies in the opposing argument (e.g., either/or thinking, broad generalization, over simplification).

   Example: Arguing that Barbie's unrealistic body hurts girls' self-esteem is logically problematic. Children have had dolls for ages…

4. **Consolidate your claim.** After expressing agreement, making concessions, and rebutting objections, you may need to regroup as you move forward with your argument. Turn back to your claim with renewed but measured energy.

   Example: Playing with Barbie need not be an unimaginative, antisocial activity that promotes conformity, materialism, and superficial ideals.

Sample Student Paper: Argumentative Research Writing

In the essay below, student writer Andrew Skogrand argues that global over-fishing is a serious ecological and cultural problem and proposes solutions that Americans can adopt to contribute to a solution. As you study his argument, explore Andrew's thinking, the structure of his argument, the tone of his writing, and his use of resources. Consider, as well, his appeals to character, emotion, and reason.

Writer's Reflection

Everyone wants to put in his or her two cents about the hot-button issues. We all have views on Social Security, U.S. energy policy, and the war in Iraq. Glamorous problems get all the attention—but what about the less flashy topics? When initially asked to investigate a problem in need of a solution, I don't believe the plight of overfishing had an amazing appeal for me. After all . . . it's just fish. Yet, as I began to realize the failing state of marine health, I found it was more than a worthy topic. Overfishing is a problem with hundreds of solutions, all offered by various interests. I felt compelled to sift through the solutions, filter out the destructive ideas and allow an articulated solution to flow forth. I didn't add to the bottleneck by adding my personal ideas; I simply became a critic [of] and [advocate] for the solutions that were already out there.   —Andrew Skogrand

Preparing to read: What do you know about ocean ecology? How does it relate to your life and the life of your community?

Argumentative Essay

The essay's title playfully establishes a theme and points to a problem-solution approach.

The first sentences creatively connect with readers, establishing common ground before presenting the essential problem.

Making Waves: Finding Keys to Success in the Failures of the Fish Industry

We are the proficient, bargain-bound consumers of America. Our wages are well earned, and our money well spent. After a hard day's work we can retire to the warm atmosphere of Red Lobster and settle down to the appetizing "Crown of Shrimp" entrée. In keeping with the American way, this meal—fit for a king—comes at the low price of $7.99 (now through January 30th). We receive a dozen delectable bamboo-skewered shrimp, and we deserve it. But the deal doesn't end at the dozen shrimp; no, we are thriftier than we thought! We pay not only for the twelve tantalizing shrimp we are served, but for every pound of shrimp we purchase, we also purchase ten pounds of assorted fish (McGinn 22). Although this fish is thrown back into the ocean, never actually making it to market because it's dead when caught alongside our now tempura-battered shellfish, we maximized our return ten-fold! Our money funds the paving of the ocean floor, turning the painfully complex ecosystem of the marine depths into a convenient underwater "parking lot" (20). And yet, remarkably, the dollar goes even further. Our kingly cuisine pays for blockades in Gulf ports and waterways by shrimp boats, for fierce conflict between fishermen and Coast Guard personnel (Margavio and Forsyth 33). All this for less than ten dollars! Yes, America is amazing, and the dollar can do so much, much more than we knew—it's practically a steal.

Andrew points to deeper issues hidden from the average reader.

Behind this innocuous act of purchasing seafood, there lurk countless consequences that remain unknown to and hidden from the average consumer. Most of the world still operates under the mindset of the 19th century professor William Carmichael M'Intosh, who stated that the "fauna of the open sea…[is] independent of man's influence" (Marx ix). People look to the overwhelmingly large oceans and deduce that the marine resources that they contain must be equally vast and impressive. We eat tuna with much concern for the safety of dolphins, but we hardly think twice about the tuna. In other words, we view the dolphin as a rare and endangered animal, but tuna is seen as an infinite, inexhaustible resource.

Using authoritative sources and indicating their credentials, the writer establishes the seriousness of the problem.

Based on the expert testimony, Andrew presents a potent truth claim at the end of his opening.

Despite popular opinion, seafood staples such as salmon and tuna are in precarious positions themselves. Currently, "11 of the world's 15 most important fishing areas and 60 percent of the major fish species are in decline, according to the U.N. Food and Agriculture Organization" (McGinn 11). Similarly, the Pew Oceans Commission, a bipartisan group composed of politicians, scientists and activists, traveled the country during 2000 and found populations of "New England cod, haddock, and yellowtail flounder [have] reached historic lows. In U.S. waters, Atlantic halibut are commercially extinct—becoming too rare to justify…commercial fishing" (5). In a letter to the President, Retired Navy Admiral James D. Watkins, chairman to the government's personal U.S. Commission on Ocean Policy, warns America's leader that "unsustainable exploitation of too many of our fishery resources" has put "our oceans and marine resources in serious trouble" (United States 5). In both the heavy reports filed by scientists, and the light catches brought in by fishermen, the truth has surfaced; America's fisheries, along with global fisheries, face an imminent collapse.

Historic Pillaging

A heading indicates the first phase of the writer's argument: the problem's history.

Recent history provides the key to a better understanding of modern fishing practices and outlooks, as well as the current crisis. Marine researcher Peter Weber reports that during this century alone "marine catch rose more than 25-fold" (11). This substantial rise can be attributed to a great increase during the 1950s and '60s in fishing activities that was so large the trends of augmented catches exceeded world population growth. This is a crucial time period; from this experience an "entire generation of managers and politicians was led to believe that launching more boats would automatically lead to higher catches" (Pauly 10). These glory days were soon to expire. The effects of the enlarged fishing fleet began to manifest and by "the 1960s, the yields from major marine fisheries…were topping out and beginning to shrink" (Weber 11). The plight of the Peruvian anchovy, a species constituting one fifth of the world's catch in 1970, quickly came to epitomize unstable fisheries when the annual catch fell from thirteen million tons to two million tons between 1970 and 1974 (McGinn 13). This bottoming out of a fishery sent shockwaves through the commercial fishing world, and the need for change became clear.

A historical example makes the analysis concrete.

Using cause-effect analysis, Andrew explains how the fishery turned to technology to solve its problems.

Sadly, the Peruvian harbinger resulted in no change in fishing policies, but rather a change in fishing practices. The crisis only spurred the industry to consolidate and modernize its fleets, thus using technological advances to make up for losses in overexploited and diminishing fish stocks. Apparently, the historic catches of the Fifties and Sixties may have died out; however, the misinformed mid-century mindset that accompanied it had not. Nonetheless, fishing industries contended that these new tools would be coupled with "models of single-species fish populations…[that provided a] 'maximum sustainable yield'" (Pauly 9). The supposed strategy was to use technology to bring in the most fish possible and—with the aid of these models—still leave enough fish for the stocks to rebound. Daniel Pauly, director of the Canadian Fisheries Centre, laments that these models were followed "only in theory" and that, even today, "fishing technologies… fail to account for ecosystem processes" (10-11). In short, to cope with increasing demand, fish equipment simply ate up everything in sight. Even today, fishermen keep what they want and casually discard the rest; unwanted fish and wildlife, or "bycatch," are sent back into the ocean dead or dying. The equipment may be proficient at catching; however, it is far from efficient in catching its target. Although this may be a small difference in adjectives, the effect is enormous. Fishing equipment not only destroyed fish populations, but it began ravage the environment in which they lived.

The writer argues that technologies exacerbated the problem.

How proficient was fishing equipment? Researcher Anne Platt McGinn with the nonprofit Worldwatch Institute, reports that when the orange roughy fish was "pitted against modern vessels, high-tech gear, and seemingly unlimited capital" the "catches of this species plummeted by 70 percent in just six years." Similarly, the 1960 introduction of commercial trawlers in the Gulf of Thailand led to an 80 percent decrease in daily catches within two decades (14). The fewer fish there are in the ocean, the more adept the fishermen became at hunting down the remaining stocks, all for the sake of keeping their nets full. This futile effort is characteristic of fishermen during the past four decades. The fishing industry's response to smaller catches has not been to allow populations to replenish, but rather to tighten its grip on fisheries by increasing productivity and further threatening the species.

Modern Plundering

The writer examines the current state of the fisheries crisis.

The idea that "more boats equal more fish" proved disastrously untrue for the industry, but with an ocean full of trawlers, fishermen have to keep working and meeting quotas. Fishermen now utilize the ominous technique of descending the food chain in order to maintain their catches. The idea behind this practice, which the industry believes to be "good and unavoidable," stems from a side-effect caused by severely limited populations of large fish, such as tuna or mackerel (10). The various fishes these predators used to eat are in greater abundance; the prey now assumes the predators' position at the top of the food chain. Fishermen do not see this abundance as a cautionary indictor that the ecosystem's scales have been dangerously tipped, but rather they view it as the next natural step in fishing. In short, the moment "top predators are fished out, we turn to their prey, for example shrimp in place of cod." Unsurprisingly, this "good" technique has led to the "unavoidable" and gradual eradication of "large, long-lived fishes from the ecosystems of the world oceans" (10). We fished for the big fish, until they were too few. Then we began to fish for the smaller fish, whose fate will be no different. When their numbers dwindle, it stands to reason that we will descend again. We will descend the food chain to catch smaller fish just as we will descend the ladder of environmental ethics to fill our appetites. We will descend.

After overfishing such species as tuna and mackerel, crippling their native populations, it hardly seems prudent to then exploit their source of food, once again hindering their chances of survival. Imagine the absurdity if hunters believed they could help endangered lions by turning their crosshairs toward shrinking populations of zebra. While the industry may feel it can relieve pressures on some species by moving down the food chain, temporarily shifting its focus to other smaller fish, realistically, we can only descend the food chain so far.

Humanity's tinkering with the marine ecosystem does not stop at the subverting of the food chain—an evolutionary and integral ocean process. Currently, in order to obtain the remaining commercially viable species, the industry utilizes "fish[ing] gear that drags along or digs into the seafloor, destroy[ing] habitat needed by marine wildlife" (Pew 8). Researcher Paul K. Dayton of the Scripps Institution of Oceanography reports that due to trawling "thousands of square kilometers of benthic habitat and invertebrate species have been obliterated…massively [altering] many coastal marine communities" (821). Once again, these communities are offered little chance to rehabilitate. Most areas of the ocean are trawled, at the least, once a year—despite the fact that most of these systems need a minimum of five years to recover (Pew 8). In order to meet demand, fishermen have not only endangered certain species, but they have begun to threaten marine biodiversity and ecosystems, that, unlike fish, don't "bounce back." These are foreign, fragile systems that science knows little about, and while reconstructing the systems remains out of the question, other possible solutions to the crisis still exist.

Future Protections

The first and most critical step in restoring our oceans lies in restoring the federal programs that protect them; without a functioning agency, any policy changes made hereafter would fail to be enforced. Today's system is plagued by an overabundance of laws and agencies that have little way of interacting. Currently there are 140 federal laws that concern the ocean and its coastlines.

In turn, these laws are under the supervision of six departments in the federal government, and more than a dozen federal agencies (Pew 14). The U.S. Commission on Ocean Policy reported the same bottleneck when

---

The writer critiques a chain-reaction process that seems destined for collapse.

Andrew uses an analogy to argue against destructive food-chain practices.

He examines the destructive contribution of modern fishing gear and practices.

With a new heading, the writer turns from arguing for the problem's seriousness to proposing specific solutions.

noting "eleven of fifteen cabinet-level departments…play important roles in the development of ocean and coastal policy" (United States XXXVI). There is no central entity in charge of creating ocean policies, enforcing ocean policies or, most importantly, studying the effects of ocean policies. Homer was right—too many kings do ruin an army.

Andrew proposes solutions that are political and institutional.

The system is buckling under the force of its own weight. Policies in the past for fishermen and coastal industries have simply been indefinite and problematic. One fisherman noted his feelings towards the current ocean administrations when complaining, "The fishermen are going fucking crazy with all the rules and regulations. Could you tell me if it is okay to use fishtraps on tilefish right now or not? How are these guys supposed to know all that crap" (Helvarg 168). Without a clear mandate, fishermen will not respond. There remains a desperate need for a single and definitive authority in the fight for ocean health and fishing sustainability, and that authority needs to be NOAA.

The National Oceanic and Atmospheric Administration, or NOAA, could merge with other appropriate ocean agencies to remove federal clutter. Consolidating the various agencies would ensure "improved communication and coordination [that] would greatly enhance the effectiveness of the nation's ocean policy" (United States XXXVI). NOAA would become an agency that consults "the scientists and resource users who know the fish stocks and appreciate the…[ocean's] complex ecosystem" (McGinn 69). It would operate as a natural resource program that would show concern for the economy in light of the environment.

It then falls on the shoulders of Congress to assign NOAA the great tasks it is to undertake and enforce. Congress would pass a new ocean policy act that would lay down clear and concise rules on how fisheries must be managed. Although this new policy would entail hundreds of regulations—as any act of Congress does—a select few would act as keystones. These vanguard policies include regulation of fishing gear, ecosystem-based planning, individual transferable quotas, and bycatch reduction and monitoring.

The writer explains how his solution would lead to particular positive results or benefits.

The regulation of fishing gear will help severely damaged areas, prohibiting the practice of trawling by indiscriminate equipment. In order to protect marine ecosystems, NOAA would allow only approved fishing gear to be used in various zones. Currently, fishermen "are not required to prove that their actions cause [no] damage" and it is up to society "to prove actual or serious impact" has occurred (Dayton 822). Under new administration, the burden of proof will be reversed, and it will be the task of the fishermen, not the society, to prove with "scientific information…[that] these activities can be conducted without altering or destroying a significant amount of habitat" (Pew 24). Once this has been accomplished, fishermen would be free to trawl. The time has come to take precautionary measures when dealing with fish stocks; practices are to be considered harmful until proven safe.

Just as gear restrictions would ensure the protection of marine habitats, ecosystem-based planning would keep marine reserves viable. Ecosystem

The solution argues for a more big-picture approach through ecosystem planning.

planning would change the way fish stocks are assessed, and thus, how many fish can be caught. Fish industries would begin to take into account the many, many factors that determine fish population, such as "age at capture, the availability of nursery or spawning areas, and the availability of critical habitat on migration routes" (Alden 27). Due to the interrelated nature of marine habitats, the industry must look at the health of the entire ecosystem, not simply the populations of targeted fish. Ecosystem planning may result in small losses for fishermen initially, but due to science's extensive scope, the health of fisheries and fishermen will be protected in the long run.

The proposal includes practical consideration of the difficulties faced by fishermen.

Once fishing limits are calculated environmentally, fishermen will be given individual transferable quotas, or ITQs. Weber describes an ITQ system that would give each boat owner "a share in the annual catch, and quota holders could buy, sell, or lease them like property" (35). The effect would be two-fold; first, fishing would become a closed system. Closing the market relieves pressure on fisheries and competing fishermen by limiting the entry of new boats. Second, ITQs would act as an immediate response system. The system would give fishermen a stake in the fisheries and encourage them to "go to greater lengths to protect the total stock, and thereby enjoy greater individual returns" (McGinn 63). In other words, the quota for each fisherman is based on total fish populations; more fish in the fishery means more fish for each fisherman. Phenomenal. Financially, it becomes advantageous for the fishermen to fish responsibly. In the past, fishermen rarely considered the long-term effects of overfishing. The ITQ system, however, would provide fishermen with immediate feedback through quota fluctuations.

Andrew anticipates the objections of skeptics and responds.

Many skeptics of the ITQ system complain that quotas encourage fishermen to discard inexpensive fish, filling their boats only with high-priced species to maximize profits. The now dead and unwanted fish is wastefully thrown back into the ocean. Bycatch reduction and monitoring would be a countermeasure against such unhealthy practices. Under the new system, it would be illegal to "discard and waste one species because [fishermen] are in a target fishery for another" (Pew 25). If the true cost remains the lives of millions of fish, then all caught fish must be brought in. If a fisherman catches it, it's part of his quota.

He turns to another important dimension of the solution.

Bycatch measures also must be taken in the case where the caught item isn't marketable, for instance sea turtles. NOAA would create mandatory program for the use of TEDs, or turtle exclusion devices. These devices allow turtles and other unwanted organisms to escape nets via a release device. Not only do TEDs "exclude 97 percent of the turtles," but also they save on "fuel costs through drag reduction—the less bycatch, the less drag" (Margavio and Forsyth 5-6). Adoption in the past of such a program has been slow, but NOAA would provide training and technical assistance to fishermen when needed. The program would emerge gradually. The program's first year would be optional and fishermen who volunteer to participate during this time would receive the TED device at no charge.

Especially in matters of equipment, fishermen must feel that they are actively participating in the ocean's rehabilitation and not unwillingly contributing to their own destruction.

Andrew includes not just government and fishermen in the solution, but also the consuming public.

NOAA would not only change the way that fish managers think, but it would also change the mindset of the public. A consumer campaign composed of "publishing cards, lists and brochures on what seafood to eat and what to avoid" (Sklandany and Vandergeest 24) would inform consumers as to what fish should be purchased. Moreover, NOAA would implement a certification system to mark which fish have come from responsibly managed fisheries, so consumers can easily identify environmentally sound choices. History has shown that a better-informed consumer will purchase the responsible product, as noted in similar successful campaigns such as "sustainable timber, dolphin-friendly tuna, organic food and fair-trade coffee" (24). The sad truth remains that until consumer demand fades, cooks like Michelle from New York will continue to purchase endangered fish as long as people want it. In her words, "Until we can't get it… I will continue to buy it" ("Still Serving" par. 8). If demand is undercut for forbidden fish, however, the industry will have little reason to evade NOAA regulations. For a solution to become effective, we must not only look at how fishermen exploit natural resources, but also why they do. The fish industry is simply folding under consumer pressure, and the system can reach equilibrium only by educating the public on what the right choices are.

Paying for Progress

The writer asks a key question: how will the solution be financed?

While certainly not expensive endeavors, the large reorganization of NOAA and the creation of many new ocean initiatives will not be free of cost. Two sources of income would provide ample resources for the new ocean policies and, notably, neither source would cause increased tax pressure on the public. The U.S. Commission on Ocean Policy readily identifies the first fiscal source as the "outer Continental Shelf oil and gas revenues that are not already committed to" other various marine initiatives. This translates into approximately four billion dollars in unclaimed revenues annually (United States LIV). Each year, this sum would be wisely placed in an ocean trust fund.

The second source of money would, again, be a redirection of already existing assets. The United States takes part in a global trend of paying out large subsidies to the fishing industry. Internationally, these figures were estimated to be $14 to $20 billion dollars in 1995. Currently, these funds encourage fishermen to continually operate at a loss and "[participate] in the downfall of their own industry" (McGinn 32). Why continue to pay for fishermen to operate unsuccessfully if there remains little hope of such subsidies reinvigorating the moribund industry? New subsidies will come under the control of NOAA; they will not encourage unsuccessful fishermen to stay in the business, but, rather, they will pay for education and training for fishermen to find new jobs in other, more open markets. Subsidies, as they were intended to do, will pay for brighter futures.

Andrew presses his readers to face the truth and to accept change.

The Power of Possibility

The time has come to face realities. The fate of the fishermen and the health of the ocean are inextricably linked. Eventually overexploited fish stocks will bottom out and, ironically, it will be the fishermen headed for certain extinction. The plight of overfishing does not simply concern marine health, but the health of the fishermen and the health of the economy. Therefore, the ocean must be treated as an investment—one that must be allowed to mature wisely; it is not a bottomless honey pot in which we can endlessly dip our hands. Although current trends are bleak, the future remains full of possibility; restructuring the system may initially upset the fishing industry, yet "300,000 related fishing jobs could be gained from better management and protection of fish stocks" (McGinn 33). Fishermen of the near future stand to increase their catch by twenty-five percent—or twenty million tons—if they simply allowed fisheries to rebuild (Weber 8). The scientists, the economists, and even the politicians have unanimously sounded a clarion call for reformation. Let us not wait until the time has passed to respond. If we fail to heed the warning, if we are slow to act, then our pockets may be full and our stomachs may be satisfied, but our oceans, our hopes, and even our futures, will be empty.

His conclusion focuses on the benefits of accepting the changes at the heart of the solutions he has proposed, but he also urges action because of the likely consequences of inaction.

The bibliography is rich with scholarly studies, trade books, and respected reports.

Works Cited

Alden, Robin. "A Troubled Transition for Fisheries." *Environment* 41 (May 1999): 25-8. Print.

Dayton, Paul K. "Reversal of the Burden of Proof in Fisheries Management." *Science* 279 (Feb. 1998): 821-2. Print.

Helvarg, David. *Blue Frontier: Saving America's Living Seas.* New York: W.H. Freeman and Company, 2001. Print.

Margavio, Anthony V. and Craig J. Forsyth. *Caught in the Net.* College Station: Texas A&M 1996. Print.

Marx, Wesly. *The Oceans: Our Last Resource.* San Francisco: Sierra Club Books, 1981. Print.

McGinn, Anne Platt. *Rocking the Boat: Conserving Fisheries and Protecting Jobs.* Worldwatch Institute. Paper 142. Washington D.C.: Worldwatch Institute, 1998. Print.

Pauly, Daniel. "Empty Nets." *Alternatives Journal* 30 (Spring 2004): 8-13. Print.

Pew Oceans Commission. 2003. *America's Living Oceans: Charting a Course for Sea Change.* Summary Report. May 2003. Pew Oceans Commission, Arlington, Virginia. Print.

Skladany, Mike and Peter Vandergeest. "Catch of the Day." *Alternatives Journal* 30 (Spring 2004): 24-26. Print.

At the writing of the essay, the sources were current and relevant.

"Still Serving Chilean Sea Bass." *Day to Day*. National Public Radio. 29 Aug. 2003. Web. 17 Nov. 2004.

United States. U.S. Commission on Ocean Policy. *An Ocean Policy for the 21st Century*. Sept. 2004. Web. 14 Nov. 2004.

Weber, Peter. *Net Loss: Fish, Jobs, and the Marine Environment*. Worldwatch Institute. Paper 120. Washington DC: Worldwatch Institute, 1994. Print.

Reading Research Writing: Questions

To deepen your understanding of argumentative research writing, consider these questions about Andrew Skogrand's paper:

1. At the beginning of his paper, what strategies does Andrew use to engage his readers and identify the problem at the heart of this argument? Do you find these strategies successful?

2. In the first sections of his paper, Andrew outlines the problem of declining fish stocks. How does he seek to help readers understand the nature of the problem and to convince readers that the problem is serious and that they should care about it?

3. The latter part of Andrew's argument is dedicated to presenting, outlining, and arguing for a solution to the problem. How successful is this part of his argument? Does the solution match the problem as he has presented it? What does Andrew do to argue that his solution is the right one and is workable?

4. Examine Andrew's conclusion: How compelling is it? How does he bring his argument to a close?

5. Examine Andrew's works-cited list and his use of sources within the paper. How strong, balanced, and compelling is his research?

6. An argument appeals to character, emotion, and reason. Identify ways or places that Andrew's paper makes these three appeals. How effectively does he do so?

 FOCUS on Research Essentials: For another example of argumentative research writing, consider the Chicago model, "A Thorn Beneath the Shining Armor: Churchill, Bishop Bell, and Area Bombing" on pages 470-481.

Practicing Your Research

1. **Respond to the model.** What is your response to Andrew Skogrand's problem-solution argument about the crisis in commercial fishing? Andrew wrote his paper in 2004. As a response to Andrew's argument, do one of the following: (a) research developments in fishing since 2004 and write a paper that looks at the current state of fish ecology, (b) examine the plight of a specific marine creature or a specific fishery, or (c) research another issue related to the health of the earth's salt-water or fresh-water ecologies.

2. **Take a cross-disciplined approach.** The perspective of multiple disciplines can help resolve debatable, controversial issues. For example, fish is one part of food culture. Choose another aspect of food culture (e.g., fast food, organic food, holiday feasting), identify a debatable issue related to that topic, and research the issue from two disciplinary perspectives (e.g., agriculture, biology, environment, nutrition, sociology, theology, history, business, literature).

3. **Make it multimedia.** A sound argument can be conveyed through many media, not only written words. Using textual, visual, and/or auditory media, develop an argument on a topic related to some problem of urban or rural living.

4. **Take it to the streets.** Argumentative activities such as taking positions and solving problems are all part of work life, public life, and family life. Identify a financial challenge related to your personal situation, your family's, a specific business, a nonprofit agency, or a government body. (Examples: spending priorities, debt reduction, saving plans, education financing, financial-system reform, corporate bailouts). Then research and write a position paper or a proposal for solving the problem.

Checklist: Use this checklist to review your argumentative research paper.

☑ **Ideas:** The thesis, the reasoning, and the evidence are sound; opposing points of view are effectively addressed.

☑ **Organization:** Whether direct or indirect, the paper's structure successfully builds a compelling argument point by point.

☑ **Voice:** The tone is appropriately urgent but measured; the attitude toward opposition is respectful.

☑ **Words:** Language is precise and energetic, but free of negative connotations, double-talk, euphemisms, and clichés.

☑ **Sentences:** Constructions are forceful but thoughtfully varied.

☑ **Correctness:** The writing is free from glaring and confusing errors in grammar, punctuation, spelling, and mechanics.

☑ **Design:** The document's design creates clarity, understanding, and conviction in readers and/or viewers (without distracting, manipulative slickness); and is formatted and documented in an appropriate style (MLA, APA, Chicago, CSE).

The IMRAD Research Report

 Q What research methods are used for primary-source research? Which of these methods have you used before? How might these methods require additional time or effort? What research tools are needed?

An IMRAD report—a form common in the social and natural sciences—is based mainly on primary research, though it may include a review of secondary sources (called a literature review—see Chapter 17). As a result, the research and writing process are somewhat different from those associated with other research writing. Generally, in such writing, (1) your connection to sources is more direct, (2) you generate most or all of your research data, and (3) you are the first person to write about the data generated.

Such primary research does happen in the humanities, taking the form, for example, of analyses of literary texts, of other artworks, or of artifacts and documents. However, in the social and natural sciences, where field research and experiments are common, primary-research reports typically follow the IMRAD format: Introduction, Methods, Results, and Discussion. The IMRAD research report is the particular focus of this chapter.

Topics to Consider: Typically, your instructor will assign your topic (e.g., through a lab manual). However, if you need to develop your own study, select a phenomenon about which you are curious, and then focus it by considering the following angles:

- Economic issues related to the topic's cost, gain, or loss
- Ethical issues related to the topic's impact on people or the environment
- Health issues related to its use, abuse, constructive effect, or destructive effect
- Historical issues related to the topic's discovery, development, or current use
- Political issues linked to related government policies, officials, or institutions
- Scientific issues related to the topic's composition, formation, or deterioration
- Sociological issues related to its impact on families, schools, or religious institutions

What's Ahead?

Guidelines for Writing an IMRAD Report

When you have chosen a topic, work through the research and writing process briefly outlined below. (As needed, go to the detailed instruction in chapters 1-11.)

1. **Review primary-research procedures such as these:**
   - **For an interview, do the following:** Determine what you want to accomplish; choose an interview medium (face-to-face, telephone, e-mail); research the interview subject and interviewee; prepare meaningful questions; politely request and schedule the interview; and gather recording equipment. (See details on pages 110-115.)
   - **For a lab experiment, review the lab manual and any handouts.** In most science courses, studies and experiments are assigned through textbooks, manuals, and handouts. Study those materials to understand what you must do and why. Read background in textbooks and other sources.
   - **For a field study, use a field or lab notebook.** Accurate, complete record keeping is crucial to doing good scientific research. Use the notebook to plan research, record what you do, collect data, make drawings, and reflect on results. For each notebook entry, record the date and your goal.
   - **For surveys, do the following:** Identify respondents, prepare the survey, distribute it, and process the results. (For detailed instructions, see pages 119-123.)

2. **Plan and complete your study or experiment by doing the following:**
   - Note whether your instructor assigned a *study* or an *experiment*: *Studies* observe what's there—by counting, measuring, sampling, and so on, whereas *experiments* test hypotheses by manipulating variables.
   - Develop key research questions. If you are conducting an experiment, then state your hypothesis, and design procedures for testing it.
   - Gather the necessary tools, equipment, and materials.
   - Carefully conduct your tests and perform your observations.
   - Take notes, being careful to record data accurately, clearly, and completely. If helpful, use a data-collection sheet. (For details, see pages 139-143.)

3. **Relying on your notes and recordings, draft the report.** Wrestle with your data. What do they mean? Were the results expected? Which factors could explain those results? What further research might be necessary? Then draft the report in the sequence outlined below (you will reorganize parts for the finished copy later):
   - **Materials and methods:** Explain what you did to study the topic or test the hypothesis. Supply essential details, being so clear that someone else could repeat the steps.
   - **Results:** Using two strategies, present the data you collected. First, share data in graphical forms—as tables, line charts, bar graphs, photographs, and so on (see pages 198-201). While full attention to graphics and statistics is beyond the scope of this book, follow this basic rule: Make your graphic independent of the written text by giving it a descriptive title, clear headings and labels, units of measurement, and footnotes. The reader should be able

to follow your study's "story" by studying your graphics. Second, draw attention to the major observations and key trends available in the data. However, do not interpret the data in your results or give your reactions to them.

- **Discussion:** Interpret the results by relating the data to your original questions and hypotheses, offering conclusions, and supporting each conclusion with details. Essentially, answer the question, "What does it all mean?" Explain which hypotheses were supported, and why. Also explore unexpected results, and suggest possible explanations. Conclude by reemphasizing the value of what you learned.
- **Introduction:** Once you have drafted the methods, results, and discussion, write an introduction that creates a framework for the report. Explain why you undertook the study, provide background information, review the literature on your topic, and state your question or hypothesis.
- **Summary or abstract:** If required, summarize your study's purpose, methods, results, and conclusions. An abstract is a one-paragraph summary that allows the reader to (1) get the report in a nutshell and (2) determine whether reading the study would be worthwhile. (See the model on page 330.)
- **Title:** Develop a precise title that captures the "story" of your study. Worry less about the length of the title and more about its clarity.
- **Front and end matter:** If required, add a title page, reference page, and appendixes.

4. **Reorder and revise the draft.** Once you have roughed out the parts, reorder them as follows: (1) front matter, (2) summary or abstract, (3) introduction, (4) materials and methods, (5) results, (6) discussion, (7) reference page, and (8) appendixes. Then revise the draft, guided by these questions:
   - Are the purpose, hypotheses, conclusions, and support clear and complete?
   - Is the traditional structure of a lab or field report followed effectively?
   - Is the voice objective, curious, and informed?

5. **Edit and proofread.** Check especially for these conventions of science writing:
   - **Measured use of passive voice:** Generally, use the passive voice only when needed—usually in the methods section to keep the focus on the action and the receiver, not the actor. (See page 221.)
   - **Past and present tenses of verbs:** Generally, use the past tense in your report. However, present tense may be appropriate when discussing published work, established theories, and your conclusions.
   - **Objectivity:** Make sure that your writing is precise (not ambiguous), specific (not vague), neutral (not biased), and concise (not wordy).
   - **Mechanics:** Follow the conventions in the discipline with respect to capitalization, abbreviations, numbers, equations, and symbols.

6. **Prepare and share your report.** Following the required format and documentation conventions, submit a polished report to your instructor. Also find ways to share your study with the scientific community (e.g., undergraduate journals).

Sample Student Paper: IMRAD Report

In the paragraph below, student writer Terri Wong describes how her writing assignment led her to complete a primary-research project that she personally found engaging and fulfilling. As you read the report (structured using IMRAD and documented in APA), note the range of tasks that it required: posing a hypothesis, designing and conducting an experiment, and gleaning and interpreting raw data.

Writer's Reflection

In Professor Brad Henderson's Scientific Writing course, I was told to write an IMRAD-style [Introduction, Methods, Research, and Discussion] paper using general principles and data to make my scientific argument. I instantly knew what topic to investigate. I grew up surrounded by pets—from the typical to the exotic praying mantis—which led me to become curious about animal behavior. More recently, I've become interested in the welfare of captive dogs and wanted to learn what makes for effective dog enrichment. Specifically, I observed whether dogs, when given the choice, had a selection preference toward a specific color of chew toy. With every scientific article I examined, it became clear that dogs could differentiate blue and red colors. Through increased interactions with certain colored toys, dogs would reveal a selection preference toward blue and red toys. Although it is a hypothetical study, writing the paper ignited my passion for scientific investigation. One day, I hope to produce authentic research through my graduate studies in animal behavior. I aim not only to research enrichment items, but more importantly to enhance the lives of captive dogs with the results of my studies.

Preparing to read: What do you know about dog behavior? What have you experienced and observed yourself?

IMRAD Report

The title identifies the topic and "story."

Chew-Toy Color Preferences in Kenneled Dogs (*Canis familiaris*)

Abstract

The writer briefly (1) identifies the problem and experiment, (2) summarizes findings of earlier studies, (3) cites her hypothesis, and (4) summarizes her findings.

Toy enrichment becomes an increasing concern for shelters seeking to purchase toys that benefit the dogs and produce long-term success. This study examines dog selection of chew toys in blue, green, yellow, and red colors, revealing whether dogs have a color preference. Previous studies have shown that dogs have peak sensitivities at 480 nm (blue) and 630 nm (red). In this study, 20 dogs were monitored on interaction rates with each colored toy. Since dogs have sensitivity toward blue and red lights, and have difficulty discriminating between 500 nm to 600 nm (green to yellow), the study hypothesizes an increase in preference for blue and red toys and an infrequent selection of green and yellow toys. The results showed that dogs did prefer blue and red over green and yellow toys. The majority of the dogs chose to interact with the blue toy. When blue was not present, dogs chose red over green and yellow; given green and yellow, subjects had no preference for one over the other. Not only do blue toys get selected more often, but the color also leads to long-term interactions. Within the hour, dogs spent a considerable amount of time interested in blue-colored toys, suggesting that dogs do have a color preference for blue.

1. Introduction: The Research Question and Its Relevance

Many dogs *(Canis familiaris)* are housed in adoption shelters from just a few days to several months. Shelters have an obligation to maintain a level of enrichment in the captive animal's environment that improves biological functioning (Newberry, 1995). Toy enrichment becomes an increasing concern as shelters, which are low in funding, must select and purchase toys that benefit the dogs and produce long-term success. The purpose of this study is to examine selection preferences of kenneled dogs when given chew toys of different colors. Popular belief about canine color vision was that it was nonexistent, that dogs were color blind. However, studies have shown that dogs have binocular, dichromatic vision and can still discriminate between colors by detecting visible wavelengths. The canine retina contains two types of cone photo pigment that have spectral peaks between 420 nm and 555 nm (Neitz et al., 1989). Jacobs et al. (1993) revealed one cone pigment with peak sensitivity at 555 nm and the second between 430nm and 435nm. Further investigation revealed that dogs have a red light sensitivity of 630 nm and a blue light sensitivity close to 480 nm (Grozdanic et al., 2007). Therefore, dogs have trouble distinguishing wavelengths from green to orange light, about 510 nm to 590 nm. So will dogs select certain colors when given the option? Do they have a color preference in toys? If so, what color catches their interest and results in extended play behavior?

Through behavioral testing, this study aims to reveal whether dogs have a selection preference in chew toys of blue, green, yellow, and red colors. During daily one-hour sessions, 20 dogs were monitored on the number of interactions (i.e., smell, lick, chew, carry, roll, touch, and guarding) that each colored toy received throughout the three-week test period. Since dogs have peak sensitivity toward blue and red lights, the study hypothesizes an increase in preference for blue and red toys. In contrast, dogs will infrequently select green and yellow toys since they have difficulty discriminating wavelengths between 500 to 600 nm. If dogs do have a color preference, adoption shelters can make cost-efficient purchases of toys with a specific color that will enrich the lives of kenneled dogs.

2. Materials and Methods

2.1 Study site. Observations were conducted at the Coyote Point SPCA, housing over 40 dogs awaiting adoption. Dog were individually housed in 4' x 6' solitary kennels (24 square feet), set 4" apart. All kennels

---

Margin notes:

The heading identifies the introduction and forecasts its content.

The writer more fully describes the problem and its importance.

As context for her own work, she identifies earlier studies and documents their findings.

She states her research questions.

The writer states her hypothesis and describes the benefits of resolving the research questions.

A detailed
explanation of
where and how
the experiment
was conducted
is given.

The subjects and
subject-selection
criteria are
identified.

Materials are
described and
their selection
criteria are
given.

Details identify
controls used
to isolate and
measure specific
responses to
specific stimuli.

Testing
conditions and
data-collection
methods are
described.

held the following: water dish, food dish, soft bed, and blanket. Two black boxes, positioned on the ground at the front of each kennel door, were installed to hold and release toys with the push of a remote-controlled trigger. The 8" x 8" x 8" black-sided boxes were placed 2' apart, orienting one on the left and the other on the right side in the subject's line of vision. Release hinges at the top of each box were triggered to open and reveal toys at the same time for every subject. Simultaneously, visual recordings started once toys were revealed and released in each kennel.

2.2 Subjects. Ten male and 10 female healthy mixed-breed dogs (*Canis familiaris*) between six months to seven years of age were used in this study (see Table 1A). All 20 subjects had prior experience with similar chew toys used in the study. These chew toys were not accounted for in the results. Subjects who showed interest in the toy by interacting and playing were observed. Subjects were excluded if they were not of age, were scheduled for adoption within the test period, were unable to interact with the toy (i.e., due to frail teeth, disability, etc.), or were fearful of the toy or black boxes.

2.3 Toy selection. A total of 40 chew toys were used: 10 blue, 10 green, 10 yellow, and 10 red. The bone-shaped toys were 6" long, weighing 10.7 oz, large enough for a medium-sized dog to hold in its mouth and light enough to be carried for an extended time. Made of natural rubber, toys were puncture resistant, nontoxic, nonabrasive, and nonsplintering. Each subject was presented two toys during daily sessions. Toy combinations for subjects followed the "Daily Toy Schedule" (DTS), where one male and one female subject received the same toy combination for that day (see Table 1A and Table 1B). The DTS allowed adequate amounts of data to be collected daily. Control-toy combinations were blue/blue, green/green, yellow/yellow, and red/red; subjects had no need to discriminate between colors since the pairs were the same color. The experimental toy combinations consisted of any combinations of two different colors (i.e., blue/red, green/yellow, red/yellow, blue/green, etc.).

2.4 Interaction and data collection. Toy combinations were presented for 60 minutes each day for a period of three weeks. The one-hour sessions occurred at 10:00 a.m., 2:00 p.m., or 7:00 p.m. For this study, exact starting times of presentations did not matter as long as all toys were presented to the 20 subjects at the same start-time for each session. Observational data of each session was collected by camcorder recordings during the test period. Recordings were digitized and filed through computer software for later analysis.

The graphic is identified by type (Table) and number (1A). In addition, the title identifies the graphic's topic and purpose.

Subjects are identified by name and gender, and toy assignments are listed.

The table shows codes used to track test conditions and results.

The test's procedure and record keeping are described.

Precautionary controls are identified.

The test's type and results are identified.

Parenthetical references indicate that details in the text are displayed in related graphics.

Table 1A: Daily Toy Schedule (DTS). The assigned toy combination each day of the week for a pair of dogs, one male and one female.

Subject		Daily Toy Schedule (Each Week)						
Male	*Female*	1	2	3	4	5	6	7
Aladdin	Jasmine	1	2	3	4	5	6	7
Peter Pan	Tinkerbell	10	1	2	3	4	5	6
Sebastian	Ariel	9	10	1	2	3	4	5
Bruno	Cinderella	8	9	10	1	2	3	4
Mushu	Mulan	7	8	9	10	1	2	3
Hercules	Meg	6	7	8	9	10	1	2
Simba	Nala	5	6	7	8	9	10	1
Mickey	Minnie	4	5	6	7	8	9	10
Pongo	Perdy	3	4	5	6	7	8	9
Tramp	Lady	2	3	4	5	6	7	8

Table 1B: Toy combinations are numbered 1 through 10: blue (B), green (G), yellow (Y), red (R)

Code	Toy Combination
1	BB
2	RG
3	GG
4	BR
5	YY
6	BG
7	RR
8	BY
9	RY
10	GY

2.5 Procedure. In preparation for each session, a technician followed the DTS and placed one toy in the left black box and one in the right black box. After all toys were in place, the technician pressed the remote-control trigger, which released the hinge of the boxes and revealed the toy combinations for each subject. Simultaneously, the cameras began recording for exactly one hour. After the session, toys were collected from each kennel and placed through a trace-free wash, removing any contaminants left over by the previous user. Toys remained in the wash overnight and were later dried for the next session. The process was repeated for three weeks.

3. Results

3.1 Color preference. A Mann-Whitney U-test revealed significant differences in rates of interaction ($U = 5.00$, $P = 0.02$) between blue, green, yellow, and red toys. Results from control toy combinations showed an equal number of interactions between the same colored toys (see Fig. 1). When paired with the same color, no one toy had significantly more interactions than the other. Every toy had an average of six interactions per hour throughout the testing period. In contrast, a significant difference was seen in experimental toy combinations (see Fig. 2). Blue toys had a total of 147 male and 151 female interactions, in comparison to green and yellow toys that averaged about 24 interactions for both genders. As for red, males interacted 120 times and females 126 times. Although lower than blue, red toys were selected more than green and yellow.

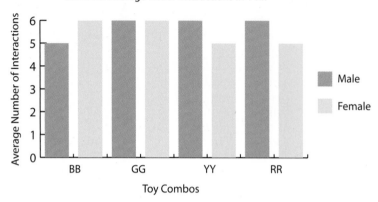

Figure 1: Average number of interactions in control groups BB, GG, YY, and RR during the one-hour sessions across the three-week testing period. All control groups resulted with dogs interacting within close range for each toy.

One-tailed Wilcoxon matched-pairs signed-rank test (T = 2.03, P = 0.02) showed a significant difference with all experimental toy combinations. Blue toys, resulting in the highest number of interactions, were compared with the other three colors (see Fig. 2).

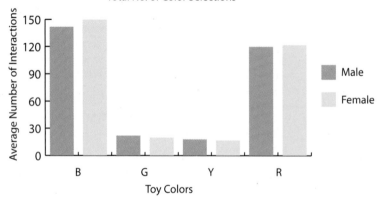

Figure 2: The total number of interactions with each color toy over the three-week test period. The 10 male and 10 female subjects showed greatest interest in blue (B) toys, followed by (R) toys. Fewer interactions occurred with green (G) and yellow (Y) toys.

The text explains details illustrated in Figures 3A, 3B, and 3C.

Toy combinations blue/green, blue/yellow, and blue/red showed higher number of blue interactions in each combination (see Fig. 3A). Blue had between 30 to 35 interactions in comparison to the following: red with 20, green with 12, and yellow with 11. When given the choice between red and another color, dogs chose red toys an average of 26 times, compared to an average of 11 times for yellow and for green (see Fig. 3B). A similar number of interactions occurred between green and yellow toys, averaging 10 interactions (see Fig. 3C).

The subheading forecasts distinctions regarding the length of time that subjects interacted with each color toy.

3.2 Length of interactions. Subjects spent an average of 47% of their time interacting with blue toys during one-hour sessions. The other colored toys had the following results: 17% red, 13% green, and 8% yellow (see Fig. 4). Subjects played with blue toys about 28 minutes each day compared to 5 to 10 minutes for the green and yellow toys. The playtime for red toys was 17 minutes higher than for green and yellow toys but significantly lower than for blue toys. Playtime for blue toys steadily increased as the experiment progressed. Although playtime for red toys was less than playtime for blue toys, playtime for red toys also steadily increased. Green and yellow toys both had similar intervals of play that continually declined. Although blue and red toys had longer play intervals, the interaction rates decreased near the end of the study.

To support her findings that dogs prefer blue toys, the writer tests for and shows that when offered a blue toy along with a green, yellow, or red toy, the subjects chose blue toys, although the frequency differed by gender.

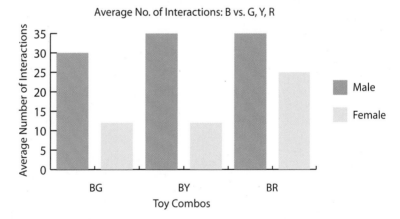

Figure 3A: Comparison of color selection per week when B is coupled with G, Y, or R toys. In these experimental combinations, B toys resulted in increased interaction when subjects were presented B and another color.

The graph and caption show that the subjects preferred red toys versus green or yellow toys.

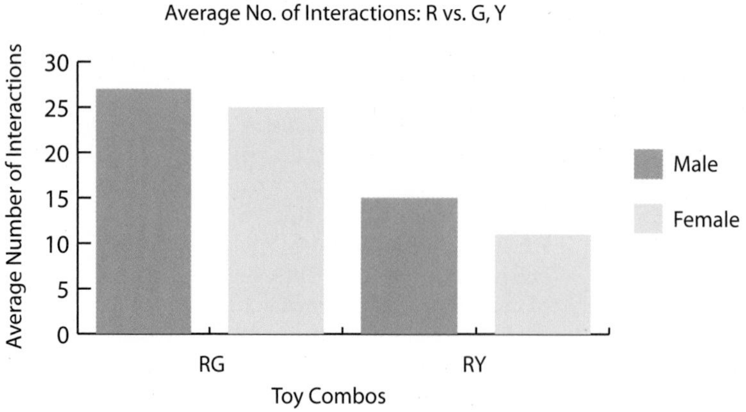

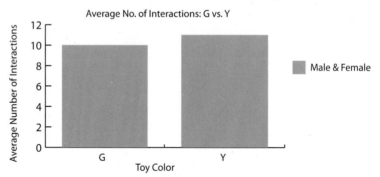

Figure 3B: Comparison of R versus G and Y toys. Average number of interactions increased for R when subjects were presented with R and another color.

4. Discussion

4.1 Color discrimination and preference. In this study, results showed blue and red toys were selected more frequently, which confirmed studies of canine retinal peak sensitivity by Neitz el al. (1989) and Jacob et al. (1993). Being more sensitive to blue and red wavelengths, subjects did prefer blue and red over green and yellow toys (see Figs. 3ABC).

The writer notes that one of her findings confirms the finding of an earlier study.

The graph indicates the subjects' preferences when offered a green toy along with a yellow toy.

Figure 3C: Comparison of G versus Y toys. When giving G and Y toy combinations, subjects selected both colors equally with no significant difference in numbers of interactions.

A pie graph shows the amount of time that subjects spent with blue, red, green, and yellow toys.

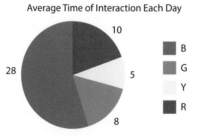

Figure 4: Graphic representation of the average time (min.) spent during daily interactions with toy combinations. Results show subjects spending the majority of their time interacting with B toys, followed by R and then G and Y.

The writer clarifies some fine points of analysis.

Blue toys were selected more than any other color. If there was a choice between a blue toy and another color, the majority of the dogs chose to interact with the blue toy. In contrast, when a blue toy was not present, dogs chose red over green and yellow. Interestingly, when given the option between green and yellow toys, subjects had no preference for one over the other; dogs were unable to discriminate between green and yellow because their eyes lack sensitivity to the wavelengths of these colors.

A new subheading introduces the writer's summary of her findings.

She cites questions for future research.

4.2 Colors' effect on length of interaction. Not only did blue toys get selected more often, but the color also led to long-term interactions. Within the hour, dogs spent a considerable amount of time with blue and red toys, particularly blue toys (see Figs. 4 and 5). Hence, their preference for blue toys results in extended toy-enriching play. Owners must consider, however, the possibility of dogs losing interest in any toy over a long period of time. Knowing that dogs prefer blue and red toys, researchers can in future studies use these colors as control variables and focus on other aspects of enrichment toys, such as shape, texture, and smell. Studies can also investigate whether rotation of blue and red toys extends a dog's interaction with enrichment items other than chew toys. And studies could compare behavioral differences between male and female dogs and publish play ethograms associated with different colors. Overall, the knowledge that dogs do have a higher preference for blue-colored toys enables adoption shelters, dog trainers, and dog owners to enrich the lives of their dogs by choosing toys that are blue, the canines' eye-catching color.

She closes by restating the benefits of her findings and combining the results in a line graph, Figure 5.

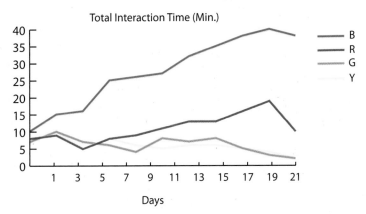

Figure 5: Average time of interaction with each colored toy over the three-week test period. Graph shows daily averages of toy interaction from all subjects. Blue and red resulted in steady increase in play that later decreased. Green and yellow continually declined in intervals of play as each day progressed.

References

Grozdanic, S. D., Matic, M., Sakaguchi, D. S., & Kardon, R. H. (2007).
Evaluation of retinal status using chromatic pupil light reflex activity
in healthy and diseased canine eyes. *Investigative Ophthalmology &*
Visual Science, 48, 5178-5184.

Jacobs G. H., Deegan, J. F., Crognale, M. A., & Fenwick, J. A. (1993).
Photo pigments of dogs and foxes and their implication for canid
vision. *Visual Neuroscience 1,* 173-180.

Neitz, J., Geist, T., & Jacobs, G. H. (1989). Color vision in the dog. *Visual*
Neuroscience 2, 119-125.

Newberry, R. C. (1995). Environmental enrichment: Increasing the
biological relevance of captive environments. *Applied Animal*
Behaviour Science, 44, 229-243.

The writer lists
her secondary
sources and
formats them
in APA style,
consistent with
IMRAD.

Reading Research Writing: Questions

To deepen your understanding of primary-research writing, consider these questions
about Terri Wong's paper:

1. Review the process Wong used to select her research topic and design her study.
   What does the process show about scientific research?

2. Compare and contrast Wong's abstract and introduction. How does she use these
   segments of the paper to introduce her study and forecast her findings?

3. Locate Wong's references to secondary sources and explain how they relate to her
   own experiment (her primary research).

4. Review the IMRAD structure of the report, exploring what this organization suggests about research and writing especially in the social and natural sciences.

5. Review the headings and subheadings of the report. What do these add to the report?

6. Study three of Wong's graphics and explain how she introduces them in the text, identifies them in the titles and captions, and uses them to illustrate her points.

7. Review Wong's hypothesis and explain how she uses it to design and direct her study.

8. Cite three choices that Wong makes to ensure that her study isolates and measures her subjects' specific behavioral traits.

 FOCUS on Your Major: If your major is in the social or natural sciences, primary-source research reports in the form of lab reports, experiment reports, survey reports, and field reports will likely be your main form of research writing. However, primary-research writing is equally common in the humanities, particularly in the form of analyzing texts, works of art, artifacts, historical records, and so on. (See for example, chapter 16, "Analysis of a Literary Text," pages 341-358.) Whatever your discipline, learn what primary research methods and forms of writing are practiced—and learn to practice them well.

Kletr/www.shutterstock.com

Practicing Your Research

1. **Respond to the model.** Review Terri Wong's paper, "Chew-Toy Color . . . ," looking for aspects of her experiment that you would like to support, challenge, or test using either dogs or some other animal. Then design your experiment, conduct it, record and analyze your results, and write your report.

2. **Take a cross-disciplined approach.** Choose a controversial topic that you believe would be better understood if readers could see how people from different occupations or academic disciplines view the topic. Then select your respondents, prepare your interview or survey questions, conduct the interviews and/or distribute the survey, record and analyze the results, and write your report. Share the report with readers from multiple occupations or disciplines.

3. **Make it multimedia.** Choose a controversial topic that people tend to view differently based on their personal data (age, ethnicity, level of education, gender, religion, or economic class). Next, select your respondents and prepare interview questions. Then conduct (and videotape) the interviews, preferably in the person's home or workplace. Finally, review your notes, analyze the results, and prepare a video report that shows and tells your findings.

4. **Take it to the street.** Interview members of a nonprofit organization about how they could better achieve their mission if the public better understood the organization's goals, challenges, participants, projects, or accomplishments. Then use primary-research strategies to research the topic. Analyze the results of your study, write your report, and donate it to the organization for its use.

Checklist: Use this checklist to review your IMRAD research report.

☑ **Ideas:** The report provides scientifically sound conclusions about accurate data.

☑ **Organization:** The report effectively follows the standard structure: abstract, introduction, materials and methods, results, and discussion.

☑ **Voice:** The tone is objective and measured throughout but also shows interest in and curiosity about the topic, issue, and hypothesis.

☑ **Words:** Terms are used accurately. The language of the specific discipline or occupation is used precisely.

☑ **Sentences:** Well-structured sentences flow smoothly from point to point. Passive voice constructions are used only when necessary.

☑ **Correctness:** The writing has no errors in grammar, punctuation, usage, and spelling.

☑ **Design:** The medium (video, audio, or print) effectively shapes and communicates the message.

Analysis of a Literary Text

Q What is the difference between reading for pleasure and reading to analyze? When you analyze a text, what do you look for? How are analyses of texts used by readers, and how should that use affect your research and writing?

Analyzing a literary text involves providing a deep reading of a poem, short story, play, or other literary work. When you research and write a literary analysis, you begin with the understanding that your reader has already read the literary text. Your aim, then, is to illuminate some not-fully-understood dimension of the work: the motivations of a particular character, the image patterns of a lyric, the historical context of a Renaissance play, and so on.

In this way, literary analysis is a special form of analytical writing (see chapter 13). In this application of analysis, your primary research is reading, rereading, and thinking through the literary text itself in order to develop a sound, insightful interpretation; secondary research supplements your primary reading by providing a range of support, from historical background to scholarly criticism. If done well, your literary analysis becomes your contribution to the academic conversation about the poem, story, or play.

Topics to Consider The literary landscape is filled with texts to analyze. Consider options like those below, clustered broadly around the issue of relationships.

- **Poetry:** Analyze a poem that explores a relationship of concern to you (e.g., people's relationship to each other, traumatic events, hopes and fears, nature and ecology, or technology). Possible poem: Robert Browning's "My Last Duchess"
- **Fiction:** Analyze a short story focusing on a troubled or changing relationship between two people (e.g., parent-child, male-female, two different ethnicities). Possible story: William Faulkner's "A Rose for Emily"
- **Drama:** Analyze a play dramatizing a relationship under strain or facing disintegration. Possible play: Henrik Ibsen's *A Doll's House*

What's Ahead?

Guidelines for Writing a Literary Analysis

When you have chosen a literary text, work through the process briefly outlined below. (As needed, go to the detailed instruction in chapters 1-11.)

1. **Explore possible analytical approaches.** One place to begin is with your questions about the text: What is unclear, funny, troubling, or challenging? A second strategy is to choose a particular literary concept as your analytical tool: irony, symbolism, plot, imagery, and so on. Finally, you can adopt one of these critical approaches, explained in more detail on page 344:

   - **Text-centered:** Focus on the formal qualities of the text.
   - **Reader-centered:** Focus on the rhetorical engagement between text and reader.
   - **History-centered:** Focus on the writer's life and/or the text's cultural context.
   - **Ideology-centered:** Apply a particular idea system (e.g., Jungian archetypes, Feminist gynocriticism) to the text.

2. **Deepen your reading of the literary text.** Your first reading of the text should have given you a sense of the whole—how the various dimensions of the text work and relate to each other, how the text flows from start to finish, and so on. Then, with your analytical approach as a guide, review and re-assess the text. If possible, annotate the text thoroughly, especially key passages illustrating your interpretation.

3. **Conduct secondary research as needed.** After studying the text carefully (your primary research), supplement and deepen your analysis by examining secondary sources like these (for details, see pages 345-346):

   - Biographical—from literary biography to author interviews
   - Cultural/historical—background studies that help you get at the text's context
   - Literary studies—from explanations of techniques and genres to literary theories
   - Critical essays—books and scholarly articles that provide "readings" of your text

4. **Develop a working thesis.** Draft a statement that encapsulates your analysis of the text. Note: your thesis should not be simply a statement of fact about the text (e.g., Hamlet hesitates to kill his stepfather, King Claudius), a summary of the plot (e.g., *Hamlet* is a tragedy in which a royal family is decimated by murder and revenge), or your opinion about the text (e.g., Hamlet's hesitation to kill Claudius is annoying). Rather, your thesis is an interpretation of what the text means and/or how it achieves this meaning. Here are examples of interpretive theses of different literary genres:

   - **Poetry:** In "Let Evening Come," Jane Kenyon takes the reader on a journey into the night, but she points to hope in the face of darkness.
   - **Fiction:** Throughout "Good Country People," Flannery O'Connor carefully links Joy-Hulga's physical impairments with deeper handicaps of the soul; then, at the closing, she strips Hulga of these physical flaws while helping her realize that her corresponding beliefs are flawed as well.
   - **Drama:** Ophelia descends into madness through the harms inflicted by the three men in her life: her father Polonius, her brother Laertes, and her lover Hamlet.

5. **Outline your paper.** Guided by your working thesis, think through how to elaborate, develop, and support that interpretation through discussion of the text and references to secondary sources. As you develop an outline, consider questions like these:

   - Should you include early in the paper a survey of critical perspectives, important background, or key definitions?
   - Should you focus on analyzing a series of key passages?
   - Should you work through the text itself from beginning to end, emphasizing how the issue is introduced, developed, and resolved?
   - Can you logically break your analysis into different textual "parts"—e.g., a comparison-contrast of two characters or settings, a series of key symbols?
   - How can you arrange your points so that your interpretation deepens or builds?

6. **Write your first draft.** Using your outline as a guide, develop the parts of your paper. Be particularly careful about accuracy of quotations:

   - **Opening:** Gain your readers' attention, identify your topic, narrow the focus to a particular issue, and state your thesis. A variety of strategies can work: starting with a quotation from the text, the author, or a critic; offering a general statement about the writer's work; or identifying the literary issue or problem at the heart of the paper. Whatever strategy you use in your introduction, do identify the title, the author, and the literary form.
   - **Middle:** Develop each point of your interpretation with well-crafted body paragraphs. Draft topic sentences that offer clear claims in support of the thesis, and expand on these statements in paragraphs that offer careful interpretations of textual elements, including direct quotations. Provide thoughtful transitions between points.
   - **Closing:** Tie key points together to focus your analysis. Assert your thesis in a fresh way, leaving readers with a sense of the larger significance of your analysis (e.g., its importance for understanding this particular author, the genre, the period, contemporary life, and so on).

7. **Revise your paper.** Set aside your first draft for a time and then come back to it. Check your paper for overall logic and completeness in your interpretation of the text. Examine whether you have sufficiently supported your analysis with evidence from the text and references to scholarly sources.

8. **Edit and proofread your draft.** After revising your essay for strong ideas and logical organization, polish your sentence style, word choice, and grammar. Make sure that your paper is free of awkward syntax, literary terms that are used vaguely or incorrectly, and errors in punctuation, spelling, and mechanics (especially with respect to quotations and documentation).

9. **Share your analysis.** In addition to submitting your paper, share your interpretation with classmates and with other readers interested in the author and text.

Literary Analysis: A Primer

If you're like most students, you've probably read many novels, poems, and plays in high school (and hopefully outside of school). At the college level, literary study becomes somewhat more scholarly, critical, and interpretive. The following instruction offers a brief introduction to literary analysis at this level.

Critical Approaches

Literary texts can be interpreted through different critical approaches or schools. Each school, with its specific foci and questions, offers a way of "conversing" about a text. While the critical approaches described below seem quite distinct, they actually share many traits: (1) a close attention to literary elements such as character, plot, symbolism, and metaphor; (2) an effort to interpret the text accurately and effectively; and (3) a desire to increase understanding of the text. Moreover, whatever approach you take will likely combine concerns of more than one school.

Formalist criticism is text-centered, focusing on how the structure of a work and the rules of its genre contribute to the text's meaning. Such criticism determines how various elements (plot, character, diction, imagery, and so on) work to build meaning, as well as how generic conventions (e.g., the rules of tragedy) function in a particular text.

> *Formalist Questions about Robert Browning's "My Last Duchess":* How do the main elements in the poem—irony, symbolism, and verse form—help develop the main theme (deception)? How does Browning use the dramatic monologue genre in this poem?

Rhetorical criticism is audience-centered, focused on the transaction between text and reader—the dynamic way that the reader interacts with the text. Often called reader-response criticism, these approaches see the text not as an object to be analyzed, but as an activity that differs from reader to reader.

> *Rhetorical Questions about "My Last Duchess":* How does the reader become aware of the duke's true nature if it's never actually stated? Do men and women read the poem differently? Who were Browning's original readers?

Historical criticism is origins-centered, focused on the author and the text's historical background. For example, an author-focused interpretation might study the text in light of the author's life—showing connections, contrasts, and conflicts. Broader historical studies explore social and intellectual currents, showing links between an author's work and the ideas, events, and institutions of that period. Finally, the literary historian might make connections between the text in question and earlier and later literary works.

> *Historical Questions about "My Last Duchess":* What were Browning's views of marriage, men and women, art, class, and wealth? As an institution, what was marriage like in Victorian England (Browning's era) or Renaissance Italy (the duke's era)? Who was the historical Duke of Ferrara?

Ideological criticism is centered on idea systems, on applying ideas outside literature to literary works. Because literature mirrors life, argues such criticism, disciplines that explore human life can help us understand literature. Here are examples:

- *Psychological criticism* applies psychological theories (Freudian, Jungian, trauma theory, and so on) to literary works by exploring dreams, symbolic meanings, character motivations, author creativity, and mental illness.
- *Myth or archetype criticism* uses insights from psychology, cultural anthropology, and classical studies to explore a text's universal appeal or recurring patterns.
- *Moral criticism,* rooted in religious studies and ethics, explores the moral dilemmas literary works raise.
- *Marxist, gender, minority,* and *postcolonial criticism* are sociological approaches to interpretation. While Marxist analysis examines the themes of class struggle, economic power, and social justice in texts, gender criticism explores the treatment of human sexuality in texts, whether the just or unjust treatment of women, the theme of homosexuality within a text, or the effects of gender on language, writing, reading, and the literary canon. Minority analysis focuses on race and ethnic identity in similar ways (e.g., African-American and aboriginal criticism), while postcolonial criticism focuses specifically on the literature of former colonies in terms of the effects of colonialism and the development of a literary culture after the end of colonial status.

  Ideological Questions about "My Last Duchess": What does the poem reveal about the duke's psychological state and his personality? How does the reference to Neptune deepen the poem? What does the poem suggest about the nature of evil and injustice? In what ways are the duke's motives class-based and economic? How does the poem present the duke's power and the duchess's victimization?

Secondary Research

Your reading of the literary text—primary research—is usually the focus of your paper. However, secondary research can serve many purposes, such as these:

Biographical research: Learning about the author's life may enrich your analysis by helping you to explore sources of inspiration, personal and literary influences, and modes of thought. Such insights might be gained through learning about the writer's childhood, cultural and ethnic background, education, writing apprenticeship, and relationships.

Caution: Be careful not to make simplistic connections between biographical details and literary texts (e.g., that the speaker of a poem or the narrator of a story is the author in a direct sense, that because the novelist grew up in the 1960s her female characters are radical feminists, that the author's intention must rule your reading of the text).

Research into historical and cultural context: Such research illuminates the text by clarifying important context and issues. These issues might be the historical realities surrounding the text's writing, its content, and its reception (past and present). Or the issues might be cultural concepts relevant to the text: class, economics, technology, transportation, religious institutions and practices, and so on.

Research into literary concepts: This type of secondary research deepens your understanding of literary issues and techniques. For example, you might read about methods and theories of irony, or you might study the nature of tragedy with the aim of enriching your analysis of the text.

Research into theory: Such research seeks to strengthen your understanding of the philosophical and ideological underpinnings of a particular literary school or theorist. Theoretical research—whether into reader-response theory, deconstruction, feminism, or the ideas of a particular theorist such as Mikhail Bakhtin—informs your thinking and directs your analysis of the literary text.

Research into scholarly interpretations: In such research, you join the critical conversation about your text, a conversation that might have been going on for a few years, a few decades, or a few centuries. Many scholarly articles and books will likely offer interpretations of your text—ways of reading, analyzing, and understanding some aspect of the text, typically from a particular point of view. Reading these sources can strengthen your own interpretation in the following ways:

- You can locate your own reading within the critical conversation, placing your interpretation in context.

- You can refine your own reading through critical engagement, exploring why different readers interpret the text as they do (comparing their perspectives and values with your own).

- You can create a critical survey early in your paper, one that reviews the interpretive schools on your issue and your text and that makes a space for your own reading.

- Within your essay, you might use the critical comment of a scholar to (a) add expert support to your interpretive argument, (b) create a starting point for further reflection and analysis, or (c) present a claim with which you disagree.

 FOCUS on Research Essentials: In a literary-analysis project, use secondary sources carefully and avoid these problems:

- Substituting your own interpretation of the text with the readings offered by secondary sources. If you find yourself continually talking about other people's interpretations or simply parroting their interpretations, you need to get back to your own interpretation in your own voice.

- Limiting your secondary research to opinions that you gather off the free Web (including sites such as Spark Notes and Cliff Notes). Instead, you need to rely on substantial sources in academic journals and scholarly books.

Literary Terms

Many, many concepts and techniques can serve as the focus or analytical tool that drives your interpretation. Below are several terms related to fiction, poetry, and drama.

Allusion is a reference to a person, a place, or an event in history or literature.

Analogy is a comparison of two or more similar objects, suggesting that if they are alike in certain respects, they will probably be alike in other ways, too.

Anecdote is a short summary of an interesting or humorous, often biographical incident or event.

Antagonist is the person or thing actively working against the protagonist, or hero, of the work.

Climax is the turning point, an intense moment characterized by a key event.

Conflict is the problem or struggle in a story that triggers the action. There are five basic types of conflict:

Person versus person: One character in a story is in conflict with one or more of the other characters.

Person versus society: A character is in conflict with some element of society: the school, the law, the accepted way of doing things, and so on.

Person versus self: A character faces conflicting inner choices.

Person versus nature: A character is in conflict with some natural happening: a snowstorm, an avalanche, the bitter cold, or any other element of nature.

Person versus fate: A character must battle what seems to be an uncontrollable problem. Whenever the conflict is a strange or unbelievable coincidence, the conflict can be attributed to fate.

Denouement is the outcome of a play or story. See *Resolution.*

Diction is an author's choice of words based on their correctness or effectiveness.

Archaic words are old-fashioned and no longer sound natural when used, such as "I believe thee not" for "I don't believe you."

Colloquialism is an expression that is usually accepted in informal situations and certain locations, as in "He really grinds my beans."

Heightened language uses vocabulary and sentence constructions that produce a stylized effect unlike that of standard speech or writing, as in much poetry and poetic prose.

Profanity is language that shows disrespect for someone or something regarded as holy or sacred.

Slang is the everyday language used by group members amongst themselves.

Trite expressions lack depth or originality, or are overworked or not worth mentioning in the first place.

Vulgarity is language that is generally considered common, crude, gross, and, at times, offensive. It is sometimes used in fiction, plays, and films to add realism.

Exposition is the introductory section of a story or play. Typically, the setting, main characters, and themes are introduced, and the action is initiated.

Falling action is the action of a play or story that follows the climax and shows the characters dealing with the climactic event or decision.

Figure of speech is a literary device used to create a special effect or to describe something in a fresh way. The most common types are antithesis, hyperbole, metaphor, metonymy, personification, simile, and understatement.

Antithesis is an opposition, or contrast, of ideas.

> "It was the best of times, it was the worst of times, it was the age of wisdom, it was the age of foolishness . . ."   —Charles Dickens, *A Tale of Two Cities*

Hyperbole (hi-pur´ ba-lee) is an extreme exaggeration or overstatement.

> "I have seen this river so wide it had only one bank."
> —Mark Twain, *Life on the Mississippi*

Metaphor is a comparison of two unlike things in which no word of comparison (as or like) is used: "Life is a banquet."

Metonymy (ma-ton´a-mee) is the substituting of one term for another that is closely related to it, but not a literal restatement.

> "Friends, Romans, countrymen, lend me your ears." (The request is for the attention of those assembled, not literally their ears.)

Personification is a device in which the author speaks of or describes an animal, object, or idea as if it were a person: "The rock stubbornly refused to move."

Simile is a comparison of two unlike things in which like or as is used.

> "She stood in front of the altar, shaking like a freshly caught trout."
> —Maya Angelou, *I Know Why the Caged Bird Sings*

Understatement is stating an idea with restraint, often for humorous effect. Mark Twain described Aunt Polly as being "prejudiced against snakes." (Because she hated snakes, this way of saying so is understatement.)

Genre refers to a category or type of literature based on its style, form, and content. The mystery novel is a literary genre.

Imagery refers to words or phrases that a writer uses to appeal to the reader's senses.

> "The sky was dark and gloomy, the air was damp and raw, the streets were wet and sloppy."   —Charles Dickens, *The Pickwick Papers*

Irony is a deliberate discrepancy in meaning or in the way something is understood. There are three kinds of irony:

Dramatic irony, in which the reader or the audience sees a character's mistakes or misunderstandings, but the character does not.

Verbal irony, in which the writer says one thing and means another ("The best substitute for experience is being sixteen").

Irony of situation, in which there is a great difference between the purpose of a particular action and the result.

Mood is the feeling that a piece of literature arouses in the reader: happiness, sadness, peacefulness, anxiety, and so forth.

Paradox is a statement that seems contrary to common sense yet may, in fact, be true: "The coach considered this a good loss."

Plot is the action or sequence of events in a story. It is usually a series of related incidents that build upon one another as the story develops. There are five basic elements in a plotline: exposition, rising action, climax, falling action, and resolution.

Point of view is the vantage point from which the story unfolds.

> *In the first-person point of view,* the story is told by one of the characters: "I stepped into the darkened room and felt myself go cold."
>
> *In the third-person point of view,* the story is told by someone outside the story: "He stepped into the darkened room and felt himself go cold."
>
> *Third-person narrations can be omniscient,* meaning that the narrator has access to the thoughts of all the characters, or limited, meaning that the narrator focuses on the inner life of one central character.

Protagonist is the main character or hero of the story.

Resolution (or denouement) is the portion of the play or story in which the problem is solved. The resolution comes after the climax and falling action and is intended to bring the story to a satisfactory end.

Rising action is the series of conflicts or struggles that build a story or play toward a fulfilling climax.

Satire is a literary tone used to ridicule or make fun of human vice or weakness, often with the intent of correcting, or changing, the subject of the satiric attack.

Setting is the time and place in which the action of a literary work occurs.

Structure is the form or organization a writer uses for her or his literary work. A great number of possible forms are used regularly in literature: parable, fable, romance, satire, farce, slapstick, and so on.

Style refers to how the author uses words, phrases, and sentences to form his or her ideas. Style is also thought of as the qualities and characteristics that distinguish one writer's work from the work of others.

Symbol is a person, a place, a thing, or an event used to represent something else. For example, the dove is a symbol of peace.

Theme is the statement about life that a particular work shares with readers. In stories written for children, the theme is often spelled out clearly at the end. In more complex literature, the theme will often be more complex and will be implied, not stated.

Tone is the overall feeling, or effect, created by a writer's use of words. This feeling may be serious, mock-serious, humorous, satiric, and so on.

Poetry Terms

While many of the terms on the previous pages can be used in poetry analysis, the terms below are specific to the formal qualities of poems.

Alliteration is the repetition of initial consonant sounds in words such as "rough and ready." An example of alliteration is underlined below:

"Our gang paces the pier like an old myth . . . "

—Anne-Marie Oomen, "Runaway Warning"

Assonance is the repetition of vowel sounds without the repetition of consonants.

"My words like silent rain drops fell . . . "   —Paul Simon, "Sounds of Silence"

Blank verse is an unrhymed form of poetry. Each line normally consists of ten syllables in which every other syllable, beginning with the second, is stressed. As blank verse is often used in very long poems, it may depart from the strict pattern from time to time.

Consonance is the repetition of consonant sounds. Although it is very similar to alliteration, consonance is not limited to the first letters of words:

" . . . and high school girls with clear-skin smiles . . . "   —Janis Ian, "At Seventeen"

Foot is the smallest repeated pattern of stressed and unstressed syllables in a poetic line. (See *Verse.*)

Iambic: an unstressed followed by a stressed syllable (re-peat´)
Anapestic: two unstressed followed by a stressed syllable (in-ter-rupt´)
Trochaic: a stressed followed by an unstressed syllable (old´-er)
Dactylic: a stressed followed by two unstressed syllables (o´-pen-ly)
Spondaic: two stressed syllables (heart´-break´)
Pyrrhic: two unstressed syllables (Pyrrhic seldom appears by itself.)

Onomatopoeia is the use of a word whose sound suggests its meaning, as in clang, buzz, and twang.

Refrain is the repetition of a line or phrase of a poem at regular intervals, especially at the end of each stanza. A song's refrain may be called the chorus.

Rhythm is the ordered or free occurrences of sound in poetry. Ordered or regular rhythm is called meter. Free occurrence of sound is called free verse.

Stanza is a division of poetry named for the number of lines it contains:

Couplet: two-line stanza   *Sestet:* six-line stanza
Triplet: three-line stanza   *Septet:* seven-line stanza
Quatrain: four-line stanza   *Octave:* eight-line stanza
Quintet: five-line stanza

Verse is a metric line of poetry. It is named according to the kind and number of feet composing it: iambic pentameter, anapestic tetrameter, and so on. (See *Foot.*)

Monometer: one foot   *Pentameter:* five feet
Dimeter: two feet   *Hexameter:* six feet
Trimeter: three feet   *Heptameter:* seven feet
Tetrameter: four feet   *Octometer:* eight feet

Sample Student Paper: Literary Analysis

In the essay below, student writer Rebecca Mombourquette analyzes the novel *A Portrait of the Artist as a Young Man* by the Irish Modernist James Joyce. Rebecca's analysis focuses on Joyce's use of the Icarus/Deadalus myth in relation to his central character, Stephen Dedalus. As you read Rebecca's analysis (documented in MLA), examine the interpretative strategies that she uses, specifically in terms of reading the novel itself and referencing secondary sources.

Writer's Reflection

Joyce's *Portrait* was not my favorite novel that we studied in Dr. Bowen's Modern English Literature class, but its connection with the Daedalus myth from ancient mythology fascinated me. The topic of my essay was of my own making. I began by asking myself: *why did Joyce use the myth?* Perhaps a simple question, but to me it seemed of utmost importance to understanding his novel. When I began the research process, at first I found very little information on my topic; it seemed that very few people had acknowledged the idea, much less dealt with it. The few sources I found I had to travel to another library to find. But it was all worth it. They confirmed my own suspicions that the myth was crucial to the novel. My research, my outlining, and my writing style came from a determination to convince myself that what I thought might be true – that the myth was the entire backdrop and bone of the novel – was actually possible and might have been Joyce's intention.

Preparing to Read: What do you know about classical mythology? How do modern writers use mythology in their work? Have you read any fiction by James Joyce?

Literary Analysis

Stephen Dedalus: Finding Identity in Myth

The paper's title identifies the paper's focus.

James Joyce's overt references to the Daedalus myth of Greek mythology in *A Portrait of the Artist as a Young Man* provide an overarching structure for his story of a man's youth and search for his identity and life's vocation. Beginning and ending with the Daedalus myth, Joyce connects Stephen Dedalus, the young aspiring artist, to the great artificer, Daedalus, and his son, Icarus. Through his epigraph, Stephen's family name, and Stephen's own considerations of the myth, Joyce skillfully weaves the ancient saga into the fabric of the novel. While many critics often overlook the deep significance of myth in Joyce's novel, others have thoughtfully engaged the material and text to uncover the implications in Stephen's life. Eugene M. Waith, in "The Calling of Stephen Dedalus," maintains that the myth is connected with Stephen's calling as an artist and Daedalus is a constant image of the courage and force necessary to be an artist; David Hayman, in "Daedalian Imagery in *A Portrait*," follows the imagery of Daedalus throughout the entire novel, suggesting the myth as the main thread connecting the whole work. What purpose, then, does the Daedalus myth play in *A Portrait* and why does Joyce use the myth? The myth is, in fact, the backdrop for the entire narrative: Stephen is Daedalus, he is Icarus, and their story provides meaning in his struggle to find his identity and vocation in life; Stephen's

The opening identifies the author, the text, and the framing issue.

Rebecca briefly surveys critical attitudes to the issue before asking the central question of her analysis and offering her thesis.

flight at the novel's end is not the culmination of his vocational search, but rather reveals his widening perception of artistic aspirations, through their relation to the Daedalus myth.

Joyce sets the Daedalus myth as the backdrop for his novel from the first lines of the epigraph quoting Ovid's story, to the last lines of the book in Stephen's appeal to Daedalus. The epigraph reads: *et ignotas animum dimittit in artes* (Jocye 5; Ovid, *Metamorphoses*, VIII.188), often translated "and so to unimagined arts he set his mind." In the Daedalus tale, King Minos commissions Daedalus, an architect famous for his skill, to designing and constructing a labyrinth on the island of Crete, to keep his wife's monster son, the Minotaur, enclosed. Ovid's story recounts: "Daedalus, an architect famous for his skill, constructed the maze, confusing the usual marks of direction, and leading the eye of the beholder astray by devious paths winding in different directions" (Scholes & Kain 266). After building the maze, Daedalus and his son, Icarus, are trapped on the island by the surrounding sea. Desiring to return home, the artificer Daedalus plans to use his skill to fabricate wings: "'The king may block my way by land or across the ocean, but the sky, surely, is open, and that is how we shall go'" (Scholes & Kain 267). Joyce's epigraph, recounting Daedalus' construction of wings, reveals his craftsmanship: "he set his mind to sciences never explored before, and altered the laws of nature" (Scholes & Kain 267). Quoting only the beginning of Ovid's line, Joyce leaves the reader with the expectation that Stephen, too, may "alter the laws of nature." Later, in the final lines of the novel, Stephen calls on Daedalus as he sets out on his life's quest as an artist: "Old father, old artificer, stand me now and ever in good stead" (Joyce 253). It is, clearly, against the backdrop of the Daedalus myth that Joyce constructs Stephen's story, the story of a young man searching for his own identity and vocation. Daedalus' myth seemingly ties the entire novel together, from beginning to end.

Joyce's links to Daedalus, at the beginning and end of the novel, inevitably signal the significance of myth to his story and, more importantly, the ties between the two stories. Throughout the novel, Joyce links Stephen with Daedalus and, in doing so, reveals Stephen's identity. Joyce's novel begins with Stephen as a young, insecure boy who wonders in childlike simplicity about the world around him. Already in the first pages of the novel, his name is noticed as strange: Stephen Dedalus; a friend asks, "What kind of a name is that?" (Joyce 9). Set apart by his name, Stephen tries to establish himself or, in modern terms, discover his identity. From the start, Joyce uses Stephen's surname, Dedalus, to connect him to the Greek myth and, inevitably, his own identity with Daedalus.

Even at such an early stage in the story, Stephen is associated with the artificer for his craftsmanship. David Hayman, in "Daedalian Imagery in *A Portrait*," suggests that Daedalus' creations are similar to ones Stephen crafts. He states: "The two principle images of the Daedalus myth are the two great inventions of the artificer: the labyrinth [...] and the wings" (Hayman 37).

The writer explains the myth behind the modern novel, using a scholarly source to do so.

Rebecca shows how both the novel's beginning and ending allude to the myth.

The writer begins to explore the links between the myth and the novel, focused on the central character.

While the wings or flight imagery in *A Portrait* may seem self-evident to any reader, less obvious are what Hayman believes to be the maze or labyrinth imagery. Hayman suggests that in the early years of Stephen's life, birds are frightening for the timid boy. He is threatened: "Stephen will apologise […] if not, the eagles will come and pull out his eyes" (Joyce 8). In response to his own fears, Stephen, claims Hayman, creates his own labyrinth by hiding under the table: "The table-cave, a miniature labyrinth and a self-made refuge is thus linked to the bird-monster" (37). Thus, Stephen can perhaps be associated with Daedalus through his own labyrinth making; Stephen, like Daedalus, hides a monster within his labyrinth, the monster of his own fear and, subsequently, reduces his identity to his fear. Thus, the initial picture of Stephen reveals an insecure boy, searching for his place and identity.

The labyrinth-like imagery in Stephen's life continues as he grows older, yet he remains equally unknown to himself. Hayman maintains that before Stephen escapes from the labyrinth into freedom he "builds an equally metaphorical labyrinth to protect him from the perils of freedom" (37). Stephen's adolescence is characterized by his fall into sinful ways of life, while still maintaining his exterior upright appearance; he himself considers the hypocrisy of his life, a life of sexual sin in contrast with his position as an admired prefect in college. The climax of Stephen's early adolescence, Hayman believes, is Stephen's wandering and first fall into sexual sin: he "explores *a maze of streets* to the end that he *encircles* himself in a ring of sensual vices" (Hayman 38). Joyce's wording, emphasized by Hayman, reveals the labyrinth quality of the life Stephen's leads, without overt reference to any labyrinth. Stephen remains trapped in sin and continues in the same route: "he would follow a devious course up and down the streets, circling always nearer and nearer in a tremor of fear and joy" (Joyce 102). Yet, for all the "dark peace" Stephen experiences, he only comes to a "cold indifferent knowledge of himself" (Joyce 103). Thus, Stephen's adolescence reveals a symbolic labyrinth in which he seeks to hide, one that ultimately leads him to grievous sin and still no true self-identity, even amidst his experiences.

Joyce artistically positions Stephen's escape from the maze or labyrinth of his hypocritical identity at the very centre of the novel: after encircling himself in a labyrinth of hypocrisy, Stephen begins a process of fleeing from false perceptions of his identity which continues throughout the rest of the novel. Thus, in the second half of the novel Daedalus' second invention, wings used for flight, identifies Stephen with Daedalus; Stephen purposes to escape impediments to his freedom and rise towards his still unknown vocation. Initially, Stephen turns to religion to free himself from his labyrinth of sin: he confesses his sins and begins a practice of severe penance. Joyce writes: "he drove his soul daily through an increasing circle of works of supererogation" (Joyce 147). In his rigorous and extreme religiosity, more

---

Rebecca bolsters her analysis with examples and quotations from the novel, but also with references to scholarly essays.

Strong transitions move the analysis forward and tie it together.

Rebecca's analysis shows insightful attention to key words and phrases in the novel.

The writer structures her analysis around the chronological development of the central character and the forward movement of the story.

As Rebecca deepens her analysis, she examines a series of longer passages from the novel, passages set off.

than duty or God required, Stephen creates for himself yet another false identity. In fact, Stephen's entire devotion to religious practices reveals that his inner maze and confusion of identity is still present. Stephen's religious aspirations lead him to consider a priestly vocation, and, in turn, reject any religious calling. Joyce writes: "the oils of ordination would never anoint his body. He had refused. Why?" (165). Intuitively, Stephen, though tempted through pride to the great dignity of a priestly office, rejects such a vocation for impeding his freedom. Instead, he believes he must find his vocation apart from religion:

> He would never swing the thurible before the tabernacle as priest. His destiny was to be elusive of social or religious orders [...] he was destined to learn his own wisdom apart from others or to learn the wisdom of others himself wandering among the snares of the world. (Joyce 162)

Stephen sees the priesthood as a static, sinless vocation which shelters priests from the world; while he once thought he desired such a life, he realizes his "soul was not there" (Joyce 162). Hayman critiques Stephen's rejections: "Just as the hero's rejection of the fleshly devils implies his dedication to the maze of theological virtues and doubts, his rejection of the priesthood implies his commitment to the 'world' in which he will have the freedom to err symbolized by the flight imagery" (41). Stephen's flight has begun, from sin, from extreme religiosity, and from a false vocation; just as Daedalus fled the labyrinth, so Stephen flees false images of his vocation and identity.

The last sentences of paragraphs effectively capture the interpretive point supporting the thesis.

Shortly after rejecting the priesthood as his vocation, Stephen dwells on the Daedalus myth, beginning in earnest to identify himself in flight. Eugene M. Waith suggests that only in flight will Stephen realize his vocation: "The images of flight relate freedom, increasing perception, and creativity [...] Stephen seeks freedom from the world and from the church as a condition necessary for new perception and for artistic creation" (260). Just as Daedalus' flight is not merely escape, neither is Stephen's: "The flight of Daedalus is not only an escape but a widening of consciousness" (Waith 260). Thus, Stephen questions his identity and vocation: if his is not to be a priest, what is his vocation? Whereas Hayman points out Stephen's fear of birds as a child, they now represent the freedom he seeks: "from slight but ominous beginnings, the references to feathered creatures and flight fan out to dominate the imagery of [...] the novel" (Hayman 45). In the novel, while Stephen meditates on his future, he hears his friends calling his name: "Hello, Stephanos! Here comes The Dedalos!" (Joyce 167). Suddenly recalling the artificer who shares his name, Stephen receives an epiphany:

Two critics offer insights that Rebecca weaves into her own analysis.

> Now, as never before, his strange name seemed to him a prophecy [...] Now, at the name of the fabulous artificer, he seemed to hear the noise of dim waves and to see a winged form flying above the waves slowly climbing the air. What did it mean? (Joyce 168-69)

Now Stephen's strange name gives meaning to his vocation and future; while Stephen does not, as yet, understand his identity, he dwells on Daedalus' flight.

Stephen begins to see his identity increasingly in myth and flight, putting aside religion to be replaced with freedom and creativity. In fact, in turning from the priesthood and religion, Stephen identifies himself increasingly with Daedalus. At the thought of Daedalus, forging wings, Stephen finds himself moved as never before:

> His heart trembled; his breath came faster and a wild spirit passed over his limbs as though he were soaring sunward. His heart trembled in an ecstasy of fear and his soul was in flight. His soul was soaring in an air beyond the world and the body he knew was purified in a breath and delivered of incertitude and made radiant and commingled with the element of the spirit. (Joyce 169)

In flight, Stephen no longer experiences confusion with his identity. Thus, Stephen is not only moved by Daedalus' flight; Joyce wants the reader to see Stephen as Daedalus. Stephen thinks and cries: "Yes! Yes! Yes! He would create proudly out of the freedom and power of his soul, as the great artificer whose name he bore, a living thing, new and soaring and beautiful, impalpable, imperishable" (Joyce 170). Religious and flight imagery shape Stephen's new discovery of himself. Turning from religion to myth to find his identity, Stephen appears to make myth and his creative vocation a type of religion. He comes across a girl standing in a stream, associating her body with a bird and the kind of "religious" creation he desires to express. Stephen's sensual desires no longer overpower him. Instead, he expresses religious awe in the girl: "Heavenly God!" (Joyce 171). Thus, Waith's suggestion is evident: "Stephen [...] has taken a beautiful body as an object of contemplation instead of the religious mysteries with which he occupied his mind after his confession" (259). Stephen "worships" the "angel" girl and in his soul feels a "holy silence" of "ecstasy" drawing him to recreate life: "To live, to err, to fall, to triumph, to recreate life out of life!" (Joyce 171-172). Thus, Stephen's religious sensibility turns from God and church to myth as religion; he flees religious norms only to make myth and his desire to create his religion.

With his newfound perception of himself and his vocation, Stephen feels no fear in failure; striving to be "The Dedalus," the artificer, Stephen accepts the possibility or reality of being Icarus as well. While Stephen experiences the thrill of imagining himself flying, Joyce's reference brings to mind the possibility of failure. The voices of his friends, which cried his name and brought to mind the great artificer, now voice the cry of Daedalus' son, Icarus, as he falls from the sky: "O, cripes, I'm drowned!" (Joyce 169). Jeri Johnson, in the introduction to *A Portrait*, connects the imagery to Stephen's Daedalus-Icarus identity:

> In placing Stephen's self-absorbed fantasy cheek-by-jowl with the boys' banter, the narrative ironically metamorphoses Stephen from

Rebecca offers her reading of the complex changes happening with the central character.

Rebecca turns to the complex Daedalus-Icarus connections in the narrative.

Daedalus, the father, into Icarus, the son, who drowned. Icarus' arrogant, ecstatic pleasure at being able to fly caused him to soar too close to the sun; the wax from which his wings were made melted, and he fell into the sea. (xxxvii)

Stephen is not just Daedalus, the successful artificer, but has the possibility of failing his flying endeavours and thereby becoming the son. Joyce's use of the myth, in the last part of the book, becomes complex: Stephen is Daedalus, he is Icarus, yet discovering his identity in them is not a final characterization, but merely an opening perception that will not end with the novel. As Waith points out, Daedalus' flight is "not only an escape but a widening of consciousness" (260). Similarly, Stephen's flight reveals his new consciousness as an aspiring artist. Stephen's desire and call to be an artist thus requires him to be unafraid to fall, as Icarus did. His own words bear witness to his surety: "I am not afraid to make a mistake, even a great mistake, a lifelong mistake and perhaps as long as eternity too" (Joyce 247). Thus, Stephen finds his identity as an artist, in the vocation to create, but ever with the possibility of failure.

In her closing, Rebecca returns to the novel's beginning and ending use of the myth, and summarizes the journey the central character has taken within the framework of that myth.

Throughout James Joyce's entire novel, from the epigraph to the final lines, the Daedalus myth provides a backdrop for Stephen Dedalus' life and calling. Joyce reveals Stephen's identity through the mythical characters of the artificer Daedalus and his son, Icarus. Just as Daedalus first fabricated a labyrinth and then wings to escape the maze, so Stephen's youth may also be seen as a labyrinth from which he takes flight in his vocation as an artist. Stephen rejects religion in favour of myth as he seeks to "forge in the smithy of [his] soul the uncreated conscience of [his] race" (Joyce 252-253). The last lines of the book, in which Stephen calls on the great artificer for his aid, signify his identification with Icarus. Johnson points out: "this novel's ending with Stephen's invocation of Daedalus leaves the 'artist' not yet having flown, not yet having created very much, but aspiring to a great deal" (xxxvii). Setting off in flight, Stephen knows his vocation as an artist, knows his identity as Daedalus, but also acknowledges himself in Icarus. Their myth gives meaning to his life and identity and so Stephen cries out to Daedalus for his artistic guidance: "Old father, old artificer, stand me now and ever in good stead" (Joyce 253).

The works-cited list shows that Rebecca consulted reliable scholarly resources.

Works Cited

Hyman, David. "Dadaelian Imagery in *A Portrait of the Artist as a Young Man.*" *Heriditas: Seven Essays on the Modern Experience of the Classical.* Ed. Frederick Will. Austin: U of Texas P, 1964. 33-54. Print.

Johnson, Jeri. "Introduction." *A Portrait of the Artist as a Young Man.* Oxford: Oxford UP, 2000. Print.

Joyce, James. *A Portrait of the Artist as a Young Man.* New York: Viking, 1968. Print.

Scholes, Robert E. and Richard M. Kain. *The Workshop of Daedalus: James Joyce and the Raw Materials for* A Portrait of the Artist as a Young Man. Evanston, IL: Northwestern UP, 1965. Print.

Waith, Eugene M. "The Calling of Stephen Dedalus." *College English* 18.5 (Feb. 1957): 256-261. JSTOR. Web. 12 Mar. 2009.

Reading Research Writing: Questions

To deepen your understanding of literary analysis, consider these questions about Rebecca's paper:

1. In her opening paragraph, what strategies does Rebecca use to introduce and focus her analysis? Do you find these strategies successful? Can you imagine a different kind of opening for her paper?

2. How would you characterize the critical approach or "school" that Rebecca uses to interpret *A Portrait of the Artist as a Young Man?* What are the strengths and limitations of this approach?

3. Overall, Rebecca's analysis unfolds chronologically; that is, she interprets the text by exploring how the issue is worked out in the novel from beginning to end. Given her focus, is this structure fitting? What other organizational strategy would work?

4. Examine a paragraph in which Rebecca quotes from the novel and refers to secondary sources. How does she combine primary and secondary research in her paper?

FOCUS on Your Major: While literary-analysis papers are obviously assigned in literature courses, such research projects are relevant elsewhere in the curriculum. First, parallel types of textual analysis are frequently assigned in Humanities courses such as history, religion, and philosophy. Second, instructors sometimes use literature in non-literature courses (e.g., history, psychology, environmental studies) to creatively extend students' learning of course content. Finally, literary analysis is paralleled in other courses by analysis of artworks, music, films, and theatrical productions, with many of the strategies of literary analysis transferable to the analysis of these other forms of imaginative expression.

Practicing Your Research

1. **Respond to the model.** What is your reaction to Rebecca Mombourquette's essay on James Joyce's *A Portrait of the Artist as a Young Man?* Does her reading of Joyce's use of myth make sense? If you have read Joyce's novel, develop your own complementary interpretation of the novel's allusions (to myths, religion, or some other knowledge). Conversely, read three short stories from Joyce's *Dubliners,* analyzing his use of myth or of religious allusions.

2. **Take a cross-disciplined approach.** As is suggested by historical criticism and by various forms of ideological criticism, multiple disciplines can make a highly helpful contribution to analysis of a literary text. Research one form of ideological criticism (e.g., psychological, feminist, Marxist, postcolonial). Then use the tenets of that critical school to interpret a poem, story, or play.

3. **Make it multimedia.** Plays, short stories, and novels are often adapted into films (e.g., Harper Lee's *To Kill a Mockingbird* and the film of the same title). Select a literary text and its film adaptation; then analyze some aspect of the works, including film shots or clips in your analysis.

4. **Take it to the street.** Select a nineteenth-century novel that would be accessible to a reading group of nonliterary experts or to a Grade 12 high school English class. After reading, analyzing, and researching the novel, develop a study guide that introduces reading groups or high school students to (a) the author, (b) key historical and cultural background for the novel, (c) three interpretive approaches, and (d) questions for discussion. Then share your study guide with your high school English teachers, with friends, or with family members interested in the novel; or post your work on the Web.

Checklist: Use this checklist to review your literary analysis prior to sharing it.

☑ **Ideas** The essay offers a solid interpretation of the text supported with direct discussion of the work plus reliable secondary research.

☑ **Organization** The interpretive argument flows logically from start to finish.

☑ **Voice** The tone is positive, confident, objective, and sensitive to competing interpretations; the attitude respects the critical conversation on the text.

☑ **Words** Literary terminology is used accurately.

☑ **Sentences** Structures read and flow smoothly, with effective variety and transitions.

☑ **Correctness** The writing is free from glaring and confusing errors in grammar, punctuation, spelling, and mechanics.

☑ **Design** The document's design is clean and attractive; the paper is formatted and documented in a fitting style (usually MLA).

17

The Literature Review

 Q What is a literature review, who writes them, and for what purposes? How is a literature review similar to or different from other research writing?

A well-written literature review guides readers through the published studies on an academic topic. In such a review, you describe key qualities in each study, but you also synthesize these articles, books, and other documents by doing such things as pointing out similarities and differences between the pieces; noting writers' research strategies, methods, or perspectives; showing connections between the works, including how studies build on each other; and identifying traits (such as gaps) in the overall collection of studies. As a result, you and readers gain a valuable overview of the topic, including scholars' treatment of the topic, the status of these studies, and the questions or issues needing more study.

Topics to Consider Because literature reviews are written in all disciplines (particularly the social sciences, natural sciences, and applied sciences), you have many topics from which to choose. To make your choice, follow these steps:

1. Select a discipline or field of study.

2. To identify topics that scholars are writing about, scan the Web sites, journals, and conference programs of professional organizations within this field. Also use your library's databases (e.g., Lexis-Nexis, EBSCOhost, or ProQuest Direct) to identify abstracts and full-text articles.

3. List three or four topics that interest you and scan a few related studies for each, noting the writers' credentials, research methods, perspectives, and findings.

4. Choose the topic about which you find at least ten current and relevant studies that you can access within your research schedule.

Note: In the social, natural, or applied sciences, studies will address current cultural or scientific issues. However, in the humanities such as history or English, writers also commonly research a person, phenomenon, text, or problem from the past.

What's Ahead?

Guidelines for Writing a Literature Review

After choosing a topic, work through the research and writing process described below. For detailed instructions on specific tasks, see chapters 1-11.

1. **Narrow your topic as needed.** Use your library's search engines to narrow your topic. For example, if your assignment requires a ten-page literature review, and you choose the topic autism, a quick search that finds three hundred studies tells you that your topic is far too broad. To narrow the topic, you could focus on one facet of the disorder, such as the link between Asperger's Syndrome (one form of autism) and low levels of cortisol. Alternatively, you could narrow the topic by focusing only on studies produced at select universities (such as England's University of Bath) that are doing leading research on Asperger's Syndrome.

2. **Find and select studies.** To find additional quality studies, use research tools such as your library's online catalogue, print indexes and databases (see list on page 66), and computer searches of other libraries' holdings (see WorldCat, page 60). Choose promising studies and preview their contents by

   - reading the titles, headings, abstracts, openings, and closings, and by scanning the rest.
   - assessing which studies would together show the span of current research on your topic.
   - looking for traits in strategies, perspectives, or findings that will help you distinguish the studies, organize your presentation, and unify the paper.
   - selecting the number of studies needed to address your topic and to fulfill your assignment.

   Finally, copy or print the literature so you can mark passages and take notes.

3. **Discern your focus.** Based on your assignment and writing purpose, decide how to approach your topic. For example, your instructor might assign a review that is

   - **theory-based**—focused on the theoretical underpinning (the *why?*) of each study's hypothesis and procedures.
   - **methodology-based**—focused on the methods (the *how?*) of each study's methods, such as research materials, experiments, and measuring strategies.
   - **function-based**—focused on each study's intended use, such as (a) free-standing informative study, (b) context for a larger study (e.g., doctoral dissertation), or (c) support in a persuasive document (e.g., research or grant proposal).
   - **history-based**—focused on how your bevy of studies represents a unique period or serves a special function in the research history of your topic.
   - **topic-based**—focused on whatever aspects of the studies that best help readers understand the topic. (Note: Instructors usually assign broad topic-based reviews, such as the model literature review on pages 362-367.)

Knowing the overall focus of your review will guide you when reading the studies, taking notes, drafting a thesis, and organizing your writing. For example, theory-based or history-based reviews are commonly organized chronologically.

4. **Read and analyze the studies.** Read each study carefully, noting its date, research site, and participants, along with the writer's description of the topic, initial hypothesis, research methods and procedures, supporting sources, and ultimate findings. Focus especially on qualities cited in your assignment. Compare and contrast these elements to assess how the studies are related.

5. **Draft a preliminary thesis.** Based on your analysis, write a thesis that asserts your core observation. For example, if you analyzed ten studies on the relationship between Asperger's Syndrome and cortisol levels, and you noted that two early studies using the same research strategy found no relationship, whereas eight subsequent studies using more current and reliable strategies did find a relationship, your thesis might assert that the findings of the later studies are more credible. (Note: A thesis based on synthesis of others' research is a valid argument when supported by relevant data in the research.)

6. **Write your review.** While the precise order of your paper may vary, most literature reviews have these parts:

   ■ **Opening:** Get the readers' attention and introduce the topic. Cite literature on the topic to describe the context or purpose of your review. State its thesis and explain the organization.

   ■ **Middle:** Briefly describe each study, especially its experiments, methodology, findings, and impact on current thinking on the topic:
   - Describe distinguishing qualities, but not the step-by-step process.
   - Cite details as needed, and summarize (but not quote) supporting passages. (For help writing summaries, see pages 238-239).
   - Analyze each study's strengths or weaknesses.

   Alternate patterns: You also might
   - describe (but not analyze) the studies,
   - describe studies individually and then analyze them collectively, or
   - group similar types of studies, explain why, and then describe and analyze each type.

   ■ **Closing:** Conclude by doing the following:
   - Briefly restate your findings, note unanswered questions, and recommend issues needing further research.
   - List the reviewed literature in an appropriately formatted bibliography.

7. **Revise the paper.** Revise your paper as needed for strong *ideas* (thesis, description, and analysis), clear and logical *organization* (clear title, headings, introduction, and closing), and an objective, academic *voice.*

8. **Edit and proofread.** Correct errors in grammar, punctuation, mechanics, and design. In addition, check (and correct as needed) documentation in your list of sources.

9. **Share your review.** In addition to submitting your literature review, find ways to share it with other students interested in the topic, perhaps by posting it on a class Web site.

Sample Student Paper: Reviewing the Literature

In the paragraph below, student-writer Dmitriy Kolesnikov describes how he chose to forego the assigned topic for writing a literature review in order to select a topic that "stimulated [his] curiosity." And what topic spurred his interest? He chose to study microRNA's possible link to cancer. As you read Dmitriy's paper, watch how he satisfies that curiosity by analyzing ten studies on the topic, and then synthesizing that literature by showing how each piece led him to conclude that microRNAs are linked to cancer and will likely help clinicians diagnose and treat the illness.

Writer's Reflection

I enrolled in Writing in the Biological Sciences in order to expand my writing abilities, which I already considered formidable prior to taking the class. However, I lacked an understanding of scientific writing methodology, and Dr. Haynes' class helped me immensely. Not only did I write several pieces of scientific writing, but I also learned how to properly read a scientific paper, a skill that had not been conveyed to me in earlier classes. "The Role of MicroRNA in Cancer" was my first successful attempt at synthesizing information found in numerous research articles. The assignment called for students to review a topic that they were familiar with, but instead I chose one that stimulated my curiosity. While the essay is intended primarily for students with college-level competence in biology, its introduction and conclusion may be comprehensible to laypeople. Since communication is crucial in science, as a prospective biologist, I appreciate the skills that I learned in Dr. Haynes' class.   —Dmitriy Kolesnikov

Preparing to Read: What do you know about the causes of cancer? How familiar are you with cancer research?

Literature Review

The Role of MicroRNA in Cancer

Introduction: MicroRNA function in cells

The titles forecast the contents of the paper and the introduction.

MicroRNAs (miRNAs) are a class of short (15-25 base long), non-protein-coding RNAs that regulate mRNA expression. They carry out this function through a variety of methods, including translational repression and mRNA cleavage. They possess complementary sequences to their target mRNAs, which allow them to carry out these functions. MiRNAs are similar to small interfering RNA (siRNA), but are less specific, and hence are capable of affecting the translation of large numbers of genes. MiRNAs have been implicated in a wide range of processes in the human body. While genomic analyses have suggested that the human genome codes for as many as 1000 miRNAs, only 300 have been extracted from human tissue and have had their function described. MiRNAs play diverse roles in cell functions, including apoptosis, angiogenesis, and cell proliferation.

The topic sentence identifies MicroRNAs as a class of non-protein-coding RNAs.

Interestingly, miRNAs tend to inhabit regions of the genome that are prone to damage or mutation. Calin et al. (2004) demonstrated that as many as 52% of the 186 sample miRNAs clustered around cancer-associated genomic regions. These findings have powerful implications for miRNAs' role in cancer.

MicroRNAs as oncogenes

One distinct type of cancer-related gene is the oncogene. Genes that merely have the potential to become involved in cancerous growth are proto-oncogenes, but they become full-fledged oncogenes when they accumulate mutations. Oncogenes actively promote tumor growth and invasion. They tend to be involved in cell proliferation, embryogenesis, and other crucial cell processes. Mutations in oncogenes are usually dominant.

Multiple miRNAs have been implicated in various cancers, including pancreatic (Bloomston et al., 2007), lung (Takamizawa et al., 2004), pituitary (Bottoni et al., 2005), and breast cancers (Ma, Teruya-Feldstein, and Weinberg, 2007). Due to their regulatory role in posttranscriptional processing, mutated miRNAs can easily lead to over- (or under-) expression of proteins. One of the earliest clusters of oncogenic microRNA, the mir-17-92 polycistron, was described by He et al. in 2005. In 65% of adenocarcinoma and lymphoma patients, pri-mir-17-92, a precursor of mir-17-92, was overexpressed compared to controls. The gene cluster was then transplanted into mice, resulting in 100% of samples displaying leukemia within 51 days. The control sample, on the other hand, showed no signs of malignancy.

Voorhoeve et al. (2006) reported that miR-372 and miR-373 act as oncogenes in testicular germ cell tumors. This particular form of cancer progressed into malignancy despite the presence of wild type p53, an important tumor suppression gene. In their experiments, miR-372/3-transformed cells displayed malignancy that is characteristic of testicular germ cell cancer, indicating that miR-372/3 probably allows the tumor to progress via a different pathway.

Another miRNA—miR-10b—has been implicated in metastasis. Ma, Teruya-Feldstein, and Weinberg (2007) demonstrated that miR-10b increases cell invasiveness *in vivo* as well as *in vitro*. This miRNA was overexpressed in secondary tumors of breast cancer. When inserted into a model organism (mouse), miR-10b interacted with HOXD10, an important gene in development, silencing it, and leading to a vast increase in invasiveness.

These results and others show that mutated miRNAs are capable of inducing a variety of steps necessary for cancer progression and development.

Margin notes:

Additional traits of this class are identified, particularly miRNA's link to cancer, the focus of the report.

Oncogenes are defined as a type of gene that promotes cancerous growth.

The writer asserts that miRNAs are linked to multiple cancers, and he supports the point by summarizing the findings of seven recent studies.

MicroRNAs as tumor suppressor genes

A second class of cancer-related genes is tumor suppressor genes. They usually regulate cell processes, but when they accumulate mutations and become inactivated, they are no longer capable of restricting uncontrolled cell growth. Mutations in tumor suppressor genes tend to be recessive, since there are two copies of them in each cell and an individual mutated copy is not sufficient for malignant growth to occur. When both copies accumulate mutations, however, active oncogenes within the cell become unrestrained.

Calin et al. (2002) hypothesized that miR-15a and miR-16-1 may be involved in tumor suppression, since their genes are found in regions that are frequently deleted in patients with chronic lymphomic leukemia (CLL). Likewise, down-regulation of the two miRNAs was chronicled in 68% of the CLL patients examined. Bottoni et al. (2005) confirmed these findings, observing that miR-15a/16-1 levels were expressed in low levels in pituitary adenomas. They also reported that miR-15a/16-1 levels correlated directly with those of p43, a known tumor-suppressor gene. Thus, they conclude, miR-15a and miR-16-1 probably regulate the expression of p43, which in turn suppresses tumorigenic growth.

Furthermore, Mayr, Hemann, and Bartel (2007) showed that the miRNA let-7 acts as a tumor suppressor gene with relation to Hmga2, an oncogene. Hmga2 is involved in proliferation during embryogenesis and development, and when it accumulates mutations, it becomes oncogenic. There are several conserved sequences between let-7 and Hmga2, further implying that the miRNA has a regulatory role.

Because they control large numbers of genes, individual miRNAs can have varying effects in different cancers. Calin et al. (2004) reported that a single miRNA, in this case miR-33b, is capable of acting either as an oncogene or a tumor-suppressor gene, depending on the sort of modifications that occur. Deletions can lead to oncogenetic properties, whereas hyper-methylation can induce loss of function, which damages the miRNA's tumor-suppressor role. Although miRNA genes tend to be short (-70 base pairs, from which the final product is cleaved) and thus usually do not accumulate gain-of-function or loss-of-function mutations, the fact that they tend to exist in clusters (Calin et al. 2004) greatly increases the likelihood that a genetic or epigenetic effect will modify miRNAs within a cluster.

Medical and diagnostic applications of microRNA

Diagnosis.

Since miRNAs tend to be over- or underexpressed in most cancers, this information can be utilized to determine which tissue may have become cancerous in the first place. Lu *et al.* (2005) demonstrated that a relatively simple method—attaching fluorescent beads to oligonucleotides complementary to miRNAs of choice—identifies miRNAs with stunning accuracy. Moreover, they sampled miRNAs from a large number of tumors and normal tissues to find that miRNA levels in tumors were found in hierarchical clusters, indicating not only whether a tissue was cancerous with near perfect accuracy, but also where the tumor itself originated. They further utilized this approach to diagnose seventeen unclassified cancers and found that miRNA analysis is considerably more reliable as a diagnostic tool than mRNA, presumably because there is a great deal of "noise" among the mRNA.

> He describes two studies in which microRNAs were successfully used to diagnose cancer.

The work of Bloomston et al. (2007) supports this application of miRNA. They sampled over 100 patients with pancreatic ductal adenocarcinoma and chronic pancreatitis, and used microarrays to detect miRNA expression level. They report that a group of miRNAs (some overexpressed and some underexpressed) could effectively differentiate between normal pancreatic cells and pancreatic tumor cells with a 90% success rate. A similar test, using a different set of miRNAs, successfully differentiated pancreatic cancer from chronic pancreatitis with a 93% accuracy rate. The ability to trace a cancer's progression throughout the body is imperative for proper diagnosis.

Prognosis.

> The subheading signals that the writer will address microRNAs use for prognosis.

While diagnosis is an important clinical tool, a parameter that can also predict survival rates is far more valuable. Bloomston et al. (2007) proposed that miRNA expression values could be used to predict the likelihood of survival over long and short terms for patients with pancreatic ductal adenocarcinoma. While diagnostic tools are currently absent for that particular disease, Takamizawa et al. (2004) reported the use of miRNAs to predict postoperative survival rates of lung cancer patients. Expression analyses of let-7 miRNA were used to group lung cancer operation patients into two groups. Patients with underexpressed let-7 had a far less promising prognosis than those with overexpressed let-7.

> The writer summarizes two studies that found microRNAs were helpful prognostic tools.

The fact that let-7 is one of the better-studied human miRNAs (particularly in lung cancer) is what allowed this prognostic application to be viable. However, much more work needs to be done with regard to other miRNAs and other human cancers. The work of Bloomston et al. (2007) on pancreatic cancer, for example, will likely inspire a number of further studies on prognosis via miRNA. However, multi-variate analyses of large clusters of miRNA will be necessary in order to have the desired prognostic effect for more complicated cancers.

The writer concludes by redefining microRNAs, reasserting their link to cancer, and projecting their future use for understanding and treating the disease.

Conclusions

MicroRNAs are a relatively new category of short regulatory RNAs that are found in chromosomal regions vulnerable to damage or rearrangement. Their role in cancers has recently been demonstrated to be very significant: over 50% of the miRNAs examined by Calin et al. (2004) were found to be in cancer-related genomic regions. Due to improved detection techniques, miRNA profiles have become an important tool in diagnosing the origin and type of certain cancers. Moreover, their expression profiles can predict survivorship over the course of years. Thus, miRNAs are likely to play an important role in the understanding and treatment of cancer in the near future.

The writer uses APA formatting to list the literature that he reviewed, though CSE would have been equally appropriate.

References

Bloomston M., Frankel W. L., Petrocca F., Volinia S., Alder H., Hagan, J. P., . . . Croce, C. M. (2007). MicroRNA expression patterns to differentiate pancreatic adenocarcinoma from normal pancreas and chronic pancreatitis. *Journal of the American Medical Association 297,* 1901-1908.

Bottoni A., Piccin D., Tagliati F., Luchin A., Zatelli M. C., & Uberti E. C. D. (2005). MiR-15a and miR-16-1 down-regulation in pituitary adenomas. *Journal of Cellular Physiology 204:* 280-285.

Calin G. A., Sevignani, C., Dumitru C. D., Hyslop, T., Noch E., Yendamuri, S., . . . Negrini, M. (2004). Human microRNA genes are frequently located at fragile sites and genomic regions involved in cancers. *Proceedings of the National Academy of Sciences 101:* 2999-3004.

Calin G. A., Dumitru C. D., Shimizu M., Bichi R., Zupo S., Noch E., . . . Rai K. (2002). Frequent deletions and down-regulation of microRNA genes miR15 and miR16 at 13q14 in chronic lymphocytic leukemia. *Proceedings of the National Academy of Sciences 99,* 15524-15529.

He L., Thomson J. M., Hemann M. T., Hernando-Monge, E., Mu D., Goodson S., . . . Hannon G. J. (2005). A microRNA polycistron as a potential human oncogene. *Nature 435:* 828-833.

Lu J., Getz G., Miska E. A. Alvarez-Saavedra E., Lamb J., Peck D., . . . Ferrando A. A. (2005). MicroRNA expression profiles classify human cancers. *Nature 435:* 834-838.

Ma L., Teruya-Feldstein J., & Weinberg R. A. (2007). Tumour invasion and metastasis initiated by microRNA-10b in breast cancer. *Nature 449:* 682-689.

Mayr C., Hemann M. T., & Bartel D. P. (2007). Disrupting the pairing between let-7 and Hmga2 enhances oncogenic transformation. *Science 315:* 1576-1579.

Takamizawa J., Konishi H., Yanagisawa K., Tomida S., Osada H., Endoh H., . . . Nimura YU. (2004). Reduced expression of the let-7 microRNAs in human lung cancers in association with shortened postoperative survival. *Cancer Research 64:* 3753-3756.

Voorhoeve P. M., Sage, C., Schrier M., Gillis A. J. M., Stoop H., Nagel R., . . . Griekspoor A., 2006. A genetic screen implicated miRNA-372 and miRNA-373 as oncogenes in testicular germ cell tumors. *Cell 124:* 1169-1181.

Reading Research Writing: Questions

To understand literature-review writing more fully, answer these questions:

1. Review Dmitriy's reflection on page 362 in which he says, "I also learned how to properly read a scientific paper, a skill that had not been conveyed to me in earlier classes." Given the literature that he reviewed in his report, what challenges might he have faced when reading the material? What tools or strategies might have helped him overcome these challenges?

2. To help readers understand the content of the literature and his synthesis of that content, Dmitriy uses five main headings and two subheadings. Review those headings and subheadings, and then explore whether they (a) help you understand the literature that he read and (b) serve as a unifying theme linking the pieces together.

3. Review three passages in which Dmitriy summarizes a source. Do these summaries effectively help you understand (a) the content of that piece of literature and (b) how the piece illustrates the idea in the heading that precedes it?

4. Review the introduction and conclusion. How do these frame Dmitriy's review of the studies?

FOCUS on Your Major: While literature reviews are commonly written in the social and natural sciences, a type of literature review is often practiced in humanities writing, as well. In longer papers and theses, writers might survey key secondary sources on their topics in order to put their own studies in context.

Practicing Your Research

1. **Respond to the model.** Read three articles that Dmitriy Kolesnikov summarizes in his literature review. Then write him an open letter in which you explain why you did or did not find that his summaries (a) accurately represented the original text and (b) warranted inclusion in his review. Share your letter with the class.

2. **Take a cross-disciplined approach.** Choose a topic that scholars in multiple disciplines research and write about: e.g., government-mandated inoculations, geothermal technologies, or a wildlife issue such as repopulating select national parks with wolves. Choose three research articles on the topic, each from a different discipline. Then write a literature review in which you compare and contrast the three studies.

3. **Make it multimedia.** Choose a topic in your discipline about which individuals write articles that include visual enhancements such as tables, graphs, charts, photographs, Web sites, or digital animations. Choose three of these articles and develop a PowerPoint literature review in which you show and explain how effectively the visuals in each article support the document's message.

4. **Take it to the street.** Choose a public policy about which people in your community are writing. Select three documents (e.g., articles, position statements) and analyze the quality of their research, arguments, and supporting data. Then write a literature review in which you aim to help the public understand the strengths and weaknesses of these documents. Finally, submit your review to your college or community newspaper, or publish it on an appropriate Web site.

Checklist: Use these seven traits to check the quality of your writing:

- ☑ **Ideas** Each summary accurately reports the content of its respective article, and the overall review logically synthesizes all articles.

- ☑ **Organization** The opening clearly introduces the topic; the body reviews the literature in a logical, coherent pattern; and the closing effectively wraps up the review.

- ☑ **Voice** The tone is energetic, but respectful of the literature and sensitive to the readers' background and needs.

- ☑ **Words** The word choice accurately communicates the literature's content and is understandable by the intended audience: e.g., where needed, technical terms are defined.

- ☑ **Sentences** Constructions are smooth, varied, and clear; transitions effectively link sentences and paragraphs.

- ☑ **Correctness** The writing includes no glaring errors in mechanics, usage, and grammar.

- ☑ **Design** The paper is correctly formatted in the assigned style, and all graphics are correctly and clearly displayed to support the document's message.

Part 3
Systems of Documentation

Chapters

> **Note:** The following chapters differ in their treatment of Web-related terms. Each chapter follows the format of the documentation style discussed therein.

18

MLA Style and Sample Paper

Because you're on this page, you've probably been told to submit your research paper in MLA style. You're looking for answers to questions like these: How do I format my paper? How do I document my research? This chapter will give you both an overview of the system (explaining its logic and principles) and specific guidelines and examples. Let's start with the basic questions below.

What Is the MLA? MLA stands for the Modern Language Association—the professional organization to which many English professors and some other humanities professors belong.

What is MLA Style? MLA style refers to a method of documenting research and formatting a research paper—a method and format used in English and some other humanities disciplines. In a nutshell, MLA style offers guidelines for the following:

1. **In-text citation**—the use of author and page-number references within parentheses
2. **Works cited**—a list of resources referred to and borrowed from in your paper
3. **Paper format**—margins, heading, pagination, indenting, paper size, and so on
4. **Punctuation and mechanics rules**—matters such as quotation marks, end punctuation, underlining, and brackets

Where can you find more information about MLA style? This chapter gives you most of what you need to know—drawn from the official *MLA Handbook for Writers of Research Papers* (7th edition), including the book's Web site at mlahandbook.org. You might also check your library's Web site, as well as other Web resources at theresearchwriter.com.

What's Ahead?

© Cengage Learning/Illustrated by Chris Krenzke

Directory to MLA Documentation

If you have a specific question about MLA style, use the directory below and on the next page to find the correct answer.

MLA Works-Cited Entries

General Guidelines for the Works-Cited Page 383
Abbreviations of Publishers' Names in Works-Cited Entries 384
Other Abbreviations for Works-Cited Entries 385
Sample Works-Cited Entries:

MLA Documentation: Quick Guide

The MLA system involves two parts: (1) an in-text citation within your paper when you use a source and (2) a matching bibliographic entry at the end of your paper. Note these features of the MLA system:

- ■ **It's minimalist.** In your paper, you provide the least amount of information needed for your reader to identify the source in the works-cited list.
- ■ **It uses signal phrases and parenthetical references** to set off source material from your own thinking and discussion. Note: A signal phrase names the author and places the material in context (e.g., "As Margaret Atwood argues in *Survival*").
- ■ **It's smooth, unobtrusive, and orderly.** MLA in-text citations identify borrowed material while keeping the paper readable. Moreover, alphabetized entries in the works-cited list at the end of the paper make locating source details easy.

You can see these features at work in the example below. "Edith Kramer" and "(28)" tell the reader that

- ■ the borrowed material came from a source written by Edith Kramer.
- ■ the specific material can be found on page 28 of the source.
- ■ full source details are in the works-cited list under the author's last name.

1. In-Text Citation in Body of Paper

Child psychologist Edith Kramer reflects that "in adult life, art . . . [is] one of the few areas of symbolic living that remain accessible" (28).

2. Matching Works-Cited Entry at End of Paper

Kramer, Edith. *Art as Therapy with Children*. New York: Schocken, 1971. Print.

In-Text Citations: The Basics

In MLA, in-text citations typically follow these guidelines:

1. Refer to the author (plus the work's title, if helpful) and a page number by using one of these methods:

Last names only in citation   No comma between names and page number

Last name and page number in parentheses:

Another reoccurring theme in the art of anorectics is an isolated figure often surrounded by dark colors or stormy weather (Acharya, Wood, and Robinson 11).

Full names in first reference

Name cited in sentence, page number in parentheses: No "p." for "page"

Psychiatrists Madushree Acharya, Michéle Wood, and Paul Robinson describe the somatic parallel between anorexia and art therapy when they write, "Like the pathological expression of [issues] through the illness, the patient is working through her body; the all-important difference is that art therapy is creative and non self-harming" (13).

2. Present and punctuate citations according to these rules:

- Place the parenthetical reference after the source material.
- Within the parentheses, normally give the author's last name only.
- Do not put a comma between the author's last name and the page reference.
- Cite the page number as a numeral, not a word.
- Don't use *p., pp.,* or *page(s)* before the page number(s).
- Place any sentence punctuation after the closed parenthesis.

Note: For many of these rules, exceptions exist. For example, classic literary texts could be cited by chapters, books, acts, scenes, or lines. Moreover, many electronic sources have no stated authors and/or no pagination. See pages 401 for complete coverage of in-text citation practices.

Works Cited: The Basics

Complete coverage of MLA works-cited issues (examples included) is offered on pages 383–400, rules for formatting the works-cited page are on page 401, and a sample works-cited page is shown on page 418. Here, however, are some templates for the most common entries:

Template for Book:

Author's Last Name, First Name. *Title of Book.* Publication City: Publisher, year of
   publication. Medium. (Other publication details are integrated as needed.)

Rabin, Murray. *Art Therapy and Eating Disorders.* New York: Columbia UP, 2003. Print.

Template for Periodical Article in an Online Database:

Author's Last Name, First Name. "Title of Article." *Journal Title* volume, issue, and/or date
   details: page numbers. *Title of Database.* Medium. Date of access.

Johnson, Karen, and Sarah Parkinson. "There's No Point Raging on Your Own: Using
   Art Therapy Groups for People with Eating Disorders." *Group Analysis* 32.1 (Mar.
   1999): 87-96. *Academic Search Premier.* Web. 16 Oct. 2010.

Note: If you read the print article, end the citation after the page numbers with "Print" as the medium.

Template for a Web Document:

Author's or Editor's Last Name, First Name (if available). "Title of Page, Posting, or
   Document." *Title of Web site* (if different from document title). Version or edition
   used. Publisher or sponsor of site (if known; if not, use N.p.), Date of publication, last
   update, or posting (if known; if not, use n.d.). Medium. Date of access.

"Frequently Asked Questions." *The Canadian Art Therapy Association.* CATA, Nov.
   2008. Web. 6 Nov. 2010.

MLA In-Text Citations

In MLA style, you give credit for your sources of information in the body of your research paper. With this method of in-text citation (sometimes called "parenthetical references"), you can indicate source material through two patterns:

1. In the text of your essay, indicate the author and/or title and then put a page reference in parentheses after the summary, paraphrase, or quotation, as needed. This first method is particularly useful when you want to stress the source's authorship because of its credibility, expertise, or particular point of view.

2. Rather than referencing the author and/or title in your discussion, simply insert the appropriate information (usually the author and page number) in parentheses after the words or ideas taken from the source. This method works when stressing authorship isn't essential, as when you are providing straightforward information rather than analysis or argument.

To avoid disrupting your writing, place citations where a pause would naturally occur (usually at the end of a sentence but sometimes within a sentence before internal punctuation such as a comma or semicolon). These in-text citations refer to sources listed on the "Works Cited" page at the end of your paper. (See page 383.)

General Guidelines for In-Text Citations

As you integrate citations into your paper, follow the guidelines below, referring to the sample citation as needed.

Sample In-Text Citation

Art therapists Wolf et. al. describe this process when they conclude, "Our clinical sense has been that patients may use art as a bridge to verbal therapies; feelings, attitudes, and conceptions can be formulated, clarified, and symbolized in art before exposing them to the potential confusion and diffusion of talk" (199).

- Make sure each in-text citation clearly points to an entry in your list of works cited. The identifying information provided (usually the author's last name) must be the word or words by which the entry is alphabetized in that list.

- Keep citations as brief as possible and integrate them smoothly.

- When paraphrasing or summarizing rather than quoting, make it clear where your borrowing begins and ends. Use stylistic cues to distinguish the source's thoughts ("Kalmbach reports . . . " / "Some critics argue . . . ") from your own ("I believe . . . " / "It seems obvious, however, . . . ").

- When using a shortened title of a work, begin with the word by which the work is alphabetized in your list of works cited (e.g., *Chase's Calendar* not *Events* for *Chase's Calendar of Events 2002*).

- For inclusive page numbers larger than ninety-nine, give only the last two digits of the second number (113-14, not 113-114).

■ When including a parenthetical citation at the end of a sentence, place it before the end punctuation. (Citations for long, indented quotations are an exception. See pages 382–383.)

Guidelines for Sources without Authorship and/or Pagination

Today, many sources, especially ones on the Web, have no stated authors and/or no pagination. For such sources, use these in-text citation strategies:

Source without a Stated Author: In a signal phrase or in the parenthetical reference, identify the source as precisely as possible by indicating the sponsoring agency, the type of document, or the title (shortened in the parenthetical reference). See page 379.

> *Example:* While the Brooklyn Museum may be best known for the recent controversy over the Sensation exhibition, it does contain a strong collection of contemporary if less controversial art, "ranging from representational to abstract to conceptual" ("Contemporary Art").

Source with No Pagination: If no pagination exists within the document, use any stable, internal divisions available—paragraph numbers, chapter titles, headings, etc. See page 380.

> *Example:* The museum's collection of Art of the Americas includes extensive holdings of works by the aboriginal peoples of North, Central, and South America, many of these gathered by archaeologist Herbert Spinden during at least seven expeditions between 1929 and 1950 ("Art of the Americas" par. 3).

In addition, follow these guidelines when referring to sources with no pagination:

■ If you refer to document divisions other than page numbers, use abbreviations: par. (paragraph), ch. (chapter), sec. (section), introd. (introduction).

■ When you have no parenthetical reference to signal the end of borrowed material, signal a shift back to your own discussion with a source-reflective statement indicating your thinking about the source.

> *Example:* . . . indicated by his recording the audio tour of the exhibit, his supporting the show financially, and his promoting Sensation at his Web site. As Welland's discussion of David Bowie's participation indicates, the controversy over the Brooklyn Museum of Art's Sensation exhibit . . .

Tip:

■ Stable pagination for many digital resources is available when you use the ".pdf" rather than ".html" version of the source.

■ For instruction on smoothly integrating source material into your paper, see pages 190–192.

■ For cautions about sources without identified authors, see pages 81, 91, and 148–149.

Sample In-Text Citations

The following entries illustrate the most common sorts of in-text citations. For convenience, we have listed parallel works-cited entries for each case.

1. **One Author: A Complete Work** (works cited 1, page 387)
   You do not need an in-text citation if you identify the author in your text. (See the first entry below.) However, you must give the author's last name in an in-text citation if it is not mentioned in the text. (See the second entry.) When a source is listed in your works-cited page with an editor, a translator, a speaker, or an artist instead of the author, use that person's name in your citation.

   > **With Author in Text** (This is the preferred way of citing a complete work.): In *No Need for Hunger,* Robert Spitzer recommends that the US government develop a new foreign policy to help Third World countries overcome poverty and hunger.

   > **Without Author in Text:** *No Need for Hunger* recommends that the US government develop a new foreign policy to help Third World countries overcome poverty and hunger (Spitzer).

   Note: Do not offer page numbers when citing complete works, articles in alphabetized encyclopedias, one-page articles, and unpaginated sources.

2. **One Author: Part of a Work** (works cited 1, page 387)
   List the necessary page numbers in parentheses if you borrow words or ideas from a particular source. Leave a space between the author's last name and the page reference. No abbreviation or punctuation is needed.

   > **With Author in Text:** Bullough writes that genetic engineering was dubbed "eugenics" by a cousin of Darwin's, Sir Francis Galton, in 1885 (5).

   > **Without Author in Text:** Genetic engineering was dubbed "eugenics" by a cousin of Darwin's, Sir Francis Galton, in 1885 (Bullough 5).

3. **Two or More Works by the Same Author(s)** (works cited 2, page 387)
   In addition to the author's last name(s) and page number(s), include a shortened version of the title of the work when you are citing two or more works by the same author(s).

   > **With Author in Text:** Wallerstein and Blakeslee claim that divorce creates an enduring identity for children of the marriage (*Unexpected Legacy* 62).

   > **Without Author in Text:** They are intensely lonely despite active social lives (Wallerstein and Blakeslee, *Second Chances* 51).

   Note: When including both author(s) and title in a parenthetical reference, separate them with a comma, as shown above, but do not put a comma between the title and the page number.

4. **Works by Authors with the Same Last Name**

   When citing different sources by authors with the same last name, it is best to use the authors' full names in the text to avoid confusion. However, if circumstances call for parenthetical references, include each author's first initial instead. If first initials are the same, use each author's full name.

   > Some critics think *Titus Andronicus* too abysmally melodramatic to be a work of Shakespeare (A. Parker 73). Others suggest that Shakespeare meant it as black comedy (D. Parker 486).

5. **A Work by Two or Three Authors** (works cited 3, page 387)

   Give the last names of every author in the same order that they appear in the works-cited section. (The correct order can be found on the book's title page.)

   > Students learned more than a full year's Spanish in ten days using the complete supermemory method (Ostrander and Schroeder 51).

6. **A Work by Four or More Authors** (works cited 4, page 387)

   Give the first author's last name as it appears in the works-cited section followed by et al. (meaning "and others").

   > Communication on the job is more than talking; it is "inseparable from your total behavior" (Culligan et al. 111).

   Note: You may instead choose to list all of the authors' last names.

7. **A Work Authored by an Agency, a Committee, or an Organization** (works cited 5, page 387) If a book or other work was written by an organization such as an agency, a committee, or a task force, it is said to have a corporate author. If the corporate name is long, include it in the text (rather than in parentheses) to avoid disrupting the flow of your writing. After the full name has been used at least once, use a shortened form of the name (common abbreviations are acceptable) in subsequent references. For example, *Task Force* may be used for *Task Force on Education for Economic Growth.*

   > The thesis of the Task Force's report is that economic success depends on our ability to improve large-scale education and training as quickly as possible (113-14).

8. **An Anonymous Work** (works cited 6, page 387)

   When no author is listed (person or group), give the title or a shortened version of the title as it appears in the works-cited section.

   > Statistics indicate that drinking water can make up 20 percent of a person's total exposure to lead (*Information* 572).

9. **Two or More Works Included in One Citation**

   To cite multiple works within a single parenthetical reference, list the references alphabetically by last name and separate them with a semicolon.

   > In Medieval Europe, Latin translations of the works of Rhazes, a Persian scholar, were a primary source of medical knowledge (Albala 22; Lewis 266).

10. **A Series of Citations from a Single Work**

    If no confusion is possible, it is not necessary to name a source repeatedly when making multiple parenthetical references to that source in a single paragraph. If all references are to the same page, identify that page in a parenthetical note after the last reference. If the references are to different pages within the same work, you need identify the work only once, and then use a parenthetical note with page number alone for the subsequent references.

    > Domesticating science meant not only spreading scientific knowledge, but also promoting it as a topic of public conversation (Heilbron 2). One way to enhance its charm was by depicting cherubic putti as "angelic research assistants" in book illustrations (5).

11. **A Work Referred to in Another Work**

    If you must cite an indirect source—that is, information in a source that is quoted from another source (e.g., a quotation within the source)—use the abbreviation *qtd. in* (quoted in) before the indirect source in your reference.

    > Paton improved the conditions in Diepkloof (a prison) by "removing all the more obvious aids to detention. The dormitories [were] open at night: the great barred gate [was] gone" (qtd. in Callan xviii).

    Note: Whenever practical, track down the original source in order to understand the quoted source in context.

12. **A One-Page Work**

    Cite a one-page work just as you would a complete work (in-text citation 1, page 378).

    > As Samantha Adams argues in her editorial, it is time for NASA "to fully commit to a manned mission to Mars."

13. **A Work without Page Numbers**

    If a work has no page numbers or other reference numbers, treat it as you would a complete work (in-text citation 1, page 378). This is commonly the case with Web resources, for example. Do not count pages to create reference numbers of your own; however, if possible, refer to stable divisions within the document, such as sections or paragraphs (see page 377).

    > Antibiotics become ineffective against such organisms through two natural processes: first, genetic mutation; and second, the subsequent transfer of this mutated genetic material to other organisms, which appears to be the main way that bacteria attain a state of resistance (Davies par. 5).

14. **A Work in an Anthology or Collection of Texts, Essays, Letters, Etc.** (works cited 7, page 387) An anthology or collection brings together shorter works, often written by different authors: poems or short stories in a literary anthology, scholarly essays in a book of criticism, the published correspondence of an author. When citing the entirety of a work that is part of an anthology or collection, if it is identified by author in your list of works cited, treat the citation as you would for any other complete work (in-text citation 1, page 378).

> In "The Canadian Postmodern," Linda Hutcheon offers a clear analysis of the self-reflexive nature of contemporary Canadian fiction.

Similarly, if you are citing particular pages of such a work, follow the directions for citing part of a work (in-text citation 2, page 378).

> According to Hutcheon, "Postmodernism seems to designate cultural practices that are fundamentally self-reflexive, in other words, art that is self-consciously artifice" (18).

Note that if you refer to two or more letters from a published collection of correspondence, that collection should be listed just once in the works-cited page. When you refer to a specific letter in your writing, cross-reference it to the correspondence collection, as shown.

> On September 12, 1918, Lewis wrote to Arthur Greves that the volume of poetry was to be called "Spirits in Prison." The book's main theme, as Lewis put it, was "that nature is wholly diabolical & malevolent and that God, if he exists, is outside of and in opposition to the cosmic arrangements" (Lewis, *Collected Letters* 397).

15. **An Item from a Reference Work** (works cited 19 and 20, page 390)
An entry from a reference work such as an encyclopedia or dictionary should be cited similarly to a work from an anthology or collection (in-text citation 14 above). For a dictionary definition, include the abbreviation *def.* followed by the particular entry designation.

> This message of moral superiority becomes a juggernaut in the truest sense, a belief that "elicits blind devotion or sacrifice" ("Juggernaut," def. 1).

Note that while many such entries are identified only by title (as above), some reference works include an author's name for each entry (as below). Others may identify the entry author by initials, with a list of full names elsewhere in the work.

> The decisions of the International Court of Justice are "based on principles of international law and cannot be appealed" (Pranger).

16. **A Part of a Multivolume Work** (works cited 10, page 388)
When citing only one volume of a multivolume work, if you identify the volume number in the works-cited list, there is no need to include it in your in-text citation. However, if you cite more than one volume of a work, each in-text reference must identify the appropriate volume. Give the volume number followed by page number, separated by a colon and a space.

> "A human being asleep," says Spengler, ". . . is leading only a plantlike existence" (2: 4).

When citing a whole volume, however, either identify the volume number in parentheses with the abbreviation *vol.* (using a comma to separate it from the author's name) or use the full word *volume* and the appropriate number in your text.

> The land of Wisconsin has shaped its many inhabitants more significantly than they ever shaped that land (Stephens, vol. 1).

17. **A Sacred Text or Famous Literary Work** (works cited 23, page 391)
    Sacred texts and famous literary works are published in many different editions.
    For that reason, it is helpful to identify sections, parts, chapters, and such instead
    of or in addition to page numbers. If using page numbers, list them first, followed
    by an abbreviation for the type of division and the division number (see page 385
    for common abbreviations).

    > The more important a person's role in society—the more apparent power
    > an individual has—the more that person is a slave to the forces of history
    > (Tolstoy 690; bk. 9, ch. 1).

    Books of the Bible and other well-known literary works may be abbreviated, if no
    confusion is possible.

    > "A generation goes, and a generation comes, but the earth remains forever"
    > (*The New Oxford Annotated Bible,* Eccles. 1.4).

    > As Shakespeare's famous Danish prince observes, "One may smile, and smile,
    > and be a villain" (*Ham.* 1.5.104).

18. **Quoting Verse**
    Do not use page numbers when referencing classic verse plays and poems. Instead,
    cite them by division (act, scene, canto, book, part) and line, using Arabic
    numerals for the various divisions unless your instructor prefers Roman numerals.
    Use periods to separate the various numbers.

    > In the first act of the play named after him, Hamlet comments, "How weary,
    > stale, flat and unprofitable, / Seem to me all the uses of this world" (1.2.133-134).

    Note: A slash, with a space on each side, shows where each new line of verse begins.

    If you are citing lines only (as with a fairly short lyric), use the word *line* or *lines* in
    your first reference and numbers only in additional references.

    > At the beginning of the sestet in Robert Frost's "Design," the speaker asks
    > this pointed question: "What had that flower to do with being white, / The
    > wayside blue and innocent heal-all?" (lines 9-10).

    Verse quotations of more than three lines should be indented one inch (ten spaces)
    and double-spaced. Do not add quotation marks. Each line of the poem or play
    begins a new line of the quotation; do not run the lines together. If a line or lines of
    poetry are dropped from the quotation, ellipses that extend the width of the stanza
    should be used to indicate the omission.

    > Bin Ramke's poem "A Little Ovid Late in the Day" tells of reading by the last
    > light of a summer day:
    >> [T]ales of incest, corruption,
    >> any big, mythic vice
    >> against the color of the sun,
    >> the sweetness of the time of day—
    >> I know the story,
    >> it is the light I care about. (3-8)

19. **Quoting Prose**

To cite prose from fiction (novels, short stories), list more than the page number if the work is available in several editions. Give the page reference first, and then add a chapter, section, or book number in abbreviated form after a semicolon.

> In *The House of the Spirits,* Isabel Allende describes Marcos, "dressed in mechanic's overalls, with huge racer's goggles and an explorer's helmet" (13; ch. 1).

When you are quoting any sort of prose that takes more than four typed lines, indent each line of the quotation one inch (ten spaces) and double-space it; do not add quotation marks. In this case, you put the parenthetical citation (the pages and chapter numbers) outside the end punctuation mark of the quotation itself.

> Allende describes the flying machine that Marcos has assembled:

> > The contraption lay with its stomach on terra firma, heavy and sluggish and looking more like a wounded duck than like one of those newfangled airplanes they were starting to produce in the United States. There was nothing in its appearance to suggest that it could move, much less take flight across the snowy peaks. (12; ch. 1)

MLA Works-Cited Entries

The works-cited section lists all of the sources you have cited (referred to) in your text. It does not include any sources you may have read or studied but did not refer to in your paper (that's a bibliography). The following pages include general guidelines for constructing your works-cited list, as well as specific instruction for most types of resources: books, periodical articles, Web pages, and other sources.

General Guidelines for the Works-Cited Page

Begin your list of works cited on a new page (the next page after the text), and number each page, continuing from the number of the last page of the text. Format your works-cited list using these guidelines:

1. Type the page number in the upper right corner, one-half inch from the top of the page, with your last name before it.

2. Center the title *Works Cited* (not in italics or underlined) one inch from the top; then double-space before the first entry.

3. Begin each entry flush with the left margin. If the entry runs more than one line, indent additional lines one-half inch (five spaces) or use the hanging indent function on your computer.

4. End each element of the entry with a period. (Elements are separated by periods in most cases, unless only a space is sufficient.) Use a single space after all punctuation.

5. Double-space lines within each entry and between entries.

6. List each entry alphabetically by the author's last name. If there is no author, alphabetize by the first word of the title (disregard *A, An,* or *The* as the first word). If there are multiple authors, alphabetize them according to which author is listed first in the publication.

7. As required by the seventh edition of the *MLA Handbook,* identify the medium of each source you use (print, Web, television, DVD, and so on). For print sources, type *Print* after the publisher and date. For Web publications, type *Web* after the publication date and before your date of access.

8. A basic entry for a book follows:

   Black, Naomi. *Virginia Woolf as Feminist.* Ithaca: Cornell UP, 2004. Print.

9. A basic entry for a journal or magazine follows:

   Stelmach, Kathryn. "From Text to Tableau: Ekphrastic Enchantment in *Mrs. Dalloway* and *To the Lighthouse.*" *Studies in the Novel* 38.3 (Fall 2006): 304-26. Print.

10. A basic entry for an online source appears below. Note that the source's URL is included only if the reader probably cannot locate the source without it, or when your instructor requires it. (See page 408.)

    Clarke, S. N. "Virginia Woolf (1882-1941): A Short Biography." *Virginia Woolf.* Virginia Woolf Society of Great Britain. 2000. Web. 12 March 2010.

Abbreviations of Publishers' Names in Works-Cited Entries

In your works-cited entries, MLA style encourages you to shorten publishers' names:

- Cut any articles (*a, an, the*), business terms (*Co., Inc., Ltd.*), and descriptive terms (*House, Press*). Exception: university presses (see below).
- For publishing houses named after one or more people, abbreviate the name to the first person's last name.
- For a publisher whose name is recognizable by initials, use the initialism (e.g., MLA, NCTE, ALA). If your reader won't recognize the organization, use standard abbreviations instead.
- For a university press, generally use *U* for *University* and *P* for *Press.*

Common Publishers

Cambridge UP	Cambridge University Press
Farrar	Farrar, Straus and Giroux, Inc.
Gale	Gale Research, Inc.
Harper	Harper and Row, Publishers, Inc.; HarperCollins Publishers, Inc.
Knopf	Alfred A. Knopf, Inc.
Macmillan	Macmillan Publishing Co., Inc.
McClelland	McClelland & Stewart, Ltd.
MLA	The Modern Language Association of America
Norton	W. W. Norton and Co., Inc.
Oxford UP	Oxford University Press
Random	Random House, Inc.
Scribner's	Charles Scribner's Sons
Simon	Simon and Schuster, Inc.
U of Toronto P	University of Toronto Press

Other Abbreviations for Works-Cited Entries

In your works-cited entries, you may be able to use a range of abbreviations besides the publisher's name. Consider these guidelines and the list below:

- Use standard month abbreviations in dates for journals, Web sites, and so on. Exceptions are May, June, and July, which are always spelled out in full.
- Jan.   Feb.   Mar.   Apr.   Aug.   Sept.   Oct.   Nov.   Dec.
- Within in-text citations, tables, illustrations, and works-cited entries, the following abbreviations may prove helpful:

anon.	anonymous
bk., bks.	book(s)
ch. (chap.), chs.	chapter(s)
comp.	compiler, compiled, compiled by
ed., eds.	edited by, editor(s), edition(s)
et al.	and others; *et alii, et aliae*
ex.	example
fig., figs.	figure(s)
ibid.	in the same place; *ibidem*
illus.	illustration, illustrated by
introd.	introduction, introduced by
lib.	library
loc. cit.	in the place cited; *loco citato*
MS, MSS	manuscript(s)
narr., narrs.	narrated by, narrator(s)
n.d.	no date given
no., nos.	number(s)
n.p.	no place of publication, no publisher given
n. pag.	no pagination
op. cit.	in the work cited; *opere citato*
p., pp.	page(s): if needed for clarity
+	plus the pages that follow
pub. (publ.)	publisher, publication, published by
qtd.	quoted
rev.	revision, revised by, review, reviewed by
rpt.	reprint, reprinted by
sc.	scene
sec. (sect.), secs.	section(s)
trans. (tr.)	translator, translation
viz.	namely; *videlicet*
vol., vols.	volume(s): capitalize when used with Roman numerals

Note: Within in-text citations, you may be able to use standard abbreviations for books of the Bible, Shakespeare's works, and other classic literature. For a table of such abbreviations, go to www.theresearchwriter.com.

Works-Cited Entries:
Print Books and Other Nonperiodical Documents

Components

The entries that follow illustrate the information needed to cite books, sections of a book, pamphlets, and government documents published in print. The possible components of these entries are listed in order below:

1. Author's name
2. Title of part of the book (an article in a reference book, foreword or afterword)
3. Title of the book, italicized (not underlined)
4. Name of editor, translator, or illustrator
5. Edition
6. Number of volume
7. Name of series
8. Place of publication, publisher, year of publication
9. Page numbers, if citation is to only a part (For page spans, use a hyphen; if clarity is maintained, you may also drop a digit from the second number—for example, 141-43, 201-334.)
10. Medium of publication (Print)

Publisher: Pat Coryell
Editor in Chief: Suzanne Phelps Weir
Senior Development Editor: Judith Fifer
Assistant Editor: Anne Leung
Editorial Associate: John McHugh
Senior Project Editor: Aileen Mason
Editorial Assistant: Susan Miscio
Manufacturing Manager: Karen B. Fawcett
Senior Marketing Manager: Cindy Graff Cohen
Marketing Assistant: Kelly Kunert

Cover Design and Interior Design: Tammy Hintz and Van Mua
Illustrations: Chris Krenzke
CD: Chris Erickson, Steve Augustyn, Jason Reynolds, Mark Fairweather
Editorial: J. Robert King, Claire Ziffer, Steven E. Schend, Stephen D. Sullivan, Janae Sebranek, Laura Bachman, Linda Presto, Joyce Becker Lee, Mariellen Hanrahan, Betsy Rasmussen, Lester Smith
Production: April Barrons, Christine Rieker, Julie Spicuzza, Susan Boehm, Kathleen Strom, Kevin Nelson, Colleen Belmont, Mark Lalumondier

Copyright © 2007 by Houghton Mifflin Company. All rights reserved.

No part of this book may be reproduced or transmitted in any form or by any means, electronic or mechanical, including photocopying and recording, or by any information storage or retrieval system without the prior written permission of Houghton Mifflin Company unless copying is expressly permitted by federal copyright law. Address inquiries to College Permissions, 222 Berkeley Street, Boston, MA 02116-3764.

Printed in the U.S.A.

Library of Congress Control Number: 2005938039

ISBN 13: 978-0-618-49169-8
ISBN 10: 0-618-49169-4

1 2 3 4 5 6 7 8 9-DOC-10 09 08 07 06

Note: In general, if any of these components do not apply, they are not included in the works-cited entry. However, in the rare instance that a book does not state publication information, use the following abbreviations in place of information you cannot supply:

n.p.	No place of publication given
n.p.	No publisher given
n.d.	No date of publication given
n. pag.	No pagination given

Additional Guidelines

- List only the city (not the accompanying state, province, or country) for the place of publication. If several cities are listed, give only the first.
- Publishers' names should be shortened by omitting articles (*a, an, the*), business

abbreviations (*Co., Inc.*), and descriptive words (*Books, Press*). If the publisher's name contains the surnames of more than one person, cite only the first of the surnames. Abbreviate *University Press* as *UP*. Also use standard abbreviations whenever possible. See pages 389-385 for more details.

1. **A Book by One Author**

   > Baghwati, Jagdish. *In Defense of Globalization.* New York: Oxford UP, 2004. Print.

2. **Two or More Books by the Same Author** List the books alphabetically according to title. After the first entry, substitute three hyphens for the author's name.

   > Dershowitz, Alan M. *Rights from Wrongs.* New York: Basic, 2005. Print.
   >
   > ---. *Supreme Injustice: How the High Court Hijacked Election 2000.* Oxford: Oxford UP, 2001. Print.

3. **A Work by Two or Three Authors** List the authors in the same order as they appear on the title page. Reverse only the name of the first author.

   > Bystydzienski, Jill M., and Estelle P. Resnik. *Women in Cross-Cultural Transitions.* Bloomington: Phi Delta Kappa Educational Foundation, 1994. Print.

4. **A Work by Four or More Authors**

   > Schulte-Peevers, Andrea, et al. *Germany.* Victoria: Lonely Planet, 2000. Print.

   Note: You may also choose to give all names in full in the order on the title page.

5. **A Work Authored by an Agency, a Committee, or an Organization**

   > Exxon Mobil Corporation. *Great Plains 2000.* Lincolnwood: Publications Intl., 2001. Print.

6. **An Anonymous Book**

   > *Chase's Calendar of Events 2002.* Chicago: Contemporary, 2002. Print.

7. **A Single Work from an Anthology or Collection of Texts, Essays, Letters, or Other Documents**

   An anthology collects a variety of texts (typically from a variety of authors)—literary works, historical documents, scholarly essays, or letters. When citing a single work from an anthology, start with the author and title of the specific piece; then follow with publication details of the anthology. For placement of an editor's name, see item 15, page 389.

   > Mitchell, Joseph. "The Bottom of the Harbor." *American Sea Writing.* Ed. Peter Neill. New York: Library of America, 2000. 584-608. Print.

   With a letter or other correspondence in a published collection, follow the format below, including the letter's date and number (if it has been given one in the collection).

   > Lewis, C. S. "To His Father (LP VI: 26-7)." 3 Sept: 1918. *The Collected Letters of C. S. Lewis, Volume 1: Family Letters, 1905-1931.* Ed. Walter Hooper. New York: HarperSanFrancisco, 2004. 395-96. Print.

8. **A Complete Anthology or Collection**

If you cite a complete anthology or collection, begin the entry with the editor(s).

> Neill, Peter, ed. *American Sea Writing.* New York: Lib. of America, 2000. Print.
>
> Smith, Rochelle, and Sharon L. Jones, eds. *The Prentice Hall Anthology of African American Literature.* Upper Saddle River: Prentice Hall, 2000. Print.

9. **Two or More Works from the Same Anthology or Collection**

To avoid unnecessary repetition when citing two or more texts from an anthology or collection, you may cite the collection once with complete publication information (see Rothfield below). The individual entries (see Becker and Cuno below) can then be cross-referenced by listing the author, title of the piece, editor of the collection, and page numbers. (See entry 16 on the next page for an explanation of the series identification in the Rothfield example below.)

> Becker, Carol. "The Brooklyn Controversy: A View from the Bridge." Rothfield 15-21.
>
> Cuno, James. "Sensation and the Ethics of Funding Exhibitions." Rothfield 162-170.
>
> Rothfield, Lawrence, ed. *Unsettling Sensation: Arts-Policy Lessons from the Brooklyn Museum of Art Controversy.* New Brunswick: Rutgers UP, 2001. Print. Rutgers Ser. on the Public Life of the Arts.

If you are citing more than one letter from a volume of correspondence, simply give one entry for the book. Then, in the body of your writing, indicate letters individually, cross-referencing them to the one text listed in your list of works cited (see pages 380–381).

10. **One or More Volumes of a Multivolume Work**

To cite a single volume, indicate the volume after the title, as shown.

> Cooke, Jacob Ernest, and Milton M. Klein, eds. *North America in Colonial Times.* Vol. 2. New York: Scribner's, 1998. Print.

If you cite two or more volumes in a multivolume work, give the total number of volumes after each title. Offer specific references to volume and page numbers in the parenthetical reference in your text, like this: (8: 112-14). (See page 381.)

> Salzman, Jack, David Lionel Smith, and Cornel West. *Encyclopedia of African-American Culture and History.* 5 vols. New York: Simon, 1996. Print.

11. **An Introduction, a Preface, a Foreword, or an Afterword**

To cite the introduction, preface, foreword, or afterword of a book, list the author of the part first. Then identify the part by type, with no quotation marks or italics, followed by the title of the book. Next, identify the author of the work, using the word *By.* (If the book author and the part's author are the same person, give just the last name after *By.*) For a book that gives cover credit to an editor instead of an author, identify the editor as usual. Finally, list any page numbers for the part being cited.

McCourt, Frank. Foreword. *Eats, Shoots, & Leaves: The Zero Tolerance Approach to Punctuation.* By Lynne Truss. New York: Gotham, 2003. xi-xiv. Print.

Atwood, Margaret. Introduction. *Alice Munro's Best: Selected Stories.* By Alice Munro. Toronto: McClelland, 2006. vii-xviii. Print.

12. A Republished Book (Reprint)

A republished book is one that has been printed again some time after its original publication (e.g., a paperback coming out some time after the hardcover). Give the original publication date after the title.

Atwood, Margaret. *Surfacing.* 1972. New York: Doubleday, 1998. Print.

13. A Book with Multiple Publishers

When a book lists more than one publisher (not just different offices of the same publisher), include all of them in the order given on the book's title page, separated by a semicolon.

Wells, H. G. *The Complete Short Stories of H. G. Wells.* New York: St. Martin's; London: A. & C. Black, 1987. Print.

14. Second and Subsequent Editions

An edition is not simply a reprinted or republished text. Rather, it refers to the particular version of the publication you are citing, as in a numbered edition (3rd ed.), a revised edition (Rev. ed.), an abridged edition (Abr. ed.), or a year's edition (2010 ed.).

Joss, Molly W. *Looking Good in Presentations.* 3rd ed. Scottsdale: Coriolis, 1999. Print.

15. An Edition with Both an Author and an Editor

The term edition also refers to the work of one person that is prepared by another person, an editor. Normally indicate the editor after the title.

Shakespeare, William. *A Midsummer Night's Dream.* Ed. Jane Bachman. Lincolnwood: NTC, 1994. Print.

16. A Book in a Series

Give the series name and number (if any) after the medium of publication.

Paradis, Adrian A. *Opportunities in Military Careers.* Lincolnwood: VGM Career Horizons, 1999. Print. VGM Opportunities Ser.

17. A Translation

Lebert, Stephan, and Norbert Lebert. *My Father's Keeper.* Trans. Julian Evans. Boston: Little, 2001. Print.

18. **An Illustrated Book or Graphic Narrative**

If a book contains significant illustrations (not merely supplemental to the text) done by someone other than the author or through collaboration, indicate the individuals' contributions as shown below.

> Moore, Alan, writer. *League of Extraordinary Gentlemen: The Black Dossier.* Art by Kevin O'Neill. Letters by Bill Oakley. La Jolla: WildStorm, 2007. Print.

19. **An Article in a Familiar Reference Book**

It is not necessary to give full publication information for familiar reference works (encyclopedias and dictionaries). For these titles, list only the edition (if available) and the publication year. If an article is initialed, check the index of authors (often in the opening section of each volume) for the author's full name.

> "Technical Education." *Encyclopedia Americana.* 2001 ed. Print.

> Lum, P. Andrea. "Computed Tomography." *World Book.* 2000 ed. Print.

When citing a single definition of several listed, add the abbreviation *Def.* and the particular number or letter for that definition.

> "Macaroni." Def. 2b. *The American Heritage College Dictionary.* 4th ed. 2002. Print.

20. **An Article in an Unfamiliar Reference Book**

For citations of lesser-known reference works, give full publication information.

> "S corporation." *The Portable MBA Desk Reference.* Ed. Paul A. Argenti. New York: Wiley, 1994. Print.

21. **A Government Publication**

State the name of the government followed by the name of the agency. Most US federal publications are published by the Government Printing Office (GPO).

> United States. Dept. of Labor. Bureau of Labor Statistics. *Occupational Outlook Handbook: 2008-09 Library Edition.* Washington: GPO, 2008. Print.

When citing the *Congressional Record,* only the date and page numbers are required.

> *Cong. Rec.* 5 Feb. 2002: S311-15. Print.

22. **A Book with a Title within Its Title**

If the title contains a title normally in quotation marks, keep the quotation marks and italicize the entire title.

> Stuckey-French, Elizabeth. *"The First Paper Girl in Red Oak, Iowa" and Other Stories.* New York: Doubleday, 2000. Print.

If the title contains a title that is normally italicized, do not italicize that title within your entry, as shown with the Dickens novel in the title below:

> Beckwith, Charles E. *Twentieth Century Interpretations of* A Tale of Two Cities: A Collection of Critical Essays. Upper Saddle River: Prentice Hall, 1972. Print.

23. A Sacred Text

The Bible and other such sacred texts are treated as anonymous books. Documentation should read exactly as it is printed on the title page.

> *The Jerusalem Bible.* Garden City: Doubleday, 1966. Print.

24. The Published Proceedings of a Conference

The published proceedings of a conference should be treated as a book. However, if the title of the publication does not identify the conference by title, date, and location, add the appropriate information immediately after the title.

> Reynolds, Patricia, and Glen GoodKnight, eds. *Proceedings of the J. R. R. Tolkien Centenary Conference.* 17-24 Aug. 1992, Oxford, England. Altadena: Mythopoeic P, 1995. Print.

To cite a particular presentation from the published proceedings of a conference, treat it as a work in an anthology.

> Greene, Deirdre. "Higher Argument: Tolkien and the Tradition of Vision, Epic and Prophecy." *Proceedings of the J. R. R. Tolkien Centenary Conference.* Ed. Patricia Reynolds and Glen GoodKnight. 17-24 Aug. 1992, Oxford, England. Altadena: Mythopoeic P, 1995. 43-52. Print.

25. A Published Dissertation

An entry for a published dissertation contains the same information as a book entry, with a few added details. Add the abbreviation *Diss.* and the degree-granting institution before the publication facts and medium. You may also add the order number at the end of the entry, if the work was published by University Microfilms International.

> Jansen, James Richard. *Images of Dostoevsky in German Literary Expressionism.* Diss. U of Utah, 2003. Ann Arbor: UMI, 2003. AAT 3084161. Microfilm.

26. An Unpublished Dissertation

The entry for an unpublished dissertation lists author, title in quotation marks, the degree-granting institution, the year of acceptance, and the medium. (For a master's thesis, use *MA thesis* or *MS thesis* rather than *Diss.*)

> Vaidhyanathan, Siva. "Unoriginal Sins: Copyright and American Culture." Diss. U of Texas, 1999. Print.

27. An Unpublished Essay

For an unpublished essay, list the author, the title of the work in quotation marks, the description *Unpublished essay,* the year it was written, and the medium.

> Carmichael, F. "Bukowski's Faith." Unpublished essay, 2010. Print.

28. A Pamphlet, Brochure, Manual, or Other Workplace Document
Treat any such publication as you would a book.

> Grayson, George W. *The North American Free Trade Agreement*. New York:
>   Foreign Policy Assn., 1993. Print.

If publication information is missing, list the country of publication [in brackets] if known. Use *n.p.* (no place) if the country or the publisher is unknown and *n.d.* if the date is unknown, just as you would for a book.

> *Pedestrian Safety*. [US]: n.p., n.d. Print.

Works-Cited Entries: Print Periodical Articles

Components

The possible components of these entries are listed in order below:

1. Author's name, last name first
2. Title of article, in quotation marks and headline style
3. Name of periodical, italicized
4. Series number or name, if relevant (not preceded by period or comma)
5. Volume number (for a scholarly journal)
6. Issue number, separated from volume with a period but no space
7. Date of publication (abbreviate all months but May, June, July)
8. Page numbers, preceded by a colon, without "p." or "pp." (For articles continued nonconsecutively, add a plus sign after the first page number.)
9. Medium of publication (Print)
10. Supplementary information, as needed

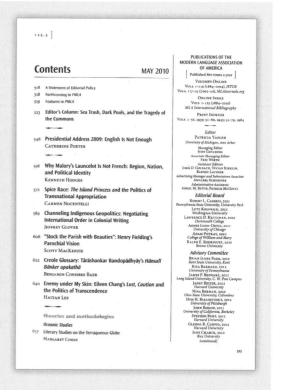

If any of these components do not apply, do not list them. The entries that follow illustrate the information and arrangement needed to cite most periodicals.

29. An Article in a Weekly or Biweekly Magazine

List the author (if identified), article title (in quotation marks), publication title (italicized), full date of publication, and page numbers for the article. Do not include volume and issue numbers.

> Green, Andy. "U2, Neil Young Films Rock Sundance." *Rolling Stone* 7 Feb. 2008: 20. Print.

30. An Article in a Monthly or Bimonthly Magazine

List the author (if identified), article title (in quotation marks), and publication title (italicized). Then identify the month(s) and year of the issue, followed by page numbers for the article. Do not give volume and issue numbers.

> Mead, Walter Russell. "Born Again." *Atlantic Monthly* Mar. 2008: 21-24. Print.

31. An Article in a Scholarly Journal

Scholarly journals are published less frequently than magazines (typically four times a year, or quarterly). Rather than using the month or full date of publication, scholarly journals are identified by volume number and issue number. List the volume number immediately after the journal title and a space, followed by a period and the issue number (with no space between). Then indicate the year of publication, with the issue month or season (all in parentheses). Follow with a colon and a space and end with the page span of the article. Finally, include the medium of publication.

> Sanchez, Melissa E. "Seduction and Service in *The Tempest*." *Studies in Philology* 105.1 (Winter 2008): 50-82. Print.

32. A Published Interview

Begin with the name of the person interviewed when that's whom you are quoting, followed by the title of the interview, the name of the interviewer (if known), and the publication details. If the interview is untitled, follow the interviewee's name with *Interview* (no italics and no quotation marks) and a period.

> Cantwell, Maria. "The New Technocrat." By Erika Rasmusson. *Working Woman* Apr. 2001: 20-21. Print.

33. A Newspaper Article

Cite the edition of a major daily newspaper (if given) after the date (3 Mar. 2008, Eastern ed.: C9). If a local paper's name does not include the city of publication, add it in brackets (not italicized) after the name. To cite an article in a lettered section of the newspaper, list the section and the page number. (For example, A4 would refer to page 4 in section A of the newspaper.) If the sections are numbered, however, use a comma after the year (or the edition); then indicate the section and follow it with a colon, the page number (sec. 1: 20), and the medium of publication you used.

> Segal, Jeff, and Lauren Silva. "Case of Art Imitating Life?" *Wall Street Journal* 3 Mar. 2008, Eastern ed.: C9. Print.

An unsigned newspaper article follows the same format:

> "Bombs—Real and Threatened—Keep Northern Ireland Edgy." *Chicago Tribune* 6 Dec. 2001, sec. 1: 20. Print.

34. A Newspaper Editorial

If an article is an unsigned editorial, put *Editorial* (no italics) and a period after the title.

> "Hospital Power." Editorial. *Bangor Daily News* 14 Sept. 2004: A6. Print.

35. A Letter to the Editor

To identify a letter to the editor, put *Letter* (no italics) and a period after the author's name.

> Sory, Forrest. Letter. *Discover* July 2001: 10. Print.

36. A Review of a Work or Event (Book, Film, CD, Concert, Art Show, etc.)

Begin with the review's author (if identified) and title. Use the notation *Rev. of* (no italics) between the title of the review and that of the original work or event. Identify the author or creator of the original work or event with the word *by.* Then follow with publication data for the review. If you cite the review of a work by an editor, translator, or director, use *ed., trans.,* or *dir.,* instead of *by.*

> Dillon, Brian. "Onion Pilfering." Rev. of *Divisadero,* by Michael Ondaatje. *London Review of Books* 13 Dec. 2007: 19-20. Print.

37. An Abstract

An abstract is a summary of a work. To cite an abstract, first give the publication information for the original work (if any); then list the publication information for the abstract itself. Add the term *Abstract* and a period between these if the journal title does not include that word. If the journal identifies abstracts by item number, include the word *item* (no italics) followed by the number. (Add the section identifier [A, B, or C] for those volumes of *Dissertation Abstracts [DA]* and *Dissertation Abstracts International [DAI]* that have one.) If no item number exists, list the page number(s).

> Faber, A. J. "Examining Remarried Couples through a Bowenian Family System Lens." *Journal of Divorce and Remarriage* 40.3/4 (2004): 121-133. *Social Work Abstracts* 40 (2004): item 1298. Print.

38. An Article with No Author Indicated (Unsigned)

If no author is identified for an article, list the entry alphabetically by title in your list of works cited (ignoring any initial *A, An,* or *The*).

> "Feeding the Hungry." *Economist* 371.8374 (2004): 74. Print.

39. An Article with a Title or Quotation within Its Title

If the article title has the title of another work within it, indicate that internal title with italics for a title normally italicized (e.g., novel, film) or with single quotation marks for a title normally put in quotation marks (e.g., a short story, a lyric poem, a song title).

Morgenstern, Joe. "Sleeper of the Year: *In the Bedroom* Is Rich Tale of Tragic Love." *Wall Street Journal* 23 Nov. 2001: W1. Print.

Lams, Victor J., Jr. "Ruth, Milton, and Keats's 'Ode to a Nightingale.'" *Modern Language Quarterly* 34.4 (Dec. 1973): 417-36. Print.

40. An Article Reprinted in a Loose-Leaf Collection

The entry begins with original publication information, including the publication medium, and ends with the name of the loose-leaf volume *(Youth)*, editor, volume number, publication information, including the name of the information service (SIRS), and the article number. (See entry 41 for an explanation of the plus sign in the example below.)

O'Connell, Loraine. "Busy Teens Feel the Beep." *Orlando Sentinel* 7 Jan. 1993: E1+. Print. *Youth.* Ed. Eleanor Goldstein. Vol. 4. Boca Raton: SIRS, 1993. Art. 41.

41. An Article with Pagination That Is Not Continuous

For articles that are continued on a nonconsecutive page, add a plus sign (+) after the page number where the article begins.

Garrett, Robyne. "Negotiating a Physical Identity: Girls, Bodies and Physical Education." *Sport, Education & Society* 9 (2004): 223+. Print.

Works-Cited Entries: Online Sources

Components

Citations for online sources follow a pattern similar to the one used for print sources. After the author's name and title of the work (either italicized or in quotes, depending on the type of work), include the title of the overall Web site in italics, and additional information as described below. Because URL's can change, the URL should be provided only if the reader probably cannot locate the source without it, or if your instructor requires it.

1. Author's name
2. Title of the article or work, italicized or in quotation marks
3. Title of the overall Web site, italicized (if different from item 2)
4. Version or edition used
5. Publisher or sponsor of the site; if not available, use *N.p.*
6. Date of publication (day, month, year, as available); if unknown, use *n.d.*
7. Medium of publication (Web)
8. Date of access (day, month, year)

42. A Site with a URL

If you must include a URL to guide the reader to a site (or because your instructor requires it), give the URL after the date of access, a period, and a space. Enclose it in angle brackets and follow it with a period. Give the complete address, including http://, for the work you are citing.

> MacLeod, Donald. "Shake-Up for Academic Publishing." *Guardian Unlimited.* Guardian News and Media Ltd., 10 Nov. 2008. Web. 6 Jan. 2010. <http://www.guardian.co.uk/Archive/>.

If the URL must be divided between two lines, break it only after a single or double slash. Do not add a hyphen.

> "Fort Frederica." *National Parks Service.* US Department of the Interior, n.d. Web. 27 Feb. 2010. <http://home.nps.gov/fofr/forteachers/curriculummaterials.htm>.

43. A Nonperiodical Publication

Most items online are not posted on a regular schedule; they are nonperiodical, unlike magazines, newspapers, and scholarly journals. Business pages, blog entries, PDF documents, online books, audio or video posts, and a host of other postings are nonperiodical publications. This includes most Web sites sponsored by magazines and newspapers. Such items can be identified following the guidelines on the previous page. (For guidelines regarding scholarly journals or periodical publications in an online database, see works-cited 46 below.)

44. A Scholarly Journal

Many scholarly journals are published only on the Web, with no print version. For such publications, follow the basic guidelines given for print periodicals (page 392), though conclude with *Web* instead of *Print,* followed by your date of access. Also, if no page numbers are given, or if each item in the journal is numbered separately, replace the normal page notation with *n. pag.*

45. A Scholarly Project or Information Database

Begin with the name of the author, compiler, or editor and follow with the title of the project or database. Next give the title of the Web site, if it is distinct from the project title, the version or edition used, the sponsor, and the posting date. Finally, include the medium of publication (Web) and your date of access.

> Salda, Michael, ed. *The Little Red Riding Hood Project.* Vers. 1.1. U of Southern Mississippi, Oct. 2005. Web. 5 Nov. 2009.

46. A Periodical Publication in an Online Database

To cite an article from a database, begin your citation with the usual information for citing print periodicals, but drop the medium of original publication (Print). Instead, include the title of the database (italicized), the medium of publication (Web), and the date of access.

> Davis, Jerome. "Massacre in Kiev." *Washington Post* 29 Nov. 1999, final ed.: C12. *ProQuest.* Web. 30 Nov. 2008.

47. Items Existing Only Online

Many publications exist only in online form. Because such publications can move unexpectedly, it is important to include enough information for your reader to locate them again regardless of their new location.

a. *A Typical Online Item*

> Booth, Philip. "Robert Frost's Prime Directive." *Poets.org.* Academy of American Poets, n.d. Web. 1 Oct. 2009.

b. *An Online Item, No Author Identified*

Begin with the title of the work, in quotation marks or italics, as appropriate. Alphabetize this entry by the first significant word of the title ("NetDay" in this case).

> "NetDay AmeriCorps Bridge Program 2001-2003." *NetDay.* Project Tomorrow, n.d. Web. 25 Nov. 2009.

c. *A Home Page*

If a nonperiodical publication has no title, identify it with a descriptor such as *Home page, Introduction,* or *Online posting* (using no italics or quotation marks). You may add the name of the publication's creator or editor after the overall site title, if it is not identified elsewhere in the entry.

> Wheaton, Wil. Home page. *Wil Wheaton dot Net.* N.p., 31 May 2006. Web. 19 Mar. 2009.

d. *An Online Item with a Compiler, an Editor, or a Translator*

When alphabetizing an entry by its compiler, editor, or translator, treat that person's name as usual, followed by an abbreviation for her or his role. If an author is identified, however, the compiler, editor, or translator follows the item title, with the abbreviation for the role preceding the compiler, editor, or translator's name.

> Webster, Michael, comp. "Books and Articles Cited in 'Notes on the Writings of E. E. Cummings.'" *Spring.* E. E. Cummings Society, n.d. Web. 4 Oct. 2009.

> Lao-tzu. *Tao Te Ching.* Trans. J. Legge. *Internet Sacred Text Archive.* John Bruno Hare, n.d. Web. 14 Apr. 2009.

e. *An Entry in an Online Reference Work*

Unless the author of the entry is identified, begin with the entry name in quotation marks. Follow with the usual online publication information.

> "Eakins, Thomas." *Encyclopaedia Britannica Online.* Encyclopaedia Britannica, 2008. Web. 26 Sept. 2008.

f. *An Online Poem*

List the poet's name, the title of the poem, and any print publication information before the electronic publication details.

> Nemerov, Howard. "Found Poem." *War Stories.* U of Chicago P: 1987. *Poets.org.* Web. 5 Oct. 2007.

48. Online Postings of Art, Other Media, and Manuscripts

For online postings of photographs, videos, sound recordings, works of art, and so on, follow the examples on pages 399–400. In place of the original medium of publication, however, include the title of the database or Web site (italicized), followed by the medium (Web) and the date of access, as for other online entries.

a. *A Work of Art*

Goya, Francisco de. *Saturn Devouring His Children.* 1819-1823. Museo Nacional del Prado, Madrid. *Museodelprado.es.* Web. 13 Dec. 2008.

b. *A Photograph*

Brumfield, William Craft. *Church of Saint Nicholas Mokryi.* 1996. Prints and Photographs Div., Lib. of Cong. *Brumfield Photograph Collection.* Web. 9 May 2009.

c. *An Audio Recording*

"Gildy Arrives in Summerfield." *The Great Gildersleeve.* NBC. 31 Aug. 1941. *EThomsen.com.* Web. 13 Apr. 2009.

d. *A Video*

Sita Sings the Blues. Prod. Nina Paley. 2008. *Internet Archive.* Web. 5 June 2008.

e. *An Unpublished Manuscript*

"The Work-for-All Plan." 1933. Mildred Hicks Papers. Manuscript, Archives, and Rare Book Lib., Emory U. *Online Manuscript Resources in Southern Women's History.* Web. 31 Jan. 2009.

Works-Cited Entries: Other Sources (Primary, Personal, and Multimedia)

The following examples of works-cited entries illustrate how to cite sources such as television or radio programs, films, live performances, works of art, e-mails, and other miscellaneous nonprint and non-Web sources.

49. A Periodically Published Database on CD-ROM or DVD-ROM

Citations for materials published on CD-ROM or DVD-ROM are similar to those for print sources, with these added considerations: (1) The contents of a work may vary from one medium to another; therefore, the citation should always identify the medium. (2) The publisher and vendor of the publication may be different, in which case both must be identified. (3) Because of periodic updates, multiple versions of the same database may exist, which calls for citation, if possible, of both the date of the document cited and the date of the database itself.

Ackley, Patricia. "Jobs of the Twenty-First Century." *New Rochelle Informer* (15 Apr. 1994): A4. CD-ROM. *New Rochelle Informer Ondisc.* Oct. 1994.

Baker, Anthony. *The New Earth Science.* Cincinnati: Freeman's P, 1991. DVD-ROM. New Media Inc. 2004.

50. Reference Work on CD-ROM

If you use an encyclopedia or other reference book recorded on CD-ROM, use the form below. If available, include publication information for the printed source.

> *The American Heritage Dictionary of the English Language.* 3rd ed. Boston: Houghton-Mifflin, 1992. CD-ROM. Cambridge: SoftKey Intl. 1994.

51. A Television or Radio Program

Include the medium (*Television* or *Radio*) at the end, followed by a period.

> "U.S. Health Care Gets Boost from Charity." *60 Minutes.* CBS. WBBM, Chicago, 28 Feb. 2008. Television.

52. A Film

The director, distributor, and year of release follow the title. Other information may be included if pertinent. End with *Film*, the medium, followed by a period.

> *Atonement.* Dir. Joe Wright. Perf. James McAvoy and Keira Knightley. Universal Pictures, 2007. Film.

53. A Video Recording or an Audio Recording

Cite a filmstrip, slide program, videocassette, or DVD as you do a film; include the medium of publication last, followed by a period.

> *Monet: Shadow & Light.* Devine Productions, 1999. Videocassette.

To cite a song on a recording, put its title in quotations before the recording title.

> Bernstein, Leonard. "Maria." *West Side Story.* Columbia, 1995. CD.

54. A Performance

Treat this similarly to a film, adding the location and date of the performance.

> *Chanticleer: An Orchestra of Voices.* Young Auditorium, Whitewater, WI. 23 Feb. 2003. Performance.

55. A Work of Art on Display

> Titian. *The Entombment.* N.d. Painting. Louvre, Paris.

56. An Unpublished E-Mail, Letter, or Memo

Include the writer, any title, the type of correspondence and recipient, the date, and the form. Use *TS* for a typescript or printout, *MS* for a work written by hand, and *E-mail* for electronic correspondence. For memos and e-mail, use the subject line as the title.

> Thomas, Bob. Letter to the author. 10 Jan. 2008. TS.

> Horvath, Andrea. "Re: Online Health Records Access." Message to the author. 21 Mar. 2010. E-mail.

57. An Interview by the Author (You)

> Brooks, Sarah. Personal interview. 15 Oct. 2008.

58. A Cartoon or Comic Strip (in Print)

Luckovich, Mike. "The Drawing Board." Cartoon. *Time* 17 Sept. 2001: 18. Print.

59. An Advertisement (in Print)

List the subject of the advertisement (product, company, organization, or such), followed by *Advertisement* and a period. Then give the usual publication information.

> Vaio Professional Notebooks. Advertisement. *Campus Technology* Oct. 2004: 45. Print.

60. A Lecture, a Speech, an Address, or a Reading

Provide the speaker's name, the title of the presentation (if known) in quotation marks, the meeting and the sponsoring organization, the location, and the date. End with an appropriate descriptive label such as *Address, Lecture,* or *Reading.*

> Annan, Kofi. "Acceptance of Nobel Peace Prize." Oslo City Hall, Oslo, Norw. 10 Dec. 2001. Speech.

61. A Legal or Historical Document

If your paper requires a number of legal citations, the MLA advises consulting the most recent edition of *The Bluebook: A Uniform System of Citation* (Cambridge: Harvard Law Rev. Assn.; Print). If you are providing only a few such citations, the MLA provides that the titles of laws, acts, and similar documents should appear in regular type (not italicized or enclosed in quotation marks), both within the text and in the list of works cited. The titles are abbreviated, and works are cited by sections, with years included if relevant. End your citation with the medium of publication followed by a period.

> 7 USC. Sec. 308a. 1928. Print.

> Do-Not-Call Implementation Act. Pub. L. 108-10. Stat. 117-557. 11 Mar. 2003. Print.

Abbreviate the names of law cases (spelling out the first important word of each party's name). Do not italicize the name in your works-cited list (although it should be italicized within the body of your paper). Follow with the case number or volume, inclusive page or reference numbers, the name of the court, the date (or year) of the decision, and the publication information for the medium consulted, including the date of access for a Web site.

> Missouri v. Seibert. 02-1371. Supreme Court of the US. 28 June 2004. *FindLaw. com.* Web. 4 June 2009.

62. A Map or Chart

Follow the format for an anonymous book, adding *Map* or *Chart* (without italics), followed by a period, the city and publisher, date, and the medium of publication.

> *Wisconsin Territory.* Map. Madison: Wisconsin Trails, 1988. Print.

MLA Format Guidelines

The MLA system offers guidelines not only for documentation but also for the paper's format. Follow the rules on the next five pages, but also check whether your instructor has other format expectations.

FOCUS on Multimedia: Use your word-processing software to preset many of these format features. Create a template for yourself or find one on our Web site at www.theresearchwriter.com.

MLA Format at a Glance

First-Page Format

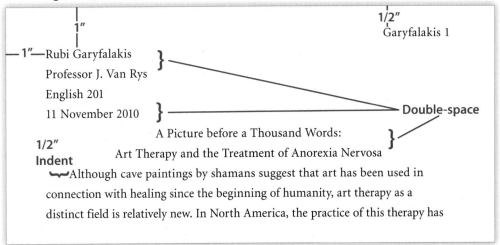

1"

1/2"
Garyfalakis 1

1"—Rubi Garyfalakis
Professor J. Van Rys
English 201
11 November 2010

} → Double-space

1/2"
Indent

A Picture before a Thousand Words:
Art Therapy and the Treatment of Anorexia Nervosa

↪Although cave paintings by shamans suggest that art has been used in connection with healing since the beginning of humanity, art therapy as a distinct field is relatively new. In North America, the practice of this therapy has

Format of Pages within the Paper

1"

1/2"
Garyfalakis 4

Double-space

{ and Paul H. Robinson describe the somatic parallel between anorexia and art therapy when they write, "Like the pathological expression of [issues] through

—1"—

Format for the Works-Cited List

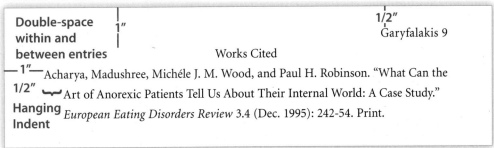

Double-space
within and
between entries

1"

1/2"
Garyfalakis 9

Works Cited

—1"—Acharya, Madushree, Michéle J. M. Wood, and Paul H. Robinson. "What Can the

1/2" ↪Art of Anorexic Patients Tell Us About Their Internal World: A Case Study."

Hanging *European Eating Disorders Review* 3.4 (Dec. 1995): 242-54. Print.
Indent

Whole-Paper Format and Printing Issues

The table below offers directions for setting up the parts of your paper and printing it for submission. Pages in the left column refer to the sample MLA paper later in this chapter.

Running Head and Pagination 410	1. Number pages consecutively in the upper-right corner, one-half inch from the top and flush with the right margin (1 inch). 2. Use numerals only—without *p.*, *page*, *#*, or any other symbol. 3. Include your last name on each page, typed one space before the page number. (Your name identifies the page if the page becomes misplaced.) Note: Your word-processing program should be able to combine the running head and pagination automatically.
Heading on First Page 410	Include the following four pieces of information, typed flush left and double-spaced, one inch from the top: 1. Your name, both first and last in regular order 2. Your professor's or instructor's name (presented as he or she prefers, with appropriate title—*Dr., Professor*) 3. The course name and number, plus the section number if appropriate (e.g., History 100-05) Follow your instructor's directions. 4. The date that you are submitting the paper, using the international format (e.g., 11 September 2010) Note the order, lack of punctuation, the complete year, and the complete spelling of the month.
Paper Title 410	1. Double-spaced below the heading, center your paper's title. 2. Do not italicize, underline, or boldface the title; do not put it in quotation marks or all caps, or use a period (though a question mark may be acceptable if warranted). 3. Follow standard capitalization practices for titles (see pages 407–408). 4. If your title has the title of a work within it, follow practices for quotation marks and italics outlined on page 407.
Works-Cited List 418	Format your works-cited list according to these guidelines: 1. Start the list on a new page immediately after your paper's conclusion (or, if applicable, after the "Notes" page—see page 405). 2. Continue the running head and pagination. 3. Center the heading "Works Cited" one inch from the top of the page; don't use quotation marks, underlining, boldface, or any other typographical markers. 4. Begin your list of works cited two spaces below the heading. Arrange all entries alphabetically by the authors' last names; for sources without identified authors, alphabetize using the work's title, ignoring *a, an*, or *the*. 5. If you are listing two or more works by the same author, alphabetize them by the titles of the works. Use the author's name for the first entry; in second and subsequent entries, replace the author's name with three hyphens.

6. Start each entry flush left; indent second and subsequent lines for specific entries one-half inch or five spaces. Use your word-processing program's hanging indent feature. (This format allows readers to easily scan the list for specific sources.)
7. Follow standard rules for capitalization, italics, quotation marks, and punctuation.
8. Double-space within and between all entries.
9. Do not repeat the "Works Cited" heading if your list runs longer than one page.

Paper Size	Print on standard 8.5- by 11-inch paper.
Paper Weight or Quality	Use quality 20 lb. bond paper. Avoid both thin, erasable paper and heavy card stock. Similarly, stick with standard white or off-white paper—no neons, pastels, letterheads, or scents.
Print Quality	1. Use a laser or inkjet printer to create a crisp, clean copy; avoid using nearly empty print cartridges. 2. Avoid submitting a paper with handwritten corrections; however, if you must make a change, make a caret symbol (^), put a single clean line through words that must be dropped, and write additions above the line.
Binding	As a first choice, use a paper clip. A single staple (upper left corner) may also be acceptable. Avoid fancy covers or bindings and never simply fold over the corners
Single-Sided Printing	Print your essay single-sided. Do double-sided printing only with your instructor's permission.
Electronic Submission or Posting	If your instructor accepts or encourages electronic submission, follow his or her guidelines concerning these issues: 1. **Mode of submission:** e-mail attachment, flash drive, and so on 2. **Pagination/reference markers:** If your document will not have stable page numbers, number the paragraphs. Place the paragraph number in brackets, follow with a space, and then begin the paragraph. 3. **Internet addresses:** If you've included URLs, reverse the MLA print practice of putting them in angle brackets; instead, make URLs live links.

Typographical Issues

Typeface	Choose a standard *serif* typeface like Times New Roman. (Serif type, for example, the type you're reading, has finishes on each letter, as opposed to sans serif, like this.) Avoid unusual, hard-to-read typefaces.
Type Size	Use a readable type size, preferably 12 points, throughout the paper.
Type Styles (underlining, italics, bold, etc.)	1. Use italics (not underlining) for titles of resources and individual words requiring this feature. An exception may be an online publication or posting; consult your instructor. 2. Avoid using boldface, yellow highlighting, all caps, and so on.

Page-Layout Issues

Margins	Set margins top and bottom, left and right at one inch, with the exception of the running head (one-half inch from top).
Line Spacing	Double-space the entire paper—including the heading and works-cited entries, as well as tables, captions, and inset quotations.
Line Justification	Use left justified throughout, except for the running head (right justified) and the title and works-cited heading (both centered). Leave the right margin ragged.
Word Hyphenation	Avoid hyphenating words at the ends of lines; in your word processor, turn off this tool.
Spacing After Punctuation	Use one space after most forms of punctuation, including end punctuation—but not before or after a dash or a hyphen.
Paragraph Indenting	Indent all paragraphs five spaces (one-half inch).
Longer (Inset) Quotations (See pages 382–383.)	1. Indent 10 spaces (one inch) verse quotations longer than three lines and prose quotations longer than four typed lines. 2. Use no quotation marks, and place the parenthetical citation after the closing punctuation. 3. With a verse quotation, make each line of the poem or play a new line; do not run the lines together. Follow the indenting and spacing in the verse itself. 4. To quote two or more paragraphs, indent the first line of each paragraph three spaces (one-quarter inch) in addition to the 10 spaces (one inch) for the whole passage. However, if the first sentence quoted does not begin a paragraph in the source, do not make the additional indent. Indent only the first lines of subsequent paragraphs.
Tables and Illustrations	Position tables, illustrations, and other visuals near your discussion of them—ideally, immediately after your first reference to the graphic, whether pasted in after a paragraph or positioned on a separate following page. Observe these rules: 1. **Tables:** Identify all tables using "Table," an arabic numeral, and a caption (descriptive title). Both the identifying headings and captions should be flush left, appropriately capitalized. Provide source information and explanatory notes below the table. Identify notes with superscript lowercase letters, not numerals. Double-space throughout the table. 2. **Illustrations:** Number and label other visuals (graphs, charts, drawings, photos, maps, etc.) using "Figure" or "Fig.," an arabic numeral (followed by a period), and a title or caption one space after the period—all flush left below the illustration, along with source information and notes.

Note: For specific rules related to capitalizing and punctuating titles of resources, see pages 407–408.

Endnotes and Footnotes in MLA Documentation

Generally, MLA in-text citation makes endnotes or footnotes unnecessary. Nevertheless, in advanced research papers, consider using two kinds of notes.

Content Notes

Develop a note to share information indirectly related to your discussion—material that would interrupt the flow of your paper, but that the curious reader might appreciate.

Sentence in Paper:

> Once bacteria have gained antibiotic resistant abilities through genetic mutations, they often pass the mutations on to other cells.[1]

Footnote or Endnote:

> [1] This transfer of mutated genetic material from antibiotic-resistant bacteria occurs by any of three bacterial mechanisms. . . .

Bibliographic Notes

Use a note that supplies extra information about sources to (1) offer evaluative comments and (2) supply additional references for your discussion.

Sentence in Paper:

> Programs like the CDC's National Campaign for Appropriate Antibiotic Use are trying to raise awareness of antibiotic resistance and its threat to health care.[2]

Footnote or Endnote:

> [2] For additional information about this program, visit <http://www.cdc.gov/drugresistance/community/#campaign>.

Format for Endnotes

MLA style recommends endnotes over footnotes. Follow these guidelines:

1. Superscript Numbers: Number notes consecutively using Arabic numerals, raised slightly and placed preferably at the end of a sentence outside the closing punctuation.
2. Endnotes: Collect notes on a separate page before the works-cited list.
   - Include your running head (last name and page number) in the upper right.
   - Center the word "Notes" (no bold, italics, etc.) one inch from the top of the page.
   - Arrange your notes sequentially (not alphabetically like works-cited entries).
   - Double-space within and between all notes.
   - For each note, indent 5 spaces or one-half inch, type the number slightly raised (as a superscript), leave one space, and then start your note. Keep second and subsequent lines of a note flush left (not indented).

Note: Within the works-cited list, include full information about any source mentioned in a note.

In-Text Abbreviations in MLA Format

Recognizable abbreviations offer writers and readers convenient shorthand for communicating information. However, in the body of your paper, restrict your use of abbreviations by following the guidelines below and using the forms that follow.

Note: For guidelines on using abbreviations in works-cited entries, see pages 384–385.

General Guidelines for In-Text Abbreviations

Follow these general guidelines for using abbreviations within the body of your research paper:

- Generally avoid abbreviations within the text of your paper: such shorthand detracts from the polish of your prose.
- Use standard abbreviations in citations, tables, illustrations, endnotes, footnotes, and your works-cited list.
- Follow appropriate punctuation and capitalization practices—which differ from one abbreviation to the next, as shown in the tables.
- Always be guided by the reader's need to clearly understand. If your reader won't recognize an abbreviation, don't use it.

Acceptable In-Text Abbreviations

The abbreviations below may be acceptable in the text of your research paper, report, or other document. To be sure, check your instructor's requirements.

Signal Abbreviations

e.g.	for example; *exempli gratia* (followed by a comma)
i.e.	that is; *id est* (preceded and followed by commas)
sic	thus in the source (used within brackets to indicate that an error in a quotation is from the original source)
vs. (v.)	versus (*v.* preferred in legal-case titles)

Temporal Terms

AD	after the birth of Christ; *anno Domini* (placed before numerals but after century references)
CE	common era (after numerals and century references)
BC	before Christ (after numerals and century references)
BCE	before the common era (after numerals and century references)
a.m.	before noon; *ante meridiem*
p.m.	after noon; *post meridiem*
c.	approximately (for date); *circa*

Tip: Avoid using *etc.* (from Latin *et cetera,* meaning *and so forth*) in your writing; this abbreviation signals incompleteness in your thinking and the discussion.

Conventions for Names, Titles, and Internet Addresses

MLA style includes a number of practices addressing the presentation of names, titles, and Internet addresses. Here are essential guidelines:

Names of People

With the names of people, whether real people or fictional characters, consider first and subsequent uses of names:

First Use: Present the person's name in full exactly as it appears in the source, generally minus any formal title (e.g., *Dr., Professor, Mr., Mrs.*). For quite famous writers and artists, you may use the last name alone, for even first references (e.g., *Shakespeare*). For literary texts, refer to the character as the text does.

Subsequent Uses: Refer to the person by last name only, not by the full name and not by first name alone (e.g., *Jane Austen* becomes *Austen,* not *Jane* or *Miss Austen*). If two people or characters have the same last name, you may use first names to distinguish persons, as needed. For literary characters, shorten the name (last or first) in a way that fits with the text's use of the character's name (e.g., *Elizabeth Bennet* becomes *Elizabeth* or *Lizzy,* not *Bennet*).

Examples:	*first use*	*subsequent uses*
	Toni Morrison	Morrison (not Toni, not Ms. Morrison)
	C. S. Lewis	Lewis (not Clive, not Professor Lewis)
	Victor J. Lams, Jr.	Lams (not Lams, Jr., not Victor)
	Miss Havisham	Havisham

Capitalization and Punctuation of Titles

Whether you use the title of a source in your paper or in the works-cited list, use the full title as it appears on a title page or in a table of contents—particularly for a first reference in your paper. (An exception would be the use of a short title in a parenthetical citation, when no author name is available.) The examples below illustrate the rules for capitalization and punctuation that follow.

Examples:	*Pride and Prejudice: An Authoritative Text, Background and Sources, Criticism*
	"The Passion Translated: Literary and Cinematic Rhetoric in *Pride and Prejudice* (2005)"
	Critical Companion to Jane Austen: A Literary Reference to Her Life and Work
	Jane Austen's Textual Lives: From Aeschylus to Bollywood
	"Trends in Adaptation: Will and Jane Go Celluloid"
	Adaptations: From Text to Screen, Screen to Text
	Flirting with Pride and Prejudice: *Fresh Perspectives on the Original Chick-Lit Masterpiece*
	"Filming Tourism, Portraying Pemberley"

1. **Capitalize all main words.** These include first and last words in both titles and subtitles, as well as nouns, pronouns, verbs, adjectives, adverbs, and subordinating conjunctions. When the title includes a hyphenated compound, capitalize the word after the hyphen as well.

2. **Do not capitalize secondary words within a title or subtitle.** These include articles, prepositions, coordinating conjunctions, and *to* in infinitives.

3. **Use punctuation consistent with these practices:**
   - Separate a title and a subtitle with a colon and one space.
   - If a title contains punctuation within it or ends with an exclamation mark or question mark, include that punctuation. Use such end punctuation between a title and subtitle rather than a colon.

4. **Italicize titles of major works.** These include books, plays, long poems published as books, all periodicals (newspapers, magazines, journals), Web sites, databases, films and broadcasts, works of art (paintings, sculptures). Note: Sacred texts such as the Bible and its books, the Koran, and the Talmud need not be italicized; however, specific editions should be italicized consistent with other published works. Similarly, important political documents, conference titles, series titles, and course titles need not be italicized. Here are common examples.

   Examples: *Pride and Prejudice* (novel or film)
   Jane Austen's Textual Lives (scholarly book)
   Eighteenth Century Fiction (journal title)

5. **Put titles of shorter works within quotation marks.** These include stories and poems published in larger works, periodical articles or articles within collections, pages within Web sites, specific episodes or broadcasts of a show or series, lecture titles, and songs (as opposed to longer musical compositions). Here are examples.

   Examples: "Ode to a Grecian Urn" (poem)
   "Carried Away" (short story)
   "From Page to Screen" (journal article)

Listing an Internet Address

In printed documents, Internet addresses and e-mail addresses should always be enclosed in angle brackets. Without these brackets, these addresses might otherwise be confusing because of their internal punctuation. <http://www.theresearchwriter.com>

Unfortunately, many modern word processors automatically convert such addresses to live hyperlinks, removing the angle brackets and adding an underline. To avoid this in your printed documents, either turn off the auto-formatting option in your word processor or cancel such formatting immediately after it occurs. (See your word processor's Help files to learn how.) If your instructor allows, live links may be used in electronic versions of your text.

Sample MLA Paper

Student writer Rubi Garyfalakis wrote "A Picture before a Thousand Words: Art Therapy and the Treatment of Anorexia Nervosa" as an analytical research paper for her expository writing class. You can use this model paper in three ways:

1. To study how a well-written humanities research paper builds a discussion from start to finish

2. To examine how sources are carefully integrated into research writing—a full-length example of the strategies discussed on pages 185-194

3. To see in detail the format and documentation practices of MLA style

 FOCUS on Multimedia: To see what Rubi's paper looks like on standard 8.5-by 11-inch pages, visit our Web site at www.theresearchwriter.com.

Writer's Reflection

When given the opportunity to write a research paper about a topic of my choice, I jumped at the chance to explore art therapy—a topic that had intrigued me since high school but that I knew little about. Once I began researching, I narrowed my focus to the use of art therapy in the treatment of anorexia nervosa, a topic that held personal significance to me as an art student with a close friend who suffers from anorexia. This complex topic taught me the importance of clarity in writing. As I struggled to explain difficult concepts, I learned that imagery and example can be applied to academic writing as effective tools for definition and explanation. Through the process of researching, organizing, and writing an analytical essay, I was forced to wrestle with the complex ideas and to seek thorough understanding. As a result of this in-depth process, I became so interested in and excited about art therapy that I decided to change my future plans and to pursue art therapy as a career.

—Rubi Garyfalakis

Preparing to Read: What do you know about eating disorders? Have you studied their causes and treatments? What have you experienced of these disorders? As for art, have you been trained to make art? In what ways do you find art meaningful?

Sample First Page

Normally, an MLA research paper does not require a title page, an outline, or an abstract (summary). Instead, the paper begins with a page like the one below—with the running head (last name and page number), the heading, and the title as key identifying information. As you review the paper, notice the margin notes with page references: these references will take you to more complete discussions of the issues involved.

The running head (page 402) and heading (page 402) supply identifying details.

The title (centered) indicates the paper's topic and theme (page 402).

The first sentence puts the topic in context.

The writer focuses her topic and asks key questions that drive her paper.

The writer provides important background information and definitions.

Garyfalakis 1

Rubi Garyfalakis

Professor J. Van Rys

English 201

11 November 2010

A Picture before a Thousand Words:

Art Therapy and the Treatment of Anorexia Nervosa

Although cave paintings by shamans suggest that art has been used in connection with healing since the beginning of humanity, art therapy as a distinct field is relatively new. In North America, the practice of this therapy has increased over the last ten years as culture adopts a more holistic approach to well-being ("Art Therapy"). Treatment of the eating disorder anorexia nervosa is one specific area where art therapy is being successfully applied. Specifically, because art therapy expresses unconscious material through symbolization and abstraction, it presents a way to reestablish healthy modes of communication. But how exactly does anorexia nervosa represent an inability to successfully communicate? How are symbols in art able to reestablish that communication? And how does this art assist in the treatment of the eating disorder?

To answer these questions, it is first necessary to examine the nature of anorexia nervosa. The Diagnostic and Statistical Manual of Mental Disorders (DSM-III) lists anorexia nervosa as a psychiatric disorder characterized by the following: intense fear of becoming obese that does not decrease or disappear as weight is lost, disturbed body image (thinking of oneself as fat even when starving), weight loss of at least 25 percent of original body weight, refusal to maintain a minimal normal body weight for height and age, and no known physical illness to explain

Garyfalakis 2

weight loss (qtd. in Rabin 7). Patients develop disturbed eating patterns (starvation often alternating with binging and purging), resulting in other symptoms such as amenorrhea, a distorted feeling of fullness, and high energy despite low caloric intake ("Anorexia Nervosa"). Although these are physical characteristics and symptoms, less apparent psychological symptoms occur as well. Distorted body image produces feelings of ineffectiveness, low self-esteem, inner emptiness, depression, and failure ("Anorexia Nervosa"). Based on this psychological dimension of the disorder, psychiatrists Jane Wolf, Mary Willmuth, Thomas Gazda, and Alice Watkins explain that many theoretical perspectives identify anorexia nervosa as a concrete or physical way "to resolve a psychological issue or conflict" (197).

Developmental psychologist J. A. Sours suggests that the central issue of anorexia nervosa is "a failure in the developmental stage of separation-individuation" (Wolf et al. 198). This stage is defined as "the process by which internal maps of the self and of others are formed," a process that occurs between birth and three years and is based on both positive and negative interactions with caregivers ("Separation-Individuation"). Because verbal communication is not yet fully understood, the child believes that language is susceptible to distortion. Differences in tone often create inconsistency between literal and implied meaning. Consequently, a child's internal understanding of dynamics and relationships is based on kinesthetic, somatic (bodily), and spatial interactions (Wolf et al. 198). For example, a parent may gently remind a child to not touch the stove because it is hot and will burn. The literal sense of the verbal communication is "no," but the encouraging tone suggests "yes." The child may try to touch the stove, and it is not until the parent quickly blocks the action or the child feels the burn of the stove that he or she fully understands. The child's perception of his or her relationship with the parent in connection to the stove is based on the somatic interaction rather than the verbal communication. The goal of separation-individuation is to "integrate frustrating and pleasurable aspects of experiences" within relationships;

When the authors are named in an attributive phrase, the in-text citation includes only the page number.

In-text citations specify authors and page numbers for borrowed material: summaries, paraphrases, and quotations.

The writer clarifies a concept with an example.

Garyfalakis 3

Two sources are listed within one in-text citation to indicate a concept from both texts.

doing so leads to the development of a stable sense of self that can deal with changing emotional states within the self and others ("Separation-Individuation"). Failure to integrate different aspects of relationships can lead to the development of a mental disorder, such as anorexia nervosa ("Separation-Individuation"; Wolf et al. 198).

Since the anorectic experienced a problem with separation-individuation, he or she understands the internal world in a physical, spatial, somatic way. The patient tries to solve abstract issues concretely, attempting to master them by manipulating food intake and body shape (Wolf et al. 198). In effect, food is used as a way to mediate between the internal and external world. The abnormal eating habits are a way of unconsciously and nonverbally attempting to deal with issues that the anorectic feels incapable of understanding or expressing in an abstract way (such as through symbol or language). For example, a case study

A case study from a source makes a concept concrete through cause-effect reasoning.

by Wolf et al. found that many female anorectics had a controlling, overbearing mother (187-88). A possible explanation for this factor could be that the patients used the eating disorder as a way of resisting their mothers' control. Instead of asserting themselves by saying something, the patients manipulated food intake to tightly control their weight and body shape—something that a mother is unable to control. This process would occur unconsciously. The patient would not recognize that she is starving herself in an attempt to claim independence from her mother; rather, she would say that she is refusing to eat because she wants to lose weight. The result of this response is that anorectics struggle to acknowledge and own their feelings, and by extension they deny their underlying psychological problems (Wolf et al. 186). This denial, combined with the distorted internal map for understanding human emotion and interaction, makes it difficult for anorectics to connect with other people, thus contributing to their sense of loneliness and emptiness (Wolf et al. 191-96).

A strong transition links main sections of the paper.

Like eating disorders, art is a nonverbal physical expression of feelings that mediates between the inner and outer worlds (Johnson and Parkinson). Psychiatrists Madushree Acharya, Michéle J. M. Wood,

Garyfalakis 4

A first reference
to authors
provides their
full names;
subsequent
references use
last names only.

and Paul H. Robinson describe the somatic parallel between anorexia and art therapy when they write, "Like the pathological expression of [issues] through the illness, the patient is working through her body; the all-important difference is that art therapy is creative and non self-harming" (254). Art materials such as paint or clay are real physical substances that can, like food, be used and manipulated in many ways (Johnson and Parkinson). Art therapy gives the anorectic an opportunity to work with materials and to spontaneously make art. At the same time, psychotherapy is combined with this creative process to help the patient to explore and better understand aspects of the self ("Frequently Asked Questions"). Ideally, the artwork becomes an object of transference between the patient and therapist, "temporarily and unconsciously becom[ing] a substitute for the use of food" (Johnson and Parkinson).

Unpaginated
Web sources
are cited without
page numbers.

Art making can be substituted for abnormal eating because it involves the unconscious and, through symbol, exposes issues hidden there. Freud suggested that the unconscious speaks in images rather than words, a concept on which he based his theories about dream analysis (Rabin 25). He identified three separate parts to a dream: the first is the latent dream content, the unconscious thoughts and desires; the second is the dream work, the unconscious mental operations that turn the latent dream into the manifest dream; and the third is the manifest dream, the conscious experience during sleep. When dreams are interpreted, it is the latent content that is understood to be the meaning and the manifest dream is interpreted symbolically as a way of expressing that meaning (Rabin 24). This same idea can be easily applied to art. Spontaneously created art produces dreamlike material that is both conscious and unconscious (or manifest and latent). The conscious content of the artwork is the actual image, and the unconscious content involves elements such as the amount of art materials used, the colors chosen, the size and placement of objects within the work, the use of the page, or the description of what the picture represents. Hence, the artwork contains both the latent and manifest content, and the dream work is ongoing and changeable as the artwork is viewed and interpreted

Using an
authoritative
source, the
writer explains
the connections
between dreams,
symbols, and art.

by different individuals (Rabin 25).

Margaret Naumburg, one of the pioneers of American art therapy, writes that "art therapy tends to release deep unconscious material [very] quickly and, in consequence, helps to speed up the therapeutic process" (qtd. in Rabin 25). This therapy acceleration occurs because, when viewed in this way, the art-making process and the artwork produced can be interpreted as symbols of what is happening on the unconscious level. Child psychologist Edith Kramer reflects that "in adult life, art . . . [is] one of the few areas of symbolic living that remain accessible" (28). Making artwork allows inner conflicts or issues to be removed from the body by symbolizing them. Understanding and using these symbols is vital to anorectics because it helps them to recognize those underlying issues and to see how they try to deal with them through their abnormal eating habits (Wolf et al. 196). For example, the way that art materials are used can symbolize the artist's relationship with food. Art therapists Karen Johnson and Sarah Parkinson noted that one of their patients consistently used vast amounts of paint to quickly make a painting. Immediately after completing the piece, the patient would throw it in the garbage and run the water in the sink as she cleaned up her work area. This pattern symbolized how the patient was bulimic: she would eat a large amount of food in a short amount of time, but immediately afterward she would "cleanse" her body by vomiting (Johnson and Parkinson).

Not only the artistic process but also the artwork itself can be symbolically interpreted. An anorexic bulimic patient treated by art therapist Michéle Wood displayed precision and a sense of restraint in the way that she made her artwork; however, the images themselves suggested passiveness and a feeling of being out of control. This contrast symbolized the patient's inner tension between a desire for control and an intense feeling of ineffectiveness, a tension that is "a definitive feature of anorexia nervosa" (Acharya, Wood, and Robinson 252). Another reoccurring theme in the art of anorectics is an isolated figure often surrounded by dark colors or stormy weather, a theme that can be

---

The citation indicates that the source was quoted in another source.

Names and attributive phrases emphasize source credibility and credentials.

Garyfalakis 6

interpreted as symbolic of the depression and feelings of isolation that are commonly associated with this eating disorder (252). For example, figures 1 and 2 below show works of art created by two different anorectics. Both images illustrate isolation and a sense of despair through the desolate scenery, the body language of the figures, and the size of the figures in proportion to their surroundings.

Fig. 1: Drawing by anorexic patient C. L. from Lara Labriola, *Art as Therapy as Art* (Chicago: Windfeld, 2010; print; 296).

Fig. 2: Drawing by anorexic patient O. P. from Lara Labriola, *Art as Therapy as Art* (Chicago: Windfeld, 2010; print; 299).

As this expressive artwork reveals, the anorectic suffers not from an inability to experience emotion but rather from an inability to effectively identify and verbalize it (Wolf et al. 198). When feelings are symbolized in art, they can be touched, seen, and acknowledged. Artwork provides a consistent, permanent, neutral representation of emotion that the

When a second reference to a source follows shortly after the first, the authors' last names don't need to be repeated; the page number suffices.

Two sample visuals are referenced in the essay, and they are correctly labeled and sourced.

A source with more than three authors is indicated with "et al."

patient can associate with and talk about without feeling confused or threatened (199). By transferring emotions to artwork, anorectics can feel like they are more in control of the discussion; instead of talking about themselves and their own feelings, they can talk about those emotions symbolized in the artwork and the possible reasons behind them. Many people use the same strategy when they confess a personal problem or concern through the guise of "I have a friend who. . . ." Separating the problem from the self allows abstraction and distance so that the problem can objectively be evaluated and analyzed, without fear of judgment.

Moreover, the opportunity to discuss artworks helps anorectics to develop relationships. Johnson and Parkinson note that patients who participate in group art therapy often struggle to understand the unconscious communication of feelings in their own artwork, but they can identify it in the work of other group members. Through discussion, anorectics can learn from each other. As they verbally interpret visual symbols, they can begin to see their own feelings, and they eventually learn to recognize and experience emotion within their own bodies and relationships (Johnson and Parkinson).

Essentially, learning to understand symbols brings the physical expression of feelings to an abstract level, whereas the eating disorder's manifestation of emotion remains at the concrete level. This disjunction blocks interpersonal communication and keeps the patient isolated. However, art therapy facilitates socialization as it teaches anorectics to acknowledge, own, and effectively express their feelings (Johnson and Parkinson). Through the physical creation of art, the patient returns to the preverbal developmental stage of individuation and separation where understanding is based on physical expression. From here, symbolization transfers unconscious material from the patient to the artwork, creating a permanent, neutral, tangible space (Acharya, Wood, and Robinson 242). In this space, verbal communication can be initiated as patients objectively view and analyze their creations. Art therapists Wolf et al. describe this process when they conclude, "Our clinical

The writer effectively integrates multiple sources to advance her discussion.

sense has been that patients may use art as a bridge to verbal therapies; feelings, attitudes, and conceptions can be formulated, clarified, and symbolized in art before exposing them to the potential confusion and diffusion of talk" (199). Thus, art therapy is a valuable first step toward addressing psychological issues within anorectics. It begins treatment at an unconscious level that goes deeper than the external symptoms of abnormal eating. Most importantly, this process is encouraging because if psychological issues can be addressed and potentially resolved, it is likely that treatment can have long-term success (Rabin 9).

Creating pictures and discussing symbols offer anorectics a way to enter into their pain and joy, and to recognize and then experience the potential beauty of relationships, a means to be assured that they are not alone. As Murray Rabin explains, "Art therapy takes a person on a pilgrimage through the dark cave of his despair into an illumination of his spiritual side. It reawakens the creative force and inspires ethical being" (159). As verbal communication is reestablished for anorectics, their pictures become narrated by a thousand words. Here, in images and words, the story of healing and restoration can begin.

Source material is correctly presented in terms of punctuation and mechanics.

In the conclusion, the writer drives home her analysis with a particularly strong quotation.

The final sentences echo the writer's title.

Garyfalakis 9

Works Cited

Acharya, Madushree, Michéle J. M. Wood, and Paul H. Robinson. "What Can the Art of Anorexic Patients Tell Us About Their Internal World: A Case Study." *European Eating Disorders Review* 3.4 (Dec. 1995): 242-54. *Academic Search Premier.* Web. 16 Oct. 2010.

"Anorexia Nervosa." *Lambton Community Health Services Department.* County of Lambton, 26 Oct. 2002. Web. 6 Nov. 2010.

"Art Therapy: History and Philosophy." *Continuum Center for Health and Healing.* Beth Israel Medical Center, 22 Apr. 2005. Web. 6 Nov. 2010.

"Frequently Asked Questions." *The Canadian Art Therapy Association.* CATA, Nov. 2008. Web. 6 Nov. 2010.

Johnson, Karen, and Sarah Parkinson. "There's No Point Raging on Your Own: Using Art Therapy Groups for People with Eating Disorders." *Group Analysis* 32.1 (Mar. 1999): 87-96. *Academic Search Premier.* Web. 16 Oct. 2010.

Kramer, Edith. *Art as Therapy with Children.* New York: Schocken, 1971. Print.

Rabin, Murray. *Art Therapy and Eating Disorders.* New York: Columbia UP, 2003. Print.

"Separation-Individuation: Precursors to Differentiation." *Marriage and Family Encyclopaedia.* 2008. Web. 9 Nov. 2010.

Wolf, Jane M., et al. "The Role of Art in the Therapy of Anorexia Nervosa." *International Journal of Eating Disorders* 4.2 (May 1985): 185-200. *Academic Search Premier.* Web. 16 Oct. 2010.

The list of works cited begins on a separate page and includes the running head and centered heading.

Sources are listed in alphabetical order by author (or by title if no author is given).

Titles are properly italicized or placed in quotation marks.

Correct abbreviations are used throughout.

All sources indicate the medium (*Print, Web*).

MLA System: Activities

1. Print a copy of a research paper that you wrote earlier in your schooling. Using the instruction and information in this chapter, carefully edit the paper so that it follows current MLA guidelines for paper format, in-text citation, and works cited.

2. Study the sample paper on pages 409-418. Explain how effectively Rubi follows the overall philosophy and style of the MLA system in her writing: does she engage her sources and present them in such a way as to successfully develop her analysis and convince you of her credibility as a researcher?

3. Using the broad topics of the sample paper (eating disorders and therapies) as a starting point, do your own research and develop a works-cited page listing at least two sources from each of the works-cited categories in this chapter: print books, print periodical articles, online sources, and other sources (primary, personal, multimedia). Make sure that your works-cited page is correctly ordered and formatted.

4. For each of the sources that you found for activity 3 above, draft a brief passage in which you use the source (either through summary, paraphrase, or quotation). Make sure that the source is correctly cited according to MLA guidelines.

© Cengage Learning/Illustrated by Chris Krenzke

MLA System: Checklist

Checklist:

☑ All borrowed material is acknowledged with an appropriate attributive phrase and/or in-text citation indicating author and page number, as appropriate.

☑ All in-text citations effectively point the reader to resources in the works-cited list.

☑ The works-cited list includes entries for all works referred to in the body of the paper: no sources are missing from the list; no extra sources are listed that have no reference within the paper.

☑ The entire works-cited list is properly alphabetized by authors' last names (or by the first main word in the title for anonymous works).

☑ Each works-cited entry (whether for a print book, a print periodical article, an online source, or any other source) contains the maximum amount of identifying and publishing information (including medium, e.g., *Print, Web*), in the proper order, using the expected abbreviations.

☑ The entire paper is properly formatted: from the running head, heading, and title on the first page to the final works-cited entry.

- Placement, spacing, and margins are correct for the paper's running head (writer's last name and page number), the heading, the title, and "Works Cited" title.

- Pagination is correct and consistent.

- First lines of paragraphs and inset quotations are properly indented; works-cited entries are properly formatted with hanging indent.

- The paper is cleanly printed single-sided on quality paper in a professional-looking typeface and in 12-point type size (without fancy typestyle features).

- The paper is properly bound with a paper clip in the upper left corner.

APA Style
and Sample Paper

19

Q How do you format a paper in APA style? How do you document your research? In what disciplines is APA style used?

Because you're looking at this page, you've probably been told to submit an assigned research paper in APA style. This chapter will give you both an overview of the system (explaining its logic and principles) and specific guidelines and examples. Let's start with the basic questions below.

What Is the APA? APA stands for the American Psychological Association—the professional organization to which psychologists and psychology professors belong.

What Is APA Style? APA style refers to a method of documenting research and formatting a research paper—a method and format used in psychology and other social science disciplines (e.g., sociology, social work, education, business). In a nutshell, APA style offers guidelines for the following:

- **In-text citation**—the use of parenthetical references indicating authorship, publication date, and page-number references.
- **References**—a list of resources that you used in your paper.
- **Paper format**—title page, abstract, running head, margins, visuals, and so on.
- **Punctuation and mechanics rules**—from capitalization practices for titles to use of ampersands.

Where Can You Find More Information About APA Style? This chapter gives you much of what you need to know—drawn from official APA resources, namely the sixth edition of the *Publication Manual of the American Psychological Association* (2009) and the manual's website (www.apastyle.org). Consider, as well, checking your library's website and ours (www.theresearchwriter.com), where you will find additional links.

What's Ahead?

Directory to APA Documentation

If you have a specific question about APA in-text citations or references, use the directory below to find the answer you need.

APA Documentation: Quick Guide

The APA system involves two parts: (1) an in-text citation within your paper when you use a source and (2) a matching bibliographic entry at the end of your paper. Note these features of the APA author-date system:

- It uses signal phrases and parenthetical references to set off source material from your own thinking and discussion. A signal phrase names the author and places the material in context (e.g., "As Jung describes it, the collective unconscious . . .").
- It's date sensitive. Because the publication dates of resources are especially important in social science research, the publication year is included in the parenthetical reference and after the authors' names in the reference entry.
- It's smooth, unobtrusive, and orderly. APA in-text citations identify borrowed material while keeping the paper readable. Moreover, alphabetized reference entries at the end of the paper make locating source details easy.

You can see these features at work in the example below. The parenthetical material "Okazaki, 2002, pp. 34-35" tells the reader these things:

- The borrowed material came from a source authored by Okazaki.
- The source was published in 2002.
- The specific material can be found on pages 34-35 of the source.
- Full source details are in the reference list under the surname Okazaki.

1. In-Text Citation in Body of Paper

Perhaps unsurprisingly, the patriarchal nature of Asian cultures enforces sexual restrictions especially strictly on women, whose public sexual disclosures "would represent a threat to the highly interdependent social order as well as to the integrity of the family" (Okazaki, 2002, pp. 34-35).

2. Matching Reference Entry at End of Paper

Okazaki, S. (2002). Influences of culture on Asian Americans' sexuality. *Journal of Sex Research, 39*(1), 34-41.

In-Text Citation: The Basics

See pages 425–428 for complete details on in-text citation. Generally, however, refer to the author(s) and date of publication by using one of these methods:

Last name(s), publication date in parentheses:
The glucostatic theory seemed logical because glucose is the brain's primary fuel (Pinel, 2000).

Last name(s) cited in text with publication date in parentheses:
Research by Green, Elliman, and Rogers (1995, 1997) has found that food deprivation up to 24 hours does not significantly impair cognition.

Present and punctuate citations according to these rules:

- Keep authors and publication dates as close together as possible in the sentence.
- Separate the author's last name, the date, and any locating detail with commas.
- If referencing part of a source, use an appropriate abbreviation—*p.* (page), *para.* (paragraph)—but do not abbreviate *chapter.*

References: The Basics

Complete coverage of reference issues is offered on pages 429–438, and a sample reference list is shown on 451–452. Here, however, are some templates for the most common entries:

Template for Periodical Article:

Author's Last Name, Initials. (Publication Year). Title of article. *Journal Title,*
volume(issue), page numbers. [Other publication details are integrated as needed.
For an online periodical article, add the DOI—digital object identifier.]

authors' names, followed by period   publication year   article title, no quotation marks, first word capitalized

Abramson, P. R., & Imai-Marquez, J. (1982). The Japanese-American: A cross-cultural, cross-sectional study of sex guilt. *Journal of Research in Personality, 16*(2), 227-237. doi:10.1016/0092-6566(82)90078-2

journal title and volume number italicized   page numbers followed by period

Template for Book:

Author's Last Name, Initials. (Publication Year). *Title of book.* Publication City: Publisher. [Other publication details are integrated as needed.]

author's name, followed by period   publication year in parentheses, followed by period   exact and full title in italics, first word capitalized, followed by period

Chow, C. S. (1998). *Leaving deep water: The lives of Asian American women at the crossroads of two cultures.* New York, NY: Dutton, Penguin.

publication location from title page, followed by colon   publisher name from title page, followed by period

Template for Online Document:

Author's Last Name, Initials. (Publication Date). *Title of work* OR Title of entry. DOI (digital object identifier) OR Retrieval statement including URL

authors' names, followed by period   publication year in parentheses, followed by period   document title

UC Davis News Service. (2004). Student headcount by ethnicity. Retrieved from the News & Information section of the UC Davis website: http://facts.ucdavis.ed /student_headcount _ethnicity.lasso

retrieval statement

APA In-Text Citations

In APA style, you must cite your source in the text (in parentheses) each time you borrow from it. Below and on the following pages you'll find general guidelines for doing in-text citation, as well as instruction and examples for specific types of sources.

Guidelines for In-Text Citations

Each in-text citation, except for those referencing personal communications, must be matched to an entry in an alphabetized "References" list at the end of your paper. Each item in the reference list should, in turn, be cited in the text.

The Form of an Entry: The APA documentation style is sometimes called the "author-date" system because both the author and the date of the publication must be mentioned in the text when citing a source. Both might appear in the flow of the text, like this:

> Children in India are being trafficked for adoption, organ transplants, and labor such as prostitution, according to a 2007 article by Nilanjana Ray.

If either the author's name or date does not appear in the text, it must be mentioned within parentheses at the most convenient place (often within the sentence rather than at the end), like this:

> According to an article by Nilanjana Ray (2007), children in India . . .

> According to a recent article (Ray, 2007), children in India . . .

Other Points to Remember

1. When paraphrasing rather than quoting, make it clear where your borrowing begins and ends. Use stylistic cues to distinguish the source's thoughts ("Kalmbach points out . . . ," "Some critics argue . . .") from your own ("I believe . . . ," "It seems obvious, however . . .").

2. When using a shortened title of a work, begin with the word by which the work is alphabetized in your reference list. For example, with the title "Measurement of Stress in Fasting Man," use "Measurement of Stress," not "Fasting Man."

3. When including a parenthetical citation at the end of a sentence, place it before the end punctuation, as in this example: (Sacks, 1964).

Sample In-Text Citations

The following entries illustrate the most common sorts of in-text citations. For convenience, we have listed parallel reference-page entries for specific cases.

1. **One Author:** A Complete Work (reference 1, page 430)
   The correct form for a parenthetical reference to a single source by a single author is parenthesis, last name, comma, space, year of publication, parenthesis. Also note that final punctuation should be placed outside the parentheses.

   > . . . in this way, the public began to connect certain childhood vaccinations with an autism epidemic (Baker, 2008).

2. **One Author: Part of a Work**
When you cite a specific part of a source, give the page number, paragraph, or chapter, using the abbreviations *p., pp.,* or *para,* but do not abbreviate *chapter.* For other abbreviations, see page 430. Always give the page number for a direct quotation.

> . . . while a variety of political and scientific forces were at work in the developing crisis, it was parents who pressed the case "that autism had become epidemic and that vaccines were its cause" (Baker, 2008, p. 251).

3. **One Author: Two or More Publications in the Same Year**
If the same author has published two or more works in the same year, a small letter *a* is added to the year of the first work listed in the reference list, *b* to the year of the next work, and so on. (Determine the order in the reference list alphabetically by title.)

> **Parenthetical Citation:**
> Reefs harbor life forms heretofore unknown (Milius, 2001a, 2001b).
>
> **References:**
> Milius, D. (2001a). Another world hides inside coral reefs. *Science News, 160*(16), 244.
>
> Milius, D. (2001b). Unknown squids—with elbows—tease science. *Science News, 160*(24), 390.

4. **Works by Authors with the Same Last Name**
When citing different sources by authors with the same last name, add the authors' initials to avoid confusion, even if the publication dates are different.

> While J. D. Wallace (2005) argued that privatizing social security would benefit only the wealthiest citizens, others such as E. S. Wallace (2006) supported greater control for individuals.

5. **Two to Five Authors** (reference 2, page 430)
In the first reference in the text, all authors—up to as many as five—must be listed, like this:

> Love changes not just who we are, but who we can become, as well (Lewis, Amini, & Lannon, 2000).

Note: The last two authors' names are always separated by a comma and an ampersand (&) when enclosed in parentheses. However, if the authors are listed in the sentence itself, use the word *and*, not an ampersand.

For works with two authors, list both in every citation. For works with three to five authors, list all names the first time; after that, use only the name of the first author followed by "et al.," like this:

> These discoveries lead to the hypothesis that love actually alters the brain's structure (Lewis et al., 2000).

6. **Six or More Authors** (reference 2, page 430)

   If your source has six or more authors, refer to the work by the first author's name followed by "et al.," both for the first in-text reference and for all references after that. However, be sure to list all the authors (up to seven) in your references list.

   > According to a recent study, post-traumatic stress disorder (PTSD) continues to dominate the lives of Vietnam veterans, though in modified forms (Trembley et al., 2010).

7. **A Work Authored by an Agency, a Committee, or Other Organization** (reference 9, page 431) Treat the name of the group as if it were the last name of the author. If the name is long and easily abbreviated, provide the abbreviation in square brackets. Use the abbreviation without brackets in subsequent references, as follows:

   > **First Text Citation:**
   > A problem for many veterans continues to be heightened sensitivity to noise (National Institute of Mental Health [NIMH], 2005).

   > **Subsequent Citations:**
   > In addition, veterans suffering from PTSD continue to have difficulty discussing their experiences (NIMH, 2005).

8. **A Work with No Author Indicated** (reference 3, page 430)

   If your source lists no author, treat the first few words of the title (capitalized normally) as you would an author's last name. A title of an article or a chapter belongs in quotation marks; the titles of books or reports should be italicized:

   > ... including a guide to low-stress postures ("How to Do It," 2001).

9. **A Work Referred to in Another Work**

   > If you need to cite a source that you have found referred to in another source (a "secondary" source), mention the original source in your text. Then, in your parenthetical citation, cite the secondary source, using the words "as cited in."

   > ... theorem given by Ullman (as cited in Hoffman, 1998).

   Note: In your reference list at the end of the paper, you would write out a full citation for Hoffman (not Ullman).

10. **A Work in an Anthology** (reference 5, page 431)

    When citing an article or a chapter in an anthology or a collection, use the authors' names for the specific article, not the names of the anthology's editors. (Similarly, the article should be listed by its authors' names in the references section.)

    > Phonological changes can be understood from a variationist perspective (Guy, 2005).

11. An Electronic or Other Internet Source

As with print sources, cite an electronic source by the author (or by shortened title if the author is unknown) and the publication date (not the date you accessed the source). If citing a specific part of the source, use an appropriate abbreviation: *p.* for page and *para.* for paragraph, but do not abbreviate chapter.

> One study compared and contrasted the use of web and touch-screen transaction log files in a hospital setting (Nicholas, Huntington, & Williams, 2001).

12. A Website

Whenever possible, cite a website by its author and posting date. In addition, refer to a specific page or document rather than to a home page or a menu page. If you are referring to a specific part of a webpage that does not have page numbers, direct your reader, if possible, with a section heading and a paragraph number.

> According to the National Multiple Sclerosis Society (2003, "Complexities" section, para. 2), understanding of MS could not begin until scientists began to research nerve transmission in the 1920s.

13. Two or More Works in a Parenthetical Reference

Sometimes, it is necessary to include several citations in one parenthetical reference (i.e., your statement contains information or ideas drawn from more than one source). In that case, cite the sources as you usually would, separating the citations with semicolons. Place the citations in alphabetical order, as in the references list:

> Others report near-death experiences (Rommer, 2000; Sabom, 1998).

14. A Sacred Text or Famous Literary Work

Sacred texts and famous literary works are published in many different editions. For that reason, the original date of publication may be unavailable or not pertinent. In these cases, use your edition's year of translation (for example, *trans. 2003*) or indicate your edition's year of publication *(2003 version)*. When you are referring to specific sections of the work, it is best to identify parts, chapters, or other divisions instead of your version's page numbers. Books of the Bible and other well-known literary works may be abbreviated, if no confusion is possible.

> An interesting literary case of such dysfunctional family behavior can be found in Franz Kafka's *The Metamorphosis,* where it becomes the commandment of family duty for Gregor's parents and sister to swallow their disgust and endure him (trans. 1972, part 3).

15. Personal Communications (E-Mails, Letters, Phone Calls)

Personal communications may include personal letters, phone calls, e-mails, memos, and so forth. Because they are not published in a permanent form, APA style does not place them among the citations in your references list. Instead, cite them only in the text of your paper in parentheses, like this:

> . . . according to M. T. Cann (personal communication, April 1, 2010).
> . . . by today (M. T. Cann, personal communication, April 1, 2010).

APA References Entries

The first part of the APA documentation system, as shown on pages 425–428, involves in-text citations within your paper when you use a source. The second part of the system is the reference list at the end of your paper—an alphabetized list of bibliographic entries for all the resources that you have cited in your paper (with the exception of personal communications such as phone calls and e-mails). What follows are general guidelines for the reference list, as well as specific instructions and examples for books, periodical articles, online sources, and other sources. For a sample reference list, go to page 451.

General Guidelines for the Reference List

Begin your reference list on a new page after the last page of your paper. Number each reference page, continuing the numbering from the text. Then format your reference list by following these guidelines:

1. Type the running head flush left and the page number flush right, approximately one-half inch from the top of the page.

2. Center the title, *References,* approximately one inch from the top; then double-space before the first entry.

3. Begin each entry flush with the left margin. If the entry runs more than one line, indent additional lines approximately one-half inch (five to seven spaces) using a hanging indent.

4. Adhere to the following conventions about spacing, capitalization, and italics:
   - Double-space between all lines on the reference pages.
   - Use one space following each word and punctuation mark.
   - With book and article titles, capitalize only the first letter of the title (and subtitle) and proper nouns. (Note that this practice differs from the presentation of titles in the body of the essay.) Example: The impact of the cold war on Asia.
   - Use italics for titles of books and periodicals, not underlining.
   - Do not use quotation marks around article or entry titles.

5. List each entry alphabetically by the last name of the author, or, if no author is given, by the title (disregarding *A, An,* or *The*). For works with multiple authors, alphabetize by the name of the first author listed in the publication. When you are listing multiple works by the same author, arrange them by the year of publication, earliest first, as shown below. If the works were published in the same year, put a lowercase *a, b,* etc., beside the year, arranging such works alphabetically by title (see in-text citation 3, page 426).

   Sacks, O. (1995). *An anthropologist on Mars: Seven paradoxical tales.* New York, NY: Alfred A. Knopf.

   Sacks, O. (2007). *Musicophilia: Tales of music and the brain.* New York, NY: Alfred A. Knopf.

6. **Follow these conventions with respect to abbreviations:**
   - With authors' names, generally shorten first and middle names to initials, leaving a space after the period. For a work with more than one author, use an ampersand (&) before the last author's name.
   - For publisher locations, use the full city name plus the two-letter U.S. Postal Service abbreviation for the state. (For international publishers, include a province and country name.)
   - Spell out "Press" and "Books" in publishers' names, but for other publishing information, use the abbreviations that follow:

p. (pp.)	page (pages)	**ed.**	edition	**Vol.**	Volume
Ed. (Eds.)	Editor (Editors)	**Rev. ed.**	Revised edition	**Pt.**	Part
Trans.	Translator(s)	**n.d.**	no date	**Vols.**	Volumes
Tech. Rep.	Technical Report	**No.**	Number		
Suppl.	Supplement	**2ⁿᵈ ed.**	Second edition		

Reference Entries: Books and Other Documents

Here is the general form for a book or brochure entry:

authors' names,   publication year in parentheses,   publisher name from title
    followed by period   followed by period   page, followed by period

Author, A. (year). *Title.* Location: Publisher.

exact and full title in italics,   publication location from title
first word capitalized,   page, followed by colon
followed by period

For a single chapter of a book, follow this form:

Author, A., & Author, B. (year). Title of chapter. In *Title of book* (pp. xx–xx). Location: Publisher.

1. A Book by One Author

Kuriansky, J. (2007). *Beyond bullets and bombs: Grassroots peacebuilding between Israelis and Palestinians.* Westport, CT: Praeger Press.

2. A Book by Two or More Authors

Follow the first author's name with a comma; then join the final author's name to the earlier names with an ampersand (&) rather than with the word "and." List up to seven authors; for eight or more authors, list the first six, insert an ellipsis, and then include the last author's name.

Hooyman, N., & Kramer, B. (2006). *Living through loss: Interventions across the life span.* New York, NY: Columbia University Press.

3. An Anonymous Book

If an author is listed as "Anonymous," treat it as the author's name. Otherwise, follow this format:

Publication manual of the American Psychological Association (6th ed.). (2009). Washington, DC: American Psychological Association.

Note: In this title, the words *American Psychological Association* are capitalized because they are a proper name. The word *manual* is not capitalized.

4. A Chapter from a Book

List the chapter title after the date of publication, followed by a period or appropriate end punctuation. Use *In* before the book title, and follow the book title with the inclusive page numbers of the chapter.

> Tattersall, I. (2002). How did we achieve humanity? In *The monkey in the mirror* (pp. 138-168). New York, NY: Harcourt.

5. A Single Work from an Anthology or Collection

Start with information about the individual work, followed by details about the collection in which it appears, including the page span. When editors' names come in the middle of an entry, follow the usual order: initial first, surname last. Note the placement of Eds. in parentheses.

> Guy, G. R. (2005). Variationist approaches to phonological change. In B. D. Joseph & R. D. Janda (Eds.), *The handbook of historical linguistics* (pp. 369-400). Malden, MA: Blackwell.

6. One Volume of a Multivolume Edited Work

Indicate the volume in parentheses after the work's title.

> Salzman, J., Smith, D. L., & West, C. (Eds.). (1996). *Encyclopedia of African-American culture and history* (Vol. 4). New York, NY: Simon & Schuster Macmillan.

7. A Separately Titled Volume in a Multivolume Work

> The Associated Press. (1995). *Twentieth-century America: Vol. 8. The crisis of national confidence: 1974-1980.* Danbury, CT: Grolier Educational.

Note: When a work is part of a larger series or collection, as with this example, make a two-part title with the series and the particular volume you are citing.

8. A Single Work within a Volume of a Series

Start the entry with the work's author, publication date, and title. Then follow with publication details about the series.

> Marshall, P. G. (2002). The impact of the cold war on Asia. In T. O'Neill (Ed.), *World history by era: Vol. 9. The nuclear age* (pp. 162-166). San Diego, CA: Greenhaven Press.

9. A Group Author as Publisher

When the author is also the publisher, simply put *Author* in the spot where you would list the publisher's name.

> Amnesty International. (2007). *Maze of injustice: The failure to protect indigenous women from sexual violence in the USA.* London, England: Author.

Note: If the publication is a brochure, identify it as such in brackets after the title.

10. An Edition Other Than the First

> Trimmer, J. (2001). *Writing with a purpose* (13th ed.). Boston, MA: Houghton Mifflin.

11. Two or More Books by the Same Author

See the discussion of multiple works by the same author under point 5 in the general guidelines for references (page 429).

12. An English Translation

> Setha, R. (1998). *Unarmed* (R. Narasimhan, Trans.). Chennai, India: Macmillan. (Original work published 1995)

Note: If you use the original work, cite the original version; the non-English title is followed by its English translation, not italicized, in square brackets.

13. An Article in a Reference Book

Start the entry with the author of the article, if identified. If no author is listed, begin the entry with the title of the article.

> Lewer, N. (1999). Non-lethal weapons. In *World encyclopedia of peace* (pp. 279-280). Oxford, England: Pergamon Press.

14. A Reprint, Different Form

> Albanov, V. (2000). *In the land of white death: An epic story of survival in the Siberian Arctic.* New York, NY: Modern Library. (Original work published 1917)

Note: This work was originally published in Russia in 1917; the 2000 reprint is the first English version. If you are citing part of a work, reprinted from another source, the parentheses would contain "Reprinted from Title, pp. xx-xx, by A. Author, year, Location: Publisher."

15. A Technical or Research Report

> Taylor, B. G., Fitzgerald, N., Hunt, D., Reardon, J. A., & Brownstein, H. H. (2001). *ADAM preliminary 2000 findings on drug use and drug markets: Adult male arrestees.* Washington, DC: National Institute of Justice.

16. A Government Publication

Generally, refer to the government agency as the author. When possible, provide an identification number for the document after the title in parentheses.

> National Institute on Drug Abuse. (2000). *Inhalant abuse* (NIH Publication No. 00-3818). Rockville, MD: National Clearinghouse on Alcohol and Drug Information.

Note: If the document is not available from the Government Printing Office (GPO), the publisher would be either "Author" or the separate government department that published it.

Reference Entries: Print Periodical Articles

Here is the general form for a periodical entry:

authors' names,
followed by period

publication year in parentheses,
followed by period

journal title (in full) and volume
number italicized

Author, A. (year). Article title. *Periodical Title, volume number*(issue number),

article title, no quotation marks,
first word capitalized

issue number in
parentheses, followed
by a comma

page numbers.

page numbers
followed by period

If the periodical does not use volume and issue numbers, include some other designation with the year, such as a date, a month, or a season. The entries that follow illustrate the information and arrangement needed to cite most types of print periodicals.

17. An Article in a Scholarly Journal

> Benson, P., Karlof, K. L., & Siperstein, G. N. (2008). Maternal involvement in the education of young children with autism spectrum disorders. *Autism: The International Journal of Research & Practice, 12*(1), 47-63.

Note: Pay attention to the features of this basic reference to a scholarly journal:

1. Provide the authors' last names and initials, as for a book reference.

2. Place the year of publication in parentheses, followed by a period.

3. Format the article's title in lowercase, except for the first word of the main title and subtitle and any proper nouns, acronyms, or initialisms; do not italicize the article title or place it in quotation marks.

4. Capitalize the first and all main words in the journal title; italicize it.

5. Include the issue number only if the journal is paginated individually by issue. Italicize the volume number but not the issue number; place the issue number in parentheses with no space between it and the volume number.

6. Provide inclusive page numbers, without "pp." or "pages."

18. An Abstract of a Scholarly Article (from a Secondary Source)

When referencing an abstract published separately from an article, provide publication details of the article followed by information about where the abstract was published.

> Shlipak, M. G., Simon, J. A., Grady, O., Lin, F., Wenger, N. K., & Furberg, C. D. (2001, September). Renal insufficiency and cardiovascular events in postmenopausal women with coronary heart disease. *Journal of the American College of Cardiology, 38*, 705-711. Abstract obtained from *Geriatrics,* 2001, *56*(12), Abstract No. 5645351.

19. **A Journal Article, More Than Seven Authors**

    > Yamada, A., Suzuki, M. [Miyoshi], Kato, M., Suzuki, M. [Mie], Tanaka, S., Shindo, T., . . . Furukawa, T. A. (2007). Emotional distress and its correlates among parents of children with pervasive developmental disorders. *Psychiatry & Clinical Neurosciences, 61*(6), 651-657.

    Note: Within your paper, abbreviate the authors like this: (Yamada et al., 2007).

20. **A Review**

    To reference a review of a book, film, exhibit, or other medium, indicate the review and the medium in brackets, along with the title of the work being reviewed.

    > Hutcheon, L., & Hutcheon, M. (2008). Turning into the mind. [Review of the book *Musicophilia: Tales of music and the brain,* by Oliver Sacks]. *Canadian Medical Association Journal, 178,* 441.

21. **A Magazine Article**

    > Weintraub, B. (2007, October). Unusual suspects. *Psychology Today, 40*(5), 80–87.

    Note: If the article is unsigned, begin the entry with the title of the article.

    > Tomatoes target toughest cancer. (2002, February). *Prevention, 54*(2), 53.

22. **A Newspaper Article**

    For newspaper articles, include the full publication date—year first followed by a comma, the month (spelled out) and the day. Identify the article's location in the newspaper using page numbers and section letters, as appropriate. If the article is a letter to the editor, identify it as such in brackets following the title. For newspapers, use *p.* or *pp.* before the page numbers; if the article is not on continuous pages, give all the page numbers, separated by commas.

    > Schmitt, E., & Shanker, T. (2008, March 18). U.S. adapts cold-war idea to fight terrorists. *The New York Times,* pp. 1A, 14A-15A.

    > Benderoff, E. (2008, March 14). Facebook sites face scrutiny for March Madness pools. *Chicago Tribune,* pp. 2C-3C.

23. **A Newsletter Article**

    Newsletter article entries are similar to newspaper article entries, but a volume number is added.

    > Teaching mainstreamed special education students. (2002, February). *The Council Chronicle, 11,* 6-8.

Reference Entries: Online Sources

Here are the guidelines for referencing online sources:

1. Whenever possible, use the final version of an electronic resource. Typically, this is called the archival version or the version of record, as opposed to a prepublished version. At this time, that final version is likely the same as the printed version of

an article, though there is a movement toward the online publication being the final version (complete with additional data, graphics, and so on).

2. In the reference entry for an electronic source, start with the same elements in the same order for print or other fixed-media resources (author, title, and so on). Then add the most reliable electronic retrieval information that will (a) clarify what version of the source you used and (b) help your reader find the source:

- Whenever possible, use the electronic document's digital object identifier (DOI). More and more, electronic publishers are using this registration code for the content of journal articles and other documents so that the document can be located on the Internet, even if the URL changes. The DOI will usually be published at the beginning of the article or be available in the article's citation.

  Author, A. A. (year). Title of article. *Title of Periodical, volume number* (issue number), pages. doi:code

- If a DOI is not available for the electronic document, give the URL (without a period at the end). Generally, a database name is not needed, except for hard-to-find documents and those accessed through subscription-only databases. Use the home- or menu-page URL for subscription-only databases and online reference works.

  Author, A. A. (year). Title of article. *Title of Periodical, volume number* (issue number), pages. Retrieved from URL

- If the content of the document is stable (e.g., archival copy or copy of record with DOI), do not include a retrieval date in your reference entry. However, if the content is likely to change or be updated, as is the case with a lot of the material on the free web, then offer a retrieval date. This would be the case for open-web material with no fixed publication date, edition, or version, or for material that is prepublished (in preparation, in press).

  Author, A. A. (year). *Title of document.* Retrieved Month day, year, from Name of website: URL

Note about URLs: When necessary, break a URL before a slash or other punctuation mark. Do not underline or italicize the URL, place it in angle brackets, or end it with a period.

24. A Journal Article with DOI

Oberg, A., Blades, D., & Thom, J. S. (2007). Untying a dreamcatcher: Coming to understand possibilities for teaching students of aboriginal inheritance. *Educational Studies, 42*(2), 111-139. doi:10.1080/00131940701513185

Note: Because the DOI references the final version of the article, the retrieval date, URL, and database name are not needed. If the online article is a preprint version, add "Advance online publication" followed by a period, and then the DOI.

25. A Journal Article without DOI

Bell, J. B., & Nye, E. C. (2007). Specific symptoms predict suicidal ideation in Vietnam combat veterans with post-traumatic stress disorder. *Military Medicine, 172,* 1144–1147. Retrieved from http://www.ebscohost.com

26. A Newspaper Article

Sengupta, S. (2008, March 18). Dalai Lama says he'll resign if violence escalates. *The New York Times.* Retrieved from http://www.nytimes.com

27. An Article in an Online Magazine (Ezine) not Published in Print

Pike, D. L. (2008, February). A boy and his dog: On Will Smith, apocalypse, and *I am legend* [Online exclusive]. *Bright Lights Film Journal.* Retrieved April 17, 2008, from http://www.brightlightsfilm.com/59/59legend.html

28. A Book Review

Shapiro, K. (2007). Mystic chords [Review of the book *Musicophilia: Tales of music and the brain,* by Oliver Sacks]. *Commentary, 124*(5), 73-77. Retrieved from http://www.ebscohost.com

29. An Electronic Book

Kafka, F. (2002). *Metamorphosis* (D. Wylie, Trans.). Available from http://www.gutenberg.org/etext/5200

Note: "Available from" indicates that the URL provides information on how to access the e-book; if the URL goes directly to the e-book, use "retrieved from."

30. Material from an Online Reference Work

Agonism. (2008). In *Encyclopaedia Britannica.* Retrieved March 18, 2008, from http://search.eb.com

Gender roles. (n.d.). Retrieved April 17, 2008, from http://psychology.wikia.com/wiki/Gender_roles

Note: For more on wikis and their fitting use in research, see pages 86-89.

31. Online Course Material

Rodriguez, N. (2000). *Unit 3, lecture 3: Sociological theories of deviance* [Lecture notes]. Retrieved from http://www.uh.edu/~nestor/lecturenotes/unit3lecture3.html

32. A Workplace Document or Other "Gray Literature"

"Gray literature" refers to informative documents (e.g., brochures, fact sheets, reports) produced by government agencies, corporations, and nonprofit groups. If possible, give a document number or identify the type of document in brackets.

Foehr, U. G. (2006). *Media multitasking among American youth: Prevalance, predictors and pairings* (Publication No. 7592). Retrieved from http://www.kff.org/entmedia/upload/7592.pdf

33. Content on Website

> National Institute of Allergy and Infectious Diseases. (2009, September 2). *Antimicrobial (drug) resistance*. Retrieved September 22, 2009, from http://www3.niaid.nih.gov/topicsAntimicrobialResistance/default.htm

34. A Podcast

> Byrd, D., & Block, J. (Producers). (2008, February 5). *Antonio Rangel: This is your brain on wine* [Audio podcast]. Retrieved from http://www.earthsky.org/clear-voices/52199

35. Message on a Newsgroup, an Online Forum, or a Discussion Group

> Avnish, J. (2008, March 18). Re: Sex education especially vital to teens nowadays [Discussion group posting]. Archived at http://groups.google.ca/group/AIDS-Beyond-Borders/topics?hl=en

36. A Weblog Post

> Koyzis, D. (2007, June 27). Re: Conservative environmentalists [Weblog posting]. Posted to http://byzantinecalvinist.blogspot.com/2007_06_01_archive.html

37. An E-Mail Message

E-mail is cited only within the paper, not in the reference list. See item 15, page 428.

Reference Entries: Other Sources (Primary, Personal, and Multimedia)

38. A Television or Radio Broadcast

List a broadcast by the show's producer or executive producer, and identify the type of broadcast in brackets after the show's title.

> Crystal, L. (Executive producer). (2002, February 11). *The NewsHour with Jim Lehrer* [Television broadcast]. New York, NY, and Washington, DC: Public Broadcasting Service.

39. A Television or Radio Series or Episode

When referencing an entire series, identify the series producer and indicate the type of series in brackets after the title.

> Bloch, A. (Producer). (2002). *Thinking allowed* [Television series]. Berkeley, CA: Public Broadcasting Service.

When identifying a specific episode in a television or radio series, indicate the episode by writers, if possible. Then follow with the airing date, the episode title, and the type of series in brackets. Complete the entry with details about the series itself.

> Berger, C. (Writer). (2001, December 19). Feederwatch [Radio series program]. In D. Byrd & J. Block (Producers), *Earth & Sky*. Austin, TX: Production Block.

40. Specialized Computer Software with Limited Distribution
Treat software as an unauthored work unless an individual has property rights to it. Show the software version in parentheses after the title and the medium in brackets. (Standard nonspecialized software doesn't require a reference entry.)

> Carreau, Stéphane. (2001). Champfoot (Version 3.3) [Computer software]. Saint Mandé, France: Author.

41. An Audio Recording
Begin the entry with the speaker's or writer's name, not the producer. Indicate the type of recording in brackets.

> Kim, E. (Author, speaker). (2000). *Ten thousand sorrows* [CD]. New York, NY: Random House.

42. A Music Recording
Give the name and function of the originators or primary contributors. Indicate the recording medium in brackets immediately following the title.

> ARS Femina Ensemble. (Performers). (1998). *Musica de la puebla de Los Angeles: Music by women of baroque Mexico, Cuba, & Europe* [CD]. Louisville, KY: Nannerl Recordings.

43. A Motion Picture
Give the name and function of the director, producer, or both.

> Cohn, J., & Cohn, E. (Directors). (2007). *No country for old men* [Motion picture]. United States: Miramax Films.

44. A Published Interview, Titled, No Author
Start the entry with the interview's title, followed by publication details.

> Stephen Harper: The Report interview. (2002, January 7). *The Report* (Alberta, BC), *29*, 10-11.

45. A Published Interview, Titled, Single Author
Start the entry with the interviewer's name, followed by the date and the title. Place the interviewee's name in brackets before other publication details.

> Fussman, C. (2002, January). What I've learned [Interview with Robert McNamara]. *Esquire, 137*(1), 85.

46. An Unpublished Paper Presented at a Meeting
Indicate when the paper was presented, at what meeting, in what location.

> Lycan, W. (2002, June). *The plurality of consciousness.* Paper presented at the meeting of the Society for Philosophy and Psychology, New York, NY.

47. An Unpublished Doctoral Dissertation
Place the dissertation's title in italics, even though the work is unpublished. Indicate the school at which the writer completed the dissertation.

> Roberts, W. (2001). *Crime amidst suburban wealth* (Unpublished doctoral dissertation). Bowling Green State University, Bowling Green, OH.

APA Format Guidelines

To submit a polished academic paper in correct APA format, follow the rules below and those shown in the model on pages 441–454, but also check whether your instructor has other format expectations. For details of in-text citation format, see 425. For details of reference-page format, see page 429–430.

Title Page (page 441)	On the first page, include three elements—your paper's title, your name, and your institution's name—on three separate lines, double-spaced, centered, and positioned in the top half of the page. Flush left at the top, type *Running head:* followed by your abbreviated title in all uppercase letters; and flush right at the top, type the page number 1. (Do not include your instructor's name or the course title unless requested by your instructor to do so.)
Abstract (page 441)	On the second page, include an abstract—a 150- to 250-word paragraph summarizing your paper. Place the title *Abstract* approximately one inch from the top of the page and center it. Place the running head and page number 2 at the top of the page.

Body (page 442)	Format the body (which begins on the third page) of your paper as follows:
	• *Margins:* Leave a one-inch margin on all four sides of each page (one and one-half inches on the left if the paper will be bound). Do not justify lines, but rather leave a jagged right margin and do not break words at the ends of lines.
	• *Line Spacing:* Double-space your entire paper, unless your instructor allows single spacing for tables and figures for the sake of readability.
	• *Page Numbers:* Place your running head and the page number flush left and flush right respectively, at the top of each page, beginning with the title page.
	• *Headings:* Like an outline, headings show the organization of your paper and the importance of each topic. All topics of equal importance should have headings of the same level, or style. Below are the various levels of headings used in APA papers.
	Level 1: **Centered, Boldface, Uppercase and Lowercase Heading**
	Level 2: **Flush Left, Boldface, Uppercase and Lowercase Side Heading**
	Level 3: **Indented, boldface, lowercase paragraph heading ending with a period.**
	Level 4: ***Indented, boldface, italicized, lowercase paragraph heading with a period.***
	Level 5: *Indented, italicized, lowercase paragraph heading with a period.*
	Examples:
	<div align="center">**Running on Empty: The Effects of Food Deprivation on Concentration and Perseverance**</div>**History of Research into Food Deprivation**
	    The global challenge of food deprivation.
	    The case of Somalia.
	    The plight of Somali children.

Appendix (pages 452–454)	Tables and figures (graphs, charts, maps, etc.) already appear on separate pages following the reference list. If necessary, one or more appendices may also supplement your text, following any tables or figures.

Sample APA Paper

Student writer Lanjun Wang wrote the following research paper on the intersection of culture and health. In the paper, written for an advanced composition class, she explores through both primary research (survey) and secondary research (articles, books, and online sources) the cultural factors impacting Asian American women's sexual health. You can use Lanjun's paper in three ways:

1. To study how a well-written research paper uses a range of resources, both primary and secondary, to build a discussion or line of reasoning that answers a research question

2. To examine how sources are used and integrated into social-sciences research writing—a full-length discussion of the strategies addressed on pages 190–192

3. To see in detail the format and documentation practices of APA style

FOCUS on Multimedia: To see what Lanjun's paper looks like on standard 8.5- by 11-inch pages, visit our website (www.theresearchwriter.com).

Writer's Reflection

In his English 101 (Advanced Composition) class, Dr. Adam Sonstegard asked us, as his students, to write a 10-page paper on a topic of our choice. The acculturation of Asian American women and sexual health had interested me since winter break, and this assignment seemed the perfect way to jump-start my research. As the statistics rolled out before me, I felt a great urgency for my female comrades. Although sexual health is a problem that is especially suppressed for Asian American women, it is an issue for every woman, regardless of generation and cultural orientation. For my female Asian American readers, I hope my paper provides knowledge that will aid them in making future choices; for everyone else, I hope they can reach out to the women in their lives and give them the information and support that they need for a healthier life. I would like to thank Dr. Sonstegard for his encouragement, and for introducing me to the many on-campus resources that were so crucial for my research. My appreciation also goes to Tony Gragg, who has provided me with countless suggestions and insights over the year, and to Lisa Yamauchi and all my survey participants, who were most generous for taking the time to lend their words and angles on such an intimate topic.

—Lanjun Wang

Preparing to Read: What is your understanding of what makes for sexual health? what forces prevent sexual health from occurring for people? What is your own cultural background, and what values and attitudes about sex and sexual health are part of your background?

Sample Title Page

Place the running head (abbreviated title) in upper left corner; page number in upper right.

Running head: ACCULTURATION OF SEX AND HEALTH   1

Full title, author(s), and school name are centered between the margins and placed in upper half of page. Include date and instructor's name only if requested.

The Acculturation of Sex and Health:

An Asian American Dilemma

Lanjun Wang

University of California Davis

Sample Abstract

ACCULTURATION OF SEX AND HEALTH   2

Abstract

Within Asian American culture, parent-child dissonance often exists regarding premarital sexuality and reproductive health. In this largely patriarchal culture where premarital sex is taboo, Asian American women seek reproductive health services at lower rates than non-Asian American women, although greater acculturation results in higher rates. This study examines the situation of Asian American women at UC Davis. Through surveys and interviews, the study confirms the findings of other research on Asian American characteristics: strong parental and cultural restrictions on premarital sex, limited parent-child discussions on the topic, discomfort when discussions do happen, and low rates of openness to sexual health practices. However, the study indicated two other conclusions: first, parental opinion does not necessarily affect young women's decisions about premarital sex; second, the greater the acculturation to American society, the higher the rate of participation in sexual health testing and screening.

The abstract summarizes the paper's central issue, its main conclusion, the key reasoning and evidence presented, and the study's significance.

APA Research Paper: The Body

As you review the body of this paper, read the side notes and examine how the writer uses and documents her sources.

The Acculturation of Sex and Health:

An Asian American Dilemma

A running head and page number top each page.

The title is centered one inch from the top, and the paper is double-spaced.

The writer begins with a thought-provoking quotation that introduces the larger issue behind her study.

Research on the topic is clearly laid out with several source references.

The writer zeros in on the more local focus of her own study, using local statistics as a starting point and stating explicitly the purpose of her study.

The great weight of parental expectations is perhaps one of the most common themes in the lives of Asian American women. From a young age, we are aware of our parents' vision for our lives. We knew what we should study, how we should act, whom we should eventually marry. . . . Even if we fail to do what was expected of us, we are always aware of the tension between parental approval and personal choice. (Chow, 1998, p. 11)

Unmentioned in Chow's statement above are perhaps the two personal issues causing the greatest parent-child dissonance of all: premarital sexuality and reproductive health. In the majority of today's societies, sex is considered the most private form of intimacy; and Asian cultures, which have traditionally been highly patriarchal and sexually restrictive, continue to view sex as taboo (Okazaki, 2002). As a consequence, Asians tend to avoid—or be disinterested in—receiving proper reproductive health services. Research has repeatedly shown that as a group, Asian American women seek both sexual or reproductive health services and screening services at a significantly lower rate than non-Asian American women (Tu, Taplin, Barlow, & Boyko, 1999; National Asian Women's Health Organization [NAWHO], 1997). However, research also shows a positive correlation between the level of acculturation of Asian American women and the likelihood they will seek sexual health services: as new generations become increasingly acculturated, more Asian American women are taking clinical reproductive health measures (Okazaki, 2002). The relationship between sexual health and culture is a factor for millions of Asian Americans nationwide, and presumably also for the thousands of Asian American students at UC Davis. As of 2004, close to 33 percent of the undergraduate student population are Asian American (UC Davis,

ACCULTURATION OF SEX AND HEALTH   4

2004a), and almost 55 percent of all students are female (UC Davis, 2004b); thus, this is an issue that potentially affects a large segment of the UC Davis population. The purpose of my study is to determine whether past findings on acculturation and sexual health apply to Asian American undergraduate women at UC Davis.

Participants and Method

The participants of this study consisted of 20 female Asian American undergraduate students at UC Davis. Undergraduates were selected for their relatively young age and their tendency to be involved in casual relationships. As many traditional Asian families remain closed to the idea of premarital sexual activity, this age group marks a critical period: although young women are not under immediate parental surveillance, they have not yet received parental consent to sexual autonomy. Thus, while they are able to make decisions about their sexual lives, the Asian American women of this group are still bound by their incomplete independence from their parents. Participants were primarily of Chinese, Vietnamese, Korean, and Cambodian national origins, with a small number of students identified as multiethnic or multicultural (i.e., with parents of differing cultures and/or nationalities). Students filled out a survey providing (1) demographic information; (2) ratings of parental, personal, and cultural attitudes toward premarital sex; and (3) self reports on sexual history and health measures. (See appendix for specifics of survey questions.) Of the 58 surveys passed out, 20 undergraduates returned completed surveys. Approximately 84 percent of the respondents were first-generation Asian Americans; of this first-generation group, 53 percent were Chinese. Of all respondents, 50 percent were sexually active.

Asian Culture and Asian Americans

Research shows that in the majority of Asian cultures, sex is directly associated with reproduction in a family setting. Open discussion about sex is highly taboo, and sexual material has traditionally been limited to "religious or fictional texts," such as the Kama Sutra (Gupta, 1994). Perhaps unsurprisingly, the patriarchal nature of Asian cultures

---

Sidebar annotations:

Headings divide the paper into clear sections.

The writer carefully outlines the primary research component of her research by describing the participants and the survey instrument she used.

Whole sources are referenced by author and date in a parenthetical citation.

enforces sexual restrictions especially strictly on women, whose public sexual disclosures and "open expression would represent a threat to the highly interdependent social order as well as to the integrity of the family" (Okazaki, 2002, pp. 34-35). Although most Asian cultures discourage sexual discussion and disclosure, each enforces this negative attitude through different beliefs and social institutions. For instance, traditional Cambodian attitudes concerning sexuality and premarital sex center around the importance of preserving family honor (Kulig, 1994), whereas traditional Filipino attitudes are strongly influenced by Catholicism (Tiongson, 1997). In the United States, despite being heavily stereotyped by the dominant White American culture, Asian Americans remain a heterogeneous group, consisting of a variety of independent traditional and cultural attitudes. However, according to a 2002 study published in the *Journal of Sex Research* (Okazaki), group members still share a number of "Asian cultural characteristics," such as the "primacy of the family," "emphasis on propriety and social codes," and "the appropriation of sexuality" only after marriage (p. 34).

The results of my study confirm the researchers' conclusions. Students participating in the surveys rated (on a scale of 1-5) both their culture's and parents' attitudes towards premarital sex on an average of 1.94 (not open at all—very negative); 64 percent of respondents gave a rating of 1 or 2. On average, students rated their personal attitude towards premarital sex as 2.63, so they were not as negative as their parents and culture in general; however, the data suggest a generally negative attitude among the participants towards the subject of premarital sexual activity. Not surprisingly, results showed a very low rate of parent-child discussions concerning sex (1.79) and a relatively low level of comfort when engaging in such discussions (2.16). Given these statistics, it was not surprising that over 80 percent of respondents asserted that they had learned about sex and its risks (e.g., sexually transmitted diseases [STDs]) from discussions with friends, from high school sex education, and from personal experiences rather than from speaking with parents. A first-generation Chinese student wrote, "I never

---

Specific details and direct quotations are referenced by page numbers as well.

The writer links her primary research with the secondary research she has just surveyed.

In her discussion of survey results, the writer offers numerical ratings, statistics, and direct quotations from respondents.

The writer offers her conclusions about the survey results.

ACCULTURATION OF SEX AND HEALTH   6

really discussed any information concerning sex and relationships. My parents are pretty traditional with their culture, [and] prefer that I do not pursue any relations (i.e., boyfriends) until I graduate from college" (original emphasis). She went on to say that she had chosen to "hide" her relationships from her parents because she did not want to "disobey," "disrespect," or "disappoint" them in "any way." The students' ratings and self reports suggest that they have, on average, remained consistent with the stereotypical cultural generalizations: that their parents and native culture are antagonistic towards premarital sex; that the students rarely have sex-based discussions with their parents; and that, when they do have such discussions, these students generally experience relatively high levels of discomfort because of their psychological struggles with parental disapproval and disappointment.

Asian Culture, Sexuality, and Health

Closely related to the issue of "sexual propriety" is the extent to which Asians are generally open to sexual health practices, such as Pap smears, pelvic examinations, and STD testing on an individual and familial basis. A survey conducted by the National Asian Women's Health Organization in 1996 reported that half of the Asian American women from six California counties had not "visited a healthcare [sic] provider within the last year for reproductive or sexual health services," and that "one fourth had never received any reproductive or sexual health information in their lives" (NAWHO, 1997; Nowrojee & Silliman, 1997, p. 74). Many Asian American women feel that by following their cultural guidelines for sexual activity (e.g. within a heterosexual marriage and for the sake of reproduction), they are not at risk for sex-related consequences other than pregnancy (Nowrojee & Silliman, 1997, p. 77).

Student survey responses do, in fact, suggest that this portrait is accurate, even for recent generations of Asian American women. Although one participant believed that it was necessary to seek reproductive health services "at least once or twice a year, just to get a checkup," she herself, after being sexually active for one year, had never received reproductive health services because she "didn't feel it was

---

A heading and transition sentence signal a shift to another aspect of the topic.

Two sources within a reference are separated by a semicolon.

The writer discusses how survey results are consistent with national trends.

necessary," and up until participating in the survey, had "never thought about it." Similarly, several participants indicated that reproductive services such as Pap smears and pelvic exams were only necessary when "switching partners" and because "college men and women tend to have multiple partners." One of the participants claimed that because she was "monogamous," she did not believe that she would "have a problem." These personal statements correspond to the common perception that only when individuals break away from a single, monogamous relationship do they find themselves at risk of infection or health problems.

Stemming from traditional expectations is a stigma toward those who contract STDs or other forms of reproductive illness, as these health problems are often associated with improper sexual activity and with shame. Thus, the sexually repressive nature of Asian cultures dissuades many Asian American young women from undertaking reproductive health services by making them fearful of personal disclosure and a lack of confidentiality on the health provider's part. Lisa Yamauchi, a Japanese American Family Nurse Practitioner at the Cowell Student Health Center (CSHC) at UC Davis, has had twenty years of experience in female reproductive health services around the Davis-Sacramento area, where she has worked in both private and campus clinics. When I asked her about this issue of confidentiality, Yamauchi asserted that although she does not feel this issue of privacy pertains exclusively to Asian Americans, she does believe that sexuality is underdiscussed in Asian American families, and that "it would be a disgrace to the family if the family knew that they were having sex before marriage or coming in for STD screening because they have multiple partners" (personal communication, May 18, 2005). Yamauchi went on to say that in some other cultures, parents may be more open in their discussion concerning reproductive measures, such as instructing their daughters to obtain birth control pills from Planned Parenthood at age sixteen (personal communication, May 18, 2005). A first-generation Vietnamese respondent specifically addressed this question of confidentiality, stating that although she felt that any method of obtaining reproductive health

Survey respondents' quotations add a personal voice to the discussion.

The writer reports on an interview with a professional who works in the field.

The interview is referenced as "personal communication," a source that does not require an entry in the reference list.

The writer paraphrases and quotes from her interview.

ACCULTURATION OF SEX AND HEALTH   8

services can be beneficial, she would "feel more comfortable going to a confidential clinic than to [her] family doctor."

Although my participants made different choices, a general trend was evident in their attitude toward parental influence on sex: although participants value their parents' concerns and beliefs, parental opinions do not necessarily influence their decisions about sex. Many young women reported that sex is a very personal decision for which they are ready to take on the consequences, and others wrote that their respect for parental values extends beyond the issue of premarital sex and into other spheres of their lives. However, it is important to note that some statistical variability exists between those who are sexually active and those who have remained abstinent. On average, students who have remained sexually abstinent gave higher ratings for (1) the importance and influence of parental opinions toward sex, (2) the level of personal agreement with parental opinions, and (3) feelings of interconnectedness between personal decisions and family reputation/well-being.

Pap Smears and Pelvic Exams: What Are They?

According to both my own respondents and researchers Nowrojee and Silliman (1997), many Asian American women do not know what a Pap smear or pelvic examination is. The culturally-embedded notion that sex "is only linked to reproduction" inevitably leads to a "failure to seek out broader health information and services for STDs, including HIV/AIDS, basic gynecology care, and sexuality education" (Nowrojee & Silliman, 1997, p. 78). Similarly, some participants reported that they did not have adequate knowledge about certain reproductive health services, such as the Pap smear. In our interview, Yamauchi also mentioned that because reproductive health services may be unavailable in some Asian countries, parents are unable to adequately inform their children of these health care options. "Women either have a fear of the Pap smear or are not aware of the importance of having one," she said. "Some of the women who have come from China, they just don't do screening like that. They don't do mammography screening and Pap smears in some of the rural cities that their families have come from, and so through the

---

The writer summarizes survey findings, including a statistical variable.

When authors are referred to in the sentence, only the year is listed in the parenthetical citation.

The writer supplies information from a reputable online source, a medical encyclopedia.

generations, it hasn't been passed on as something that's as important" (personal communication, May 18, 2005).

According to *Kaiser Permanente,* the Pap test is used to screen women for cervical cancer. During the examination, women lie on an examination table with their legs supported by stirrups, which raises a woman's legs and allows a certified health professional to examine the vagina and genital area. The examiner uses a lubricated vaginal speculum to ease the vaginal walls apart before taking small samples of cells from the surface of the cervix using a cotton swab, brush, or small spatula. The samples are then smeared onto slides (Pap smear) or mixed in a liquid fixative before being examined under microscopes in the laboratory. Women may feel uncomfortable during the speculum insertion and/or during the cervical scrapings, but the discomfort can decrease if both the examiner and the woman are relaxed (Payne & Spengler, December 10, 2003).

Different publication dates (within parenthetical citations) indicate two separate articles by the same authors.

Unlike the Pap test, pelvic examinations include both external and internal examinations of a woman's reproductive organs. According to *Kaiser Permanente,* a typical pelvic examination may consist of four components: (1) An external examination of the vulva (i.e., the area and structures surrounding the vagina, including the clitoris, labia, and urethral opening); (2) an internal examination of the vagina and reproductive organs, which may include a Pap smear and an STD test; (3) a bimanual internal examination during which the examiner inserts two lubricated and gloved fingers into the vagina while pressing on the abdomen, and occasionally (4) a rectovaginal examination during which the examiner "inserts the lubricated first finger of one hand into the vagina, and second finger of the same hand into the rectum," while also pressing on the abdomen. Some women may feel slight pain during the bimanual examination as the health professional physically feels the ovaries, and in some cases women may feel sensations suggesting bowel movement when the health professional extracts his/her finger from the rectum during the rectovaginal examination. This feeling is completely normal and will last only a few seconds (Payne & Spengler, September 26, 2003).

ACCULTURATION OF SEX AND HEALTH   10

Asian American Acculturation, Sexuality, and Health

Some research has indicated that Asian American sexual conservatism has eroded with increasing exposure to the more sexually open American ideology (Okazaki, 2002). Results show that as younger generations become increasingly acculturated into the White American culture, Asian American youths show a decrease in both guilty thoughts and feelings about sexual activity (Abramson & Imai-Marquez, 1982) and an increase in premarital sexual intercourse in college. What is particularly interesting is that Asian Americans who "consistently" date "White Americans" have "more sexual experience than those dating only Asian Americans" (Huang & Uba, 1992) and that Asian American high school students who speak English as their primary language are more likely to be "non-virgins than other Asian American peers" (Schuster, Bell, Nakajima, & Kanouse, 1998). It is hard to say whether a casual relationship exists between English-speaking Asian families, White American partners, and increased sexuality. However, these results may suggest that the Asian American youths who have primarily engaged in intimate relationships with White American individuals or who are from families who employ English as their primary mode of communication may have reached a higher level of acculturation, thereby leading to higher rates of sexual activity.

Judging from my study, sexual activity does seem to correlate with acculturation, as a greater percentage of second-generation Asian American students (66.6 percent) are sexually active compared to first-generation Asian American students (50 percent). Sexual activity aside, the data reveal some interesting trends and relationships in other areas of personal choice and of parental influence. While both first- and second-generation Asian American students rated their parents' attitudes and opinions toward premarital sex as fairly important (3.43 and 3.75, respectively) and somewhat influential (2.94 and 2.74, respectively), their self-reported ratings for agreement with parental opinions on sex and connectedness between personal choices and family well-being showed an interesting contradiction. Although first-generation Asian Americans rated their agreement with their parents' opinions lower (3.25) than

With a new heading, the writer pulls together the strands of the previous discussion and moves her paper toward its conclusion.

The writer weaves together information from several sources, showing how she has thought through the material.

The writer discusses ways that her survey results relate to the larger body of secondary source material.

did their second- generation counterparts (3.5), first-generation Asian American young women reported that their personal choices were more strongly tied to their family's reputation and well-being (3.75) than did second-generation Asian American young women (3.5). When it comes to sexual and reproductive health services, the difference between generations was more pronounced. Of the first-generation students who were sexually active, only 38 percent had taken some sort of testing or screening, whereas with the second-generation students, the percentage reached a surprising 100 percent.

In her final remarks, the writer furthers the connection between her survey results and past research.

With increasing exposure to Western, White American values, Asian American women face cultural dissonance with their parents. For many young women, growing up under a traditionally sexually restrictive family atmosphere allowed them to internalize some of their parents' values, which sometimes conflict with their newly acquired, more Westernized attitudes. Researchers have found that with acculturation, Asian Americans become more likely to engage in premarital sexual activities (Huang & Uba, 1992; Schuster, Bell, Nakajima, & Kanouse, 1998), and the present study suggests that alongside this increase in openness to sexuality, younger generations of Asian American women are—on average—also seeking reproductive health services more often.

Finally, while qualifying her findings, the writer offers a firm conclusion.

It is important to note that these conclusions were drawn from averaged ratings/generalizations provided by a small sample of UC Davis students, and do not necessarily apply equally to all Asian American women. However, results from both the current study and past research unveil that an alarmingly low number of Asian American women are knowledgeable about and/or seeking sexual and reproductive health services. Such disregard for receiving health services can lead to critical health problems, such as STDs, cervical and ovarian cancer, and infertility. Coupled with the effect of acculturation (i.e., greater rate of sexual activity in younger generations), this lack of knowledge places Asian American women at increased risk of reproductive health problems, and so it is increasingly critical to educate this population before they are endangered by the bind of tradition.

ACCULTURATION OF SEX AND HEALTH   12

References

Abramson, P. R., & Imai-Marquez, J. (1982). The Japanese-American: A cross-cultural, cross-sectional study of sex guilt. *Journal of Research in Personality, 16*(2), 227-237. doi:10.1016/0092-6566(82)90078-2

Chow, C. S. (1998). *Leaving deep water: The lives of Asian American women at the crossroads of two cultures.* New York, NY: Dutton, Penguin.

Gupta, M. (1994). Sexuality in the Indian subcontinent. *Sexual and Relationship Therapy, 9*(1), 57-69.

Huang, K., & Uba, L. (1992). Premarital sexual behavior among Chinese college students in the United States. *Archives of Sexual Behavior, 21*(3), 227-240. doi:10.1007/BF01542994

Kulig, J. C. (1994). Sexuality beliefs among Cambodians: Implications for health care professionals. *Health Care for Women Intl., 15*(1), 69-76.

National Asian Women's Health Organization (NAWHO). (1997). *Expanding options: A reproductive and sexual health survey of Asian American women.* San Francisco, CA: Author.

Nowrojee, S., & Silliman, J. (1997). Asian women's health: Organizing a movement. In S. Shah (Ed.), *Dragon ladies: Asian American feminists breathe fire* (pp. 74-77). Boston, MA: South End Press.

Okazaki, S. (2002). Influences of culture on Asian Americans' sexuality. *Journal of Sex Research, 39*(1), 34-41.

Payne, K., & Spengler, R. (Eds.). (2003, September 26). Pelvic examination. In *Kaiser Permanente: Health encyclopedia.* Retrieved May 18, 2005, from http://www.kaiserpermanente.org

Payne, K., & Spengler, R. (Eds.). (2003, December 10). Pap test. *In Kaiser Permanente: Health encyclopedia.* Retrieved May 18, 2005, from http://www.kaiserpermanente.org

Shuster, M. A., Bell, R. M., Nakajima, G. A, & Kanouse, D. E. (1998). The sexual practices of Asian and Pacific Islander high school students. *Journal of Adolescent Health, 23*(4), 221-231. doi:10.1016/S1054-139X(97)00210-3

All works referred to in the paper (with the exception of a personal communication) appear in the reference list, alphabetized by author (or title).

Each entry follows APA guidelines for listing authors, dates, titles, and publishing information.

Retrieval dates are included when source material may change over time.

Tiongson, A. T., Jr. (1997). Throwing the baby out with the bathwater: Situating young Filipino mothers and fathers beyond the dominant discourse on adolescent pregnancy. In M. P. P. Root (Ed.), *Filipino Americans: Transformation and identity* (pp. 257-271). Thousand Oaks, CA: Sage.

Tu, S., Taplin, S. H., Barlow, W. E., & Boyko, E. J. (1999). Breast cancer screening by Asian American women in a managed care environment. *American Journal of Preventive Medicine,* 17(1), 55-61.

UC Davis News Service. (2004a). Student headcount by ethnicity. Retrieved from http://facts.ucdavis.edu/student_headcount _ethnicity.lasso

UC Davis News Service. (2004b). Student headcount by gender. Retrieved from http://facts.ucdavis.edu/student_headcount_gender .lasso

Capitalization, punctuation, and hanging indentation are consistent with APA format.

Entries with identical authors and publication dates are further alphabetized by title. A letter suffix (a, b) is added to the year.

Appendix

Survey of UC Davis Asian American Female Students

Name: _____
Age: _____

Class Standing: _____

Ethnicity/Nation   Generation: _____
    Chinese
    Japanese
    Vietnamese
    Filipino
    Indian
    Other:_____

The appendix contains a copy of the survey used in the study.

ACCULTURATION OF SEX AND HEALTH   15

All participants must answer questions 1-10. If you are presently sexually active or have been at some point in the past, please answer questions 11-15. If you have never been sexually active, please answer questions 16-18. Please answer these questions as fully and accurately as you can. Thank you very much for your help!

Note: The information gathered will be kept confidential. Should your responses be published, a false name will be used to protect your privacy.

All Participants

1. Rate how open your culture is about premarital sex.

1	2	3	4	5
Not open at all		Somewhat open		Very open

2. Rate how traditional you feel your parents are in general.

1	2	3	4	5
Not traditional		Somewhat traditional		Very traditional

3. Rate how negative or positive you feel your parents are concerning premarital sex.

1	2	3	4	5
Very negative		Indifferent		Very positive

4. Rate how negative or positive you feel about premarital sex.

1	2	3	4	5
Very negative		Indifferent		Very positive

5. Rate how often you and your parents have discussed the topic of sex.

1	2	3	4	5
Very rarely		Sometimes		Very often

6. Rate how comfortable you are about discussing sex with your parents.

1	2	3	4	5
Very uncomfortable		Indifferent		Very comfortable

7. Rate how important your parents' opinions are to you in general.

1	2	3	4	5
Very unimportant		Indifferent		Very important

8. Rate how influential your parents' opinions about sex are on you.

1	2	3	4	5
No influence at all		Mixed		Very influential

ACCULTURATION OF SEX AND HEALTH   16

9. Rate how much you agree with your parents' attitudes toward sex.

1	2	3	4	5
Do not agree at all		Mixed		Very much agree

10. Rate how closely you tie your personal choices to your family's
    reputation and well-being.

1	2	3	4	5
No connection at all	Somewhat connected			Very connected

Respondents who are or have been sexually active:

11. How long have you been sexually active? Or, if you were sexually
    active at some point in the past, for how long?

12. During the time of your sexual activity, did you at any point seek
    pelvic examinations, Pap smears, or other reproductive health tests
    from a clinic? If so, how often and why? If not, why not?

13. How necessary do you feel it is for you to seek reproductive health
    tests through a clinic? Why or why not?

14. Do you think you are very knowledgeable about reproductive health?
    If so, why? Where did you get your knowledge? If not, why not?

15. How influential has your cultural background, traditions, or family
    been on your decisions concerning sexual activity and reproductive
    health?

Respondents who have never been sexually active:

16. Why have you not engaged in sexual activity so far?

17. How necessary do you feel PAP smears, Pelvic examinations, and
    other reproductive health tests/measures are? Why or why not?

18. How influential has your cultural background, traditions, or family
    been on your decisions concerning sexual activity and reproductive
    health?

APA System: Activities

1. Print a copy of a research paper that you wrote earlier in your schooling. Using the instruction and information in this chapter, carefully edit the paper so that it follows current APA guidelines for paper format, in-text citation, and references.

2. Study the sample paper on pages 440-454. Explain how effectively Lanjun follows the overall philosophy and style of the APA system in her writing: does she engage her sources and present them in such a way as to successfully develop her analysis and convince you of her credibility as a researcher?

3. Using the broad topics of the sample paper (ethnic identity and sexual health) as a starting point, do your own research and develop a references page listing at least two sources from each of the references categories in this chapter: print books, print periodical articles, online sources, and other sources (primary, personal, multimedia). Make sure that your references page is correctly ordered and formatted.

4. For each of the sources that you found for activity 3 above, draft a brief passage in which you use the source (either through summary, paraphrase, or quotation). Make sure that the source is correctly cited according to APA guidelines.

APA System: Checklist

Checklist:

☑ All borrowed material is acknowledged with an appropriate attributive phrase and/or in-text citation indicating author(s), publication date, and page number, as appropriate.

☑ All in-text citations effectively point the reader to resources in the reference list or to personal communication.

☑ The reference list includes entries for all works referred to in the body of the paper: no sources are missing from the list; no extra sources are listed that are not cited within the paper. Exception: Personal communications are identified in in-text citations but not in the reference list.

☑ The entire reference list is properly alphabetized by authors' last names (or by the first main word in the title for anonymous works); multiple works by the same author are listed chronologically, earliest first.

☑ Each reference entry (whether for an article, a book, an online document, or other source) contains the maximum amount of identifying and publication information, in the proper order, using the expected abbreviations.

☑ The entire paper is properly formatted: from the title page to any appendix.

- Placement, spacing, and margins are correct for the title page, abstract, report, and reference list.

- Pagination is correct and consistent, as is the paper's running head.

- First lines of paragraphs, including paragraphs under headings, and inset quotations, are properly indented; reference entries are properly formatted with hanging indent.

- The paper is cleanly printed single-sided on quality paper in a professional-looking typeface and in 12-point type size (without fancy typestyle features).

- Rules for capitalization, lowercase, quotation marks, and italics are observed throughout the text, especially with names and titles.

© Cengage Learning/Illustrated by Chris Krenzke

Chicago/Turabian Style and Sample Paper

If you need to submit an assigned paper in Chicago (CMS) or Turabian format, you're looking for answers to questions like these: How do I format my paper? How do I document my research? This chapter offers answers, starting with the questions below.

What's the CMS, and who is Turabian? *The Chicago Manual of Style* is published by the University of Chicago Press, a leading academic publisher. This manual has established widely accepted rules and conventions for academic book publishing. Kate Turabian has published a Chicago manual for students writing college-level papers.

What is the Chicago/Turabian Style? Chicago/Turabian style refers to a method of documenting research and formatting a research paper—a method and format used in humanities courses outside English (e.g., history, philosophy, the fine arts) and in some social science disciplines (e.g., journalism, economics). While the Chicago system does offer an author-date plus bibliography option (parallel to APA, chapter 19), it is best known as a note-based system with these features:

- **In-text citation**—superscript numbers indicating source material.
- **Footnotes or endnotes**—explanatory and bibliographic notes supplying complete information when a source is first used, plus shortened information for subsequent references.

Where Can You Find More Information? This chapter offers an overview of CMS/Turabian. For more information, consult the following:

- *The Chicago Manual of Style: The Essential Guide for Writer's, Editors, and Publishers* (15th edition), along with the University of Chicago Press Web site www.press.uchicago.edu, which offers an online subscription to the guide.
- Kate Turabian, *A Manual for Writers of Term Papers, Theses, and Dissertations* (7th edition): check your library's reference section.
- Our Web site www.theresearchwriter.com, where you'll find additional help .

What's Ahead?

Directory to Chicago Style

If you have a specific question about Chicago/Turabian style, use the directory below to find the answer within this chapter.

Chicago Documentation: Quick Guide

Chicago style involves (1) a superscript or raised number within your paper when you use a source, and (2) a matching footnote or endnote. Note these features:

- **It uses signal phrases and superscript numbers** to set off source material from your own thinking and discussion. Note: a signal phrase names the author and places the material in context (e.g., "As Paul Ricoeur argues in *The Symbolism of Evil*").

- **It's flexible and unobtrusive.** Bibliographic notes corresponding to the superscript numbers can be placed at the bottom of the page on which the number appears (footnotes) or collected sequentially on a "Notes" page at the end of the paper (endnotes). As a result, the paper's flow is relatively uninterrupted by references. Chicago style offers further flexibility in that notes can serve explanatory as well as bibliographic purposes.

You can see these features at work in the example below. The reference to Loyal Jones and the superscript number "1" tell the reader that

- the borrowed material came from a source authored by Loyal Jones.
- bibliographic information can be found under note "1" on the endnotes page.

In-Text Citation

As Loyal Jones points out, many of country music's influences came from German, English, French, Irish, and Scottish immigrants.[1]

Matching Endnote

1. Loyal Jones, "Singing Cowboys and Musical Mountaineers: Southern Culture and the Roots of Country Music," *The Journal of Southern History* 60, no. 4 (1994): 849-850. http://www.jstor.org (accessed March 26, 2010).

In-Text Citation: The Basics

With Chicago documentation, the placement of in-text citations follows these simple rules:

- **Signal the beginning of source material.** Typically, you can use a reference to the author or the work's title. Example: "Louise Pound, author of *The "Uniformity" of the Ballad Style,* explains ballads. . . ." For straightforward citations of information, the signal phrase isn't needed.
- **Insert a superscript number after the source material.** Typically, your word-processing program will allow you to create superscripts and the accompanying footnote or endnote automatically. For example, in Microsoft Word, follow the instructions under "Insert" followed by "Reference." Except when used with dashes, place superscript numbers after punctuation marks (e.g., periods, commas, quotation marks, closed parenthesis). Place a superscript number before a dash (two hyphens).
- **Number notes consecutively.** As your paper unfolds, number each source reference in order, starting with 1. Again, your word-processing program likely handles this task automatically.

Footnotes and Endnotes: The Basics

Placed at the bottom of the page on which the reference appears, a footnote has the advantage of proximity: when a superscript number appears in the essay, your reader can jump down to study the note easily. An endnote page, conversely, gathers all notes on a separate page (or pages) after your essay, making access to all of your source information convenient for readers. While your word-processing program may format footnotes and endnotes automatically, you should follow these practices:

Footnote Format

- Place notes at the bottom of the page, separated from the text either by a triple space or by a short horizontal line (about two inches or twelve spaces).
- Indent five spaces, give the number (not in superscript) followed by a period, a space, and then the source information.
- Keep second and subsequent lines of a note flush left.
- Single-space within each note; double space between notes.

Endnote Format

- Create a separate page after the last page of your essay, centering the heading "Notes" (no bold or italics) one inch from the top.
- Triple space down from the heading.
- Indent five spaces, give the number (not in superscript) followed by a period, a space, and then the source information. Keep second and subsequent lines flush left.
- Double-space within and between each note.

Typical Information in Notes: A sample endnote page is shown on page 480, and examples of entries for various types of resources are on pages 462–469. Generally, however, a note contains the following information in this order:

1. note number (not superscript)
2. author's name (first followed by last name)
3. title of work (plus title of larger work for sources that are articles, chapters, or other shorter works within the larger work)
4. publication information (e.g., city, publisher, journal title)
5. publication date
6. page(s) referenced, if the note refers to a direct quotation or part of the source

Template for Book:

Number. Author's First and Last Name, *Full Title of Book* (Publication City: Publisher, publication year), page number(s). [Other publication details are integrated as needed. For an e-book, include the specific type, service, number, and/or online address.]

4. Garry Wills, *Lincoln at Gettysburg: The Words That Remade America* (New York: Simon and Schuster, 1992), 135.

Template for Periodical Article:

Number. Author's First and Last Name, "Title of Article," *Journal Title* volume, number (year): page number(s). [Other publication details are integrated as needed. For an online periodical article, add the Internet address followed by the access date in parentheses.]

12. Charlie Seemann, "The Cowboys Poetry Gathering," *The Journal of American Folklore* 104, no. 414 (1991): 505.

Template for Online Document:

Number. Author's First and Last Name [if available], "Document Title," *Journal or Site Title*, publication information [e.g., volume, posting date], Internet address (access date).

7. Len Green, "Trail of Tears," *The Choctaw Nation of Oklahoma Home Page,* July 1, 2002, http://www.choctawnation.com/trailoftears.htm (accessed May 17, 2010).

Second and Subsequent Notes for Sources: After your first reference to a source, you create notes with shortened information for second and subsequent references to the source. Doing so takes two forms, depending on the situation:

- For a reference that is to the same work as the reference note that came immediately before it, use the Latin abbreviation *Ibid.*
  - ***Example:*** 16. Ibid., 43.
- For subsequent references to a source separated in sequence from a previous reference to that source, provide the author's last name, a shortened title, and a page number.
  - ***Example:*** 17. Wills, *Lincoln at Gettysburg,* 43.

Content Notes: In Chicago style, notes can also offer commentary—on a given source, on related sources that readers might find helpful, on your research methods, or on interesting issues that are nevertheless tangential to your main discussion. Here is an example:

> *Sentence in Essay:* Morality conflated with anything but the honor of God is a recipe for human vengeance.[10]

> *Corresponding Content Note:* 10. For an interesting study of the German side of this issue, consult *The Holy Reich: Nazi Conceptions of Christianity, 1919-1945,* by Richard Steigmann-Gall.

Bibliographic Entries: The Basics

A bibliography in addition to notes is not absolutely needed in Chicago style, as notes provide complete bibliographic information for sources. However, your instructor may request one in order to see an alphabetized list of all the sources that you cited or consulted. Follow this format:

- On a separate page after your essay (if you used footnotes) or after your endnotes page(s), center the heading *Bibliography* (or *Sources Consulted, Selected Bibliography,* etc.) one inch from the top.
- Begin your first bibliographic entry three lines down from the heading.
- Double-space within and between each entry.
- Begin each entry flush left, with second and subsequent lines indented five spaces.
- Alphabetize entries by author's last name.

While sample bibliography entries for specific resources are shown on pages 462–469, templates for common entries are shown below:

Template for Print Book:

Author's Last Name, First Name. *Full Title of Book.* Publication City: Publisher, publication year. [Other publication details are integrated as needed.]

Wills, Gary. *Lincoln at Gettysburg: The Words That Remade America.* New York: Simon and Schuster, 1992.

Template for Periodical Article:

Author's Last Name, First Name. "Title of Article." *Journal Title* volume, number (year): page numbers. [Other publication details are integrated as needed. For an online article, add the Internet address followed by the access date in parentheses.]

Allen, Michael. "'I Just Want to Be a Cosmic Cowboy': Hippies, Cowboy Code, and the Culture of a Counterculture." *The Western Historical Quarterly* 36, no. 3 (Autumn 2005): 275-299.

Template for Online Document:

Author's Last Name, First Name [if available]. "Document Title." *Journal or Site Title,* publication information [e.g., volume, posting date]. Internet address (access date).

Green, Len. "Trail of Tears." *The Choctaw Nation of Oklahoma Home Page,* July 1, 2002. http://www.choctawnation.com/trailoftears.htm (accessed May 17, 2010).

Sample Chicago Notes and Bibliographic Entries

As shown on the previous pages, in the Chicago/Turabian system, research is documented through footnotes or endnotes keyed to superscript numbers in the body of paper. Sometimes, a bibliography supplements that documentation, as requested or required. Basic guidelines for notes and bibliographies are covered on pages 459–461. The following pages add to that instruction by offering sample notes and bibliographic entries for the most common types of resources.

Books and Other Nonperiodical Sources (Print and Digital)

1. Book, One Author
Note:

> 1. Denis Dutton, *The Art Instinct: Beauty, Pleasure, and Human Evolution* (New York: Bloomsbury Press, 2009), 221.

Bibliography:

> Dutton, Denis. *The Art Instinct: Beauty, Pleasure, and Human Evolution.* New York: Bloomsbury Press, 2009.

2. More Than One Book by the Same Author
Note:

> 2. Paul Ricoeur, *The Symbolism of Evil* (New York: Harper & Row, 1967), 245.

> 3. Paul Ricoeur, *History and Truth* (Evanston, IL: Northwestern University Press, 1965), 24.

Bibliography: When you reference two or more works by the same author, alphabetize the works using the title (ignoring initial articles *A*, *An*, or *The*). For second or subsequent works, replace the author's name with a dash (three hyphens).

> Ricoeur, Paul. *History and Truth.* Evanston, IL: Northwestern University Press, 1965.

> ---. *The Symbolism of Evil.* New York: Harper & Row, 1967.

3. Book, More Than One Author
Note: With two or three authors, list them all. With four or more, follow the first author's name with "and others" or "et al."

> 4. Alasdair C. MacIntyre and Paul Ricoeur, *The Religious Significance of Atheism* (New York: Columbia University Press, 1969), 63.

Bibliography: Invert only the first author's name. List all coauthors if the book has ten or fewer authors; if the book has more than ten authors, list the first seven only, followed by "and others" or "et al."

> MacIntyre, Alasdair, and Paul Ricoeur. *The Religious Significance of Atheism.* New York: Columbia University Press, 1969.

4. **Book with Editor**
Note:

> 5. Joshua Dressler, ed., *Encyclopedia of Crime and Justice,* 2nd ed., 4 vols. (New York: Macmillan Reference USA, 2002), 3:256.

Bibliography:

> Dressler, Joshua, ed. *Encyclopedia of Crime and Justice.* 2nd ed. 4 vols. New York: Macmillan Reference USA, 2002.

5. **An Edition of a Book**
Note:

> 6. Friedrich Nietzsche, *The Use and Abuse of History,* 2nd rev. ed., trans. Adrian Collins (Indianapolis: Bobbs-Merrill Educational Publishing, 1957), 24.

Bibliography:

> Nietzsche, Friedrich. *The Use and Abuse of History.* 2nd rev. ed. Translated by Adrian Collins. Indianapolis: Bobbs-Merrill Educational Publishing, 1957.

6. **An Anonymous Publication**
Note:

> 7. Anonymous, *Primary Colors: A Novel of Politics* (New York: Random House, 1996), 295.

Bibliography: If "Anonymous" appears as the author on the title page, use this term. If no author is indicated, you may start with the work's title or insert "Anonymous."

> Anonymous. *Primary Colors: A Novel of Politics.* New York: Random House, 1996.

7. **An E-Book or Online Edition** After indicating the author, title, and publishing information, add details about the e-book service, as well as other identifiers such as a URL.
Note:

> 8. Junius P. Rodriguez and Orlando Patterson, *Chronology of World Slavery* (Santa Barbara, CA: ABC-CLIO, 1999), NetLibrary, http://www.netLibrary.com.

Bibliography:

> Rodriguez, Junius P., and Orlando Patterson. *Chronology of World Slavery.* Santa Barbara, CA: ABC-CLIO, 1999. NetLibrary. http://www.netLibrary.com.

8. **A Multivolume Work**
Note:

> 9. Bruno Nettl, Ruth M. Stone, James Porter, and Timothy Rice, *The Garland Encyclopedia of World Music,* 10 vols. (New York: Garland Publishing, 1998-2002), 8: 98.

Bibliography:

> Nettl, Bruno, Ruth M. Stone, James Porter, and Timothy Rice. *The Garland Encyclopedia of World Music.* 10 vols. New York: Garland Publishing, 1998-2002.

9. A Work (Chapter, etc.) within an Edited Collection or Anthology

Note:

> 10. Robin Morgan, "Goodbye to All That," in *Masculine/Feminine: Readings in Sexual Mythology and the Liberation of Women,* ed. Betty Roszak and Theodore Roszak (New York: Harper & Row, 1969), 245.

Bibliography:

> Morgan, Robin. "Goodbye to All That." In *Masculine/Feminine: Readings in Sexual Mythology and the Liberation of Women,* ed. Betty Roszak and Theodore Roszak, 241-250. New York: Harper & Row, 1969.

10. Classical Works and Sacred Texts

Note: Books of the Bible may be abbreviated. For a classical Greek or Latin work, the text may be identified in a parenthetical citation rather than a note.

> 11. Luke 20:1-3 (New International Version).
>
> 12. Homer, *The Odyssey,* trans. E.V. Rieu (New York: Penguin Books, 1946), 85.

Bibliography: References to sacred texts and classical Greek and Latin works do not require bibliographic entries, unless you wish to indicate the specific edition.

> *The NIV Study Bible: New International Version.* Gen. ed. Kenneth Barker. Grand Rapids, MI: Zondervan Bible Publishers, 1985.
>
> Homer. *The Odyssey.* Translated by E.V. Rieu. New York: Penguin Books, 1946.

11. A Translation

Note: If the translator's name appears alone on the title page (e.g., for an anonymous work), put the name first followed by *trans.* In all other cases, place the translator's name as shown.

> 13. Friedrich Nietzsche, *The Birth of Tragedy and the Genealogy of Morals,* trans. Francis Golffing (Garden City, NY: Doubleday, 1956), 144.

Bibliography:

> Nietzsche, Friedrich. *The Birth of Tragedy and the Genealogy of Morals.* Translated by Francis Golffing. Garden City, NY: Doubleday, 1956.

12. A Reference Work

Note: For well-known reference works (e.g., major dictionaries or general encyclopedias), include the edition but exclude details about the publisher and page numbers.

> 14. "Women: Historical and Cross Cultural Perspectives," in *Encyclopedia of Bioethics,* rev. ed., 5 vols., ed. Warren T. Reich (New York: Macmillan Publishing, 1995), 5: 415.

Bibliography: While more specialized reference works should be included, standard dictionaries need not be listed in your bibliography.

> "Women: Historical and Cross Cultural Perspective." In *Encyclopedia of Bioethics.* Rev. ed. 5 vols., edited by Warren T. Reich. 5: 415-418. New York: Macmillan Publishing, 1995.

13. An Unpublished Dissertation, Thesis, or Essay
Note:

> 15. Timothy Lewis, "The Political Economy of Debt and Deficit Politics in Canada" (PhD diss., University of Toronto, 1999), 445-456.

Bibliography:

> Lewis, Timothy. "The Political Economy of Debt and Deficit Politics in Canada." PhD diss., University of Toronto, 1999.

Periodical Articles (Print and Digital)

While specific types of articles are discussed below, here are some general principles:

- **Notes:** For an article written by four or more authors, give the first author's name followed by "and others" or "et al." If you are referring to an online version of an article, add the URL followed by the access date in parentheses.
- **Bibliography:** For an article written by ten or fewer authors, list all names, with only the first inverted. For eleven or more authors, list only the first seven, followed by "and others" or "et al." If you are referring to an online version of an article, add the URL followed by the access date in parentheses.

14. Article in Scholarly Journal
Note:

> 16. William Moul, "Power Parity, Preponderance, and War between the Great Powers, 1816-1989," *The Journal of Conflict Resolution* 47, no. 4 (Aug. 2003), 475.

Bibliography:

> Moul, William. "Power Parity, Preponderance, and War between the Great Powers, 1816-1989." *The Journal of Conflict Resolution* 47, no. 4 (Aug. 2003): 468-489.

15. Article in Magazine (Monthly or Weekly)
Note:

> 17. Leanda de Lisle, "Katherine Grey: Heir to Elizabeth," *History Today,* September 2009, 26.

> 18. Andrew Coyne, "Inside the Meeting That Saved the World," *Maclean's,* October 19, 2009, 42.

Bibliography:

> de Lisle, Leanda. "Katherine Grey: Heir to Elizabeth." *History Today,* September 2009, 23-29.

Coyne, Andrew. "Inside the Meeting That Saved the World." *Maclean's,*
October 19, 2009, 40-47.

16. Newspaper Article

Note: Include full bibliographic information in the first reference, since newspaper articles are normally omitted from a bibliography.

19. Jeff Segal and Lauren Silva, "Case of Art Imitating Life?" *Wall Street Journal,* March 3, 2008, Eastern ed., C9.

Bibliography: Newspaper articles are generally not included in a bibliography, though you may include a particularly important one. Page numbers are optional, since they often differ from edition to edition.

Segal, Jeff, and Lauren Silva. "Case of Art Imitating Life?" *Wall Street Journal,*
March 3, 2008, Eastern ed., C9.

17. Anonymous Article

Note:

20. "Feeding the Hungry," *Economist* 371, no. 8374 (2004): 74.

Bibliography:

"Feeding the Hungry." *Economist* 371, no. 8374 (2004): 74.

18. A Review (of a Book, Film, CD, Exhibit, Etc.)

Note:

21. Anne Enright, "Come to Read Alice, Not to Praise Her," review of *Too Much Happiness,* by Alice Munro, *The Globe and Mail,* September 2, 2009, http://www.theglobeandmail.com/books/too-much-happiness-by-alice-munro (accessed October 8, 2009).

Bibliography:

Enright, Anne. "Come to Read Alice, Not to Praise Her." Review of *Too Much Happiness,* by Alice Munro. *The Globe and Mail,* September 2, 2009, http://www.theglobeandmail.com/books/too-much-happiness-by-alice-munro (accessed October 8, 2009).

Online Sources

19. Web Page

If you are referencing a Web site, start with the name of the site. When referencing a specific page, start with the page author, or if no author is indicated, the Web page title.

Note:

22. Companion Web site for *The Great War and the Shaping of the Twentieth Century,* http://www.pbs.org/greatwar (accessed October 8, 2009).

23. "Slaughter," Companion Web site for *The Great War and the Shaping of the Twentieth Century,* http://www.pbs.org/greatwar/chapters/ch2_slaughter .html (accessed October 8, 2009).

Bibliography:

> "Slaughter." Companion Web site for *The Great War and the Shaping of the Twentieth Century.* http://www.pbs.org/greatwar/chapters/ch2_slaughter .html (accessed October 8, 2009).

20. E-Mail or Discussion Group Posting

If a posting has been archived at a stable URL, include the address and your access date. Unless an e-mail, IM, or posting can be accessed by your reader on his or her own, do not include it in your bibliography.

Note:

> 24. Raymond Bolting, e-mail message to author, October 14, 2009.

> 25. J. Cubby, "Re: Connecting Playwrights & Theatre Companies," posting to AACT Online Forums: Playwriting & Playwrights, January 12, 2008, http:// www.aact.org/cgi-bin/yabb/YaBB.cgi (accessed October 14, 2009).

Bibliography:

> Cubby, J. "Re: Connecting Playwrights and Theatre Companies." Posting to AACT Online Forums: Playwriting & Playwrights. January 12, 2008. http:// www.aact.org/cgi-bin/yabb/YaBB.cgi (accessed October 14, 2009).

21. A Blog Entry

Note:

> 26. "On This Day in History: Jim Hines Won Olympic 100m Final, 1968," The Modern Historian Weblog, entry posted October 14, 2009. http:// modernhistorian.blogspot.com/2009/10/on-this-day-in-history-jim-hines -won.html (accessed October 30, 2009).

Bibliography:

> "On This Day in History: Jim Hines Won Olympic 100m Final, 1968." The Modern Historian Weblog. Entry posted October 14, 2009. http:// modernhistorian.blogspot.com/2009/10/on-this-day-in-history-jim-hines -won.html (accessed October 30, 2009).

22. A Podcast

Note:

> 27. Nick Lippis, "The Post Great Recession IT Industry Structure," *The Lippis Report Podcasts,* n.d. http://lippisreport.com/2009/09/the-post-great -recession-it-industry-structure (accessed October 14, 2009).

Bibliography:

> Lippis, Nick. "The Post Great Recession IT Industry Structure." *The Lippis Report Podcasts.* n.d. http://lippisreport.com/2009/09/the-post-great -recession-it-industry-structure (accessed October 14, 2009).

Other Sources (Primary, Personal, and Multimedia)

23. Material from an Archive or a Special Collection

When referencing material from a physical archive or an online archive, provide as much of the following information as possible in this order: author and item description, date of item, identification number for item, collection title, and library location and/or online site.

Note:

> 28. Program of PROGRESS, Oldest Negro Publication in Canada, ca. 1901, Alvin D. McCurdy Fonds, Archives of Ontario, http://www.archives.gov.on.ca/ english/on-line-exhibits/alvin-mccurdy/community.aspx (accessed October 14, 2009).

Bibliography: Generally list the collection first because of its primary importance, unless in your paper you reference only one item from the collection.

> Alvin D. McCurdy Fonds, Archives of Ontario, http://www.archives.gov .on.ca/english/on-line-exhibits/alvin-mccurdy/community.aspx (accessed October 14, 2009).

24. An Interview (Published or Personal)

For interviews that you conduct, indicate the type of interview (personal, telephone).

Note:

> 29. Alice Munro, personal interview, October 15, 2009.

> 30. Maria Cantwell, "The New Technocrat," interview by Erika Rasmusson, *Working Woman,* April 2001, 20.

Bibliography: Include published interviews but not personal interviews in your bibliography.

> Cantwell, Maria. "The New Technocrat." Interview by Erika Rasmusson. *Working Woman,* April 2001, 20–21.

25. Artwork or Photograph

Note: For original artworks and photographs, give a date (approximate, if necessary, preceded by ca., meaning circa or around) and location (e.g., museum, institute, gallery). For works reproduced in books or accessed online, provide publication information after the artist, title of the work, and date, as shown.

> 31. El Greco, *The Assumption of the Virgin,* 1577–1579, Art Institute of Chicago.

> 32. Yousuf Karsh, *Winston Churchill,* 1941, Estate of Yousuf Karsh, http:// www.karsh.org/#/the_work/portraits/winston_churchill (accessed February 14, 2010).

> 33. Henri Matisse, *Venus in the Shell,* 1930, in Gilles Néret, *Henri Matisse,* trans. Josephine Bacon (Köln, Germany: Taschen, 1996), 163.

Bibliography: Artworks and photographs are not listed in your bibliography.

26. **A Performance, Film, Video, or Television Program**

For performances, recordings, and broadcasts, include essential identifying information. If you are featuring specific elements, add these to your reference.

Note:

> 34. *The Devil's Disciple,* by Bernard Shaw, directed by Tadeusz Bradecki, performed by Evan Buliung, Donna Belleville, Guy Bannerman, Fiona Byrne, Peter Krantz, Shaw Festival Theatre, Niagara-on-the-Lake, Ontario, October 3, 2009.
>
> 35. *Mr. Smith Goes to Washington,* DVD, directed by Frank Capra (1939; Culver City, CA: Columbia Pictures, 2008).
>
> 36. *Monty Python's Flying Circus,* "Whither Canada?" season 1, episode 1, directed by Ian MacNaughton, performed by Graham Chapman, John Cleese, Terry Gilliam, Eric Idle, Terry Jones, Michael Palin, BBC, October 5, 1969.

Bibliography:

> *Mr. Smith Goes to Washington,* DVD. Directed by Frank Capra. Performed by Jean Arthur and James Stewart. Screenplay by Sidney Buchman. 1939; Touchstone Pictures, 2008.

27. **Musical Recording**

For a typical recording, follow the pattern below. However, if you are referencing a music video or liner notes, identify the source as such: *music video* after the title, *liner notes for* placed before the title. If you accessed the music online, indicate the online vendor and/or URL, along with your access date in parentheses.

Note:

> 37. Michael Bublé, "Cry Me a River," *Crazy Love,* Reprise Records 143, 2009.

Bibliography:

> Bublé, Michael. "Cry Me a River." *Crazy Love.* Reprise Records 143, 2009.

Sample Chicago Paper

Student writer Robert Minto wrote "A Thorn Beneath the Shining Armor: Churchill, Bishop Bell, and Area Bombing" in a history course focused on Great Britain. You can use this model paper in three ways:

1. To study how a well-written humanities research paper builds a discussion from start to finish.

2. To examine how sources are carefully integrated into research writing—a full-length example of the strategies discussed on pages 190-192.

3. To see in detail the format and documentation practices of Chicago/Turabian style.

 FOCUS on Multimedia: To see what Robert's paper looks like on standard 8.5 by 11 inch pages, visit our Web site at www.theresearchwriter.com.

Writer's Reflection

"I wrote this essay for a class on the History of the British Isles. One of the primary sources my professor, Keith Sewell, encouraged us to read was the wartime speeches of Winston Churchill. Because I enjoyed his speeches, I decided to delve deeper into the life of Churchill. But I was appalled at what I found there. Though Churchill was a great man in many respects, the pervasive comparative evaluation of Churchill with Hitler emerges from a triumphalist example of selective listening to history. I decided that in my final essay, I would try to puncture this evaluation with a particularly lurid example of one of the ways Churchill even exceeded Hitler in savagery: area bombing."

—Robert Minto

Preparing to Read: What have you studied of WWII in the past? What do you know about bombing practices? What about Winston Churchill and Adolph Hitler as contrasting leaders?

Sample First Page

Flush left, create a heading with your name, your professor's name, the course number, and the date.

Place page numbers in the upper right corner, along with your last name.

Minto 1

In the introduction, Robert introduces his focus on the moral issues associated with aerial bombing in WWII and offers his thesis.

Robert M. D. Minto

Professor Keith Sewell

History 212: History of the British Isles

April 17, 2010

Center the title below the heading and above the text.

A Thorn Beneath the Shining Armor:

Churchill, Bishop Bell, and Area Bombing

No one cares to challenge the idea that Adolph Hitler needed to be stopped. I cannot think of an intellectual cow more popularly sacred than the righteousness of World War II. The enemy of the Allies was so ghastly, that even much-deplored developments on the part of the "good guys"—the atomic bomb, for example—cannot dethrone Hitler from his place as the exemplary villain of our age. In moral terms, Hitler has been held up as the paragon of evil, a case study for everything from the dangers of the gospel of self-esteem to the spirit of the Antichrist. If this is the case now, in North America in 2010, then how much more villainous did he appear, for example, to the citizens of Britain, victims of his bombs, an isolated people whose nation trembled but remained firm before the force of the Nazi wave? In fact, Hitler appeared so evil that the ones who opposed him could hardly help but appear good. WWII is historically the closest thing to a post-Middle Ages crusade.

Double-space everything in the paper.

Use one-inch margins on all sides (except with the page number, which is ½ inch from the top). Leave the right margin ragged.

For this reason, it is difficult to poke a hole in the shining armor of British involvement in WWII. However, I propose to do so by way of illustrating the dangers of a crusade grounded on a secular morality. The dramatic figures we will follow are Winston Churchill and Bishop Bell, as the former fights his crusade and the latter questions the holiness of it.

The Gradual Descent of Bomber Command

Centered headings divide the paper into sections.

On September 3, 1939, Bomber Command authorized its first operation in World War II. Bomber planes executed a strike upon Bremen, Hamburg, and several other smaller cities in Germany. The

Minto 2

payload? Pamphlets urging the German people to rebel against Nazi rule.[1]

Eight months of quiet followed before Bomber Command sent out anything against civilians more lethal than these pamphlets. Legend has it that the pamphlet paper supplied Germans with toilet paper for the entire first year of the war.[2] Bombs were simply too imprecise, and Prime Minister Chamberlain was strongly against any suggestion that their inaccurate destructiveness could work for good. In a Parliamentary debate on July 21, 1938, he had said the following:

> We can strongly condemn any declaration on the part of anybody, wherever it may be made, that it should be part of a deliberate policy to try to win a war by the demoralization of the civilian population through the process of bombing from the air. This is absolutely contrary to international law, and I would add that, in my opinion, it is a mistaken policy from the point of view of those who adopt it, but I do not believe that deliberate attacks upon a civilian population will ever win a war for those who make them.[3]

Chamberlain could argue that this sort of bombing was "absolutely contrary to international law" not because any particular law against aerial bombing of civilians existed but because of a precedent established at the Hague Conference. In 1907, according to Geoffrey Best, Britain, "leading the list of signatories,"[4] signed a Declaration at the Hague Conference agreeing to "prohibit the discharge of projectiles and explosives from balloons or by other new methods of similar nature."[5] However, because this document was only a "'Declaration', not a proper Convention, it quickly became nothing more than a historical curiosity."[6] The 1907 *Hague Land War Regulations* prohibited "'the attack or bombardment, by any means whatever, of towns, villages, habitations, or buildings which are not defended.'"[7]

Then, on September 10, 1940, Hitler began an aerial bombardment of London that would last for 57 days, killing nearly 50,000 civilians and destroying nearly 1,000,000 houses.

A source reference is indicated with a superscript number.

Citations are numbered sequentially.

The writer offers a long quotation from a primary source, indenting the whole passage.

A series of direct quotations is carefully documented.

Minto 3

The writer advances his argument through a key quotation.

What becomes of international law when one party violates it so viciously? Nations bring out their enforcers. And that is precisely what happened, in the person of Winston Churchill, who became Prime Minister soon after 6:00 p.m. that same day. Churchill described his feelings on this occasion as ones of "walking with destiny."[8] The sense of destiny in wartime has often been felt by humanity with dire consequences. It is often a key ingredient in a crusade.

Churchill moved the issue of the war with Germany out of the realm of defensive violence onto an altogether more epic and spiritual plane in his very first public speech to the House of Commons as Prime Minister:

A second long quotation from a primary source effectively contrasts the first inset quotation.

> You ask, what is our aim? I can answer in one word: Victory—victory at all costs, victory in spite of all terror, victory, however long and hard the road may be, for without victory, there is no survival. Let that be realized; no survival for the British Empire; no survival for all that the British empire has stood for, no survival for the urge and impulse of the ages, that mankind will move forward towards its goal. But I take up my task with buoyancy and hope. I feel sure that our cause will not be suffered to fail among men. At this time I feel entitled to claim the aid of all, and I say, "Come, then, let us go forward together with our united strength."[9]

In light of what we will shortly be considering, "victory at all costs" sounds more ominous than glorious. The spirit that Churchill here begins to prod to life—the spirit of British nationalism—demonstrates just how his appointment as chief executive in the war was a fire-against-fire measure. Something that is rarely done is to compare the respective grounds on which the war was fought at first—and these grounds were very much a myth of German nationalism against a myth of British nationalism. And it could be argued that Churchill was as successful in rallying greater Britain through his rhetoric and statesmanship as Hitler was in raising the Third Reich with his.

Minto 4

The key phrase in the above quotation is this: "all that the British empire has stood for [...] the urge and impulse of the ages, that mankind will move forward towards its goal." Setting up the British Empire as the "urge and impulse" toward mankind's "goal" can hardly be considered less than a declaration that the authority behind Churchill's war making was a providence-directed force. Already we can see the subtle confusion that would eventually allow Churchill's administration to sanction retaliatory area bombing with a clear conscience: the morality that opposition to the immorality of Hitler signified is here conflated with the honor of the British nation. Morality conflated with anything but the honor of God is a recipe for human vengeance.[10]

Early in 1940, Churchill addressed his war cabinet in these words: "[T]he civilian populations around the target areas [of precision bombing] must be made to feel the weight of the war."[11] As he began to survey Britain's chances in this war, Churchill found very little hope for progress on any front. The prospect was bleak. The blitz on London continued unabated, and the humanity of its perpetrators began to fade away from British consciousness as the bombs fell. In December, 1940, Churchill authorized an air-strike on Mannheim "specifically described as a retaliation for the earlier German assault on Coventry."[12] Stephen Garrett claims that, "in effect, Churchill's argument seemed to be that in order to sustain the nation's morale, it was necessary to do unto others as they were doing to Britain."[13] Geoffrey Best categorizes this decision as one with many precedents in the history of land and sea bombardments:

> The most short and easy method to avert criticism was to admit the illegality of the whole thing at once by announcing it plainly as a reprisal; as was often done by all the bombing powers in both world wars. Reprisals by definition are unlawful acts deliberately done to punish and deter an unlawfully behaving enemy. Wars being what they are, and the business of propaganda being what it is, there was never much difficulty in finding pretexts for reprisals, and much

---

The writer deepens and extends his analysis of the inset quotation by closely examining the language.

A content note points to a source that readers might find useful.

Changes and clarifications in a quotation are placed in brackets.

Robert balances his analysis of quotations from primary sources with support from recognized and respected scholars (his secondary sources).

Minto 5

advantage in doing so, no further justification being called for, and the moral responsibility being thrown back upon the enemy.[14] However, on Feb. 14, 1942, Churchill moved beyond this reprisal argument toward more specific aggressions. All wavering between an "ostensible program of precision bombing and an increasing tendency toward area bombing" ended with *Directive No. 22,* issued to Bomber Command.[15] This directive stated that now the bombing offensive was to be "focused on the morale of the enemy civil population and in particular of the industrial workers."[16] The chief of Air Staff added in a memo the next day, "the aiming points are to be the built-up areas, not, for instance, the dockyards or aircraft factories."[17] Over the next three years, about three quarters of the bombs dropped on Germany by Great Britain were against densely populated civilian targets.[18]

The Rationale for Area Bombing

In war it is always easy to find excuses for successful violence. The immediate and unspoken reason for Churchill's huge support of the Bombing Offensive in general is that it was a satisfying, devastating return for the sufferings of the British people at a time when no other military front could boast such success. Area bombing was a natural step from this position because it was virtually impossible to be precise when bombing at night. Germany's anti-air defenses were too good for daylight approaches, so the only way for the Bombing Offensive to continue was via area bombing—in the early 1940s it was one of very few ways Britain seemed to be taking the war to the enemy.

Gradually, and later, other factors joined this one to justify area bombing. For example, Lord Cherwell, in a minute to the Prime Minister on March 30, 1942, suggested from an analysis of German bombing of British cities that house damage was even more demoralizing than loss of relatives, so the idea of "the shattering of the German people's morale, and thus of Germany's will or ability to continue her war," became one of Bomber Command's guiding principles.[19] It may be

---

With a new heading to signal a shift, the writer explores and critiques the rationale given for aerial bombing.

Minto 6

unnecessary to point out that this rationale ignored the nearest example of the effect of area bombing upon national morale: Britain itself. The blitz, far from shutting down the British spirit, was exactly the fuel that Churchill's righteous indignation needed to fire the fighting spirit of his fellow citizens. British area bombing served up far more destruction of lives than the blitz did—it is estimated that over 500,000 German civilians died in these bombardments [20]—with just as little effect from dampened morale.

However, perhaps the most ironic and deceptive rationale for area bombing involved collateral damage to factories and military installations. Martin Middlebrook describes the public relations of the Bomber Offensive in this way:

> In some ways, area bombing was a three-year period of deceit practiced upon the British public and upon world opinion. It was felt to be necessary that the exact nature of R.A.F. Bombing should not be revealed [...] the impression usually given was that the industry was the main target and that any bombing of worker's housing was an unavoidable necessity. Charges of "indiscriminate bombing" were consistently denied. The deceit lay in the concealment of the fact that the areas being most heavily bombed were nearly always either city centers or densely populated residential areas, which rarely contained any industry. [21]

Geoffrey Best also comments upon the deceitfulness of this rationale:

> [J]ustification [...] was facilitated by the very nature of "indiscriminate" bombing itself. It was, necessarily, the bombing of inhabited areas; if not sizeable towns and cities, then at any rate "industrial areas"; areas where "every bomb would count." But hardly ever was there nothing within such areas that could not be construed as a military target, and often civilian premises in such urban/industrial areas lay close to very obvious military targets indeed. It could therefore truthfully enough be claimed

Two inset quotations from scholars lend authority to the writer's argument.

Minto 7

that "military targets were hit," without mentioning how much else besides military targets was hit or (as became the case with indiscriminate bombardment *par excellence* in the second world war) that the civilians and their houses—the "collateral damage," to use one of the standard phrases for it—are what you had really been interested in.[22]

The Preacher Against the Crusade

One might expect the church in England to have something to say to such ethically questionable policies as area bombing. However, for the most part, the church partook of the general atmosphere of resolute British nationalism and anti-Germanic sentiment. One churchman, however, stands out. Bishop Bell, a cleric of the Anglican Church, saw clearly the situation of his contemporaries with respect to Germany— and feared as much for a war won as for a war lost.

Bell was a humanitarian activist in many ways. He made the issue of area bombing his own personal issue, and before that, he had engaged in such humanitarian ventures as visiting German refugee camps, lobbying for better conditions for them, and chairing the Famine Relief Committee. He was also connected, by way of Dietrich Bonhoeffer, with the conspiracy that could have overthrown Hitler from within the Führer's own ranks. In 1942, Bell met with Bonhoeffer and relayed from him to the British government news of this conspiracy. The British government paid no attention, and eventually the conspiracy was foiled.

All of this activity prepared Bell for his biggest stand—a stand larger than just against area bombing, a stand for the humanity of the German people despite their own belligerent leaders. In a speech to the House of Lords, on February 11, 1943, where he brought the inhumanity of area bombing into focus—to the consternation of all—he made the following remarks:

A new heading indicates a shift to a new figure in the story.

The writer introduces and offers background on Bell that prepares for the discussion of Bell's critique of aerial bombing.

Using statements by Bell in a speech and in a magazine article, the writer contrasts Bell's thinking with the stance of those supporting aerial bombing.

To line up the Nazi assassins in the same row with the people of Germany whom they have outraged is to make for more barbarism, possibly to postpone peace, and to make certain an incredible worsening of the conditions of all Europe when at last peace comes. [...] The remedy is to tell those inside Germany who are anti-Fascist that we want their help, that we are willing to help them in getting rid of the common enemy, and that we intend that a Germany delivered from Hitlerism shall have fair play and a proper place in the family of Europe.[23]

Here we have a profound contrast to Churchill's whipping up of the British spirit of nationalism—instead, a moral stance based upon openly Christian principles. Bell was profoundly aware of a transnational community—the church—and of its ecumenical commitments. British Christians could not abandon German Christians. Certainly British Christians could not condone the massacre of Germans by the area bombing of their civil centers. In the *Chichester Diocesan Gazette,* January 1940, Bell wrote the following:

Robert asks pointed questions about religion and war as a way of focusing Bell's critique.

It is our task to make the European tradition, a tradition animated by the Christian spirit, prevail: to interpret its character: to show it reintegrating a dying civilization, by a rekindling of the old strength at the ancient sources: to set it forth in all its implications, derived from an all-embracing Christian faith: and reveal it embodied in the political and economic order, in the relation of nations, and in the collective life, as well as in the experience of the individual personality.[24]

This declaration points to the unavoidable conclusion that a holy or just war must not be pursued merely with the fanaticism of a crusade but rather with virtues of all-embracing holiness and justice that alone merit such fanatical resistance. Can war ever be pursued in this way? Can justice and mercy ever meet in such a world?

Minto 9

In his conclusion, Robert returns to his beginning and presses readers to connect his analysis with current affairs.

For many, WWII is characterized by iconic images and memories of evil. However, we are all too apt to be kind to those who write the histories—an uncritical tendency that can very easily lead to the repetition of history. A close examination of Britain's aerial bombardment of civilian Germany suggests that some icons need to be approached more thoughtfully. Without applying this historical story of nationalist bombardment to a particular current event, this question needs to be asked: Will we side with the Churchills or the Bishop Bells of our generation?

Sample Endnotes Page

Notes

Start the Endnotes page on a new page after the text, paginated consecutively.

1. Stephen A. Garrett, *Ethics and Airpower in WWII* (New York: St. Martin's Press, 1993), 9.

2. Ibid., 10.

3. Neville Chamberlain, Parliamentary Debates, Vol. 337 (London: British House of Commons, 1938).

Center the title "Notes" at the top of the page.

4. Geoffrey Best, *Humanity In Warfare: The Modern History of International Law of Armed Conflicts* (Bristol: Methuen Press, 1983), 262.

5. Ibid., 262.

6. Ibid., 262.

Double-space within and between notes.

7. Ibid., 263.

8. Geoffrey Best, *Churchill: A Study in Greatness* (London: Oxford University Press, 2003), 165.

9. Winston Churchill, "Blood, Toil, Tears, and Sweat,'" in *Blood, Toil, Tears, and Sweat: the Great Speeches,* ed. David Cannadine (London: Penguin Books, 2002), 149.

In your notes, include all sources summarized, paraphrased, or quoted in your paper—in the order used in the paper.

10. For an interesting study of the German side of this issue, consult *The Holy Reich: Nazi Conceptions of Christianity, 1919-1945,* by Richard Steigmann-Gall.

11. Charles Messenger, *Bounder Harris* (New York: St. Martin's Press, 1984), 40.

12. Garrett, *Ethics and Airpower,* 12.

13. Ibid., 12.

14. Best, *Humanity in Warfare,* 267-268.

Indent the first line of each entry, type the number (not superscript) plus a period and a space. Keep second and subsequent lines flush left.

15. John Colville, *The Fringes of Power* (New York: W.W. Norton, 1985), 311.

16. Ibid., 311.

17. Ibid., 312.

18. Garrett, *Ethics and Airpower,* 11-12.

Minto 11

For subsequent notes to a source, use the author's last name, a shortened title, and page numbers. For successive notes on the same source, use *Ibid.*

19. Ibid., 13.

20. Ibid., 21.

21. Martin Middlebrook, *The Battle of Hamburg* (London: Allen Lane Publishing, 1980), 343-344.

22. Best, *Humanity in Warfare,* 268.

23. George Bell, Parliamentary Debates, Vol. 125 (London: British House of Lords, 1943), 31.

24. George Bell, *Chichester Diocesan Gazette* (January 1940); quoted in Ronald Jasper, *George Bell: Bishop of Chichester* (New York: Oxford University Press, 1968), 259.

Follow capitalization and punctuation as shown.

Chicago Style: Activities

1. Print a copy of a research paper that you wrote earlier in your schooling. Using the instruction and information in this chapter, carefully edit the paper so that it follows current Chicago guidelines for paper format, citation, endnotes, and bibliography.

2. Study the sample paper on pages 470-481. Explain how effectively Robert follows the overall philosophy and style of the Chicago system in his writing: does he engage his sources and present them in such a way as to successfully develop his argument and convince you of his credibility as a researcher?

3. Using the broad topic of the sample paper (the ethics of certain practices in war) as a starting point, develop your own focused topic, do research for a variety of resources, and put together a bibliography of eight quality sources. Make sure that your bibliography is correctly ordered and formatted. Then, for each source, draft a brief passage in which you use the source (either through summary, paraphrase, or quotation) and create a correct endnote.

4. For the writing project that you are currently working on, develop a working bibliography of fitting resources properly ordered and formatted in Chicago style. Exchange your working bibliography with a classmate, and edit each other's lists.

Chicago Style: Checklist

Checklist:

☑ All borrowed material is acknowledged with an appropriate attributive phrase and/or a superscript number.

☑ Source references are numbered sequentially from the beginning to the end of the paper.

☑ Each superscript number has a corresponding footnote (bottom of page) or endnote (separate page at end of paper) that correctly identifies the source of the information (bibliographic note) or that offers supplemental information to the paper's discussion (a content note).

☑ Each footnote or endnote supplies correct source information:

- The first reference to a source supplies complete identifying information: author, title, publication details, and page number(s).

- Subsequent references to the source (references separated from the first reference by references to other sources) use the author's last name, a shortened title, and the page number(s).

- When subsequent references come immediately after a previous reference to the source, the source information is shortened to *Ibid.* plus page number(s).

☑ The entire paper is properly formatted: from the title page to any bibliography.

- Placement, spacing, and margins are correct for the essay and endnotes, as well as any title page, outline, or bibliography included.

- Pagination is correct and consistent.

- First lines of paragraphs and notes are properly indented; bibliographic entries are properly formatted with hanging indent.

- The paper is cleanly printed single-sided on quality paper in a professional-looking typeface and in 12-point type size (without fancy type style features).

- Rules for capitalization, lowercase, quotation marks, and italics are observed throughout the text, especially with names and titles.

Illustrated by Chris Krenzke
© Cengage Learning/

21

CSE Style
and Sample Paper

Q How do you document research in the natural and applied sciences? How are sources treated in science writing?

In the natural and applied sciences, documentation practices differ discipline by discipline. If you are a student in one of these sciences, you need to learn the appropriate documentation system by talking to your professors and studying the right style manuals. (Go to www.theresearchwriter.com for examples.) Nevertheless, the most common documentation style in the sciences is the CSE format. This chapter offers a brief introduction to this system.

What's the CSE? CSE stands for the Council of Science Editors—the primary professional organization of authors, editors, and publishers in the natural and applied sciences.

What is CSE Style? In a nutshell, CSE style offers three choices: the name-year system of in-text citation, the citation-name sequence system, or the citation-sequence system, each accompanied by a references list. Because the name-year system is similar to APA format (chapter 19) and the citation-name system is similar to MLA format (chapter 18), we'll focus on the citation-sequence option, which has these features:

- **In-text citation**—the use of a number (in superscript) corresponding to a numbered entry in a References list.
- **References**—a list of numbered resources sequenced according to the first reference to the source in the paper (not arranged alphabetically).

Where Can You Find More Information about CSE Style? This chapter offers a brief introduction to CSE style. For further information, consult the following:

- *Scientific Style and Format: The CSE Manual for Authors, Editors, and Publishers* (7th edition, 2006): check your library's reference section.
- The CSE Web site (http://www.councilscienceeditors.org).
- Web resources at our Web site (http://www.theresearchwriter.com).

What's Ahead?

Directory to CSE Style

If you have a specific question about CSE style, use the directory below to find the answer within this chapter.

CSE Documentation: Quick Guide

The CSE citation-sequence system involves two parts: (1) a numbered in-text citation within your paper when you use a source; and (2) a bibliographic entry keyed by the number at the end of your paper. Note these features of the CSE system:

■ **It typically refers to entire sources** through the use of the numbers. Each number is assigned sequentially as sources are used within the text. When the source is referred to again in the paper, the assigned number is re-used.

■ **It lists sources by number, not by alphabet.** Unlike other systems that arrange references in the end-of-paper list alphabetically by authors' last names, CSE lists sources in the order that they first appear in the text.

You can see these features at work in the example below.

In-Text Citation in Body of Paper

Three main types of genetic mutations can provide bacteria with a means of antibiotic resistance [4]. First, mutations can produce "plugs" that block an antibiotic from entering the bacterial cell. . . .

Matching References Entry at End of Paper

4.   Kairys DJ. The science behind antibiotic resistance. Rev of Optometry 2002 Oct 15:39-44.

In the example on the previous page, the superscripted [4] tells the reader that

- the information prior to the number is borrowed from a source.
- publication information for that source is listed under *4* in the references page.
- the discussion after the number summarizes the source or provides further information from it.

In-Text Citation: The Basics

With the citation-sequence approach, the placement of the numbered citation follows these straightforward rules:

- Place the number immediately after the words to which they refer. Whether you are referencing a specific author or a topic, place the number immediately after the word, not at the end of a sentence or passage. In addition, place the number within any punctuation mark (e.g., comma or period).
- Use a superscript (raised) number. To insert a superscript number, check your word-processing program's "insert" function. (Your instructor may allow use of a number in parentheses or brackets instead.)
- Number sources consecutively, according to first references. Number sources in the order that they initially appear in your writing; for second and subsequent references to a source, use the originally assigned number.
- For references to multiple sources, use hyphens and commas. When referring, for example, to sources 3, 4, and 5, use *3-5*; when referring to sources 7 and 9, use *7, 9*.

Reference Entries: The Basics

A sample references page is shown on pages 494–495, while sample references for the most common resources are found on pages 486–488. Below, however, are some templates for common entries. (Note that in the references page each entry is double spaced and that second and subsequent lines line up under the first letter of the first word (not under the number).

Template for Print Book:

Source Number. Author's Last Name Initials. Title of book. Publication City (State or Country): Publisher; publication year.

1. Tortora GJ, Funke BR, Case CL. Microbiology: An introduction. San Francisco (CA): Benjamin Cummings; 2002.

Template for Print Periodical Article:

Source Number. Author's Last Name Initials. Title of article. Journal Title abbreviated year;volume(issue):page numbers.

Note: Do not include a space between year, volume, issue, and page numbers.

3. Wenzel RP, Edmond MB. Managing antibiotic resistance. New Engl J Med 2000;343:1961-3.

Template for an Online Document:

Source Number. Author's Last Name Initials. Title of work. [Medium]. Place of publication or [place unknown]: Publisher or [publisher unknown]. Date of publication [plus date last updated or modified; date cited, accessed, or retrieved]; page, document, volume, and issue numbers. Pages or approximate length [lines, paragraphs, screens]. Available from: URL doi:number

6. Davies PD. Does increased use of antibiotics result in increased antibiotic resistance? Clin Infect Dis [database on the Internet]. 2004 [cited 2010 Apr 3];39(1):11-17. Available from: http://www.ncbi.nlm.nih.gov/entrez/query.fcgi

CSE References

While templates for the main types of resources (books, journal articles, and online sources) are outlined above and on the previous page, the following pages offer models for a range of specific sources within those categories.

Books and Other Nonperiodical Sources (Print)

1. A Book with One Author

1. Bargagli R. Antarctic ecosystems: Environmental contamination, climate change, and human impact. Berlin (Germany). Springer; 2005.

2. A Book with More Than One Author

2. Stern N, Sager A, Stern RA. Assembler language programming for IBM and IBM compatible computers. Indianapolis (IN): Wiley; 1986.

3. A Book with an Editor

3. Kyrala GA, editor. High energy density laboratory astrophysics. Houten (Netherlands). Springer; 2005.

4. An Anonymous Publication

4. Environmental Fact Sheet. Lincoln (NE): Nebraska Dept. of Environmental Quality; 2001.

5. A Multivolume Work

5. Hobson KA, Wassenaar LI, editors. Tracking animal migration with stable isotopes. London (England). Academic Press; 2008. (Terrestrial ecology; vol. 2).

6. A Work (Chapter, etc.) within Edited Collections, Anthologies, or Conference Proceedings

6. Ndubisi F. Landscape ecological planning. In: Thompson GF, Steiner FR, editors. Ecological design and planning. New York (NY): Wiley; 1997.

7. A Translation

7. Gürlebeck K, Habetha K, Sprößig W. Holomorphic functions in the plane and n-dimensional space. Venturino E, Schneider M, Schlichting A, translators. Basel (Switzerland). Birkhäuser Verlag; 2008.

8. **An Unpublished Dissertation or Thesis**

   8. Tewg JY. Zirconium-doped tantalum oxide high-k gate dielectric films [dissertation]. [Bryan/College Station (TX)]: Texas A&M University; 2005.

9. **A Database (Non-Internet)** After the title, include the medium in brackets. End with notes of physical format and any other pertinent information

   9. PowerOne medical combo [CD-ROM]. Beaverton (OR). Infinity Softworks; 2005. 1 CD-ROM: 5 1/4 in. System Requirements: Windows 98/XP Tablet PC Edition/2000/Me/XP/XP Professional/XP Home Edition, Pocket PC 2000/2002/2003/Windows Mobile 3 or Palm OS 3.1 or later, 2MB of Windows or Macintosh computer memory for manual and installer.

Periodical Articles (Print)

10. **An Article in a Scholarly Journal**

    10. Hu G, Shen J, Cheng L, Xiang D, Zhang Z, He M, Lu H, Zhu S, Wu M, Yu Y, et al. Purification of a bioactive recombinant human Reg IV expressed in Escherichia coli. Protein Expr Purif. 2010;69(2):186-90.

Note: List the first ten authors, followed by et al. for "and others."

11. **An Article in a Magazine (Monthly or Weekly)**

    11. Seiffert ER, Perry JM, Simons EL, Boyer DM. Convergent evolution of anthropoid-like adaptations in Eocene adapiform primates. Nature. 2009 Oct 22:1118-1121.

12. **A Newspaper Article**

    12. Hamilton, T. It's only a letdown if you expected something better. Washington Post; 2009 Oct 12;Sect. D:1.

13. **An Anonymous Article**

    13. International pact needed to prevent organ trafficking, UN-backed study says. Arabia 2000. 2009 Oct 14;Sect. A:1,3.

Internet Sources

Besides the usual information for a print source, include the designator [Internet] after the primary title; add any update and your date of access in brackets after the publication date; and conclude with an "Available from:" statement, including the doi if available.

14. **A Book on the Internet**

    14. Model ML. Bioinformatics programming using python [Internet]. Sebastopol (CA). O'Reilly Media; 2009 [cited 2010 Jan 31]. Available from: http://my.safaribooksonline.com/9780596804725

15. **A Journal Article on the Internet**

    15. Kiriharaa M, Yamamotoa J, Noguchia T, Itoua A, Naitoa S, Hiraib Y. Tantalum(V) or niobium(V) catalyzed oxidation of sulfides with 30% hydrogen peroxide. Tetrahedron [Internet]. 2009 Dec [cited 2010 Feb 19];65(50)10477-10484. Available from: http://www.sciencedirect.com doi:10.1016/j.tet.2009.10.007

16. An Internet Homepage

16. The Carl Sagan portal [Internet]. [place unknown] Druyan - Sagan Associates; c2009 [cited 2010 Mar 28]. Available from: http://www.carlsagan.com

Note: The "c" beginning the date indicates that this is a copyright date.

17. An Anonymous Portion of an Internet Site Begin by citing all but the URL of the Internet homepage (see above). Then include specific information for the section cited, as shown here.

17. Harvard University: Office of the Vice Provost for Research [Internet]. [Cambridge (MA)]: Harvard Univ.; c2009. Harvard university and federal stimulus funding: Alert! Assurances and compliances [cited 2010 Feb 8]; [1 paragraph]. Available from: http://research.harvard.edu/content/ harvard-university-and-federal-stimulus-funding

Note: In this example, the section title includes both page title (before the colon) and subheading on the page (after the colon). The square brackets around the place of publication indicate that the location is inferred by the researcher, not actually stated in the source.

Audiovisual Sources

Add the medium in brackets just after the title, and end with a physical description. (For journals in audiovisual media, place the medium after the journal title, not the article title.)

18. A Videocassette

18. Standard Deviants. Organic chemistry, part 3 [videocassette]. San Francisco (CA). Cerebellum Corp., 2000. 1 videocassette, 120 min.

19. An Audiodisc

19. Scivision, editor. Scilogp [audiodisc]. San Diego (CA). Academic Press; 1999. 1 audiodisc: 196 min.

Sample CSE Paper

Because paper format in the natural sciences is typically specified by the form (e.g., lab report, field report, literature review) and the submission requirements of specific journals, the CSE does not advocate for a strict format (unlike MLA, for example). However, science papers and reports should share general characteristics of format, layout, and typography. While you can study these characteristics in the model literature review on pages 362-367 and the model IMRAD report on pages 330-338, you can also see this format and documentation at work in "Human Papillomavirus Infection in Males: Penile Carcinoma" by student writer Aurora Seaton Cruz.

 FOCUS on Multimedia: To see what Aurora's paper looks like on standard 8.5 by 11 inch pages, visit our Web site at (http://www.theresearchwriter.com).

Writer's Reflection

When I was assigned a research paper on a health topic of my choosing, my first thought was human papillomavirus. I've seen the devastating effects of HPV in women and girls while working in a gynecology practice, but with all the excitement and press surrounding the HPV vaccine (FDA approved only for women), I decided to research the effects of HPV in males. The research process was more interesting and intellectually empowering than I had imagined. I'd like to thank my professor Dr. James McElroy for pushing me beyond my comfort zone and making me a better writer. I'd also like to thank Dr. Karen Callen, who first gave me the opportunity to love medicine, and who demonstrates what is required to be an exceptional physician. I hope others find the result of my research paper to be interesting and informative.

—Aurora Seaton Cruz

Preparing to Read: What do you know about cancer as it impacts women and men? In what ways is cancer related to gender? How comfortable are you with reading and understanding cancer studies? How are such scientific studies popularized within society?

Sample First Page

Place page numbers in the upper right corner.

Center the report's title, your name as the writer, and the date.

Use one-inch margins on all sides.

Use headings to help readers quickly grasp information.

Indent paragraphs and double-space throughout the text.

Indicate source references with citations numbered by the order in which sources are used in the paper. Numbers may be superscript or placed within parentheses or brackets.

1

Human Papillomavirus Infection in Males:

Penile Carcinoma

Aurora Seaton Cruz

2010 Apr 17

Abstract

Although Human Papillomavirus (HPV) is responsible for nearly all cervical cancers in women, infected men are almost universally asymptomatic. Studies reveal that more than 60% of college-aged men are infected, compared to under 40% of college-aged women. These facts indicate that infected men are unwitting carriers of the disease. Those few men who suffer penile cancer linked to HPV typically do so decades later. Risks for infection increase among uncircumcised men, those with many sexual partners, and smokers. Gardasil has proven extremely effective against HPV infection in women, and early tests suggest the same in men. Further public awareness of the disease could help to defeat it by promoting safer choices and more widespread identification and treatment.

Introduction

Human Papillomavirus (HPV) is the most prevalent sexually transmitted infection worldwide, causing 92.9% of all cervical cancers in women [1]. Much has been learned about the prevalence and etiology of oncogenic (high-risk) HPV infection in females, but little is known about HPV infection in males, other than that they are typically carriers of human papillomavirus, unknowingly spreading the infection, and thus playing a pivotal role in the viral lifecycle. Nononcogenic HPVs cause genital condylomata, the common clinical indicator of male HPV infection [2], but HPV-infected males are often asymptomatic, and clinical testing is scarcely available.

HPV Infection Rates

Recent studies have found HPV infection in males to be both common and multifocal. A 24-month University of Washington study

Sample Middle Pages

2

Numbers zero and one are spelled out in text; numbers 2 and up use digits.

revealed a 62.4% incidence of oncogenic and nononcogenic HPV infection in college-aged males. Females in the same age group and population were found to have a considerably lower incidence (38.8%) of HPV. The 2 most common HPV types found in males were HPV-16 (19.5%) and HPV-84 (23.3%). HPV-16 is oncogenic, causing 51.5% of cervical cancers in women [1]. Of 240 study subjects, 47.9% tested positive for high-risk HPV types, etiologic agents for cervical cancer and anogenital cancers in both men and women [3].

A second reference to a source uses the originally assigned number.

The high incidence of oncogenic HPV infection in males is surprising, considering many are clinically asymptomatic. Nononcogenic (low-risk) HPV types are largely responsible for condylomata (genital warts), though some oncogenic HPV types cause condylomata as well. HPV DNA testing in not clinically available, so most men are unaware of oncogenic HPV infection. HPV is transmitted through genital contact; therefore, higher infection rates are expected in male partners of HPV-infected women [3]. In a 2005 study, oncogenic HPV was found in 60% of males with HPV-infected female sexual partners [4].

Relation of HPV to Penile Cancers

Though uncommon (0.3/100,000 men) in the United States and Europe, penile carcinoma is often caused by oncogenic human papillomavirus types [5]. Penile cancer tends to have a late onset, with a mean age of 60 at time of diagnosis [5]. A 2005 study found HPV DNA in 79.8% of all penile cancer tumors. HPV-16 was found in 69.1% of penile tumors, suggesting a strong correlation between oncogenic HPV and penile carcinoma [6]. These results indicate the most common type of oncogenic HPV (HPV-16) is also responsible for 69.1% of human papillomavirus-associated penile cancers, and a similar percentage of cervical cancers (51.5%) [3, 6]. This strong association between HPV and penile cancer has been found in other studies [6].

A reference to two sources places both numbers in the citation, separated by a comma.

Lack of neonatal circumcision is traditionally considered to be the greatest risk factor for both male HPV infection and penile carcinoma.

3

Sources are
generally
identified by
study and year,
not by authors.

A 2008 study found an increased oncogenic HPV infection rate among uncircumcised males. Swabbings from different genital regions revealed a higher HPV prevalence (49%) in the glans/corna of uncircumcised males than circumcised males (29%) [7]. Oncogenic HPV infection in the glans/corona of uncircumcised males was found to be 19% higher than circumcised males [7]. The reason for this higher prevalence is unknown, but may be due to tissue tears and abrasions during sexual intercourse. The foreskin absence in circumcised males reduces skin abrasions and basal cell exposure to HPV, possibly lowering infection rates [7].

Studies have found similar associations between lack of circumcision and penile carcinoma. Men not circumcised as neonates were found to have an increased risk (odds ration = 2.3) of invasive penile cancer [6]. A history of phimosis—inability to fully retract the foreskin—increased the risk of penile cancer (OR = 11.4) considerably. It is unclear why phimosis increases penile cancer risk, but phimosis-associated tissue trauma may increase basal cell exposure to HPV6. Neonatal circumcision removes the possibility of phimosis and appears to reduce HPV and penile cancer risk. With the foreskin surgically removed, phimosis-related trauma and other foreskin abrasions are not possible, reducing basal cell exposure and possible infection.

Additional Risk Factors in Males

Other risk factors—number of female sexual partners, condom use, and smoking—have also been found to contribute to human papillomavirus infection in males. Lifetime number of female sexual partners (FSPs) has a significant effect on risk of HPV infection in males. Men with 11-21 and 21 or more life FSPs are at an increased risk of oncogenic HPV infection (OR = 3.7 and 5.3, respectively) than men with 5 or fewer FSPs [8]. This association confirms that each FSP increases risk of exposure and infection. Previously noted infection rates for males may be higher than females due to greater lifetime number of sexual partners. Using condoms at least half the time appeared to decrease (OR = 0.5) the risk of oncogenic HPV infection by limiting viral exposure [8].

4

Because only genital contact is required for infection, condoms are not considered absolute protection from HPV. Cigarette use increased oncogenic HPV risk (OR = 2.1). Smoking 10 or more cigarettes per day increased the risk significantly (OR = 3.7) [8]. It is unknown why smoking increases HPV infection risk, so further studies must be done to address this interesting risk association [8]. Reduction of lifetime FSPs, increased condom use, and not smoking appear to effectively reduce oncogenic HPV infection risk.

Effectiveness of Gardasil

The U.S. Food and Drug Administration approved Gardasil, a quadrivalent HPV vaccine, on 8 June 2006. The vaccine was approved for females aged 9 to 26 against HPV types 6, 11, 16, and 18 [9]. The vaccine was found to have 95-100% efficacy against anogenital and cervical lesions related to HPV-6, 11, and 18, cellular precursors to cervical and vulvar cancers [10]. Since approval, legislation has been introduced to require adolescent Gardasil vaccination as a preventative measure against HPV infection in women, but the vaccine is not yet universally required. The quadrivalent HPV vaccine has the potential to reduce male HPV infection rates, male-to-female viral transmission, and HPV-related anogenital disease in males, though it is not currently available for males. Gardasil has not yet received FDA approval for use in men, but young males were shown to have effective immunity in clinical trials [10]. Merck, the pharmaceutical company offering Gardasil, is currently seeking FDA approval for vaccine use in males and older adult women [10].

Conclusions

Vaccinating prior to HPV exposure is important for reducing HPV transmission and HPV-related diseases, but little attention is paid to the personal and societal risks of the unvaccinated male population. As research reveals associations between human papillomavirus and anogenital cancers, public awareness of this dangerous and widespread virus will encourage women and men to protect themselves through lifestyle choice and vaccination.

Sample References Page

5

References

1. Bosch FX, Manos MM, Muñoz N, Sherman M, Jansen AM, Peto J, Schiffman MH, Moreno V, Kurman R, Shan KV, et al. Prevalence of human papillomavirus in cervical cancer: A worldwide perspective. International biological study on cervical cancer (IBSCC) Study Group. J Natl Cancer Inst. 1995;87(11):796-802.

2. Nielson CM, Flores R, Harris RB, Abrahamsen M, Papenfuss MR, Dunne EF, Markowitz LE, Giuliano AR. Human papillomavirus prevalence and type distribution in male anogenital sites and semen. Cancer Epidemiol Biomarkers Prev. 2007;16(6):1107-1114.

3. Partridge JM, Hughes JP, Feng Q, Winer RL, Weaver BA, Xi LF, Stern ME, Lee SK, O'Reilly SF, et al. Genital human papillomavirus infection in men: Incidence and risk factors in a cohort of university students. J Infect Dis. 2007;196(8):1128-1136.

4. Nicolau SM, Camargo CG, Stávale JN, Castelo A, Dôres GB, Lörincz A, de Lima GR. Human papillomavirus DNA detection in male sexual partners of women with genital human papillomavirus infection. Urology. 2005;65(2):251-255.

5. Heideman DA, Waterboer T, Pawlita M, Delis-van Diemen P, Nindl I, Leijte JA, Bonfrer JM, Horenblas S, Meijer CJ, Snijders PJ. Human papillomavirus-16 is the predominant type etiologically involved in penile squamous cell carcinoma. J Clin Oncol. 2007;25(29):4550-4556.

6. Daling JR, Madeleine MM, Johnson LG, Schwartz SM, Shera KA, Wurscher MA, Carter JJ, Porter PL, Galloway DA, McDougall JK, et al. Penile cancer: Importance of circumcision, human papillomavirus and smoking in situ and invasive disease. Int J Cancer. 2005;116(4):606-616.

7. Hernandez BY, Wilkens LR, Zhu X, McDuffie K, Thompson P, Shvetsov YB, Ning L, Goodman MT. Circumcision and human papillomavirus infection in men: A site-specific comparison. J Infect Dis. 2008;197(6):781-783.

6

8. Nielson CM, Harris RB, Dunne EF, Abrahamsen M, Papenfuss MR, Flores R, Markowitz LE, Giuliano AR. Risk factors for anogenital human papillomaviurs infection in men. J Infect Dis. 2007;196(8):1137-1145.

9. US Food and Drug Administration [Internet]. Silver Spring (MD): US Dept. of Health and Human Services; [date unknown]. Vaccines, Blood & Biologics: Gardasil [last updated 2009 Nov 17; cited 2010 Mar 20]; [1 screen]. Available from: http://www.fda.gov/cber/products/gardasil.htm

10. Villa LL. Overview of the clinical development and results of a quadrivalent HPV (types 6, 11, 16, 18) vaccine. Int J Infect Dis. 2007 Nov; 11 Suppl

Use double-spacing between and within all entries.

For entries longer than one line, align second and subsequent lines beneath the first letter of the first word (not the number).

Use initials and abbreviations as shown.

CSE System: Activities

1. Print a copy of a research paper that you wrote earlier in your schooling. Using the instruction and information in this chapter, carefully edit the paper so that it follows current CSE guidelines for documentation.

2. Study the sample paper on pages 489-495. Explain how effectively Aurora follows the approach and practices of science writing in general and of CSE style in particular: does she work with her sources in ways that make for a credible discussion of the research and its significance?

3. Using the broad topic of the sample paper (cancer research) as a starting point, select a specific form of cancer and a specific line of research on that cancer. Then track down a variety of studies, read them carefully, and write up a review of this literature following the documentation rules of CSE style.

CSE Checklist

Checklist:

☑ All borrowed material is acknowledged with an appropriate number either in superscript or placed within brackets or parentheses.

☑ Sources are numbered in the order in which they are referenced in the paper.

☑ Second and subsequent references to a given source use the original number given the source.

☑ Each resource number is keyed to a references page where resources are listed in the order in which they are cited in the paper (not in alphabetical order).

☑ Each reference entry contains complete information on the source:

- Up to 10 authors (last name followed by initials), plus *et al* if needed.

- Title and subtitle for the source (including journal or site title, if appropriate)—with correct capitalization and abbreviations.

- Publication details (e.g., publication city and publisher; journal volume and issue; date of publication; page numbers).

☑ The entire paper is properly formatted according to the specifications of the assignment, the form (e.g., lab report, field report, literature review), and the discipline.

Index

Models: